Praise for *America's Fiscal Constitution*

"Something remarkable . . . a fascinating book about our economic history. . . . *America's Fiscal Constitution* tells the story of how America has dealt with its debt since its founding, and in doing so provides a compelling roadmap to a more responsible fiscal future."
—*President Bill Clinton*

"Our nation cannot be strong militarily, diplomatically, or politically unless it is strong economically, and we cannot remain strong economically unless we deal with our massive debt burden. . . . A must read for those who believe that we should get our economic house in order."
—*James A. Baker, III, former Secretary of the Treasury and Secretary of State*

"In order to understand our fiscal plight, it's crucial to appreciate how carefully America has dealt with debt in the past. Bill White makes that tale fascinating."
—*Walter Isaacson, bestselling author and former CEO of CNN and managing editor of* Time *magazine*

"Lucid and pioneering . . . a compelling and illuminating formula for both economic growth and fiscal restraint."
—*James MacGregor Burns, Pulitzer Prize–winning historian and Professor Emeritus at Williams College*

"There are few Americans I trust more than Bill White. With history as his guide, White trail-blazes through the Washington, DC, bureaucratic jungle, revealing Big Truths that are bolstered with Hard Facts."
—*Douglas Brinkley, professor at Rice University and CBS News historian*

"A thought-provoking and well-told history of our nation's traditional financial principles. Every citizen can benefit from this book's practical insights."
—*Ross Perot*

AMERICA'S
FISCAL
CONSTITUTION

BILL WHITE

AMERICA'S FISCAL CONSTITUTION

ITS TRIUMPH
and
COLLAPSE

PUBLICAFFAIRS
New York

Published in the United States by PublicAffairs™, a Member of the Perseus Books Group
All rights reserved.

Printed in the United States of America.

PublicAffairs books are available at special discounts for bulk purchases in the U.S. by corporations, institutions, and other organizations. For more information, please contact the Special Markets Department at the Perseus Books Group, 2300 Chestnut Street, Suite 200, Philadelphia, PA 19103, call (800) 810-4145, ext. 5000, or e-mail special.markets@perseusbooks.com.

Book design by Trish Wilkinson
Set in 11-point Adobe Garamond Pro

Library of Congress Cataloging-in-Publication Data
White, William H., 1954–
America's fiscal constitution : its triumph and collapse / Bill White. —
First edition.
     pages cm
Includes bibliographical references and index.
ISBN 978-1-61039-343-0 (hardcover) — ISBN 978-1-61039-344-7 (e-book)
1. Debts, Public—United States—History. 2. Budget—United States—History.
3. Fiscal policy—United States. 4. United States—Appropriations and expenditures. 5. United States—Economic policy—2009– I. Title.
HJ8119.W45   2014
336.73—dc23
2013042841

First Edition

10 9 8 7 6 5 4 3 2 1

To my parents—and others in their generation—who worked to create a brighter future for their children and limited federal debt for decades after World War II

Contents

Author's Note

THE ARCHITECT OF the written Constitution, James Madison, hoped that federal leaders would limit debt with principles that would be clearly "visible to the naked eye of the ordinary politician." For almost two centuries ordinary American politicians followed well-defined principles—an unwritten fiscal constitution—to make budget decisions that now seem extraordinary. They incurred debt for only four well-defined purposes. That achievement appears more remarkable every year, as the federal government now lurches from one budget crisis to another.

The size and nature of federal borrowing changed when the nation's traditional limits on debt collapsed at the beginning of the twenty-first century. Never before had the federal government waged major wars without raising taxes. Never before had it so heavily relied on foreign creditors. Never before had the president and Congress financed a permanent new domestic program entirely with debt. Never before had progressives accepted, much less insisted on, the substitution of federal debt for payroll contributions supporting the Social Security trust fund. Never before had many conservatives organized the fight against a constitutional amendment requiring a balanced budget. Never before had so many leaders of each major political party claimed that balancing the budget—even with national income at an all-time high—would impair sustainable economic growth. After 2000 the federal government borrowed increasing amounts to pay for routine operating expenses in addition to debt incurred to pay for wars and recession-related stimulus.

The collapse of traditional budget practices occurred quietly, unaccompanied by some notable shift in public opinion or ideology. Americans did not wake up one morning and decide to mortgage their children's future. No mandate to borrow arose from the photo-finish 2000 election. The federal government borrowed large amounts with a Republican president and Republican Congress, a Republican president and Democratic House, a Democratic president and Democratic Congress, and a Democratic president and Republican House.

The twenty-first century borrowing binge cannot simply be blamed on some defect in the character of federal elected officials. For two decades I have known our presidents and many congressional leaders in each party. They and others willing to endure the ordeal of elections care at least as much about their country's future as do others who sit on the sidelines. In the 1990s, as a chief operating officer of a federal cabinet department, I found that leaders in both parties respected good faith efforts to balance budgets.

I am more optimistic than those cynics who doubt that the federal government can balance its budget once more. For much of the last decade I served as the mayor of Houston, the nation's fourth largest city, with a population greater than that of many states. Like most other state and local governments, Houston cannot use debt to fund routine operating expenses. Almost daily I explained to citizens tradeoffs between various levels of taxation and spending. People with diverse backgrounds and beliefs were (and are) able to recognize the need to balance public obligations and tax revenues.

To understand what has recently gone wrong with federal debt, it helps to know what had once gone right. We can learn much from America's exceptional history, which we often treat as almost a form of secular scripture. American elected officials limited debt when facing far harder budget trade-offs after the Revolution, the Civil War, and sixteen tough years of the Great Depression and World War II. Thomas Jefferson hoped that fiscal discipline would become "habitual" and that future voters would use the fiscal records of "different epochs" to hold officials accountable. This book's description of historical limits on federal debt—the American Fiscal Tradition—is written with Jefferson's vision in mind.

1

THE AMERICAN FISCAL TRADITION

FIFTY-FIVE CITIZENS OF TWELVE STATES GATHERED TO DECIDE HOW to pay past due bills from the War of Independence. They solved that problem by creating a new nation, the United States of America.

George Washington worried about public debt that could grow "like a snowball . . . rolling."[1] When leaving the presidency he cautioned his countrymen to avoid "throwing upon posterity the burden which we ourselves ought to bear."[2] The first American citizens did not treat "posterity" as an abstraction. Most had endured the hardship of untamed wilderness in order to create a better future for their children. Farmers and merchants realized that private investment suffered when public debt absorbed more credit. Even Americans with little formal education understood that government paid for on an installment plan would ultimately cost more. Early Americans valued freedom, including national independence from foreign creditors. Their sacrifices transformed the world's first modern democracy into the first major nation to become debt-free.

The Constitution required Congress to authorize any debt, but it did not prescribe the use of borrowed funds. Early federal leaders remedied that lack of clarity—and several others—by creating an informal constitution to supplement the written one. Great Britain had an unwritten constitution, and one of its principles—taxation imposed only by the consent of some body of taxpayers—had spawned the American Revolution.

By 1820 America's unwritten fiscal constitution included principles for limiting debt. This book refers to those limits on debt as the American Fiscal Tradition. That tradition was more than a simple belief in balanced

1

budgets, since federal leaders were allowed to borrow for certain extraordinary purposes.

Budget practices instituted by the Founding Fathers helped generations of federal leaders resist the temptation to borrow excessively. Those practices included clear accounting, "pay as you go" budget planning, and the use of trust funds with spending confined to the level of tax revenues dedicated for a particular purpose. Congress clearly defined the amount and use of each debt incurred.

Limits on debt strengthened democracy itself. "Pay as you go" budgets helped voters to weigh the benefits of each new federal financial commitment against the palpable price paid in the form of taxes.

The role of political parties would, in time, also become embedded in the nation's unwritten constitution. The original Democratic and Republican parties incorporated traditional budget principles into their early platforms. Each party tried to persuade voters that it was the most trustworthy steward of the public purse. The competitive pressure to balance budgets forced party leaders to resolve conflicts among the varied priorities of their constituencies.

In the first year of the Washington administration, two Founding Fathers considered how to prevent government officials from using debt to provide services that were more costly than available tax revenue. Thomas Jefferson feared that public officials might try to use debt to hide the actual cost of government. He asked James Madison to minimize that risk by drafting a constitutional amendment that would limit debt, but Madison suggested that principles based on experience—rather than abstract philosophy—would yield more effective restraints.[3]

Budget experiences in the nation's first several decades helped define only four acceptable uses of debt.

The United States *borrowed to preserve the union* when it assumed state debts from the Revolution and brought states back into the Union after the Civil War.

The nation *borrowed to expand and connect the nation's borders* with the Louisiana Purchase. The United States later incurred modest debts to extend its boundaries to the South and the West and to better link its territory with intercontinental railroads and the Panama Canal.

The United States *borrowed to wage war* beginning with the War of 1812. In that war, the Civil War, World War I, and World War II, the federal government incurred debt and adopted extensive new tax systems that facilitated debt service after the wars. The federal government used debt to finance wars with Mexico, Spain, North Korea, and North Vietnam. Only after the collapse of the American Fiscal Tradition in the twenty-first century did the United States finance prolonged wars solely with debt.

The federal government *borrowed during severe economic downturns* beginning with the Panic of 1819. The United States also incurred debt during three major depressions and severe recessions. Federal debt plugged holes in budgets occasioned by sharp drops in forecasted revenue, and it helped pay for some expenditures directly related to the downturns.

The federal government promptly balanced its budget after each temporary use of debt. Until the Cold War, federal leaders used surpluses to steadily retire debt after its emergency use. Occasionally they did borrow when revenues fell short of mistaken estimates. But for almost two centuries the president and Congress never planned to incur debt simply to reduce taxes or to pay for routine annual spending.

Generations of Americans took the American fiscal constitution for granted. President John F. Kennedy did not have to spell out its details in a 1962 commencement address challenging young Americans to adapt the nation's fiscal tradition to the modern economy. Weeks after that speech, a poll showed that three out of four Americans preferred to be taxed at high rates during the Cold War rather than have the nation incur debt. The most powerful member of Congress in the late twentieth century, Wilbur Mills, told Kennedy that voters adhered to "this old concept that they've grown up with: if you're gonna cut taxes . . . you better cut your spending."[4]

The American Fiscal Tradition collapsed in 2001. Afterwards the federal government regularly borrowed a third or more of its expenses. Only part of the debt was used for the traditional purposes during war and a severe downturn. By 2014 federal debt had soared to almost $120,000 per working American.[5]

Debt now casts a dark shadow over the nation's economy. After 2008 debt was nine times greater than revenues available to pay for the debt, a level higher than in any multiyear period of time before Thomas Jefferson became president in 1801.[6] Bankers commonly use such a similar "debt coverage ratio" to evaluate the creditworthiness of debtors. A business typically considers bankruptcy before its debt rises to nine times annual revenues. Few people would feel comfortable incurring home equity debt with an existing mortgage nine times their annual income.

Many Americans and foreign leaders question the capacity of the nation's current political system to restore fiscal discipline. As interest rates rise and the federal government begins to pay the Medicare bills of the vast Baby Boom generation, the United States continues to borrow. After each of the nation's five prior spikes in debt—following the Revolution, the War of 1812, the Civil War, World War I, and World War II—borrowing ceased entirely once the emergency ended. Today debt funds much of the federal government's routine costs, even with national income at an all-time high.

Events during two pivotal years in budget history, 1950 and 2003, illustrate the triumph and collapse of the American Fiscal Tradition. In 1950 the requirements of the unwritten fiscal constitution forced federal leaders to weigh spending and taxes for global security and minimum pensions for older Americans. In 2003 debt helped disguise the costs of tax reduction, reconstruction of foreign nations, and a vast expansion of federal medical services. The battle in each milestone budget year began with a State of the Union address delivered by a president often underestimated by his political opponents.

1950: The Power of the American Fiscal Tradition

While addressing a joint session of Congress in January 1950, President Harry Truman complained that "the ill-considered tax reduction" three years earlier had resulted in a shortfall in revenue needed to pay for "necessary expenditures." Loud moans from Republican members of Congress caused Truman to stumble over his next line, which he then repeated: "To meet this situation, I am proposing that Federal expenditures be held to the lowest levels consistent with our international requirements and the essential needs of economic growth, and the wellbeing of our people."[7] Neither the Democratic president nor any congressional leader in either party at that time proposed using debt to fund routine spending.

Truman spoke to Congress in an era of fierce partisan rivalry. In February 1950 many Republicans applauded when a senator claimed to have evidence that communist traitors had infiltrated the Truman administration. Truman's campaign speeches in 1948 had been the most partisan ever delivered by a sitting president. Many of those campaign speeches attacked Senator Robert Taft of Ohio, who set the Washington agenda of the Republican Party. Taft and Truman had fought over the size and scope of a normal federal budget since the end of World War II.

Truman and Taft were a study in contrasts. Truman never attended college; Taft graduated at the top of his class at Yale and Harvard Law School. Truman grew up in a modest home in a small Missouri town; young Taft lived in the White House during his father's presidency. Truman was not considered a serious candidate for the presidency until well after he became president following the death of President Franklin Roosevelt in 1945; Taft was a leading presidential candidate within months of his first election to the Senate in 1938.

Both, however, were decisive, plainspoken, and ready to fight over matters of principle. Senator Taft had no quarrel with the president's belief that "pay as you go" was the "soundest principle of financing I know." Both Truman and Taft made hard choices in defense of that principle while they reduced federal debt from its World War II peak.

Taft demanded aggressive cuts in spending in order to lower federal income tax rates. Though Republican activists loathed communism, Taft opposed efforts to fund the deployment of troops in Europe to counter Soviet forces. While attempting to cut the Marshall Plan, which assisted allies resisting internal communist threats, Taft candidly explained: "Why not? I want to save us a tax increase."[8]

Truman and a bipartisan coalition in Congress blocked Taft's attempts to cut military spending, close bases abroad, and prevent America's participation in the North Atlantic Treaty Organization. The president also fought Pentagon demands to spend more than anticipated federal revenues. The stress between "pay as you go" budgets and military leaders who demanded higher spending took its toll on Truman's subordinates. In 1949 it drove the nation's first secretary of defense, James Forrestal, to depression and eventual suicide and forced another proponent of spending restraint, General Dwight Eisenhower, to take an extended medical leave.

In the summer of 1950, despite intense partisanship, Truman, Taft, and almost every single member of Congress agreed on two major federal commitments and the taxes to pay for them. Those decisions—on federally administered pensions for older Americans and a global security umbrella—would shape all future federal budgets.

The chairman of the House Ways and Means Committee, Robert Lee Doughton—"Muley Bob" or just "Muley" to his rural constituents in North Carolina—kept out of the headlines. He had worked across party lines to create a tax system for financing World War II and servicing debt afterward. That new tax system, embodied in the Revenue Act of 1942, served as the principal source of federal revenues for at least the next seventy years. After the war, Doughton labored to build a consensus on the future of an old-age pension program, which many people referred to using the title of a bill he had sponsored in 1935—the Social Security Act. The Social Security pension system had since atrophied. Most older Americans lived in poverty after losing much of their savings as a result of the Great Depression and wartime inflation. The minimum pension benefit of $35 a month, supported by a 2 percent tax on payrolls, had never increased and was not enough to live on after World War II. As a result, Congress—with virtually no dissent—annually approved higher funding to states for public assistance, or "welfare," for more than a fifth of Americans over sixty-five without other means of support.

Federal leaders in each party worried about the rising cost of those grants, but no one wanted to revert to the earlier practice of cramming destitute older Americans into local poorhouses. Workers in a far more mobile society had often moved away from aging relatives who were living longer; women—who had been the traditional caretakers—poured into the paid workforce in record numbers. Without additional revenues, the budgetary problem of funding public assistance with general revenues would only get worse. Personal and corporate income tax rates were already at extraordinarily high levels, needed to pay for interest on wartime debt, the armed forces, and benefits promised to over ten million veterans.

Doughton found widespread support for an expanded old-age pension system funded entirely with higher taxes dedicated for that purpose. Groups that once opposed the original Social Security Act—including insurance companies and many employers and labor unions—had since changed their views. A portable minimum federal pension could play a useful role in corporate pension planning. Civic leaders in rural areas, who had once insisted on the exemption of nonindustrial employees from the pension system, now wanted some means of defraying the rising cost of welfare payments for older Americans.

Doughton's amendments to the Social Security Act extended pension coverage to most American workers, raised minimum benefits by 70 percent (just above subsistence), and increased the payroll tax supporting the Old Age and Survivors Trust Fund. Congressman Wilbur Mills assured his colleagues that a viable pension system financed with contributions from workers would relieve the growing expense of "welfare" and was better than doling out "something . . . for nothing."[9] The bill passed the House in 1949 with a 333–14 vote.

By financing a pension trust fund using a schedule of gradually rising payroll tax rates to maintain its actuarial balance, the House bill avoided the replay of a heated debate in the 1930s concerning the size of a pension reserve. President Franklin Roosevelt—a former insurance executive— believed that the pension system was consistent with traditional limits on debt so long as trustees maintained benefits and contributions at levels determined by actuaries. That practice, which was standard for private insurers, would require a large reserve as the population aged. Roosevelt asserted that it would be "dishonest to build up an accumulated deficit for the Congress of the United States to meet in 1980."[10]

Republicans shared Roosevelt's unwillingness to impose debt on a future generation, but feared that building a large pension reserve could magnify that very risk. The GOP leader on the issue, Senator Arthur Vandenberg of Michigan, argued that future leaders might be tempted to disguise debt incurred by the normal federal budget—now called the federal funds budget—by combining it with a Social Security system with large reserves. The conservative Vandenberg preferred a "pay as you go" pension system with only modest reserves. He rejected the alternative of investing pension reserves in corporate securities rather than federal debt, an idea he called "socialism."[11]

Doughton's bill incorporated part of Taft's Republican plan for medical care—a federal program for grants to states for use in paying hospital bills of low-income Americans, the precursor of modern Medicaid. The bill passed the Senate in June 1950 by a vote of 81–2. From that day on, a system of pension benefits, sustained by payroll taxes and without debt, allowed most Americans to retire with a measure of dignity.

Five days after the Senate passed the Social Security Act Amendments of 1950, North Korean soldiers invaded South Korea, and only US soldiers in South Korea could stop them. The United States accepted the burden of global leadership, ending a four-year partisan debate within and between leaders of each party concerning international military commitments. Months before the North Korean invasion, the Truman administration had blocked a Republican-led attempt in the House to cut military assistance to Korea. At the same time, in order to balance a budget, Truman had declined to approve his National Security Council's recommendation that the United States raise taxes and triple its military spending. After the North Korean invasion, Truman signed the recommendation and asked Congress to suspend consideration of any new domestic spending. Congress raised taxes three times within eighteen months, to the highest levels in history, and vastly increased military spending even apart from the direct costs of the Korean War. In the first year of the war, during which the United States led U.N. forces against a larger Chinese army, the federal budget ran a surplus.

Federal income tax collections rose from $35.7 billion in 1951 to $51 billion in 1953, the last year of combat in Korea. By then federal funds taxes—those not dedicated to support specific trust funds—consumed 16.6 percent of national income, just shy of the record 18.8 percent in the last year of World War II and far greater than the average level of 10.3 percent during the period 2001–2010.[12]

In 1950 the American Fiscal Tradition forced the federal government to balance its responsibilities and resources for pensions and international security. The nation had borrowed for war before, but federal leaders in 1950 realized that total federal debt was already too high. The president and Congress made hard choices in order to avoid an additional mortgage on future tax revenues.

The new consensus on global commitments and a balanced trust fund for pensions survived after Republicans gained control of Congress and the White House in 1953. President Dwight Eisenhower argued that balanced budgets preserved the future of the nation's children, the burgeoning Baby Boom generation. Like Truman, Eisenhower fought to maintain military spending at a level far less than that requested by the armed forces, though more than the amount urged by Taft. Faced with Pentagon protests about budget cuts, he quipped that the National Security Council should study "whether national bankruptcy or national destruction would get us first."[13]

Also like Truman, Eisenhower backed a pension system funded fully with dedicated taxes outside the normal federal budget. By a voice vote with no dissent, the Senate passed Eisenhower's proposal to broaden the Social Security system. Eisenhower remarked to his brother that a system of minimum pensions completely funded by broad-based taxation was opposed only by "Texas oil millionaires and an occasional politician or business man" whose "number is negligible and . . . stupid."[14]

2003: THE COLLAPSE OF THE TRADITION

Newly elected president George W. Bush displayed a portrait of Eisenhower in the Oval Office. In his first State of the Union address Bush echoed a favorite theme of both Eisenhower and Truman. Bush pledged to reduce federal debt by $2 trillion and keep $1 trillion in reserve. He reminded the public that "we owe it to our children and grandchildren to act now."[15]

Bush's goal for debt reduction appeared within reach at that time. Inflation-adjusted average income had tripled since Truman's 1950 State of the Union address. President Bill Clinton and congressional Republicans had implemented a multiyear plan to balance the budget and then produce a surplus. That plan rested in part on the continuation of annual spending ceilings and procedural rules that his father, President George H. W. Bush, had fought to obtain in 1990. Moreover, George W. Bush was the first Republican president since Eisenhower who could count on a Republican majority in the House and Senate. Six years before Bush's inauguration in 2001, all but one Republican member of Congress and many Democrats had voted for a constitutional amendment to balance the budget by 2002.

Bush's goal of a $2 trillion reduction in federal debt would require Congress to maintain large surpluses in the federal funds budget—federal spending and revenues outside of trust funds. Achieving that goal would take discipline, since there had been only a slight federal funds surplus in the fiscal year before Bush took office. Economic growth had already begun to slow. In the months following Bush's budget address, however, neither the president nor Congress tried to confine spending to available revenues.

Within twenty-four months of Bush's first State of the Union address, the federal government was borrowing at a rate of half a trillion dollars per year—almost $5000 annually for every American household. Federal funds spending had soared by $200 billion a year while federal funds tax revenues plummeted by more than $300 billion a year.[16] Only a very small portion of the rise in spending was related to the military response to the terrorist attacks on September 11, 2001.

President George W. Bush made no mention of his earlier goals for debt reduction during his State of the Union address in 2003. Instead, he asked Congress to reduce tax revenues again—by more than $2 trillion—and called for the most costly expansion of Medicare since 1972. The White House then submitted to Congress a budget with sharply higher levels of domestic and defense spending.[17] The war in Afghanistan accounted for only a small portion of the additional funding.

The federal budget disguised the extent of total debt by subtracting the surplus in Social Security trust funds, the precise form of manipulation once feared by traditional fiscal conservatives like Vandenberg. Bush's predecessor, Bill Clinton, had separated trust fund revenues in his last budgets in order to avoid hiding any deficit.

In March 2003 the United States invaded Iraq. During prior major wars, Congress had raised taxes in order to reduce the need for borrowing and to demonstrate civilian support. Majority Leader Tom DeLay of Texas, then the most powerful member in the House, was adamant that "nothing is more important in the face of a war than cutting taxes."[18] Popular Republican senator John McCain opposed cutting taxes during war, but only two other Republicans in Congress joined him in voting against the large tax cut enacted in the spring of 2003. Congressional budget experts calculated that within ten years the 2003 tax cut would add $2.7 trillion, or about $20,000 per working American, to the federal debt.[19] After the planned expiration of the tax cuts in 2010 federal borrowing was projected to skyrocket, as the first of seventy-five million Baby Boomers began to qualify for Medicare. Projected debt would be even greater with an extension of those tax cuts.

President Truman had repeatedly championed federal medical insurance even though he never included it in his budgets. He refused to plan for domestic spending greater than the level of taxes that Congress would impose. In 2003, freed of constraints imposed by traditional budget practices—"pay as you go" budget planning, the use of dedicated taxes paid into trust funds to finance new programs, and congressional authorizations of debt for defined purposes—Congress borrowed to finance an expansion of Medicare and suspended the limit on the annual Medicare costs that had been crafted by President Clinton and Republican congressional leaders just six years earlier.

The idea of expanding Medicare to cover prescription drugs was nothing new; its cost had always been the problem. The original architect of Medicare, Wilbur Mills, had excluded coverage of prescription drugs used outside of hospitals because of his concern that the cost would exceed available federal revenues. In 1988 President Reagan and Congress had tried to tax high-income Medicare recipients in part to allow coverage of expensive prescription drugs, but Congress quickly repealed the program following a backlash against the tax.

In 2003 President Bush asked Senator Ted Kennedy of Massachusetts to help him obtain coverage for prescription drugs. Kennedy had participated in every significant legislative initiative concerning medical services since the creation of Medicare and Medicaid thirty-eight years earlier. With Kennedy's help, the bill expanding Medicare passed the Senate by a lopsided, bipartisan margin. While many Democrats had objected to the large debt financing of a tax cut passed in May of the same year, few voted against a debt-financed expansion of Medicare.

House Republicans who previously bridled at passing a new spending program tried to secure new debt-financed tax breaks as the price of their support. When the Senate rejected those tax reductions, House Republicans instead obtained new debt-financed federal subsidies for privately administered Medicare insurance. The estimated cost of the new program for prescription drugs rose sharply after its enactment.

The Medicare Prescription Drug Improvement and Modernization Act was the first major new domestic program in history that the White House and Congress planned from the outset to finance almost entirely with debt. Congressman John Boehner of Ohio, who chaired the Republican Policy Committee, explained to Republican House members that "the American people did not want a major reduction in government" and that they should accept "such realities as the burdens of majority governance."[20]

Analysts warned of the risks of a debt-financed expansion of Medicare. Baby Boomers—children born from 1946 through 1964—were in their prime earning years. Medicare costs would begin to soar when the first of their generation became eligible for Medicare in 2010. From 2000 to 2010 the growth in the number of Americans age forty-five to sixty-four—the Baby Boomers—equaled three-quarters of the growth in the entire population.

The 2003 spending spree did not end with the expansion of Medicare. In September the president requested $87 billion for military operations in Iraq and Afghanistan and efforts to reconstruct those nations.[21] Republicans defeated an attempt in the Senate to delay a planned tax cut in order to defray the amount of debt used to finance the war.

Never before in American history had federal leaders financed a major war entirely with debt. Federal officials did not even ask the general public to contribute to war efforts by lending money. When the nation made a commitment to a global security umbrella in 1950, tens of millions of American citizens purchased savings bonds to fund a fifth of the total federal debt. American insurance companies and banks purchased most of the rest. From 2001 to 2004, in contrast, foreign creditors financed almost the entire rise in Treasury debt, apart from the amounts sold to federal trust funds or the Federal Reserve.

MYTHS CONCERNING FEDERAL DEBT

The foregoing sketches of budget history in two pivotal years *describe* but do not *explain* what happened to the traditional limits on federal debt. There was no official announcement that federal leaders abandoned the traditional fiscal constitution. Partisan or cynical explanations of what happened gave rise to influential myths. Examples of common myths include "the federal government almost never balances its budget" and "they always used to balance the budget." In fact, for 180 years the federal government never set out to borrow to support routine spending, though at times it did borrow quite a bit for the four extraordinary purposes identified earlier.

Consider the following common budget myths.

Myth: *"It's an old story: liberals always spend more, and conservatives tax less."* "Conservatives" once supported a stronger central government. In the late nineteenth century, "liberal" referred to Republicans and Democrats who supported policies akin to those of Gladstone's British Liberal Party—competitive markets and balanced public budgets. Throughout most of American history progressive politicians refrained from the use of debt in order to avoid mortgaging the future, and conservatives strongly opposed debt-financed tax cuts.

Myth: *"Ultimately, the federal government just inflates the dollar to reduce the burden of the debt."* Federal officials have never intentionally inflated the currency for the principal purpose of reducing the burden of debt. Following every spike in debt occurring from the War of 1812 to World War II, the federal government restricted credit in order to curb inflation.

Myth: *"Keynesian economics led federal leaders to believe that balanced budgets stifle economic growth."* Members of Congress rarely defer to economists when crafting legislation on taxes or appropriations, though politicians often cite the opinions of economists who agree with their actions.

John Maynard Keynes argued that debt incurred during downturns should be repaid with future surpluses.

Myth: *"It all started with the New Deal."* Franklin Roosevelt began his presidency by cutting "normal" federal spending, including federal civilian and military salaries and veterans' benefits. He sought to restrain debt by vetoing a record 665 bills.

Myth: *"It all started with the Great Society programs in the 1960s."* Spending on new social programs amounted to a small fraction of the federal funds budget during the Johnson administration. Since 1977 federal funds domestic spending, apart from medical services, has not grown significantly as a share of national income.

Myth: *"It all started with Reagan, who thought he could cut taxes without a loss of revenue."* Neither President Reagan nor his senior White House economic advisors believed that the 1981 reduction in tax rates, in itself, would raise federal revenue as a share of national income. They explicitly assumed that federal revenues would grow rapidly as high rates of inflation persisted and pushed Americans into higher tax brackets.

Myth: *"The real problem is Social Security."* The Social Security trust funds are in great shape compared to the federal funds budget, which is the only budget capable of incurring debt. Reforms enacted in 1983 created large reserves for the pensions of Baby Boomers. Modest changes in future benefits or payroll taxation would balance Social Security's long-term revenues and payments.

Myth: *"The real problem is partisanship and gridlock."* Democratic and Republican leaders blamed each other for the death of much of the nation's population in the decades immediately after the Civil War. Yet they worked together to pay down debt. After 2000 federal elected officials often compromised on budget issues, typically by raising spending, cutting revenues, and increasing debt. From 2001 through 2006 debt-financed appropriations bills sailed through Congress with lopsided bipartisan majorities.

Myth: *"The debt crisis is the unfortunate result of the War on Terror and the Great Recession."* Traditional uses of borrowed funds—fighting two wars and filling budget holes during a severe downturn—account for no more than half the debt incurred during 2001–2013.

Myth: *"We cannot balance the budget without hurting the economy."* Long run economic growth results from a growing and productive workforce, not greater debt. The United States has experienced sustainable economic growth principally at times when the federal government repaid debt or borrowed very little in relation to the size of the economy. From 2000 through 2007, even before the Great Recession, private sector job growth lagged far behind twentieth-century averages despite a massive federal borrowing binge.

———————

In hindsight it is easy to describe what happened: After 2000, members of Congress and two presidents made commitments that resulted in a large gap between spending and tax revenues. In short, they behaved like many government officials in many nations throughout history who descended down the slippery slope of debt—to use Washington's phrase—"like a snowball . . . rolling."

Debt-financed spending has a powerful allure. It disguises the perceived cost of government, what economists call a "fiscal illusion." In fact, this very illusion is critical to the notion that debt-financed spending or tax cuts can stimulate the economy; people would be reluctant to spend or invest more if their share of higher federal debt showed up on their credit card balance.

Traditional budget practices—clear accounting, "pay as you go" budget planning, trust fund spending confined to dedicated revenues, and specific congressional authorizations of the amount and use of each new debt—had been eroding for years before the link between taxes and spending broke in 2001.

Rosy projections, creative accounting for trust funds, and traditional borrowing during wars and recessions made it difficult for voters, and sometimes even elected officials, to appreciate the extent of the nation's dependence on debt. Benjamin Franklin had once noted the plight of debtors in denial: "The second vice is lying, the first is running in debt. . . . lying rides upon debt's back."[22]

American history after 2000 is not the most promising place to find a solution to the current debt crisis. It is more useful to seek guidance from lessons learned from prior generations of American leaders who matched federal commitments and resources—and still managed to get reelected.

Too often budget battles often appear as minor subplots in historical narratives constructed around the drama of elections and wars. Some say that politicians campaign in poetry and govern in prose. Frequently, however, numbers rather than words yield greater insight concerning hard decisions. Political rhetoric can gloss over the difference between the ideal and the possible. Libraries contain hundreds of books describing Civil War military campaigns, yet few volumes shed light on budget battles extending over two centuries. Just as peacekeepers leave lighter footprints in history than do soldiers marching in war, so too has the legacy of budget heroes faded from popular memory. Nonetheless, their success in limiting debt preserved the nation's future and independence.

This book narrates a journey along a tested trail of fiscal safety. Earlier generations who persevered along that path overcame partisan, regional, and ethnic obstacles far greater than those today. They built a great nation without mortgaging its future. They opened doors of opportunity, created the first generation of older Americans with financial security, and set a standard of living that remains the envy of much of the world. They fended off an invasion from the world's strongest military power, secured possession of much of North America, endured a civil war, financed two world wars, and relieved human suffering during three severe economic depressions.

The story of Americans who crafted and respected America's fiscal constitution can inspire as well as instruct. It begins with a weary Virginian who traveled on horseback toward his first Christmas at home in eight years. He was troubled by debts owed to the soldiers he led, some of whom had chased Congress out of town because it could not honor its financial commitments.

PART I

A NEW NATION AND
DEMOCRATIC PARTY LIMIT
FEDERAL DEBT: 1789–1853

2

DEBT GIVES RISE TO A
NEW NATION AND POLITICAL PARTY

1789–1802: Years when deficits exceeded debt service = 0

A NATION CONCEIVED IN DEBT

More than two hundred guests gathered for a sentimental evening at Mann's Tavern in Annapolis, Maryland, on December 21, 1783. Some had journeyed long distances over rough roads to pay their respects to General George Washington, who had led an improvised Continental Army to victory against the world's greatest military power. Grateful citizens had greeted the general throughout his sixteen-day trip from New York to the Maryland tavern. Washington looked forward to relinquishing his command in Annapolis before completing the ride to his Mt. Vernon home.

Guests at the farewell dinner lifted their glasses for thirteen toasts, each punctuated by the boom of a cannon blast from outside. The crowd grew quiet as the dignified general rose to offer a toast that sounded more like a plea than a benediction. He expressed hope that the states would give the Congress of the Confederation "competent powers," which it would need to pay debts to the soldiers and suppliers who had sacrificed so much during the long war for independence.[1]

Washington had requested a payment plan nine months before this farewell dinner, when he had acted to quell a rebellion by unpaid soldiers who waited in camp for news of a peace treaty with Great Britain. He had denounced agitators in his army who urged the "dreadful alternative of deserting our country, or turning our arms against it."[2] Those veterans, often dressed in rags, had good reason to worry about whether the Continental Congress would pay their back wages. Congress had no taxing authority, and Great Britain had compelled the states to give assurances, soon broken, that former colonists would honor debts owed to British commercial creditors.

Congress appointed a committee led by Alexander Hamilton, then twenty-nine years old, and James Madison, only four years older, to respond to Washington's demand that his troops receive three months' pay when they were released from duty. Madison and Hamilton sympathized with the request but could authorize only partial payment, in the form of bank notes with little value. In June 1783 angry veterans chased Congress out of Philadelphia. General Washington appealed in vain to the governors of all the states: "Where is the man to be found who wishes to remain indebted for the defense of his own person and property, to the exertions, the bravery, and the blood of others, without making one generous effort to pay the debt of honor and gratitude?"[3]

The morning after the farewell dinner, Washington formally resigned his military commission in a ceremony choreographed by his friend Thomas Jefferson. Jefferson was not the only one who recognized that Washington's voluntary return to private life might endure as a symbol of democratic public service. George III, ruler of Great Britain and former monarch of the colonists, noted that Washington's willing departure from official power made him the "greatest character of the age."[4]

No one, however, lauded the greatness of the insolvent Congress of the Confederation. It took four months just to clear the farewell dinner bill from Mann's Tavern. And for five years thereafter, Congress lacked the "competent powers" to repay the principal or interest on debts remaining from the Revolution.[5]

Hamilton of New York and Madison of Virginia unsuccessfully argued that Congress should tax imported goods to repay its debt. The Articles of Confederation required the consent of all states for the imposition of any tax. In 1785 New York objected to this import tax, as Rhode Island and Virginia had done two years earlier. Meanwhile, compound interest accumulated on the debt.

Some states printed paper money and threatened to compel creditors to accept it in payment of debts, but one state's paper money would not satisfy creditors in other states or countries. Creditors who had lent money to pay for the Revolution expected debts to be repaid in some form of currency equivalent to the dollar's value relative to British, French, or Spanish coins.

Dutch bankers, whose credit remained vital for the states' economic independence from Great Britain, grew impatient.[6] Twenty-eight-year-old Congressman James Monroe, a veteran of the Revolution and close friend of Hamilton and Madison, heard that some citizens of Northern states were considering a withdrawal from the Confederation, which would leave the remaining states with the full burden of congressional war debt.

Without the power to tax, Congress could only "requisition," or beg, states to pay their share of debt service. In 1786 it billed the states for a total of $3.8 million and repeatedly warned each state that failure to pay would be "a breach of public faith and a violation of the principles of justice." Existing records show that the states paid, at most, $663.[7] Delegates from some states even tried to dodge the issue of taxation by avoiding meetings of Congress.

In August 1786 Washington, who called the requisitions "little better than a jest," mused glumly that "we have probably had too good an opinion of human nature in forming our confederation."[8] Hamilton and Madison, however, had not quite given up hope. Weeks after Washington expressed his frustrations, the two traveled to the same tavern at which the general's retirement from military service had been honored nearly three years earlier. They would try once more to resolve the debt crisis.

Ten delegates from three other states joined them at Mann's Tavern for a meeting originally called for the modest purpose of resolving various disputes among states over water boundaries, seaborne trade, and coordinated collection of state taxes on imports. Madison and Hamilton, each of whom stood barely five feet tall, had larger purposes in mind. Madison later wrote—in the formal English he had acquired from reading all the books in his father's substantial library by the time he was eleven—that they "did not scruple to decline the limited task assigned."[9] Madison and Hamilton convinced the other delegates to call for yet another meeting, in Philadelphia the following spring, to consider issues transcending coastal trade. They hoped to enlist participation by the most influential citizens from each state, so that the Philadelphia meeting would have "powers adequate" to decide how to satisfy the Congress of the Confederation's outstanding financial obligations.[10]

The ambitious purpose of the Philadelphia meeting was deemphasized in Hamilton's written invitation, which suggested that the resolution of commercial issues might require "a correspondent adjustment of other parts of the Federal System."[11] Madison and Hamilton were more forthright with close friends in sounding the alarm that the Congress of the Confederation had run out of options to repay its debts. To break the deadlock over debt, Hamilton and Madison needed greater authority than they or any state could muster. That task, they believed, required the unique prestige of General Washington.

Madison, along with Virginia governor Edmund Randolph, persuaded Virginia's legislature to quickly choose the members of the delegation it would send to Philadelphia. They named Washington as the head of the delegation, even though the nation's most distinguished citizen had not yet been persuaded to attend the meeting. Madison explained to the retired general why his participation would demonstrate "the magnitude of the occasion," but Washington begged off. After all, Washington protested, he had just declined to attend an annual reunion of veteran army officers in Philadelphia on the grounds that he had withdrawn from public life.[12] In spite of his reluctance, Virginians publicized the fact that Washington would lead their delegation.

Pennsylvania also promptly selected its delegation, which included the state's two leading citizens: Benjamin Franklin, the famous inventor, writer, and merchant, and Robert Morris, the most prominent businessman in the thirteen states. Franklin and Morris had each played critical roles in financing the Revolution; Franklin secured grants and loans from France, while Morris managed extensive borrowing from American merchants and large planters. News of the attendance of Washington, Franklin, and Morris impressed leaders in the other states. Eventually, every state except Rhode Island sent delegates to Philadelphia.

The meticulous Madison prepared for the meeting by studying how various nations throughout history had collected taxes, regulated commerce, organized defense, and resolved disputes. Meanwhile, Hamilton had made estimates of potential revenues from national taxation.

In February 1787 Congress had been unable to attract a single subscriber for a $500,000 loan, an amount of only about 1 percent of its outstanding debt. Weeks later Washington agreed to attend the Philadelphia meeting. He wrote to a friend that the impotent Confederation was like "a house on fire" that was "reduced to ashes" while people debated "the most regular mode of extinguishing" the blaze.[13]

Tensions mounted in the months before the delegates left for Philadelphia. They heard reports that armed farmers in Western Massachusetts had refused to pay property taxes designed to retire the state's war debts. Samuel Adams of Massachusetts, organizer of the original Tea Party, supported the taxes and thought that those encouraging the tax revolt should be hanged for treason. Henry Lee, Washington's able cavalry commander during the Revolutionary War, warned that the tax rebellion might spread to other states.

By May 1787, when the Philadelphia meeting convened, Madison observed that "it was seen that the public debt rendered so sacred by the cause in which it had been incurred remained without any provision for its payment."[14] John Marshall, an incisive young lawyer and Revolutionary War veteran from Virginia, described the situation in plainer language: "The public creditors had lost faith in the old government."[15]

The delegates in Philadelphia unanimously elected Washington to preside over the proceedings. On May 30, 1787, the fourth day of deliberations with a quorum, they adopted a resolution that reflected the essence of Madison's plan for establishing a national government "consisting of a supreme Legislative, Executive & Judiciary."[16] For several months they fleshed out a plan to create a new organization capable of servicing existing debt and any future debt occasioned by emergencies. The assembled delegates called it "the United States of America" and set forth its powers in the Constitution.

Benjamin Franklin, then eighty-one, had to be carried to the convention meetings and rarely spoke. He listened carefully to the extended debate about whether senators, who were expected to be wealthier than most members of the House of Representatives, should be allowed to propose or amend any "money bills," that is, legislation affecting spending or taxes. Franklin blessed the final compromise, which allowed only the House to originate bills, by repeating the maxim "Those who feel can best judge." Decades earlier, in the colonies' first request for greater financial independence from the Crown, Franklin had made a related point: taxation would be more acceptable when those who paid taxes could direct how the money would be spent. From the outset the nation's founders understood the importance of the link between spending and taxation.

Franklin delivered the Philadelphia convention's closing remarks, in which he urged that all delegates "act heartily," despite any personal reservations about the text of the Constitution, to obtain its ratification.[17] No one heeded that advice more than Madison and Hamilton, who each worked tirelessly to overcome opposition from certain powerful politicians in their states. They wrote essays, now known as the Federalist Papers, designed to persuade New Yorkers to ratify the document. The essays stressed the need for a federal power that could levy taxes to repay existing debt and support national defense. Many citizens in New York and Massachusetts feared the loss of state revenues if the federal government had the exclusive right to tax imports through their busy ports. Connecticut and New Jersey were among the first to ratify the Constitution, since each sought to curtail New York's ability to tax imports shipped through its port and purchased by citizens of neighboring states.

Some Virginians led by Patrick Henry, the famous orator and a perennial power in the state's government, argued against the new taxing power granted to the federal government by the Constitution. Madison responded that states could not defend themselves without a reliable source of revenues capable of supporting a national military. If war came, who "could be expected to lend to a government which depended on the punctuality of a dozen or more governments for the means of discharging even the annual interest of the loan?"[18]

Hamilton battled opposition from his state's governor and told Madison that the prospect for ratification in New York was "infinitely slender, and none at all," unless Virginia first approved the document. In the summer of 1789 Virginia and New York finally ratified the Constitution, by narrow margins, though only after enough states had already done so to form a union without them.

Many state conventions sought to condition their ratification on the adoption of various amendments. Madison, already recognized as an authority on the Constitution, asserted that no state could conditionally join the Union. He did, however, pledge that Congress would carefully consider suggested amendments after ratification. This argument failed to persuade North Carolina's political leaders or Madison's fellow Virginian James Monroe, who believed that their states should join the Union only after the Constitution incorporated a bill of rights. New York recommended a constitutional amendment requiring a two-thirds majority vote in Congress for any authorization of new federal debt.

Washington's election as president was a foregone conclusion. Each state chose electors to cast their ballots for the nation's first chief executive, and even those electors who had opposed the Constitution cast their votes for the American most responsible for securing their independence from Great Britain. Madison ran for a seat in the House of Representatives, and the ultimate outcome of that election was less clear, as some Virginians had recruited Madison's neighbor Monroe to run against him. That winter of 1788 the two candidates traveled together frequently on a campaign trail that then, as now, exacted a heavy toll on candidates. One night, on the long ride home after a debate at a small Lutheran church, Madison's nose became permanently scarred from frostbite. Madison ultimately won by a margin of three hundred votes after a campaign dominated by two issues—taxes and religion—that would become familiar sources of discord in American politics. That election result surely altered US history. Monroe had natural leadership skills, but he lacked Madison's ability to craft legislation, which was vital for securing passage of the Bill of Rights and various laws organizing the government.

Federal leaders such as Washington and Madison were well aware that every action by the new federal government might establish a precedent. The Constitution itself sketched the federal government in broad strokes, including only essential principles and allowing operating procedures to be filled in later. Even the very first minutes of Washington's administration established an enduring tradition, in the form of an inaugural address that the president drafted with Madison's help.

The Constitution made the debt of the Confederation "valid against the United States." That debt's size—more than $54 million—was enormous in relation to the scale of a national economy consisting of only four hundred thousand free households, whose principal source of wealth was land.[19] The debt was equivalent to the value of over a hundred acres of prime land per family. Total debt far exceeded the value of several millions of dollars of foreign coins circulating as currency. Even citizens considered wealthy by virtue of large land holdings, like George Washington, had little cash. He had to borrow money at 6 percent interest to pay for the cost of his travel to the inauguration. The burden of debt before 1800, measured as a share of national income, would be greater than at any time before national income collapsed at the depths of the Great Depression in 1933.

When Congress first convened, in March 1789, Madison introduced a tax bill he drafted with help from Hamilton. Madison quickly became the de facto leader of the House of Representatives. Representative Fisher Ames of Massachusetts, who would later become an opponent of the Virginia congressman, offered this description of Madison during the first session of Congress: "He is possessed of a sound judgment, which perceives truth with great clearness, and can trace it through the maze of debate. . . . He is a studious man, devoted to public business, and a thorough master of almost every public question that can arise."[20]

On July 4, 1789, the thirteenth anniversary of publication of the Declaration of Independence, Congress passed legislation that taxed imports at 5 percent of their value, with discounts for goods arriving on American vessels. Various luxury items such as lace, carriages, playing cards, and liquors were taxed at higher rates.[21] In the early years, these taxes produced enough revenue to pay annual interest but were insufficient to retire principal on outstanding debt.

Madison then managed the passage of a bill creating the Department of the Treasury, despite objections from members of Congress who feared the potential concentration of power in its secretary. Washington's close friend Robert Morris declined that job and recommended that the president offer the post to Hamilton, who had served as the general's chief of staff during the Revolution. Madison also believed that Hamilton was best suited for "that species of business."[22] Secretary of the Treasury Hamilton promptly borrowed $50,000 from a bank to pay the federal government's expenses, including the salaries of the president and members of Congress.

Hamilton faced an enormous task. He would have to calculate the amount of the debt, develop systems for accounting and tax collection, and estimate the level of projected tax revenues. The federal government would have difficulty paying its bills until it had an organization capable of collecting the new import taxes when ships pulled into harbors.

Meanwhile, Madison fulfilled a promise to his constituents and various states when he shepherded through Congress twelve constitutional amendments, ten of which were approved by states and became known as the Bill of Rights. The task took patience, since congressmen who had opposed ratification pressed for more extensive revisions, while strong supporters of ratification saw no need to solve theoretical problems. After passage of the Bill of Rights, Madison believed he had completed, at least for awhile, his labors on the language and structure of the Constitution that he had begun three years earlier with the assistance of books sent from Paris by his friend Thomas Jefferson. Madison was ready to get on with the practical business of governance. Jefferson, still serving as the country's minister to France, was not yet satisfied with the Constitution. He pressed Madison to consider another constitutional amendment imposing a limit on federal debt.

Jefferson had focused on the question of public debt when the National Assembly in France debated a plan to deal with the nation's enormous debts. Some of those debts had resulted from financial support of the American Revolution, which former French finance minister Anne-Robert-Jacques Turgot had unsuccessfully argued France could not afford.

According to Jefferson, some French leaders he consulted treated the US Constitution "like . . . the bible, open to explanation but not to question."[23] Yet Jefferson did question the document's lack of an explicit limitation on debt. The French monarchy had accumulated large debts, and Jefferson hoped that his nation would not impose similar mortgages on future generations. Throughout his adult life, Jefferson had opposed laws that allowed one generation of free citizens to restrict the freedom of the next, such as the British laws of entail (limiting rights to inherit land to a defined category of descendants, e.g., eldest male heirs) and mortmain (vesting permanent, nontransferable rights in land to a church or corporation). In 1776, he had helped abolish entail in Virginia and viewed independence from Great Britain as an opportunity to rid the New World of feudal legal doctrines.[24]

Jefferson preferred to write rather than make speeches, as he found it easier to organize his thoughts on paper and desired to conceal a slight lisp. He expressed concerns about federal debt financing in an essay he wrote to Madison, a fellow Virginia planter, in September 1789. Jefferson acknowledged that existing debts would have to be paid as a matter of honor. "But with respect to future debts," he wrote, "would it not be wise and just for [a] nation to declare, in the constitution they are forming, that neither the legislature, nor the nation itself, can validly contract more debt than they may pay within their own age, or within the term of 19 years?" Jefferson illustrated his point with the hypothetical example of a king who borrowed from foreign bankers an amount equal to the annual income of the kingdom's economy and then sought favor by distributing the borrowed money to his subjects. If that king allowed interest at 5 percent to compound rather than be paid each year from tax collections, Jefferson calculated that after nineteen years the debt would be 2.5414 times the amount originally borrowed. He considered placing that type of burden on the next generation "an act of force, and not of right."[25]

Jefferson also noted that limits on debt might help place a leash on "the Dog of war."[26] Like Scotch economist Adam Smith, Jefferson believed that financing a war with debt rather than taxes might disguise the war's true cost. He concluded his letter by asking Madison to consider how to craft a constitutional limitation of debt.

Madison sympathized with his friend's goal but had doubts about the use of a constitutional amendment to accomplish it. Debt may be needed for some purposes—like the Revolutionary War itself—that could benefit "posterity." Furthermore, he cautioned that any principles used to limit debt should be grounded in practical experience rather than theory. Madison placed great faith in the lessons of historical experience and had explained in a Federalist essay that "experience is the oracle of truth."[27] He agreed with the notion that "the living generation" should not impose "unjust or unnecessary burdens on their successors." He suggested that this truth, based in "Philosophy," required principles grounded in practical experience in order to be "visible to the naked eye of the ordinary politician."[28]

Nonetheless, Jefferson's warning about the risks of debt, expressed during the Republic's first year, continued to weigh on Madison. In an essay a few years later, Madison concluded that each generation should pay "its own debts" and that government should be financed with "more palpable" taxation rather than the more "imperceptible mode" of debt. Madison's essay attempted to distill the proper limits on debt in the form of a Socratic dialogue with a "republican philosopher." In response to the potential objection that "the benefits of war descend to succeeding generations, and the burdens ought also to descend," Madison's philosopher responded that it was better to sacrifice reasonable exceptions to the rule against borrowing than to open the door for "converting exceptions into general rules."[29]

Joseph Jones, a member of the Continental Congress and James Monroe's uncle, used plainer language when counseling Madison on the appropriate budget principle: "Pay as you go is the best policy. The next best is to settle and pay as soon as you can [so] that the interest may not gradually devour the capital."[30]

Shortly after Jefferson returned from France to begin serving as Washington's secretary of state, Treasury Secretary Hamilton gave a report to Congress on the nation's credit. This report, which contained many practical details, also included Hamilton's articulation of a principle for avoiding "dangerous abuse" of debt. He posited that it ought to be "a fundamental maxim, in the system of public credit of the United States, that the creation of debt should always be accompanied by the means of extinguishment and principal payments on the debt."[31] In short, Hamilton believed that taxes should always be high enough and spending low enough to allow taxes, rather than additional borrowing, to service both interest and principal payments on debt. Jefferson and Madison had no quarrel with that concept. They were alarmed, however, by one of Hamilton's specific recommendations: the creation of a national bank.

Adding Debt to Preserve the Union

Hamilton and Madison had reached an impasse in early 1790 over two issues referred to by Jefferson as "the most irritating questions that ever can be raised . . . funding of the public debt, and . . . fixing on a more central residence [for the federal government]."[32]

Federal funding of the debts incurred by state governments during the Revolution generated the greatest controversy. Hamilton initially estimated that those debts totaled $25 million.[33] The Constitution only obligated the nation to assume the debts of the Continental Congress. Massachusetts adamantly insisted on the federal assumption of debts incurred in the fight for independence; its delegates had ratified the Constitution by a narrow margin, and now the state feared being shortchanged if it remained liable for debt after the Constitution removed its ability to tax imports into its busy Boston port. Its citizens had already rebelled against attempts to retire state war debts with property taxes. Other states, in contrast, worried that federal assumption of state debts would force them to pay more than their fair share.

Apprehensions were heightened by complex accounting.[34] Some states contributed financially to the Revolution principally by sending funds to the Continental Congress, while others had borrowed money to pay directly for their militias. Several states, including Virginia, had already repaid their war debts and, along with North Carolina, strongly resisted the idea of imposing a new federal tax on landowning citizens who had little cash.

Madison surprised Hamilton by abandoning his earlier belief that "justice" required a common responsibility for state debts during the Revolution.[35] Madison worried that "an increase of the federal debt" would "prolong the evil" of the debt itself.[36] He also objected to paying the full face amount of debt to speculators who had purchased debts at a discount. This concern was not hypothetical, since Madison learned that James Reynolds, an agent for a New York bond dealer, had obtained the Treasury's confidential list of debts owed to veterans and used that knowledge to buy their claims at a deep discount. Madison brought that fact to Hamilton's attention, and Hamilton agreed to make public the lists of creditors. (A year later, the unscrupulous Reynolds arranged for his wife to have an affair with Hamilton and then tried to blackmail him.)

Hamilton believed, as Madison once had, that each state incurred Revolutionary War debts for a common benefit and that it was impractical to adjust the payments due to each bondholder based on the price paid for the bond. More significantly, some leaders in Massachusetts threatened to impede the collection of federal import taxes without a commitment from the federal government to pay their state's war debts. Even before the Constitutional Convention Madison recognized that a state's refusal to allow collection of federal taxes—which could lead to federal military action against the state—subverted the very rationale of the Union.[37]

On June 19, 1790, Hamilton encountered Jefferson on the street outside the president's office and complained that gridlock over state debts threatened the Union. Jefferson listened to the "somber, haggard and dejected" Hamilton and responded by inviting him to "a friendly conversation" with Madison over dinner at his house on Maiden Lane in New York, then a city of about thirty thousand people.[38] Jefferson was well practiced in the French custom of negotiations over a multicourse meal with wine.

Jefferson's hospitality diffused tensions between his two guests, both of whom respected their host, who was several years older and had earned an international reputation by virtue of his authorship of the Declaration of Independence and various writings on North America's natural history.

While drinking wine and dining with friends, the reserved Jefferson could become charming, humorous, informal, and provocative. Jefferson preferred to converse rather than argue because he had observed that words could rarely change an opinion already formed. Years later as president, he would scandalize the European diplomatic corps, who were accustomed to strict court protocol, by hosting dinners in casual dress at tables without seating plans.

It is likely that Jefferson began the evening on a personal note. Madison was a close and trusted friend, and the host must have asked Hamilton about his wife, Eliza, whose sister Jefferson, a widower, had fallen in love with in Paris during his years as minister to France.

Madison and Hamilton each appreciated how difficult it would be for the other to compromise on the issue of state debts. Madison was in a position to be reminded by his former political opponent, Monroe, that the congressman had once assured Virginians that the Constitution imposed no obligation to pay state debts. Hamilton, on the other hand, would have to explain the loss of New York as the temporary capital to his wealthy father-in-law, who had raised funds to pay for federal offices there.

The issue of state debt seemed far more important to Hamilton than did the location of the capital. Just ten days earlier, at a meeting with Pennsylvania senator Robert Morris on a foggy morning at the southern tip of Manhattan, Hamilton had offered to support a temporary capital in Morris's preferred location of Philadelphia as long as Morris delivered the votes necessary for the federal government to assume state debts. But Morris could not overcome the opposition of Virginia's House delegation to the assumption of state debts. To do so might require Jefferson's influence with Virginians such as James Monroe and members of the powerful Lee family.

Jefferson had already anticipated that a deal with Virginians on the capital might engender opposition from Pennsylvanians. Shortly before his dinner with Madison and Hamilton, Jefferson met with Morris to float the idea of a temporary capital in Philadelphia.

Madison himself shared Hamilton's concerns that the issue of state debts had to be resolved in order to avoid impediments to tax collection in Massachusetts. Just days before his dinner with Jefferson and Hamilton, Madison had written to Monroe with alarm about the "prophetic menaces" of debtor states.[39]

Jefferson's dinner meeting served his desired purpose. The three resolved to locate the new, permanent capital on the Potomac, close to Washington's plantation home, with a temporary capital in Philadelphia. Jefferson would help bolster support for the federal assumption of state debts, while Hamilton would work with Morris to bring Pennsylvania on board and mollify disappointed New Yorkers. After the dinner, Jefferson wrote to Monroe, who had once served as his law clerk, to explain "the necessity of yielding for this time to the cries of the creditors in certain parts of the union, for the sake of union, and to save us from the greatest of all calamities, the total extinction of our credit in Europe."[40]

Jefferson wrote to his brother-in-law that the failure to assume state debts could interfere with "the funding of the debt altogether, which would be tantamount to a dissolution of the government."[41] In July Congress approved the location of the new capital on the Potomac, where it would move after ten years in Philadelphia. President Washington would use the home of the status-conscious Morris as his official mansion. Morris himself, who unsuccessfully speculated in land development within the boundaries of the new capital, would spend three years of the Washington administration housed nearby, at the Prune Street jail, for nonpayment of debts.

In August Congress passed the Funding Act, which authorized the assumption of state debts and raised the estimated federal debt to $75.4 million.[42] Once freed of debt, many states slashed their property taxes. This assumption of debt was the first of many occasions on which the states would demand the federal government shoulder various financial responsibilities while at the same time protesting the related intrusion of federal authority.

Of the $52 million in obligations directly inherited from the Confederation, $40.3 million was owed to American citizens, amounting to $27.3 million in principal and $13 million in accumulated interest. The balance, $11.7 million, was owed to foreigners, principally in the Netherlands, Spain, and France. The Funding Act gave priority to payment of interest owed abroad, in order to preserve the nation's international credit. It also gave interest payments priority over all federal expenditures except for an annual sum of $600,000 earmarked for general administration, including tax collection.[43]

Hamilton then refinanced, at a lower average interest rate, the principal amount of all domestic debt and accrued interest. Hamilton expected to be able to pay interest but not retire principal for the foreseeable future.

The total debt after the assumption of state debts imposed a great burden on the young nation, whose economy in 1790 produced goods and services with an estimated value of $200 million and which had a population of 807,094 free white males and eight million acres of culti-vated land trading at little more than $2 per acre.[44] Much of the popula-tion lived outside the cash economy.

In February 1792, after Hamilton's refinancing, Treasury debt bearing the highest interest rate sold for $1 for every dollar of face value, a sharp rise from its value of 45 cents per dollar two years earlier. Many merchants considered that appreciation to be a remarkable achievement. Both Ham-ilton's supporters and critics compared US debt to the familiar benchmark of British sovereign debt. Even Great Britain at times would receive less than a pound sterling for every pound of face value of its standard bonds, known as "consols." Hamilton's detractors were aware that those consols were often purchased by the English landed gentry, who treated them as a perpetual annuity financed by taxes.

Stable pricing of federal debt in relation to gold coins helped provide liquidity. To understand the importance of federal paper notes worth their "face value," consider today's ten dollar bill, on which Hamilton's picture appears. Creditors and vendors accept it in payment for $10 owed, with-out the need to negotiate its "real value." Hamilton wanted US Treasury notes, or notes from a bank with Treasury notes in reserve, to serve as a na-tional standard of value and thereby facilitate trade within the new nation.

Even when the United States began circulating its own coins, the quan-tity of these coins was insufficient to serve the needs for "hand-to-hand" money and bank reserves. Gold and silver tended to be drained abroad, since the United States typically imported goods of greater value than it exported.[45] Federal debt obligations backed by federal taxing power served as an alternative standard of commercial value. That value depended, of course, on the creditors' confidence that federal revenues would be avail-able to pay debt service. After the destruction of finances in other devel-oped nations following World War II, US debt became—as Hamilton could only dream—the worldwide standard of commercial value.

DEBT AND POLITICAL OPPOSITION

The spirit of cooperation at Jefferson's 1790 dinner did not last long. The following year, during the third and final session of the First Congress, Hamilton pushed through legislation chartering a national bank, the Bank of the United States. Private investors supplied 80 percent of the bank's original funding. The new Bank of the United States assumed responsibility for handling the deposits and disbursements of the US government.

Scholars often revisit the bank controversy in order to discern the origins of the nation's competing political doctrines. However, Hamilton's defense of the bank was grounded less in ideology than in his practical need for help in collecting taxes at distant ports and disbursing payments to scattered vendors and creditors. The overworked Hamilton had few competent staff members and only a crude accounting system.

Hamilton also understood, as has virtually every secretary of the treasury since, that properly regulated banks could support short-term federal borrowing. The government's cash flow inevitably fluctuates over the course of a budget year, and the revenues of a new tax system were especially difficult to predict. Bank credit could smooth the cash flow and assist when revenues fell short of estimates. Not even a handful of the nation's wealthiest citizens had much gold to lend during the nation's first dozen years, so the Bank of the United States provided a vehicle for pooling funds from a large number of investors and depositors. Moreover, Hamilton believed that oversight by a broad group of investors might reduce the risk of political influence over the bank's credit decisions.

Jefferson and Madison's intense opposition to the bank likewise rested on a practical objection to monopoly. English law treated chartered corporations as having the exclusive or monopoly right to engage in a defined line of business.[46] In fact, it was not until 1837 that the Supreme Court decided, by only a slim majority, that a state could legally charter more than one corporation for a particular purpose. Jefferson and Madison's opposition to the bank also reflected their antipathy toward the concentration of power in a financial institution controlled by the executive branch and a group of wealthy private investors that included more than thirty members of Congress.

The bank controversy initiated more than a century of national debate concerning the responsibility for functions now described as "central banking." The Constitution gave Congress the power "to coin money [and] regulate the value thereof" but did not specify *who* ultimately would make decisions on the supply of money and credit or *how* enough would be supplied to accommodate the reasonable public and commercial credit needs without inflation. Jefferson sought to limit private influence over these decisions, while Hamilton wanted to curb future interference by elected officials who might lack the competence, discipline, integrity, and access to private capital required to effectively manage the nation's banks and currency. This essential debate over central banking continued until an agreement was reached between the Treasury Department and the Federal Reserve in 1951.

By 1792 Jefferson and Madison had organized like-minded political leaders in opposition to the bank and some of Hamilton's other initiatives. They began referring to their anti-Hamilton coalition as one of two "parties," and, like modern partisans, they stereotyped their opponents as an elitist minority. In a letter to Madison, Jefferson offered one description of the party alignment:

> On one side, 1. the fashionable circles of Phila, N. York, Boston, & Charleston (natural aristocrats), 2. merchants trading on British capitals, 3. paper [money] men. . . . On the other side are 1. merchants trading on their own capitals, 2. Irish merchants, 3. tradesmen, mechanics, farmers, & every other possible description of our citizens.[47]

Madison was even less generous. He described the opposition as being "partial to the opulent" and as "having debauched themselves into a persuasion that mankind are incapable of governing themselves."[48]

Jefferson and Madison called their group "republicans." Like-minded citizens in various cities gathered as "democratic" clubs or societies. Their opponents often called them antifederalists or Jacobins. For the next forty years, the party operated as a coalition without an official organization, platform, or name.

Though the written Constitution did not explicitly refer to political parties, eventually a party system would become part of the nation's unwritten constitution and an accepted means of expressing political opposition. This prospect did not sit well with President Washington, for reasons often misunderstood. Washington was a superb politician who listened to public opinion and paid attention to details affecting his public image. For example, he designed his frequent walks in New York to help cultivate his identity as a man of the people. Yet he also knew how to set himself apart; he chose to ride on horses whose white color he enhanced with powders he specially prescribed. Washington felt that federal elected officials derived their authority based on a direct relationship with voters or the electors who chose them. Accordingly, he suspected that parties might undermine the direct accountability of elected officials to voters, their ultimate source of authority.

Though Washington's views on parties did not ultimately prevail, his crucial decisions about executive power did set precedents incorporated in the nation's unwritten constitution. Washington believed that federal appointees should be loyal to the president and his policies. The written Constitution did not state whether the president could discharge senior appointees who had been confirmed by the Senate, especially for differences with the president arising from policy or politics rather than competence in executing the law. Paradoxically, Washington's idea that presidential appointees should adhere to an administration program served to accelerate partisan groupings that could be used to identify people sharing common policy preferences.

Budget issues—especially opposition to Hamilton's attitude toward spending, taxes, and debt—energized Jefferson's coalition. Jefferson showed Madison his own calculations of national debt, divided by public revenue, for the United States and ten European countries. Great Britain, with debt at sixteen times the public revenue, had the greatest burden of debt in Europe. Jefferson estimated that US debt amounted to "about 20 years of revenue, and consequently that though the youngest nation in the world we are the most indebted nation also."[49] Jefferson's comparison of total debt to total tax revenue available to service debt is similar to what is now known as the "debt coverage ratio," one of the most significant tools used by modern banks and investors in analyzing the creditworthiness of any debtor.[50] In September 1792 Jefferson complained to Washington: "this exactly marks the difference between Colonel Hamilton's views and mine, that I would wish the debt be repaid tomorrow; he wishes it never to be paid, but always to be a thing wherewith to corrupt and manage the Legislature."[51]

Jefferson and Madison did not like Hamilton's financial policies, but they seemed incapable of presenting a concrete alternative. That type of criticism angered Hamilton and his supporters. Hamilton protested to Washington that, for Jefferson, "creditor and enemy appear to be synonymous."[52] Everyone knew that the nation had financed its struggle for independence with debt, a stark reality that Hamilton characterized as "the price of liberty." No one besides Hamilton offered a plan to pay that price. No one, that is, until Albert Gallatin, a Swiss immigrant who lived in a valley on the nation's remote frontier.

Gallatin Develops a Fiscal Policy

Gallatin had emerged from his trading post in Western Pennsylvania as a spokesman for citizens opposing a tax on whiskey production. In 1791 Madison and Hamilton had persuaded Congress to impose that tax for the purpose of servicing state debts assumed by the federal government. Federal leaders received a petition in protest from settlers in the isolated valleys of Western Pennsylvania, a petition written using crisp logic rather than the hyperbolic rhetoric typical of the era. The petition acknowledged the need for federal revenues but argued against taxing "the common drink of a nation, [which,] instead of taxing the citizens in proportion to their property, falls as heavy on the poorest class as on the rich."[53] It also pointed out that the tax encouraged fraud, since whiskey stills could be easily hidden. The petition concluded by noting that many distillers did not have the cash to pay the tax; whiskey itself, not coins, often served as the region's currency.

Federal leaders learned that the articulate brief against the whiskey tax had been written by Albert Gallatin. Just who was this Gallatin?

Many in Congress asked that question when thirty-three-year-old Gallatin appeared in the nation's capital in Philadelphia as a new senator from Pennsylvania in 1793. Within days of joining the Senate, the frontiersman who spoke with a heavy French accent sponsored a resolution that passed unanimously. It called for Secretary Hamilton to report on the terms of all federal debt, to account for all debts repaid and those held by foreign creditors, and to list itemized categories of receipts and expenditures for each of the prior years.

On its face the resolution made sense, but Hamilton angrily complained that it would force him to hire an additional clerk at an expense of $850 to $900. He asserted that he was already working "to the utmost of my faculties and the injury of my heath," and objected to "distressing calls for lengthy and complicated statements."[54] Hamilton's supporters, including his mentor and Gallatin's fellow Pennsylvania senator Robert Morris, asked the upstart immigrant to prove that he had been a citizen for nine years, a constitutional requirement for election to the Senate. Gallatin had enlisted briefly in a Revolutionary militia promptly after his arrival in 1780 and used much of his modest savings to procure military supplies. He believed that he had nothing to prove. The Senate disagreed and promptly ejected Gallatin, who returned to his store in Western

Pennsylvania. Hamilton ignored the earlier resolution, though Gallatin's probing questions would soon return.

Gallatin's erudition set him apart from his rough-edged Scotch-Irish neighbors, who nonetheless respected his principled independence. After leaving the Senate, the unpretentious Gallatin joined residents from nearby valleys in a meeting at a local ferry crossing. The organizers of the gathering intended to form a militia to resist the collection of the federal tax on whiskey distillers. Gallatin disagreed with their position and offered a motion to instead appoint a delegation to negotiate a satisfactory outcome. An angry citizen at the meeting posed a question designed to discredit Gallatin's more conciliatory approach: Did he also object to the recent burning of a barn belonging to an arrogant and unpopular federal official? Gallatin replied matter-of-factly: "If you had burned him in it, it might have been something, but the barn had done no harm."[55] This disarming reply seemed to win over the majority, who approved Gallatin's proposal.

Collection of the tax proved difficult, and Hamilton convinced President Washington to take aggressive action to discipline the Western Pennsylvanians. In October 1794 Henry Lee—father of the future rebel general Robert E. Lee—led thirteen thousand soldiers to Western Pennsylvania and brought around twenty alleged rebels back to Philadelphia in chains. Jefferson considered the military response in Pennsylvania as a sign that Hamilton had lost touch with reality: the "insurrection was announced . . . and armed against, but could never be found."[56] It was a pyrrhic victory at best. A generation of Western Pennsylvanians, who did not forget the strong-armed response to their protest, would make their region into a political stronghold for Jefferson's party. Western Pennsylvanians elected Gallatin to the House of Representatives in 1794, less than a year after the Senate had expelled him. Soon most Americans learned much more about this remarkable Mr. Gallatin.

Gallatin was uniquely prepared for public financial leadership. Born into an elite merchant family in Geneva, he graduated with top grades from the city-state's schools and colleges, then the finest in the world. Many in the Revolutionary generation admired from a distance the great Enlightenment philosophers Voltaire and Rousseau; Voltaire was a close friend of Gallatin's family, and Rousseau was part of their social circle. Gallatin, who was orphaned at a young age, emigrated to the rebelling colonies after finishing his education in spite of being warned of the dangers there by Benjamin Franklin, who furnished a letter of reference for the young man at the request of Gallatin's prominent relatives. He improved his English while teaching French for a time at Harvard. Gallatin spoke calmly and politely, with an authority conveyed by his poised, penetrating gaze. Virginia's most talented lawyer, John Marshall, offered to tutor him in law after they became acquainted on one of Gallatin's journeys to purchase supplies for his isolated mountain store. Gallatin was always polite, and he brandished a wit that was ironic but never sarcastic. Though he spoke with an accent, he could write in clear and forceful English. He communicated even better in the language of numbers.

Gallatin shared Jefferson and Madison's aversion to debt, though his attitude arose from a different personal experience. Jefferson never managed to escape the debts he inherited from his father and father-in-law, while Gallatin simply avoided personal debt. In Gallatin's native Geneva, failure to pay debts resulted in the loss of the right to exercise the privileges of citizenship for both the debtor and his children.

Gallatin respected Jefferson and Madison despite having occasional differences of opinion with the two slave owners from Virginia. The Pennsylvanian joined a group advocating the abolition of slavery and supported Hamilton's Bank of the United States, an institution that Madison and Jefferson had fought. Gallatin's most severe criticism of Hamilton rested more on the sloppiness of cost controls and his accounting rather than on some grand philosophical difference. Hamilton left his post as secretary of the treasury in January 1795, shortly before Gallatin returned to Congress. Before his departure, the nation's first treasury secretary had published projections showing how the federal debt might be paid off in thirty years. He also called for higher taxes while noting that Americans strongly supported debt reduction, though not always the taxes required to do it. Hamilton left the Treasury Department in order to practice law to support his family financially. He continued to advise his successor and others allied against Jefferson and Madison.

Gallatin correctly suspected that Hamilton had borrowed more than many realized. He did so largely to fund shortfalls that resulted principally from faulty estimates rather than deliberate policy.[57] Days after Gallatin began his first term in the House of Representatives, the body unanimously passed his resolution to establish a committee to examine the federal finances and determine "whether further measures [were] necessary" to balance the budget and repay the debt.[58] A few days later, the House asked this Committee on Ways and Means to report on the "Public Debt, revenues, and expenditures."[59] An ad hoc committee of this nature had existed from time to time, but its responsibilities became more formal after Gallatin's resolution.

The following year Jefferson requested that Gallatin "reduce this [budget] chaos to order" and "present us with a clear view of our finances."[60] The congressman personally reviewed the Treasury's records and prepared the comprehensive "Sketch of the Finances of the United States," a two-hundred-page treatise that included detailed appendices.

Gallatin's "Sketch," published in 1796, served as the foundation for the budget policies of Jefferson's party. Higher interest payments, Gallatin argued, redistributed national wealth but did not increase it. A larger debt required interest payments paid for with either higher taxes or a reduction in other useful public spending. Moreover, federal debt reduced the amount of national savings that could be invested to build the new nation's economy, including needed manufacturing. If the nation used import taxes to pay down interest-bearing debt, the interest rate on the remaining debt would decline while savings available for investment would increase.

He described lessons from other nations "enfeebled by a public debt. Spain . . . and . . . Holland . . . still feel the effects of the debts they began to contract two centuries ago, and their present political weakness stands as a monument of the unavoidable consequences of that fatal system. . . . France, where the public debt . . . has at last overwhelmed government itself . . . Taxes in Great Britain, would, if unencumbered [by interest,] discharge the yearly expenses even of the war in which she is now engaged."[61]

Madison and Jefferson exulted in the financial genius of their young partner. Madison described Gallatin to Jefferson as "an absolute treasure . . . sound in his principles, accurate in his calculations, and indefatigable in his researches."[62] At last they had found an ally who could translate into actual budget math the ideas they could only describe in prose. The rustic folk in the hill country of Pennsylvania had sent to Congress a man who, for almost two decades, knew the budget by memory and, after he became Jefferson's secretary of treasury in 1801, would serve longer in that position than any other American. Gallatin attributed his rapid rise in influence, despite speaking "in a foreign language with a very bad pronunciation," to "laborious investigation, habits of analysis, thorough knowledge of the subjects under discussion, and more extensive general information, due to an excellent early education."[63]

Although Washington had come to believe that Jefferson treated Hamilton's administration unfairly, he shared his concern about debt. The first president's farewell address asked his fellow citizens to "discharge the debts," rather than "ungenerously throwing upon posterity the burdens which we ourselves ought to bear."

Vice President John Adams narrowly defeated his old friend Jefferson in the election to succeed Washington. In his inaugural address, the nation's second president warned that the "accumulation of public debts in other countries ought to admonish us to be careful to prevent their growth in our own." Adams advocated federal spending only of an amount that could be supported "by immediate taxes, and as little as possible by loans." A French insult to American pride soon tested that resolve.

When Adams took office in March 1797, both Europe and American policy toward various European nations were in disarray. The ruling French Directory lashed out at foreign and domestic enemies, funded its government by printing currency, and plundered other nations to supply needed revenue. France declared its freedom to attack ships trading with Great Britain, the dominant American trading partner. When the United States sent a delegation to France for the purpose of negotiating an end to attacks on American commercial vessels, French foreign minister Maurice Talleyrand conditioned negotiations on the payment of a bribe and demanded a $10 million loan to France.[64]

Americans were outraged by the requested bribe. Robert Goodloe Harper, a member of the Ways and Means Committee, expressed the public's attitude: "Millions for defense, sir, but not one cent for tribute!" Congress increased military spending, principally for the construction of naval vessels. Gallatin thought it foolish to arm against a French invasion, and reasoned that "if the sums to be expended to build and maintain the frigates were applied to paying a part of our national debt, the payment would make us more respectable in the eyes of foreign nations than all the frigates we can build." Like many in future generations, Gallatin was resigned to having his motives for opposing the military buildup questioned, but he pledged to persist even when "branded with the usual epithets[:] Jacobins and tools of foreign influence."[65]

Once the military spending measures passed, however, Gallatin took the lead in arguing for the use of higher taxes rather than debt to pay for it. It would not be the last time that some in Congress were more willing to vote to increase military spending than to vote for taxes needed to pay for that spending. President Adams sided with Gallatin. One of the unpopular taxes imposed at the time was the "window tax," based on the size of houses as determined in part by the number of windows.

If contemporary Americans seek to divine the budget policy of participants in the original Boston Tea Party, organized by John Adams's cousin, then they need look no further than the views of President Adams. He believed that taxes should be raised as needed to pay for spending appropriated by Congress.

Congress authorized $5 million in debt to fund the building of naval ships, though the net debt of the nation did not increase by this amount, since the Treasury paid down other debt shortly after the bonds were issued.[66] Maritime hostilities with France, conducted on each side principally through contractors—"privateers" working on a commission—provided little precedent for future budget policy. American policy during this Quasi-War was, at best, muddled. Vice President Jefferson at times hoped for a French invasion of Great Britain, while Secretary of State Timothy Pickering urged a formal alliance with Great Britain and declaration of war against France. Alexander Hamilton organized an army to resist a potential invasion by France. President Adams grew tired of the military frenzy and developed reservations about the military buildup he had requested.

Critics of Jefferson labeled him a traitor on account of his opposition to military preparations. Jefferson, however, believed that public opinion would vindicate his stance. He likened the war fever to a disease, arguing that "the doctor" was "on his way to cure it, in the guise of a tax gatherer." The vice president predicted that "excessive taxation" for military spending would soon "carry reason and reflection to every man's door, particularly in the hour of the election."[67]

That election victory came soon enough. Jefferson, Madison, Gallatin, and their allies won the presidency and a congressional majority in an election they would call the "Revolution of 1800." Hamilton, though he had been frequently at odds with Jefferson, ultimately helped facilitate his election to the presidency. He believed that Jefferson was opportunistic but honorable and that the other candidates, President Adams and Senator Aaron Burr, were temperamentally unfit for the office. Hamilton also correctly believed that Jefferson, with Gallatin's assistance, would preserve his national bank, whose notes served as an unofficial currency.

Pillars Supporting Limits on Debt

Though Jefferson had once criticized Hamilton's strong use of executive power, Jefferson's administration exerted more influence over Congress than did the Washington or Adams administrations. After all, President Jefferson, Secretary of State James Madison, and Secretary of the Treasury Albert Gallatin also functioned as acknowledged leaders of a party with a congressional majority. That party—originally formed as a means of organizing opposition to federal policies—now provided cohesion between the White House and Congress. President Jefferson dined twice a week with his party's congressional leaders. When Congress was in session, Gallatin invited key congressional budget allies, including House Speaker Nathanial Macon and Ways and Means Chairman John Randolph, to nightly dinners at his home on Capitol Hill. For years, this close cooperation resulted in a predictable budget process.

Treasury Secretary Gallatin instituted several commonsense budget practices that would serve as structural pillars for the American Fiscal Tradition. He shared Jefferson's commitment to presenting a budget "as clear and intelligible as merchants' books, so that every member of Congress and every man of any mind in the Union should be able to comprehend them, to investigate abuses, and consequently to control them."[68] Jefferson believed that lucid accounting allowed the public to judge the "comparative [budgets] . . . of different epochs."[69]

Gallatin prepared detailed reports of each year's spending.[70] He asked Congress to authorize funds for purposes more specific than the four broad budget categories that had been used during the Washington and Adams administrations. To enhance transparency, Gallatin also eliminated the secret operations of a "sinking fund" committee, instituted by Hamilton, that traded federal debt in public markets. Clear budget accounting became the first budget practice, or pillar, supporting limits on borrowing.

Gallatin also initiated the nation's first transparent "pay as you go" budget planning. He estimated the tax collections for the next fiscal year, subtracted all interest to be paid on debt, and then allocated the amount remaining into various, detailed categories of spending. This budget practice served to link the level of estimated taxes and spending. Secretary Gallatin's first budget draft, in 1801, dedicated about two-thirds of all tax revenues to interest payments and debt reduction, and cut everything else—primarily spending on the army and navy—to fit within the remaining third.[71] "Pay as you go" budget planning became another pillar supporting limitation of debt.

Congress in 1802 eliminated the unpopular taxes on whiskey and salt. However, Gallatin persuaded Congress to raise import taxes and place these revenues in a new Mediterranean Fund for use in the financing of naval protection of American shipping from pirates based in Tripoli. The dedication of taxes to a fund for a specific purpose tightened the link between spending and taxes. In fact, revenues from the original whiskey tax were earmarked for the specified purpose of debt service and reduction. This practice, used extensively in the twentieth century, became a third pillar supporting limitation of debt.

Gallatin's Treasury Department also performed some functions of a central bank. His planned retirement of debt expanded the nation's money supply without inflation, a practice with an effect similar to later purchases of debt by the Federal Reserve. In 1801 he became the first treasury secretary to bolster bank credit by shifting $50,000 in federal deposits to a sound bank that had a temporary liquidity problem.[72]

Americans supported Gallatin's goal of reducing debt. One report of the House Ways and Means Committee noted that the need to reduce debt was "too obviously true to require any illustration."[73] Jefferson observed that, apart from some past differences on foreign policy, "the bulk of both parties had the same principles fundamentally."[74]

Gallatin's drive to reduce federal debt benefited from rising import tax revenues. Most Americans lived on subsistence farms, and one in six was enslaved, but the nation's maritime industry blossomed. Gallatin reduced the debt from $83,038,050 to $77,054,686 in the first two years of the Jefferson administration.[75] By 1803, the debt represented less than a sixth of the annual output of the nation—half what it had been in 1790. While Europeans teetered on the precipice of the Napoleonic Wars and massive related debts, the United States refinanced its debt with lower interest rates. Almost all of its federal debt had been incurred to finance the War for Independence and to preserve the Union. The nation's federal leaders would soon decide whether to allow the use of debt for another purpose: securing borders and room to grow.

3

JEFFERSON'S PARTY DEFINES
THE LIMITS ON DEBT

1803–1824: Years when deficits exceeded debt service = 4
(1812–1815, War of 1812)

BORROWING FOR ROOM TO GROW

First Consul of France Napoleon Bonaparte spent his Easter Sunday, April 10, 1803, preparing for war. The de facto dictator, then only thirty-three, was considering how best to use French territory in North America to finance a likely war against Great Britain.

France had acquired—but not yet occupied—a vast amount of Spanish territory west of the Mississippi and north of the Rio Grande. Americans were still angry that Spain had temporarily limited their ability to store goods in the Port of New Orleans. In response the US ambassador to France, Robert Livingston, informed French officials that President Jefferson might seek help from the British navy to guarantee free access to the port.

Jefferson's threat signaled a new low in relations between the former English colonies and France. Just twenty years earlier the French fleet had forced the surrender of British forces at the decisive Battle of Yorktown. Jefferson never forgot France's crucial help during the Revolution, but he considered any nation that possessed New Orleans as the "natural and habitual enemy" of the United States because "the produce of three-eighths of our territory" had to pass through that city's port.[1] Americans in the new states of Kentucky and Tennessee were especially vulnerable to shipping disruptions on the routes from the Ohio and Mississippi Rivers to New Orleans.

Napoleon did not relish a battle with the United States, whose "numerous, warlike, and frugal population" he regarded as "an enemy to be feared."[2] He was also haunted by the loss of more than sixty thousand French soldiers, including his own brother-in-law, in an unsuccessful effort to suppress a slave revolt in the colony of Saint-Domingue, present-day Haiti, in 1802. France could not afford a similar diversion of resources during a war with Great Britain.

French diplomat Pierre Samuel du Pont de Nemours had formulated a means to resolve the issues troubling his friends Bonaparte and Jefferson. Du Pont was an early member of a group of French intellectuals who the English called "economists." In 1802 Du Pont counseled Jefferson to dispense with military threats and instead just offer to buy New Orleans. He advised Jefferson to calculate the cost of war and agree to pay "a part—a half, let us say," of that sum. Du Pont urged prompt action, since the price might rise if French soldiers took possession of New Orleans. Du Pont also knew that Albert Gallatin planned to retire all federal debt within fifteen years and noted in a letter to Jefferson that the United States would get "an excellent bargain . . . from a pecuniary point of view" by extending the federal debt another "three or four years" to purchase New Orleans.[3]

Du Pont, in this same letter to Jefferson, mentioned that he had just set up a factory in Delaware that might satisfy the American need for gunpowder and wryly implored the president to "not burn it against" France. Jefferson authorized Du Pont to explore with Napoleon the idea of the United States purchasing New Orleans, but also insisted that Du Pont convey the threat of a potential American alliance with Great Britain.

Napoleon listened to Du Pont carefully. On New Year's Eve 1802 Jefferson received a letter from Du Pont recommending a price of about $6 million.

Jefferson never referred publicly to Du Pont's advice, but he did ask Congress in January 1803 to delay military preparations against France and to send James Monroe to the country for the purpose of negotiating a settlement. Seventeen years earlier Monroe had led the fight against a proposed Confederation treaty that would have recognized Spanish control of the Mississippi, earning him credibility among settlers in the West who demanded military preparations to secure their access to the Port of New Orleans. Monroe also commanded respect in France, where he had arrived as the American minister in 1794, when many other nations had withdrawn their embassies because of the chaos of the French Revolution.

Gallatin asked Congress to set aside $2 million for a potential monetary settlement, while Jefferson secretly authorized Monroe to pay up to 50 million livres, or $9 million, for New Orleans and the part of Spanish Florida around Mobile Bay.[4] In light of the Jefferson administration's frugality, Monroe arranged to pay for his own trip to France by selling his silverware to Secretary of State Madison.

On Easter 1803, with Monroe due to arrive any day in Paris, Napoleon knew he had to decide quickly how best to use his vast New World claims. Great Britain was not going to relinquish Malta, as demanded in an ultimatum from Napoleon, so the young French ruler's attention turned to war. France lacked the domestic bond market that enabled the British to ramp up military spending quickly. Excessive taxation had resulted in the protests that incited the French Revolution, and Bonaparte had avoided similar unrest only by financing his prior military campaigns with loot from conquests.

The Port of New Orleans remained closed to free storage of American exports, and Napoleon was aware that the US Congress had grown impatient with diplomatic approaches to that problem. He did not assign resolution of this issue to Foreign Minister Talleyrand, whose demand for bribes had precipitated the Quasi-War with the United States only six years earlier.[5] Napoleon turned instead to his finance and naval ministers. Finance minister Francois Barbé-Marbois, a friend of President Jefferson who had married an American woman, argued in favor of a quick sale. Minister of the Navy Denis Decrès, however, wanted to retain New Orleans because he believed the city could become a major world port if a canal was ever built to cross the Isthmus of Panama.

It was time for Napoleon to make a decision.

Talleyrand believed that "speech was given to man to disguise his thoughts," but Napoleon announced his decision unambiguously to Barbé-Marbois on April 11, 1803: "It is not only New Orleans that I cede; it is the whole colony, without reserve. I know the price of what I abandon. . . . I renounce it with the greatest regret; to attempt obstinately to retain it would be folly. . . . Have an interview this very day with Mr. Livingston."[6]

Ambassador Livingston, a proud, nearly deaf New Yorker who had administered the first inaugural oath to President Washington, expressed interest in France's offer while explaining that his instructions only concerned New Orleans and perhaps the portion of Florida around Mobile Bay. Though the French offered 100 million francs, Livingston speculated that his country might not object to paying 20 million francs, or less than $4 million.[7] Talleyrand, who had insinuated himself in the negotiations, rejected the low price, and Livingston responded that he would present the French proposal to Monroe, who had just arrived in Paris.

Livingston resented Monroe's role in the negotiations, but nonetheless graciously invited the Virginian and his clerk to dine at his home in Paris. During dessert, they noticed someone watching them through the dining room window. Livingston recognized the man as the French finance minister and invited him inside. The anxious Barbé-Marbois told the Americans that Napoleon made decisions "like lightning" and warned them to conclude the deal quickly.

Napoleon did indeed act decisively when Barbé-Marbois advised him that the United States could not afford the price of 100 million francs. Napoleon cut his price for the half a billion acres of French territory to 50 million francs, in cash.[8] It was, Talleyrand commented, history's greatest drop in the value of real estate.

On April 24 Barbé-Marbois called on Monroe, who was lying on a couch incapacitated by back pain from the long voyage, and presented him with an agreement drafted by Napoleon himself. After brief negotiations, they settled on a price: a note for 60 million francs for all French territory in North America and an additional 20 million francs in cash earmarked to pay claims against France by influential merchants whose cargoes had been lost to French privateers.[9] One can detect the hidden hand of Du Pont in the deal; the 50 million franc sum that Napoleon had "pulled out of the air" was the same amount that Jefferson had previously authorized. It was the same amount that bankers were offering to pay for a 60 million franc note payable by the United States over fifteen years.

Napoleon intended to transfer to the United States all of the territorial rights France had acquired from Spain, but he refused the American request for a more detailed description of the territory being sold. France had acquired the land by a secret treaty in 1800 in which Napoleon had made a promise that he had not yet kept. The transfer was also complicated by the fact that Spain had arguably ceded control to France of a region now called Texas, an area where Spanish citizens lived. Gallatin later discouraged Jefferson from trying to occupy that portion of the territory, "the miserable establishments of Santa Fe and San Antonio."[10] Aware that

Spain might still claim ownership of some of the Louisiana territory, Napoleon insisted on the equivalent of what lawyers call a quitclaim deed—a legal instrument conveying any rights of the holder without guarantying the legal validity of those rights.

Within weeks of signing the agreement with the United States, Napoleon declared war on Great Britain.

The Louisiana Purchase was paid for with a bond, at the time referred to as "stock," for $11,250,000, accruing annual interest at 6 percent.[11] The final principal payment was not due for fifteen years, which was consistent with the estimated date for the retirement of all other federal debt. The American assumption of private claims against France, valued at $3,750,000, seemed far more important to Livingston and his merchant friends in New York than it did to either France or the Jefferson administration.[12] Gallatin could pay that amount out of cash balances.

Napoleon needed the cash immediately, so France sold the bond to a Dutch bank and its British partner, Baring Brothers. They paid 78.5 cents on each dollar of the principal amount of the American debt. Gallatin perceived something a bit strange about the transaction, since American 6 percent notes traded in European markets at a smaller discount. The Dutch bankers, in fact, repackaged the bonds in smaller denominations and sold them at face value, netting a large profit. History does not record all the details of the dealings between the bankers and French officials, but one might draw conclusions from the fact that the corrupt Talleyrand had investment bankers in place to purchase the debt for less than market value. Barbé-Marbois received cash from the sale in the form of a commission set by Napoleon.

The United States could not have afforded the Louisiana Purchase without incurring long-term debt; its entire annual budget, exclusive of interest, was only $4 million in 1802.[13] The Louisiana Purchase doubled the nation's territory, secured the nation's borders, and allowed for future growth, all at the price of pennies an acre. Yet one aspect of the transaction troubled President Jefferson. He and Madison had opposed Hamilton's use of powers not explicitly granted in the Constitution, which said nothing about buying vast new territories. Jefferson quickly drafted a constitutional amendment authorizing the purchase.

Bankers would not provide funds to France until the Senate ratified the treaty and Congress authorized the debt. When warned by Gallatin and Livingston that further delays could lead Spain to challenge the legality of the sale, Jefferson dropped the idea of a constitutional amendment and characterized the Louisiana Purchase as an implied use of the power to make treaties and defend the nation.

Jefferson did, however, articulate a principle to justify this use of federal debt. Incurring debt to acquire territory directly benefited the next generation. As Jefferson explained in August 1803: "It is the case of a guardian, investing the money of his ward in purchasing an important adjacent territory; and saying to him when of age, I did this for your good. . . . I thought it my duty to risk myself for you."[14]

Most Americans rejoiced at news of the Louisiana Purchase, though critics of the Jefferson administration decried the potential cost of protecting the new territories. Years later, the historian Henry Adams described public reaction: "the Federalist [anti-Administration] orators of July 4, 1803, set about their annual task of foreboding the ruin of society amid the cheers and congratulations of the happiest society the world then knew."[15] Adams's grandfather, John Quincy Adams, was the only Federalist member of Congress from New England to vote for the ratification of the Louisiana Purchase, although he unsuccessfully fought to resolve the issue of the rights and future governance of the people residing in the new territory. Americans in the West celebrated the loudest. On hearing of the Louisiana Purchase a young Tennessee politician, Andrew Jackson, wrote to Jefferson about how it put smiles on the faces of everyone he saw. Even Virginian John Taylor, the most doctrinaire philosopher of limited government, defended the Louisiana Purchase as a means of providing an outlet for healthy growth away from cities.

Jefferson's party crushed its opposition in the 1804 elections. In the president's second term, his administration used budget surpluses to steadily pay down debt. Gallatin had warned Jefferson years earlier that if the federal government could not generate enough revenues from land sales and import taxes, their administration would have to cut spending, forestall plans to reduce unpopular taxes on whiskey, or delay planned annual reductions in the debt. He argued strenuously against delaying debt reduction, which would push debt onto "ensuing generations."[16]

Fortunately, flourishing trade during the initial years of the Napoleonic Wars produced revenues from import taxation that consistently exceeded estimates. Warring nations refused to trade with one another, and US merchants and ships often filled the gap. The fledgling democracy became one of the world's leaders in maritime commerce. Import taxes averaged $12.2 million annually from 1801 through 1811, up sharply from the previous high of $7.5 million in 1797. The amount of outstanding debt fell from $86.4 million in 1803 to $45.2 million in 1811.[17]

Treasury Secretary Gallatin understood that the nation needed to conserve its credit capacity for use in an emergency. So, unlike the practice in more recent history, Gallatin used bonds with long maturities—even if that meant paying somewhat higher interest rates. Long maturities on federal debt gave the United States more flexibility in dealing with the unknown.

In 1806, after learning of a larger federal budget surplus than had been originally projected, the president urged Congress to begin considering investments for the "great purposes of the public education, roads, rivers, canals."[18] Jefferson asked Gallatin whether the country could afford to fund a great national university, though Gallatin had his own dreams for federal investments, with roads and canals topping the list. His store in Pennsylvania was located near the intersection of the headwaters of the Potomac and Ohio Rivers, so he appreciated the need for a road linking the markets east and west of the Appalachian Mountains.

Jefferson and Gallatin refrained from pushing for spending on projects they personally favored so long as they doubted the public's willingness to pay for them with higher taxes. Instead, they endorsed various long-run goals—like funding for higher education and roads—without rushing to gain credit for implementing them until the Treasury paid down more debt. Gallatin began to devote half of the annual federal budget to a sinking fund or reserve to ensure debt reduction, a use of funds that decreased annual interest expense and preserved national credit for use in response to a serious threat.

One such threat loomed on the horizon. As France and Great Britain tightened trade embargoes against each other, they intensified their attacks on US ships.[19] Napoleon seemed to back off when confronted with American protests, but Great Britain's navy did not. Against Gallatin's advice in 1807, Jefferson persuaded Congress to respond to these attacks with an embargo on trade with Great Britain. That trade embargo illustrates how the law of unintended consequences preys on minds distracted by lofty ideals. The embargo hurt the nation's economy far worse than British naval attacks. It crippled port cities and caused a sharp drop in the import tax revenues that sustained federal budgets. Gallatin used the Treasury's cash reserves to cover the shortfall. Congress repealed the embargo on the last day of Jefferson's presidency.

The naval budgets in Jefferson's second term provide a valuable lesson on the perils of detaching defense spending from the practical requirements of a military mission. Everyone at the time recognized that the United States could not afford a navy capable of fully protecting its commerce against the massive British navy. Against Gallatin's advice, Jefferson yielded to congressional pressure for a naval response by supporting construction of a fleet of small coastal gunboats, an affordable alternative to a full oceangoing fleet. Yet the gunboats proved useless, since they could be sunk by a single cannon shot from British warships.

Near the close of his presidency, Jefferson expressed to Gallatin his pride in how they had subordinated other policy goals—including ones they highly valued—in favor of debt reduction. He hoped that future federal leaders would follow their example and entertained little doubt that his friend James Madison, the country's next president, would do so. Madison took the oath of office on March 4, 1809, almost twenty years after he and Jefferson had discussed the need for strong and practical principles to limit the burden of federal debt. Jefferson offered budget advice to the nation's fourth president: "extinguishment of our public debt [would] open upon us the noblest application of revenue that has ever been exhibited by any nation."[20]

Gallatin, who stayed on as secretary of the treasury, also counseled Madison that they should pay off more debt before participating in military combat. By early 1811 Gallatin battled Secretary of State Robert Smith and his brother, Maryland senator Samuel Smith, over the amount spent on the navy. The Smiths controlled Maryland's electoral votes and pressed for higher naval spending to support a stronger response to attacks on US shipping and to bolster employment in their state's shipyards. Gallatin grew weary of fighting the Smiths' demands and offered to resign. Gallatin's steady budget leadership had become invaluable, however. The president asked James Monroe, his former rival in his first congressional race and more recent competitor for succeeding Jefferson in the White House, to replace Robert Smith as secretary of state.

Monroe became convinced that the United States should retaliate against attacks on its shipping. Former President Jefferson remained skeptical. In April 1811 he expressed to Du Pont his "hopes that, if war be avoided, Mr. Madison will be able to compleat the paiment of debt with his term." Jefferson also shared with Du Pont his vision for future federal finances: "We are all the more reconciled to the tax on importations, because it falls exclusively on the rich. . . . Our revenues once liberated by the discharge of the public debt, and its surplus applied to canals, roads, schools, etc., . . . the farmer will see his government supported, his children educated, and the face of his country made a paradise by contributions of the rich alone. . . . The path we are now pursuing leads directly to this end."[21]

THE WAR OF 1812

Voters defeated more than half of the incumbents in the House of Representatives in 1810. Young "war hawks" like Kentucky's Henry Clay and South Carolina's John C. Calhoun dominated a new House majority after the election. Congress was not yet willing to raise taxes to build a navy to protect US shipping against British attacks. Ezekiel Bacon of Massachusetts, chairman of the House Ways and Means Committee, observed: "If the people will not bear the necessary taxes, it cannot with propriety be said that they will bear the contemplated war, and the sooner we know it the better."

Jefferson's friend Jean-Baptiste Say, the most influential economist at the beginning of the nineteenth century, wrote in his 1803 *Treatise on Political Economy* that "the whole skill of government . . . consists in the continual and judicious comparison of the sacrifice about to be incurred, with the expected benefit to the community."[22] The War of 1812 forced federal leaders to weigh carefully the mix of debt and taxation to pay for war. Until the twenty-first century, the federal government would never consider waging a prolonged war without asking for public support in the form of higher taxes to finance it.

When the House finally voted to raise taxes in February 1812, President Madison wrote to Jefferson that the resolve to take "the dose of taxes" showed that people "would not flinch from the contest" with Great Britain.[23] In March, Congress authorized $11 million in debt, at 6 percent interest, to prepare for combat, though the Senate delayed action on the tax increase.

The ostensible reasons for the War of 1812 seem odd to modern eyes. New England merchants and shippers adamantly opposed a war declared for the official purpose of protecting their shipping from naval attacks. They were far more willing to endure occasional losses than a potential British trade embargo. Meanwhile, politicians from states in the South and West, which suffered least from maritime attacks, clamored for war. In reality, many residents of those states saw the war to be both a means of defending national honor and a pretext for occupying Canada and taking territory from Native Americans they had identified as British allies. On June 1, 1812, President Madison sent Congress a message detailing America's grievances against Britain, which included predation on American trade, the kidnapping ("impressment") of American sailors for service on British vessels, and the alleged support of Native American attacks on Western settlers.

The House—under the leadership of Speaker Henry Clay—voted quickly for war. The Senate passed the declaration of war by a margin of 19 to 13 following an initial tied vote and lengthy debate. From the outset critics labeled the conflict "Mr. Madison's War" and predicted defeat. The US Navy had five old frigates and none of the large ships of the line that formed the backbone of the Royal Navy. The US Army consisted of only six thousand soldiers—most paid a dollar a day—and assorted state militias. In contrast, Great Britain fielded a quarter of a million professional soldiers and possessed a navy of over a thousand warships. Moreover, Great Britain reacted with anger in response to the American attempt to invade Canada at a time when British forces were fighting Napoleon in Europe.

The divisive war wounded Madison politically. He was barely reelected in 1812, when most of the nation's merchants supported the rival candidacy of DeWitt Clinton, mayor of the nation's commercial center, New York City. Madison would have lost without the support of Gallatin's former constituents in Western Pennsylvania.

Before 1812 the new nation had added significant amounts of debt for only two purposes: to strengthen the Union by assuming state debts from the American Revolution in 1790 and to expand and secure the nation's borders in 1803. Congress had authorized debt for naval construction in the 1790s, but the political chaos surrounding the Quasi-War made it difficult to treat that action as a lasting precedent. Funding for the War of 1812, however, *did* set a precedent for a third use of debt: financing war.

Creditors were reluctant to lend as much money as Congress sought to borrow. Of the $11 million in bonds authorized by Congress in March 1812, Gallatin managed to sell only $6.2 million, a third to individuals and the rest to banks.[24] Many New England banks, some of the nation's strongest, refused to buy Treasury debt issued to finance a war they vehemently opposed. In June 1812 Congress authorized the Treasury Department to issue $5 million in notes.

By 1813, with bank credit exhausted, Gallatin asked for help from three of the nation's wealthiest businessmen. Each of the three—shipping magnate Stephen Girard, fur trader John Jacob Astor, and international financier David Parish—had immigrated to the United States and made fortunes from trade during the preceding decade. They bought some bonds on their own account and resold some bonds to others. On March 24, 1814, Congress authorized a new $25 million loan, which prompted a lively public debate on the nation's capacity to sustain a debt of that size.[25] Opponents of the loan questioned whether the nation could ever repay it, while its supporters argued that the nation's economy provided a sufficient potential tax base, comprising $2.567 billion in property and an estimated annual national income of $237 million.[26] To facilitate commerce, advocates of the loan estimated that the nation needed currency—in the form of bank notes—totaling no more than $47 million, which would leave about $53 million in remaining bank notes.[27]

Modern politicians frequently make exaggerated claims along the lines of: "The United States faces a great challenge, perhaps its greatest ever." When doing so, they ought to consider the situation confronting President Madison in the fall of 1814. By October 1814 Secretary of the Treasury George Campbell reported that the federal government had collected only half the revenue it needed for that year and was $50 million short of future requirements.[28] Worse still, the federal government could not find anyone to lend it more money and would soon be unable to pay interest on existing debt. Merchants accepted Treasury notes only at a deep discount, and the government's gold supply was exhausted. Treasury Secretary Campbell concluded this gloomy report by resigning after only eight months on the job. Secretary of the Navy William Jones advised Alexander Dallas, whom Madison nominated to be the new secretary of the treasury: "Something must be done speedily or we shall have an opportunity of trying the experiment of maintaining an army and navy and carrying on a vigorous war without money."[29]

Just weeks earlier, British soldiers had burned down much of official Washington, including the White House and Capitol. President Madison only narrowly escaped after Secretary Monroe rode in from the front lines near midnight to warn of the British approach. The president, armed with dueling pistols, left town the next morning on a horse he had to borrow when his own mount went lame.

Madison implored Congress to raise taxes in the wake of the occupation. He argued that "in offering their blood Americans give the surest pledge that no other tribute will be withheld."[30] Congress increased all taxes and began imposing new or higher taxes on luxury goods such as carriages, gold and silver watches, and household furniture. In September Monroe, serving as both secretary of state and secretary of war, borrowed $5 million on behalf of the government on his own signature and credit to supply troops led by General Andrew Jackson.[31]

Peace prospects seemed slim during that grim autumn of 1814. Gallatin had made little progress after traveling to Europe the preceding year for the purpose of negotiating a peace treaty. He and other American negotiators, including John Quincy Adams, had little bargaining power when British officials eventually agreed to meet with them. America's attempts to invade Canada had failed, and British troops occupied parts of Massachusetts. President Madison instructed the American delegation to seek peace without a resolution of the issues giving rise to the war.

Time was not on the side of an insolvent United States. Days later Madison received word that British negotiators were demanding part of Maine, control of the Great Lakes, and swaths of territory for their tribal allies in exchange for peace. The weary but determined president worried about domestic opponents of war who threatened to dissolve the Union. Gouverneur Morris, who drafted much of the Constitution, urged a "union of commercial [Northern] states to take care of themselves, leaving the War, its Expense, its Debt" to Madison.[32] On October 17, 1814, Massachusetts called for a convention of the New England states to discuss how to end the war, with or without the existing federal government. That same day Alexander Dallas, the capable new secretary of the treasury, told Congress that the United States could incur more debt without increasing taxes.

Like his predecessors Hamilton and Gallatin, Dallas had immigrated to the United States as a young man. He received a fine education in Edinburgh, Scotland, and he and Gallatin had gravitated toward one another early in their careers, when Dallas introduced Gallatin to the woman he later married. Secretary Dallas found that imports—the foundation of the prewar tax system—had shrunk to $13 million in 1814, less than a tenth of the level in 1807.[33] In late 1814 Dallas notified creditors that the United States might default on its debt—the first and last notice in American history of a potential default or a failure to pay interest when due. Dallas recommended a balanced budget consisting of $21 million in tax revenues and spending.[34]

The effective interest rate on federal debt had already soared to double-digit levels. Bonds could be sold for merely 88 percent of their face value, and even at that discount the federal government had to accept paper notes valued by merchants at 80 percent or so of their face value. A congressional investigation conducted years later concluded that Treasury obligations with the face value of $80 million yielded just $34 million gold dollars during the war.[35]

Secretary Dallas requested the formation of a new national bank. Jefferson disagreed, arguing that the Treasury Department should continue issuing interest-bearing notes. President Madison sided with Dallas and explained to Jefferson that a bank with private capital at risk could impose greater discipline than a Treasury controlled by the White House. In December 1814, however, Madison vetoed legislation creating a national bank because the bill prohibited the bank from lending to the government.

Delays in communications across the Atlantic forced Madison to speculate about the status of peace negotiations. He did not learn until later that his most trusted negotiator, Gallatin, experienced the peril inherent in federal indebtedness to foreign creditors. Alexander Baring, a banker and member of Parliament, had served for years as the agent for the US government's payment of European creditors. Before the next installment on the bond from the Louisiana Purchase came due in January 1815, Baring asked Gallatin how he could be expected to "advanc[e] sums for the service of a Government with which we are at war?"[36]

Yet, when things looked the worst for the United States in the fall of 1814, Great Britain's own excessive debt undermined that nation's will to continue the war. Its debt approached 800 million pounds, or nearly $4 billion—twice the size of British annual national income after a decade of wars with Napoleon and the United States.[37] British bonds, once the most creditworthy in the world, sold at only 55 percent of face value. Parliamentary debate on the war with America centered on its costs and related taxes.

Prime Minister Robert Banks Jenkinson, Earl of Liverpool, sought to end the conflict. In October 1814 the British cabinet asked the nation's preeminent military hero—Arthur Wellesley, Duke of Wellington—to consider taking command in America to end the conflict with either decisive victory or negotiation. He declined the post, explaining that he "would have great reluctance in undertaking the command, unless we made a serious effort to obtain peace."[38] Wellington privately urged Gallatin to remain patient. The duke knew, however, that some veteran soldiers from his Spanish campaign, commanded by his brother-in-law General Edward Pakenham, had already sailed to capture New Orleans.

Lord Liverpool, the prime minister, informed his foreign secretary, Lord Castlereagh, that they should "bring the American War to conclusion," impress the pro-American Russian czar, and "pay serious attention to the state of our finances, and to the difficulties we shall have with the property tax" in Parliament.[39]

On December 24, 1814, the British and American delegations in Ghent signed a peace treaty, news of which took weeks to travel across the Atlantic. The same day Gallatin noted that Baring Brothers agreed to disburse funds due to satisfy the Dutch bondholders who had financed the Louisiana Purchase.

The War of 1812 was a financial fiasco for the United States and Great Britain. Both nations had to pay exorbitant interest rates and had reached the limit of publicly acceptable taxation. That financial reality was imprinted on the memory of a new generation of American leaders, who would seek a more sustainable system of financing for national security.

Most Americans preferred to remember the Battle of New Orleans rather than the nation's wartime financial crisis. Ten days before the peace treaty was signed, more than eight thousand British soldiers on sixty ships entered Lake Borgne, a dozen miles from New Orleans. Even after signing the treaty, Lord Liverpool privately expressed to Wellington his hope that "the American war should terminate with a brilliant success on our part." General Andrew Jackson—who had been abused by British soldiers when he was captured during the Revolutionary War—had a different outcome in mind.

General Jackson's regular army consisted of seven hundred soldiers, and he enlisted various residents in the New Orleans area—including free blacks and a gang of pirates—to form a militia. Volunteers from Tennessee and Kentucky arrived daily to join them. His makeshift force prepared for battle by building a dirt wall along the banks of a dry canal that crossed the British approach to New Orleans. General Pakenham planned a frontal assault to break the American line and panic the volunteer militia.

On January 8, 1815, Jackson rose from bed at one a.m. and told his subordinates to prepare for battle. Columns of British redcoats fell before volleys from American cannons and rotating lines of fire from frontier soldiers whose marksmanship had been honed by hunting. Eight hundred Scottish Highlanders, the royal regiment whose bagpipes and discipline under fire had struck fear in the hearts of Napoleon's veteran armies, advanced steadily toward the American line despite heavy losses. American cannon fire cut down General Pakenham and his staff just as they saluted the Highlanders, who then retreated. When the smoke cleared, Jackson's army had suffered seventy-one casualties, while the British force had lost more than two thousand soldiers.

Word of the astonishing victory in New Orleans arrived on the East Coast at the same time as news of the peace treaty. Suddenly Mr. Madison's War became everyone's victory. In Gallatin's words, the war's final outcome made citizens feel "more American." Jackson's parting words to his victorious troops summarized the new spirit of nationalism: "Natives of different states, acting together, for the first time, in this camp; differing in habits and in language, instead of viewing in these circumstances the germ of distrust and division . . . have reaped the fruits of an honorable union."[40] The reputation Jackson earned from the brief but decisive battle made him the nation's foremost hero since Washington.

In 1815 Treasury Secretary Dallas found it easier to sell bonds.[41] He raised $9.3 million by selling bonds for 95 percent of their face value, or par, yielding 7 percent.[42] National debt peaked at $127.3 million, and the Treasury rapidly paid off notes issued during the war as imports and tax collections soared.[43]

Madison and Monroe—and a younger generation of congressional war leaders including Henry Clay, John C. Calhoun, and William Crawford—emerged from the conflict with enhanced stature and a new conception of federal taxation and responsibilities. They resolved to strengthen the federal tax system and the nation's army and navy.

Greater Federal Commitments and Taxation

The war forged a new consensus about the responsibilities of the federal government. Deprivation caused by wartime British trade embargoes spurred support for a stronger federal role in economic development. Pennsylvania writer and economist Mathew Carey sold more than ten thousand copies—a huge number at the time—of a tract that called for Jefferson's party to endorse a more professional peacetime army, improved transportation, a sound currency, a central bank, and a tax system that encouraged domestic manufacturing.

The Treasury Department reached similar conclusions in its 1814 "Report on Manufacturing." The report's author, Tench Coxe, had attended the fateful Mann's Tavern gathering in 1786 that spawned the Constitutional Convention. He later worked for Alexander Hamilton at the Treasury Department, where he helped research Hamilton's celebrated 1791 "Report on Manufactures." Coxe respected Hamilton's intellect but ultimately left the Treasury to support financial policies championed by Gallatin. In his 1814 report Coxe described how mechanized looms could allow a population less than half the size of New York City or Philadelphia, the nation's biggest cities, to produce enough textiles to clothe the nation's eight million residents. "To neglect, in our country, the due use of such an advantage, would evince a destitution of common sense."[44] Modern machines could help "every farmer and hamlet" to participate in the "profits of the woolen branch" of commerce. Domestic distilleries could likewise produce enough whiskey to eliminate the need for imports. Like Mathew Carey, Coxe advocated investing in roads and canals to transport raw materials to the Atlantic Coast and manufactured goods to the country's interior.

Madison's annual message to Congress in December 1815 proposed federal programs along the lines outlined by Carey and Coxe. Madison's nationalist message echoed some of Hamilton's themes, though the nation could now afford the cost of a standing army and public infrastructure without additional debt.

On April 27, 1816, Congress increased the level of import taxes to 20 percent on most goods and 25 percent on cotton and wool textiles. Congressman John C. Calhoun vigorously defended these higher taxes in the House, arguing that strong domestic manufacturing benefited even agricultural centers like his own state of South Carolina: "The farmer will find a ready market for his surplus produce . . . and . . . a certain and cheap supply of all of his wants."[45] Calhoun, a forceful speaker, explained that without domestic production and internal transportation, the nation could be victimized again by a foreign-imposed embargo. Calhoun also joined the majority in Congress who voted to charter a new Bank of the United States.

Interest and principal payments on debt absorbed at least half of tax revenues during Madison's administration after the war. In the last full fiscal year of Madison's presidency, the Treasury collected $36 million in import fees—roughly $15 million more than budgeted—and applied a $20 million surplus to debt reduction.[46]

Secretary of the Treasury Dallas adeptly refinanced debt after the war. Treasury gold reserves rose, as cotton prices and production soared in response to demand from British textile mills. A few days before the end of the Madison administration, Dallas resumed the prewar requirement that Treasury funds be deposited solely in banks that paid depositors gold on request. By then the nation's credit and currency had recovered from their 1814 collapse.

Madison concluded his presidency in 1817 by quietly vetoing a bill, sponsored by Calhoun, that created a new trust fund to finance roads and canals. Though Madison cited constitutional reasons for the veto, he had signed earlier legislation to fund roads. As a result, his veto of Calhoun's bill is best interpreted as an attempt by the president to draw a line on spending. Until later in the century, presidents cited constitutional issues in their veto messages as a means of trying to sidestep the question of whether a president should veto legislation simply because of a policy difference with an elected majority in Congress.

James Madison left the White House almost three decades after his work to retire Revolutionary War debts had culminated in the adoption of the Constitution. He and Jefferson had carefully justified each exceptional new use of federal debt. Though Madison's intellectual detachment at times seemed ill-suited for a wartime leader, he emerged from the War of 1812 with a reputation for perseverance and the ability to withstand criticism—traits one might expect from the author of the First Amendment. In 1817 John Adams mused to Jefferson that history would judge Madison's administration as greater than all of the previous administrations combined. Madison's success in defending national honor during the War of 1812 virtually ended organized opposition in the form of a Federalist Party.

In contrast, the public held Congress in low regard shortly before Madison left office. Voters who had accepted higher taxes to reduce debt and pay for defense were outraged when House members converted their pay from $6 a day during sessions to an annual stipend of $1,500.[47] The backlash from this raise swept 70 percent of incumbent House members out of office in the election of 1816.

Great Britain emerged from the Napoleonic Wars with an enormous national debt, high interest and tax rates, and a paper currency trading at a discount to its official value in gold and silver coin. American political, business, and academic leaders kept abreast of issues that arose during heated British budget debates of the time, including the ideas of Member of Parliament David Ricardo, who had made a fortune trading in British debt during the Napoleonic Wars. Ricardo's influential 1817 treatise on economics and public finance, *On the Principles of Political Economy and Taxation*, employed mathematical rigor to prove a point familiar to Jefferson, Madison, Gallatin, and most people in business: high tax revenues required to service high debts inhibit investment and economic growth. Ricardo asserted that the use of debt rather than taxes to finance public spending ought to cause citizens to save more money in anticipation of higher taxes to follow. However, he later clarified that concept by noting that people would likely fail to save more because their tendency to think of the expense of debt "only in proportion to what we are at the moment called to pay for it in taxes, without reflecting on the probable duration of such taxes."[48]

Parliament rejected Ricardo's plan to retire debt by purchasing it at market value—an almost 50 percent discount from face value—with funds provided by an immense, one-time tax on all national wealth. For the first half of the nineteenth century, debt service consumed half of the British budget and provided a salient reminder concerning the risks of excessive public debt.

Borrowing During a Recession

A surprisingly slim majority of the congressional caucus endorsed James Monroe as Madison's successor. Monroe had the aura of authority conferred on those considered Founding Fathers. Nonetheless, many members of Congress instead supported Secretary of the Treasury William Crawford in order to signal their weariness of Virginia's perceived monopoly on the presidency.

Since the controversies that marked the tension between Jefferson and Hamilton had ended, Monroe believed that the United States had outgrown its need for political parties. He sought to achieve unity by appointing to federal offices both former supporters and opponents of Jefferson's coalition. He asked his rival, Crawford, to continue to serve as secretary of the treasury—a decision President Monroe would eventually regret.

Crawford attempted to fill the vacuum of leadership in the Jeffersonian party organization. The handsome and personable politician exploited his powerful office to build a national political base outside his home state of Georgia. Crawford courted an older generation of political power brokers, including Thomas Jefferson, by extolling the virtues of limited government. At the same time, he endorsed higher spending for frontier fortifications, a stronger navy, an expanded postal service, and new pensions for veterans.

Early in the Monroe administration, rising revenues from import taxes helped Secretary Crawford juggle conflicting commitments to higher spending and limited government. Various branches of the new Bank of the United States extended easy credit, especially for the purchase of federal lands. The official books of the bank showed a substantial net worth until 1819. But, as in 2008, the bank had a low amount of liquid reserves in relation to its liabilities. It would prosper only so long as its loans were repaid and nothing prompted depositors and note holders to demand immediate payment in gold and silver.[49]

Easy bank credit fueled an enormous boom in the sale of federal lands. Buyers stood in lines extending beyond the doors of many US Treasury Land Offices; the phrase "land office business" came to be used as a synonym for any boom. Some land purchasers planned to plant cotton for export, while others sought to resell their new land for a profit. In Jefferson's first term, the president and Gallatin had set a minimum price of $2 an acre and allowed payment over four years.[50] That policy continued through Monroe's first term. Buyers could pay the Treasury by tendering bank promissory notes. Debt owed to the federal government for land purchases soared from $3 million in 1815 to $23 million in 1819.[51] Cash receipts for land sales in 1819, however, amounted to less than $4 million.[52]

From 1816 through 1818 the federal government sold tens of millions of acres of land, principally in Alabama, Mississippi, Louisiana, Arkansas, Missouri, Illinois, and Indiana. The mass migration of Americans into these territories resulted in the admission of a new state to the Union during each of six consecutive years after 1815. One action by these new state governments—expanding the right to vote to white males regardless of land ownership or wealth—would soon make national politics more popular.

The land rush during 1816–1818 in certain respects resembles the real estate bubble preceding the Great Recession of 2008. In each period, citizens borrowed vast amounts to purchase real estate based on the assumption of ever-rising values, while politicians relaxed credit in support of greater home ownership. When land prices fell in 1819, the federal government and the Bank of the United States were left with a large portfolio of uncollectible loans.

Crawford's friend William Jones ran the second Bank of the United States. Jones had a fondness for hard drink and an aversion to detail. He did not understand the role of the Treasury and Bank of the United States in managing credit to prevent excessive monetary expansion.

In December 1818 the federal government asked to withdraw $2 million in gold from its deposits at the bank in order to pay the final installment on the bonds issued for the Louisiana Purchase.[53] When Jones could not find sufficient funds in the bank's vaults, he had to borrow gold from European banks. Audits revealed more problems after Jones resigned. The reserves of the bank's Baltimore branch had disappeared. Its cashier, James W. McCulloch, had lent to Western land speculators, to bank officers, to himself, and to a business owned by the bank's patron and Gallatin antagonist, Samuel Smith—then chairman of the House Ways and Means Committee. McCulloch also made history by refusing to pay state taxes on federal bank notes. His refusal led to the Supreme Court's decision of *McCulloch v. Maryland*, which established the supremacy of federal law and the right of the federal government to undertake actions necessary and proper to discharge its duties.

When Secretary Crawford and the bank's new management belatedly tightened credit in 1819, state banks failed, and the prices of goods and services fell. Cotton production increased while demand declined as a result of a sharp downturn in the British economy. The price of cotton—the principal export of the United States—dropped sharply.

During the Panic of 1819, the nation's first major recession, revenues from import taxes—the lifeblood of the federal budget—fell from $26 million in 1817 to $15 million in 1820.[54] Crawford faced a difficult choice when Congress asked him for a report on monetary policy. Congressmen from frontier states with many insolvent debtors pressed him to issue paper money to counter deflation and fill the federal budget gap, while those from East Coast merchant centers adamantly opposed any policy that could risk future inflation. Crawford's charm was not sufficient to finesse the dilemma faced by all central bankers during credit contractions. The Treasury's report acknowledged that a limited circulation of paper money might curb deflation, but recommended against setting a precedent that might permit future federal leaders to unleash inflation with the federal printing press.

In 1820 former president Madison weighed in, asserting that "a paper currency rigidly limited in its quantity to purposes absolutely necessary, may be made equal and even superior in value to specie [i.e., gold or silver]. But experience does not favor a reliance on such experiments. Whenever the paper has not been convertible into specie, and its quantity has depended on the policy of the government, a depreciation [i.e., loss of purchasing power through inflation] has been produced by an undue increase, or an apprehension of it."[55] The 1820 debate over expanding the money supply to stimulate the economy during a severe credit contraction was the first of many in the nation's next two centuries.

The modest borrowing to offset sharp drops in revenue during the Panic of 1819 also presaged a feature typical of federal borrowing during later downturns: federal revenues almost always drop more than anticipated. Exuberant markets and mistaken forecasts often precede severe downturns. Budget planning is difficult because economic cycles do not conform to federal fiscal years. And until the Great Depression, the federal government compiled little "real time" economic information, making projections more uncertain. In short, the American Fiscal Tradition's final refinement—allowing federal borrowing during downturns—in part reflected the inevitable effect of any unanticipated drop in revenues.

Secretary Crawford belatedly informed President Monroe and Congress of the looming budget deficit. Congress authorized a $3 million bank loan in 1820 and an additional $5 million loan in 1821.[56] The amount of approved debt turned out to be far greater than the federal deficits, which amounted to only $1.7 million, or 5 percent of the total federal spending during those two years.[57] Moreover, in 1820 and 1821 the federal government expended far more in debt service than the amount of its deficits, and it borrowed primarily to refinance some principal and interest due on war debt. The 1820–1821 policy of borrowing during recession bears little resemblance to the post-2000 practice of *adding* recession-related borrowing to large "normal" deficits.

Thomas Jefferson faulted Congress for the budget deficit in 1820. Even before the downturn, he wrote to his friend, publisher Thomas Ritchie, that Congress seemed "to be at a loss for objects whereon to throw away the supposed fathomless funds of the Treasury." He further noted that "the people were themselves betrayed into the same frenzy" and expressed hope that "the deficit produced, and [the] heavy tax to supply it" would "bring both to their sober senses."[58]

In 1820 James Monroe became the last president to be reelected without facing significant opposition and the only one ever reelected during a severe downturn that began after he took office. Monroe warned in his inaugural address of the need to raise taxes if federal revenues continued to fall short of spending. Following an acrimonious debate in 1821, Congress slashed spending for the army and fortifications along the nation's borders. Critics of the cuts in military spending, such as Secretary of War John C. Calhoun, complained of the "economizers."

The Panic of 1819 marked the first, but not the last, time that the federal government would incur debt to offset the loss of revenues during a downturn. Because only 6 percent of the population lived in cities, and farms of the era were largely self-sufficient, there was no perceived need for any kind of federal effort to prevent starvation.

The federal government did, however, provide a social safety net by blocking foreclosures. The Relief Act of 1821 reduced the debts of hundreds of thousands of citizens who had borrowed to buy federal land.[59] Land was then the principal route to self-sufficiency and opportunity, in much the same way education and specialized skills would be later in the nation's history. Since loan forgiveness did not require cash outlays, a review of budgets alone can understate the impact of this federal power in the nineteenth century.

In 1824 Congress raised import taxes, less to pay for new spending than to counter the competitive threat of Great Britain's robust wool and iron industries. The tax bill passed over opposition from the cotton-growing South and with the support of wool-producing states—New

York, Pennsylvania, and Ohio—that could determine the outcome of a presidential vote in the Electoral College.

Monroe had become a symbol of the nation's historical transformation by the time he left office in March 1825. The former Revolutionary War captain and friend of Washington evoked the traditions of an earlier era. He wore the outdated knee-length pants of the colonial period. He led the nation from the depths of a debt crisis at the Constitutional Convention to a point at which he could express, in his last annual message to Congress, "a well-founded hope" that the national debt could be paid off when the last outstanding bond matured in 1834. Without the burden of debt, he argued, the nation could use its tax revenue on "objects as may be most conducive to the public security and welfare."[60]

Monroe was the last of three presidents from Virginia who guided the nation for the first quarter of the nineteenth century. For each of them, the danger of debt was not merely theoretical. After the Panic of 1819 Jefferson, Madison, and Monroe were each forced to consider selling their farms to pay off personal debts.

Since President Washington's inauguration, the federal government had added debt only for four identified purposes. It did so to preserve the Union (1790), secure and extend the nation's borders (1803), fight a war (1812–1815), and fund deficits during a recession (1820–1821). Americans clearly understood the reason for incurring each of these debts. After 1821 the federal government would not borrow again until the onset of the nation's first full-scale depression, eighteen years later.

These and other precedents established during the Republic's first decades soon evolved into traditions with the authority of an informal constitution. Other such traditions, apart from the use of debt, included a two-term limit for presidents, the use of presidential power to remove appointees, a standing army led by professional officers, and the committee organization of Congress.

Jefferson had once expressed to his friend Du Pont the importance of setting budget precedents: "I hope we shall be able by degrees to introduce sound principles and make them habitual. What is practicable must often controul what is pure theory; and the habits of the governed determine in a great degree what is practicable."[61] By 1824 the principle of limited debt had grown to rely on habitual budget practices—clear accounting, "pay as you go" budget planning, the use of trust funds to link new spending and taxes, and congressional approval of the amount and purpose of any new debt. Those practices served as pillars of the American Fiscal Tradition of borrowing for limited purposes.

After the close of Monroe's presidency in 1825, Americans began to develop another critical feature of the unwritten constitution. Their nation would soon embrace a more formal and organized system of political parties.

4

A Revived Democratic Party Pays Off the Debt

1825–1853: Years when deficits exceeded debt service = 9
(1838–1843, Depression after the Panic of 1837;
1846–1848, Mexican War)

The Crisis of Presidential Authority

President John Quincy Adams made an astonishing request in his annual message to Congress on December 6, 1825. He asked congressmen to enact his ambitious spending program without being "palsied by the will of their constituents."[1] Politically savvy senator Martin Van Buren found the president's attitude hard to believe. Members of Congress should ignore the will of the voters? Van Buren, a disciple of Thomas Jefferson, noted that even Alexander Hamilton had respected the need for representatives "to conduct the government on the principles" of their constituency.[2]

Since Van Buren himself helped block the Adams spending plan, he recognized the source of the president's frustration. Adams's had outlined an ambitious agenda for the construction of roads, canals, lighthouses, universities, and even "lighthouses of the skies" (national astronomical observatories).[3] Citizens easily grasped the usefulness of public works projects but loathed the cost of higher taxes. "Pay as you go" budget planning limited federal spending to no more than the amount voters were willing to pay in taxes. That limit was a matter of high principle, not—as Adams suggested—a form of palsy or paralysis.

While prior presidents had tried to *persuade* the public of the desirability of a given program, they had never lectured Congress on the need to spend more money than could be generated by a publicly acceptable level of taxes. Few congressmen, if any, heard that their constituents were willing to be taxed at a higher rate to build "lighthouses of the skies."

Van Buren felt that something had gone wrong with the American presidential selection system that had placed a person with Adams's attitude in the White House. The veteran politician from New York had earned the nicknames "the Little Magician" and "the Red Fox" because of his skill in exploiting political opportunities before others did. After the election of 1824 he moved quickly to change the presidential selection process by building the nation's first modern national political organization, a party with a platform grounded in traditional fiscal principles.

Adams had entered the White House in 1825 after winning 31 percent of the popular vote, less than the votes cast for retired General Andrew Jackson. Since none of the four major candidates—each of whom professed loyalty to the ideals of Jefferson—won a majority in the Electoral College, the House of Representatives had the constitutional responsibility for choosing the next president from among the top three candidates. Adams won the presidency only with help from the fourth-place candidate, powerful Speaker of the House Henry Clay. Jackson's followers called their political alliance a "corrupt bargain" when Clay became Adams's secretary of state.

Delegates at the Constitutional Convention in 1787 had found it difficult to devise a satisfactory means of presidential succession. It appeared at the time that no one besides George Washington and a handful of other leaders from the Revolution were famous enough to command an Electoral College majority in such a geographically dispersed nation. Toward the end of the convention, weary delegates voted to let the House of Representatives—with each state casting one vote—select the president if no candidate won a majority in the Electoral College. This means of selecting a new president could inevitably lead to compromise candidates who lacked the authority of a broad democratic mandate.

That adverse outcome was avoided for decades as a result of presidencies of a pantheon of Founding Fathers. They included a virtual dynasty of Virginia tobacco farmers—Washington, Jefferson, Madison, and Monroe—who led the nation for all but four of its first thirty-six years. Along with John Adams, each of them could personally remember the collapse of the Confederation under the weight of crushing Revolutionary War debt.

Flaws in the process for choosing a new president were exposed during President Monroe's second term, from 1821 to 1825, when the administration split into factions supporting rival candidates. Monroe, the last of the Founding Fathers available to serve as president, rejected even the informal party leadership role. In 1822 he wrote to Madison that "surely our government may go on and prosper without the existence of parties."[4] Yet, without a more established party system, the nation lacked a means for narrowing the field of presidential nominees.

Changes in the nation's electorate made it more difficult for an elite to designate the nation's chief executive. Propelled by extraordinary birth rates, the population of the United States had tripled since President Washington's inauguration. Waves of settlers poured into new states that had extended the right to vote to all free, tax-paying white males regardless of whether they owned property.

This geographic expansion generated more intense competition for federal resources, especially for transportation improvements. Great Britain replaced its imports of raw cotton from India with cotton produced largely by slave labor in Southern states. In turn, thriving cotton farms and growing coastal cities became potential markets for corn, wheat, and pork produced in the country's interior. Farmers sought more efficient ways to ship their products to distant markets. Many states envied the success of the Erie Canal, which had strengthened the role of New York City as the nation's foremost commercial hub.

Regional conflicts concerning import taxes also intensified in the early 1820s. Iron producers, strongest in Pennsylvania, welcomed taxes offering protection from iron produced in Britain by firms that used more efficient technology. New England textile mills feared competition from modern British textile looms. Southern cotton producers, however, resisted higher import taxes that raised the prices of goods such as iron farm tools and the coarse British wool used to clothe slaves.

Martin Van Buren had learned how to use a political organization to resolve festering conflicts. He grew up on a small farm in upstate New York. The area was dominated by Dutch American aristocrats who owned massive estates cultivated by tenant farmers and who—along with New York City's merchant class—controlled much of the state government.

Van Buren fought that elite by forming a disciplined coalition consisting of small farmers and merchants in upstate New York and middle-class citizens in New York City. As New York extended the right to vote to tax-paying white males who did not own land, Van Buren integrated them into his organization.

Like many interest groups today, Van Buren's coalition enhanced its power with the ability to deliver a bloc of votes. After resolving conflicts among its constituency through negotiation, the organization expected its individual members to unite behind the final decision. Silas Wright, a key Van Buren lieutenant, described what was required of members of the party once it took a position on an issue: "The first man we see step to the rear, we cut down. . . . They must not falter, or they perish."[5] By 1822 Van Buren's coalition—known as the Albany Regency—was no longer a group of outsiders. It won control of the legislature and filled most political appointments in what had become the nation's most populous state and dominant commercial center.

Van Buren believed that the practice of resolving internal differences in order to create a large, powerful voting bloc could be used to nominate a national presidential candidate.[6]

A New Democratic Party

Adams, a former professor and diplomat, lacked the interpersonal skills and political organization required to rally Congress behind his administration. It would be daunting, however, for Van Buren and his allies to unseat a sitting president at a time of national peace and prosperity. To prevail over Adams in the election of 1828, Van Buren would need to find a marketable candidate, craft a unifying platform, and neutralize an issue that could energize opponents in the swing states critical to victory in the Electoral College. This three-part strategy today would hardly seem innovative, but it was bold in the 1820s, when many Americans still viewed party organizations as unnecessary or even subversive.

Van Buren shared his vision with potential allies, beginning with Vice President Calhoun, whom Van Buren's organization would back for the vice presidency.[7] He also enlisted support from the leader of Jefferson's disciplined Virginia organization, publisher John Ritchie. In January 1827 Van Buren described to Ritchie how Jackson's election based on military service rather than shared principles "would be one thing. His election as the result of a combined and concerted effort of a political party, holding in the main to certain tenets & opposed to certain prevailing principles, might be another and far different thing." Van Buren urged Ritchie to help forge an alliance between Southern planters and "plain" citizens in the North, who together would agree politically "in the main to certain tenets."[8] They began to refer to themselves as Democratic Republicans.

Andrew Jackson—the candidate favored by Van Buren, Calhoun, and Ritchie—posed some risks. The venerated Jefferson had considered Jackson "one of the most unfit men" he could think of for the presidency.[9] In 1821 Jackson himself had remarked to a journalist: "Do they think that I am such a damned fool as to think myself fit for President of the United States? No, sir; I know what I am fit for. I can command a body of men in a rough way, but I am not fit to be President."[10]

Yet no other American—apart from former presidents—rivaled Jackson's fame. Even though Jackson lived on a plantation maintained by slave labor, many voters of modest means could identify with a frontiersman who rose from penniless Revolutionary War private to become a general who had defeated Europe's best.[11] In contrast, Van Buren and his allies portrayed Adams as a pampered elitist, even though the president lived a spartan existence that included brisk morning walks before the president swam across the Potomac's chilly waters naked.

Throughout 1828 Van Buren labored to elect Jackson, even though he did not meet the general until after the election. He did know, however, that Jackson rewarded supporters and punished opponents. That type of loyalty would be essential for maintaining discipline in a national party organization.

There were few policies that would serve as what Van Buren had described to Ritchie as "common tenets"—in modern parlance, a party platform. The diverse factions within Van Buren's broad coalition could agree on little more than the need to balance the budget and pay off the national debt. Accordingly, the party attacked Adams for proposing extravagant federal outlays for a national university, naval academy, new department to manage federal lands, and, of course, the astronomical observatory.

Though he was equipped with both a candidate and a unifying budget principle, Van Buren still had to resolve the divisive issue of import taxes. Henry Clay, who led Adams's reelection campaign, would use that issue to try to capture critical electoral votes. Most Americans supported at least some import taxes on *manufactured* goods as a means of paying federal bills. Taxes on imported *raw materials* posed a greater political challenge. Manufacturers sought to obtain raw materials as cheaply as possible, while woolgrowers sought protection against imported raw wool. Shepherds and farmers in the hills of upstate New York, Western Pennsylvania, and Eastern Ohio would eventually breed herds that could yield fine wool, but in the meantime they sought some cost advantage over wool imported from Scotland.

Twenty-first-century journalists report on targeted appeals from presidential campaigns to the voters of Pennsylvania and Ohio, states that often swing the balance in the Electoral College. Van Buren and Clay battled intensely for voters in those states in 1828. To prevail, Van Buren had to convince enough voters in Western Pennsylvania, Eastern Ohio, and his own upstate New York that Jackson's election would not threaten import taxes on iron and raw wool. He had to thread a needle, by conveying that message without alienating Jackson's core base of Southern supporters, who opposed those very taxes. The result was the Machiavellian Tariff of 1828, soon to be called the Tariff of Abominations.

Van Buren's friend and political ally, Congressman Silas Wright of New York, initiated the legislative ploy by bringing to the House floor a bill raising import taxes on imported iron, textiles, and raw materials like wool, molasses, and rope. Molasses was used by New England distillers and rope by shipbuilders in Massachusetts. With support from the large delegations of New York, Pennsylvania, and Ohio, a House majority passed Wright's bill. States in the South and New England commanded a majority in the Senate. Van Buren reassured Jackson's Southern supporters that they could defeat Wright's bill in the Senate so long as it retained high taxes on materials essential to New England's merchants. Accordingly, "Jackson men"—including those opposed to higher import taxes—voted against all amendments to reduce the harsh taxes on New England's raw materials.

Then Van Buren sprang a trap. Some New England textile mills sought to avoid the economic impact of high taxes on raw wool by supporting even higher taxes on woven wool. Unexpectedly, Senator Van Buren and another Jackson loyalist voted with New England and the Adams men. Calhoun and other foes of higher import taxes realized only afterwards that the last-minute addition of a higher import tax on finished woolen textiles had captured the votes of Massachusetts senator Daniel Webster and enough other New Englanders to secure the passage of Wright's legislation.

Van Buren's scheme to neutralize the issue of import taxes worked. Van Buren and Wright could now reassure proponents of higher import taxes in Pennsylvania, Ohio, and New York that they had nothing to fear from a Jackson presidency. Southern congressmen attacked President Adams for signing it into law. Jackson himself remained silent on the issue. Congressional veteran John Randolph of Virginia opined that a bill touted as protecting domestic manufacturing in fact "served principally to manufacture . . . a President."[12]

Van Buren had completed his three-part plan for melding diverse regional constituencies into a national organization. He backed a popular candidate, highlighted the unifying goals of paying down debt and curbing extravagant spending, and deprived Adams of an economic issue—import taxes—that could have rallied support in swing states.

The "Democratic Republicans" were better organized than the "Adams men," also known as "National Republicans." In 1828 Jackson handily won both the Electoral College and a popular vote swollen by a flood of newly enfranchised voters. Voter participation had tripled from its level four years earlier. The United States had a new system for nominating presidents, which Van Buren would refine four years later with use of a convention. Within a dozen years a formal party system soon would become an essential feature of the unwritten American constitution. For the next century and a half, parties would serve as the most powerful means of enforcing the American Fiscal Tradition's limits on debt.

PAYING OFF DEBT

Andrew Jackson formed opinions based on personal experience rather than scholarship, which explains his particular hostility toward debt. When Jackson first arrived in the nation's capital as a young congressman from Tennessee in 1795, he tried to make a fortune by selling land in the wilderness back home. Finding few buyers, he finally managed to sell fifty thousand acres in exchange for a $10,000 note.[13] Jackson promptly endorsed that note over to a merchant in payment for goods destined for

Jackson's general store in Tennessee. The maker of the note failed to pay and landed in debtor's prison, leaving Jackson—as endorser—liable for the amount due. Jackson worked for over a decade to pay it off and afterwards viewed freedom from debt as an essential element of independence. In Jackson's first inaugural address, in 1829, he pledged to work for "the extinguishment of the national debt, the unnecessary duration of which is incompatible with real independence."[14]

Jackson's secretary of the treasury made the populist case for paying off debt in terms that: "Interest is now paid to capitalists, out of the profits of labor; not only will this labor be released from the burden, but the capital, thus thrown out of an unproductive use, will seek a productive employment; giving thereby a new impetus to enterprise . . . at a lower charge for interest than before."[15] The American policy of paying off its debts contrasted with that of Great Britain, where debt service from its wars—including the War of 1812—consumed over half of all tax revenues for decades following the Napoleonic Wars.

The Jackson administration, like Jefferson's, subordinated all other goals to its drive to retire the federal debt. For that reason the president did not quickly repeal the unpopular Tariff of Abominations. His position surprised and disappointed Vice President Calhoun and many among the South's planter aristocracy. High import taxes generally functioned to limit the growth of imports, but the booming demand for cotton exports bolstered the ability of merchants to pay for greater volumes of imports even with the tax burden. Import tax revenues rose steadily during Jackson's presidency, which allowed the administration to retire debt while funding popular improvements in public transportation at record levels.[16]

Jackson and Secretary of State Van Buren buttressed party discipline by rewarding political allies with appointments and retaliating against opponents. Henry Clay, whom Jackson blamed for blocking his election to the presidency in 1825, was singled out for harsh treatment. Jackson's veto in 1830 of a project favored by Clay established a powerful and enduring budgetary precedent. The drama began without fanfare, when Congress voted to fund the Maysville road connecting Clay's home state of Kentucky with the Ohio leg of the National Road. Van Buren later bragged to a friend that he worked hard to hide the president's views on the road bill in order to enhance the impact of Jackson's veto. James Madison had downplayed his 1817 veto of a public works bill, while Jackson's 1830 veto message was strongly worded and widely publicized.

The veto was a political masterstroke. Jackson, like Madison in 1817, justified the veto in part based on constitutional objections to public works. But Jackson's constitutional objection was transparently a ruse. While Madison objected to an open-ended fund for public improvements, Jackson vetoed a project that was similar to many others already in existence. Members of Congress were dismayed that the president would use an unexpected veto to blame them for wasteful spending. Meanwhile, voters applauded the president's role as the guardian of tax dollars.

Vetoes of spending bills by future presidents would anger Congress while earning respect from taxpayers. A century after Jackson's presidency, Franklin Roosevelt—a careful student of history—would ask his staff to actively search for spending bills that he could veto as a sign of his financial stewardship. Presidents rarely vetoed spending bills after traditional limits on debt collapsed in the twenty-first century.

Jackson's use of the presidential veto and attacks on the independence of the Bank of the United States accelerated the organization of political opposition. That opposition coalesced around state organizations comprised of Jackson's adversaries. They began to call themselves "Whigs," a name used by a party of the English gentry who had fought for limits on the power of the king, particularly limits on spending and taxes. Though Whig leaders Henry Clay and Daniel Webster tried to flesh out a political platform, the issues that motivated that anti-Jackson coalition were frequently grounded in the personality-based politics within each state.

Vice President Calhoun did not call himself a Whig, but he rallied South Carolina against the 1828 Tariff of Abominations by claiming that a state had the right to nullify, or disregard, federal laws it considered unconstitutional. Jackson considered this idea to be a form of treason. "Nowhere can it be found where the right to nullify a law, or to secede from this Union, has been retained by the state[s]. . . . This," he affirmed in an 1832 letter, "is my creed."[17] The plainspoken president warned a congressman from South Carolina that if anyone blocked the enforcement of federal laws, Jackson would personally "hang the first man I can lay my hand on engaged in such treasonable conduct, upon the first tree I can reach."[18] Advocates of nullification in South Carolina backed down.

Vice President Calhoun also joined Senators Henry Clay and Daniel Webster in blocking confirmation of Van Buren's appointment to the position of US ambassador to Great Britain. Van Buren exacted revenge by replacing Calhoun as the vice presidential nominee at his party's first national nominating convention, held in 1832. By then people referred to members of the party of Jackson and Van Buren as Democrats. The Jackson–Van Buren ticket won the election of 1832 by a lopsided margin, though their Southern support had eroded.

The apogee of Jackson's eight years in office occurred on January 8, 1835, in a festive gathering of more than two hundred national leaders at Brown's Hotel in Washington. They celebrated both the anniversary of the Battle of New Orleans and the final payment on the national debt. Van Buren read a toast on behalf of the president: "The Payment of the Public Debt: Let us commemorate it as an event which gives us increased power as a nation." Senator Thomas Hart Benton of Missouri—whose brother had shot Jackson twice in a brawl twenty-two years earlier—led off almost a hundred other toasts. "In the 58th year of the republic," Benton pronounced, "Andrew Jackson being President, the national debt is paid and the apparition, so long unseen on earth, a great nation without a national debt!"[19]

Five days after the banquet, someone tried to shoot the president outside the US Capitol. The aging but frontier-hardened Jackson beat his assailant to the ground with a cane.

While Americans shared a common pride in the nation's ability to pay off its debt, they argued about how to handle budget surpluses. From 1829 until the end of Jackson's administration in 1836, the federal government collected $250 million—including extraordinary payments for the sale of public lands—and spent $153 million.[20] The Treasury could not hoard gold and silver coins without depriving the nation of much of its currency.[21] Senators Calhoun and Clay lined up a congressional majority in support of distributing tens of millions of surplus federal dollars to the states. Jackson vetoed that bill but ultimately allowed a new version of the popular concept to become law ahead of the 1836 election. This would be the first, but not the last, of several instances in American history—including in 1857 and 2001—when Congress made plans to spend a surplus just as it began to disappear.

Federal funds distributed to states in 1836 and early 1837 were invested by state governments in banks, canals, and railroads. Many state governments supplemented those investments with state debt, principally obtained from foreign creditors.[22]

The Panic of 1837

Martin Van Buren tried to nurture a more populist image during the 1836 election campaign. Democrats used the slogan "Vote for OK," based on the initials for Van Buren's Old Kinderhook farm on the Hudson River. These initials would eventually become part of American English, signifying assent without enthusiasm.

Some Democrats sought to appeal to frontier voters by nominating a folksy vice presidential candidate, Richard M. Johnson of Kentucky. Johnson's fame rested in part on his claim of having killed the Native American leader Tecumseh during the War of 1812. Johnson's personal life itself reflected the frontier's unique mixture of bigotry and individualism. He married a slave, Julia Chinn, and took responsibility for raising their two children. When she died, Vice President Johnson lived with another slave and worked as a bartender when he was not presiding over the Senate.

Van Buren prevailed in the election, though by a narrower margin than in Jackson's two triumphs. The Whigs might have won had the contest occurred a year or so later. Van Buren, the first president born as an American citizen, was also the first president to take office at the onset of an economic depression.

Like the Great Recession of 2008, the multiyear downturn called the Panic of 1837 followed a real estate bubble fueled by easy credit. A land rush had started two years earlier, when federal and state-chartered banks lent vast amounts to purchasers of federal land, mostly in regions around the Mississippi River and Great Lakes. The bubble burst when the British central bank began accumulating gold and pushed Great Britain into recession with rising interest rates.[23] As British demand for cotton fell, so did US farm income. Credit contracted when American banks failed. Many bank notes became worthless, and bank depositors often lost their savings. By 1840, the prices of thirty basic commodities had fallen 25 percent below levels in 1837. From 1837 to 1840 the amount of the principal currency—bank notes—dropped from $149 million to $106 million.[24]

Eight state governments defaulted on their debts to foreign creditors when property tax revenues declined during the Panic of 1837. Van Buren's administration refused state requests for federal grants. During the

following decades the vast majority of state governments adopted constitutional limits on their ability to incur debt. Limitations on debt were
routinely inserted in the constitutions of new states. All but a handful of
states still retain these limits.

Van Buren and many Democrats blamed banks for the Panic of 1837,
while Whigs blamed the policies of the Jackson administration, especially
Jackson's "war" on Nicholas Biddle's Bank of the United States. However,
modern economic historian Peter Temin persuasively attributes the 1837
downturn to international events like the British recession and a contraction in the US money supply that was precipitated by the diversion of
Mexican silver exports. US banks had imported Mexican silver to enhance
their reserves, but by the late 1830s China had absorbed Mexican silver
to finance its imports. The nation's first depression—preceded by a real
estate bubble and prolonged by a European debt crisis and Chinese trade
policy—provides valuable lessons forgotten by many political leaders after
2000.

The 1837 depression gutted federal revenues. Federal land sales had
soared from $4.8 million in 1834 to $14.7 million in 1835 to a record
$24.8 million in 1836. Land sales then dropped to $6.7 million in 1837
and even lower thereafter.[25] Import tax revenues plummeted as well. When
the value of cotton exports declined, the nation could afford fewer imports, and import tax collections fell from $23.4 million in 1836 to $11.1
million in 1837.[26]

As a result, in 1837 the federal government experienced an unprecedented peacetime deficit of $12.3 million, about one-third of federal spend-
ing.[27] Cash balances from surpluses after Jackson's debt repayment in 1835
might have been sufficient to cover this shortfall without borrowing, but
Congress had already distributed $28 million to the states pursuant to leg-
islation adopted in 1836. The Van Buren administration and Congress
slashed spending, principally for the army. They cut federal outlays by a
third between 1837 and 1840, which was still not by enough to offset the
decline in revenue from import taxes and land sales.[28] With the exception
of a brief period in 1839, during which a European drought boosted demand for farm products, federal deficits continued until the end of 1843.

Van Buren resisted occasional calls for federal spending to stimulate the
economy. In a September 4, 1837, message to Congress, he decried the
fact that "all communities are apt to look to government for too much . . .
especially at periods of sudden embarrassment and distress."[29]

Financing the budget shortfall posed a challenge to a Democratic ideology so grounded in opposition to debt. The Van Buren administration refused to borrow from a banking system that it blamed for the downturn. Senator Calhoun, who had not spoken to Van Buren for years, made peace with the administration and came to its aid with an alternative to selling long-term bonds to banks. He proposed that the Treasury meet its obligations by issuing short-term notes, bearing little or no interest. To Calhoun, "the elements of a true and stable currency" consisted "partly of gold and silver, and of paper, resting not on the credit and authority of banks, but of the Government itself."[30] The notes with little or no interest issued in the Panic of 1837 had some characteristics of "paper money," though they were not legal tender, that is, currency that law required creditors to accept at face value in payment of debt. The notes, however, could be used to satisfy federal tax obligations.[31]

Calhoun instinctively understood how monetary expansion might counter deflation. During a credit contraction, the United States could finance deficits with short-term notes and manage to avoid inflation, since the supply of these notes satisfied the need for circulating currency and liquid bank reserves.

The concept of expanding currency to cover deficits was nothing new. For thousands of years governments had generated income by taking the difference between the amount paid by an official mint for metal used in coins and the face value of coins in mints. This source of income—called seigniorage—could be abused whenever it significantly lowered the purchasing power of the coin. On occasion, monarchs had collected taxes by clipping off a portion of all outstanding coins. Modern seigniorage or monetization of debt occurs when the Federal Reserve buys Treasury debt for the long term in exchange for cash or Federal Reserve credit convertible to cash.

Throughout American history, federal leaders have used short-term debt with low interest rates to help minimize interest expense or the stigma associated with higher long-term debt. They did so at the beginning of the Civil War and during the first six years of the Vietnam War. When federal leaders began their borrowing binge in 2001, the Treasury lowered the interest cost in part by shortening maturities. In 2011 the Federal Reserve monetized debt in an amount offsetting all federal borrowing that year.

The issuance of short-term notes might have helped curb deflation, but the Van Buren administration neutralized that effect by hoarding coins it had received for taxes and land sales. Van Buren ignored former Treasury Secretary Albert Gallatin's warning that the Treasury's accumulation of metal currency depleted bank reserves needed to support foreign trade. Van Buren tried to appease monetary conservatives in his party who insisted on conducting transactions using coins of gold and silver rather than commercial bank notes.

Borrowing for Recession and War and Paying Down Debt

No American president—other than Monroe—has ever been reelected after annual national income fell below the level at which he took office. In 1840 Van Buren became the first casualty of this political reality. Before retiring to New York after losing the presidency, Van Buren—the architect of the first modern American political party—warned of the dangers inherent in borrowing with long-term bonds, which he said would have a tendency to "concentrate ultimately in the coffers of foreign stockholders."[32]

Like modern opposition politicians who promise to bring prosperity when elected during a downturn, Whig leaders were ill prepared to deal with the economic crisis that continued after their election victory. The party itself was a heterogeneous association that included old New England federalists, like Daniel Webster; Southern advocates of states' rights, like John Tyler; and advocates of higher import taxes being used to finance a national system of transportation, like Henry Clay.

William Henry Harrison, the Whig candidate for president in 1840, had served as governor of the Ohio territory during the Jefferson administration. At the time of his election to the White House, he was serving as a local court clerk. Whigs mounted a symbol-laden campaign that emphasized Harrison's "log cabin" values and fondness for hard cider, the cheap drink of the frontier. They cast Van Buren as a pampered Eastern aristocrat, the same way Jackson supporters had depicted John Quincy Adams a dozen years earlier, and they blamed the depression on "Martin Van Ruin."

The sixty-eight-year-old Harrison died of pneumonia a month after delivering the longest inaugural address in history during a bone-chilling snowstorm. Harrison's vice president, John Tyler, inherited the budget crisis. Though Tyler disliked taxes, he abhorred deficits and reluctantly signed a bill preventing a scheduled reduction in import taxes.

Tyler's secretary of the treasury, Tom Ewing of Ohio, tried to distance the Tyler administration from Van Buren's reliance on short-term notes.

He attempted to sell $12 million in bonds, an amount greater than the capacity of the fragile banking system. Ewing wrote and Congress passed legislation chartering the Fiscal Bank of the United States. Tyler vetoed it as an infringement on the rights of state-chartered banks. Ewing tried to avoid that problem with a new bill creating the Fiscal Corporation of the United States, an entity that had the sole function of accepting deposits and purchasing federal debt. At Calhoun's urging, Tyler also vetoed that bill. Treasury Secretary Ewing subsequently resigned, and frustrated Whigs expelled the president from their party.

Though federal leaders had argued about how to borrow during the depression, the nation's track record of paying down debt served it well when the economy recovered in 1843. The Treasury was able to market a long-term bond at a modest effective yield of 4.82 percent.

Van Buren's political party prepared for a comeback in 1844, the year in which it officially adopted the "Democratic Party" name. Van Buren himself steadily lined up support for another presidential nomination. He was confident in his ability to find common ground within a party. In 1844 that familiar ground experienced the tremors of an earthquake that would eventually shatter its foundation and national unity. Party politics began dividing along the fault line of slavery.

Van Buren sought to stifle the very discussion of the emotional topic of slavery. Neither he nor anyone else could silence John Quincy Adams, however. Adams had returned to Washington as an independent member of the House of Representatives in 1830. Since then, his impolitic voice—one that had once urged members of Congress not to be "palsied" by the will of constituents—repeatedly reminded citizens that slavery violated the ideals of Christian morality and democratic equality. He frustrated Democratic and Whig leaders with a long and ultimately successful fight against congressional rules that prohibited legislative debate over slavery. Every year Adams's message gained resonance, particularly among devout Christians in the North, a group whose numbers grew during that era's Great Awakening. Appeals to widely shared moral values tend to prevail in American politics when they are not countered by some other deep conviction. That fact explains the historical aversion to saddling future generations with debt. In 1844 Calhoun felt compelled to defend slavery by writing a racist tract that claimed enslavement was the only "moral" way to incorporate Africans and their descendants into American society.

Moral issues brook little compromise. Adams and Calhoun turned the debate over whether to annex Texas into a national referendum on the extension of slavery. The Democratic and Whig frontrunners for the presidential nomination in 1844, Van Buren and Henry Clay, tried to separate the issues of Texas and slavery by embracing the concept of territorial expansion while opposing the annexation of Texas on the grounds that it would provoke war with Mexico. Many Texans invited annexation, since their republic had been unable to balance its budget or pay its debts.

Jackson's strong endorsement of the annexation of Texas undermined Van Buren's position in the days leading up to the Democratic nominating convention. Van Buren, the Little Magician, ran out of tricks after unsuccessfully trying to eliminate a convention rule—that he had once endorsed—requiring a two-thirds majority vote for the nomination of a presidential candidate. After numerous ballots, a tired and deadlocked convention abandoned Van Buren and nominated the first "dark horse" presidential candidate, James Knox Polk of Tennessee.

Polk proceeded to win a very close election and then appointed the unusual Robert Walker, who had led the fight to preserve the two-thirds rule at the convention, as secretary of treasury. A tiny man with a quick mind and acerbic wit, Walker combined elite East Coast credentials with frontier sensibilities. He had been educated at the University of Pennsylvania and married Benjamin Franklin's granddaughter before moving to Mississippi to seek his fortune. As a senator from Mississippi, he became the most vocal advocate for annexing Texas.

Polk and Walker's relentless pursuit to annex the state led to war with Mexico, a war Walker financed with debt and taxes imposed on Mexican commerce. With a strong economy and good credit history, the federal government was able to sell bonds in exchange for amounts paid entirely in gold and silver coins. To pay for their war, Polk's government issued net debt of $49 million in bonds and Treasury notes.[33] The Treasury received bids totaling $57.7 million for an $18 million bond issue. President Polk also encouraged Congress to economize on spending unrelated to the conflict, "a high duty which . . . becomes the more imperative in a period of war."[34]

The Mexican Cession of 1848 and the acquisition of territory in the northwest from Great Britain extended the nation's borders to the Pacific Ocean. The 1.2 million square miles of new territory obtained by the Polk administration exceeded even the size of the Louisiana Purchase. In

1850 the United States assumed $10 million in debts of the Republic of Texas—which previously had traded at 10 cents on the dollar—in return for a large portion of Texas's territory that included much of present-day New Mexico and parts of other states to the north. Texas received $5 million in 1852, and another $5 million was paid to bondholders, who included prominent political and financial figures in Washington.[35]

Secretary Walker initiated the first comprehensive federal tax reform in American history. The Walker Tariff of 1846 attempted to set import tax rates based on the principle that they should be simplified and fixed at the "the lowest rate which will yield the largest amount of revenue."[36] It imposed three different rates that would be applied to goods in three basic categories, with luxuries such as whiskey and cigars being taxed at the highest rate.

Walker's reform of import taxes was one of the few "tax reforms" in federal history that did not sacrifice revenue. Whigs complained about lower import taxes, but the nation's iron and textile industries continued to thrive.

Thirteen years of astounding economic growth—1844 through 1856—followed the recovery from the Panic of 1837. A tide of immigration—which rose steadily from 114,371 new residents in 1845 to 427,833 in 1854—helped fuel this growth. The almost 2.9 million immigrants who arrived in America during those years equaled a sixth of the entire national population in 1840. More Germans arrived in 1854 than the total number of immigrants from all countries during the period between 1820 and 1832.[37] The number of Irish immigrants arriving in 1851 alone exceeded the entire population of Florida, Delaware, Rhode Island, or Iowa.

Farm output soared. The value of wheat, corn, and beef production doubled in the ten years beginning in 1844, as did the value of cotton exports. Railroad construction exploded in Ohio, Indiana, and Illinois. Railroads integrated those states—the Old Northwest territory—into the economy of the Northeast. The use of anthracite coal also boosted iron production dramatically in this period.

Gold discoveries increased national production of the world's most precious commodity. The population of California, which exported more than $45 million worth of gold annually by the mid-1850s, rose twentyfold, giving rise to new needs for transportation and communication to connect the new state to the rest of the nation.[38] Gold production permitted the United States, for the first time, to rely on its own coins rather than those imported from Spain and Mexico. Credit expanded as banks accumulated gold reserves.

Federal revenues and surpluses grew apace. Sales of public lands soared to $9 million per year by the mid-1850s.[39] From 1844 to 1854, the value of exports increased from $105 million to $237 million, while imports rose from $104 million to $309 million.[40] Import tax revenues climbed steadily from $17 million in 1843 to a high of $64 million in 1854, which allowed the government to pay off much of the debt incurred during the Panic of 1837 and the Mexican-American War.[41] In 1854 the federal debt of $42 million was no greater than it had been just before the War of 1812, when the country's economy was much smaller.[42] Since the federal government would have to buy back additional debt at a sharp premium over its face value, cash balances accumulated in the Treasury. Congress raised spending to subsidize postal service to the West Coast and to deploy military forces to counter hostility from displaced Native Americans.

This remarkable period of economic expansion is just one example of many throughout American history when no one seriously entertained the idea that the federal government needed to spend borrowed money in order for the economy to grow.

By the 1850s the national political debate focused on social rather than economic issues. The massive wave of foreign immigration sparked a nativist backlash. Above all, a rising population in the Western territories forced the United States to confront choices about the future of slavery outside the South.

THE LITTLE MAGICIAN AND SALMON CHASE

Martin Van Buren was not content to sit on the sidelines and let Polk, Walker, and Calhoun run the party he had done so much to build. Within a few years of his loss of the Democratic nomination in 1844, Van Buren emerged as a catalyst for the formation of a new political party opposed to the extension of slavery into the territories. They called themselves Free Soilers and, eventually, many of the new party's members became the first Republicans.

For awhile after 1844 Van Buren was content to watch with pride as his loyal lieutenant, Silas Wright, developed a national following. As New York's governor, Wright helped break up the Old World property laws that perpetuated the Hudson River aristocracy. Polk and other party leaders offered the vice presidential nomination to the popular Wright after the South turned against Van Buren at the 1844 convention. Wright curtly declined the invitation in a message transmitted from the Baltimore Democratic convention to Washington, DC, by the nation's first major telegraph line. Wright would not abandon Van Buren or serve in an administration that advocated the addition of states permitting slavery.

Van Buren's political prowess commanded respect; Wright's forthright principles earned affection. Northern Democrats grieved when Wright died while working on his farm in 1847. Even more mourned after John Quincy Adams died early the following year. No death of a public figure affected Northern citizens so greatly since the passing of Adams's father and Thomas Jefferson on the fiftieth anniversary of the Declaration of Independence in 1826. The irascible former president, who had once urged members of Congress not to be swayed by the will of their constituents, had strengthened the will of many Americans on the issue of slavery.

Van Buren returned to the political fray as his old adversary was laid to rest. He rallied a faction within the New York Democratic Party in opposition to the extension of slavery. People called members of this group "Barnburners" because they fought in the spirit of a stubborn Dutch farmer who, according to legend, had burned down his barn to kill a detested rat.

John Van Buren, the former president's son and a powerful orator, excited a Barnburner convention in 1848 with a slogan adopted in part by a new political movement: "Free Trade, Free Labor, Free Soil, Free Speech, and Free Men." Martin Van Buren himself wrote a well-publicized "Barnburner Manifesto," which declared that "free labor and slave labor . . . cannot flourish under the same laws."[43]

Antislavery activist Salmon Chase of Ohio wrote excitedly to his friend Charles Sumner that the Barnburners' stand on slavery represented a turning point "in the History of Parties in the Country."[44] The Barnburners asked for Chase's help in organizing a new national party, a task that Chase had spent a lifetime preparing for.

Chase was one of eight children left destitute in New Hampshire after his father's death. After being raised by a relative in the clergy on the Ohio frontier, Chase studied law under William Wirt, who served as attorney general for a record twelve years during the Monroe and Adams administrations. He then practiced law in the boomtown of Cincinnati, the heart of the nation's slaughterhouse industry and home to the West's most active Christian abolitionists.

There, in 1834, the scholarly young Chase prepared the first standard text on Ohio law, in which he argued that the Northwest Ordinance of

1787 showed the intention of the Founding Fathers to prohibit slavery in all states created from federal territories. Chase also believed that federal fugitive slave laws infringed on the constitutional right of states to ban slavery within their boundaries, an argument he put to the test when representing a runaway slave named Matilda. Matilda escaped to Cincinnati when her white father and "master" brought her on a trip across the river from Kentucky. She found refuge in the household of James Birney, an antislavery publisher in Cincinnati. Though Chase lost the trial and Matilda was ultimately returned to slavery, the young lawyer's stature grew in the national antislavery movement.

Chase then worked to raise the profile of the miniscule Liberty Party, founded by Matilda's patron, James Birney. Chase labored in hopes of creating a vehicle for Northern Democrats whom he expected to break from their national party on the issue of slavery. As a result, Chase aligned his views with Democratic opposition to debt and bank notes. He framed his opposition to slavery as a populist attack on "the Slave Power" in the form of Southern plantation owners who often dominated their region's politics. Years of relentless effort by Chase failed to enlist a single established Northern Democratic leader, and by 1848 his dream of finding a new antislavery party seemed quixotic.

Chase's political isolation ended when the Barnburners asked for his help. Chase helped author a Free Soil party platform stating that "the obligations of honor and patriotism require the earliest practical payment of the national debt," supporting import taxes only for the purpose of balancing the budget, and proposing "a retrenchment of the expenses and patronage of the federal government." In addition to these traditional Jeffersonian goals, the Free Soil platform endorsed a new law entitling "actual settlers" to free grants of public land.[45] The Free Soilers rallied around a slogan—"free soil, free men"—that within several years would be adopted as the banner of a new Republican Party.

Delegates to the Free Soil convention in 1848 nominated Martin Van Buren for president and Charles Francis Adams, the son of John Quincy Adams, for vice president. In a first for a national political convention, they welcomed participation from African Americans.[46]

Free Soilers—principally antislavery Democrats—had a significant impact on the 1848 election. In a three-way contest, a plurality of voters elected the slave-owning Whig presidential candidate, General Zachary Taylor, who declined to comment on federal issues until after the election. Voters in Massachusetts, Vermont, New York, and Ohio elected a significant number of Free Soilers to their state legislatures, which selected US senators until a constitutional amendment adopted in 1913 required their direct election. A coalition of Democrats and Free Soilers in the Ohio legislature elected Salmon Chase to the Senate by a one-vote margin in 1848. He was joined in the Senate by Charles Sumner, who was elected by a similar one-vote margin in Massachusetts. Chase and Sumner identified themselves as "Independent Democrats," though the Senate Democratic caucus promptly expelled them because of their views on slavery.

The Free Soil Party lost momentum when many of the New York Barnburners moved back into the Democratic Party. By 1852 the Whig Party was also disintegrating as a result of the deaths of its two founders—Henry Clay and Daniel Webster. That year Democratic leaders finessed the issue of slavery in the territories by running distinct campaigns in the North and South. Their modest and obscure candidate Franklin Pierce assisted that strategy by saying little. The Whig's proud candidate, General Winfield Scott, simply could not hold his tongue. Pierce won the votes of all but four states in the Electoral College.

The 1853 municipal election in Chase's Cincinnati—the nation's major immigrant gateway to the Ohio River—served as both a microcosm of and a fulcrum for Northern politics. The city's Whig Party almost vanished, and its historic Democratic majority receded. They were replaced by local parties built around single issues, such as opposition to the influence of Catholic immigrants, aid to Catholic schools, and the public sale of alcohol. Anti-immigrant groups throughout the nation coalesced into a new political organization, the Native American Party, more commonly known as the "Know-Nothing Party" because of its secretive strategy.

As memories of Jefferson and Jackson began to fade into legend, Senator Stephen A. Douglas of Illinois tried to modernize the Democratic Party with a vision of a railroad that would link the East and West Coasts and open the interior for settlement. That type of progress would require some form of government that could administer property laws in the Western territories. Douglas introduced a bill creating the Kansas-Nebraska Territory on January 4, 1853. To enlist support for the bill from Southern Whigs in Congress, Douglas and President Pierce agreed to amend the bill to void the prohibition of slavery in territory north of a line enshrined in the Missouri Compromise of 1820.

Northern opposition to that amendment spread like wildfire. Salmon Chase fanned those flames with a nationally publicized "Appeal of the Independent Democrats in Congress to the People of the United States."[47] Chase and his colleague Charles Sumner called on all citizens opposed to the extension of slavery to fight together against the Kansas-Nebraska Act.

Half of the Northern Democrats in Congress defied the views of their constituents by voting with Southern Democrats and Whigs for passage of that legislation. Northern Democrats felt betrayed by their representatives in Congress who supported the measure, while Northern Whigs distanced themselves from Southern Whigs who voted for the bill.

The Kansas-Nebraska Act made Chase's repeated warnings about a conspiratorial Slave Power appear prophetic. A new generation of Northern civic leaders prepared to run against incumbents in 1854. These "Anti-Nebraska" men would form the nation's second enduring political party and adopt the American Fiscal Tradition as the group's unifying economic platform.

PART II

THE TRADITION SUSTAINS A GROWING NATION AND THE REPUBLICAN PARTY: 1854–1900

5

REPUBLICANS EMBRACE THE TRADITION

1854–1860: Years when deficits exceeded debt service = 3
(1858–1860, recession after Panic of 1857)

TRIBUTARIES FLOWING
INTO A REPUBLICAN RIVER

Tracing the origin of the early Republican Party is like charting the source of a river with many tributaries. Northerners in 1854 elected a new House majority consisting of congressmen who had campaigned against the extension of either slavery or open immigration and, frequently, both. These winning candidates had used a variety of party names: Whig, Democrat, Anti-Nebraska, People's Party, Free Soil, Fusion, Independent Democrat, Native American or Know-Nothing, and Republican. Only after Ohio voters elected Salmon Chase as their governor in 1855 and House members selected a Speaker in 1856 did various groups that opposed the extension of slavery agree to share a common name: "Republican."

Anti-Nebraska men such as House members John Sherman of Ohio and Justin Morrill of Vermont had little time to consider an economic or budgetary platform in 1855 and 1856. Yet within a few years they—along with Salmon Chase, William Fessenden of Maine, and Thaddeus Stevens of Pennsylvania—would craft the tax and spending policies that preserved the nation during the Civil War. Sherman and Morrill would manage federal budgets for decades afterwards. Their stories explain how the Republican Party came to embrace the American Fiscal Tradition.

John Sherman learned the value of a dollar at an early age. He was six years old, one of eleven children, when his father died in 1819 on the Ohio frontier. A local lawyer, Tom Ewing, raised his brother William—nicknamed "Cump"—whom Mary Sherman considered to be her "smartest boy." Mary sent John to live with the family of another frontier lawyer. Cump left for the US Military Academy at West Point, while his younger brother John, at age fourteen, went to work on the construction of a lock and dam on a canal between the Ohio River and Gallatin's Cumberland Road. Ohio's Democratic governor gave John's job to a political supporter, leading Sherman to wryly reminisce that he "was a Whig of sixteen" who felt like "it was glorious to be a victim of persecution."[1] Sherman then studied law, a promising field in the nation's fastest growing state.

The young lawyer was among the hundreds of Ohioans who responded to Chase's 1854 Anti-Nebraska "Appeal" by attending a statewide meeting of citizens opposed to the extension of slavery. They adopted a resolution proclaiming that they were not "a mere old-time Abolition convention. . . . We are not here to construct a Free Soil, a Whig or a Democratic platform. Our duty is a higher and nobler one."[2] Calling themselves "Anti-Nebraska men" or "the People's Party," they backed a slate of candidates—including thirty-three-year-old John Sherman—for the House of Representatives. With rallies often held in churches, their slate swept the 1854 Ohio congressional elections.

Vermont voters that year also elected a political newcomer, Justin Morrill, to the House of Representatives. Like Chase and Sherman, his parents had many children, though most of Justin's siblings died young. Morrill's blacksmith father could not afford college tuition for his studious son Justin, who worked at a general store and learned the merchant's skills of accounting and managing credit for customers who could not pay in full until after the harvest. Over time Morrill bought several Vermont general stores. His knack for math, encyclopedic memory, and reputation for fairness helped him thrive as a trader of promissory notes, the unofficial paper money that circulated before John Sherman and Salmon Chase helped create the first official paper currency in 1862.

Morrill, like the vast majority of people in Vermont, loathed slavery. Even Chase's Liberty Party had flourished in the state, though its Vermont branch had passed resolutions containing antislavery language so aggressive that the national party refused to publish them out of fear of reprisals.

Vermont's voters also strongly believed in the use of import taxes to nurture American businesses. Since the state's economy depended so heavily on herds of sheep, its citizens enthusiastically backed high import fees on wool.

Morrill paid more attention to politics after he sold his business in 1848. He also spent more time in his treasured library, where his reading turned to history and economics. In 1854, at age forty-four, he ran for Congress as an Anti-Nebraska Whig, though he did not follow the example of Maine's William Fessenden, who combined Whigs with Free Soil Democrats to create a "fusion" majority. Morrill won by a narrow margin in a contest against both Democratic and Free Soil candidates. The 1854 campaign was Morrill's last close election for four decades and his last election as a Whig.

Seasoned politicians wondered whether the tide propelling the Anti-Nebraska and Know-Nothing movements had crested during the 1854 elections. They sought to discern the answer in the nation's third-largest state, Ohio, which elected its governor and other state officials in October 1855.

Some veterans of Ohio politics expected the Anti-Nebraska men to either rejuvenate the state's Whig Party or try to form a new Northern Democratic Party. Conservative Whig leader Tom Ewing, Tyler's former treasury secretary and mentor as well as father-in-law to William "Cump" Sherman, urged Anti-Nebraska Whigs to keep away from controversial issues that might offend "wise and conservative southern men."[3] In contrast, Independent Democrat Salmon Chase thought there "must be . . . a Democratic Party & a Conservative Party under some name," and he hoped to recruit the Anti-Nebraska men in his efforts to take over the Democratic Party.[4]

Anti-Nebraska Democrats, Whigs, Know-Nothings, and Free Soilers in Ohio convened in Columbus in July 1855 to decide their next steps. They chose young Congressman-elect John Sherman, to chair the meeting and another lawyer, William Boyd Allison, to serve as secretary. Along with Morrill, Sherman would chair the tax-writing Senate Finance Committee for most of the years between the Civil War and turn of the century. Allison would chair the Senate Appropriations Committee during much of that era. Their budgets helped define the fiscal principles of the new party taking root in 1855.

Budgets were far from Sherman's mind as he presided over the Columbus convention. His job was to convince factions with disparate views on economics and immigration to work as a team. The convention ultimately endorsed a slate of candidates that included Independent Democrat

Salmon Chase for governor and Know-Nothing sympathizers for all of the other state offices. The convention charged a committee with the task of contacting like-minded groups in other states in hopes of organizing a national convention for a new Republican Party. Salmon Chase agreed to call himself a Republican and won a narrow victory that October to become the first Republican governor of a large state.

Congressman John Sherman joined other Anti-Nebraska men who, by a bare majority, elected an Anti-Nebraska Democrat with Know-Nothing sympathies as the new Speaker in early 1856. Sherman explained to his colleagues that he was willing to "act in concert with men of all parties and opinions who will steadily aid in preserving our Western territories for free labor."[5] Sherman later wrote that "the Whig Party had disappeared. . . . The Republican party then represented the progressive tendency of the age."[6]

Delegates to the first Republican National Convention, held in Philadelphia in 1856, could agree only on a skeletal platform: they opposed slavery in the territories and supported the construction of a rail line to the Pacific. Their nominee for president, John Frémont of California, was a famed mapmaker whose cartography skills could be helpful in charting the route for a transcontinental railroad. His skills as a presidential candidate were weaker. The Ohio delegation to the national convention of Know-Nothings led many others from the North to bolt from their party and join the Republicans.

Frémont's spotty military record became a liability during the campaign, in which he seemed to have little interest. His 1856 Electoral College loss to a Democratic politician with decades of experience, James Buchanan, was less surprising than the fact that Frémont had managed to carry most Northern states.

Republicans hoped to prevail in the Electoral College in 1860 by keeping the votes of states won by Frémont and adding the votes of at least two other states that he had lost—Pennsylvania and either Illinois or Indiana. To demonstrate their capacity for national governance, Republicans also needed a better presidential candidate and a more complete economic platform.

REPUBLICANS UPHOLD THE TRADITION

In his 1857 inaugural address President Buchanan bragged that the federal government's financial strength was "without a parallel in history. No nation has ever before been embarrassed from too large a surplus in its treasury."[7] He called for a reduction in import taxes, the steady retirement of federal debt, and a larger navy. That surplus disappeared quickly after Buchanan spoke, as the United States entered a severe recession known as the Panic of 1857.

The downturn originated in part due to events in Europe, where central banks in Great Britain and France raised interest rates in order to replenish gold supplies exhausted during the costly Crimean War. Rising British interest rates interrupted the flow of the capital that had financed US railroad construction. Without capital inflows to offset the American balance-of-trade deficit, the value of US exports—still dominated by cotton—fell. The 1857 collapse of the New York branch of an Ohio financial firm prompted a cascading series of bank failures. Bank deposits in New York fell by one-third, and many banks suspended payment of deposits in gold or silver. The American credit contraction, in turn, accelerated a recession in the nation's principal trading partner, Great Britain.

Treasury Secretary Howell Cobb warned of the need to borrow $20 million, which was almost 40 percent of the previous year's spending.[8] Federal expenses had grown almost as quickly as federal revenues in the prosperous prior decade. Growing subsidies supported postal service for citizens scattered all the way to the West Coast.[9] For awhile the Treasury used accumulated cash balances and short-term notes to offset lost revenues.

In May 1858 Congressman Sherman demanded action to reduce the gap between spending and tax revenues. He condemned spending for the type of local projects known today as "earmarks" and faulted the House Ways and Means Committee for its unwillingness to raise taxes. His friend Justin Morrill was appointed to the House Ways and Means Committee in May 1858 and spent the balance of the year studying the historical tax and debt policies of the various governments.

A deep sectional split handicapped the ability of the Democratic Party to offer a coherent budget plan. The success of Republicans in Northern states had given Southern Democrats a congressional majority within their party. They used that new power to oppose higher import taxes. Yet, in a pattern that would become familiar a century and a half later, some anti-tax Southerners such as Mississippi senator Jefferson Davis also opposed a cut in a large category of federal spending, outlays for the salaries of military officers.

President Buchanan had always walked a fine line on the issue of import taxes. Import taxes opposed by his party's Southern base were quite popular among the wool and iron industries in Buchanan's Western Pennsylvania stronghold, a region that had been responsible for the swing margin of victory in many national elections since 1800. When Buchanan proposed to increase import tax revenues, Secretary of the Treasury Cobb, a Georgian, dismissed the president's views as being inconsistent with the policy of "the Administration."[10]

In a reverse mirror image of the brinksmanship over the debt ceiling in the summer of 2011, some Northern Democratic congressmen vowed to block any additional federal debt to fund ongoing expenses unless Congress also raised taxes. In March 1859 a thin congressional majority authorized $20 million in new debt in the last hour on the last day of the regular session.[11]

When a frustrated Sherman ran for Speaker of the House, Southern congressmen attacked him for endorsing an economics book that blamed slavery for the low wages of white Southern workers. Sherman fell one vote short in the Speaker's race, but a new Republican-backed Speaker made Sherman the chairman of the Ways and Means Committee. Sherman, in turn, charged Morrill with the task of preparing the first Republican budget plan.

It was difficult for Republicans to craft fiscal policy, since the new party included both historic advocates and opponents of import taxes designed to limit foreign competition. In the words of one scholar, "the Panic of 1857, therefore, exposed the disorganization of the Republicans on issues other than slavery."[12] Yet the severity of the budget crisis did not give Sherman and Morrill the luxury of waiting for their party to devise its economic platform. They relied, instead, on the authority of that old pillar of the American Fiscal Tradition—"pay as you go"—to find common ground. In explaining his plan Morrill employed the same words—"pay as you go"—used by Joseph Jones, James Monroe's uncle, when he explained his conception of the desired fiscal policy to James Madison.

Morrill proposed that the federal government finance the deficit with long-term loans or bonds rather than short-term notes, reduce spending ("retrace our steps of extravagance"), and increase import taxes.[13] The earnest Morrill told his House members that their nation should not "'go to bed without its supper' every time the imports of the week fall short."[14]

Drafting a comprehensive tax bill required at least some knowledge of trade in all types of imported goods. Months of study and years of business experience equipped Morrill for the task. His legislation set tax rates at levels designed to yield higher revenue rather than block entirely the import of some categories of goods. He gave the Republican Party a merchant's perspective, similar to the one Gallatin had imparted to the early Democrats. The Morrill tax bill earned almost unanimous support from Republican members in the House, whose ranks included former Democrats, Whigs, and Know-Nothings. It passed the House, but a deadlocked Senate refused to bring it to the floor.

Early Republicans even wove their political philosophy of "free men, free soil" into the fabric of their new fiscal policy. They argued that "free men" with economic independence should support taxes that discouraged competition from goods produced by cheap foreign labor. Republicans would use that argument effectively with industrial workers and wool producers in Western Pennsylvania during the 1860 presidential election.

Many Republicans of the period also linked freedom to public education. Like Jefferson and Gallatin, Morrill believed that accessible education was vital to the nation's future. The Vermont merchant, whose family had not been able to afford to send him to college, introduced a bill granting large tracts of federal land to each state for the purpose of financing public colleges. That bill was one of the few contested measures to pass both the House and the Senate during the legislative stalemate preceding the election of 1860. Morrill described to his colleagues how Prussia's system of public universities had undergirded innovation in industry and agriculture, and he explained how universities could be crucial to achieving competitive advantages. Buchanan, citing the need for a more limited role for federal government, vetoed the bill. Several years later President Lincoln signed the Morrill Act, which boosted the development of state universities.

By 1860 gridlock over slavery and the federal budget prompted foreign lenders to withdraw credit from the United States. Sherman estimated that the Treasury's cash balance would fall that summer to less than $2 million, a tenth of the reserves available at the beginning of the Buchanan administration.[15] The Treasury could not even pay congressional salaries on time. When seeking to borrow $5 million at a competitive auction in late 1860, the Treasury received bids for only $1,831,000 at interest rates of up to 12 percent.[16] The federal government accepted all offers, and a New York bank funded the balance at 12 percent interest—by far the highest interest rate since the War of 1812. In January 1861 the Buchanan administration desperately and ineffectively pleaded with states to return the distributions of federal surpluses they had received in 1836.

The downturn associated with the Panic of 1857 paralyzed British politics in a manner that reverberated across the Atlantic. In 1859 a coalition of British politicians who favored more efficient public spending, a broader tax base, and public education formed a new Liberal Party. Like many Americans who became active in the movement against the extension of slavery, British Liberals tended to view public policy issues through the prism of Christian ethics.

THE REPUBLICANS FIND A CANDIDATE

The Republican Party had originated as an opposition movement, as had Jefferson's coalition in the early 1790s. Republicans who worked to balance the budget in the late 1850s did not shy away from carrying the Jeffersonian torch of fiscal stewardship.

The new party searched for a presidential candidate who could compete effectively in Illinois and Indiana, states where Whigs had been slow to combine with Free Soil Democrats. Maine senator William Fessenden was typical of many party leaders in his hope for a presidential nominee who had "no particular following, and while a decided Republican, would not be obnoxious to any branch of the party—provided such a man can be found."[17]

Republicans gambled by nominating Abraham Lincoln, an Illinois railroad lawyer who had lost his last two elections. They expected that Lincoln's log cabin childhood and service in a frontier militia could appeal to Western voters. Lincoln was best known for his distinctive style of speaking, which combined humor, logic, and emotion, though no one had yet been elected to the presidency based on the power of his oratory.

Lincoln won a solid electoral majority in 1860, and days after his inauguration the Senate finally passed the Morrill Tariff. Rebel soldiers shelled Ft. Sumter in Charleston Bay two weeks later.

Stephen A. Douglas, a Northern Democratic leader, had prompted many Americans to abandon older party organizations when he put together a coalition to pass the Kansas-Nebraska Act seven years earlier. In March 1861 Senator Douglas now lectured his Republican colleagues, the new majority, on the need to compromise with slave states. Douglas considered the secession of Southern states to be treason, yet he announced that Northerners would somehow have to find an alternative to war. He explained that higher import taxes simply could not produce more than $100 million a year, less than a third of the amount needed to pay for an army capable of suppressing the rebellious South.[18] The first generation of Republicans rose to meet Douglas's challenge.

6

BORROWING AND TAXING TO RESTORE THE UNION

1861–1879: Years when deficits exceeded debt service = 5
(1861–1865, Civil War)

EARLY DENIAL

In the Civil War's first year, 1861, the United States of America and Confederate States of America both relied on bank loans and short-term notes. For the remainder of the war, the United States imposed much higher taxes and sold bonds to the general public and to a new banking system. The Confederacy lost the financial battle well before the last shot in the war was fired. High taxes and national banks violated the dominant ideology of Confederate states. The Confederate economy drowned in a flood of paper notes. Twenty-first-century politicians who advocate paying for war entirely with debt rather than with higher taxes have more in common with leaders of the Confederacy than Lincoln's Republicans.

In early 1861 few people anticipated the length and ferocity of the Civil War. One who did was William T. "Cump" Sherman, whose brother had filled the Ohio Senate seat vacated after Salmon Chase resigned to serve as Lincoln's secretary of the treasury. In March 1861 Senator Sherman arranged for Cump to brief the president on Southern military preparations. To the dismay of both Sherman brothers, Lincoln responded to their alarm by making a wisecrack. Only later was the president's casual demeanor under stress recognized as a source of strength.

Several months later Cump Sherman, who by then was a Union general, warned Secretary of War Simon Cameron that the North would need an army of two hundred thousand trained professionals to invade the South and end the war.[1] Secretary Cameron could not imagine paying for an army of that size and remarked to a reporter that stress had driven the general "insane."[2] Sherman eventually received the resources he needed, invaded the South, and ended the war by cutting off supplies to Lee's army. During his March to the Sea through Georgia, General Sherman passed by the plantation home of Buchanan's former Treasury secretary, Howell Cobb, and remembered how Cobb had depleted the Treasury through deficit spending in the years preceding the war. General Sherman burned Cobb's home to the ground.

Cobb also helped create a problem for Confederate finances. He had presided over the Confederate constitutional convention that had limited the ability of the new government to levy taxes. In the war's first twelve months the Confederacy spent $347 million while receiving tax revenue of only $14 million and bank loans and bonds of $38 million.[3]

PAPER MONEY AND TAXES, 1861–1862

Salmon Chase, whom Lincoln had asked to serve as Secretary of the Treasury, inherited from Cobb a federal budget in shambles. For the fiscal year ending on June 30, 1861, the United States borrowed $25 million to finance $66 million in spending.[4]

President Lincoln asked Congress to authorize a budget that would "make this contest a short and decisive one." Secretary Chase requested a budget of $320 million in the next fiscal year.[5] Chase asked Congress to raise taxes to pay for a quarter of that amount and authorize debt to pay for the rest. The entire US money supply at the beginning of the war consisted of $414 million in gold coin and circulating bank notes.[6] Secretary Chase hoped that a show of Union resolve would lead to prompt reunification. General George McClellan assembled a large army in the hopes of forcing the Confederate capital, Richmond, to surrender.

In July 1861 Congress authorized $250 million in debt, imposed new taxes on domestic sales, and increased some import taxes.[7] As Senator

Stephen A. Douglas had predicted, these import revenues could not cover much of the war's cost. Congressman Justin Morrill concluded that the nation needed a new tax on incomes to help finance the war effort. Congressman Thaddeus Stevens of Pennsylvania rammed Morrill's income tax bill through the House, while Senators John Sherman and William Fessenden guided it through the Senate. Since Chase's Treasury Department lacked the organizational capacity required to collect federal taxes on incomes, collection was delayed until the summer of 1862.

By December 1861 Chase had raised the projected cost of the war's first year to $543 million and lowered projections of tax revenues from $80 million to $35 million.[8] Chase met in New York with the nation's leading bankers, who agreed to make three consecutive $50 million loans in late 1861.[9] Chase insisted that banks loan the full amount in gold, not bank notes, a request tantamount to transferring to the Treasury all gold then held as bank reserves. James Gallatin, son of former treasury secretary Albert Gallatin and spokesman for the New York bankers, respectfully declined Chase's request. Chase questioned the patriotism of those bankers, who felt that a loss of all gold reserves would cripple their ability to finance needed international trade. Their disagreement paralleled the dispute between Albert Gallatin and the Van Buren administration more than two decades earlier, when Van Buren weakened commercial banking by building the Treasury's gold reserves. Those episodes offer a lesson with contemporary relevance: large federal borrowing can reduce funds needed for commercial activity unless accompanied by an overall expansion of credit.

By the end of 1861, commercial banks and the Treasury had to suspend payments in gold. Chase's Jacksonian fealty to the ideal of a gold standard yielded to the extraordinary reality of wartime finances. The federal government had not even been able to borrow the full $250 million Congress had authorized; the US Treasury ran out of money. Senator Sherman summarized the dilemma: "At the beginning of the year 1862 we were physically strong but financially weak. . . . There was great wealth in the country but how could it be promptly utilized?"[10]

Lincoln delegated wartime budgets to Chase, though the secretary preferred to spend his time conferring with the cabinet and Congress on broader issues of wartime strategy. Strong congressional leaders—Senators John Sherman and William Fessenden and Representatives Justin Morrill and Thaddeus Stevens—filled the vacuum of budget leadership. Though they usually worked as an effective team, they disagreed on how to proceed once Chase's Treasury had exhausted currency reserves and bank credit in the winter of 1861–1862.

Sherman and Stevens saw no alternative to issuing some paper money with the status of legal tender. The Treasury had already circulated non–interest-bearing demand notes, but so far in the nation's history only metal coins had served as legal tender—a status that required people to accept money at face value in payment for amounts owed. Today one still finds on American paper money the words: "This note is legal tender for all debts, public and private." Sherman and Stevens worried about "debts public." Sherman argued that the hoarding of coins during wartime artificially restricted the supply of hand-to-hand currency. He also invoked the authority of Jefferson, who had urged President Madison to issue Treasury notes backed by future taxes during the War of 1812 to finance deficits.

The concept of paying bills with paper money ran counter to deeply held beliefs. Democrats associated paper notes with the type of hardships experienced when bank notes became worthless during downturns, while many former Whigs—including Fessenden and Morrill—believed that printed legal tender opened the door to inflation. Sherman urged them to minimize these risks by making a national commitment to redeem the paper money in gold after the war's end. Stevens and Sherman prevailed on the issue because of the lack of any viable alternative for paying the mountain of military bills accumulating in 1862. In early 1862 Congress authorized $150 million in green paper dollars, or "greenbacks." By March 1863 Congress had raised the total amount of authorized paper money to $450 million.[11]

During the Civil War, Secretary of Treasury Chase welcomed the paper money and even put his picture on the bills. Chase returned to his Jacksonian opposition to paper money after the war and declared, as chief justice of the United States, that it was unconstitutional to require their acceptance as legal tender.

In 1862 and early 1863 greenbacks temporarily helped close the gap between revenues and spending. They ultimately financed about 15 percent of total federal war expenses. Though the new currency did create sharp double-digit increases in prices, the Union avoided the ruinous price inflation that haunted the Confederacy, which relied far more heavily on currency and short-term notes. The use of greenbacks bought time for the federal government to develop a new system of bond financing.

In early 1862 Chase hired financier Jay Cooke, then thirty-one, to develop new markets for federal bonds.[12] Cooke's brother Harry, Ohio's leading Republican newspaper publisher, was one of Chase's most loyal political supporters. The younger Cooke turned out to be a marketing genius. He hired over 2,500 salesmen to create the world's largest retail brokerage firm and used patriotic appeals to sell $500 million in bonds bearing 6 percent interest. The sheer quantity of new federal notes and bonds overwhelmed private printers, prompting Congress to federalize the printing function by creating the Bureau of Printing and Engraving.

Secretary Chase boasted after the war that he had avoided dependence on foreign creditors, though in reality he had had no choice. At the war's outset he had asked Augustus Belmont, the chief representative of the Rothschild family's banking interests, about the prospects of foreign borrowing. "Not a chance," Belmont replied.[13]

Confederate financial leaders could not overcome their states' ideological resistance to taxation. That resistance was one of the grievances some used to justify the rebellion. Confederate vice president Alexander Stephens of Georgia argued that Republican opposition to secession rested more on fiscal interests than on moral opposition to slavery. If Northern leaders objected to the extension of slavery in US territory, Stephens asked, why should they oppose the departure of slave states? Why did many Northerners resist the annexation of Texas as a slave state and then oppose its secession? Republicans, concluded Stephens, sought only "one object, and that is a collection of taxes, raised by slave labor, to swell the fund necessary to meet their heavy appropriations."[14] Stephens advocated the use of loans rather than taxes to finance the Confederate military.

Frustrated Confederate leaders such as President Jefferson Davis and Treasury Secretary Christopher Memminger understood that tax revenues would eventually be needed in order to show the capacity to repay loans.[15] "Cotton certificates" were used to obtain goods from Great Britain early in the war but had limited value after the Union's naval embargo of cotton exports. Smugglers who successfully evaded the embargo on imports and exports rarely complied with tax laws. The struggle of the Confederacy to finance the war illustrates the plight of any nation that spends far more than its available tax revenues. In order to supply the war effort, the "conservative" Confederate government began confiscating agricultural produce in exchange for paper notes.

NEW TAXES AND BANKS, 1863–1865

Congress raised taxes throughout the war, leading some to joke that it "taxed everything except coffins." A congressman warned against repeating that phrase to Morrill, who might just respond by passing a coffin tax. Imports were taxed at an average rate of 47 percent of their total value.[16] Congress also taxed sales of domestic manufactured goods, raw materials, railroad services, dividends, legal transactions, occupations, and licenses.

In July 1861 Morrill proposed a 3 percent tax rate on personal incomes above a standard exemption of $800, which was about the average household income.[17] In the debate over the nation's first income tax bill, he asked his colleagues: "Ought not men . . . with large incomes . . . pay more in proportion to what they have than those with limited means, who live by the work of their own hands, or that of their families?"[18] By the war's end, Congress had raised this rate to 5 percent of incomes between $600 and $5,000 and 10 percent of incomes above $5,000.[19] Since most taxpayers with high incomes lived in a small number of commercial hubs, the residents of just three states—New York, Massachusetts, and Pennsylvania—paid about 60 cents of each dollar of federal revenues generated by the Civil War income tax.[20] In 1865 income taxes produced more revenue than import taxes and yielded a quarter of the total federal revenues during the war.

Wartime internal revenue—that is, revenue exclusive of import taxes—peaked in the fiscal year ending on June 30, 1866, at $309 million, an amount five times greater than the entire prewar federal budget and more than all Confederate tax revenues collected during the entire war.[21] Tax revenue had also peaked in the last year of the War of 1812 and would do so again in the final years of World War I, World War II, and the Korean War. Taxes during the Civil War's last year covered about 40 percent of its total cost, almost the same percentage as in the last years of World War I and World War II.

By the end of 1862 Jay Cooke had exhausted his ability to sell bonds to existing businesses and banks. He needed a broader market for federal debt. Treasury Secretary Chase, once an opponent of national banking, asked Congress to create a new system of federal banks that would be capable of buying more debt. Since those banks could accumulate more of the nation's wealth by attracting deposits and equity investment, their investment in federal bonds would absorb some purchasing power, thereby moderating wartime inflation.

In early 1863 the exigency of Civil War financing forced a resolution of the national banking issue that had been debated since early in the Washington administration. Some state-chartered banks continued to lobby against new competition, and Northern Democrats had not forgotten Jackson's storied battle with the national bank. Jackson disciple and Polk secretary of the treasury Robert Walker eventually implemented a "subtreasury" system as the Democratic alternative to a national bank. The Lincoln administration, therefore, welcomed help from Walker in overcoming Democratic opposition to a new national banking system.[22] Walker warned Northern Democrats that federal debt would continue to rise by at least half a billion dollars a year for the duration of the war. He saw no alternative to chartering well-regulated banks that issued notes in exchange for federal debt that could be held as a form of reserve.

Sherman confided to his wife in early 1863 that he could "scarcely sleep" until he passed the National Bank Act, which he described as "indispensable to create a demand for our bonds."[23] It took Sherman only a week to pass the bill that March. The National Bank Act created an enduring new banking system, initially with a three-tier structure of "country," regional, and New York City banks. Country and regional banks could satisfy reserve requirements with deposits in New York City banks, thereby elevating Wall Street's status as the nation's financial center.

Cooke sold much of the Treasury debt to the newly chartered national banks. State banks continued to exist, though by 1866 the federal government had taxed their notes out of existence. The fate of the nation's credit system after the war would depend on the ability of the federal government to maintain the value of bank reserves by repaying its debts with a dollar of roughly equivalent value.

The war effectively ended with General Robert E. Lee's surrender of the Army of Northern Virginia in April 1865. The war's human and economic costs persisted long afterwards. In just four fiscal years—July 1861 through June 1865—the federal government spent over $3.3 billion on the military, almost double the total of all federal outlays since President Washington's inauguration.[24] About $2 billion was funded with outstanding interest-bearing bonds or notes.[25]

At the war's conclusion Congress resolved—with only one dissenting vote—that "the public debt created during the late rebellion was contracted upon the faith and honor of the Nation; that it is sacred and inviolate, and must and ought to be paid, principal and interest."[26] In explaining his determination to pay down the debt, President Lincoln's last treasury secretary, former Indiana banker Hugh McCulloch, evoked the American Fiscal Tradition's most powerful, underlying value: "As all true men desire to leave to their heirs unencumbered estates, so should it be the ambition of the people of the United States to relieve their descendants of this national mortgage." Anticipating the argument that the debt was too high to pay off within a generation and that "future generations [should] be asked to share the burden," McCulloch observed that "wars are not at an end, and posterity will have enough to do to take care of the debts of their own creation."[27]

"Free Soil, Free Men," but Not Free Government

The emergence of the Republican Party marked the advent of a stable two-party system that soon became embedded in the nation's unwritten constitution. That system would be incorporated in a variety of practices and laws that governed primary elections, campaign financing, and the organization of the legislative branches of state governments. The Civil War itself interrupted the evolution of a Republican consensus concerning the proper size and scope of the federal government. However, two decisions made by Republican leaders during the war—on railroad subsidies and political activities by federal employees—would shape the party's attitude toward the breadth of federal activities until the 1920s.

The Republican platforms of 1856 and 1860 had promised to expand economic opportunity by providing federal aid for railroad construction. Since the war absorbed all tax revenues, Congress subsidized rail lines with exclusive licenses and grants of public lands to corporations that committed to raise private dollars to build them. The Pacific Railway Act of 1862 also authorized loans to build the intercontinental Union Pacific line. Agents for railroad promoters in Washington pressed members of Congress to obtain more land and loan guarantees. In meetings in the lobbies of the Capitol and nearby hotels, this outpouring of "lobbyists" gave cash, stock, and campaign contributions to members of Congress they referred to as "friends."

Congress granted to railroads the rights to over 130 million Western acres, a total area about the size of Ohio, Illinois, New York, and Michigan combined. The Union Pacific's linking of the East and West Coasts, completed in 1869, opened the country's vast interior for settlement. The warm relationship between politicians and rail owners marked the beginning of a new era of greater influence of corporate money on federal politics.

Public land grants also served as a means of "off balance sheet" financing for other wartime domestic initiatives. Ultimately seventy million acres would be granted to homesteaders while seventeen million helped sustain state colleges.[28] Though today some Republicans question the federal government's role in education or support of home ownership, the party's founders viewed support for expanded opportunity as consistent with their values of "free soil, free men."

The Republican campaign in 1864 planted another seed that would later blossom into both corruption and support for a larger federal government. Until General William T. Sherman's capture of Atlanta in September 1864, the outcome of the presidential election was uncertain. Lincoln ran as a "National Union" candidate rather than as a Republican in hopes of wooing support from pro-war Democrats. His running mate, Andrew Johnson of Tennessee, was an old-school Jacksonian Democrat. Lincoln's bipartisan campaign required Republican candidates down ballot to scramble to put together their own state organizations capable of competing with the established structure of the Democratic Party.

Senator Zachariah Chandler of Michigan, a gruff pragmatist, took charge of the Republican congressional campaign. For the next dozen years, Chandler effectively divided up campaign assignments among party members. At the time most of the Republican Party's natural leaders labored as soldiers or civilians in public office. Many held jobs that depended on appointments by their patrons in Congress. Chandler directed members of Congress to assign fundraising and get-out-the-vote goals to federal employees. After Lincoln's death, Congress stripped President Andrew Johnson of much his executive authority and exercised even more control over federal employees. Incumbent Republican leaders began to identify their party with the federal government that employed much of the rank-and-file party organization.

Military veterans emerged as a major new force in the Republican politics after the war. They favored the presidential nomination of a former Democrat with no political experience, General Ulysses Grant. He won the popular vote in 1868 by a surprisingly small margin. Senator Sherman naively hoped "that our candidate Grant should be so independent of party politics as to be a guarantee of peace and quiet."[29]

As a field commander Grant quickly assimilated information and issued clear orders, a style of leadership not suited for the White House. In September 1869 congressional leaders and members of Grant's cabinet were startled to learn that the president's personal secretary had negotiated—with the help of cash and federal gunboats—a treaty to annex the Dominican Republic. Congress refused to go along with this plan, and afterwards, Grant gave more control over federal appointments to key senators in return for their cooperation with other White House initiatives. Senators Simon Cameron of Pennsylvania and Roscoe Conkling of New York, among others, exploited this system to build their own powerful political machines. Many of the late president Lincoln's friends and cabinet secretaries began drifting to the minority Liberal Republican faction or the Democratic Party.

PLANNING THE RETIREMENT OF CIVIL WAR DEBT

While some Republicans worked to reconstruct Confederate states, John Sherman and Justin Morrill were more concerned with the reconstruction of precarious federal finances. They easily rebuffed President Johnson's idea that enormous debt could not be paid in full and that the interest paid each year should "be applied to the reduction of the principal in semi-annual installments"—in effect defaulting on at least part of the principal.[30] To no one's surprise, the Fourteenth Amendment to the Constitution voided obligations to repay Confederate debt. That amendment also sought to reassure creditors that the "validity of the public debt . . . shall not be questioned."

Congressional leaders in each party also resolved to reduce debt using tax revenues rather than perpetually rolling it over, as would become the practice in the twenty-first century. In his annual report to Congress in 1865, Treasury Secretary McCulloch forcefully asserted the advantage of retiring debt while taxpayers remembered clearly why it had been incurred: "The people of the United States will never be so willing to be taxed for the purpose of reducing the debt as at the present time. . . . Now, it is regarded by a large majority of taxpayers as a . . . sacred debt."[31] A member of the

British embassy in Washington reported with admiration that "the majority of Americans would appear disposed to endure any amount of sacrifice rather than bequeath a portion of their debt to future generations."[32]

John Sherman, chairman of the Senate Finance Committee, and Justin Morrill, chairman of the House Republican Caucus and the Ways and Means Committee, shared those sentiments. They also understood reducing the debt required a careful balance between monetary and fiscal policy. In general, monetary policy concerns the regulation of credit markets and currency, while fiscal policy refers to the level and nature of spending and revenues. (The term "fiscal policy" was used sparingly to refer to federal budgets until the 1940s.) In order to reduce debt, Sherman, Morrill, and their allies sought to lower interest rates in order to free more tax revenues for principal reduction and to promote the long-term economic growth on which debt reduction depended. Creditors might refinance Civil War debt at lower rates of interest if they felt the Treasury would make timely payments for debt service using dollars that had retained their purchasing power. The alternative of higher interest rates—and the corresponding decline in the value of outstanding bonds—posed a threat to the nation's banking and credit system that held federal debt as its principal reserve.

Since the Treasury lacked large gold reserves, an immediate return to the gold standard was impractical. An eventual return, however, was more than an ideological obsession. Since early in the war people struggled to cope with a dual set of pricing for many goods: a gold dollar could purchase more than a greenback dollar. In addition, international trade required credit that could be converted to gold at fixed rates for various currencies. A firm deadline for returning to the gold standard might stabilize prices; that deadline had to be soon enough to comfort bondholders and late enough to allow the Treasury to accumulate gold reserves.

Secretary of the Treasury Hugh McCulloch unintentionally jeopardized an orderly restoration of the gold standard when he tried to rapidly eliminate the greenbacks issued in 1862 and 1863. In 1866 Congress authorized the Treasury to exchange new interest-bearing Treasury debt for paper money. Sherman was able to repeal that measure by arguing that some amount of paper money was needed to sustain commercial activity and avoid deflation. Furthermore, currency—which did not bear interest—encumbered federal tax revenue less than interest-bearing bonds.

In 1867 to 1869 Secretary McCulloch refinanced Civil War bonds at lower interest rates based on a promise of payment in gold.[33] McCulloch noted that the United States needed to bring down its trade deficit through productivity growth and steadily retire its debt through an estimated annual debt service of $200 million a year over three decades.[34]

Several corrupt Wall Street speculators tried to force the Treasury to hoard excessive amounts of gold in the postwar period. Financier Jay Gould, President Grant's brother-in-law Abel Corbin, and a senior Treasury official were part of a group that attempted to corner the gold market in 1869. Grant ordered the Treasury to sell gold and squeeze the speculators once he discovered their scheme.

Congress slowly dismantled wartime levels of internal taxation but retained taxes high enough to service the debt.[35] When taxes on whiskey fell from $2 per gallon to 50 cents per gallon, revenues skyrocketed from $18 million to $55 million in two years, a stark reminder that excessive taxation can lead to tax evasion.[36]

In 1870 Sherman fought hard to retain the personal income tax, arguing that it broadened the federal tax base and provided a source of revenues for retiring the debt. That year, when the Senate voted to allow the income tax to expire, Sherman forced consideration of a bill to offset the loss of income tax revenues by raising taxes on sugar and the gross receipts of businesses. In response, the Senate reversed its position and agreed to extend the income tax—though at lower rates—until 1872. The majority of senators were not swayed by Sherman's early Republican idealism, which led him to argue that Congress should "retain the income tax on all incomes above one thousand dollars . . . and then throw off these taxes on consumption that oppress the poor."[37]

Justin Morrill's system of import taxes remained largely intact after the war. Frank Taussig, the preeminent historian of import taxation, noted that if immediately after the war "the question had been put to almost any public man, whether the tariff system of the war was to be continued, the answer would certainly have been in the negative, that in due time the import duties were to be lowered." Nonetheless, wartime levels of import fees persisted because "the country [had] adapted itself more closely to the tariff as it was."[38] Congress did not, however, extend high taxation to growing new categories of imported goods, which kept import tax revenues at a fairly steady level in the decades following the war, even though the size of the economy and the value of imports rose steadily. Textiles and sugar, the two workhorses of federal import tax revenues, declined as a share of all imports.

Lower Interest Rates
and a Stable Currency

Many Americans blamed the long recession following the Panic of 1873 on the collapse in the market value of railroad stocks and bonds.[39] Investors had speculated on the economic potential of railroads, even though railroad income did not keep up with railroad investment, in a manner similar to the Internet bubble in the late 1990s. Jay Cooke's business collapsed when the Northern Pacific Railroad defaulted on bond payments in 1873. Cooke blamed the downturn on the federal government's tight money policies, while many Americans blamed Cooke and Wall Street. Banks failed and credit contracted—first in the United States and then in Europe.[40]

The federal government balanced its budget throughout the downturn despite the heavy burden of interest payments. In 1874, for example, the federal government collected $163.1 million in import duties, $102.2 million in sales taxes, and $39.4 million in other taxes and proceeds from public land sales.[41] It used those revenues to pay for $107 million in interest on the debt, $73 million in military expenses, $29 million in military pensions, and $93 million for everything else.[42] Often commentators on the post-2000 debt crisis treat formula-based "entitlement" expenses as a recent innovation, but in the era following the Civil War—as during much of the nation's history—most federal spending consisted of interest payments fixed by contract, military salaries, and pensions for veterans set by statute.

Some Americans promoted creative schemes for paying off the enormous debt. When Congressman Thaddeus Stevens called for confiscation of all large plantations owned by rebels in the former Confederate states, his constituent mail showed that "the most popular argument in favor of the confiscation was that the proceeds from the land sales could be used to reduce the public debt and thus to reduce taxes."[43]

Other citizens hoped that gold discoveries would reduce the burden of national debt. In his first inaugural address, President Grant highlighted the fact that "Providence had bestowed upon us a strong box in the precious metals locked up in the sterile mountains of the far West."[44] Many of his countrymen headed for those mountains in search of gold. That group included Colonel George Custer, who abandoned his assigned post in Washington to lead the Seventh Cavalry into the Black Hills of South Dakota, a land considered sacred rather than sterile by the Northern Sioux. A newspaper headline in the Dakota Territory proclaimed: "The National

Debt to Be Repaid When Custer Returns."[45] Custer never returned, so Senator Sherman worked on a more conventional plan to repay the debt, while General Sherman sent forces to vanquish the Sioux.

Republican control over federal economic policy was threatened when voters, tired of recession and corruption, elected a Democratic House majority in 1874. After the election—but before the new Congress took office—the lame duck Congress passed Sherman's Specie Resumption Act, which committed the federal government to make payments in gold on request beginning on January 1, 1879. Many farmers protested that a scarcity of gold might accelerate the decline in the prices of cotton and wheat.

The Specie Resumption Act gave the federal government four years in which to accumulate gold reserves. It conferred broad discretion on the secretary of the treasury to manage the transition to an open "gold window" at banks. The election of 1876 would determine who held that office.

On November 7, 1876, John Sherman somberly monitored election returns at the Ohio home of his friend, Rutherford Hayes. Sherman had helped Hayes, the pious governor of Ohio, obtain the Republican presidential nomination. Democrats had nominated Samuel Tilden, a successful businessman, reformer, public intellectual, and governor of New York. Hayes and Tilden differed little in their views on the need to reduce debt and return to the gold standard. Tilden blamed wasteful Republican spending for the delay in accomplishing those goals.

Telegrams arriving at the Hayes home that day brought news of a Tilden landslide. Eighty-eight percent of eligible voters cast ballots in the election of 1876, the highest percentage in American history. The Democrat from New York had received a quarter of a million more popular votes than Hayes and over seven hundred thousand more votes than any previous candidate. Hayes confided to his diary that he had lost the election.

All but one newspaper—the *New York Times*—proclaimed Tilden the winner. On the night of the election, the partisan Republican editor of the *Times* sent a telegram signed by Republican national chairman Zachariah Chandler to the party leaders in several states still occupied by federal reconstruction forces, including Louisiana, Florida, and South Carolina. Chandler's telegrams and the next morning's *Times* stated that the election was not yet over. South Carolina's vote was close, and though Tilden won the reported popular vote in Louisiana and Florida by significant margins, Republican canvassing boards in those states had not yet certified the vote.

Tilden would have only 184 electoral votes out of the 185 needed for election if a recount reversed his popular vote victories in those three states.

John Sherman and Congressman James Garfield of Ohio left for Louisiana in an effort to find irregularities that might alter the count of that state's popular vote. President Grant dispatched General William T. Sherman and federal troops to Florida. Chandler sent large amounts of cash to each disputed state. Republicans were not able to count the votes of African Americans who had been improperly disqualified from casting ballots, but they could disqualify votes that had actually been cast. For the first—but not the last—time in US election history, a recount of Florida's votes pushed the Republican candidate over the top in the Electoral College tally. After an investigation by a commission that split along partisan lines, Tilden conceded with grace instead of creating another national crisis so soon after the Civil War.

Hayes quietly slipped into Washington to avoid protests and stayed at Sherman's home before taking the oath of office in a private ceremony. He promptly appointed the Ohio senator as his secretary of the treasury.

Secretary Sherman worked long hours to prepare for the opening of the gold window in 1879. In the words of one leading nineteenth-century economic historian, Sherman "was unwavering in pursuit of the resumption goal; practical, resolute, and adroit in the means employed."[46] He issued new bonds in exchange for gold, stockpiled gold collected from import taxes, and played New York banks against foreign banks in order to refinance federal debt on better terms. The average interest rate on debt fell from 6.26 percent in 1874 to 5.74 percent in 1879, even with an extension of maturities.[47] Sherman's Department of the Treasury joined the New York Bank Clearing House Association, a private group organized to maintain liquidity among banks in the nation's financial center. That membership gave the Treasury more immediate access to the reserves of the nation's largest banks, and began a collaboration that laid the foundation of the future Federal Reserve Bank of New York.

Some members of Congress tried to derail Sherman's economic plan. The House passed a bill—sponsored by Lincoln Republican turned Democrat Tom Ewing Jr., son of the Sherman brothers' mentor—repealing the Specie Resumption Act. Secretary Sherman's allies in the Senate blocked passage of the bill but could not prevent passage of legislation designed to increase the coinage of silver.

Silver coins from Mexico had once served as much of the nation's circulating currency, but silver coins had largely disappeared before 1873. The amount of silver in a dollar tended to be worth more than a dollar in Europe.[48] In 1873, however, Germany moved to a gold standard and began liquidating its silver reserves just as massive new silver deposits began to be mined in Nevada. When the value of the metal in a silver dollar dropped to less than the value of a gold dollar, members of Congress—including most from mining and farming states—demanded that the Treasury increase its purchase of silver. Miners welcomed a new outlet for their product, while farmers hoped that a devalued currency would raise agricultural prices. Congress overrode President Hayes's veto of a bill, cosponsored by Senator William Allison, that required the government to purchase silver and issue more currency in the form of certificates backed by a dollar of silver at market value. Sherman was content to issue silver certificates so long as the Treasury could collect import taxes in gold and give federal creditors the option of being paid in gold.

1879: A TURNING POINT

William Tecumseh Sherman helped end the Civil War with a famous March to the Sea that cut off Lee's supplies. His brother John's fight to restore federal finances had taken longer. Since 1866 the federal government had paid more than $1 billion in interest but had not managed to pay down principal due on the debt. With the opening of the gold window only a year away, many doubted the viability of any plan to reduce the burden of debt without devaluing the currency.

By late 1878 Secretary Sherman had stockpiled gold worth $114 million in Treasury vaults, yet these reserves represented only a fraction of the outstanding paper money that potentially could be redeemed.[49] Along with many other Americans, he was nervous about whether people would rush to exchange their greenbacks for gold.

The drama climaxed on January 2, 1879, when the federal government allowed the conversion of paper currency into gold. To the relief of the public and financial markets, only a few people showed up to exchange currency for gold. Surprisingly, the public deposited more gold that day than they received in exchange for greenbacks. Sherman later likened the date to the final day of a recovery from a long illness. Creditors no longer worried about receiving payment in the form of a devalued currency.

The opening of the gold window coincided with three years of spectacular American economic growth and the emergence of the United States as a global economic superpower. Industrial production increased by 52 percent in physical unit volume, a level three times larger than at the beginning of the Civil War.[50] The population surpassed fifty million people, an increase of almost nineteen million since 1860. Immigration reached almost eight hundred thousand people in 1882.[51] The nation also became a net exporter. For its first ninety years, America's appetite for imported iron—along with consumer staples such as sugar, salt, and tea—had resulted in chronic trade deficits that made it difficult to stabilize international credit. When the trade balance turned positive in 1879, the nation's exports were more diversified than in the preceding decades, when cotton had been king. Farmers exported large quantities of wheat and corn, while mills exported iron and steel. An extensive new rail system connected coastal ports to the interior, and the first oil pipeline reached the Atlantic.

In 1880 alone the United States paid down over $200 million in debt, four times more than the total federal budget before the Civil War and more than the total that Secretary Chase had been able to borrow from banks in 1861.[52] Debt reduction, not debt-financed stimulus, lowered interest rates and freed savings for private investment.[53] As the Treasury retired federal debt, credit expanded. The banking system became more efficient with the greater use of bank drafts, or checks, that replaced the unstable antebellum reliance on bank notes.[54] In 1881 interest rates on US debt fell to the same level as British debt, which for much of the nineteenth century had commanded the lowest interest rates in the world.

Not all Americans experienced the benefit of this growth. Farm income suffered because soaring levels of production depressed farm prices. The struggles of farmers with personal debt, while reinforcing their antipathy toward public debt, fomented discontent. The nation's industrial boom and pride in debt reduction did, however, help revive the fortunes of the Republican Party immediately ahead of the 1880 election. The unyielding commitment of Sherman and others to debt reduction had become embedded in the young party's political DNA.

The reduction in Civil War debt was more than a partisan achievement. The Democratic candidate for president in 1876 had won a large majority of the popular vote after campaigning for a more rapid reduction in debt. To an academic theorist it may seem odd that large European nations ruled by monarchs serving for life had far more trouble paying down debt than did a volatile democracy with no institutionalized process for long-term budget planning.

In fact, the attitude toward the reduction of debt after the Civil War showed the strength of a fiscal constitution that was grounded on fundamental and shared values. Hundreds of thousands of Americans had sacrificed their lives in service of a more perfect Union. Those who endured the war honored the dead on both sides by working to protect the nation's future. A generation that had already borne the wounds of war made the sacrifices required to reduce their country's debt. President Hayes himself had been shot four times. This moral commitment to the American Fiscal Tradition resembled the earlier commitment of the Founding Fathers, who considered paying down debt to be the culmination of the work of the American Revolution and War of 1812.

7

SHRINKING DEBT AND DRIFTING PARTIES

*1880–1900: Years when deficits exceeded debt service = 3
(1894–1895, depression after Panic of 1893;
1899, Spanish-American War)*

REPUBLICANS SPLINTER AND DEMOCRATS UNITE

Federal budget battles in the 1880s centered on large surpluses rather than deficits. Progressive reformers within each party condemned federal spending on padded payrolls. By 1912 that spirit of reform—which encompassed "efficient" spending and taxation based on the ability to pay—would dominate the American political mainstream.

The triumph of reform seemed like a distant dream in 1880. John Sherman occupied a lonely position between Republican reformers and the more powerful group of "Stalwarts" that included New York's machine politician Roscoe Conkling. Treasury Secretary Sherman had backed President Hayes's attempt to break Conkling's hold on thousands of jobs at the New York Custom House, the largest single source of federal revenues. Conkling succeeded in blocking Hayes's nomination of a reform-oriented businessman, Theodore Roosevelt Sr., to replace Chester Arthur, a Conkling man, for the post.

Conkling exacted his revenge at the 1880 Republican National Convention. President Hayes, humbled by his tainted election in 1876, declined to run and backed Sherman as his successor. House Appropriations chairman James Garfield of Ohio gave a memorable nomination speech for Sherman. After describing Sherman's successful fight to pay down war debt and restore the currency, Garfield urged delegates to cast votes on the basis of "the destiny of the Republic" rather than political calculation. When Conkling failed to secure the nomination for former President Grant after thirty deadlocked ballots, the exhausted delegates nominated Garfield for president and Chester Arthur for vice president. Garfield served only two hundred days in office before dying of gunshot wounds inflicted by an office-seeking assassin who proclaimed that his action had made the Stalwart, Chester Arthur, president.

Republican reformers slowly gained political strength, particularly in New York and Massachusetts, states that contained 15 percent of the nation's population. Reformers prevailed in their fight for the creation of a professional civil service to replace the patronage system used then to staff the federal government. They made little headway, however, when calling for tighter controls on pensions for the families of Civil War veterans or effective regulation of the business of railroad tycoons such as Jay Gould.

Reformers also gained momentum in the Democratic Party. In Northern cities they fought Democratic machines that provided social services to a flood of immigrants and padded city payrolls with campaign workers. Samuel Tilden of New York galvanized support from reformers throughout the nation with his fight against Tammany Hall leader "Boss" Tweed, the most corrupt machine politician of all. Tilden would also provide the Democratic Party with a fiscal platform that endured for two decades.

The soft-spoken Tilden's record of public service, spanning almost half of the nation's history, exemplified the liberal mainstream in the mid-nineteenth century. After the Panic of 1837, he articulated a Democratic economic ideology based on competitive markets, balanced budgets, and a stable currency. In 1846 he crafted a novel New York state law that allowed businesses to pool the money of shareholders in a corporation without the need for legislative action or any implied grant of monopoly. Other states copied the law, which gave rise to the modern corporation as the distinctive form of American business organization. After helping Salmon Chase write the Free Soil platform in 1848, Tilden set up corporations that built railroads and then rallied most New York Democrats behind the Lincoln administration's war efforts.

After his election as governor of New York in 1874, Tilden prosecuted "Boss" Tweed for bribery. Governor Tilden cut the state's padded payrolls, which permitted him to balance the budget while slashing state property taxes. Tilden's 1876 presidential campaign slogan—"retrenchment and reform"—signified honest government with lower taxes and more efficient spending, a theme embraced by future Democratic Party platforms.[1]

Tilden earned the respect of British Liberals who shared his belief in efficient spending and balanced budgets. After the Civil War, Liberal leader Gladstone commended US leadership for "braving a large burden of taxation" in their belief "that the true secret of their future power lies in the steady and rapid reduction of their debt."[2] Gladstone and Tilden viewed universal public education and debt reduction as means to enhance upward mobility and create opportunities for the next generation.[3]

Tilden's large victory in the popular vote for the presidency in 1876 election showed that Democrats could win the White House with a candidate capable of carrying the South, New York, New Jersey, and at least one other Northern state. The aging Tilden would not run again, and Democrats longed for a reformer in his mold.

Enter Grover Cleveland.

Cleveland, a three-hundred-pound, forty-four-year-old bachelor, regularly ate dinner—usually sausage and beer—at one of the many taverns in Buffalo, New York. One Saturday night in October 1881, while dining at Billy Dranger's bar, three other patrons invited him to their table and shared their troubles. Those three had repeatedly been turned down in their attempts to recruit a Democratic candidate for mayor. Buffalo, after all, was a Republican town. Why not nominate Grover? Within weeks of that meeting, Buffalo voters elected Cleveland as their mayor.

Cleveland compensated for his lack of political experience by carefully reading every measure considered by Buffalo's city council. Buffalo politicians had routinely made grants to various small civic organizations. Cleveland vetoed these grants as well as a street cleaning contract that he considered overpriced. These vetoes stunned city hall insiders but impressed voters. State party leader Daniel Manning, a publisher and friend of Tilden, began thinking about the future of this newcomer who many called "the veto mayor."

Nine months after Cleveland's election, New York Democrats reached a deadlock in their balloting to nominate a candidate for governor. Manning and other reform-oriented party leaders gambled by arranging for the nomination of Cleveland. In the general election the veto mayor received support from Republicans who were repelled by their nominee's ties to Senator Conkling and rail tycoon Jay Gould. A number of Republican reformers, including young Theodore Roosevelt Jr., were also elected to the state legislature.

Governor Cleveland vetoed eight bills passed by the legislature during his first three months in office. Those vetoes encompassed more than just wasteful spending. Democrats and Republican reformers succeeded in passing a popular bill that lowered the fees of a New York City transit line from 10 cents to 5 cents. The transit line's owner, Jay Gould, had made generous campaign contributions to Cleveland's Republican opponent in the governor's race, and no one liked to pay higher fares. In vetoing the bill Cleveland explained that he could not discern any consistent principle to justify the use of state power to override valid municipal contracts. Cleveland's reliance on principle even when vetoing a popular bill earned national attention. The day after the veto, Theodore Roosevelt Jr. publicly apologized for backing the bill for political purposes and applauded Governor Cleveland's courage.[4]

The Veto President

Only three years after Cleveland walked into Billy Dranger's bar, Americans elected him to serve as the first Democratic president since the Civil War. In the bitter 1884 presidential campaign, GOP operatives accused the religiously devout Cleveland of being an alcoholic who kept a harem of young women. Republican reformers in New York again crossed party lines to give Cleveland the electoral victory.

In the six years before Cleveland took office in 1885, the federal government retired over half of the $2 billion in interest-bearing Civil War debt.[5] All that remained was $250 million in bonds yielding 4.5 percent, which would mature in 1891, and $737 million in bonds yielding 4 percent, maturing in 1907.[6] Federal bonds sold at a premium to face value that ranged from 10 to 24 percent, reflecting the strength of the nation's credit and currency.[7] After 1883 the federal government refused to pay market premiums to retire more debt, so budget surpluses led to a rise in the cash balances in the Treasury.[8]

Since the end of the Civil War the federal government ran a surplus despite its padded payrolls and increased spending on pensions for military veterans and their families. The nation spent little on its army and navy compared to European nations. Lower debt and interest rates had reduced the annual federal interest expense.

As president, Cleveland diligently read each bill passed by Congress and vetoed hundreds of spending bills intended to curry favor with particular constituencies. He rejected legislation that would have extended generous veterans benefits to all soldiers with at least ninety days of service, regardless of whether they saw combat or suffered from a disability. The president called the "race for pensions" an incentive for "pretended incapacity" and "dishonesty."[9] In vetoing the Texas Seed Bill, which authorized $10,000 to help drought-stricken farmers, Cleveland criticized the use of federal tax dollars for "relief of individual suffering." His veto message proclaimed that "though the people support the Government, the Government should not support the people."[10]

The president also championed efficient use of public dollars and assets. He eliminated half the jobs at the Bureau of Printing and Engraving. When an audit showed that railroad companies had received land grants despite failing to meet contractual deadlines, the Cleveland administration forced them to relinquish eighty million acres.[11]

CLEVELAND'S FIGHT TO LOWER TAXES

Continuing federal surpluses had long encouraged the type of spending opposed by Cleveland. Treasury Secretary Daniel Manning continued to advise the president that it would be wasteful to use surplus revenues to buy back federal debt at a market value that included a large premium over the face value. As a result, Cleveland had to find another means of eliminating the surplus.

In the fall of 1887, Cleveland discussed the issue with key Democratic leaders at his farm, Oak View, now the site of the upscale Cleveland Park neighborhood in Washington, DC. Afterwards the president toured the country to participate in a series of "Oak View Conferences" with civil and political leaders. He observed a nation in the throes of rapid change.

Rail transportation reduced the significance of the country's vast distances. Immigrants used these rail lines to settle the interior's federal lands. The population of the Dakotas, Kansas, and Nebraska tripled in the 1870s and doubled during the 1880s. By 1890 the population of these four states approached three million, double the size of New York City.[12] Railroad corporations financed their expansion with large amounts of debt, and by the end of the 1880s they had issued bonds of over $5 billion, an amount far exceeding the amount of federal debt.[13]

The rail lines spawned both growth and discontent. Farmers worked hard and produced more, but larger harvests yielded lower prices and farm income. From 1886 to 1889 the average price of wheat had fallen by a third from its average during the years between 1870 and 1873.[14] Cotton and cattle prices had declined by almost half in the same period. Farmers borrowed to purchase mechanized equipment and then struggled to service their debt when wheat prices fell after production outstripped domestic demand. Wheat, like cotton, was a cash crop; corn producers fared better because their surpluses could be fed to livestock and poultry. Agrarian frustration erupted where the wheat and cotton belts began.

The cost of rail transportation reduced the net price received by farmers for their crop. Rail lines had been financed with help from public land grants. Since powerful industrialists and the federal postal service had secured volume discounts on their rail rates, farmers demanded that federal, state, and local officials obtain lower rail rates for agricultural products.

American farmers longed for both the independence of business owners and the secure income of hard-working employees. Federal import taxes had been used for generations to protect the interests of producers of textiles and other goods. Farmers now demanded similar help and took a keen interest in monetary policy.

The amount of circulating paper currency—greenbacks—remained fixed at the level set by John Sherman and Congress in 1878. Gold supplies would not increase until new gold discoveries in the late 1890s. The total money supply, including bank credit and federal silver certificates, rose almost in line with economic growth from 1870 to 1890. Yet distressed farmers demanded even greater amounts of currency in the form of silver dollars or greenbacks. Because the market price of silver declined relative to gold, farm prices fell less when expressed in silver rather than gold. In agricultural areas, many voters believed that an increased amount of silver dollars would lead to higher prices.

Farmers had been organizing long before Cleveland's 1887 national tour, and their organizations began to realign the constituencies of Democratic and Republican parties. It may seem surprising today that ranchers in Texas gave birth to a populist movement that is considered a precursor to twentieth-century liberalism. Several ranchers who met in 1876 at John R. Allen's ranch and called themselves the Pleasant Valley Farmers Alliance No. 1 had modest goals: recovering missing livestock and discouraging legal challenges to land titles. Farmers Alliances soon spread throughout rural Texas and began protesting railroad freight rates and the prices charged by monopolies such as the Barbed Wire Trust. The alliances spread like wildfire and spilled over into the cotton-growing Southern states. In 1880 Chicago publisher Milton George founded the Northern Farmers Alliance, and six years later a Texas minister began assembling the Colored Farmers Alliance.

The growing industrial economy posed other challenges. Deposits of coal and iron ore near Lake Superior powered rapid growth in steel production and related employment. Chicago and Minneapolis doubled in population during the 1880s, while Cleveland, Detroit, and Milwaukee grew by more than 50 percent.[15] The wages of laborers, however, did not rise as fast as the fortunes of the powerful men who dominated ownership of certain industries. Andrew Carnegie consolidated steel mills, improved production technology, and minimized costs. John D. Rockefeller built the country's dominant oil company in the same manner.

Younger writers such as Woodrow Wilson and Theodore Roosevelt idealized the virtues of political life in the early republic. Utopian authors offered a vision of the future rooted in the modern experience of industrial efficiency. Edward Bellamy's novel, *Looking Backward*, became a bestseller shortly after Cleveland's 1887 national tour. Bellamy depicted the United States in the year 2000 as a technologically advanced nation with universal public education, gender equality, pensions for seniors, greater access to medical care, shorter working hours, credit cards, discount stores, home delivery of goods, and even a music and information delivery system linked to homes through a "cable-telephone." Competent managers rather than corrupt politicians guided the public sector in *Looking Backward*. Bellamy's ideal inspired millions of Americans to join Nationalist Clubs committed to greater cooperation and economic justice.

Prairie populists and urban reformers applauded Cleveland's efforts to reduce wasteful spending, but the president had not addressed their concerns over growing industrial monopolies and declining farm income. The president did not believe he could raise the price of farm commodities or prohibit the sale of one business to another, but he sensed he had to do something.

Cleveland's search for a new Democratic program culminated in an extraordinary message to Congress in December 1887. Ordinarily the annual presidential message surveyed a broad range of federal policies, but Cleveland decided to focus entirely on a single, transformative issue. The Democratic president intended to spur a tax revolt.

He began with a simple fact: "The amount of money annually exacted, through the operation of present laws, from the industries and necessities of the people largely exceeds the sum necessary to meet the expenses of the Government." The president then branded excess tax revenues as "extortion and a culpable betrayal of American fairness and justice."[16] Import taxes, he argued, also imposed a cost on consumers greater than the revenues collected. Cleveland demanded that Congress cut import taxes.

Out of a total US workforce of 17,392,099 people, Cleveland noted that only 2,623,089 were employed in manufacturing industries that "claimed to be benefited by a high tariff." The federal government would continue to need some import tax revenue to pay federal expenses, including the repayment of all debt, so the president denied that his proposed tax cut was simply a cry for "so-called free trade."[17]

Twenty-first-century observers may find it hard to understand America's nineteenth-century attachment to import taxes and disdain for "so-called free trade." American officials viewed the use of trade barriers in the same manner as did the leadership of developing nations such as Japan and Korea after World War II. They believed that emerging domestic industries needed help to overcome the initial advantage of leading foreign competitors.

In reality, by the 1880s the federal government applied high import taxes to a steadily decreasing share of total imports. Taxes on sugar, molasses, wool products, and silk produced most revenues. Silk was taxed as a luxury, since the United States had no domestic industry to protect. The strongest economic pressure for import fees came from owners of Louisiana's sugar plantations, the refined Sugar Trust, and wool growers. However, import taxes—"tariffs"—had become a powerful symbol for federal commitment to industrial development.[18]

In the 1880s Republican leadership on tax issues had shifted from Senator Justin Morrill to his younger colleague, Senator Nelson Aldrich of Rhode Island. Aldrich seemed to know the purpose and effect of import duties on each of the more than four thousand categories of goods. He used that knowledge to build coalitions. More significantly, Aldrich understood that import taxes were an important symbolic commitment to domestic industrial growth.

The Senate blocked Cleveland's 1887 attempt to reduce import taxes. Democrats would need a strong public mandate in the 1888 election in order to overcome Aldrich's control of the Senate. It initially appeared that Cleveland would run against the old Republican warhorse John Sherman. Mark Hanna, an Ohio industrialist and political tactician, mounted an energetic national campaign on behalf of the aging statesman. The New York political machine once again blocked Sherman's nomination, and Republican delegates, as in 1876 and 1880, instead nominated another "dark horse" former Civil War general, Senator Benjamin Harrison of Indiana.

Aldrich's industrial allies spent unprecedented sums on behalf of Republican candidates in the fall campaign, especially in the swing states of Pennsylvania and New York. Though the proud and stubborn Cleveland considered campaigning to be beneath the dignity of a sitting president, he won the popular vote. Cleveland's Democratic enemies in Tammany Hall helped Harrison secure a narrow victory in New York and an Electoral College majority.

Before leaving the White House, Cleveland expressed the frustration of reformers: "The communism of combined wealth and capital . . . is not less dangerous than the communism of oppressed poverty and toil."[19]

THE LAST STAND OF
THE ORIGINAL REPUBLICANS

The eventful congressional session of 1889–1890 spawned a nickname: the Billion Dollar Congress. As in 2001, Republicans controlled the White House and both houses of Congress for the first time in many years and used that power to increase federal spending. The Congress that met in 1889–1890 marked the final passing of the leadership torch from Sherman's generation of Civil War Republicans to business-oriented pragmatists like Aldrich.

Aldrich considered politics to be a form of competition among varied economic interests. Though prairie populists cast their political agenda in the language of Christian virtue, Aldrich viewed them as an interest group trying to raise their income through inflation, artificially low rail rates, and a shift of federal taxation from imports to incomes. Aldrich and his allies aligned the Republican Party with industrial growth, a principal engine of future prosperity. Aldrich's ideology and leadership were well suited for a Senate containing many millionaires, a fact that Senator George Hearst of

California viewed as proof that senators were "the survivors of the fittest." Aldrich kept his word, compromised when necessary, and worked closely with another shrewd and powerful leader, House Speaker Thomas Reed of Maine.

Sherman was unwilling to yield to Aldrich on one issue. The aging Ohioan who had entered Congress in 1855 in order to break the power of slaveholders thought that his colleagues should challenge the power of monopolists who were consolidating their hold on American industry. The Senate's best lawyers questioned whether Congress could write a law preserving competition. They asked how Congress could prohibit an owner of stock from selling to the highest bidder or avoid penalizing gains obtained through greater efficiency.

Despite those questions, in 1889 Sherman introduced a bill challenging the legality of the trust combinations. Populist Democrats like Senator John Reagan of Texas, a former Confederate cabinet member, applauded Sherman's courage.[20] After being rewritten by two other pre–Civil War Republicans, George Hoar of Massachusetts and George Edmunds of Vermont, the Sherman Antitrust Act passed Congress in 1890. It still serves as the foundation of federal laws that preserve competition. Sherman, Hoar, and Edmunds tried but failed to enact federal legislation protecting the voting rights of African Americans. A voting rights bill passed the House before being killed in the Senate. It would take more than seventy years for the next voting rights bill to come to the Senate floor.

More Republicans in the Billion Dollar Congress supported higher federal spending and taxes than did Democrats. To reduce the surplus, Republicans increased spending on pensions for veterans and their surviving relatives—even while the number of living Civil War veterans declined. By 1890 those pensions amounted to a full third of the federal budget. The Billion Dollar Congress also passed a tax bill—the McKinley Tariff—that raised taxes on some manufactured goods while eliminating the unpopular tax on raw sugar that had previously yielded substantial federal revenue. Only in the 1920s would the Republican Party begin to be widely perceived as an advocate of smaller federal government.

The Billion Dollar Congress outraged prairie populists. In 1890 various Farmers Alliances and the Knights of Labor gathered at a national convention in Ocala, Florida, and framed a platform—the Ocala Demands—that endorsed a graduated income tax, an increase in the money supply, the "rigid and just" regulation of companies involved in public communications and transportation, and the direct election of US senators.[21] The Ocala platform, which many consider to be a precursor to the liberal agenda of the twentieth century, also called for a reduction in taxes and spending only for "necessary expenses of government economically and honestly administered."[22] These ancestral liberals would never have supported the use of debt to finance routine federal expenses.

Members of the Farmers Alliance won control of the legislatures of at least six states in the 1890 election. The election results two years later, in the first election conducted by secret ballot throughout the nation, shocked political pundits. Grover Cleveland trounced President Harrison in both the popular vote and the Electoral College, while Democrats won three-quarters of the seats in the House of Representatives. One out of twelve voters cast ballots for the candidate of a new Populist Party. Democrats won elections in Iowa, which was considered the most Republican state outside of New England. William McKinley, the affable chairman of the House Ways and Means Committee, was defeated in his previously Republican district in Ohio. Sixteen years after some Republicans coined the nickname "Grand Old Party," the party seemed old but not so grand.

THE DEPRESSION OF 1893

Democrats did not have long to savor their triumph. Ten days before President Cleveland's inauguration, the Philadelphia and Reading Railroad— one of the country's largest—filed for bankruptcy. Banks failed and output declined throughout 1893, signaling the onset of the nation's second severe depression. The Panic of 1893, the worst downturn since 1837, lasted for almost the entire length of Cleveland's second term.

Though most politicians looked for domestic explanations for the Panic of 1893, in fact the US economy was buffeted by global trends. Great Britain had experienced a banking crisis. When European demand for gold increased, some US commercial banks suspended gold payments to depositors.

When the Treasury experienced a run on its gold reserves, President Cleveland asked Congress for the authority to incur debt in order to buy gold reserves. Congress refused to do so. The Treasury had stockpiles of silver, and most Democrats and many Republicans thought that the federal government should just issue silver certificates to monetize any debt. This impasse over borrowing authority was more an issue of monetary policy (the use of new currency or gold) than fiscal policy (the level of spending and taxes). Congress had always prescribed the use, amount, and terms of new debt, a practice that had long served as one of the pillars of the American Fiscal Tradition.

When the Treasury's gold reserve fell to $50 million in early 1895, Cleveland bypassed Congress, relied on laws passed decades earlier, and exchanged new bonds for gold gathered by a J. P. Morgan consortium.[23] The use of debt to fill budget holes during a downturn was consistent with the American Fiscal Tradition, but Congress—including members of the president's own party—recoiled at the president's blatant disregard for the traditional practice of specific congressional authorization for new debt. Cleveland deepened the wound by instructing his cabinet to withhold political patronage from members of Congress who opposed his monetary policy. Sherman predicted that the president would "destroy his party" if he failed to compromise with Democratic congressional leaders.[24] That prophecy came true in the next election.

Attitudes concerning the use of debt during depressions in the nineteenth century differed from those in the twentieth century. In the Panics of 1837 and 1893 federal leaders were divided on their willingness to monetize debt using short-term notes or currency. By contrast, in 1933—the trough of the Great Depression—the Federal Reserve monetized debt aggressively with dollars used to purchase Treasury obligations. Nineteenth-century federal leaders also rejected using debt to invest in public works to boost employment. During the Panic of 1893 a successful businessman, John Coxey of Ohio, proposed that Congress authorize interest-free bonds to finance $500 million in roads constructed by workers paid $1.50 a day.[25] Coxey led an "army" of unemployed workers to Washington to press for congressional action. His proposal, however, ran counter to a deeply held value underlying the American Fiscal Tradition: the desire to protect the nation's future by minimizing debt. Not until the Hoover administration accelerated public works in 1929 did the nation incur debt during a downturn to provide temporary employment.

The political turmoil of the early 1890s loosened partisan bonds forged in the Civil War. That transition created opportunities for a new generation of Democratic and Republican leaders that included two young lawyers who had moved to the boomtown of Omaha, Nebraska. William Jennings Bryan and Charles Dawes lived on the same block, worked in law offices in the same small building, and even sued the same rail lines. Both of their fathers had been active in Midwestern politics. Bryan, a Democrat, escaped the routine of a small-town law practice by running for Congress. Dawes, a Republican, felt more comfortable working behind the scenes and—after moving to Chicago in 1893—became active in the reform movement. Bryan and Dawes each made their mark during their respective party's 1896 national conventions and would later help reshape the economic policies of their parties.

Bryan burst on the national political scene when supporters of a personal income tax chose him to make a closing argument following a long congressional debate in 1894. Congress sought to generate more revenue to reduce the recession-related budget deficit and lower certain import taxes. Since most of the wealthy Americans who would be subject to the tax lived in New York, Massachusetts, and a few adjoining states, congressional support for the income tax broke down principally along regional lines.

The thirty-three-year-old Bryan's powerful voice was a great asset in the era before microphones. He laced his speech with Christian and patriotic imagery. Responding to the argument that taxes on citizens with high incomes undermined the moral claim to civic participation by other Americans, Bryan replied, "Oh, sirs, is it not enough to betray the cause of the poor—must it be done with a kiss?" In response to a prominent business leader's argument that the income tax might force wealthy citizens to move their residences abroad, Bryan bellowed: "If we have people who value free government so little that they prefer to live under monarchial institutions, even without an income tax, rather than live under the stars and stripes and pay a two percent tax, we can better afford to lose them and their fortunes than risk the contaminating influence of their presence."[26] The House gave Bryan a standing ovation and passed the new income tax by a lopsided margin.

The Supreme Court declared key features of the new tax unconstitutional with an opinion that modern scholars consider an expression of ideology rather than law. A Supreme Court justice who concurred with the majority labeled a personal income tax a form of "class legislation."[27] Secretary of the Treasury John Carlisle blamed the Supreme Court's invalidation of the income tax for the budget deficit in fiscal year 1895.

With a depressed economy and divided party, Democrats suffered an election disaster in 1894 as severe as the Republican debacle two years earlier. Democrats lost 130 House seats, one of the largest swings in the nation's history.

THE GOP BUILDS A
NEW COALITION AND FUNDS A WAR

Mark Hanna had managed to make John Sherman the Republican front-runner in 1888 despite the candidate's stern personality, which had led some to call him the "Ohio Icicle." In 1893 Hanna found a more engaging candidate: William McKinley, a former congressman and Civil War veteran. To circumvent the control of state political machines, Hanna launched a grassroots presidential campaign that transformed national politics.

Hanna needed to polish McKinley's résumé. Buried in the voluminous 1890 tariff bill produced by McKinley's Ways and Means Committee was a prohibitively high tax on imported tin plates—a product not manufactured in the United States. McKinley guaranteed the debt of a startup manufacturer of tin plates, which later failed and could not pay its debts. To prevent McKinley from going bankrupt, Hanna quietly arranged for wealthy industrialists to pay off these debts and managed the Ohioan's victorious campaign for governor in 1894. Hanna then organized a national presidential campaign with the efficiency of a modern business enterprise.

Hanna urged powerful state leaders to back a potential winner early and threatened to create state organizations to compete with anyone who resisted. Charles Dawes put together a McKinley slate that fought the existing party leaders in Illinois. As Hanna's delegate count mounted, opposition began to fold.

Like Hanna, William Jennings Bryan ran an unconventional campaign that became a model for future campaigns of outsider candidates. Bryan bypassed traditional power brokers and directly courted delegates. He planned to pick a fight over the platform when he got to the nominating convention and correctly predicted to his wife that he would make a historic speech there. After an initial deadlock, delegates nominated the thirty-six-year-old Bryan for the presidency. The two-party system had become deeply embedded in the nation's unwritten constitution, and the Democratic Party largely absorbed the Populist Party. Other strong third parties would either atrophy or be absorbed by one of the two major parties after strong showings in 1912, 1968, and 1992.

Bryan embraced traditional Democratic fiscal policies such as cutting wasteful spending, balancing the budget, and lowering import taxes. Hanna tailored McKinley's campaign to a more industrialized nation. To voters struggling to recover from depression, he offered a clear and simple message: Republicans would restore prosperity. Though some historians treat the election as a referendum on Bryan's advocacy of more silver-backed currency, McKinley largely sidestepped the issue by supporting greater use of silver only on terms unlikely to be set in an international monetary treaty. Bryan's tributes to farmers and swipes at cities endeared him to rural voters but alienated many urban voters.

McKinley's win in 1896 represented less a shift in ideology than a continuation of the historic pattern of change following the onset of a severe downturn. Almost on cue, the economy began an extended period of strong growth immediately following McKinley's election. Gold supplies increased as a result of more efficient mining techniques and discoveries in the Yukon, Australia, and South Africa. With deflation checked, the movement to expand silver currency faded. Farm prices began a twenty-year rebound, sustained by increased demand for food among rapidly growing urban populations.

A massive wave of immigration that began in the mid-1880s boosted US population in 1900 to over seventy-six million, more than the combined population of Great Britain and France.[28] By then federal debt had been paid down to about $1 billion, and the Treasury held a large balance of surplus cash.[29] In 1900 the federal government paid only $40 million in interest on the debt, less than a third of the annual amount thirty years earlier.[30]

President McKinley reluctantly bowed to populist pressure to intervene in favor of rebels in Spain's colony of Cuba. McKinley and most business leaders allied with Hanna, and Aldrich viewed the war fever—which was inflamed by some newspaper chains—as an expensive distraction. After the battleship *Maine* exploded and sank in Havana's harbor on February 15, 1898, it appeared Congress would declare war with or without White House approval. Spain had met all the conditions demanded by US diplomats, and John Sherman was so dismayed by the declaration of war that he ended his public career by resigning as secretary of state.

Most Americans took pride in the nation's easy victory in the brief Spanish-American War, which lasted only until August 1898. The United

States had a population almost four times than Spain's and a somewhat larger navy. The nation easily financed the early war preparations with excess cash in the Treasury. An issue of bonds bearing a modest 3 percent interest rate was oversubscribed.[31]

The White House and Congress continued the traditional practice of raising taxes to limit war-related debt. Populist Democrats and reformers in each party resumed their call for taxes on incomes and estates rather than higher import taxes. Aldrich compromised with them by by agreeing to legislation that imposed new taxes on estates over $10,000 and a tax of 1 percent on the revenues of large oil and sugar refiners.[32] Congress also raised taxes on tobacco, beer, whiskey, banks, brokers, bowling alleys, patent medicines, and toiletries. Revenues from these taxes facilitated rapid debt reduction after the war.

Budget issues played only a minor role in the 1900 presidential election, in which each party's populists and reformers flexed their muscles. Most senior Democratic leaders believed that Bryan's call for more silver-backed currency had lost its luster. Yet Bryan, who controlled a majority of delegates, insisted that the party platform endorse a dubious plan for the Treasury to coin silver dollars minted with only about 70 cents of silver in each coin.

Mark Hanna, who chaired the national Republican party, also lost some control of his convention's delegates in 1900. Since it was a foregone conclusion that the convention would again nominate President McKinley, delegates focused on the nomination of the vice presidential candidate following the death of the incumbent. McKinley preferred Sherman's old friend, Senator William Allison, but Allison had no interest in leaving his chairmanship of the Senate Appropriations Committee. New York party boss Senator Tom Platt, sensing an opportunity to rid himself of a troublesome rival in state politics, began lining up support for his state's governor, Theodore Roosevelt Jr. Roosevelt's command of the colorful Rough Riders in the Spanish-American War and reform credentials made him a national hero.

Roosevelt genuinely did not want the job, which suited Hanna just fine. Hanna tried to put an end to Platt's plan by holding a press conference in which Hanna announced Roosevelt's refusal to be considered for the vice presidency. The reaction of delegates startled both Hanna and Roosevelt. Western delegates seemed determined to nominate the Rough Rider, regardless of the views of McKinley, party leaders, or even Roosevelt himself.

Charles Dawes, who had become a close advisor to McKinley, asked the president to head off a split in the party over the issue. Roosevelt, Dawes said, would strengthen the ticket in populist Western states and give the delegates someone new to celebrate. After McKinley asked Hanna to invite Roosevelt to be on the ticket, Hanna grumbled that the president would have to serve out his term to protect their party from "that cowboy."[33] That cowboy would soon define the public's expectations of the modern presidency and inaugurate a new and costly American role in international affairs.

PART III

PROGRESSIVE REFORMERS EMBRACE THE TRADITION: 1901–1940

8

REFORMERS REDEFINE THE
PARTIES AND GOVERNMENT

*1901–1915: Years when deficits exceeded debt service = 3
(1904 and 1909, Panama Canal; 1915,
brief downturn caused by the Great War)*

1902: THEODORE ROOSEVELT AND THE
ROLE OF THE FEDERAL GOVERNMENT

Theodore Roosevelt Jr. entered the White House following the death of President McKinley in 1901. Though other vice presidents who had become president upon the death of their predecessor wielded little influence, no one expected Roosevelt to keep quiet; he never had.

The forty-two-year-old Roosevelt was a national celebrity with an unusual biography: political reformer, war hero, cowboy, and author. He was also a natural campaigner. Grover Cleveland remarked that Roosevelt was "the most perfectly equipped and the most effective politician thus far seen in the presidency."[1] Many wondered, however, how an unabashed reformer could effectively assume leadership of a Republican Party dominated by Mark Hanna and a congressional "old guard" led by Senator Nelson Aldrich and Speaker of the House Joe Cannon of Illinois.

In 1902, his first full year in office, Roosevelt answered that question decisively. Several of his actions that year—regarding the Panama Canal, antitrust issues, labor relations, and foreign policy—fit the mood of early-twentieth-century America like custom-made boxing gloves.

Roosevelt helped Senator Hanna obtain congressional approval for American construction of a canal through Panama. Hanna grasped the significance of the canal to commerce, while Roosevelt appreciated its potential naval benefits. Hanna's leadership of his national party and sponsorship of the popular McKinley conferred unique authority on the squat, cigar-smoking senator from Ohio. He generally let senatorial colleagues such as Aldrich and Allison take the lead in crafting legislation. So members of both parties paid attention when Hanna gave his first and only major Senate speech. That 1902 speech described the advantages of building a canal through the Colombian province of Panama and persuaded Congress to abandon its earlier preference for a Nicaraguan route. Congress passed the Spooner Act, which gave the president responsibility for managing the project. Roosevelt used the US Navy to embolden rebels in Colombia's Panamanian territory, which the United States recognized as an independent government and paid to obtain rights to build a canal.

The Panama Canal facilitated trade between the East and West Coasts and the transit of American naval vessels. Congress authorized $375 million for the project. It was an enormous amount, more than half the annual spending in prior federal budgets. The Treasury used cash balances to finance the first large payment, totaling $50 million in fiscal year 1904. When the Panic of 1907 drained federal surpluses, the federal government issued bonds totaling $136.6 million for the specified purpose of completing the canal. That debt ultimately financed more than a third of the total cost of the largest public project yet undertaken.[2] Debt used to finish the canal—like debt incurred for the Louisiana Purchase and Union Pacific rail line—helped connect and secure the nation's borders.

While Roosevelt worked as an effective partner with Hanna on the Panama Canal, he demonstrated his independence from Republican leaders by filing an antitrust suit against some of the party's largest donors. In February 1902 Hanna and the party's other congressional leaders were stunned to learn that the president had authorized the Justice Department to sue banker J. P. Morgan and the Northern Trust Company, a combination of the Northern Pacific and Great Northern railroads. The federal government accused them of violating the Sherman Antitrust Act, a law that had been largely unused since its passage in 1890.

After hearing of the lawsuit, Morgan and other financiers traveled by private rail car to Washington to plan a response. Roosevelt disarmed the agitated tycoons by inviting them to share a drink at the White House when their train arrived at ten p.m. The next morning Roosevelt met with Morgan, who wanted to determine whether other attacks on his interests—particularly the Steel Trust—would follow. Roosevelt assured him that the legal action was not personal and that the Steel Trust had nothing to worry about unless it had "done something that we regard as wrong."[3] Morgan and his colleagues realized that while they could talk frankly with the new president, he was subservient to no one. Americans applauded their president's courage in taking action against some of the nation's most powerful businessmen.

Roosevelt also broke new ground in labor relations in 1902. Previous administrations had deployed federal marshals—armed with injunctions issued by federal courts—against striking workers. In the fall of 1902, during a crippling and violent coal miners' strike, Roosevelt invited mine operators and union leaders to meet with him to find common ground. Many in Congress called for the federal government to take over the mines to avoid a winter coal shortage. Roosevelt instead suggested arbitration by a neutral party, such as former Democratic president Grover Cleveland. After the coal companies rebuffed Roosevelt's offer, J. P. Morgan showed the president that he, too, knew how to wield power. Morgan, whose partners controlled many of the largest customers of the mine owners, brought the owners to the negotiating table.

Roosevelt's antitrust and labor initiatives were bold but not expensive. His vision of a larger navy and more assertive foreign policy had a higher price tag. The president previewed his new foreign policy in 1902, when England and Germany, the world's two greatest naval powers, sent warships to Venezuela in order to collect a past-due debt of $70 million. The president dispatched an American naval fleet to Venezuela, informed the German ambassador to the United States that an occupation of that country would lead to war, and then offered to personally arbitrate the dispute. The ambassador politely explained that Kaiser Wilhelm had already considered and rejected that alternative. The president, who considered the German ruler an insecure bully, curtly responded by giving Germany a deadline to comply with the American "offer."

The rattled German ambassador called a mutual friend to ask whether this inexperienced American leader could possibly be serious about declaring war over Venezuela. Yes, he was told, Roosevelt was a new sort of American president. The night before Roosevelt's deadline, the German Reichstag met in special session, reversed the kaiser's position, and consented to arbitration. Immediately after the Germans backed down, Roosevelt welcomed a high-level German delegation to Washington and impressed its members by reciting—from memory—entire passages from German literature. Roosevelt began to define a new, global role for the United States, one supported by a stronger military.

TEDDY'S NAVY

When he was just twenty-four years old, Roosevelt wrote *The Naval War of 1812*, which criticized Albert Gallatin's limitations on the navy. As recently as 1879, when the United States considered influencing the outcome of a war between Peru and Chile, some wondered whether Chile's navy was stronger than that of the United States. A naval buildup started when Roosevelt served as McKinley's assistant secretary of the navy. Total military spending in 1897 was $84 million, about the same level it had been for the previous twenty years. By 1908, Roosevelt's last full year in office, spending had soared to $115 million for the navy and $156 million for the army.[4]

Roosevelt requested more battleships in his message to Congress in December 1902. The Venezuelan crisis and Roosevelt's popularity prompted Congress to fund five new battleships, a substantial increase. In March 1905 Roosevelt managed to obtain funding for a fleet consisting of twenty-eight battleships, which he said would allow the country "to rest and merely replace the ships which are worn out."[5] The president, however, did not rest long in his pursuit of a stronger navy. In 1906 he asked Congress to fund new battleships that could compete with a the superior, turbine-driven British design. Roosevelt also instructed a skeptical War Department to purchase several airplanes, a recent invention, to test their military potential.

In 1907 a fleet of sixteen modern American battleships headed out to sea from the Chesapeake Bay.[6] Roosevelt directed the battleships—referred to as the Great White Fleet on account of their fresh coats of white paint—to display American strength abroad after showing the flag at major US port cities. Congress had not approved funds to finance that voyage, but Roosevelt reckoned it would be forced to pay for the return of the fleet. Because of the enduring power of the American Fiscal Tradition, no federal leader even considered borrowing money to pay for the fleet or its routine operating expenses. Within thirty-eight years of the Great White Fleet's tour, the US Navy would dominate the world's oceans and continue to do so—at great cost—until the present.

Many congressional leaders indulged Roosevelt's naval and foreign policy on account of his popularity. He weakened Bryan's hold on populists and elevated the influence of progressive reformers within the Republican Party. The president handpicked the 1908 Republican presidential nominee, William Howard Taft. Taft had been his loyal lieutenant but had never previously been elected to public office.

THE CHANGING ROLE OF
IMPORT TAXES AND THE PANIC OF 1907

Import tax revenues had steadily declined for decades in relation to the total value of imports and the size of the US economy. Ever since the nation had become a net exporter, business leaders realized the benefits of lower barriers to international trade. Pressures to alter the GOP's historical view of import taxes had begun shortly before Roosevelt entered the White House. In 1901 Republican leaders in Iowa had unanimously endorsed reductions in import taxes obtained through reciprocal trade agreements with other nations. In a speech delivered the day before he was assassinated, President McKinley noted that "the period of exclusiveness has passed. The expansion of our trade and commerce is the . . . problem."[7]

Since import taxes represented 40 percent of federal revenue, lowering these taxes would require new offsetting sources of federal income.[8] Taxes—who pays them and how much—are often at the heart of any party's budget policy, and Republican leaders found it awkward to shift from their historical defense of import taxes. It would also be difficult to cut import taxes without reducing outlays for the emblematic Republican program of pensions for the families of Union Civil War veterans. By 1902 these pensions cost $138 million, an amount greater than outlays for the army or navy.[9]

The Senate's Republican old guard worried that a reduction in import taxes would open the door for an income tax, which was favored by Democratic populists and a rising number of Republican reformers. Republican congressional leaders sought to reach an understanding with Roosevelt on tax policy. They could not dictate to the popular president; they needed his help in the West before the 1902 midterm elections, especially to compensate for expected Republican losses in urban areas populated by ethnic Democratic majorities. Roosevelt, in turn, sought cooperation from his party's Senate leadership in order to pass legislation.

On September 16, 1902, the president hosted a meeting with Aldrich, Allison, and Hanna. No one took notes, but Roosevelt's words on his campaign tour after the meeting describe their compromise on tax policy. He said the federal government should "treat the tariff as a business proposition and not from the standpoint of any political party. . . . But neither our nation nor any other can stand the ruinous policy of readjusting its business to radical changes of the tariff at short intervals."[10] Roosevelt proposed no major tax bill during his eight years in the White House. However, the days of raising revenue using higher import taxes were over.

After his landslide election victory in 1904, Roosevelt outlined his vision of a tax system that included a "progressive tax on all fortunes."[11] Two years later, he endorsed a "graduated inheritance tax, and, if possible, a graduated income tax."[12] According to the most popular Republican president thus far in the nation's history, "the man of great wealth owes a peculiar obligation . . . because he derives special advantages from the mere existence of government."[13]

Aldrich did not bring serious tax legislation to the Senate floor until after Roosevelt left office. To a degree unanticipated by Aldrich, public opinion on tax issues by then had shifted dramatically in Roosevelt's direction. Aldrich's tax bill was prompted by the need to offset federal revenue lost during a brief recession, the Panic of 1907.

The first major downturn in the Panic of 1893 also demonstrated the need to modernize the nation's monetary and budgetary system. The recession began with a fall in copper prices, which severely affected some Latin American economies, their European creditors, and investors in copper stocks. These investors included the president of the Knickerbocker Trust Company, one of many large trust companies that had constituted a parallel and unregulated banking system, similar to the largely unregulated financial institutions that played a leading role in the Great Recession of 2008. National banks in New York in 1907 had assets of $1.8 billion compared to the $1.4 billion in trust companies.[14] News of copper speculation by Knickerbocker's president caused a run on its deposits.

Depositors lined up to withdraw funds from other New York trust companies and banks. News of the financial panic reached J. P. Morgan at a church retreat in Virginia and Roosevelt at a bear hunt in Louisiana. Roosevelt continued hunting, while the seventy-year-old Morgan returned to New York. Morgan convened the nation's leading bankers and assigned them tasks such as auditing the strength of various banks. Treasury Secretary George Cortelyou, who attended Morgan's New York meetings, used Treasury deposits to strengthen the liquidity of certain banks. Morgan was a whirlwind of activity, raising more than $25 million for loans to brokers, keeping the New York City government solvent, and enlisting New York's clergy to urge depositors to remain calm.

These prompt actions facilitated a swift recovery from the recession, but not before the downturn lowered federal revenues and produced the first federal budget deficit in years. The federal government used its cash reserves to avoid incurring debt. The Panic of 1907 led to reforms of the tax, monetary, and budgeting systems that would provide policy tools of vital importance to future federal leaders.

Immediately after Taft's inauguration in March 1909, the president met with Senator Aldrich and House Speaker Cannon to discuss the need to close the budget deficit. That month Congress passed a resolution instructing the "Secretary of the Treasury [to] advise Congress how . . . the estimated appropriations could with the least injury to the public served be reduced or . . . new taxes as may be necessary to cover the deficiency."[15]

Even though his party held sixty of the ninety-two seats in the Senate, Aldrich lost control of the debate over his bill that raised import taxes. A group of Republican senators—led by Senator Robert La Follette of Wisconsin and Allison's successor, Albert Cummins of Iowa—lined up support in both parties for the addition of an income tax to Aldrich's bill. Aldrich sought President Taft's advice. Taft and William Jennings Bryan, his Democratic opponent for the presidency, both supported a federal personal income tax and lower import taxes during their 1908 campaigns.

Aldrich agreed to Taft's recommendation of a new corporate income tax and a constitutional amendment permitting a personal income tax, subject to state ratification. Within days a corporate income tax bill passed the Senate, by a vote of 59 to 11. Aldrich's resolution for a constitutional amendment that allowed a personal income tax passed the Senate unanimously.

Progressive leaders resented that Taft had refused to lead their fight for the income tax. The president was far more forceful in fighting on behalf of another progressive cause: establishing a modern and transparent federal budget process. This initiative began in 1909, when Congress requested a report from the administration about how to balance the next budget. Treasury secretaries since Albert Gallatin had annually reported on the prior year's spending and revenues, while various executive departments provided information about estimated future needs directly to congressional committees. Treasury Secretary Franklin MacVeagh recommended the use of a formal budget process that included annual total spending and revenue targets. He explained that budgets based solely on informal coordination between the executive and legislative branches, as they had been during Hamilton's tenure, "could never have lasted and cannot now be instituted."[16]

The Commission on Economy and Efficiency, authorized by Congress and appointed by Taft, urged the White House to prepare an annual budget proposal for submission to Congress at the beginning of each calendar year. Fearing a loss of power to the executive branch, Congress rejected this recommendation. Taft complained in 1912 that the "United States is the only great Nation whose Government is operating without a budget."[17] It may seem odd to many citizens a century later that the federal government rarely borrowed before it had a formal presidential budget submission, a distinct congressional budget, or any legal ceiling on total federal debt. Such was the power of the American Fiscal Tradition.

THE NEED FOR A CENTRAL BANK

The Panic of 1907 also highlighted the need for an institutionalized system of central banking. Some combination of the US Treasury, commercial banks, and, occasionally, Congress had exercised control over the money supply since 1790. Nineteenth-century politicians tended to blame downturns on various aspects of the banking system.

Classical economists of the nineteenth century thought that the supply of money played a relatively small role in the shaping of business cycles. They attributed market swings to the influence of "animal spirits," notably greed and fear. Yet no one could dispute the fact that bank failures contracted credit and prolonged each of the nation's two depressions, beginning in 1837 and 1893. Banks by their very nature were leveraged. As a result, bank failures during downturns caused credit to contract by more than simply the loss of equity in banks.

The Constitution gave Congress responsibility for the currency. As with the congressional power to authorize debt, the Constitution itself provided no guidance about how that power should be exercised. Until the Civil War most commerce was conducted with bank notes and foreign coins. By the late nineteenth century, commercial transactions depended on entries in bank ledgers rather than "hand-to-hand" currency. Borrowers relied on bank credit. Since banks could make loans many times the value of their deposits held as reserves, any bank could be vulnerable to a run that jeopardized the security of deposits and availability of credit unless the bank could turn to some lender of last resort.

The federal government had long used its cash balances to bolster the reserves of the commercial banking system. Treasury Secretary Gallatin had shored up the reserves of a vulnerable bank in 1801, his first year in office. A subtreasury system—proposed by Van Buren and Calhoun and implemented by Treasury Secretary Walker during the Polk administration—institutionalized the Department of the Treasury's role in performing some functions of a central bank. John Sherman used that power when he deliberately strengthened liquid bank reserves by exchanging gold for bank-held federal debt. Throughout the late nineteenth century and early twentieth century, the Treasury shifted its deposits to agricultural regions to support the capacity to make loans that came due after harvests. Roosevelt's treasury secretaries, Leslie M. Shaw and George Cortelyou, aggressively used the Treasury Department's control over federal deposits to strengthen reserves supporting bank credit. In fact, some reformers viewed a new central bank as a means of diffusing the treasury secretary's enormous power over the entire banking system.

Private bankers themselves performed the functions of a central bank. Regional bank clearinghouses facilitated the daily clearing of drafts, or checks, as well as providing a means for clearinghouse members to boost their short-run liquidity. However, there was no formal mechanism for coordinating monetary actions across the regional clearinghouses.

Since 1790 national leaders had had difficulty balancing the roles of elected officials and private bankers in regulating the supply of money and credit. Placing this power exclusively with the president or his chosen treasury secretary could result in political abuse or the instability inherent in election cycles, while delegating this power to an association of private bankers could create conflicts of interest and lead to a concentration of power largely unaccountable to elected officials. Congress itself was a large and part-time legislative body that lacked the capacity and expertise to administer a central bank. The improvised response to the Panic of 1907 showed the benefits of having a "lender of last resort" that could call on the credit of the federal government and large pools of bank assets.

In 1908 Senator Aldrich—who was only the third chairman of the Senate Finance Committee in forty years, following Sherman and Morrill—decided to define the proper balance between federal and private control of central banking. No one was better prepared for the task than the Rhode Island Republican whom Taft admired for his "effectiveness, straightforwardness and clearheadedness."[18] Even those who disagreed with Aldrich respected his intelligence and candor. Powerful business tycoons, who treated most elected officials as supplicants, considered Aldrich a peer. The nation's two most powerful businessmen, J. P. Morgan and John Rockefeller, detested each other, but both admired Aldrich. Aldrich vacationed with Morgan, and in 1901—at the year's premier society wedding—the senator's daughter Abby married Rockefeller's sole heir.

The Aldrich-Vreeland Act of 1908 allowed banks to pool certain reserves to raise their capital, granted the Treasury additional authority to issue notes, and created the National Monetary Commission to recommend reforms. Aldrich chaired this commission and recruited an outstanding team of advisors to assist him. He spent months studying banking and meeting with European central bankers.

Other financial leaders of the era had also been studying the national banking system. Two respected New York bankers—Paul Warburg and Frank Vanderlip—criticized the lack of a US central bank with the power to call on bank reserves and public credit during a downturn. Vanderlip headed the City Bank of New York, which had underwritten the bond issue financing the Spanish-American War and served as the bank for Rockefeller interests. Warburg had moved to New York from Germany to manage his father-in-law's Kuhn Loeb investment bank. Vanderlip and Warburg appreciated the long-standing political impediments to a central bank. For more than a century many Democrats had resisted a privately led central bank, while early-twentieth-century Republican congressmen often echoed the views of regional bankers who feared central control of their operations. Warburg proposed makeshift alternatives to a modern central bank in order to navigate around those perceived political barriers. Aldrich agreed with Warburg's critique of the existing banking system but rejected his recommendations as being too "timid." Aldrich bluntly told him, "You say that we cannot have a central bank, and I say we can."[19]

In 1920 Warburg, Vanderlip, and other bankers traveled in secrecy, using assumed names, to meet with Aldrich at a remote resort on Jekyll Island off Georgia's coast. There they fleshed out a plan for a National Reserve Association, which would consist of regional bank groups and a central governing board with the power to guide national interest rates. When leading bankers heard the details of that plan, they objected to the recommendation that the president be given the power to appoint the chairman of the national board. William Jennings Bryan, still a force to be reckoned with among rural Democrats, criticized the plan for giving bankers too large a role on the governing board. Perhaps Warburg had perceived the political hurdles better than Aldrich, who exited the Senate at the end of his term in 1910.

Reformers Triumph

Voters gave reformers control of the federal government and the two major political parties in the pivotal election of 1912. The two leading candidates—Theodore Roosevelt and Woodrow Wilson—ran as progressive reformers. Along with socialist Eugene Debs, they received 77 percent of the popular vote.

The new mainstream political current that swept that election shaped the perspectives of a new generation of federal leaders. Some of them—including William McAdoo, Calvin Coolidge, John Nance Garner, Robert Doughton, Herbert Hoover, and Franklin Roosevelt—would make budget policy for decades. A younger group who came of age during the Progressive Era—like Robert Taft, Arthur Vandenberg, and Harry Truman—would set budget priorities until the early 1950s. They all believed in the limits on the use of debt embedded in the American Fiscal Tradition. Except for the traditional uses of debt during the Panic of 1893, the Spanish-American War, and the Panama Canal, the federal government had not borrowed during their lifetimes. The prevailing attitude of the era was expressed in 1888 by a young scholar, Woodrow Wilson: "Appropriation without accompanying taxation is as bad as taxation without representation."[20]

William Gibbs McAdoo exuded the confidence of a businessman who had overcome setbacks and persevered until he succeeded. He emerged as a public figure in New York City by constructing two parallel subway tunnels that linked the city with New Jersey in 1908. Owners of other local rail lines had often shared the attitude of Cornelius Vanderbilt, famous for the maxim "The customer be damned." McAdoo, however, trained his employees to treat riders according to his company's motto, "The customer is king."

The restless and ambitious McAdoo undertook a new type of challenge when helping build the political career of Woodrow Wilson, a political scientist, historian, and president of nearby Princeton University. In a 1907 series of lectures on constitutional government in the United States, Wilson described the president's power of leadership as anything that "he has the sagacity or force to make it."[21] Professor Wilson marveled at Roosevelt's use of that power, though he personally preferred the older spirit of reform exemplified by former Democratic president Grover Cleveland. Wilson believed in a strong chief executive, but by 1908 Princeton University's board—including Grover Cleveland—reined in Wilson's authority as the school's president. Wilson, like McAdoo, yearned to play on a larger stage.

McAdoo and Wilson had much in common. They were both Southerners who left small-town law practices to seek their fortunes in the Northeast, the nation's financial and academic center. They were both tall, slender, courteous, well spoken, and disciplined. Though they rubbed shoulders with the nation's wealthy business elite, they respected great deeds more than great fortunes. Each took pride in adapting traditional values to modern circumstances. Wilson had championed a more egalitarian culture at a college that had long been dominated by private clubs, while McAdoo implemented the novel practice of paying women the same wage as men for the same job.

New Jersey, the home of Wilson's Princeton, was rapidly changing. During the nation's largest wave of immigration, the state's population swelled from 1.4 million in 1890 to 2.5 million in 1910.[22] Urban bosses battled reformers within the state's Democratic and Republican parties. A majority of New Jersey voters had supported Grover Cleveland in his three elections, but rejected the agrarian populism of William Jennings Bryan in all three of his presidential campaigns. New Jersey's electoral votes could swing the outcome of a close presidential election.

National magazines and large newspaper chains often served as effective vehicles for mobilizing national opinion. McAdoo's friend, publisher George Harvey, used *Harper's Magazine* to promote a public career for Woodrow Wilson. New Jersey Democrats recruited Wilson to run for the governorship, a move that Wilson described to a friend as "the mere preliminary of a plan to nominate [him] in 1912 for the presidency."[23] A

Democratic landslide in 1910 gave Democrats control of the House of Representatives for the first time since 1892 and helped Wilson become governor of New Jersey.

The rising tide of reform had reached Capitol Hill even before the November 1910 midterm elections. That spring Democrats and progressive Republicans had limited the enormous power of Speaker Joseph Cannon. The House Ways and Means Committee was given responsibility for making committee assignments. This power, combined with the committee's jurisdiction over all tax legislation, gave those who chaired the committee extraordinary influence on federal budgets for much of the twentieth century.

Roosevelt's departure for a tour of Europe and an African safari created a political vacuum in the GOP after Taft entered the White House. Taft attempted to implement Roosevelt's agenda without his predecessor's characteristic sweeping rhetoric. When Roosevelt returned from abroad in June 1910, he was not impressed with Taft's progress. In August 1910 Roosevelt returned to the public arena with a passionate speech promoting a "New Nationalism." The senators who had led the charge on the income tax formed the National Progressive Republican Caucus.

Taft provoked Roosevelt's anger in late 1911 by filing an antitrust action that claimed his predecessor had been duped into approving an antitrust violation. The former president, an amateur boxer, announced he would throw his hat "in the ring" for the next Republican presidential nomination. After the power of patronage allowed Taft to retain the Republican nomination, Roosevelt bolted from the GOP to head the ticket of the new Progressive Party.

Delegates to the 1912 Democratic National Convention in Baltimore arrived in high spirits after hearing of the GOP split. Many Democratic leaders, however, worried about their party's own division between rural populists who still admired Bryan and urban voters represented by organizations such as New York's Tammany Hall. House Speaker Champ Clark, who tried to keep Bryan at a distance, won most of the primaries against an amateurish Wilson campaign.

Bryan's booming voice unexpectedly challenged the convention's leadership on the first, largely ceremonial order of business: the designation of a temporary presiding officer. He narrowly lost that vote but made his presence felt as he greeted delegates—most of whom he knew personally— while seated in the convention's front row as he fanned himself with a large palm leaf. Though it became apparent only in hindsight, the battle for the direction of the Democratic Party for most of the twentieth century would be decided in that sweltering convention hall.

Large delegations from states dominated by urban organizations—New York, Illinois, and Massachusetts—sought to maximize their strength by supporting minor candidates and then switching that support to create momentum for a candidate who would subsequently be in their debt. On the tenth ballot the large New York delegation controlled by Tammany Hall chief Charles Murphy swung its votes to the front-runner Clark, giving him a clear majority. Clark delegates began a long demonstration to celebrate their anticipated victory. McAdoo persuaded Wilson not to send a prepared telegram conceding defeat, since party rules still required a nomination by a two-thirds majority.

Then Bryan announced to the delegates that he could not back Clark, since Bryan interpreted New York's support as a sign that Clark might be a candidate beholden to Wall Street. Support for Clark slipped away over numerous ballots until the delegates finally nominated Wilson on the forty-sixth ballot. A professor with barely eighteen months experience in public office had become the presidential nominee of the world's oldest political party.

Roosevelt's platform—the "Contract with the People"—called for "a modern industrial society" with minimum wages, the abolition of child labor, and a social insurance that could mitigate the "hazards of sickness, accident, invalidism, involuntary unemployment, and old age."[24] Wilson endorsed many of Roosevelt's proposed policies, although he expressed that support in language that also conveyed a Jeffersonian skepticism of federal power. The aloof Democratic nominee agonized privately over his failure to match Roosevelt's magnetism on the campaign trail. After being shot at close range three weeks before the election, the former president proceeded to give an hour-long speech with a bullet lodged an inch from his heart.

Roosevelt's stamina and popularity were not sufficient to overcome the strength of a two-party system that had become embedded in the nation's unwritten constitution. This system was every bit as powerful as traditional limits on debt. The defection of Roosevelt progressives from the Republican Party gave Wilson an easy victory in the Electoral College. Taft received only 23 percent of the national popular vote. In several states the incumbent president trailed the Socialist candidate, Eugene Debs.

The 1912 election completed the thirty-year ascendency of populist and progressive reformers. Roosevelt returned to the Republican Party, which in turn realized it needed to bring many of the former president's supporters back into the fold. Wilson made the urban reformer McAdoo his secretary of the treasury and the rural populist Bryan his secretary of state.

Wilson trusted McAdoo's economic and political judgment, and the two became even closer after McAdoo married one of Wilson's daughters. Assisted by a talented staff, McAdoo became the most powerful treasury secretary since John Sherman.

A CENTRAL BANK AND AN INCOME TAX

The Democratic platform in 1912 explicitly opposed the "Aldrich plan" for a central bank. During the election, McAdoo and Wilson's largest donor, the moderate Republican Cleveland Dodge, quietly assured Wall Street firms that Bryan's rural populists would not control the monetary policy of a Wilson administration.

Carter Glass, a fiscally conservative Democrat from Virginia, chaired the House Banking Committee. He had concluded that the nation needed a central bank. Glass traveled to the president-elect's New Jersey home to learn Wilson's views on the controversial issue. Wilson, who had studied the history of American banking and monetary policy, agreed with Glass. In the following months they worked as a team to overcome opposition from Democratic populists led by Bryan, regional bankers who resisted central control, and other bankers who insisted that a central bank be controlled only by bankers.

Glass's initial bill merely created regional associations. As Glass anticipated, many bankers came forward to make the case for at least some measure of central authority. In order to rebut Bryan's claim that a central bank would allow private bankers too much influence, Wilson told Glass to amend his bill to give obligations of the new central bank the backing of the full faith and credit of the federal government. Glass argued that would be unnecessary because the proposed reserve system pooled most of the nation's commercial banking reserves. Wilson persuaded Glass by turning the argument around: if federal credit was redundant, then a federal guaranty would do no harm and might reassure populists that the federal government would control a central bank that exercised a constitutional power ultimately derived from Congress.

Wilson understood that Democratic opposition to a central bank had always rested more on distrust of bankers than of federal authority. Wilson and Glass eventually agreed to Bryan's demand that the president be given the power to select the members of the national governing board. By giving board members staggered, fourteen-year terms, they sought to preserve the central bank's independence from any particular administration. After passage by the House, 287 to 85, and the Senate, in a closer vote, Wilson signed the Federal Reserve Act into law on December 23, 1913. The perennial controversy over "paper money" faded into history. The Federal Reserve's green paper notes became the nation's principal hand-to-hand currency and paper money no longer appeared as debt on the national balance sheet.[25]

American history before the Federal Reserve yields a straightforward answer to the question of whether the federal government had "printed money" to cover budget deficits. The United States printed $450 million during the Civil War to pay its bills.[26] Between the Civil War and the creation of the Federal Reserve, the Treasury issued bonds—instead of currency—to refinance Civil War debt and to fund debt incurred during the Panic of 1893, the Spanish-American War, and the construction of the Panama Canal.

The new Federal Reserve did, of course, have the authority to use cash—that is, Federal Reserve notes or credits—to purchase federal debt from the Treasury or in the open market. The Federal Reserve ordinarily has monetized debt as a means of expanding the money supply in order to provide liquidity and accommodate growth. When the Federal Reserve was created, no one anticipated how quickly it would be called on to monetize debt used to finance World War I.

The Federal Reserve was not the only innovation in 1913 that forever altered the management of federal debt and budgets. That year, after state ratification of the sixteenth amendment to the Constitution, Congress enacted a personal income tax applicable to individuals with the highest incomes. The tax was included in eight pages of an import tax bill totaling more than eight hundred pages. Congress taxed 1 percent of all "gains, profits, and income" for people with incomes above a $3,000 standard deduction and an extra $1,000 deduction for a married taxpayer. Higher rates, then called surtaxes, were applied to those in higher income brackets. Annual taxable income of over $500,000 was taxed at the maximum rate of 7 percent. The bill excluded from taxation all interest on state and local bonds and allowed taxpayers to deduct "necessary" business expenses, including tax and interest payments. In its first years, only 2 percent of American households paid the federal income tax.[27]

Wilson's early legislative agenda consisted of regulatory and tax reforms rather than large new spending programs. The budget was in surplus. For the first time in years, postal service was paid for entirely with dedicated user fees.

The triumph of rural populists and urban progressives did not alter the power of the nation's unwritten fiscal constitution. From 1902 through 1915, the level of federal interest-bearing debt was stable for longer than at any other time in the nation's history, before or since. Debt in this period began at $931 million and ended at $962 million.[28] In fact, in 1915 the total debt differed little from when Grover Cleveland had taken office in 1884, even though national income had quadrupled. Two-thirds of the debt in 1915 represented refinanced Civil War debt, while the remainder consisted of bonds used to finance either the Panama Canal or the Spanish-American War. Congress authorized each issue of debt, and the public could easily identify precisely why the federal government had borrowed.

9

FINANCING A WORLD WAR
AND PAYING DOWN DEBT

*1916–1928: Years when deficits exceeded debt service = 2
(1917–1918, World War I)*

DEBATING MILITARY PREPAREDNESS

President Wilson went to bed on election night in 1916 believing that
he had lost. His narrow margin of victory, despite the strong economy,
reflected the close partisan balance that existed once Theodore Roosevelt
returned to the GOP. The war in Europe cast a shadow over the election.
Wilson had kept the United States out of Europe's tragic conflict, but
found—as had Jefferson and Madison—that it was difficult to navigate a
policy of neutrality in the perilous waters of trade embargoes, particularly
after the advent of submarine warfare.

The war actually seemed to help the US economy after an initial financial panic in 1914. American products replaced European exports to Asia
and Latin America. Gold flowed in as exports flowed out, and New York
City displaced London as the center of global finance.

The red ink of European debt rose in tandem with the river of blood
flowing from a generation of European soldiers. In contrast, the federal
government ran a surplus in the fiscal year ending June 30, 1916. Though
Congress had enacted an income tax, consumption taxes—the traditional
staple of federal taxation—accounted for 80 percent of federal revenues.

Taxes on alcohol and tobacco alone generated more revenue than did the new personal income tax, which was paid in 1916 by only 437,000 wealthy American families out of a total population of about 100 million.[1] That mix of tax revenue would soon change forever.

Democratic Ways and Means Committee Chairman Claude Kitchin opposed calls for higher military spending in response to the German submarine threat. Kitchin, who also served as the Democratic majority leader in 1915, largely controlled federal tax policy. He could count on help from his home state ally, Furnifold Simmons of North Carolina, then chairman of the Senate Finance Committee. An audience often filled the galleries in the House when the eloquent Kitchin, a master of budget detail, engaged in debate.

Kitchin's political heritage and views on World War I shed light on the sudden and irrevocable emergence of a federal tax system based largely on the ability to pay. His family had helped lead the wing of North Carolina's Democratic Party that had emerged from the Farmers Alliance in the 1890s. North Carolina Democrats channeled agrarian populism into a mainstream program of reforms. Kitchin had supported the Wilson administration until he disagreed with the president's request for more battleships in the wake of a German submarine attack on the ocean liner *Lusitania* in 1915. Majority Leader Kitchin thought the purchase of new battleships would be more effective in raising the profits of steelmakers than sinking submarines. Congress nonetheless increased naval funding, prompting the forty-seven-year-old Kitchin to complain to William Jennings Bryan about the influence of "the jingoes and war traffickers."[2]

The American Fiscal Tradition was so strong that no mainstream American leader in 1915 argued that debt rather than taxes should fund this military buildup. Chairman Kitchin succeeded in doubling—from 1 to 2 percent—the basic tax rate applied to incomes above a standard exemption. That exemption was set at a level higher than the incomes of a vast majority of households. Graduated rates of up to 13 percent applied to the highest incomes.[3] Like Jefferson in the 1790s, Kitchin hoped that the burden of taxation would dampen enthusiasm for war, which ran especially strong in financial centers with commercial ties to Great Britain. He anticipated that "when the New York people are thoroughly convinced that the income tax will have to pay for the increases in the army and navy . . . preparedness will not be so popular with them as it now is."[4]

After his reelection the professorial Wilson asked each warring European nation to give a written description of its goals in continuing war. The war cabinets in London, Paris, and Berlin dreamed that victory would enable them to acquire territory and force their enemy to pay reparations. Yet the government of each belligerent power was reluctant to admit those objectives in a war justified to citizens as a matter of national survival.

By 1916 the war had taken a horrific turn. More than two million soldiers had died during failed offensives intended by each side to obtain a decisive victory on the Western Front. At the beginning of 1917, Allied and Central leaders had become desperate. They faced the potential loss of an entire generation of young men while their civilian populations grew restless and experienced economic hardships.

Germany's military command rested its hopes on a decisive battle in France. To maximize their chance of success on that front following a peacy treaty with Russia, they planned to disrupt Allied supply lines. On February 1, 1917, Germany announced its intention to begin unrestricted submarine warfare against all ships in a zone around Great Britain, France, Italy, and the Eastern Mediterranean. Some German leaders hoped to delay an effective American military response by initiating covert schemes to influence Congress with campaign contributions and to encourage Mexico to invade the United States. German opposition leaders complained that these bizarre plots made their government an international laughingstock. Americans were not amused, and most agreed with McAdoo's conclusion that "it was not possible to avoid war with honor."[5]

The precipitous shift in American public opinion in favor of war sheds light on a perennial tension underlying American foreign policy and military spending. A majority of Americans are loath to sacrifice their tax dollars and American lives on causes not clearly related to the security of the United States itself. An influential minority, however, believes that their nation should assume the responsibility for broader international leadership, backed in part by a strong military. As Germany found out in 1917, the two groups coalesce against credible threats to the lives of Americans.

The Senate overwhelmingly passed a declaration of war on April 4, 1917. Two days later Democratic leader Claude Kitchin pleaded with his colleagues in the House to vote against a war "to which we were and are utter strangers."[6] Kitchin's position lost by an overwhelming margin, and he immediately began working to minimize the amount of wartime debt by raising taxes on "wealth, and not poverty."[7] Kitchin's tax legislation permanently ended the federal government's primary reliance on consumption taxes. From 1917 on, federal taxation would be based largely on the ability to pay.

FINANCING THE WAR

President Wilson, on April 5, 1917, asked that "so far as practicable the burden of the war should be borne by taxation of the present generation rather than by loans."[8] McAdoo requested that Congress appropriate $3.5 billion for American military preparations and $3 billion for loans to the Allies.[9] Congress promptly authorized debt of $5 billion, five times more than the federal government's normal annual budget.[10]

McAdoo surveyed financial leaders concerning the nation's debt capacity and set the goal of using tax revenues to pay for half of the first year's estimated war cost of $8.5 billion.[11] McAdoo observed that "one of the most fatal mistakes that governments have made in all countries has been the failure to impose fearlessly and promptly upon the existing generation a fair burden of the cost of war."[12] The treasury secretary's analysis of the improvised early financing of the Civil War gave him "a pretty clear idea of what not to do."[13]

Kitchin quickly moved a tax bill to the House floor, where he noted— to the applause of House members—that no man should protest higher taxes if he "remains at home while the boys are at the front."[14] Young males were conscripted to serve in the nation's military, with low pay, because they were considered the most physically able to do so. Using similar logic, Kitchin's tax bill imposed the war's cost on profitable corporations and wealthy citizens with the greatest ability to pay.[15]

In October 1917 Congress passed the War Revenue Act. By then, six months after the declaration of war, the Treasury was borrowing at a rate of over $400 million a month.[16]

The War Revenue Act of 1917 was the most fundamental change in the federal tax system since the end of the Civil War. It lowered the threshold of income exempt from taxation, tripled corporate tax rates, and raised excise taxes and postal rates. The lowest personal income tax rate was 4 percent, and additional rates, or "surtaxes," of 13 percent to 50 percent were imposed on higher income brackets.[17] The act also taxed "excess profits" as measured by extraordinary returns on investment in an attempt to capture some wartime profits of industrial firms with few competitors, such as US Steel and the progeny of the Standard Oil Trust.

It was difficult for McAdoo to estimate revenues generated by a tax system based largely on self-reporting of income by individual taxpayers. The idea of financing government largely by citizens who calculated their own taxable income and then mailed in checks was almost inconceivable in other nations. But most Americans complied with the law. During the months of the initial large tax payments—May, June, and July 1918—the Treasury received $2.626 billion, double the level received from all federal taxation collected previously during any fiscal year.[18]

The United States sorely needed those revenues. McAdoo had raised his estimate for the first year's cost of war to $12.3 billion by the end of 1917.[19] By that time he had also concluded that tax revenues could only be expected to pay for a third of the total cost of the war. McAdoo reasoned that "if you take the whole of a man's surplus income through taxes, you cannot expect him to buy bonds, nor can you expect industry to expand."[20] The American Fiscal Tradition had sanctioned the use of debt to pay for war, but had not defined a guideline for the split between wartime taxes and debt. McAdoo's two-thirds rule was the first attempt to do so in the twentieth century.

Kitchin's Democrats and the remaining Progressive Party members worried about the level of wartime debt, leading them to raise taxes again even after combat ended in November 1918. The Revenue Act of 1919 also reflected congressional concerns about the high levels of wartime profits and the need to replace revenues from federal taxes on alcohol after the ratification that year of a constitutional amendment banning commerce in alcoholic beverages.

The Revenue Act of 1919 set the highest personal income tax rate at 77 percent of personal income and phased it out over two years.[21] The Wilson administration warned Congress that the highest tax rates were counterproductive and encouraged tax shelters. Industrialist Andrew Mellon noted that many high-income Americans had not lawfully sought to reduce their taxes during war, but afterwards they looked on high tax rates "as a business expense" and "treated them accordingly by avoiding payment as much as possible."[22]

The corporate income tax yielded far more revenue than did the personal income tax. The standard exemption from personal income taxation remained at a level above the incomes of most workers. During and immediately after the war surtaxes on high income, paid by a very small percentage of all taxpayers, accounted for approximately 70 percent of personal income tax revenues.[23] In 1919 only half of personal income tax revenue came from taxes paid on wages and salaries; the rest came from dividends, interest, and unincorporated business income. Though the nation's partisan balance shifted significantly in the years after the war, a tax system based on the principle of ability to pay endured.

WARTIME BORROWING AND A DEBT CEILING

The federal government borrowed $21.5 billion in five separate bond issues—four Liberty Bonds and a Victory Bond—between May 1917 and April 1919. Short-term debt at the war's end amounted to another $5 billion. Most bonds matured in ten or fifteen years and paid interest ranging from 3.5 percent for the first bond issue to 4.7 percent for the fourth.[24]

Slogans used to sell bonds left little to the imagination: "You who are not called upon to die—subscribe" and "A man who can't lend his government $1.25 at the rate of 4% is not entitled to be an American citizen."[25] Popular entertainers helped sell Liberty Bonds issued in small denominations. Each of the bond issues was oversubscribed. More than twenty-two million Americans bought Liberty Bonds, though more than 70 percent of the value of bonds sold at face values of $1,000 or more, amounts that only banks, corporations, and wealthy investors could afford.[26]

Congress specifically defined the amount and terms of wartime borrowing. Congress initiated the use of an overall debt ceiling when Secretary McAdoo sought to market a second bond issue before he had sold the full $5 billion authorized for the first bond issue.[27] Since the Treasury could not predict exactly how much would be sold under each of the two bond authorizations, Congress allowed the Treasury to sell bonds with a ceiling on total debt from the two bonds.

A legislated ceiling on debt remained in effect after the war. It was never intended to replace the traditional requirement for congressional authorization of debt for defined purposes. The reason for borrowing up to the ceiling was crystal clear—the nation incurred debt to fund its war efforts. The final 1919 debt ceiling remained on the books even while the federal government in the 1920s steadily retired World War I debt. Federal leaders in the Hoover and Roosevelt administrations would work within this World War I debt ceiling, with minor adjustments, to offset revenue shortfalls and fund emergency relief during the Great Depression. In 1939 Congress did consolidate the ceilings on bonds and notes into a total debt ceiling of $45 billion.[28] Afterwards it raised the ceiling—eventually to $300 billion—for World War II. That level of debt was not exceeded until the Cold War's Berlin Crisis of 1961. Federal leaders rarely differed in their perception of why the nation incurred more debt until the 1980s. Today many federal leaders appear to have forgotten the modest original purpose of the debt ceiling. Congress did not use it to control spending, since Congress could more directly cut outlays with limits on appropriations.

The World War I banking system absorbed federal debt far more smoothly than it had during prior major wars. The Treasury borrowed from banks at low rates by issuing short-term "anticipation" certificates that were paid off after the sale of each bond issue. The Federal Reserve also extended credit to support bank purchases of Treasury obligations. The Federal Reserve sharply increased the amount of circulating currency, in the form of Federal Reserve notes—modern American paper money—up to a total of $2.5 billion by 1919.[29] By the end of the war, the Federal Reserve Act of 1913 required the issuance of paper money to be backed by gold reserves of at least 40 percent, but that posed no serious limit at a time when much of the world's gold supply poured into the United States. The Federal Reserve Bank of New York alone had gold reserves greater than those of all European central banks.

The federal government wielded extraordinary wartime economic power, often at McAdoo's direction. It guaranteed future wheat prices to secure needed supplies, assumed control of the rail system, and directly financed investments in the arms industry.

American economic and military power turned the tide of battle in France from August 1918 until the Armistice of Compiègne on November 11. German leaders, who had miscalculated the speed at which the United States could field its forces in Europe, sought a peace treaty along the lines of the plan outlined by President Wilson. The president had become a hero to many Europeans, though his relations with leaders of wartime allies soured. Allied nations that had begged for American loans protested that they could not repay them. The United States had loaned its allies $10 billion: Great Britain, $4.3 billion; France, $3 billion; Italy, $1.6 billion; and the balance to others. Interest accrued at the rate of $475 million a year, payable in gold.[30]

These and other war debts of Great Britain, Germany, France, and Russia reached a crippling level of more than 150 percent of their annual prewar national income. Great Britain was the only country—besides the United States—that financed a substantial amount of war-related costs through taxation. Great Britain and France both tried to transfer much of the burden of their debts onto Germany, just as Germany had done to France after its victory in 1871 in the Franco-Prussian War. Reparations and other punitive measures angered Germans, whose nation had still occupied parts of France when it agreed to end the war. Ultimately Germany would wash away much of its domestic debt with hyperinflation. Russia simply repudiated its war debts and lost its international credit. The United States eventually recovered only 15 percent of all amounts loaned to its allies.[31] Only Finland paid off its debt to the United States in full.

For twenty months, from the declaration of war until the armistice, the US government had prepared for a long conflict by ramping up its military forces and related contracts for armaments, food, and transportation. After hostilities ended, the Wilson administration seemed incapable of managing an orderly demobilization. An exhausted McAdoo resigned within weeks of the war's end. President Wilson spent months in Europe negotiating a peace treaty and suffered an incapacitating stroke after his return.

High wartime taxes allowed the budget to return to a surplus, despite the fact that federal spending remained higher than it had been before the war. In fiscal year 1920, which began almost eight months after the armistice, the federal government spent $6.3 billion—six times the prewar level.[32] Treasury Secretary David Houston warned that "we have demobilized many groups, but we have not demobilized those whose gaze is concentrated on the Treasury."[33]

DISILLUSIONMENT

The expense of the federal government became a central issue in postwar politics marred by the bitter aftertaste of the costly war. Historian Richard Hofstadter noted that "the war was justified to the American public—perhaps had to be justified—in the Progressive rhetoric and on Progressive terms."[34] Wilson had argued for US entry into the nationalistic conflict based on the heady morality of making the world "safe for democracy" and sought to conclude it with a peace treaty he claimed was accomplished "by no plan of our conceiving, but by the hand of God, who led us in this way."[35] Many Americans, including veterans, blamed the Wilson administration, rather than God, for a war that they viewed in hindsight as accomplishing little.

The momentum of progressive reformers was still strong enough in 1919 to allow them to gain ratification of constitutional amendments giving women the right to vote and prohibiting the sale of alcoholic beverages. Disillusionment with the war did, however, alter the course of the progressive movement. The moral authority of progressive idealism had been wounded, along with so many Americans, by the brutal reality of war. The intense war also exacted a physical toll on federal leaders. Congress toiled without air conditioning through hot summers. Many senators died. Theodore Roosevelt, a symbol of national vigor and champion of military strength, aged rapidly after losing a son in combat. The strong-willed Kitchin collapsed with a stroke on the House floor in 1920.

President Wilson's stroke in September 1919 left him isolated in the White House with his wife and physician. He lost touch with public sentiment. His arrogant response to criticism of the Treaty of Versailles—including a refusal to answer questions about its terms from the Senate—exemplified a general decline in the civility of public life. Many immigrants felt targeted by campaigns against suspected traitors and communists after the war. Military veterans resented their sacrifices in light of civilians whose wages had risen to ten times the pay of most soldiers. Farmers who had been encouraged to expand production to feed wartime allies watched anxiously as bumper crops led to a sharp decline in produce prices.

A postwar recession resulted in part from the Federal Reserve Bank of New York's policy of curbing inflation with an innovative "open market operation" that soaked up liquidity by selling bonds in exchange for cash. That first experience with the policy of slowing growth and inflation by selling debt undermines any assumption that rising unmonetized debt leads to growth.

Progressives suffered setbacks at the 1920 nominating conventions of each major political party. McAdoo, with Bryan's help, attempted to fill the political vacuum resulting from his father-in-law's physical decline. He led the early balloting for the Democratic presidential nomination until Tammany boss Charles Murphy rallied urban delegations behind the party's nominee, Ohio Governor James Cox. General Leonard Wood, a Roosevelt protégé and former Rough Rider, took an early lead among Republican convention delegates. Senators, weary of strong presidential leadership, blocked Wood's nomination and arranged for the selection of a personable but nondescript colleague, Warren Harding of Ohio.

The 1920 vice presidential nominees foreshadowed each party's future. Cox picked Theodore Roosevelt's thirty-nine-year-old cousin, Franklin Roosevelt, explaining that "his name is good, he's right geographically, and he's anti-Tammany."[36] The Democratic Roosevelt, a former New York state senator and assistant secretary of the navy, campaigned in favor of greater fiscal discipline. The convention hall erupted with overwhelming approval when a delegate rose to nominate Massachusetts governor Calvin Coolidge as Harding's running mate. The modest Coolidge had supported progressive reforms while also symbolizing traditional authority after he broke an unlawful strike by Boston police.

The backlash against the war, inflation, and the postwar economic downturn led to a Republican landslide in 1920. The GOP won the White House and a solid majority in the House and Senate. Republican candidates even prevailed in some urban ethnic precincts considered to be Democratic strongholds. The Republican triumph hardly indicated a major shift in national ideology; neither party's platform repudiated the fruits of progressive reforms. Though many commentators stereotype the 1920s as "conservative," Harding described himself as a "rational progressive."[37] State governments continued to enact much of the old progressive agenda, including laws protecting employees and funding large-scale construction of roads, schools, and hospitals. Harding's election did, however, promote a measure of political reconciliation, as exemplified by his pardon of socialist labor organizer Eugene Debs. (The Wilson administration had imprisoned Debs for condoning wartime labor unrest.)

THE DRIVE FOR EFFICIENCY

The United States entered the 1920s with economic growth spurred by a remarkable technological revolution in automobiles, aviation, electricity, radios, and telephones. American corporations had lowered costs with new techniques of mass production, and many taxpayers longed for that type of efficiency in government. Progressive ideals of expertise and efficiency moved to center stage in the 1920s. Many cities responded by adopting charter amendments that gave nonpartisan professional managers authority over their budgets and operations.

President Harding preferred to delegate management responsibility. He marred his reputation by putting his corrupt Ohio political gang in charge of law enforcement and veterans' benefits. In contrast, he assigned power over budgets, taxation, and economic policy to honest and seasoned corporate managers, most notably Charles Dawes, Herbert Hoover, and Andrew Mellon. They and their expert staffs refined Kitchin's tax system, institutionalized a new federal budget process, and paid down federal debt. Dawes, Hoover, Mellon, and Harding's successor, Calvin Coolidge, approached government in a manner that defined a new "conservative" Republican mainstream. Before the 1920s Democrats—not Republicans—were generally identified with the cause of smaller government. That would change by the end of the decade.

Herbert Hoover and Charles Dawes emerged from the war with reputations as brilliant managers. Hoover, a forty-six-year-old former mining executive, achieved international renown by alleviating war-related starvation in Europe. Dawes, a Chicago banker and utility executive nine years older than Hoover, excelled in his role as a brigadier general in charge of army logistics.

Harding initially had trouble bringing Hoover and Dawes into his administration. Republican senators objected to a cabinet post for Hoover, a hero to reformers in both parties who was being touted as a possible presidential candidate. Harding asked Dawes to manage the budget as secretary of the treasury, but Dawes declined on the grounds that he would need more authority in order to manage budgets across departmental lines.

A role for Andrew Mellon, one of the country's wealthiest people, posed an even greater challenge. Mellon made his fortune as a banker and owner of a steel company that he sold to J. P. Morgan's US Steel and an oil company that he sold to Rockefeller's Standard Oil. His wealth continued to grow as a result of investments in the Aluminum Corporation of America and in Gulf Oil's early entry into petroleum production and refining in Texas.

Powerful Pennsylvania senator Philander Knox suggested that Harding tap Mellon for the Treasury position that Dawes had turned down. Harding agreed to the appointment on the condition that Knox would clear the way for Hoover's confirmation as secretary of commerce. The president correctly anticipated that Mellon's appointment would generate public criticism, "as bad as appointing J. P. Morgan."

Yet Secretary of the Treasury Mellon's solid performance eventually won over most skeptics. They found that he was neither an ideologue nor a dilettante. He mastered the details of tax policy and articulated clear budget goals. Those goals remained intact for eleven years, during which

Mellon served as the treasury secretary under three presidents. First and foremost, he said, the nation should balance its budget and reduce its debt, a goal he described as "the fundamental policy of the Government since its beginning." Second, he called for a tax system that would produce sufficient revenue to pay for spending, eliminate the burden on those least able to pay, and remove "those influences which might retard the continued steady development of business."[38] He referred to this approach as "scientific taxation."

In contrast to some twenty-first-century Republicans, Mellon strongly defended the graduated personal income tax. The pragmatic tycoon found it "incredible" that "men of moderate incomes" paid income taxes on their salaries, while tax-exempt investments allowed "a man with an income of $1,000,000 a year to pay not one cent to the support of his Government."[39] Mellon's advocacy of corporate taxation and progressive personal income taxation ensured the survival of Kitchin's tax system.

A MODERN FEDERAL BUDGET

Charles Dawes and his colleague, fellow army general Herbert Lord, first implemented the modern federal budget process. Before 1921 no law authorized the president to propose an annual budget. Traditional budget practices such as clear accounting and "pay as you go" budget planning had allowed a well-informed elite, largely within Congress, to manage budgets within the limitations of the nation's unwritten fiscal constitution. Powerful House and Senate leaders helped confine spending to the level of estimated revenues. Continuity was provided by long-serving senators such as John Sherman, Justin Morrill, and Nelson Aldrich. The scale and complexity of budgets for World War I exposed the flaws of that old, informal system.

Chambers of commerce, editorial writers, and academic experts championed budget reform. The report of Taft's Commission on Economy and Efficiency, entitled "The Need for a National Budget," urged "that the executive branch submit [an annual] statement to the Legislature which would be its account of stewardship as well as its proposals for the future."[40] Many in Congress remained wary of shifting budget power to the White House, which some likened to an attempt to impose the British political system on the United States. In 1912 Congress had ignored the recommendations of the Taft Commission, eliminated funding for the commission, and objected to the submission of a detailed presidential budget. Former members of the commission obtained private funding to continue their work, giving rise to the first think tank, known today as the Brookings Institution. Its budget experts, Frederick Cleveland and Arthur Willoughby, stressed the benefit of incorporating all spending and revenues into a consistent plan.

The reliance on personal and corporate income taxation also accelerated momentum toward budget reform. After a bitter internal struggle, the House consolidated spending power in a thirty-five-member Appropriations Committee.[41] The House resolution noted that "people took little interest in appropriations" funded with import taxes but that the burden of income taxes centered more political attention on "the problems of economy [i.e., spending] as reflected in the appropriations made by Congress."[42] Two years later the Senate vested its Appropriations Committee with similar power.

The Budget and Accounting Act of 1921 established the Bureau of the Budget within the executive branch and mandated the submission of a presidential budget early in each calendar year. President Wilson vetoed similar legislation based on a constitutional objection to an unrelated provision, and Congress passed it again after the 1920 election. President Harding signed the bill shortly after his inauguration in 1921 and made Dawes the new budget director.

Dawes commanded respect from politicians in both parties. Even an important twenty-first-century political strategist, Karl Rove, would study Dawes's brilliant management of McKinley's campaigns in 1896 and 1900. Dawes's network of friends included William Jennings Bryan, war hero General John "Black Jack" Pershing, and many of the nation's leading bankers and businessmen. General Dawes, while a consummate insider, had become a public celebrity after his outburst at a congressional hearing on the cost of supplies ordered during World War I. Dawes lost patience with congressional second-guessing: "Hell'n Maria! We weren't trying to keep a set of books, we were trying to win the war! . . . I'd have paid horse prices for sheep if the sheep could have hauled artillery."[43]

In August 1921 Budget Director "Hell'n Maria" Dawes inaugurated modern budget process at a meeting attended by President Harding, Vice President Coolidge, all cabinet secretaries, the senior military brass, and the top twelve hundred senior managers in the federal government. Following a pep talk by the president, Dawes urged all executive branch leaders to root out savings. He asked those committed to the task to rise from their seats. Everyone stood.

The Budget Bureau standardized accounting, purchasing, logistics, inventory, and other business systems across the federal government. The bureau's deputy director, General Herbert Lord, was cut from the same no-nonsense cloth as Dawes. Lord had served as chief staff member of the Ways and Means Committee before a long army career culminating in his service as finance director of the War Department. Dawes and Lord, sometimes joined by Secretary Mellon, summoned cabinet members and senior military officers to answer detailed questions on their budgets. In 1921 they quickly racked up $305 million in savings, almost a tenth of the total amount Congress had appropriated for the entire year.[44] Only the Navy Department failed to identify savings, though Dawes and other federal officials managed to reduce demand for naval spending by negotiating international treaties that limited the size of naval forces. From 1922 to 1929, the United States authorized the construction of only 11 naval vessels, compared to 125 for Japan and 74 for Great Britain.[45]

Dawes dramatized his push for efficiency at a second administration-wide budget meeting, in February 1922, attended again by the president, the cabinet, and all other senior federal officials. He illustrated the desired attention to detail by holding up an army broom and navy broom, which differed only by the army's use of twine rather than the navy's wire to wrap the bristles. He chastised the navy for ordering more of its wire-wrapped brooms even though the army had an inventory of 350,000 of its brooms.[46] A well-run business, Dawes lectured, "would drive the guilty man out of his position in disgrace."[47] In the presence of the president and cabinet secretaries, Dawes then compared each department's year-to-date spending with a pro-rata apportionment of its annual appropriations.

By the end of 1921 the Bureau submitted the first official presidential budget to Congress. That budget, for the fiscal year beginning on July 1, 1922, offers a clear snapshot of federal responsibilities and revenue sources at the time. Dawes balanced projected revenues of $3.9 billion with the same amount of outlays, including expenses of $975 million for interest and $387 million to reduce principal on the debt.[48] Less than a sixth of the total represented spending on items other than debt reduction, interest, defense, veterans, and some wartime demobilization. Corporate and personal income taxes provided the bulk of federal revenue, which amounted to almost 5 percent of national income in 1921.[49] By 2012, when the nation had global military commitments, personal and corporate income taxes supporting the federal funds budget had grown to 8.9 percent of national income.[50]

Dawes earned a Nobel Prize for restructuring European debt after he left the Bureau of the Budget. His successor, Herbert Lord, served until 1930 and continued to manage "pay as you go" budget planning by convening biannual meetings with all senior officials in the executive branch. Sixteen of those meetings occurred from 1921 through the end of the Coolidge presidency in early 1929.

Federal budget accounting in the 1920s was straighforward. Budgets confined all spending, including planned debt reductions, to the limit set by estimated revenues. Congress treated annual debt reduction as a budgeted expense similar to defense, benefits for veterans, and interest. Federal officials did not claim a surplus until revenues exceeded a spending level that included a substantial annual amount of debt reduction. Secretary Gallatin had effectively employed a similar system 120 years earlier. Budget practices used in the 1920s would have made it difficult for the president and Congress in 2001 to claim that their budget reduced federal debt even though they allocated no revenue for that purpose.

By 1929 the federal government had retired $8.1 billion in debt, a third of the total a decade earlier.[51] Annual appropriations accounted for three-quarters of that debt reduction, and additional surpluses paid down the rest. Even without the authority of the Budget Act of 1921, by the late 1920s the chief executive played a critical role in shaping federal budgets. The Constitution itself permitted Congress to ignore any budget submitted by a president, but the unwritten constitution evolved to include the White House as an active partner in the annual budget process.

In the 1920s most of the growth of the public sector occurred in state and local governments. Local governments financed sanitary water and wastewater treatment systems, the most radical effective public health reform in US history. Cities and states borrowed record amounts—with voter-approved bonds issues for specific purposes—to finance these improvements and others, such as new roads and hospitals. State and local debt grew from $4.5 billion in 1913 to $19.5 billion in 1932. By 1930, New York City's net debt was $1.6 billion, far more than interest-bearing federal debt before World War I.[52]

Demands for efficiency rose alongside the cost of state and local services. Popular Democratic governor Al Smith of New York implemented management reforms and imposed fiscal discipline on a Republican legislature. With bipartisan support from business leaders, Smith obtained broad powers to manage the budget of the nation's most populous state. He consolidated overlapping operations and cut income tax rates twice. New York permitted debt only for voter-approved bonds used for capital improvements that were accounted for apart from the state's operating budget.

Tax Reform

Treasury Secretary Andrew Mellon "agree[d] perfectly with those who wish to relieve the small taxpayer by getting the largest possible contribution from the people with large incomes."[53] One historian of the early income tax notes with wonder that while many Republicans had complained about the progressive income tax, "there was not, however, one serious utterance about repeal."[54]

Mellon's tax policies are instructive for those searching for lessons from budget history. Populists such as Senator Robert La Follette claimed that Mellon's reforms favored wealthy citizens. In recent decades Mellon has been embraced by advocates of "supply side economics" who seek precedents for the debt-financed tax cuts in 1981, 2001, and 2003. Both perspectives distort the original intent and effect of Mellon's policies.

The extraordinary tax increase adopted in 1919 ended within two years, after which tax rates fell back to the level imposed at the outset of the war. With the help of his twenty-nine-year-old assistant, S. Parker Gilbert, Mellon crafted a plan to increase federal revenues from corporations and Americans with the highest incomes while relieving millions of Americans in the lowest brackets from paying any income taxes at all. He strongly objected to debt-financed tax reduction.

In 1921 the top marginal personal income tax rate applied to 1 percent of Americans, most of whose taxable earnings came from interest and capital gains. Those taxpayers could avoid taxable income by investing in tax-exempt bonds or deferring the sale of investments for a gain. State and local bonds with interest exempt from taxation totaled at least $10 billion by 1924, a substantial amount in relation to all corporate bonds.[55] Mellon failed in his efforts to end the tax-exempt status of interest on state and local bonds.

Tax returns showed clearly that high income tax rates combined with tax avoidance served to reduce the total, *taxable* income of wealthy Americans. In 1916, when the highest income tax rate was 15 percent, Americans who reported taxable income in excess of $300,000 paid $81 million, almost half of all personal income tax revenue.[56] By 1921, with the top rate at 73 percent, they reported about the same taxable income, but their share of the total taxable income had dropped to 10 percent.[57] Between 1919 and 1921, the total tax revenue from the "surcharge," the term used for tax rates applicable to higher brackets, dropped from $802 million to $411 million.[58] Investors moved to tax-exempt bonds, deferred selling for capital gains, and retained income within corporations taxable at lower rates. High tax rates also contributed to tax evasion in an era in which many Americans routinely violated federal criminal laws against alcoholic beverages.

Congress acted slowly at first on Mellon's recommendations concerning "scientific taxation." In 1922 Congress increased corporate tax rates, reduced the maximum personal surcharge on high incomes to 50 percent above the base rate, and raised the personal exemption.[59] Mellon's arguments steadily gained converts. Congress cut tax rates and raised personal exemptions in 1924 and 1926, until the maximum personal tax rate fell to the level recommended by Mellon: 25 percent.[60]

As Mellon predicted, wealthy Americans shifted their investments to taxable bonds and dividends.[61] By the late 1920s only corporations and the wealthiest 2 to 3 percent of Americans paid federal income taxes. The share of all federal taxes paid by the wealthiest Americans and corporations was immensely higher in the late 1920s, a supposed high-water mark of conservative power, than at any later time in the nation's history.

After the adoption of Mellon's tax program, some Democrats in Congress led by House Minority Leader John Nance Garner of Texas sought to lower corporate tax rates. With the backing of the US Chamber of Commerce, Garner proposed to cut the corporate tax rate from 13.5 percent to 11 percent. Along with the old Roosevelt Progressives still in Congress, Mellon fought Garner's initiative on the grounds that it would reduce federal revenue and slow debt reduction, arguing that "as long as I am Secretary of the Treasury Department" he would "resist [any] undermining of the principle" of balanced budgets.[62] Throughout Mellon's tenure, corporations paid far more income taxes than individuals; in 1926, for example, individuals paid $732 million out of total income tax revenues of $1.974 billion, with corporations accounting for the balance.[63]

In later decades Mellon's policies would be invoked by Republican leaders, such as Congressman Jack Kemp, in support of debt-financed tax cuts. Yet Mellon himself flatly disagreed with the idea that new borrowings with reduced taxes were "preferable to higher taxes with reduced debts." He said that "a moment's reflection will convince anyone that prosperity cannot come from continued plunging into debt."[64] Mellon pressed only for tax rate reduction designed to promptly increase federal revenues as a share of national income. Those who cited Mellon's policies in justification of tax reductions in 1981 and 2001 did so without evidence that tax revenues would promptly rise as a result of a tax cut.

The six years following both 1920 and 2000 offer some interesting contrasts, as they were the only six-year periods in the last century in which Republicans controlled both the White House and the House of Representatives. New Republican presidents pledged to pay down the debt. After 1920 the federal government retired debt, while after 2000 debt soared, even excluding war-related borrowing. From 1921 to 1926 Republican presidents frequently vetoed spending bills, something that did not occur from 2001 to 2006.

The cuts in the top personal income tax rate enacted in 1964 and 1986 offer a better parallel to the Mellon-era tax cuts. Mellon's business experience led him to believe that the maximum personal tax rate that would avoid economic distortions was 31 percent.[65] After passage of the Tax Reform Act of 1986, the top tax rate was 28 percent, though for many high-income taxpayers the effective tax rate was actually 33 percent, as deductions were phased out with income. This initiative, led by congressional Democrats with support from the Reagan White House, explicitly accepted another of Mellon's arguments—that a lower maximum tax rate would lead to a less distorted or tax-driven economic decisions.

It is difficult to believe, as some do, that Mellon's reductions in personal tax rates were responsible for the growth in national income from $73 billion in 1921 to $103 billion in 1929. Though lower taxes on investment income removed some perverse incentives, tax rates affecting 1 or 2 percent of the population had less impact on the economy than did a reduction of over $8 billion in federal debt. Wealthy Americans paid more to the federal government by the end of the decade, and state and local spending and taxes increased. Steady annual economic growth in the 1920s is better explained by the impact of construction and technological innovation.

Similarly, Mellon's liberal critics, including New Deal Democrats and historians such as Arthur Schlesinger, are incorrect to blame Mellon's tax cuts for stock market speculation in the 1920s. Federal and state policies permitting high leverage on margin loans contributed more to the bubble that burst in 1929. Since interest on loans could be deducted, lower tax rates actually reduced incentives for the purchase of stock in margin accounts.

In the 1920s Congress and Mellon's Treasury resolved an obscure issue that would have a profound effect on the federal tax system later in the century. Very few companies—with the notable exception of Sears, Roebuck and Company and the Eastman Kodak Company—made annual contributions to investment accounts held in trust for future pension obligations. They deducted those expenses in calculating taxable income. Tax accountants within the Treasury tried to treat income from pension trusts as if it belonged to a single wealthy person, but that made no sense because the ultimate beneficiaries were likely to have incomes lower than the standard exemption. Moreover, it was considered arbitrary and unfair to attempt to allocate taxable income to workers before they were entitled to receive it. Congress and the Treasury agreed to exempt employer pension contributions from personal income taxation. Future retirees would pay any taxes when they actually received a pension. That commonsense solution, later applied by analogy to noncash medical benefits, seemed fair and reasonable throughout the twentieth century.

Mellon abhorred tax loopholes. He helped close one that had long been used to avoid payment of estate or inheritance taxes. States relied on estate taxes to pay for essential services such as public education and roads. Florida, for the avowed purpose of attracting wealthy retirees from other states, banned all estate taxation. It seemed unfair that residents of other states could benefit from services paid for with inheritance taxes and then avoid those taxes by retiring to Florida. Mellon and Congress solved the problem by imposing a federal estate tax and agreeing to credit 80 percent of the federal tax to states that imposed their own estate taxation.

TWO AMERICAS

The urban economy flourished in the 1920s. The share of households with cars rose from about a quarter to three-fifths; households with electric lighting rose from a third to two-thirds; and households with radios rose from very few to two-fifths.[66] This progress, along with the expanded use of telephones, flush toilets, central heating, and washing machines, defined a new middle-class standard of living. Private debt—which grew from 119 percent of national income in 1920 to 157 percent in 1930—helped finance this growth in consumption.[67]

Americans on farms borrowed simply to try to preserve a minimum standard of living. Farm income declined in the 1920s. Farm productivity rose faster than the demand for farm products, thereby driving down commodity prices and the value of farm land. In 1920 the value of all manufactured products was triple the $21.4 billion produced from farming and ranching activities. A decade later the value of manufactured products had increased, but the value of agricultural products had fallen by $11.8 billion.[68] Farm foreclosures surged, and hundreds of rural banks failed throughout the 1920s.

Many farmers looked to the federal government for help. A strong congressional Farm Bloc included both Republicans and Democrats. Secretary of Agriculture Harry C. Wallace, a Republican from Iowa, publicly supported federal assistance to deal with chronic overproduction. He and his Farm Bureau allies proposed that the federal government buy farm products, export them at lower prices, and pay for the export subsidy with a tax on domestic farm sales. They viewed this program, embodied in the McNary-Haugen bill, as the equivalent of nurturing domestic industries with protective import taxation.

Calvin Coolidge, who became president after Warren Harding's death in 1923, defied the Farm Bloc. Coolidge was obsessed with the efficient use of tax dollars. In his first inaugural address he identified spending discipline as the "soundest method" of restraining taxes.[69] He embraced Mellon's approach to scientific taxation and the Bureau of the Budget's push for spending discipline. Coolidge would become an icon for later twentieth-century Republican conservatives, though he remained distant from the Senate's traditional Republican leadership. He identified more with the independent-minded Idaho senator William Borah, a self-described liberal, whom Coolidge tried to recruit as his running mate in 1924. Coolidge and Borah both loathed wasteful spending while unequivocally embracing Prohibition, the most intrusive of all progressive initiatives. Dawes, considered a moderate, joined the Coolidge ticket after Borah declined.

Coolidge twice vetoed the McNary-Haugen farm bill. Mellon strongly supported those vetoes, as did Secretary of Commerce Hoover, who helped Coolidge draft a veto message explaining that other nations would not sit idly by while subsidized farm exports were dumped in their domestic markets. Even if the bill temporarily raised farm prices, Coolidge and Hoover argued that higher prices would spur higher production. Lower prices would eventually follow, leading to demands for even higher subsidies and taxation. Coolidge and Hoover encouraged farmers to join cooperatives in order to become more efficient. That recommendation did not satisfy the Farm Bloc, and the plight of agriculture created an unstable fault line in American politics.

Another fierce budget divide arose from the attempt of a bipartisan congressional majority to raise pensions for World War I veterans. Citing the need to maintain budget discipline, Presidents Harding, Coolidge, and Hoover opposed bills raising benefits for veterans, especially those without service-related disabilities. Many of the three million Americans who had served in the military sometime during World War I had earned little more than a dollar a day as soldiers, a small fraction of civilian wage levels. Like Vietnam veterans in a later generation, they felt unappreciated by a nation whose citizens just wanted to forget the war. President Coolidge shared the attitude of an earlier generation of reformers who had considered escalating Civil War pensions to be a form of political corruption. Progressives, particularly strong in Coolidge's Massachusetts, instead favored pension systems in which employees contributed alongside employers.

In 1924 Congress overrode Coolidge's veto of legislation that promised World War I veterans a bonus, which would be paid in 1945 (or sooner to the surviving family of a veteran who died earlier). By delaying payment until 1945, Congress sought to avoid interfering with the planned retirement of World War I debt. In fact, the obligation could be considered a form of "off the balance sheet" financing. Payment was based on a formula—$1 per day of service and $1.25 per foreign deployment, minus discharge payment, plus 4 percent interest until payment—that was estimated to yield approximately $1,000 per veteran.[70]

Coolidge, Mellon, and Hoover were of one mind in opposition to farm subsidies and bonuses for veterans, but Coolidge and Mellon were wary of

Hoover's approach to reducing unemployment that would inevitably accompany future economic downturns. Laid-off industrial workers lacked the historical safety net of a subsistence farm. The National Conference on Unemployment in 1921, convened by Hoover, had recommended the creation of a trust fund—financed with some amount of annual tax revenues—that could pay for large-scale public works during severe downturns. Neither the White House nor Congress embraced that idea. Federal debt reduction during the 1920s, however, accomplished much the same purpose by freeing debt capacity to support future extraordinary spending during downturns. Put another way, Mellon's policy of debt reduction was the economic equivalent of designating a reserve fund to purchase and hold Treasury debt that could be sold back into the market in an emergency. The notion of balancing a budget across a business cycle became a refinement to traditional "pay as you go" budget planning only in the late twentieth century.

Republicans nominated Hoover for the presidency when Coolidge declined to seek reelection in 1928. Hoover had never held elected office or been a military general, unlike prior presidents except Taft. He did, however, represent the 1920s ideal of a pragmatic progressive interested in results rather than rhetoric. Both business organizations and labor unions backed the corporate executive known for his humanitarian relief efforts during World War I and the severe flooding of the Mississippi River in 1927. Hoover's inaugural address, which identified problems and listed solutions, read like a business briefing.

The American Fiscal Tradition had become deeply ingrained as part of the unwritten constitution. Political leaders in each party helped retire wartime debt. They had adapted an old tradition to a modern age.

A political figure with the most appealing family pedigree in politics, Franklin Roosevelt, feared that his Democratic Party had neglected other values of the party's founders. After disastrous Democratic losses in the 1924 election, the former vice presidential candidate wrote a letter to Democratic leaders and newspaper publishers urging them to revive the party by attacking the alignment of business with political power. Roosevelt's advice, inspired by his reading of Jefferson's collected works, was largely ignored. As most of Theodore Roosevelt's old Bull Moose Progressives returned to the Republican fold, those who still clung to the minor Progressive Party commanded little attention when they called for a "new deal" in 1928.

For 130 years federal leaders had confined the use of planned debt to only four purposes. The limits of borrowing for one of those purposes would soon be tested when the progressive tax system, designed by Kitchin and reformed by Mellon, failed to produce revenues covering even minimal federal expenses during the Great Depression.

10

DEBT DURING THE GREAT DEPRESSION

1929–1940: Years when deficits exceeded debt service = 10
(1931–1940, Great Depression)

HOOVER ATTEMPTS TO RESTORE
CONFIDENCE AND LIMIT BORROWING

British political leader Winston Churchill expected to observe the mechanics of the world's most robust financial market when he arrived at the New York Stock Exchange on October 24, 1929. He witnessed instead the chaos of panicked selling. The Exchange closed its public galleries to hide the disaster called "Black Thursday."

The stock market crash in the last months of 1929 eliminated $26 billion in paper wealth, approximately 40 percent of the value of public stocks.[1] Stocks appear overvalued in hindsight; unsold inventories of goods had begun to rise months earlier. Yet the future had once seemed boundless for technology-driven companies such as General Motors, American Telephone & Telegraph, Radio Corporation of America, and General Electric.

By early 1930, four million American workers—out of a total workforce of fifty million—were unemployed.[2] Farm foreclosures and bank failures climbed to record highs each successive month. Construction ground to a halt. The world's other industrial leaders, Great Britain and Germany, also staggered.

Recessions, of course, had always been part of the economic cycle. Civic and business leaders hoped this one would be relatively brief, like the two that began in 1907 and 1920. They looked for signs that the economy had bottomed out. President Hoover tried to inspire confidence; he told the US Chamber of Commerce in May 1930 that the country had "passed the worst."[3] Yet local charities and governments still struggled to provide food and shelter to a vast number of families of unemployed workers.

Banks failed when borrowers could not make their payments. Surviving banks preserved their capital by curtailing new lending. The collapse of prominent regional banks precipitated other bank failures when depositors raced to withdraw funds. Runs on deposits resulted in four distinct waves of bank failures over several years, culminating with the most severe convulsion in early 1933.

It was impossible to accurately estimate federal revenue after 1929. Since income taxes were paid the year after income was earned, a surplus persisted well into the downturn. In December 1930 Americans paid quarterly income taxes of nearly half a billion dollars, an amount greater than they had paid in December 1928. A year later, in December 1931, income receipts fell by half.[4] The president and Congress were unprepared for the speed and size of the drop in revenues. Writing in 1934, the first great historian of the federal budget, Davis Dewey, described the budget disaster:

> The fiscal year ending June 30, 1931 marked a turn in the fortunes of federal finance. For eleven years, the Treasury had enjoyed a surplus averaging annually $760,000,000. . . . Writing on November 20, 1930, Secretary Mellon declared that "the finances of the Federal Government for the fiscal year 1930 continued the favorable record of recent years." . . . Six months later, in June 1931, the deficit for the year amounted to $903,000,000.[5]

Most Americans had supported the federal shift toward reliance on income taxation. Yet that very dependence exacerbated the decline in federal revenues. In fiscal year 1930 the United States collected $2.9 billion from personal and corporate income taxes and import duties. Three years later, revenues from those sources fell to just less than $1 billion, even after Congress raised tax rates.[6] Federal tobacco taxes, which produced a fifth the revenue of income taxes in 1930, generated more revenue than either personal or corporate income taxation three years later. The New Deal would soon be celebrated by progressives, but New Deal budgets relied more heavily on more stable revenues from regressive sales taxes.

Secretary of the Treasury Mellon, who was once treated as a financial genius, became a symbol of callous wealth. The seventy-one-year-old industrialist told President Hoover that the downturn served as a needed reminder of the virtues of hard work and thrift. He blamed the downturn on debtors who borrowed too much and the banks that extended too much credit.

President Hoover was quite willing to innovate in order to revive the economy. He reassured Congress, in December 1930, that the nation could balance the budget across an economic cycle: "We can confidently look forward to the restoration of . . . surpluses with the general recovery of the economic situation, and thus the absorption of any temporary borrowing that may be necessary."[7] Hoover directed federal departments to accelerate planned public works projects and assigned priority to those that could produce future revenues, like hydroelectric dams. The president also pleaded with business leaders to maintain capital spending and wage levels.

The economy appeared to bottom out in early 1931. By then output had declined by 40 percent from the all-time high reached in July 1929.[8] Hopes faded that spring in the wake of another bank panic. More than eight million Americans still could not find work.[9] Many families exhausted their savings.

Economists, bankers, and business leaders searched for ways to end the pervasive gloom. A chorus of economists and business leaders urged President Hoover to boost confidence by reducing the budget deficit. Hoover, who had cut taxes modestly at the outset of the downturn in order to demonstrate such confidence, tried to follow their advice. In an attempt to balance the budget, he asked Congress to raise taxes, including a national sales tax, higher estate taxes ("the most economically and socially desirable—or even necessary—of all taxes"), and personal income taxes (on "upper brackets . . . to 45 percent as compared to the present 23 percent").[10] Mellon also supported a reversal of the cuts in income tax rates.

Hoover sought cooperation from Democrats, who held a House majority after 1930. Bushy eyebrows, pink cheeks, and a mischievous smile gave a benign appearance to their leader, Speaker John Nance Garner. Garner, who amused his colleagues with profane wit, treated the rising debt as a serious matter. In early 1932 the Speaker descended from his rostrum to make an unusual personal appeal for bipartisan cooperation in efforts to balance the budget. When he asked House members to stand up to show their resolve to support higher taxes, almost everyone rose.

In early 1932 the Ways and Means Committee endorsed a bill containing a mix of higher sales and income taxes. All but one of the members of the powerful committee voted for the bill. The dissenting vote belonged to Robert Lee Doughton, a polite sixty-eight-year-old farmer and small-town banker from North Carolina. Doughton once described tax legislation as getting "the most feathers you can with the fewest squawks from the goose."[11] Doughton himself squawked at higher sales taxes championed by both President Hoover and Speaker Garner. His constituents, mostly farmers who were struggling even before the onset of the Great Depression, had experienced a collapse of the cash economy and feared higher sales taxes. The constituents of progressive Republican Fiorello La Guardia from New York shared those fears. Doughton and La Guardia persuaded House members to increase sales taxes by less than the amount proposed by the Hoover administration and House leadership. Congress passed the tax bill in the summer of 1932 with hopes that it would produce a billion dollars in additional revenue.

Hoover blamed Congress for delaying the tax cut and prolonging the deficit. Critics later blamed the tax bill for deepening the Great Depression, but in fact the new taxes took little purchasing power out of the economy. Incomes and purchasing power had already plummeted so much that higher taxes on anything other than tobacco yielded only minimal revenue.

Members of the Federal Reserve Board of Governors and its regional banking associations did not know how to slow the economic descent or preserve the nation's banking system. They interpreted low interest rates as a sign of sufficient availability of credit. The Federal Reserve also believed that it lacked the legal authority to inject liquidity directly into banks by monetizing federal debt or other loans in bank portfolios.

The Federal Reserve worried about the nation's gold reserves. A run on gold in Germany and Austria spread to Great Britain, where many worried that the government would devalue the pound in order to monetize its large budget deficits. Great Britain shocked the world by departing from the gold standard in September 1931, while France's central bank began hoarding gold. The run on gold further imperiled US national banks, which were required to maintain reserves in the form of gold and short-term commercial paper.[12]

On the advice of Federal Reserve Chairman Eugene Meyer, President Hoover asked Congress to create the Reconstruction Finance Corporation (RFC) for the purpose of lending money to banks, many of which lacked the liquidity to extend mortgages that typically matured in five years. Hoover observed how congressional leaders "seemed shocked at the revelation that our government for the first time in peacetime history might have to intervene to support private enterprise."[13]

Garner sympathized with the RFC's purpose, though he worried about whether it might "linger on as a pipeline to the United States Treasury for chiselers and drone businesses, which . . . partisan favor will give them."[14] Garner insisted that the president appoint sound bankers—including former vice president Charles Dawes and Texan Jesse Jones—to lead the RFC. In January 1932 Congress created the RFC, appropriated $500 million for its capital, and authorized it to borrow $1.5 billion.[15] Like the Troubled Asset Relief Program created during the Great Recession of 2008, the RFC tried to bolster bank balance sheets.

In early 1932 Senator Carter Glass helped pass the first of two Glass-Steagall Acts, which allowed the Federal Reserve to buy federal debt with new currency. The Federal Reserve used that power to monetize more federal debt in 1932 than in any other year between World War I and World War II. By then, however, creditworthy consumers and businesses were reluctant to borrow, and banks were reluctant to lend. The second and better known Glass-Steagall Act, passed in June 1933, separated commercial and investment banking and authorized the RFC to buy loans from troubled banks.

As is typical during troubled economic times, partisan leaders blamed their political opponents for the severity of the downturn. Their rhetoric contributed to decades of partisan lore that blamed federal tax and spending policies—too much or little—for the sharp downward slide in production, prices, credit, and employment from 1929 to 1933. In fact, federal budget policies had far less impact on economic activity than did a variety of other factors leading to the collapse of a private debt bubble, a fragile farm economy, and the consequences of a severe European downturn. The money supply fell sharply, characterized by what economist Milton Friedman later called "the Great Credit Contraction." Another economist, Ben Bernanke, demonstrated decades later that the collapse of commercial banking deepened and prolonged the Great Depression. Economists would eventually come to describe the stagnation as a "liquidity trap," in which a belated expansion of credit failed to stimulate economic activity once consumers were too fearful to spend and businesses too nervous to invest.

THE CRISIS OF LEADERSHIP

By 1932 the reaction to the economic tragedy—fear itself—ripped apart the nation's social fabric. Cities struggled to keep schools open. Angry mobs stormed courthouses to block foreclosure sales of family farms. Gaunt, hungry men filled urban streets. The normally resilient Calvin Coolidge articulated the mood of the country before his death in January 1933: "In other periods of depression it has always been possible to see some things which were solid and upon which you could base hope, but . . . I see nothing to give ground for hope."[16]

Despair nurtured radicalism. Union leaders worried aloud about a groundswell of support for socialism. A Farm Bureau leader observed that one could not "find a conservative farmer today," while the American Legion passed an ominous resolution declaring that the economic crisis could not be resolved "by existing political methods."[17] When Congress cut the pay of federal employees in 1932, President Hoover quietly urged it to exempt soldiers who might be needed to maintain domestic order. An ambitious army officer, Douglas MacArthur, led cavalry and tanks to disperse a gathering of unemployed World War I veterans encamped in the nation's capital.

Americans anxiously watched other nations lurch toward extremes. Japan's Prime Minister Osachi Hamaguchi was killed when he attempted to curb the nation's deficit by reducing defense spending, while communist and fascist militias battled in the streets of Germany.

Since the nineteenth century, American cities and counties had provided some "outdoor relief" in the form of food delivered to "paupers." Older Americans and disabled citizens without subsistence income received "indoor relief" in crowded poorhouses or poor farms. The weight of the Great Depression's hardship tore holes in this traditional safety net. City officials formed the US Conference of Mayors to seek federal assistance in preventing starvation and restoring employment.

State governments stepped in to supplement local humanitarian efforts. Voters in fifteen states approved bond issues for relief. Governor Franklin Roosevelt of New York funded local relief efforts with a voter-authorized bond issue backed by a large increase in the state income tax.[18] Where state constitutions did not allow voter-authorized bonds to fund public assistance, state officials tried to frame bond issues in other terms. Voters in Michigan declined to approve a bond issue for relief to prevent "incipient insurrection," while the state of Washington incurred emergency debt for that very purpose.[19]

In July 1932 President Hoover vetoed an appropriation of $322 million for loans to fund state and local relief agencies and $2 billion for public works.[20] He believed that the new spending would undermine the deficit reduction from the tax bill passed that summer. In August, facing an override of his veto, the president allowed a similar bill to become law. That legislation funded much of the early emergency relief attributed to his successor's New Deal.

The Hearst newspapers promoted Speaker Garner for the 1932 Democratic presidential nomination. Garner had difficulty blaming Hoover for failing to balance the budget, since the Congress he led controlled the nation's spending and taxes. Governor Roosevelt felt free to attack federal borrowing, and he did so with a vengeance. The outcome of the elections would not turn on policy platforms. Many Americans yearned for what one progressive Republican supporter of the New York governor called "another Roosevelt." The tide of public support for the Democratic Roosevelt allowed his party to avoid the bitter nomination fights that had marred most of their conventions since the turn of the century. Garner withdrew from the contest and became Roosevelt's running mate.

A NEW DEAL

Franklin Roosevelt always tried to maintain a balance between bold innovation and humble respect for fiscal traditions. The 1932 Democratic platform endorsed a 25 percent reduction in normal federal spending and the "maintenance of national credit by a federal budget annually balanced on the basis of accurate executive estimates within revenues."[21] Roosevelt called for a "stern and unremitting administration policy of living within our income."[22] His warm voice reminded radio listeners in July 1932 that temporary borrowing was sometimes necessary but chronic borrowing invariably led to the "poorhouse."

The Democratic presidential nominee finessed the issue of federal spending required to prevent starvation. Weeks before the election he told a Pittsburgh audience that the "reduction in federal spending" was "one of the most important issues in this campaign," while noting that "if starvation and dire need on the part of any of our citizens makes necessary the appropriation of additional funds which would keep the budget out of balance, I shall not hesitate to tell the American people the full truth."[23]

Hoover distinguished federal outlays for emergency relief from other, routine expenses. He pointed out that the federal government had cut expenditures for normal activities and challenged Roosevelt to show how he could reduce routine spending by 25 percent. Budgeted spending totaled $3.647 billion, including $2 billion for debt service and the military and $946 million for veterans.[24] "If he stopped all public works, [Roosevelt] would finally have to take $500 million" from the veterans, Hoover asserted, calling that idea "a gross injustice."[25]

The banking system imploded between Roosevelt's landslide victory in November 1932 and his inauguration in March 1933. In three and a half years employment had dropped by a devastating 25 percent, leaving 13 to 15 million workers without jobs.[26] Many people could only find part-time work. Economic output had fallen by 50 percent.[27] In March 1933 one out of six American families depended on some sort of relief provided by public programs and, to a lesser extent, private charities.

In the fiscal year ending months after Roosevelt's inauguration, the federal government borrowed far more than Hoover and Congress had ever imagined possible. Briefly in 1933, for the only time since the presidency of John Adams, federal revenues dropped to less than 10 percent of outstanding debt.[28] A low ratio of revenues to debt squeezed the ability to both service the debt and continue to provide essential services such as an army and navy and pensions for veterans. Revenues available to service federal debt would never again be so low in relation to total debt until after the collapse of the American Fiscal Tradition in the twenty-first century.

Roosevelt paid homage to "pay as you go" budget planning during his first weeks in office. Within a week of his inauguration he asked Congress to slash normal federal spending, including civilian and military pay and all benefits for veterans without service-related disabilities. The president hoped that the spending cuts offered "a reasonable prospect that within a year the income of the government will be sufficient to cover the expenditures," at least for normal functions apart from extraordinary relief.[29] Over the dissent of ninety-two House Democrats, Congress quickly passed Roosevelt's Economy Act, which was officially titled "A Bill to Maintain the Credit of the United States Government." In 1934 Congress repealed many of the bill's draconian cuts, such as those for veterans' benefits, and then overrode Roosevelt's subsequent veto.

A strong mother, celebrated name, financial security, patrician charm, and curious intellect imbued Franklin Roosevelt with unusual self-confidence. Years of physical therapy to regain use of his polio-stricken legs in the 1920s gave him time to read and reflect on political history. He wrote his only book review, a glowing endorsement of *Jefferson and Hamilton: The Struggle for Democracy in America* by Claude Bowers. Like Bowers, Roosevelt sympathized with Thomas Jefferson and James Madison in their battles with Hamilton in the 1790s over fiscal policy. Roosevelt shared the belief of his party's founders that excessive debt compromised the nation's future.

President Roosevelt would build a memorial to Jefferson in the nation's capital. He also followed the Jeffersonian obsession with clearly articulating the purpose of debt. Like Hoover, Roosevelt carefully distinguished between spending for emergency relief and spending for normal government operations. In one of his first radio "fireside chats," the Democratic Roosevelt noted that it "may seem inconsistent for a government to cut down its regular expense and at the same time to borrow and to spend billions for an emergency." He then explained that the government had "imposed taxes to pay the interest and installments on [the emergency] part of the debt."[30]

Congress passed major legislation at an unprecedented pace during Roosevelt's first months in office, beginning in March 1933. For several months old battle lines faded. The prohibition of alcoholic beverages had been one of the most contentious public issues. Yet Congress quickly passed Roosevelt's bill to legalize the sale of beer and wine as a means of raising revenues, which would soon almost equal those produced by the personal income tax.

Members of Congress from both parties indulged Roosevelt's experiments. When the president ordered reluctant cabinet officials to quickly draft legislation creating an organization of uniformed civilian workers to perform hard labor on public lands, the head of the American Federation of Labor denounced the plan as "Hitlerism." Within days in April 1933, however, Congress had authorized creation of the Civilian Conservation Corps. In the following months, 1,300 camps would employ 275,000 workers—mostly young men—who sent a significant portion of the $1 per day they earned back to family members.[31]

Other elected officials also felt free to innovate. Senator Arthur Vandenberg, a Republican newspaper publisher from Michigan, worried that the RFC would save only large banks and proposed the creation of a trust fund, financed with a tax on bank deposits, to insure some amount of all bank deposits. Senior Roosevelt administration officials opposed Vandenberg's idea because of concerns about the impact of a tax on banks. Because the program was intended to be permanent, no one considered paying for it with debt. Vice President Garner liked Vandenberg's idea and lined up support from Senate banking expert Carter Glass. Garner prompted Vandenberg to offer his program as an amendment to the second Glass-Steagall bill. Bank panics ceased and deposits began flowing back into banks after the establishment of the new Federal Deposit Insurance Corporation, the FDIC.

The FDIC's use of a trust fund financed with dedicated taxes was nothing new, of course. That sort of financing solidified the bond between new taxes and new obligations. In the defense of his Albany Plan of 1754, Benjamin Franklin noted that higher taxes would "fare better when [people] . . . have some share in their direction."[32] Hamilton and Madison had originally earmarked new whiskey taxes for retiring debt assumed from the states, while Gallatin placed revenues from higher import taxes into the Mediterranean Fund that was dedicated to defraying naval expenses for combating piracy. The traditional concept of trust funds that linked specific spending and taxes would be used more extensively than ever in the 1930s.

THE DRIVE TO BALANCE THE BUDGET

Two actions in 1935—one by Congress and the other by the Supreme Court—thwarted the Roosevelt administration's goal of balancing the budget as the economy bounced back from its low two years earlier.

Congress passed and then overrode Roosevelt's veto of a bill that required the federal government to pay over $2 billion to citizens who had served in the military during World War I. Eleven years earlier Congress had overridden Coolidge's veto of legislation that gave veterans a bonus due with accrued interest in 1945. The certificate documenting this obligation had since become the most valuable possession of many veterans. Veterans demanded that the federal government cash out those obligations at a reasonable discount. Roosevelt agreed to that demand only if Congress passed a new tax, such as a higher inheritance or estate tax, to fully offset the cost. Congress instead instructed the Treasury to pay for the bonus to veterans with new currency. When Roosevelt strongly objected to any attempt to make federal spending "free," Congress passed the bill without that particular requirement.

The president believed that the veterans' bonus was not an appropriate use of debt during a downturn, since the program did not condition payment on a specific hardship or work requirement. Every emergency appropriation so far, he said, had been "predicated not on the mere spending of money to hasten recovery, but on the sounder principle of preventing the loss of homes and farms, of saving industry from bankruptcy, of safeguarding bank deposits, and most important of all, of giving relief and jobs through public work to individuals and families faced with starvation."[33] Roosevelt raised the political stakes by delivering that message before a joint session of Congress at which he signed the veto with dramatic flair. Congress nonetheless overrode the veto with a lopsided, bipartisan vote. Even this use of debt was consistent with historical principles, as it merely substituted balance sheet debt for an existing obligation that had been created off the balance sheet.

The Supreme Court also undermined Roosevelt's drive to balance the budget when it invalidated a tax dedicated to pay for a farm program designed by Roosevelt's agriculture secretary, Henry A. Wallace. Wallace, whose father had served Harding and Coolidge in the same position in the 1920s, crafted legislation that taxed food processing in order to finance payments to farmers who limited their production to "allocated" acreage. He hoped that restriction on production would raise farm prices.

Roosevelt was furious at the Supreme Court's action, which he considered an overreaching interference with domestic policy. The president viewed the food processing tax as far more conservative than the radical farm program favored by Senator Huey Long of Louisiana. Roosevelt was determined to show conservatives on the Supreme Court the consequences of their insistence on more established forms of taxation. He asked Congress to fill the budget hole with higher taxes on millionaires, large businesses, and estates.

The veterans' bonus cost the federal government $1.77 billion in fiscal year 1936 and $556 million the next. In fiscal year 1935, before being struck down by the Supreme Court, the food processing tax had produced $526 million—14 percent of all federal revenue—a share equal to all personal income taxes.[34] Without the veterans' bonus and with revenues from the processing tax, the fiscal year 1936–1937 budgets, excluding relief spending, would have balanced even though unemployment remained high.[35]

Pragmatic administrators stretched the value of limited federal dollars. They included Jesse Jones, chairman of the Reconstruction Finance Corporation; Henry Morgenthau Jr., secretary of the treasury; and Harold Ickes, secretary of the interior and leader of the Public Works Administration.

Jones, a conservative Texas banker and businessman, leveraged the RFC's public dollars with project financing in the form of bonds backed by mortgages, banks, and revenue from infrastructure projects instead of Treasury credit. By 1939 the RFC had made $10 billion in loans, an amount equivalent to all other Depression-era federal emergency efforts combined. By that time all but $1.9 billion had been repaid.[36]

While Jesse Jones wielded power derived solely from congressional confidence in his business acumen, Secretary Morgenthau's influence rested on his personal relationship with the president. Morgenthau was Roosevelt's neighbor in New York's rural Dutchess County, and the two families had vacationed together for years. Morgenthau, whose somber and precise manner projected the image of a conservative banker, pressed Roosevelt to balance the budget once the worst of the Depression had passed. In 1937 he told his polio-afflicted friend that it was time to "throw away the crutches and see if American enterprise could stand on its own feet."[37]

Secretary of the Interior Harold Ickes worked to ensure that the federal government financed only public works projects that had enduring value. Ickes, a former Theodore Roosevelt Progressive, met with Roosevelt weekly to review the details of each project recommended for federal funding. Roosevelt and Ickes approved grants to help local governments finance hundreds of water and sewer improvements, schools, roads, and hospitals. Contractors for federal agencies built hydroelectric dams and naval vessels, including the aircraft carriers *Enterprise* and *Yorktown* that years later played a critical role in the decisive Battle of Midway.

Roosevelt urged Ickes not to rush the construction of public works. After all, if the economy recovered, they could avoid spending borrowed funds. The president also directed Ickes and others to refrain from claiming that public works created indirect jobs as a result of spending by construction workers. Roosevelt wanted to prevent creating the false impression that the federal government could create prosperity by spending vast amounts of borrowed money. Modern construction required specialized skills and could not efficiently employ more than a small fraction of unemployed Americans.

SOCIAL INSURANCE

Emergency grants from the Federal Relief Administration, at the cost of less than 2 percent of national income, helped prevent starvation and homelessness during the winters of 1933 and 1934.[38] The Civilian Works Administration financed temporary jobs. Four million of those jobs ended in the spring of 1934, when Roosevelt argued that no one would "starve during the warm weather." The president objected to putting able-bodied citizens "on the dole" of long-term public assistance, which he likened to a "narcotic." In November 1934 he told Woodrow Wilson's former advisor, Colonel Edward House, that he was "seeking . . . the abolition of relief altogether."[39]

The president's views about "the dole" reflected the American political mainstream, as did his commitment to assist people who had lost their savings and were too old to work. Huey Long's "Share the Wealth" plan suggested confiscating the wealth of the richest Americans and redistributing part of it to pay old-age pensions. A mild-mannered California physician, Dr. Francis Townsend, generated a groundswell of support for his plan for the federal government to pay $200 a month—enough to support a comfortable standard of living—to everyone over the age of sixty.[40] Townsend claimed his pension plan would stimulate the economy and proposed the program be paid for using revenues from sales taxes.

Townsend had hold of a potent issue. Americans of all ages feared the grim fate of elderly citizens who had exhausted their savings during the Great Depression. Employers of the era typically did not provide pensions for retirees. By 1934 dues-paying members supported several thousand "Townsend Clubs," which could swing the balance in a close congressional election.

State and local governments also sought federal help in providing services to indigent older Americans. The federal government had unintentionally already borne a portion of these costs when some states—most notably in the South—diverted grants intended for the relief of laid-off workers in order to support citizens who were too old or disabled to work.

Fifteen months after taking office the president appointed the Committee on Economic Security to recommend "some safeguards against misfortunes which cannot be wholly eliminated in this man-made world." Roosevelt endorsed plans paid for "by contribution rather than an increase in general taxation" to provide for future retirees and temporarily unemployed workers. He asked Congress in January 1935 to enact the committee's recommendations in part to help "quit this business of relief."[41]

The committee recommended that pensions be funded with a tax on some percentage of the pay of employees who would later become eligible to receive a pension. A payroll tax for pensions would be split between the employer and employee, while a payroll tax for temporary unemployment insurance would be paid directly by employers. The administrative or federal funds budget would continue to provide matching grants to states for poor children, blind people, and older Americans who did not qualify for benefits under the new contributory pension program. That form of public assistance, or welfare, was the least controversial part of the House Ways and Means Committee's bill that was entitled the Social Security Act.

The Social Security Act gave states the responsibility for administering the unemployment insurance program. To prevent states from abandoning the program in order to lower taxes and attract new employers, the federal government imposed a federal tax on payrolls and credited amounts back to states that maintained unemployment insurance. The system of contributory unemployment insurance was not intended or financed to sustain unemployed workers over long periods of time.

The proposed old-age pension system could not help the 6 percent of Americans already over sixty-five in 1935, since they had no history of contributions that qualified them to receive benefits. The new pension system could, however, satisfy the widely perceived need for minimal and portable pensions for future retirees. President Hoover had earlier offered the rationale for a pension system funded half by employers and half by employees: "Medical science and work in public health controls had so prolonged the average life of the population that, instead of the two or three percent living beyond 60 years of age a century earlier, we now had 10 or 12 percent. The burden of the destitute and old people was too great to be met by the old-fashioned county commissioners with their 'poor-houses.'"[42]

The Committee on Economic Security concluded that it would be a bureaucratic nightmare to require each state to track the work histories and payroll tax payments of everyone employed within its borders. As a result, few saw any alternative to a national organization capable of assigning each worker a unique identifying number and compiling the information needed to determine each person's eligibility and benefits.

Secretary of Labor Frances Perkins, who chaired the Committee on Economic Security, hoped to use some amount of general revenues to supplement payroll taxation as a means for financing the pension system. General revenues could provide some capacity to give pensions to older Americans who would have little or no chance to earn a pension based on payroll contributions. Roosevelt and Morgenthau disagreed. The president insisted that actuaries design a system that was fully funded by a dedicated new tax. When Perkins explained that it would be many decades before the pension fund might need general revenues to offset the cost of early benefits, Roosevelt curtly told her that it would be "dishonest to build up an accumulated deficit for the Congress of the United States to meet in 1980." The president referred to any reliance on general revenues as "the same old dole under another name."[43] No one even considered borrowing to pay for pensions, since the very purpose of a pension system was to save, rather than borrow, in order to defray the future costs associated with an aging population.

Doughton convinced the president to bless the bill's assignment to his Ways and Means Committee. With advice from Morgenthau, Doughton's committee drafted the bill in a manner designed to maintain actuarial balance. That is, the estimated future stream of income from payroll taxes plus interest earned on trust would have to cover the cost of future benefits. The Ways and Means Committee excluded agricultural and domestic workers, whose wages Morgenthau said would be hard to track. Though payroll withholding began on January 1, 1937, the first benefit payments would not be made until five years later. A reserve would accumulate as workers earned the right to participate.

The Social Security Act—passed by Congress in August 1935 by an overwhelming, bipartisan majority—included a plan for state-administered unemployment insurance, a national old-age pension program, and state-administered matching grants for public assistance supporting impoverished older Americans, blind people, and single mothers with young children.

Most workers subject to the payroll tax had never before paid directly to the federal government a tax that was based on their earnings. Even though the average income of many Depression-era workers covered little more than subsistence, the program for minimum Social Security pensions was enormously popular from the outset. Future amendments to the Social Security Act—adopted in 1939, 1950, 1965, 1972, 1983, and 2003—would authorize much of federal domestic spending by the twenty-first century.

Accounting for Social Insurance

Almost immediately the new federal pension system posed a challenge to clear budget accounting, one of the pillars of the American Fiscal Tradition. Jefferson had "hope[d] to see the finances of the Union as clear and intelligible as merchants' books, so that . . . every man of any mind . . . should be able to comprehend them, to investigate abuses, and consequently to control them."[44] Proper actuarial accounting for social insurance required both economic and demographic projections reflecting the valuation of future streams of revenues and outlays. Traditional accounting would be misleading to the extent it failed to account for future liabilities related to present contributions.

President Roosevelt and Senator Arthur Vandenberg developed well-reasoned but starkly different solutions to the problem of accounting for future pension assets and liabilities. Roosevelt, a former insurance executive, believed that established principles used by actuaries in accounting for annuities should be used to link future liabilities with current payroll contributions. Independent trustees could be charged with maintaining the trust fund—held apart from the federal budget—in actuarial balance. Trustees could invest any reserve in interest-bearing Treasury obligations. Banks, private life insurers, and pension funds bought most federal bonds from 1933 through 1936. By 1936 bank investments in federal debt began to exceed the amount of their private loans. Between 1936 and 1940, debt held by federal trust funds increased from $2.3 billion to $7.1 billion, representing about half of the net increase in debt during this period.[45]

Senator Vandenberg, who voted for the Social Security Act, was troubled by the potential size of the pension reserves. Vandenberg noted that Social Security reserves could grow to an estimated $47 billion by 1980. He feared that the federal government sometime in the future might use that reserve to disguise the size and annual expense of federal debt.[46] The conservative Vandenberg dismissed the alternative of investing reserves in corporate bonds as "socialism." He preferred a pension system operating on a "pay-as-you-go basis, with only a modest contingent reserve."[47] A smaller initial reserve would also allow the trust fund to begin distributions earlier and include benefits to surviving spouses.

Vandenberg's position largely prevailed when Congress passed the Social Security Act Amendments of 1939. The legislation did, however, salvage some of the private sector insurance practices favored by Roosevelt. The bill more explicitly linked eligibility, benefit levels, and contributions; moved Social Security accounts from the Treasury to an independent trust fund; and required trustees to monitor and report the actuarial balance between projected obligations and revenues.

For thirty years after the 1939 amendments, Congress avoided the danger of misleading pension accounting that had so troubled Roosevelt and Vandenberg. The trust fund remained apart from the federal budget and was not used to conceal the amount of federal debt or annual borrowing. The fifty-year actuarial balance remained sound, even without a large reserve, because of the slow rise in benefits until the late 1960s and rapid growth in the workforce. Then, in 1969, the threats of unfunded liabilities (Roosevelt's concern) and the use of reserves to disguise borrowing (Vandenberg's concern) became more concrete. That year the federal government consolidated the Social Security trust fund with the administrative or federal funds budget. Muddled and opaque accounting for the Social Security and Medicare trust funds would eventually create an illusion of surplus that facilitated the collapse of the American Fiscal Tradition.

REELECTION AND ANOTHER DOWNTURN

Roosevelt was reelected in 1936 in a landslide so large that many Republicans—including Vandenberg and the other twelve remaining GOP senators—began to question the future survival of their party. No one had predicted such a lopsided outcome just a year earlier, when polls showed that Roosevelt's public approval ratings, once sky high, had dipped to 50 percent. Even many Democrats cringed at Roosevelt's National Recovery Administration, which attempted to restore corporate profits using price fixing. Left-wing populists had also criticized Roosevelt for being too cautious with his legislative agenda.

The president managed his 1936 campaign brilliantly. He largely ignored his progressive Republican opponent, Kansas Governor Alf Landon, and aimed his attacks on the well-funded American Liberty League, which accused Roosevelt of encouraging class warfare.

Roosevelt relished the opportunity to voice the concerns of the millions of Americans who had lost their life savings or worked for low wages. He labeled his opponents "economic royalists" and courted former Theodore Roosevelt Progressives. Roosevelt, in a radio broadcast, asked voters to cast their ballots based on whether they thought things were better than they had been four years earlier, when the unemployment rate was far higher.

Democrats won control of all but eight state houses in the 1936 election. Landon, who had picked one of Theodore Roosevelt's friends as his running mate, blamed his defeat on the GOP's failure to showcase his "really liberal stand on many questions."[48] Hoover agreed with Landon and blamed the American Liberty League for highlighting Roosevelt's popular willingness to stand up to big business.

Though the president showed respect for the American Fiscal Tradition, he lost much of his political capital with Congress by threatening another part of the nation's unwritten constitution. The Constitution did not confine the Supreme Court to the nine positions established by statute in 1869, but the size and independence of the court had since evolved into a sacrosanct tradition. In 1937 Roosevelt proposed to expand the size of the Supreme Court that had invalidated parts of his New Deal legislative program, a ploy that quickly became known as the "court-packing scheme."

The Republican Party was so weak in 1937 that its leaders kept quiet in order to allow Democrats in Congress to lead the assault on the court-packing scheme. Even Vice President Garner expressed his unease with such a challenge to the traditional balance of power. Roosevelt's brash proposal may have accomplished one of his purposes, as the court subsequently became less aggressive in restraining New Deal legislation. However, the president's defiance of the nation's traditional constitution permanently alienated many conservative Democrats in Congress, who developed an effective partnership with congressional Republicans during the remainder of Roosevelt's presidency.

The president never underestimated the power of the American Fiscal Tradition. He submitted a budget for fiscal year 1938 that projected a surplus apart from the cost of work relief programs.[49] Roosevelt assured Vice President Garner of his continued commitment to balancing the budget and told him that he would say so publicly "fifty times."[50] In the calendar year 1937 estimated revenues would have exceeded spending had they been calculated based on normal levels of employment, a measure used by economists later in the century.

The economy's steady recovery ended in late 1937. After the nation's money supply shrank between 1929 and 1933, it expanded from 1933 to 1936. The Federal Reserve nurtured this trend. Then—in 1937—it tightened credit in order to avoid inflation.

The president persisted in emphasizing the theme of budget discipline even as employment continued to decline in early 1938. Though many commentators now blame that recession on the drive to balance the federal budget, the fault clearly lay with the 1937 monetary contraction. When the Federal Reserve relaxed credit and the Treasury stopped purchasing gold flowing in from Europe, the economy began to grow again. The president explained to the public that the federal government would borrow only an amount equivalent to its investment in durable public works projects or sound loans made by the RFC.

The American people clearly supported traditional limits on federal debt. A Roper poll in 1939 asked: "If you were a member of the incoming Congress, would you vote yes or no on a bill to reduce federal spending to a point where the national budget is balanced?" An overwhelming 61.3 percent said yes; only 17.4 percent replied no.[51] Budget cutters had a three-to-one margin in every income group.

The economy had fully recovered from the 1938 downturn by the time Germany invaded Poland in September 1939. Unmonetized federal debt had grown to 40 percent of national income, a level only 9 percent higher than that of two decades earlier.[52]

Presidents Hoover and Roosevelt, who served as icons of opposing political philosophies, had articulated similar principles for limiting debt during downturns. They both supported debt-financed spending on public works that had a clear benefit to posterity. Though they approved some debt-financed emergency relief to prevent starvation and homelessness, they both opposed longer-term programs that might encourage dependency. Both favored pensions and temporary unemployment insurance financed by self-sustaining trust funds.

Unlike federal leaders in the twenty-first century, Hoover and Roosevelt tried to preserve traditional limits on debt by articulating clearly what borrowed funds should and should not pay for. Senior federal officials in the 1930s never lost sight of the ceiling on debt authorized during World War I.

By the late 1930s some economists came to believe that federal fiscal restraint had prolonged the Great Depression. In hindsight, however, it seems implausible that several billions of dollars in additional borrowing in an economy with an annual income of $55 billion to $75 billion would have cured unemployment.

Twentieth-century labor markets had changed in a manner not easily altered by debt-financed federal spending. The productivity and real wages (wages and salaries adjusted for purchasing power) of Americans with full time jobs *rose* during most of the Great Depression. The gap widened between incomes of workers with specialized skills and all others. By 1939 national output and income had been restored to 1928 levels, though unemployment was far higher than before. The issue of jobless recoveries from downturns would haunt the economy in the wake of many future downturns. For example, the number of private sector jobs grew more slowly in the twenty-first century than at any time since the Depression, despite massive federal borrowing and credit expansion.

The fact that full employment levels returned during World War II does not justify the conclusion that the federal government should have borrowed more aggressively in the 1930s. World War II was no picnic, and wartime employment came at a high price. The nation did not relish sending much of its young population off to war or coping with shortages of civilian goods.

The unwillingness of Americans to mortgage the nation's future tax revenues for the purpose of stimulating the economy disturbed British economist John Maynard Keynes, whom Roosevelt thought had little understanding of democratic governance. Keynes's celebrated book, *The General Theory of Employment, Interest and Money*, described how debt-financed stimulus could potentially raise employment in an economy with few imports, excess capacity and savings, and high unemployment. In these circumstances, Keynes prescribed public spending financed with debt that could be fully monetized. In the preface to the German edition of his book and his correspondence with economist Frederick Hayek, Keynes acknowledged that his prescriptions might be more suited to a nation guided by an expert elite. In 1940 Keynes presciently predicted that it might take a war to encourage Americans to borrow more.

When that war came the following year, the federal government needed every single dollar of available credit and savings. After World War II federal leaders were thankful that the taxpayers had not been saddled with even higher debt service in the 1930s. The American Fiscal Tradition had survived the Great Depression intact.

PART IV

CONTAINING THE
BURDEN OF WORLD WAR II DEBT
WHILE INCREASING COMMITMENTS:
1941–1976

11

War and Taxes

1941–1949: Years when deficits exceeded debt service = 5
(1941–1945, World War II)

A New Tax System

When Adolf Hitler's armies occupied much of Europe in the summer of 1940, Congress appropriated $5 billion to strengthen the nation's army and navy. It authorized a national defense bond and raised taxes. Federal military spending grew steadily from $199 million per month in July 1940 to $1.9 billion per month in November 1941.[1]

Republican Senate leaders Arthur Vandenberg and Robert Taft opposed what they perceived as a White House agenda to lead the United States into war. As a result, President Roosevelt had difficulty obtaining congressional approval to register young Americans to prepare for a future military draft.

Public attitudes changed completely on December 7, 1941, when Japanese aircraft attacked Pearl Harbor. Four days later, when Germany declared war on the United States, Hitler gave a speech disparaging American racial diversity and asked how "a state like that can hold together—a country where everything is built on the dollar."[2] Americans responded with one voice, and their elected officials spent dollars like never before. In 1942 the German sphere of control in Europe had a population and national income greater than those of the United States. That year it managed to produce fifteen thousand aircraft and five thousand tanks. The

United States produced forty-eight thousand aircraft and seventeen thousand tanks in 1942 and vastly more each of the next several years.[3]

President Roosevelt did not mince words in his 1942 State of the Union address: "War costs money. That means taxes and bonds and bonds and taxes."[4] Treasury Secretary Henry Morgenthau initially proposed that tax revenues pay for half the war's costs—the same goal articulated by Secretary William McAdoo when the United States entered World War I.[5] High levels of taxation allowed the nation to borrow at a low interest rate during World War II and service the debt after the war. By 1943 Roosevelt told Morgenthau that paying a third of the war's cost with new taxes was a more realistic goal.

In April 1942 Roosevelt asked Congress to tax 100 percent of personal incomes over $25,000 per individual and $50,000 per family. Senator Taft, who emerged as the Republican leader on fiscal issues, expressed the prevailing sense of the members of Congress in both parties: "The rate might be 90 percent, but it should never be 100 percent."[6]

Congress imposed high tax rates on wealthy citizens and corporations. Memories of high inflation during World War I led to bipartisan support for taxes that would restrict the purchasing power of most Americans, including families with middle incomes who had never paid income tax. The White House and members of Congress could not immediately agree, however, on the best form of broad-based taxation. Some—including Roosevelt's budget director and most Republicans—favored a national sales tax. Morgenthau and Ways and Means Committee Chairman Robert Doughton preferred to lower the standard exemption from the income tax and raise all income tax rates.

The Revenue Act of 1942 passed with only two dissenting votes in the House and none in the Senate. It helped finance the war and laid the foundation of the future federal income tax system. The Revenue Act's high taxes on corporate income and its broad-based tax on personal income soon yielded federal revenues amounting to almost a fifth of national income. Surtax rates applicable to various income brackets ranged from 13 percent to 82 percent. Corporate tax rates rose from 31 percent to 40 percent.[7] Taxes on extraordinary returns on investment supplemented taxes on corporate income.

The taxation of middle-income Americans imposed by the Revenue Act marked a turning point in the federal fiscal system. In the nineteenth century import taxes produced most of the federal revenue. Income taxes had not touched the majority of Americans during the Civil War and World War I.

The Revenue Act of 1942, in contrast, reached middle incomes by lowering the standard exemption, which fell to $500 even while inflation and a tight labor market pushed up wages.[8] In 1939, 7.6 million Americans filed federal income tax returns and reported gross income—the top line on tax returns—totaling 27 percent of national income.[9] The $929 million they paid in income taxes equaled just 3.66 percent of total reported gross income.[10] By 1943, 43.7 million Americans filed tax returns and reported gross income equal to 54 percent of total national income. They paid $14.6 billion—13.7 percent of reported gross income—in income taxes.[11]

While World War II marked the beginning of the broad-based personal income tax, an even higher percentage of the workforce would pay federal income taxes later in the twentieth century. In the 1940s, the standard deduction amounted to a higher percentage of average income than it would be in later decades. In 1948 the personal deduction was almost half of average income, while by 1981 it ranged from 30 percent of average income for single filers to 16 percent for married filers with two dependents.[12]

During the 2012 election, Republican presidential nominee Mitt Romney sparked a controversy by noting that "47 percent" of the workforce paid no net income tax. In fact, because of the erosion in the value of the standard deduction, a higher share of American households paid income taxes at the end of the twentieth century than during World War II. The top 1 percent of taxpayers paid almost a third of all personal income taxes during World War II, a share substantially lower than in the "conservative" 1920s and greater than the share they paid in the twenty-first century.

Certain features of personal income taxation have been remarkably stable ever since passage of the Revenue Act of 1942. Personal income tax revenues have generally remained in the range of 7 to 9 percent of national income. Since its enactment American taxpayers have reported gross taxable income in a narrow band around 60 percent of the total value of national income. In other words, if total national income were depicted as a pie chart, about three-fifths would be labeled gross personal income subject to taxation and reported on tax forms.

EXCLUSIONS, DEDUCTIONS, AND WITHHOLDING

Because a relatively stable 60 percent or so of national income has been subject to federal personal income taxation since World War II, federal officials and commentators naturally turn to the other 40 percent when considering how to raise additional revenue. The reasoning underlying the structure of the World War II tax system—created at a time when virtually all Americans understood the need for higher taxes and higher tax revenues—sheds light on various exclusions and deductions from personal income taxation.

Ways and Means Committee Chairman Robert Doughton and Senator Robert Taft struggled with how best to handle a category of noncash compensation—pension contributions—that was excluded from personal income taxation until the receipt of pensions by the beneficiary. Their resolution of that issue had a profound long-term effect on the American economy and tax revenues.

Although Doughton and Taft had very different backgrounds, they worked together to find common ground during the war. Whereas Muley Bob Doughton's father was a rural populist active in the Farmers Alliance that rallied around William Jennings Bryan, Taft's father, William Howard Taft, beat Bryan in the 1908 presidential race. Few employers had pension plans before World War II. Since the 1920s it had been clear that employer contributions to pension trust funds and earnings on those trust funds would not be taxed until the employee received the pension distribution. Doughton and Secretary Morgenthau feared that managers would try to escape paying high wartime tax rates by diverting part of their compensation into custom-designed pension plans. Taft acknowledged this risk of abuse but resisted standardized pensions that would reduce the flexibility of individual firms to craft their own pension plans. Doughton and Taft settled the matter by agreeing that employer pension contributions would be taxed only when employees received their pensions, but only so long as a pension plan was available to a broad base of employees. Tax lawyers interpreted that policy in a manner that excluded employer-funded medical insurance from the taxable income of employees.

Wartime shortages of skilled labor and federal wage ceilings prompted many large employers to offer pension and medical insurance plans during World War II.[13] The exclusion of that form of compensation from taxable income began to significantly limit the share of national income appearing on personal tax returns. By 2005, for example, the $7.4 trillion in gross income that appeared on the top line of personal income tax returns excluded $900 billion in the estimated value of pension and insurance contributions and related investment income.[14]

Interest payments had always been deductible from gross taxable income. The income tax had originally applied to wealthy Americans, for whom interest payments were typically a business expense. Then, after World War II, many Americans bought houses and deducted the interest they paid on home mortgages. Since interest was cost for landlords, it seemed only fair that Americans who invested in their own housing should also be able to deduct mortgage interest. That deduction did, however, narrow the base of net taxable income.

After passage of the Revenue Act of 1942, those far-reaching decisions concerning exclusions and deductions seemed far less pressing to Secretary Morgenthau than did the practical issue of tax collection. Tens of millions of Americans at the time had never filed a tax form. Beardsley Ruml, CEO of R. H. Macy & Company, urged Secretary Morgenthau to withhold an estimated amount of income taxes from paychecks. Congress engaged in a spirited fight about whether to forgive some amount of taxes for 1942—which were due in April 1943—if withholding began in 1943. Doughton compromised on the issue with Senator Arthur Vandenberg, clearing the way for broad-based withholding of income tax from wages and salaries.

Even withholding did not end Secretary Morgenthau's challenge in collecting the broad-based income tax. A Gallup poll showed that most Americans thought withholding dispensed with the requirement to file annual tax returns. The Treasury Department did not have the personnel to audit tens of millions of tax forms, much less discover all those who should have filed them but did not do so. Morgenthau feared that even innocent noncompliance would erode the moral force of a tax system dependent on self-reporting.

So Morgenthau and his staff enlisted the power of mass media. Radio stations frequently aired an upbeat jingle by Irving Berlin, "I Paid My Federal Income Taxes Today." Radio personality Roy Rogers promoted income taxes as an expression of wartime patriotism. A Donald Duck cartoon shown to more than thirty million moviegoers demonstrated how to fill out tax forms. By the end of the war, forty-nine million households were filing tax returns, more than ten times the number in 1939.[15]

President Roosevelt favored even higher taxes. Because Congress dismissed his idea of taxing all income over a certain level, in March 1943 he signed an executive order banning salaries of more than $25,000. Congress superseded that executive order when it raised the debt ceiling to $210 billion, the first—but far from the last—use of congressional power over the debt ceiling to accomplish another purpose.[16]

The tax dispute between the president and congressional leaders in both parties grew bitter by 1944. In February Roosevelt vetoed a tax bill on the grounds that it failed to raise more revenue from corporate taxation. His veto message accused Congress of passing a tax bill "not for the needy, but for the greedy."[17] Irate members of Congress overrode Roosevelt's veto. By 1944 tax revenues supporting the federal funds budget exceeded 20 percent of national income. Even Doughton, a stalwart supporter of Roosevelt's New Deal programs, concluded that federal taxation had reached the maximum level that individual taxpayers could take. Doughton—who owed nothing to big business—and a majority in Congress believed that an additional increase in corporate taxation would impair the investment required to support war-related production and to retool factories after the war.

RECORD BORROWING

The scale of wartime borrowing and the desire to avoid inflationary pressures led most of the president's senior economic advisors to conclude that citizens should be forced to buy bonds. Roosevelt and Morgenthau disagreed. They felt that voluntary bond purchases allowed citizens to take pride in their participation in the war effort. Morgenthau instructed Treasury bond salesmen to forgo "intimidation . . . of any kind to induce people to sign pledges." He thought the government had to "persuade people to buy . . . willingly and enthusiastically, by bringing them to realize that in doing so they serve[d] their country today and themselves tomorrow."[18] People from a variety of backgrounds, including active duty military personnel, made this pitch during bond drives. The federal government even enlisted allied leaders Winston Churchill and Joseph Stalin in campaigns to market savings bonds. By the end of the war, Americans had purchased savings bonds totaling almost $50 billion, an amount greater than prewar federal debt.[19] Almost twenty-eight million workers earmarked some portion of their salaries and wages for the purchase of bonds.[20]

Morgenthau and Federal Reserve Chairman Marriner Eccles, who had battled over economic policy in the 1930s, worked as a seamless team during World War II. The Federal Reserve directly bought over $20 billion of debt and offered banks credit certificates at low interest rates to support bond purchases.[21] The federal government sold vast amounts of debt at extraordinarily low interest rates. Amazingly, the average interest rate on the debt declined from 2.52 percent in 1941 to 1.94 percent in 1945.[22] Because of a high rate of national savings, consumer prices rose far less than the expansion of the nation's money supply.

At the height of the war, in fiscal years 1944 and 1945, debt financed only 56 percent of federal spending, a lower percentage than at the end of World War I (72 percent from 1918 to 1919); the Civil War (72 percent in 1864 to 1865); and the War of 1812 (62 percent in 1814 to 1815).[23] Nonetheless, debt rose to record levels. A comparison of debt to federal funds revenues available for debt service provides a reliable measure of how far the nation stretched its debt capacity. At the end of World War II those revenues covered only 15 percent of total debt, the same level as at the end of the Civil War.[24] At the end of the War of 1812, when the federal government missed a payment on debt, tax revenues had dropped to 12 percent of outstanding debt.[25] Only after the collapse of the American Fiscal Tradition in the twenty-first century would federal funds tax revenues cover a lower share of outstanding debt.

With the war's conclusion in sight, American political leaders began to consider the scope of future federal responsibilities. Millions of Americans read Secretary of Commerce Henry Wallace's best-selling book *Sixty Million Jobs*, published shortly after Roosevelt's death in April 1945. The president had replaced the popular Wallace as his running mate with Senator Harry Truman before the 1944 election. Wallace, who was adept at statistical analysis, concluded that by 1950 the American economy could employ sixty million people—full employment—and maintain an output of $200 billion. At that level of national income, he projected that the United States could cut wartime tax rates and balance a federal budget with spending of $25 billion, and "approach, with a lighter heart and heavier purse, the retirement of national debt."[26]

While Wallace embodied the aspirations of many liberals at the conclusion of World War II, Senator Robert Taft shaped the expectations of many conservatives. Both Wallace and Taft assumed that the atomic bomb and America's geographical distance from Europe and Asia would allow the federal government to balance its budget by slashing military spending. Americans across the political spectrum wanted life to return to normal after the surrender of Germany and Japan. They hoped that "normal" would not include a permanently high level of military spending and related taxes.

THE DEBATE OVER MILITARY SPENDING

Harry Truman lacked Roosevelt's wealth, education, and magic last name. He did, however, reflect the values and attitudes of many middle-class Americans.

Truman disagreed with Senator Taft on many issues, though he respected the fact that there "was nothing devious about him."[27] Taft, in turn, considered Truman to be a "straightforward man" who also had "the quality of decision" necessary for executive leadership.[28] The two partisan adversaries shared a commitment to the traditional limits on debt.

After Major Harry Truman returned from World War I, he worked hard for a dozen years to pay off debts from the failure of a retail store he owned in Missouri. As a county executive, he balanced his operating budget. These life experiences and his thorough knowledge of American history shaped his belief that "the pay as you go idea . . . represents the soundest principle of financing that I know."[29] This principle, guided President Truman's response to the nation's greatest postwar budget challenge: balancing the desire to reduce wartime tax rates with the goal of maintaining a military capable of meeting commitments to allies. A person at the center of that conflict—Secretary of Defense James Forrestal— noted that Truman was "a hard-money man" who believed that America could not "afford to wreck our economy in the process of trying to fight the 'cold war.'"[30]

Congress rapidly cut military spending and a portion of wartime taxes after Japan surrendered in September 1945. The United States could not, however, cut its spending to prewar levels while American troops were still occupying Germany and Japan. The war in Europe ended with Germany's surrender, not a comprehensive peace treaty. The struggle between communist and democratic forces for power continued within many European nations, and Soviet leader Joseph Stalin refused to withdraw his army from Eastern Europe.

President Truman's first budget message, delivered in January 1946, declared that the federal government should retire debt with planned surpluses. The president urged "a continuation of our present policy, which is to maintain the existing tax structure for the present, and to avoid nonessential expenditures."[31]

There was no clear benchmark for estimating normal federal budgets after the sixteen years spanning the Great Depression and World War II. Truman used basic rules of thumb as part of traditional "pay as you go" budget planning. His Budget Bureau began by estimating revenues from existing taxes, apart from those dedicated to trust funds. It then subtracted debt service and devoted a third of the remaining revenues to the military. The remaining funds were allocated to cover all other expenses, including substantial sums for veterans and military assistance to allies.

International affairs, however, did not abide by White House budget priorities. In the words of historian John Gaddis, "the period of late February and early March, 1946, marked a decisive turning point in American policy toward the Soviet Union."[32] In February 1946 an official at the US embassy in Moscow, George Kennan, gave senior Washington officials a thoughtful analysis of a belligerent speech delivered by Stalin. Kennan predicted that the Soviet regime would attempt to dominate other nations in order to preserve its own ideological authority and only American military strength could check that tendency.

Senator Arthur Vandenberg called for American preparations to protect Europe from Soviet aggression. Secretary of State James Byrnes expressed alarm at the Soviet Union's "unilateral gnawing away at the status quo."[33] In Truman's home state of Missouri, former British prime minister Churchill likened the Soviet police state to an "Iron Curtain" descending over Eastern Europe. In April 1946 Truman told Americans that it would be "a tragic breach of national duty" if the United States declined to accept its responsibility as "the world's strongest nation."[34]

Fierce debates occurred within each of the two major parties concerning the appropriate level of postwar military spending and taxes. Secretary of Commerce Henry Wallace, a potential Truman rival for the 1948 Democratic presidential nomination, thought that the United States could avoid costly military competition if it simply recognized the inevitable reality of a Soviet sphere of influence. The president disagreed and asked Wallace to leave the cabinet in September 1946.

The congressional budget debate following the 1946 midterm elections exposed a parallel conflict within the Republican Party. Senator Taft and Representative Harold Knutson, ranking member of the House Ways and Means Committee, had crafted a GOP election platform that promised a 20 percent tax cut. Republicans believed they had a mandate for that tax cut after winning a majority in the Senate and House for the first time since 1928.

The Legislative Reorganization Act of 1946 tried to institutionalize "pay as you go" budget planning by requiring Congress to vote on spending limits and revenues before each new fiscal year. The new Republican-led Congress, in February 1947, adopted a budget that cut taxes and limited spending to $31.5 billion for fiscal year 1948. Truman had proposed a budget with higher military spending, a surplus, and $37.7 billion in revenues without a tax cut.[35]

Despite the significant difference of opinion concerning the overall level of federal spending and taxes, Truman and congressional Republicans agreed on the need for an orderly reduction in debt. On March 3, 1947, with Truman's support, the Senate voted to use the surplus in the existing fiscal year to retire at least $2.6 billion of the national debt.[36]

Events in Europe gave a sense of urgency to the debate over military spending in the budget for the fiscal year beginning on July 1, 1947. After the House cut spending to far less than the Truman administration had requested, congressional leaders from both parties met at the White House with George Marshall, the nation's ranking general since the beginning of World War II. The respected soldier asked for military assistance for Turkey and Greece in order to counter imminent communist takeovers. Heavily indebted Great Britain could no longer afford to maintain an armed presence in those countries. Deputy Secretary of State Dean Acheson starkly described the potential isolation of the United States in a world dominated by communist dictatorships.

The nation's unwritten fiscal constitution did not allow Congress to evade a hard budget choice by opting to use debt to fund security-related spending. Senator Vandenberg, who chaired the Senate Foreign Relations Committee, agreed to help the administration raise defense spending. He insisted, however, that Truman clearly express to the public the threat posed by Soviet expansion.

The president then urged a joint session of Congress "to support free people who are resisting attempted subjugation by armed minorities or by outside pressures."[37] After Truman's appeal, Vandenberg restored some defense cuts made by the House. Like many Americans, Vandenberg had no trouble reconciling his former isolationism with his new internationalism. He explained why his views had changed: modern aviation and new weapons dramatically reduced the effectiveness of the buffer once provided by the Atlantic and Pacific Oceans.

The United States was then the only nation that had the economic capacity to pay for the defense of Western Europe. At the conclusion of the war, the United States produced half of the world's industrial output. It had the world's only large grain surpluses and its only strong gold-backed currency and banking system.

At the beginning of 1946—as in 2013, for example—most economists worried that a sharp contraction of debt-financed federal spending would harm economic growth. They were mistaken. Though federal outlays dropped from the wartime high of $98 billion in 1945 to $34.5 billion in 1947, federal tax collections fell only 10 percent from their wartime peak even after the enactment of modest reductions from wartime tax rates.[38] By 1947 the nation was experiencing strong economic growth.

Despite the robust economy, in 1947 Truman vetoed tax cuts that he thought would endanger the nation's ability to retire debt. By late 1947, halfway through fiscal year 1948, the White House announced a projected surplus of approximately $7 billion.[39] By the end of that fiscal year, the federal funds budget was running a surplus amounting to an unprecedented quarter of all revenues. The size of the surplus moved Congressman Robert Doughton to join Republicans in passing legislation to cut tax rates and then overriding the president's subsequent veto of the bill.

Secretary of Defense James Forrestal worried about the gap between America's new global commitments and its military capabilities. A humorless and hardworking federal executive who had served as secretary of the navy after a brilliant career on Wall Street, Forrestal respected Truman's commitment to a balanced budget. He also believed that the Soviets could only be restrained by the credible threat of American intervention. The Pentagon's senior military brass pushed the secretary to obtain more funding.

Truman gave Forrestal a March 1, 1948, deadline to prepare the first budget request for the new Department of Defense, which had been created to facilitate more efficient and coordinated spending by the armed forces. In the meantime, the president presented Congress with a budget for fiscal year 1949 that limited spending to $39.7 billion, including $11 billion for the military and $4 billion for an economic aid package to rebuild Europe—the Marshall Plan. That budget proposed a 13 percent reduction in troops and a projected surplus of $4 billion.[40]

Meanwhile, Stalin continued to incorporate Eastern Europe satellite nations into the orbit of the Soviet police state. His troops brutally suppressed opposition in Czechoslovakia in February 1948, prompting the commander of American forces in Europe, General Lucius Clay, to warn that further Soviet military aggression could come "with dramatic suddenness."[41] Truman reluctantly authorized $3.1 billion in additional military spending, less than the $8.8 billion—principally for greater air power—requested by Forrestal.[42]

Because Congress refused to raise taxes, a balanced budget depended in large part on confining military spending within available tax revenues. The president met with Forrestal in the Oval Office in May 1948 and instructed him to develop a multiyear plan for defense outlays of no more than $15 billion annually, including $600 million per year in stockpiled supplies.[43] The president knew that some military leaders would second-guess his decision, and he presented Forrestal with a memorandum, prepared in advance, that recorded their conclusions. Truman wrote in his diary that he worked to obtain a "balanced sensible request for which the country can pay."[44]

The Joint Chiefs of Staff, the nation's ranking military officers, could not agree on how to allocate spending among the branches of the armed services. All acknowledged the need for greater investment in the air force, but neither the army nor the navy agreed to take a corresponding cut in its funding. The Joint Chiefs insisted that they needed at least $4 billion more. Forrestal pressed them to specify how the additional spending would affect the outcome of a potential conflict. In October 1948 he reported their conclusions to the president: if the Soviets moved into Western Europe, a $15 billion budget could support a bombing campaign based in Great Britain, while an additional $4 billion would strengthen control of the Mediterranean.[45] Since Truman believed that Congress would not raise taxes to cover that cost, he declined to authorize the supplementary funds.

Neither Forrestal nor congressional leaders in either party expected Truman to be reelected in 1948. The Democratic Party had splintered. Some liberals supported the third-party candidacy of former vice president

Henry Wallace, while many Southern Democrats backed a third-party bid by Governor Strom Thurmond of South Carolina. Republicans presented a more unified front. Their platform promised lower taxes and a balanced budget while maintaining a strong defense, commitments to veterans, and popular domestic programs.

Truman thought the budget could not be balanced with the enactment of the program endorsed by the Republican platform. To emphasize that fact, he called Congress back into session and challenged Republicans to enact their platform's tax and spending policies. To the surprise of many observers, the president was reelected. Democratic congressional candidates fared well, and their party regained control of Congress.

Political histories of the 1948 election tend to focus on the contrasting campaign styles of Truman and his Republican opponent, New York governor Thomas Dewey. The American Fiscal Tradition, however, framed the trade-off between spending and taxes. In the farm belt Truman reversed the partisan results of the election two years earlier. Federal support for agricultural prices was one of the few New Deal spending programs that remained in effect. Lower tax rates would require lower outlays for defense and farm programs. Taft and other Republican budget leaders knew that, so they were slow to deny the intent to cut agricultural spending.

After the election Forrestal flew to West Berlin, where Soviet forces had blockaded land access to sectors of the city under Allied administration. He asked General Lucius Clay whether "he would be willing to accept deficits in the federal budget over the next several years" to build up American military strength. Clay said no, because "an unbalanced budget in the United States would have a serious impact in Europe, where it would be taken as a signal that even the United States was unable to cope with its fiscal problems."[46]

Squeezed between pressure for budget discipline and the demands of the professional military, Forrestal became severely depressed. He jumped to his death from a hospital window shortly after the president requested his resignation. Retired general Eisenhower had tried to help Forrestal mediate the dispute between the military services and develop operational plans tied back to budget numbers. That effort physically exhausted Eisenhower, whose doctor insisted that he take time off. The United States balanced its budget after World War II, but it had yet to bridge the gap between international commitments and capabilities that had vexed Forrestal and Eisenhower.

THE REPUBLICAN BUDGET DILEMMA

Republicans in Congress never resolved the tension between Taft's emphasis on reduced taxes and Vandenberg's support for the Truman administration's level of military spending. America's unwritten fiscal constitution
precluded the illusion of "free" debt-financed spending or tax cuts. Corporate managers and small business owners, a core GOP constituency, firmly
backed "pay as you go" budgets.

Republicans hoped to find some fiscal room to maneuver when Congress appointed former president Herbert Hoover, an expert on management and a harsh New Deal critic, to identify waste and inefficiency.
Truman also loathed inefficiency and welcomed Hoover's help. Congress
passed the Hoover Commission's most ambitious recommendations. That
experience yielded a result similar to future drives for efficiency: the effort
was worthwhile, but the savings were small when compared to the size of
the federal budget and the level of tax cuts desired by many conservatives.

Despite his loss in two presidential elections, Governor Dewey was a
talented politician who continued to be reelected, with lopsided margins,
as the governor of the nation's largest state. He believed the GOP would
be "buried" if it opposed "farm price supports, unemployment insurance,
old-age benefits, slum clearance, and other social programs."[47] In reality,
federal spending on domestic programs, other than for veterans, constituted a small portion of the federal funds budget.

Senator Taft faulted Dewey for not defining his differences with the
Truman administration more sharply. Some of those differences—notably
concerning labor-management relations—had little budget impact. Moreover, Taft himself had championed some new spending programs. Taft,
one of the most influential senators in the twentieth century, had the rare
gift of being able to articulate a broad political vision and then apply it to
the details of varied legislation. His conservative beliefs may surprise many
twenty-first-century Republicans. The senator journalists called "Mr. Republican" explained that "under a free system we are bound to have much
greater inequality than under a socialistic system, although in the end I
believe the socialistic system would level everybody down. . . . I believe,
however, that we must accept the inequalities and then do our best to
improve the condition of the people at the lower end . . . by economic
measures like minimum wage laws, and to an extent by direct assistance
to health, education, housing and the like."[48] In short, Taft thought that

a competitive market economy should be accompanied by a social safety net for Americans who were unable to work or make ends meet even when they worked hard.

Taft sponsored legislation to create public housing for working Americans who could not otherwise afford it. He endorsed federal grants to states in support of improved housing, health, and education. Taft felt that states alone could not fund these essential services without losing business to other states that maintained lower taxes by shirking those responsibilities.

While Taft set the Republican tone on domestic policy, Vandenberg prevailed on foreign policy. Vandenberg fought Taft's efforts to cut the military budget and reduce foreign military deployments and economic assistance—such as the Marshall Plan—to allies. Vandenberg wrote in his diary that he got "so damned sick of the little band of GOP isolationists . . . that [he] could scream."[49] Republicans in Congress shifted toward Vandenberg and away from Taft on international security after the 1948 election. Younger party members such as Richard Nixon and Joseph McCarthy scored points by attacking Democrats for being "soft" on communism. In June 1949 Taft was one of only thirteen senators to vote against the North Atlantic Treaty, the agreement that established NATO and committed US forces to the defense of Western Europe.

International developments in the fall of 1949 made it more difficult to restrain military spending. In October President Truman announced that the Soviets had successfully detonated an atomic bomb. Later that month the Soviet Union recognized the communist People's Republic of China. Those events evoked memories of Pearl Harbor and Munich, yet Truman held the line on defense spending. He wrote to an old friend that it remained his "ambition to reduce the national debt below Two Hundred Billion Dollars."[50]

DOWNTURNS AND LIMITS ON DEBT

W. Elliot Brownlee, a leading historian of federal taxation, observed that immediately after World War II, "for the first time since the early nineteenth century, the two political parties agreed on the essential elements of the nation's fiscal policy."[51] Those essential elements included a broad-based, graduated tax on personal income; a flat percentage tax on corporate income; and a flat percentage payroll tax earmarked for social insurance. During fiscal years 1947 to 1950, that tax system—exclusive of trust funds—produced revenues of $157.4 billion, which more than covered the government's $153.4 billion in spending.[52] Outlays for defense, international commitments to allies, veterans' benefits, and interest on the public debt accounted for $120.6 billion, almost 80 percent of the total.[53]

Concerns about high unemployment led to a spirited contest in Congress that shed light on the post–World War II concept of the federal budget. The Employment Act of 1946 arose from bills filed, debated, and passed by the House and Senate in 1945. The original bills declared the national goal of full employment. The text of the Full Employment Act was negotiated in the context of a political dialogue in the United States and Western Europe over whether people seeking work had a right to be employed. Americans across the political spectrum respected the dignity and self-sufficiency accompanying gainful employment, but many elected officials—especially conservatives in both parties—rejected the implication that the federal government needed to finance employment as a last resort.

The Senate passed the Employment Act with a lopsided vote, 71 to 10, after it was strongly endorsed by Senator Joseph O'Mahoney of Wyoming, a centrist Democrat considered by his colleagues to be an economic expert. He assured other senators that he staunchly opposed planned deficit spending, although deficits tended to follow a downturn. The Senate unanimously voted for an amendment to the bill, drafted by Taft and Radcliffe, stating that any program designed to boost employment would have to be linked to taxation "calculated to prevent any net increase in the national debt" over a reasonable period.[54] The bill that passed by the House and emerged from the conference committee stripped out most language in the Senate version that required federal spending and full employment. It passed by overwhelming margins in the House and Senate.[55]

The Employment Act of 1946 could be interpreted as no more than a hollow endorsement of the goal of high employment, but it did demonstrate a heightened awareness of the relationship between the federal budget and the economy as a whole. In that spirit, the bill created the White House Council of Economic Advisers. The White House Bureau of the Budget, then managed by Harold Smith, had already added economists to its growing fiscal division. Federal leaders since 1789 had considered the impact of federal spending and taxes on economic growth. In the immediate aftermath of the Great Depression and World War II, elected officials more frequently referred to the budget's impact on the economy by using a term borrowed from economists: "fiscal policy."

The Employment Act of 1946 coincided with a debate within the economics profession concerning the appropriate limit of borrowing during downturns. In 1948 two young economists, Milton Friedman and Paul Samuelson, outlined those limits in a manner that influenced debates among budget experts for the balance of the twentieth century. They each recognized that recessions would cause federal income tax revenues to decline and rejected the notion of raising tax rates in order to balance the budget during a downturn.

In 1948 the thirty-six-year-old Milton Friedman, a professor at the University of Chicago with a gift for statistical research, spelled out his approach to balanced budgets in his influential article, "A Monetary and Fiscal Framework for Economic Stability." Friedman proposed that the federal government should try to balance its budget across each multiyear economic cycle with tax rates set at a level expected to balance the budget in average economic circumstances. He envisioned that the federal government would "keep two budgets: the stable budget, in which all figures refer to the hypothetical [or projected] income [at a normal level of employment], and the actual budget."[56] Since Friedman recommended the reduction of downturn-related debt after the economy recovered, any such could be financed by short-term borrowing supported by the Federal Reserve. As a result, the net burden of unmonetized debt would not increase.

Thirty-three-year-old Paul Samuelson authored the first edition of his influential introductory text, *Economics*, in 1948. Like Friedman, Samuelson had a gift for clear communication in both English and math. His book described the depth of the Great Depression as a "liquidity trap" characterized by high unemployment, increased savings, and excess capacity. In that circumstance, debt-financed public spending or tax cuts could potentially stimulate economic activity that otherwise has stalled at a level accompanied by high unemployment. Debt used for that purpose could either be monetized or financed from unutilized savings. Samuelson agreed with Friedman that debt could be repaid when the economy recovered.

The two economists disagreed about the appropriate limit on federal spending during downturns. Friedman thought borrowing during downturns should be limited to the amount needed to finance the drop in revenues and any rise in downturn-related outlays such as public assistance. Samuelson thought that federal officials could spend even more or tax less to accelerate recovery, though he warned in the first edition of his text that this prescription was "controversial." Friedman identified himself as a libertarian; Samuelson referred to himself as a liberal. Each would advise future presidents on budget issues. In reality, very few economists have ever actually changed federal spending and tax decisions, which are typically made by powerful members of congressional committees. After 1945, however, politicians more frequently cited the authority of economists who agreed with them.

The views of the business-oriented and privately funded Committee for Economic Development may have had a greater immediate impact on postwar policy. The committee consisted principally of corporate executives, with the balance made up of prominent bankers and scholars. In 1947 it recommended a rule similar to Friedman's: budgets should be balanced across each economic cycle, and tax rates should be stable and set at a level designed to produce a slight surplus at normal or full employment.

The Committee for Economic Development considered it impractical to fine-tune spending and tax rates in an attempt to precisely balance each budget, since economic conditions rarely conformed to projections made well before the beginning of each fiscal year. Frequent changes in tax rates also undermined the desirable predictability of taxation. Because expenditures tended to "resist downward change and taxes . . . resist upwards change," the committee warned that the surpluses needed to retire debt for "compensatory" or stimulus spending during downturns might never materialize—especially because advocates of federal spending for certain programs tended to exaggerate the need for such spending.[57]

12

CONTAINING DEBT WHILE FUNDING DEFENSE, PENSIONS, AND HIGHWAYS

*1950–1962: Years when deficits exceeded debt service = 3
(1953, Korean War; 1959, recession; 1962, Cold War)*

THE COST OF GLOBAL LEADERSHIP

Harry Truman, Robert Taft, Arthur Vandenberg, and James Forrestal struggled for years to define the new normal level of military spending and income taxes following sixteen years of the Great Depression and World War II. Someone far outside the federal government, Joseph Stalin, ultimately served as a catalyst in forging an American consensus on that balance. In the spring of 1950 Stalin approved Kim Il Sung's plan to invade the UN protectorate of South Korea. North Korea's crossing of the thirty-eighth parallel in June 1950 gave rise to a bipartisan commitment to high levels of military spending and taxation to maintain a worldwide security perimeter.

Until that invasion President Truman had persisted in cutting the Pentagon's spending requests in order to balance the budget within the revenues produced by the tax rates set in Congress. When the Joint Chiefs of Staff warned that America's military capabilities were "inadequate in light of present commitments," the president's chief economic advisor countered that additional debt would weaken the nation's ability to respond to a future security emergency. Truman's planned defense budget for fiscal year of 1951 represented slightly more than 5 percent of national income—a level higher than the 1 percent average before World War II and roughly in line with defense spending in 2013.

As Kim Il Sung prepared for war in the spring of 1950, the National Security Council (NSC) presented its recommendations for defense policy and military budgets to Truman. The NSC, organized several years earlier, counted among its members the secretaries of state and defense departments and the chairman of the Joint Chiefs of Staff. In a classified document designated NSC-68, the high-powered group argued for a "substantial increase" in military spending and military assistance programs. To pay for these initiatives, it suggested "the deferment of certain desirable domestic programs" and "increased taxes."[1] Truman would not sign the recommended policy; he was willing to support higher taxes but understood that Congress would not. His assessment was correct. Taft and his allies in Congress fought to restrain military spending in order to balance the budget with lower tax rates. That spring, before the North Korean invasion, the House blocked $100 million in military assistance to South Korea but ultimately reversed the vote after heavy administration lobbying.[2] Then, in the words of Secretary of State Dean Acheson, the June invasion "removed the recommendations of NSC 68 from the realm of theory and made them immediate budget issues."[3]

The American-led United Nations force desperately battled to retain a foothold in the Korean peninsula. By September 1950, when the United States and other UN forces reversed North Korea's initial military gains, Truman signed NSC-68 and approved a rapid buildup of the national security budget: $69.5 billion in fiscal year 1951 and $56 billion in each of the next three fiscal years—a level of spending that was more than half the nominal amount at the height of World War II.[4] General Eisenhower accepted Truman's request that he organize forces within the European-based North American Treaty Organization (NATO). The president agreed to Eisenhower's request for a sustained financial commitment to an American military presence in Europe.

The financing of the Korean War highlights the influence of traditional fiscal doctrine in striking a balance between spending and taxation. Congress raised taxes three times within eighteen months to pay for the Korean War. Personal and corporate income tax collections rose from $37.8 billion in 1951 to $54.4 billion in 1953.[5] During the thirty-six months from fiscal year 1952 through fiscal year 1954, revenues supporting the federal funds spending rose to 16.6 percent of national income, a higher share than at any time in the nation's history except the final two years of World War II.[6] This level of federal funds taxation was double the average during the three years at the height of the wars in Iraq and Afghanistan in the early twenty-first century. By the end of the war in 1953, federal debt had risen only 3 percent from the amount in 1950, though military outlays had grown by 300 percent.

Truman acknowledged that some Americans were wondering "how high we can push taxes without having serious effects" on economic growth, and opined that such a limit still had not been reached.[7] High tax rates, Truman noted, had not prevented rapid economic growth since the end of World War II.

Following Roosevelt's example during World War II, Truman deferred requests for new domestic spending, remarking that "many of the things we would normally do must be curtailed or postponed."[8] The widespread desire to avoid excessive debt forced both Republican and Democratic leaders to delay legislation dear to their constituents. Americans with high incomes—a wellspring of GOP support—chafed at personal income tax rates that they considered punitive. For decades the cost of the Cold War undermined the ability to lower these rates without risking a loss in tax revenue and corresponding increase in debt.

Meanwhile, the White House and the Democratic congressional major- ity realized that federal tax revenues were insufficient to pay for both mili- tary commitments and Truman's proposal to provide medical insurance for families without access to employer-based plans. While Truman embraced the vision of federal medical insurance, his administration never offered specific legislation to implement it. Various plans for expanded medical insurance never made it past Truman's White House Budget Office.

Americans did not enjoy paying higher taxes in the 1950s, and feared high medical bills. Federal officials at the time did not care less about their favored domestic agendas than those in power during the post-2001 wars in Iraq and Afghanistan; they simply subordinated these agendas to the principle of limiting debt in order to avoid mortgaging future tax revenues. Even after the end of the Korean War, the White House and Congress strived to fund major domestic initiatives—like an expansion of Social Security pensions and a new federal program for highway construction— with dedicated taxes paid into trust funds kept apart from the administra- tive or federal funds budget.

Numerous battles in the Korean War, particularly those against Chinese forces, demonstrated the importance of sustained investment in military technology. It became obvious the United States could not hope to prevail in future wars by simply trading casualties. When North Korean leaders complained about the dearth of Soviet support in 1953, Stalin told Chinese premier Zhou Enlai that the North Koreans "have lost nothing, except for casualties."[9] Elected officials in America could not be so cavalier about the loss of life.

Even though senior federal officials agreed to higher spending and taxes consistent with the new American role in the world, the nation could not afford everything the Pentagon requested. In March 1951, for example, the various military services compiled estimates of their requirements for the next fiscal year totaling $104 billion, an amount that would have absorbed much of the national economy. Within a month, Truman forced them to pare that estimate back to $60.7 billion.[10]

The post-1950 Cold War ushered in a new era in federal budget history. Before World War II, the United States invested only a small share of national income in its military except during war. For years after 1950 spending for global security, veterans, and interest on the debt dwarfed the cost of all other commitments in the federal funds budget and delayed plans to pay down the remaining debt from World War II.

SUSTAINABLE SOCIAL SECURITY PENSIONS

Many Americans who had lost their savings during the Great Depression struggled to make ends meet after their retirement. The erosion of purchasing power as a result of wartime inflation had undermined the value of Social Security pension benefits, which had not increased from the levels set in 1935. The average Social Security pension of $25 a month was too small to survive on.[11] As a result, a vast number of older Americans lived on state-administered public assistance—supported by matching grants authorized in the Social Security Act of 1935—rather than contributory pensions. A fifth of older Americans received Social Security pensions in 1949, while even more were forced to rely on monthly welfare checks. Social Security offered a weak safety net in rural America, where most retirees were ineligible for its benefits. In Louisiana, for example, more than half of the elderly population relied on welfare payments for subsistence. Relatively few retired Americans received employer-funded pensions.

House Ways and Means Chairman Robert Doughton was in a unique position to craft a consensus on the future of Social Security pensions. The eighty-six-year-old dean of the House had worked effectively across party lines to finance World War II. The powerful House Speaker, Sam Rayburn of Texas, respected the chairman and was one of the few who still called him by his old nickname, "Muley." Doughton still arrived at the Capitol at six a.m. each weekday, and he used those morning hours in 1949 to prepare for hearings on pensions at which more than 250 witnesses testified about the future of the pension system.

A decade earlier, President Roosevelt and Senator Vandenberg had wrestled with the issue of how best to account for pension liabilities far into the future within a federal budget that had historically been managed by comparing of annual revenues and expenses. Estimating the level of benefits that could be sustained for decades required complex calculations based on economics, statistics, and actuarial accounting. Doughton and other House members began to rely heavily on the judgment of Congressman Wilbur Mills of Arkansas, a graduate of Harvard Law and the soft-spoken son of a small-town banker. Mills, forty years old in 1949, had entered Congress a decade earlier and had served on Doughton's Ways and Means Committee since 1943. The fiscally conservative Mills mastered the details of pension accounting, forming an enduring partnership with Social Security's actuary, Robert Myers. During the next decades the two would craft modern Social Security, Medicare, and Medicaid, programs that guided the trajectory of much of the federal budget through the present day.

By early 1950 Doughton, Mills, and Myers had developed a plan for Social Security reform that satisfied critics in both parties. Some liberals such as Henry A. Wallace, disliked the regressive nature of Social Security payroll taxes, which were assessed at a flat percentage rate up to a wage ceiling. Insurance executive Albert Linton, one of the leading Republican voices on federal pension programs since the mid-1930s, feared the loss of control over a program administered apart from annual appropriations. Linton had persuaded some Republicans to back a plan for a flat, standard pension for all older Americans. No mainstream federal elected official supported the abolition of a federal pension system or a return to locally funded poorhouses. Similarly, no one entertained the notion of borrowing to pay for the retirement expenses of the growing population of seniors, a form of financing that would be utilized by Congress in legislation enacted in 2003 and 2010.

The cost of the Cold War and the interests of the business community undergirded the new consensus on Social Security. Congress needed every dollar of revenues from income taxes to balance Cold War budgets. A contributory pension system financed with payroll taxes prevented income tax revenues from being consumed by the rising cost of old-age assistance grants. By the late 1940s, even business organizations and labor unions that had opposed federal pensions in 1935 appreciated how portable pension benefits could be integrated into a system of employer-based retirement benefits.

A pension system based on employees' contributions was a conservative alternative to welfare. If an older American had paid into a fund while employed, Mills said their pensions were not a form of receiving "something . . . for nothing."[12] It did not seem unfair that benefit formulas provided a higher return for those contributing workers who lived longer or earned less. After all, most Americans had some form of life insurance, and the relationship between total premiums paid and the benefit received varied greatly among families. In late 1949, the House—by a vote of 333 to 14—passed the legislation amending the Social Security Act. Only two senators voted against the Senate version in 1950, and President Truman signed it into law just weeks after the North Korean invasion.[13]

The act increased the minimum monthly benefit by 77 percent to offset the impact of inflation since 1935.[14] Congress raised payroll taxes to 3 percent of wages and the ceiling on wages subject to the payroll tax. Most American workers, including self-employed Americans, were included in the Social Security system. The act almost immediately relieved pressure for higher public assistance grants; in 1951, for the first time, more seniors received Social Security pension payments than checks for public assistance.

By separating the Social Security trust fund—officially referred to as the Old Age and Survivors Trust Fund—from the rest of the budget, Congress avoided the problems inherent in combining actuarial and traditional budget accounting. A unified annual budget that counted pension fund revenues without an accrual of future liabilities would have been misleading, while one that attempted to do so would have been difficult for non-experts to comprehend or reconcile with cash accounts. Though the trust fund did not build up a cash reserve to the extent originally envisioned in 1935, the trustees reported on its annual actuarial balance. Their reports rested on a conservative "flat wage" assumption, which produced a steady cushion of reserves so long as wages grew steadily over time. In essence,

Robert Myers compared the value of future payments at existing benefit levels with the value of future revenues from payroll contributions based on the assumption of no increase over existing wage levels. Mills and Meyers realized that this assumption would result in an actual surplus so long as the level of wages and salaries continued to grow. This method gave Congress a margin of error when deciding the levels of benefits and corresponding tax rates.

The Social Security Act Amendments of 1950 also authorized federal matching grants that states could use to reimburse medical expenses for patients unable to pay, a critical feature of the plan sponsored by Senator Taft as an alternative to proposals for national medical insurance. The cost of the program, the precursor to modern Medicaid, would rise sixfold, to over half a billion dollars, during the next decade.[15]

Oscar Ewing, a skilled lawyer and political confidante of Truman who led the agency overseeing the Social Security system, looked for an affordable alternative for expanding health insurance. Leonard Pink, who headed New York's nonprofit Blue Cross program, recommended that the federal government administer an insurance pool that could reimburse hospitals for up to sixty days of care for older Americans. Blue Cross and other insurers offered employer-based hospital insurance, and retired Americans did not qualify as part of an employee group. Private insurers, Pink said, would find it hard to estimate medical costs in a pool for retirees. Ewing convinced Truman to embrace Pink's idea. The plan made little immediate headway because of the cost of the Korean War and the preference of medical associations for state grants. It began to gain momentum as hospital costs soared in the late 1950s.

After passage of the Social Security Act Amendments of 1950, elected officials in both political parties almost universally accepted the concept of federal old-age pensions. Dwight Eisenhower, the first Republican president elected since Herbert Hoover, called for an expansion of Social Security pensions during his 1953 inaugural address. He characterized worker-supported pensions as a form of self-reliance and "domestic security."[16]

His administration rejected the US Chamber of Commerce's proposed plan for the federal government to guarantee a flat minimum pension to all retirees, regardless of whether they had contributed payroll taxes. Instead, in 1954 Congress passed—with only eight dissenting votes—a bill expanding coverage and payroll taxation to many agricultural and public sector workers.

Social Security pensions, like pensions for veterans, incorporated a historic ideal of reformers in both parties: benefits should be earned and distributed based on formulas rather than discretionary decisions subject to patronage politics or ethnic discrimination. In 2001 President George W. Bush's chief economic advisor explained why payroll taxes were unlike other taxes: "When I pay another dollar for Social Security tax, I buy an explicit, legislated amount of benefits. . . . It is purely a private good."[17] George W. Bush himself, in his second inaugural address, referred to the Social Security Act as an expression of "economic independence."[18]

Like the acceptance of a global leadership role, the commitment to maintaining a minimum standard of dignity for older citizens became part of the American "way of life." This promise reflected changes in culture rather than ideology. By the 1950s, more Americans had moved away from their families, and more women worked outside the home. A portable national pension allowed women, who frequently cared for aging relatives, to balance other responsibilities at work and with children. Between 1950 and 2000, females accounted for 60 percent of the growth in the workforce, while the birth rate soared during the Baby Boom from 1945 to 1965.[19] In 1957 the United States set its all-time record for births: 4.3 million babies joined a population of 172 million.[20]

Retired Americans lived longer. The average remaining life expectancy of thirty-year-old male workers rose from 38.86 years in 1945 to 46.87 years in 2010.[21] In 1950 people over the age of sixty-five represented 8 percent of the population, an increase from 3 percent in 1900.[22] By 2010, 13 percent of the population exceeded age sixty-five.[23] With the retirement of Baby Boomers, Americans over sixty-five are expected to constitute a fifth of the population by 2030.

Social Security pension benefits have always remained at modest levels in relation to average working incomes. In June 2013 the average beneficiary received $1,158 a month, and for most elderly Americans, the Social Security pension remained their largest source of income.[24] Until 2010 the federal government never incurred long-term debt to pay for Social Security benefits.

THE INDEPENDENCE OF MONETARY POLICY

Federal Reserve Chairman Marriner Eccles had supported the Treasury's insistence on low interest rates during World War II. After the war he fought to regain the central bank's control of monetary policy. A monetary policy capable of sustaining growth without inflationary pressures on interest rates would be critical, Eccles believed, in managing postwar debt, just as it had been after the Civil War. Though Truman replaced Eccles with Thomas McCabe as head of the Federal Reserve, Eccles continued to serve on the board and enlisted a majority of its members, including the new chairman, in support of his position.

Truman's Treasury Department insisted that the nation's central bank continue its support of low interest rates even after the war's end. Since income tax rates were considered to have reached their practical limit, any spike in interest rates would require corresponding cuts in military and other types of spending in order to balance the budget. For example, if the interest rate on federal debt had averaged 5.2 percent rather than the actual 2.2 percent in 1947, the extra cost would have exceeded half the amount of the nation's military spending. Growing private sector loan demand could exert upward pressure on interest rates without continued support by the Federal Reserve. Eccles and other Federal Reserve officials realized that unlimited monetary expansion could spark inflation. Yet Eccles was repeatedly rebuffed by the Treasury when he attempted to negotiate an agreement recognizing the Federal Reserve's independence. The concept of an autonomous Federal Reserve had not yet become part of the nation's unwritten constitution.

The Federal Reserve unilaterally broke the impasse on August 18, 1950, when it decided to raise interest rates on short-term debt without the Treasury's permission. Many members of Congress and the administration, including Truman personally, failed to corral the Fed.[25] The Federal Reserve felt even greater urgency to curb inflation when consumer prices spiked in early 1950, after Chinese intervention in Korea threatened to prolong the war indefinitely. Eccles explained to Congress that "as long as the Federal Reserve is required to buy government securities . . . for the purpose of defending a fixed pattern of interest rates established by the Treasury, it must stand ready to increase bank reserves in unlimited amounts." He condemned that requirement as an "engine of inflation."[26]

On March 3, 1951, the Federal Reserve and Treasury announced that they had "reached full accord with respect to debt-management and monetary policies" for the common goal of assuring "the successful financing of the Government's requirements and, at the same time, to minimize monetization of the public debt."[27] The Federal Reserve agreed to credit to the Treasury any interest on its investments in federal debt and thereby avoid future tension over whether the central bank profited from its open market operations. The 1951 agreement, frequently referred to as the Accord, concluded a 160-year national struggle to define the power of federal elected officials, the Treasury, and financial market participants over monetary policy, even after the great compromise of 1913 that created a Federal Reserve, an organ of the executive branch during the crises of two world wars and much of the Great Depression.

Within days of the Accord, the Federal Reserve's Open Market Committee allowed interest rates on five-year notes to climb. President Truman promptly replaced Federal Reserve Board Chairman Thomas McCabe with William McChesney Martin, an assistant treasury secretary and former Wall Street prodigy who had once served as president of the New York Stock Exchange. Martin had negotiated the Accord on behalf of the Treasury, but, to Truman's dismay, he defended the Federal Reserve's independence after becoming chairman. Interest rates on Treasury debt rose slowly during the 1950s, from 2.27 percent in 1950 to 2.51 percent in 1956 to 3.25 percent in 1960.[28] During his nineteen years as chairman, Martin used his keen intellect and political skills to define the modern role of the Federal Reserve. The Federal Reserve's role as guardian of the currency gave it great influence on financial markets, a power that it sometimes used to reinforce traditional limits on debt.

The independent Federal Reserve became a virtual fourth branch of government, with power over the money supply. Money, which principally consists of electronic ledger entries in a modern economy, performs several functions. It serves as a medium of exchange, which an economy needs in sufficient quantity to facilitate standardized pricing and settlement of amounts owed. Money is also a means of storing wealth. The Federal Reserve, like most central banks, tries to maintain the level of money to serve effectively as both a medium of exchange and a store of value. At times these functions may conflict, like when an excessive supply of money reduces its usefulness as a store of value and constricts savings. An inadequate supply of money, in turn, can result in deflation, which puts a premium on money as a store of value and reduces the willingness to spend and invest. Since adequate investment requires both saving and lending or investing, either deflation or inflation can destabilize the investment and consumption needed to fuel economic growth. Central bankers are principally concerned with managing the money supply at a level that supports the dual objectives of stable prices and economic growth that fosters employment.

The Federal Reserve can create money by purchasing federal debt. The Accord obligates the Federal Reserve to credit interest it receives back to the Treasury. An amount of debt likely to be held permanently is effectively monetized by the Federal Reserve. For this reason, an accurate measure of the burden of Treasury debt—as shown in Appendix A—is gross debt minus amounts held by the Federal Reserve.

EISENHOWER'S COMMITMENT TO BALANCED BUDGETS

Herb Brownell, who managed Thomas Dewey's successful races for the Republican presidential nomination in 1944 and 1948, knew how to line up votes for the Republican National Convention. Before committing to help Eisenhower in the 1952 election, Brownell probed the general's views—largely unknown to the public or anyone else—on domestic policy. For most of his life Eisenhower had not even voted. Eisenhower relayed to Brownell his central political philosophy: the budget should be balanced.

Eisenhower had emerged from World War II as a national military hero. He secured the nomination with a come-from-behind convention victory over Senator Taft, and then soundly defeated the Democratic nominee, Illinois Governor Adlai Stevenson, in the November election. Differences over the federal budget did not play a significant role in the contest because Stevenson shared Eisenhower's loathing of federal deficits. Eisenhower's coattails swept Republicans to majorities in the House and Senate.

When Eisenhower took office in January 1953, the United States serviced an unmonetized debt of almost $240 billion, an amount just shy of the record level reached in fiscal year 1946.[29] The expense of the Cold War and large interest payments on that debt had prevented sharp cuts to the tax rates of World War II. Revenues from personal income taxes rose from $18.4 billion a year at the end of World War II to $27.9 billion in the fiscal year when Eisenhower was elected. During that period corporate income tax revenues grew from $16.4 billion to $21.2 billion.[30]

Eisenhower's 1956 State of the Union address reminded Americans of "our enormous national debt and of the obligation we have toward future Americans to reduce that debt whenever we can appropriately do so.

Under conditions of high peacetime prosperity, such as now exist, we can never justify going further into debt to give ourselves a tax cut at the expense of our children."[31]

The four traditional pillars of fiscal discipline remained intact throughout the Eisenhower presidency. First, budgets presented by the White House and adopted by Congress were clear and understandable. The administration rejected advice from economists to consider trust fund surpluses in deciding whether the budget balanced. Second, "pay as you go" planning confined proposed spending to a level within projected revenue in the annual budget proposed to Congress. Third, trust funds linked taxes and spending on specific programs, most notably for expanded Social Security pensions and federal highway construction. Fourth, when borrowing occurred to offset revenue shortfalls during downturns in 1954 and 1958, federal officials worked within a debt ceiling no greater than the one set at the peak of World War II.

As the Korean War wound down early in Eisenhower's presidency, Eisenhower faced pressure from Republicans in Congress to cut tax rates quickly. The president understood that high tax rates could distort economic decisions. He had personally attained financial security by publishing a best-selling memoir under a contract deliberately structured to avoid the application of the top tax rate. When Eisenhower asked Congress to delay scheduled tax reductions in order to balance the budget, Senator Taft exploded in anger. The Republican chairman of the Ways and Means Committee refused to allow a vote on the delay. The US Chamber of Commerce and the National Association of Manufacturers heeded the president's call for fiscal discipline and reluctantly agreed with the administration. President Eisenhower ultimately prevailed with Congress to postpone tax cuts.

Two years later, Eisenhower opposed a proposal from some congressional Democrats to reduce taxes by $20 per taxpayer. "Every political party likes to cut taxes; there is no question about that," Eisenhower assured the press. "So we will do it as soon as we can."[32] The president also condemned any use of debt to raise the standard deduction, which he also feared might "excuse millions of taxpayers from paying income tax at all."[33]

Secretary of the Treasury George Humphrey spoke for the administration on fiscal policy. Before joining the Eisenhower administration, Humphrey had headed the nation's second largest steelmaker, M. A. Hanna Company, which was named after the famed organizer of the Republican

Party at the turn of the twentieth century. Humphrey expressed himself with a candor that seems quaint in comparison with the twenty-first-century practice of contrived political "messaging." Humphrey outright dismissed the idea of borrowing for a tax cut in order to stimulate growth: "I will contest a tax cut out of deficits as long as I am able. . . . I don't believe in this idea that you can cut taxes out of deficits, and then build up from that."[34]

When conservatives questioned the level of spending in the president's proposed budget in 1957, Secretary Humphrey invited them to find places to cut. Senator Harry Byrd of Virginia, chairman of the Senate Finance Committee, accepted that invitation. He cut $4 billion, about 5 percent, from the administration's budget request, mostly by paring down the economic and military assistance to Cold War allies, a White House priority.[35] The White House could, however, count on Byrd and about a dozen other conservative Democrats who would vote with the administration in defeating debt-financed tax cuts. In opposing the effort to give every American a $20 income tax cut, Byrd pointedly remarked: "We are not engaged in war. If we cannot balance the budget now, I ask when can we balance it?"[36]

Senator Barry Goldwater became a hero to many conservative Republicans in the late 1950s. The former city councilman from Phoenix and heir to a retail fortune had ridden Eisenhower's coattails to the Senate in 1952. Like Byrd, Goldwater believed that "spending cuts should come before tax cuts."[37] He suggested that reducing taxes without making careful choices about government expenditures was tantamount to courting "deficit spending."

As the economy slowed in late 1957, Eisenhower explained to former economic advisor Arthur Burns that he was "against vast and unwise public works programs . . . as well as the slash-bang kinds of tax-cutting from which the proponents want nothing so much as immediate political advantage."[38] Yet as employment continued to fall in early 1958, the ambitious vice president, Richard Nixon, publicly mentioned the possibility of a tax cut. Wilbur Mills, who by then had become chairman of the House Ways and Means Committee, warned House Speaker Rayburn that falling tax revenues during the recession would inevitably lead to a deficit even without a tax cut.

Rayburn, Mills, and Senate Majority Leader Lyndon Johnson worked to avoid either being blamed for the deficit or allowing Republicans to take credit for any tax cut initiative. Days after Nixon's off-the-cuff public statement, Treasury Secretary Robert Anderson met with senior Democratic congressional leaders and agreed that neither Congress nor the administration would move unilaterally to cut taxes. Within days Johnson mustered a bipartisan majority to defeat—by a 71–14 vote—a tax cut offered by Senate liberals.

In the wake of the recession, Democrats enlarged their congressional majority during the 1958 midterm election. Eisenhower worried that Congress would try to stimulate the economy using debt-financed spending. In 1959, for the first time, the president presented his budget on national television. He aggressively vetoed spending bills, though Congress overrode the veto of an appropriation for water projects.

Secretary Anderson commanded the unqualified respect of the president and the two most powerful Democrats in Congress, Speaker Rayburn and Majority Leader Johnson. Anderson had served in various federal positions after selling his Texas radio station to Lady Bird Johnson, Congressman Johnson's wife, in early 1943. Eisenhower considered Anderson to be his most qualified potential successor. Anderson believed in the values underlying the American Fiscal Tradition and helped cast one of its traditional pillars—"pay as you go" budget planning—in modern terms. He identified the true burden of debt as "the impact of the taxes that must be levied to service it." Anderson thought that federal leaders should nurture "sustainable growth" with budgets that usually contained a modest surplus for use in retiring debt incurred during recessions. He urged that "variations in tax rates or spending programs for cyclical purposes [should] be kept to a minimum," since federal outlays could not be timed to coincide beneficially with the rise and fall in economic activity. Furthermore, he recognized that it would be politically easier to "achieve a deficit in a recession than a surplus in a boom."[39]

Eisenhower took pride in the large surplus obtained in the fiscal year of 1960. In his final State of the Union address, Eisenhower asked the nation to forgo tax cuts until it had paid down some debt with several years of surpluses, an action he termed a "reduction on our children's inherited mortgage." He added that "once we have established such payments as a normal practice, we can profitably make improvements in our tax structure and thereby truly reduce the heavy burdens of taxation."[40] Federal funds spending in fiscal year 1960 included large amounts for defense ($48.13

billion); interest on the debt ($7.51 billion); veterans' benefits ($5.44 billion); and agriculture ($2.62 billion).[41]

"Pay as You Go" Highway Funding

In the five years following the end of World War II, the number of registered vehicles rose from thirty-one million to forty-nine million. Each day more Americans experienced the aggravation of being stuck in traffic.[42] President Eisenhower viewed enhanced mobility as a key to both economic growth and "greater standards of living."[43] As a young officer in 1919, he had participated in an army convoy that tested how long it took to transport materials by truck across the country: sixty-three days from the East to the West Coast. As president, he proposed a $50 billion highway program to link the nation's major urban centers.[44] The Eisenhower administration insisted that any highway plan had to pay for itself through tolls or new, dedicated taxes on fuel, automobiles, and tires.

Eisenhower lobbied Congress for his highway program with atypical fervor. Retired general Lucius Clay, a friend of Eisenhower's, helped develop the details of the plan. Clay, a national hero honored with a ticker-tape parade in New York for leading the airlift that broke the blockade of Berlin, encountered some stiff political resistance. Members of Congress from rural states feared changes in the existing program that financed farm-to-market roads. Trucking companies that supported better highways had historically opposed financing them with user taxes. The traditional link between new spending and taxes forced the trucking industry to change its position and accept transportation-related taxes so long as the revenues were dedicated solely to the proposed Highway Trust Fund.

A shrewd Democratic populist, Senator Al Gore Sr. of Tennessee, tested the link between spending and new taxes by convincing a Senate majority to back his plan to accelerate highway construction using some general revenues to supplement the resources of the proposed Highway Trust Fund. Byrd believed that there were no spare revenues and blocked Gore's efforts.

Byrd also killed General Clay's attempt to expedite construction through the sale of bonds serviced by future trust fund revenues. Byrd favored federal support for highways but opposed the use of debt to build them. In his twenties he had headed a nonprofit organization that built a road through the Shenandoah Valley and then led a successful push to defeat a proposal by Virginia's state government to use bonds to accelerate road construction. A few years later, as the state's governor, he relied on tax revenues not debt to build hundreds of miles of roads. Byrd was personally polite with Senate colleagues, but no one could bend his iron-willed adherence to "pay as you go."

The Federal Aid Highway Act of 1956 imposed new taxes on motor fuels, tires, and vehicle sales to finance the world's most ambitious public works program. The "pay as you go" budget practice had forced federal officials to weigh the benefits of highway construction against the tolerable cost of new taxes. The tough debate on financing had produced a consensus on the scope of highway funding. The act passed the Senate with one dissenting vote and the House on a voice vote. By the early 1960s, the Highway Trust Fund accounted for more than 3 percent of federal spending. Like the other trust funds—for old-age and disability pensions, bank deposit insurance, unemployment insurance, federal civilian and military employee retirement, and airport construction—the Highway Trust Fund fell outside the administrative or federal funds budget.

Byrd's opposition to borrowing for highways planted the seed of a debate among academic economists concerning limits on public debt. The corporate-funded Council on Economic Development commissioned a talented young economist, James Buchanan, to study the merits of Byrd's contention that highways and all other federal functions should be paid for on a "pay as you go" basis. Most economists, including Buchanan initially, viewed the "pay as you go" tradition as dogma unjustified by economic analysis. Many economists after the Great Depression focused on the effect of debt-financed public spending during severe downturns rather than debt's resulting mortgage on future tax revenues. Buchanan expressed the logic of Byrd's stand against borrowing for highways in the language of modern economics.

Two problems with the routine use of public debt bothered Buchanan. Public debt could both divert savings from private investment and suppress information about the true cost of public spending. Thomas Jefferson and James Madison, though not many modern economists, had recognized the benefits of allowing the public to weigh the cost of federal spending against the felt burden of current taxation.[45] Economists, however, had shown how markets allowed consumers to measure the benefit they associated with a particular service against its cost. While some voters might reasonably expect to shift the ultimate cost of debt to other taxpayers, an entire nation could not transfer its debt to others. Buchanan's "theory of public choice" later earned him a Nobel Prize in economics. He also noted that the United States had long avoided the slippery financial slope of excessive debt because of what he called its "fiscal constitution."

EISENHOWER'S LIMITS ON MILITARY SPENDING

Eisenhower struggled to define the level and nature of spending for global security that could be sustained without borrowing. He believed that limits on debt preserved the nation's credit for use during future military emergencies. The president decried the inefficiency of the nation's long history of starving defense budgets during peacetime and then giving military professionals whatever they asked for, at high cost, after the shooting began. He also appreciated the fact that modern warfare required steady annual spending designed to preserve a technological superiority. Eisenhower's approach to Pentagon budgeting would endure and preserve a unique role for the United States in international affairs.

Eisenhower's first budget, for fiscal year 1954, included spending of slightly more than $63 billion—an almost 10 percent cut from Truman's draft budget for that year.[46] Most of the savings came from proposed Pentagon spending. Eisenhower reminded citizens of the opportunity costs of an arms race by remarking that the price of a modern bomber was equal to the expense of a "modern brick school in more than 30 cities."[47] In October 1953 the president signed NSC-162, which prescribed a steady level of defense spending within a balanced budget and noted that a "strong, healthy and expanding national economy is essential to the security and stability of the free world."[48]

Eisenhower's "New Look" Pentagon budgets reduced the number of American soldiers, increased investment in research and the procurement of new weapons, and shifted spending from the army to the navy and air force. The president replaced some military commanders who continued to insist on larger budgets. Army Chief of Staff Maxwell Taylor, once a stellar field commander, continued to push for more conventional forces suitable to a "flexible response" in regional wars.[49] Taylor's ideas impressed Senator John F. Kennedy and many others in Congress, but not Eisenhower, who thought American forces should be designed to fight the Soviets or Chinese rather than their proxies.

The Presidium of the Supreme Soviet briefly sought to relieve tensions with the United States after Stalin's death in 1953. This approach ended abruptly after party leader Nikita Khrushchev executed the political rival who led the initiative. Khrushchev consolidated his power and then publicly exaggerated the Soviet Union's technological strength and ability to withstand millions of casualties. He asserted that the Soviet Union produced intercontinental missiles like "sausages from an automatic machine," when in reality it possessed only a handful.[50] Chinese strongman Mao Zedong responded to Khrushchev's bluster by mentioning his own willingness to sustain three hundred million wartime casualties, a negotiating tactic that was not available to democratically elected leaders like Eisenhower.

Members of the Congress, however, could reply to such threats by spending unparalleled amounts of money on defense and related research. Senators Lyndon Johnson and John F. Kennedy criticized the state of American military preparedness after the Soviet Union successfully launched *Sputnik* in 1957. Eisenhower complained that he was "tired" of reminding critics that defense should not be cited as "an excuse for wasting dollars."[51] The United States already had more than nine thousand nuclear devices that could be delivered by aircraft, missiles, and field artillery. In 1960 Congress added $700 million to the president's defense spending request, including money for the development of two new types of missiles and a B-70 bomber program that Eisenhower had previously cut.[52]

Eisenhower's last defense budget, exclusive of costs for veterans and some intelligence activities, was equivalent to $388 billion in 2012 dollars adjusted for inflation. This level of military spending would eventually serve as a floor for the level of real—inflation-adjusted—military spending. By 2012, the inflation-adjusted base military budget—apart from direct spending for war—exceeded Eisenhower's final one by $180 billion.[53]

Eisenhower personally edited almost thirty drafts of a farewell speech that he delivered to a large national television audience. In the intervening years, many have quoted his observation that "an immense military establishment and a large arms industry" was then something "new in the American experience." As always, he placed this warning in a fiscal context: "We cannot mortgage the material assets of our grandchildren without asking the loss also of their political and spiritual heritage."[54]

Senator John F. Kennedy supported the goal of balancing budgets throughout his 1960 presidential campaign. Three weeks before the election he pledged to balance the budget across the economic cycle, a fiscal policy he described at the time as "conservative." He concluded the presidential race by making a commitment "to maintain a balanced budget except in times of national emergency or severe recession."[55]

THE BURDEN OF COLD WAR TAX RATES

Soviet actions made it difficult for President Kennedy to keep his budget pledge. Khrushchev threatened to use military force to establish East Germany's control over sectors in Berlin entrusted to the United States, Great Britain, and France. When Khrushchev boosted Soviet military spending in the spring of 1961, Kennedy asked Congress for a corresponding increase. The president and his brother, Attorney General Robert Kennedy, considered imposing a one-year tax surcharge for the explicit purpose of demonstrating public support for sustained military spending. In Kennedy's mind, the Berlin crisis exposed a flaw in military capabilities based so heavily on nuclear arms, since he was the first of many presidents who believed that the United States would not credibly be able to threaten first use of nuclear weapons.

Republican Douglas Dillon, Kennedy's secretary of the treasury, stressed the importance of balanced budgets. Assistant Treasury Secretary for Tax Policy Stanley Surrey, a respected former tax professor, persuaded Dillon that income tax rates could be cut without a loss in revenue as long as Congress also eliminated certain deductions. Meanwhile, Kennedy's chief economist, Walter Heller, proposed modest debt-financed tax cuts to spur investment and employment. Average unemployment had remained at about 6 percent from 1959 to 1961, compared to an average of little more than 4 percent for the decade before the 1958 recession.[56]

Tax policy in the era depended less on the Kennedy administration than on the House Ways and Means Committee and its powerful chairman, Wilbur Mills. Senate Finance Committee Chairman Byrd maintained a minimal staff for his committee and waited for the House to originate tax bills.

No one ever doubted Mills's mastery of legislative detail, but his initial years as chairman of the Ways and Means Committee gave little indication of the qualities that would soon make him the most powerful member of Congress. At times during the 1950s, Mills seemed more interested in policy than politics. His hearings featured testimony from economists and law professors instead of the standard fare of lobbyists and business executives. The failure of two of his legislative initiatives early in his chairmanship demonstrated the power of the budget practices that had served as pillars of the American Fiscal Tradition.

Mills tried to reform eligibility for unemployment insurance in response to the 1958 recession. Professional policy analysts questioned why benefits for laid-off workers should depend on their employers' payments to the Unemployment Insurance Trust Fund, a circumstance beyond the control of the employees themselves. Conservatives rebuffed Mills and insisted on retaining the basic contributory trust fund principle that linked taxes and spending. Another bill proposed by Mills sought to ease restrictions imposed by Congress on interest rates on federal bond issues. Treasury Secretary Anderson believed that the Treasury should extend the average life of debt with staggered maturities and sought relief from legislated interest rate limits in order to sell long-term bonds. This bill was also eviscerated on the House floor because Congress was reluctant to relinquish its traditional control over the terms of debt.

By the early 1960s Mills used lessons gleaned from those experiences to solidify his power. He made the Ways and Means Committee's ranking Republican, John Byrnes of Wisconsin, a virtual partner. Together they filled vacancies on their committee with members of Congress who were willing to work as a team. Throughout the Mills chairmanship, only one freshman congressman—the promising George H. W. Bush—was selected to serve on the committee. By 1972 every single member of the committee had joined it while Mills was chairman. Committee members often demonstrated greater loyalty to Ways and Means than to their party leaders in the House.

Mills abolished subcommittees, so only the full committee—for which he set the agenda—could hold hearings and consider legislation. He reached an agreement with the Rules Committee that prevented the House from amending bills brought to the floor by the Ways and Means Committee. Mills enhanced his power by keeping score on whether members of Congress favored his legislation. He was willing to consider minor changes in the tax code requested by those he could count on.

Mills agreed to pass two modest tax changes requested by the Kennedy administration in 1961. One allowed businesses a tax credit for some types of new investments, while the other required companies to withhold federal income taxes when they paid dividends and interest. Senate Finance

Committee Chairman Byrd blocked the withholding proposal but failed to kill the tax credit despite uncharacteristic support from liberals on the issue. The ultraconservative Byrd pointedly asked American corporate executives why they needed the "help" of government in order to make good investments. In a sharp contrast with the attitudes of post-2000 conservatives, the Virginian considered tax breaks financed with debt as a type of federal subsidy.

Except for these modest tax changes and somewhat higher spending for the space program and military readiness, Kennedy's budgets differed little from those of the Eisenhower administration. One budget expert noted that federal spending, including trust funds, remained at "an almost constant level of 19.7 percent" of the economy for a decade.[57]

President Kennedy, in an erudite commencement speech delivered at Yale University on June 11, 1962, called attention to the power of the nation's fiscal tradition. He characterized fiscal policy as a field in which "myths are legion and the truth hard to find." As an example, he noted that many believed "debt is growing at a dangerously rapid rate," even though "debt as a proportion to our national product [had] declined sharply" since World War II. Kennedy challenged young Americans to develop fiscal principles based on "technical answers, not political answers." Nothing in his speech suggested that the federal government should ever borrow to pay for routine annual spending. In fact, Kennedy ended the speech with an homage to history. He quoted Thomas Jefferson's call for the marriage of time-honored values to modern circumstances by the application of "old words to new objects."

Weeks after this speech on fiscal policy, a reporter confronted Kennedy with a Gallup Poll showing that 72 percent of Americans opposed a tax cut financed with debt.[58] The president recognized the power of the American Fiscal Tradition and the advantage of peacetime balanced budgets. But he worried that he had not fulfilled his campaign promise to get the economy "moving."[59]

Kennedy inherited a budget for fiscal year 1961 with an initial projected surplus that turned into a modest deficit when economic growth slowed and interest rates on World War II debts rose. That deficit gave Kennedy little opportunity to cut tax rates. When economist Paul Samuelson suggested that Kennedy intentionally propose tax cuts that Congress would not enact, the president rejected the idea as "vanity, not politics."[60] In early 1962 Treasury Secretary Dillon publicly warned against a "massive reduction in tax rates, without any provision for compensating revenue," since a loss of tax revenue "would leave us no alternative but withdrawal from our world commitments and neglect of our pressing needs at home."[61] Everyone realized that it would be easier to cut tax rates than to raise revenues by eliminating deductions or exclusions. In August Kennedy assured Mills that he would delay the introduction of any tax proposal until after the November 1962 midterm elections. In a White House meeting concerning the economy, Dillon offered an insightful prediction: long-term economic growth would pick up when the Baby Boomers began entering the workforce in 1965.

Kennedy and Mills both appreciated the problems caused by high Cold War tax rates. A study conducted by the Treasury Department and the Ways and Means Committee found that few Americans paid the highest tax rate and that those in the highest bracket lawfully sheltered taxable income. The highest tax rates also resulted in a loss of revenue from outright noncompliance.

After the 1962 midterm elections, with the unemployment rate still at the same level as when he had taken office, the president made the case for lowering personal income tax rates to spur savings and investment. At the insistence of Mills, Kennedy acknowledged that spending would have to be trimmed to try to balance the loss of revenue. The historical link between tax and spending policies remained intact.

13

MEDICAL NEEDS, WAR, AND RECESSION

*1963–1979: Years when deficits exceeded debt service = 10
(1968, Vietnam; 1970–1973
and 1975–1979, recession and stimulus)*

TAX CUTS AND SPENDING RESTRAINT

When Chairman Wilbur Mills brought a tax bill to the House floor in September 1963, he circulated a letter from President Kennedy noting that tax reduction must "be accompanied by the exercise of even tighter rein on Government expenditures, limiting outlays to those expenditures which meet strict criteria of national need."[1] That commitment to traditional discipline helped secure House passage of the tax bill, though most Republicans voted against it.

Senate Finance Committee Chairman Harry Byrd and all but four of the seventeen Finance Committee members insisted that the administration submit a budget that actually cut total spending, not just freeze spending on everything except defense and space, *before* they would consider a reduction in tax rates. Byrd wanted to reduce spending for fiscal year 1965 to $100 billion, less than had been appropriated for fiscal year 1964.[2] Byrd sharply questioned the commitment of some Kennedy administration officials to the traditional practice of "pay as you go."

President Kennedy never witnessed the outcome of his tax initiative. The nation grieved for weeks after he was killed in late November 1963.

His successor, Lyndon Johnson, had little time for mourning. Johnson utilized his well-honed legislative skills after taking charge of the budget within weeks of Kennedy's assassination. The new president told the senior White House staff that they would have to cut spending in the existing budget draft or relinquish any hope of Senate action on the tax cut. He said that asking "Congress to reduce taxes in the face of a budget imbalance" was akin to asking it "to pass a joint resolution endorsing sin."[3] The new president recounted how a bipartisan coalition of fiscal conservatives in the Senate had dictated budgets even when Franklin Roosevelt enjoyed unprecedented popularity after the 1936 election.

Johnson spent weeks reviewing potential budget cuts with each cabinet secretary. Secretary of Defense Robert McNamara identified the largest amount of spending cuts.

Days after taking office Johnson pressed Byrd to let the tax bill get to the floor. One evening he invited the seventy-three-year-old chairman to the White House and poured him a double shot of his favorite Old Grand-Dad bourbon. Then Johnson complained to Byrd that his failure to allow a vote on the tax bill dishonored the memory of the slain Kennedy. The elderly chairman, one of the few people who continued to address the president as Lyndon, agreed to let the tax bill out of the Finance Committee so long as its staff could review the president's budget and confirm that it would actually cut spending. A reduction in total federal spending from one year to the next had rarely occurred except after the conclusion of major wars.

In early January 1964 Johnson phoned Byrd to share a surprise: the president had sent a budget to the printer with spending of $97.9 billion, less than the prior year and below the ceiling that Byrd had insisted on.[4] Johnson used his first State of the Union address, delivered in January 1964, to highlight the fact that his budget would reduce federal spending to the smallest percentage of national income since 1951. Newspaper headlines about the president's speech echoed its dominant theme of budget discipline. To make sure that executives of the nation's largest corporations appreciated his resolve to balance the budget, Johnson briefed them at a private White House dinner. Only later did others begin to focus on another portion of the speech that declared a "war on poverty."[5]

Byrd would not personally vote for a tax cut before there was an actual—not merely proposed—budget surplus. He did, however, move the tax bill to the Senate floor, where it drew fire from conservative Republicans, such as Barry Goldwater, and populist Democrats, such as Al Gore Sr. Senator Gore had warned Kennedy against cutting tax rates to stimulate growth because "the beautiful economic theory about moving taxes up and down" was "utterly impractical, since Congress would always be ready to cut taxes, never to raise them."[6] Johnson also prepared to fend off efforts to amend the bill to cut excise taxes and thereby jeopardize the goal of a balanced budget.

Johnson counted on the bill's floor manager, Finance Committee member Russell Long of Louisiana, to pass the bill intact. The forty-six-year-old Long, whose playful grin made him look even younger, was known principally for his quick wit.

Senator John McClellan of Arkansas, supported by Republican Minority Leader Everett Dirksen, tried to amend the bill to condition the tax cut on a spending limit of $98 billion.[7] Few senators cared to confront McClellan, the stern conservative Democrat who chaired the Permanent Subcommittee on Investigations. Senator Long surprised colleagues by responding with humor. With exaggerated humility, Long asked how he and other senators could possibly support an amendment that would impugn the judgment of the conservative majority on the Senate Appropriations Committee, which set the level of federal spending. To the laughter of various senators, as well as visitors in the gallery, Long slowly named and respectfully defended the honor of each member of the Appropriations Committee, including McClellan himself.

Long succeeded in ridiculing the idea that a majority in Congress would vote in favor of appropriations that set one level of federal spending and also vote not to spend that very amount. An idea that seemed laughable in 1965 would unfortunately become commonplace later on. Most recently, the Budget Control Act of 2011 allowed a majority to vote to appropriate one level of spending and then require that the federal government not spend those very amounts. In 1964, however, the Senate soundly defeated McClellan's amendment and passed the Revenue Act of 1964, which phased in lower income tax rates. The highest rate fell from 91 percent to 70 percent; the lowest rate dropped from 20 percent to 14 percent.[8]

Long's 1964 performance marked the beginning of his powerful influence on the federal budget. In January 1965 he succeeded Harry Byrd as chairman of the Senate Finance Committee and replaced Hubert Humphrey, the newly elected vice president, as Senate majority whip.

In fiscal year 1965 federal funds outlays dropped by $2 billion from the prior year, the only year since 1948 that annual federal funds spending actually declined.[9] In the late 1970s Republican congressman Jack Kemp would cite the "Kennedy tax cut" as a precedent for his influential proposal to cut tax rates, the precursor of the major reduction in Cold War tax rates in 1981. Yet, in fiscal year 1965, defense spending—the largest component of the administrative or federal funds budget—fell by almost 10 percent, while in 1981 that spending rose by more than 10 percent.[10]

Barry Goldwater's 1964 presidential campaign shifted the geographic balance of power within the Republican Party. The passage of the Civil Rights Act of 1964 spurred a steady partisan realignment in the South, but it did not change the broad consensus in support of the American Fiscal Tradition. The square-jawed, candid Goldwater found it difficult to identify cuts in the largest categories of federal funds spending: defense, veterans, and interest on outstanding debt. The Republican platform fashioned by conservative activists in 1964 actually endorsed larger defense spending. Johnson beat Goldwater in a landslide in 1964, a year in which the budget roughly balanced and all federal funds spending apart from interest and national security (including space and veterans programs) represented 3 percent of the national income.[11]

MEDICAL CARE FOR OLDER AMERICANS

By the early 1960s medical advances had greatly improved the effectiveness of hospital care. Innovations in serology, antiseptic practices, anesthesia, diagnostic practices, pharmaceuticals, and medical specialization had a high price tag. An overwhelming Democratic victory in 1964 increased the pressure on Chairman Mills to ease the burden of rising hospital costs on older Americans.

A federal role in public health was nothing new. By 1950 Congress had adopted all elements of Senator Taft's plan for state grants to fund hospital construction, medical research and education, and payment of some medical bills of citizens with low incomes. The exclusion of health insurance premiums from federal taxable income had indirectly supported employer-based insurance for workers. By 1960 most industrial employees had some type of medical insurance.

Premiums for employer-based medical coverage were based on the average estimated cost for each group of covered employees. Retired people—who typically had lower average incomes and higher average medical costs than people who were still employed—often found themselves priced out of the market for private insurance. Social Security benefits had only been raised twice during the preceding decade, while hospital room rates had escalated at nearly 10 percent annually. State and local governments and nonprofits, which operated most hospitals, struggled to cover the costs of charity hospital services for older Americans.

In 1960 Mills and Senator Robert Kerr sponsored legislation authorizing federal grants to match state funding for hospital bills of the "medically indigent."[12] The Kerr-Mills Act was roughly similar to the Eisenhower administration's proposal that some called "medicare." State budgets had already been stretched thin in satisfying the demand for education of the enormous Baby Boom generation, so many states found it hard to meet the Kerr-Mills requirement for matching funds. The American Medical Association (AMA) strongly objected to the reimbursement of hospital bills that included charges for salaried physicians. The son-in-law of the AMA's president, motivational speaker Ronald Reagan, helped the organization fight "socialized medicine."[13]

Wilbur Mills had another type of concern about proposals to use Social Security payroll taxes to pay for hospital bills. Pension costs would increase as the population aged, and Mills worried that Social Security would lose public support if payroll taxes reached an upper limit, which Mills and others believed to be about 10 percent of wages. Because of the bipartisan respect for fiscal discipline, both supporters and opponents of federal health insurance expected that the program would require an increase in payroll taxes. Concerns about the level of payroll taxes led to a confrontation that could hardly be imagined after the collapse of limits on debt in the twenty-first-century. In 1964 most Democrats on the Ways and Means Committee blocked an attempt by conservatives, including Mills and all but one Republican, to raise Social Security pension benefits by 6 percent.[14] Liberal opponents of the pension increase realized that the higher payroll taxation required to support higher pensions might preclude funding needed for a new medical benefit.

Mills treated medical care for older Americans as a practical rather than an ideological challenge. He once explained to an Arkansas chamber of commerce group that sound public policy differed from televised Westerns in which the "good guys" fought the "bad guys." His job was "understanding . . . problems and picking and choosing among the many solutions proposed," an approach he called "the true conservative yet progressive tradition."[15]

In "picking and choosing among the many solutions" for medical insurance, Mills sought to identify a sustainable source of funding and give physicians an incentive to participate in the program. By 1965 the president and most Senate Democrats embraced a plan that would raise payroll taxes to pay for most of the hospital bills of older Americans, though that coverage would not extend to medical services rendered outside of hospitals. House Republicans, meanwhile, gravitated toward an alternative that would subsidize half the cost of premiums paid by older Americans.

President Johnson encouraged Mills to develop his own plan. He and other Washington observers tried to discern the intention of the powerful chairman during weeks of hearings on the issue. Their speculation ended on March 2, 1965. Mills invited John Byrnes, the ranking Republican on the Ways and Means Committee, to publicly repeat the arguments for the GOP's alternative of a premium subsidy. After Byrnes finished speaking, Mills stunned those in the room by instructing the committee's staff to draft a bill with three elements: (1) a new trust fund, financed entirely with payroll taxes, to pay for up to sixty days of hospitalization; (2) subsidized but voluntary premiums paid by older Americans for insurance to cover their fees for physicians—essentially the Byrnes plan; and (3) matching grants to states, like in the Kerr-Mills program, to cover a portion of the medical costs of Americans of various ages without the ability to pay. These three components of the bill were later referred to as Medicare Part A, Medicare Part B, and Medicaid.

Mills believed that this financing plan could fit within a balanced budget. He emphasized the value of the traditional link between new services and new revenues: "Whenever you have a program financed by a specific tax, the willingness of people to pay that tax, that specific tax, limits the benefits of that specific program . . . if you put a program, then, into the general fund of the Treasury, there is less likelihood that you control the package of benefits initially enacted."[16] The most costly feature of the program at the time of its enactment—Medicare Part A's hospitalization insurance—was fully paid for by payroll taxes earmarked for the new Medicare trust fund. By requiring beneficiaries to pay half the cost of Medicare Part B and states to match federal Medicaid grants, the program provided an incentive to restrain the escalation of costs.

Mills described his legislation as "a satisfactory and reasonable solution of the entire problem [of medical insurance], not just a partial solution."[17] To limit upward pressure on costs, Mills rejected coverage of prescription drugs dispensed outside of hospitals, a benefit that had been included in the Republican alternative.

The bill allowed doctors to set their "customary fees," without a regulated price ceiling, in order to overcome threats of a boycott. Mills countered the emotional charge of "socialized medicine" by making Medicare Part B voluntary for patients and physicians and requiring that fees be paid directly to doctors. The requirement of direct payment to physicians changed the business model of hospitals that had previously employed a variety of specialists.

Mills and House Speaker John McCormack called to brief President Johnson on the potential budget impact of the federal funds subsidy for physician fees, an idea that Johnson said Mills "stole from Byrnes."[18] Mills highlighted the estimated federal funds cost of $450 million for the first year, and the president assured him that it could be offset by savings found in other programs.[19] House members gave Mills a standing ovation when he brought the Social Security Act Amendments of 1965 to the floor. It passed the House and Senate with bipartisan backing.

The part of the bill entitled "Grants to the States for Medical Assistance"—Medicaid—generated the least controversy and media attention in 1965. Relatively few states had aggressively pursued grants under the earlier Kerr-Mills Act, and few could argue with the chairman's desire to help states meet "the medical needs of the aged, blind, and disabled or the mothers and children receiving aid for dependent children."[20] By 2013 Medicaid would become the principal ground of contention between Republican and Democratic budget plans.

Since the adoption of Medicare in 1965, Americans have lived longer. Deaths from heart disease fell by 5 percent between 1963 and 1968, and another 15 percent by 1975.[21] Americans with low incomes utilized hospital services more frequently. In the words of President Johnson, young families no longer had to "see their own incomes, and their own hopes, eaten away" because they were committed to "carrying out their deep moral obligations to their parents, to their uncles, and to their aunts."[22] Medicare became immensely popular. Even opposition from the AMA vanished.

The great compromise on medical services orchestrated by Mills in 1965 did not, however, anticipate four trends that would severely strain federal funds budgets in the future.

First, medical costs grew at double digit annual rates rather than the assumed growth rate of slightly more than the rate of inflation. Mills and actuary Robert Myers did not predict the emergence of expensive new outpatient services, the rapid rise in physicians' fees, or the cost of greater medical specialization.[23] By 1969 rising medical costs, in turn, caused Congress to relax the original requirement that beneficiaries pay premiums covering half the annual cost of outpatient services.

Second, states expanded Medicaid services more aggressively than originally projected. A handful of states with Republican governors—California (Ronald Reagan), New York (Nelson Rockefeller), Massachusetts (John Volpe), and Michigan (George Romney)—led the way. New York made Medicaid available to families with incomes of $6,000 or less—fully half of the state's population.[24] Even after Mills amended Medicaid to limit the eligibility of individuals receiving public assistance, costs continued to soar in part because of the sharp rise in the population of nursing homes. Mills had rejected the use of Medicare to pay for nursing home care, which he called "a bottomless budgetary pit."[25] Demographic trends such as greater mobility of family members, climbing divorce rates, increasing employment of women, and growth in the population over age seventy propelled the growth in assisted living facilities. By 2010 Medicaid paid for the services provided to 9.4 million disabled and 4.3 million older Americans, 3.1 million of whom lived in residential facilities.[26]

Third, complex accounting and funding for Medicare began to undermine two important pillars of the American Fiscal Tradition: the use of clear budgets and self-sufficient trust funds. Unreliable estimates of medical costs confounded budget planning, and the federal funds budget did not account for liabilities related to current payroll contributions. Private insurers annually adjust premiums in an effort to maintain their plans in actuarial balance. The annual ceiling on Social Security payroll taxes rises for that same reason, but Medicare has no such annual adjustment mechanism.

Fourth, federal leaders would not act decisively based on the advice of Medicare actuaries. Two decades of extraordinarily high birth rates preceded the implementation of Medicare. Then, in 1965—the very year

Medicare was enacted—the number of children born in the United States fell below four million for the first time in a decade. That number would not be exceeded again for a quarter of a century.[27]

Contrary to popular belief, the rising costs of Medicare and Medicaid are unrelated to their status as "entitlements," a legal concept embodying the commitment to fair and nondiscriminatory decisions concerning eligibility.[28] Each session of Congress can prospectively change the criteria for eligibility and scope of services rendered and lower the annual appropriation by a corresponding amount.

The Vietnam War

Problems with financing future medical costs were not apparent in the hot summer days in Washington in 1965, when Mills and Senate Finance Chairman Long put the finishing touches on the Medicare bill. The bill's initial claim on federal funds revenues appeared manageable in light of strong economic growth and tight limits on other spending in the Johnson administration's first fiscal year. The budget outlook began to change within days of the bill's final passage, however, when President Johnson agreed to a request from the American field commander in Vietnam to expand his mission and increase the number of American ground forces. The Cold War suddenly became hot and more expensive. The Vietnam War ultimately resulted in direct costs of $111 billion, an amount almost equal to the entire annual federal budget when the escalation began.[29]

Little more than a month into fiscal year 1966, Secretary of Defense McNamara urged the president to seek a supplemental appropriation for $10 billion and a tax increase to pay for the military costs in Vietnam. Johnson told him to test the waters in Congress, but then decided not to seek additional funds until January 1966. As the administration complied with General William Westmoreland's requests for more troops in late 1965, some members of Congress became frustrated with the administration's unwillingness to provide an estimate of the war's cost.

Except for fiscal years 1953 (the height of Korean War), 1958 (severe recession), and 1962 (the Kennedy defense and space buildup), since World War II the nation had paid more each year in interest on its debt than it had borrowed. By fiscal year 1967, however, debt incurred for war-related costs grew rapidly. The Vietnam War propelled defense spending from $50 billion in fiscal 1965 to $81 billion in fiscal 1968.[30] With federal funds tax revenues increasing from $101 billion to $114 billion, the budget could have balanced without the cost of war.

Mills urged the president to tell the public that he had been forced to choose between paying for the war and domestic spending. Federal Reserve Chairman Martin recommended higher taxes and cuts in domestic spending in order to reduce wartime borrowing. When the administration was slow to respond, Martin raised interest rates.

Almost eighteen months after the decision to escalate combat operations in Vietnam, President Johnson proposed a tax surcharge—an across-the-board tax increase. The budget deficit for fiscal 1968 was projected to be 3 percent of national income, equivalent to the shortfall caused by the recession in 1958 and far lower than those incurred during the post-2000 wars in Afghanistan and Iraq. The president, famous for his strong-armed "Johnson treatment," began to receive similar treatment from Mills. The Ways and Means chairman had once remarked, "You don't need the title [of president] to run things in Washington."[31] He made that point by refusing to bring a tax bill to the floor until the president made large, specific commitments to reduce spending. Mills received the backing of most business organizations and House Republicans led by a new minority leader, Gerald Ford.

The impasse between the president and Mills persisted into early 1968. In Johnson's words, "The issue was never whether the people should like the tax or not. Of course they would not like it; I did not like it either. The issue was whether they would dislike it as much as the consequences of not enacting the tax."[32] Several years earlier Mills had expressed the essence of his position: "You can't form tax policy in a vacuum. You have to connect it with your spending policy."[33]

Matters came to a head at a lunch on March 22, 1968, attended by Mills, House Appropriations Chairman George Mahon, Treasury Secretary Henry Fowler, and Federal Reserve Chairman Martin. Mills expressed disgust at the lack of a more formal process to link total spending and estimated revenues.[34] Mahon, a soft-spoken, dignified West Texan who towered over Mills, resented Mills's attempt to control the entire federal budget.[35] Martin once described his job as "taking away the punch bowl just when the party gets going."[36] He would relieve pressure on interest rates only if Congress reduced federal borrowing.

Secretary Fowler had loyally defended the administration's position that Congress should raise taxes and decide where to cut spending. After the March meeting, however, he informed the president that Congress would not pass the tax bill until Johnson asked for domestic spending cuts. He also told the president that without prompt action on the tax bill, they would have to ask Congress to raise the legal debt ceiling.

Days later, Johnson delivered a nationally televised speech in which he pledged that as "part of fiscal restraint that includes a surcharge" he would "approve appropriations reductions in the January budget."[37] He called on Congress to pass a tax bill "together with expenditure control that Congress may desire and dictate."[38] Then the president stunned the nation, as well as his staff, by concluding his fiscal message with the announcement that he would not seek reelection. Johnson later explained that by sacrificing any political advantage, he hoped to be more effective in breaking the budget impasse.

Although the Constitution required that "money bills" originate in the House, the Senate promptly voted for a tax increase accompanied by a cut in spending. Mills had prevailed. Congress passed the Revenue and Expenditures Control Act of 1968, which imposed a 10 percent surcharge on personal income taxes for most taxpayers and also mandated a $6 billion cut in projected spending.[39] By requiring the president to cut spending that had already been appropriated by a majority vote in Congress, that legislation represented a turning point in budget history. When signing the bill Johnson chided Congress for shifting "to the President the responsibility for making reductions in programs which the Congress itself is unwilling to do."[40] Congress would also employ a similar mechanism—a "sequester"—in attempts to control spending that its own majority voted for in the late 1980s and after 2011.

Although the last federal budget in Johnson's presidency required only very modest borrowing in the administrative or federal funds budget—no more than half of 1 percent of national income—an unheralded change in federal accounting created the illusion of a slight surplus. In fiscal year 1969 the federal government adopted a "unified budget," which consolidated the federal funds and trust fund budgets. The change reflected advice from economists who sought to shape budget accounting in a manner that could be used to estimate the short-run impact of federal outlays and receipts on the economy as a whole. For that limited purpose, it made little difference whether federal spending was paid for with taxes dedicated to trust obligations or taxes that could be used to service debt.

The unified budget also had the deceptive allure of simplification, since federal officials had previously used three different versions of the budget, each for distinct purposes. Elected officials and journalists usually referred to the administrative budget—similar to what is now referred to as the federal funds budget—which could be used to compare annual spending appropriations with annual revenues apart from the trust funds. That budget served the traditional purpose of aligning federal commitments and related taxation. Another version of the budget—the "consolidated cash budget"—was used to manage the timing and amount of sales of Treasury debt. The consolidated cash budget included the administrative, or federal funds, budget and all trust fund budgets. Economists relied on yet another budget, the "national income accounts budget," which was modified to conform with the economic accounting used to estimate national income. If the federal funds budget borrowed $5 billion entirely from trust funds, the net borrowing in the national income accounts budget appeared to be zero since there was no net change in total economic activity resulting from that transaction. The President's Commission on Budget Concepts recommended that these three disparate versions of the budget be collapsed into one.

Though economic calculations of the budget's impact on employment and inflation did not depend on whether revenues and spending occurred inside or outside the trust funds, the unified budget undermined an important rationale for separating trust funds from the rest of the budget. It made it more difficult to tell whether federal resources and commitments balanced *within* the federal funds budget. Revenues accumulating in the trust funds—principally for Social Security pensions, Medicare, highways, airports, and various federal employee retirement plans—could not be used to pay the interest and principal on the debt. Private businesses would be engaging in fraud if they counted trust fund reserves as income. Three decades later President Clinton sought unsuccessfully to remedy this distortion.

In 1969, however, future threats to fiscal discipline appeared only as clouds on a distant horizon. The parents of the Baby Boom generation could take pride in having reduced their children's burden of federal debt. The federal funds budget when Johnson left office consisted of tax revenues at 14.6 percent of national income, somewhat less than outlays amounting to 15.1 percent.[41] This relatively small gap did not seem particularly risky in light of the twenty-four-year decline in total federal debt as a share of national income. Unmonetized federal debt, $298 billion in 1969, had grown by only $54 billion since the end of World War II.[42] Debt held by creditors outside the federal trust funds was virtually unchanged from the end of that war. American citizens held about 15 percent of the debt, or $52.2 billion, in savings bonds.[43] The inflation-adjusted value of federal debt had decreased by about a third, the same scale of reduction achieved in the quarter of a century following World War II. Tax revenues could pay for debt service and much more. By 1969 unmonetized federal debt was only double the amount of annual federal funds revenue. In contrast, at the end of World War II debt was seven times the revenue available to service debt. Debt rose to nine times that amount by 2013.[44]

THE LIMITS OF TAX REFORM

Johnson's successor, Richard Nixon, referred to the economy only once in his 1969 inaugural address, when he asserted that the nation had "learned to manage its continued growth."[45] The economy appeared strong, with the unemployment rate at a fifteen-year low of 3.3 percent and inflation hovering at 4.7 percent.[46]

Nixon had lost two elections in eight years before being elected to the presidency with only 43 percent of the popular vote, and these experiences contributed to his obsession with reelection. The president understood the breadth of public support for domestic commitments such as Medicare. He sought to govern as a progressive on domestic spending programs and a conservative on what his staff called "the social issue," a cultural agenda that called for slowing down desegregation, appointing conservative judges, and backing public aid to Catholic schools.[47] Nixon confided to his staff that he would secure his place in history by easing Cold War tensions, an aspiration based in part on the president's belief that Americans had tired of the Cold War's tax burden.

Nixon respected the political power of traditional values, including those undergirding limits on debt. Even with the continuing expense of the Vietnam War, he intended to balance the budget unless the economy faltered. The president had to choose between extending Johnson's surtax, which was set to expire in mid-1969, or running a deficit. He chose the surtax and garnered congressional support for its extension by assuring

Democratic leaders that he would support tax reform. Political momentum for the reform of tax laws had gained ground after publication of a report showing that more than one hundred Americans with very high incomes paid no income taxes.

A bipartisan coalition of centrists and conservatives in Congress extended the surtax until the end of the year. Congress then incorporated an additional extension as part of a separate bill, the Tax Reform Act of 1969. The Nixon White House hoped that tax reforms would raise revenues to assist in financing its new domestic initiatives such as "revenue sharing" with states and the Family Assistance Plan, which guaranteed a minimum income to poor families. But the Ways and Means Committee changed the tax code without any projected increase in tax revenues.

Mills was accustomed to bringing his committee's bills to the House floor with a special "closed rule" that prevented amendments. In late 1969, however, the Rules Committee refused to grant that closed rule unless the Ways and Means Committee amended its tax bill to reduce taxes for Americans with low and middle incomes. Within hours the committee altered its bill to comply with that requirement, even though the change resulted in a significant net loss in estimated revenue. The Tax Reform Act of 1969, as passed by the House, increased some deductions while extending the war surtax, raising the tax rate on capital gains, limiting deductions for oil producers, and initiating the Alternative Minimum Tax.

Senate debate on the Tax Reform Act mirrored public discontent with high Cold War taxes. Democratic Senator Al Gore Sr., who was facing a tough battle for reelection in 1970, sponsored a populist tax cut. He initially proposed to raise the standard personal exemption or standard deduction to $1,250, up from the $600 that had been in place since 1948. After a Treasury official estimated that his proposal would result in an enormous loss in tax revenues, the Senate Finance Committee rejected even a scaled-back version of Gore's amendment. On the Senate floor, however, ten Republicans joined forty-eight Democrats to raise the standard deduction to $800. Nixon threatened to veto the bill but signed it after the conference committee raised the standard deduction to $750, phased in over three years.[48]

President Johnson's former budget director, Charles Schultze, criticized Democratic support for the Tax Reform Act. Schultze argued that the revenue reductions would ultimately force Congress to cut funding for programs valued by Democrats in order to balance the budget. Gore lost his reelection, but his challenge to the Cold War income tax foreshadowed an intense debate a decade later.

BORROWING WHEN UNEMPLOYMENT RISES

A slowing economy in early 1970 eliminated the slight surplus that had been projected for the next fiscal year. That prompted White House Budget Director Charles Mayo to recommend various spending cuts. Mayo, a nonpartisan budget expert, had been hired by Nixon based on the recommendation of chairmen Mills and Mahon. Rather than paring down federal spending, Nixon replaced Mayo with George Shultz, who had been serving as labor secretary. The president acknowledged that the downturn would result in a modest deficit, but on July 18, 1970—with Shultz's encouragement—he explained his rule for budget planning: "Except in emergency conditions, expenditures should never be allowed to outrun the revenues that the tax system would produce at reasonably full employment."[49]

Herbert Stein, the chairman of the Council of Economic Advisers in Nixon's White House, had championed the concept of the budget balanced at "reasonably full employment." The rule blended the traditional practice of "pay as you go" budget planning with the more pragmatic goal of balancing the budget across economic cycles. After all, it was impractical to change tax rates and spending within each budget year based on fluctuations in economic activity. Declaring the budget balanced at "reasonably full employment" also served Nixon's political desire to rationalize the existence of a modest deficit. The president claimed that borrowing to offset revenues lost from higher unemployment served as a "self-fulfilling prophecy" that would lead to higher employment and a balanced budget. The theory did not impress many traditional conservatives, including a Nixon cabinet member who called it "economic bullshit."[50]

Stein believed that a "balanced budget at full employment" provided an acceptable criterion for limiting deficits during downturns. It was not not a prescription for ending the business cycle. Since temporary borrowing was to be repaid out of surpluses once the economy rebounded, the president asked Congress for only a "temporary" increase in the debt ceiling in 1971. Through the troubled economy of the next dozen years, Congress did not alter the permanent debt ceiling of $400 billion—largely representing debt from World War II and Vietnam—and labeled each increase in the ceiling as "temporary."[51]

Nixon counted on aggressive expansion of the money supply to boost economic growth before the 1972 election. For that purpose he turned to Arthur Burns, whom he nominated in 1970 to be the chairman of the Federal Reserve Board. When Nixon appointed Burns, he expressed hope that the new Federal Reserve chairman would "independently" conclude that the president's views "are the ones that should be followed."[52] Burns quickly leaned on his colleagues on the board to expand the money supply and ease interest rates through aggressive purchases of federal debt. From 1970 to 1971 the Federal Reserve bought $13.6 billion in Treasury obligations, monetizing more debt than in any two-year period since World War II.[53] Afterwards the Federal Reserve carried on its balance sheet almost 17 percent of Treasury debt, a higher share than at any previous time.[54]

That monetary expansion continued for years and ultimately led to the nation's most severe peacetime inflation. Shortly after leaving the chairmanship, Burns admitted that the Federal Reserve could have restricted the money supply and slowed the economy "to terminate inflation with little delay. It did not do so because the Federal Reserve was itself caught up in the philosophic and political currents that were transforming American life and culture."[55]

The shift in monetary policy coincided with another economic transition. In 1971 the value of US imports exceeded the value of its exports for the first time in seventy-four years. President Nixon privately predicted a long-term decline in the competitive position of American manufacturing. The trade deficit and monetary growth posed an immediate threat to the Treasury's gold supply.

Chronic trade deficits also signaled a trend that weakened the federal tax system. As taxable corporate profits declined under the pressure of international competition, so too did the share of national income paid as corporate income taxes. By 1971 many American business leaders and economists began advocating lighter corporate taxation as a means of encouraging domestic investment.

Nixon and Treasury Secretary John Connally, a former Texas governor, announced in August 1971 that the United States would abandon the gold standard, levy a fee on imports, and impose mandatory wage and price controls. Before the 1972 election Nixon tried to boost spending by accelerating the rate of outlays by various federal departments. The economy grew, and price controls temporarily suppressed price inflation.

Nixon's unorthodox approach to economic policy coincided with an innovative foreign policy, symbolized by the president's trip to the People's Republic of China. The president's popularity soared along with the tantalizing possibility of an end to the costly Cold War.

The Social Security Act Amendments of 1972

Neither President Nixon nor the American people desired to scale back Medicare despite its soaring costs. In Medicare's first five years, the number of enrolled Americans had increased slowly, while the cost of hospitalization rose by an annual average of 13.2 percent and medical fees by an annual average of 7.5 percent.[56] Private insurers experienced an equivalent jump in costs.

Federal medical costs were still relatively small compared to federal funds outlays for defense and for several domestic programs. In 1970 general (or federal funds) revenues paid for only 24.6 percent of the $7.5 billion spent for Medicare.[57] In 1970 federal funds revenues for Medicare and Medicaid amounted to less than four-tenths of 1 percent of national income, roughly equivalent to the level of federal transportation grants.[58] Dedicated payroll taxes funded the entire $5.3 billion cost for Medicare's hospitalization coverage.

Federal leaders offered competing plans to expand medical coverage. Many Democrats, led by Senator Ted Kennedy of Massachusetts, sought to raise payroll taxes to fund greater medical insurance for working Americans. Nixon's alternative required employers to offer medical coverage through managed care plans with federal subsidies for premiums. Senate Finance Chairman Long and House Ways and Means Chairman Mills resisted the cost of these proposals. Then, in 1972, Congress undertook sweeping changes in Social Security pensions and Medicare. Those changes would largely exhaust the perceived capacity of the payroll tax to fund further expansions of federal medical coverage.

Between November 1954 and March 1968 Congress had raised pension benefits just three times—by 7 percent in February 1959, 7 percent in February 1965, and 13 percent in March 1968.[59] Payroll tax rates supporting old-age and disability pensions rose from 2 percent of covered payroll in 1954 to 8.4 percent in 1970.[60] According to actuaries, benefits at those levels could be sustained at defined and predictable rates of payroll taxation. After 1968, however, Mills began to lose control of benefit levels.

Led by Long, Congress increased pensions by 15 percent in 1969 and then by another 10 percent in 1970.[61] Long added the latter increase to a bill that raised the legislated ceiling on federal debt, making it difficult to veto without shutting down the federal government. The veteran actuary of Social Security, Robert Myers, quit in disgust. Long and Nixon pushed for legislation creating a formula that automatically adjusted pension benefits to account for changes in the cost of living.

Mills blocked that effort, which he feared would put excessive pressure on payroll tax rates and diminish congressional control of the program. When the automatic inflation adjustment passed both the House and the Senate in 1971, Mills used his extraordinary power to kill the bill by refusing to schedule a conference committee meeting. This action reinforced the chairman's credibility as a fiscal conservative, a credibility he soon exploited to the detriment of long-term budget discipline.

In early 1972 Mills announced his candidacy for president and introduced House Bill 1, the Social Security Amendments of 1972. The ultimate congressional insider had caught a severe case of presidential fever. He proposed the most ambitious expansion of federal services since the Social Security Amendments of 1965, which created Medicare and Medicaid. Mills sought to raise pension benefits and link them to future rates of inflation, expand Medicare coverage to disabled Americans, limit the premiums paid by beneficiaries for Medicare Part B, remove copayments for certain types of home health care, raise the payroll tax and wage ceiling, and convert many state-based public assistance grants into a new program of direct payments, called Supplemental Security Income.

The legislation increased the number of Medicare beneficiaries by 10 percent by making disabled Americans eligible for the program.[62] The related cost, however, would rise even more because people with disabilities incurred higher than average medical costs.[63] The bill was amended to require Medicare reimbursement for the high costs of dialysis used in the treatment of kidney failure. In addition, Congress passed a 20 percent hike in the level of monthly Social Security pensions, an increase that—on top of prior pension increases—doubled the level of pension benefits compared to those in 1967.[64]

In 1972 Mills abandoned his long-standing opposition to the use of projections of future wage growth in setting pension benefits. Because wages and employment had consistently grown faster than inflation up to that time, many economists had criticized the flat wage assumption. Unfortunately, within two years of the passage of House Bill 1, inflation and inflation-adjusted pension benefits began to rise faster than both employment and productivity. The prudence of the old flat wage assumption was vindicated too late. To remain self-sustaining, trust funds for pensions and Medicare hospitalization required sharply higher payroll tax rates, which would climb to 15.3 percent of payroll in 1990.[65]

The Social Security Commission had good reason to call the Social Security Act Amendments of 1972 "a new social security program."[66] The number of older Americans living in poverty would be cut in half. The next generation of conservative federal leaders would begin to decry the emergence of a "welfare state," often pejoratively associated with Johnson's War on Poverty and Great Society programs. In fact, the largest expansion of the social safety net occurred with the passage of the Social Security Act Amendments of 1972. The final bill emerging from the conference committee sailed through the House with a vote of 305–1 and the Senate unanimously.

Mills received little political benefit from that new social safety net. His quixotic presidential campaign floundered, and Nixon attempted to take credit for the new program. The first checks with higher monthly pension payments were mailed in October, right before the election. The White House tried to mail those payments along with a presidential message and Nixon's picture, but this plan was dropped after Social Security officials threatened to resign in protest.

NIXON FIGHTS CONGRESS ON THE BUDGET

Nixon won reelection in 1972 with a record Electoral College margin for a Republican president. In the final weeks before the election he campaigned as a traditional fiscal conservative. He told voters that his opponent's spending programs meant higher taxes down the road. After his election he lectured Congress: "Some people have forgotten the crucial point that the full-employment principle requires that deficits be reduced as the economy approaches full employment."[67] Like many of his predecessors, Nixon wanted to leave office with a balanced budget. He used traditional language when submitting his next budget to Congress along with a reminder that "the only way to restrain taxes" was "to restrain spending."[68]

Even though deficits remained modest in relation to national income, the president announced plans to impound, or refuse to spend, amounts appropriated. Congress bridled at being blamed for deficits and responded by passing the Congressional Budget and Impoundment Control Act of 1974, which created new budget committees and the Congressional Budget Office. The legislation required Congress to adopt resolutions each spring that set ceilings on estimated spending. The new budget process was intended to reduce congressional dependence on the presidential budget.

By 1974 the Nixon White House was severely weakened by the investigation of the president's role in the Watergate burglary. In July, after an economic downturn reduced expected revenues, Nixon proposed cuts in spending. Eleven days later, following Nixon's resignation, Vice President Gerald Ford took the oath of office.

By the time Nixon resigned, the claim in his first inaugural address that federal leaders had learned how to manage the economy was as discredited as the president himself. A simultaneous rise in unemployment and inflation baffled many economists. Gasoline was rationed and oil prices soared after many large oil exporters embargoed shipments to the United States. By the end of 1974 the Dow Jones Industrial Average had fallen to half its level two years earlier.

Rising inflation, Nixon's disgrace, and dashed hopes of victory in the War on Poverty and in Vietnam had battered the public's confidence in federal leadership, but not public support for balanced budgets.

SEVERE RECESSION AND PRESIDENTIAL VETOES

Hours after Ford took the presidential oath, the White House economic team and Federal Reserve Chairman Burns advised him that the economy showed signs of recovery from the inflation and unemployment experienced earlier in the year. They urged a cut in federal spending to close the anticipated budget gap.[69] Ford—who described himself as a fiscal conservative—understood the federal budget well. His years of service on the House Appropriations Committee led Deputy Chief of Staff Dick Cheney to observe that the president grasped details of the budget better than anyone else in the White House.

Two months after taking office, in his first major address to Congress and the nation, Ford proposed to cut spending and raise revenues with a temporary 5 percent surcharge on most income taxes. After the speech the economy slid into its most severe recession since 1938. In the last three months of 1974, inflation-adjusted income fell by 7.5 percent, and unemployment rose steadily to 7.2 percent at the end of the year.[70] A continued rise in consumer prices confounded forecasts generated using economic models.

Debt filled the gap when federal tax revenues plunged. A Republican Party still haunted by the aura of failure associated with the Hoover administration felt compelled to "do something" to curb the economic slide. Democrats, meanwhile, invoked the New Deal. When a fiscally conservative Democrat, Senator Ernest Hollings of South Carolina, offered an amendment to limit spending to estimated tax revenues, the Senate defeated it by a two-to-one margin.

Since Ford had been appointed rather than elected to the vice presidency before Nixon's resignation, he lacked the political capital conferred by an election victory. He dropped his request for a tax surcharge and in January 1975 proposed a one-time $16 billion tax rebate linked to a ceiling on federal spending.[71] As unemployment swelled to almost 9 percent in May 1975, Congress passed a temporary tax cut and a $5.3 billion "jobs" bill funded through Nixon's 1973 Comprehensive Employment and Training Act (CETA).[72] Congress failed to override Ford's veto of the jobs bill despite pressure from Democratic leadership, who made the vote a test of party loyalty.

Ford vetoed sixty-six bills during his presidency in an attempt to maintain spending discipline. Congress overrode only his vetoes of appropriations for education, health care, and child nutrition.

In October 1975 the president proposed a tax cut conditioned on a spending ceiling of $395 billion, roughly the level of spending during the prior twelve months plus a cost of living increase for Social Security.[73] Ford's proposal was crafted with help from White House staff members who would play crucial roles in fiscal policy in the early twenty-first century: Chief of Staff Donald Rumsfeld, Deputy Budget Director Paul O'Neill, Deputy Chief of Staff Dick Cheney, and Council of Economic Advisers Chairman Alan Greenspan. When a Republican congressional leader warned Ford about the political danger of vetoing a tax cut simply because it did not include a spending ceiling, the president cited the example of Truman, who had vetoed a tax cut to balance the budget in 1947 and was reelected the following year. Congress passed the tax cut without a spending ceiling and failed by a narrow margin to override Ford's veto on December 17, 1975.

Before Christmas Day, Long convinced Ford to sign a new bill that contained both the tax cut and unenforceable language that pledged spending restraint. Ford's political advisors were relieved to have a tax cut to counter promises made by the president's opponent in the primaries, former California governor Ronald Reagan.

The battle between Ford and Reagan for the presidential nomination continued until the 1976 Republican National Convention. Reagan had kicked off his campaign the previous year by announcing an ambitious program to lower federal spending by $90 billion—almost a quarter—in order to balance the budget with lower tax rates.[74] His budget plan called for an end to Medicaid as well as most domestic programs except for Social Security, Medicare, and "some aspects of agriculture, transportation and the environment."[75] Ford gained ground in early primaries by pointing out that Reagan's proposal would shift the burden of financing the established social safety net to the states. Reagan regained momentum after he deemphasized his budget plan and focused his attacks on Ford's foreign policy. The GOP platform of 1976 expressed traditional conservative doctrine: the nation could not "responsibly cut back taxes" without "spending restraint."[76]

Former governor of Georgia Jimmy Carter surprised his party's leaders with his strong showing in the Democratic primaries. Carter had always identified himself as a fiscal conservative. He pledged to improve efficiency, cut waste, and balance the budget as employment recovered from the deep recession. The onetime peanut farmer quipped that he had "never known an unbalanced budget—in my business, on my farm, as Governor of Georgia."[77] The economy had revived by the November election, even though unemployment remained above the level previously considered normal. Carter defeated Ford by a miniscule margin.

The American Fiscal Tradition appeared to be as strong as ever after an election between two presidential candidates committed to traditional limits on debt. Nonetheless, the budget had not balanced during a decade that had included the final years of the war in Vietnam and a severe recession. A growing public movement sought to amend the nation's *written* Constitution to include the traditional limits on debt.

PART V

THE EROSION, REVIVAL, AND
COLLAPSE OF THE TRADITION:
1977–2013

14

STRUCTURAL DEFICIT: PRESSURES FOR TAX CUTS AND A REVIVED COLD WAR

1977–1981: Years when deficits exceeded debt service = 5
(1977–1981, soaring interest rates and military costs)

RISING INTEREST EXPENSE

Jimmy Carter's status as a Washington outsider was a campaign asset that became a liability when he had to prepare a budget within weeks of taking office. His staff's lack of experience with budgets and Congress made his task difficult.

Carter searched for wasteful spending and decided to cut nineteen hydroelectric power projects. Members of Congress in both parties objected to the potential loss of those infrastructure investments, which had been planned for years. Some members also objected to the president's deferral of investments in several new weapons systems. Carter's tax proposal—a one-time tax rebate of $50 per taxpayer—was slow to gain traction, and the administration dropped its initiative after only a few months in office.[1] From then on, Carter later reflected, his "major economic battle would be against inflation," a fight in which he tried to "stay on the side of fiscal prudence, restricted budgets."[2]

The emphasis on fiscal discipline limited the Carter administration's ability to undertake new domestic initiatives. Carter's annual budgets—like

271

those of his predecessor, Gerald Ford—contained few new programs apart from those intended to enhance energy security.

Rising interest expense made it even harder to balance the budget. When Carter took office in January 1977, the Treasury sold long-term bonds at an effective interest rate of 7.63 percent. By 1979 Treasury bonds were sold at a yield of 10.44 percent, a level reached previously only during the War of 1812 and the Civil War.[3] Higher interest rates soaked up revenues that otherwise could have been used to fund expanded medical services, tax reduction, or more robust Cold War military budgets.

Consumer prices increased 13 percent in 1979.[4] Monetarist economists marshaled persuasive evidence showing price levels rose principally to the extent that the supply of money grew faster than did the output of the economy. Carter's appointee as chairman of the Federal Reserve, Paul Volcker, began throttling back growth in the money supply in October 1979. The combination of restricted credit and inflationary expectations propelled the prime lending rate offered by banks to an unprecedented level of 21 percent.[5]

For all that, however, by the end of fiscal year 1979, the deficit in the federal funds budget had fallen to 2.3 percent of national income, almost half the level of the deficit in the last full fiscal year in the Ford administration.[6] The budget probably would have satisfied the criterion of balance at "reasonably full employment." Nonetheless, the public grew impatient with the seeming inability of elected officials to restore traditional fiscal discipline.

By 1979 a majority of state legislatures had passed resolutions calling for a constitutional amendment that required a balanced federal budget. According to polls, more than 70 percent of Americans supported such an amendment.[7]

BUDGET CHAOS IN 1980

Carter sought to balance the budget by the end of his term. There was more at stake than fulfilling a campaign promise or securing his legacy. The Federal Reserve had been contracting the supply of credit in order to curb inflation. Democratic and Republican leaders in Washington believed that the federal government should assist that effort by reducing its demand on credit.

In January 1980 Carter submitted a budget with a projected deficit of $15 billion, the lowest in years.[8] Days later budget experts raised the estimate of required federal borrowing. The bond market began to crash. The market value of long-term Treasury bonds fell by more than 20 percent in the first seven weeks of 1980, and interest rates on Treasury debt soared to 12 percent.[9] The Dow Jones Industrial Average fell to its lowest level in eighteen years.

In March 1980 Carter invited congressional leaders from both parties, the administration's senior economic officials, and Federal Reserve Chairman Paul Volcker to daily White House meetings convened for the purpose of rewriting the administration's budget. Volcker described Carter during those meetings as "a president with basically conservative instincts making preliminary decisions challenged by advisors sensitive to both particular interests and to the more liberal traditions of his party."[10] Most of the group agreed to cut federal grants, withhold estimated taxes on interest and dividends, and levy a new tax on oil imports. Volcker's Federal Reserve restricted credit card lending in an attempt to curb price inflation, triggering an abrupt fall in consumer spending and economic output. The harsh monetary medicine resulted in a slow but steady reduction in price inflation.

Shortly after the White House meetings, bipartisan budget cooperation ended. Members of Congress nervously eyed the November election, and Congress refused to authorize a fee on imported oil that bipartisan leadership had endorsed just weeks earlier. Senate Republicans even endorsed a 10 percent reduction in income tax rates. Gridlock ensued. Procedures enacted in 1974 required Congress to pass a budget resolution by the spring *before* the fiscal year that began each October. In 1980 Congress missed that deadline and was unable to pass a budget resolution until October 1—the first day of fiscal year 1981—just as the administration prepared to shut down the government due to lack of funding.

The belated budget resolution included a feature that offered some solace for advocates of traditional "pay as you go" budget planning. Congress revised its budget procedures to give a voting majority the power to order committees to amend legislation affecting taxes and spending so as to fit within—be "reconciled with"—the annual budget resolution's spending ceiling and revenues estimates. Congressional leaders hoped that this broad "reconciliation" power would be used to restrain formula-based spending.

The budget resolution adopted on October 1, 1980, also projected a lower operating deficit—federal funds outlays minus receipts before counting the interest expense—than any budget since the recession from 1974 to 1975. No one had quite figured out how to pay for those rising interest rates. By the end of fiscal year 1981, gross interest expense rose to $95 billion, more than double the amount paid in the year Carter had taken office.[11]

Even the apparent discipline—before interest expense—for fiscal year 1981 would turn out to be an illusion, however. Revenue projections assumed that rapid economic growth and high rates of inflation would push taxpayers into higher tax brackets, and that the resulting flood of revenues would allow Congress to raise future defense spending and still balance the budget.

The budget prepared in 1980 did, however, include two hard choices. The Carter administration beat back an attempt by some Democratic leaders to expand federal medical services, and ended a signature Democratic jobs initiative.

After his election in 1976, Carter had asked for time to consider how to deal with Senator Ted Kennedy's proposal to expand access to medical insurance with an employer mandate and some premium subsidies, an approach endorsed earlier by President Nixon and later by President Clinton. Carter could not find room for the new program within a balanced budget, especially after Congress defeated his initiative to cap the annual rise in costs for Medicare hospitalization. Senator Kennedy proceeded— without the White House—to line up support for his plan. Polling showed that about 60 percent of Americans in the 1970s said "too little" was spent on health programs, a percentage much higher than those who felt "too little" was spent on defense.[12] Senate Finance Committee Chairman Russell Long and House Ways and Means Committee Chairman Al Ullman blocked action on the insurance legislation, prompting Kennedy's supporters to organize a challenge to Carter's renomination.

The drive to balance the budget also forced cuts in a Democratic jobs program. In 1977 Congress had increased funding for public service jobs administered under the Comprehensive Employment and Assistance Act, known as CETA, enacted during the Nixon administration.[13] Congress required more than four hundred grant recipients, principally local governments, to create hundreds of thousands of jobs by the spring of 1978. The number of subsidized jobs grew from 300,000 in May 1977 to 725,000 in March 1978.[14] Local governments hired unemployed people to fill temporary jobs in schools and parks and to perform street maintenance. Occasionally they shifted parts of their existing workforce to CETA grants. Under media scrutiny, Congress blamed grant recipients for mismanagement, while local governments recoiled at new CETA mandates and audits.

In fiscal years 1977–1979, Congress appropriated more than $27 billion for employment and training programs.[15] In 1980 Congress pared down the program, over the objection of Senator Kennedy.

THE COLD WAR DILEMMA

The years following the withdrawal from Vietnam, unlike those after other major wars, evinced no drop in military spending. The end of conscription raised personnel costs. At the same time, the Ford administration endorsed an expensive five-year plan of investments to modernize military hardware. Carter delayed that plan's contemplated outlays for new nuclear delivery systems. He and Secretary of Defense Harold Brown placed more emphasis on upgrading conventional forces with improved technology and precision-guided missiles. Carter and Brown challenged NATO allies to share the burden of Cold War expense by making a multiyear commitment to increase military spending by 3 percent annually after inflation—a level the president hoped would serve as a ceiling as well as a floor on US defense costs.[16]

Senator Henry "Scoop" Jackson demanded substantially higher military outlays. Jackson had never agreed with Nixon and Ford's policy of détente with the Soviet Union. Jackson was an unapologetic Truman Democrat who had served in Congress since World War II. The Soviet Union's economy appeared vulnerable. For that reason, the down-to-earth liberal senator from Washington opposed popular nuclear arms control treaties. Jackson believed that Americans should be willing to pay the tax rates sufficient to challenge the Soviet Union's brutal suppression of human rights and control of Eastern European nations.

In 1978 Carter vetoed a military spending resolution crafted by Jackson and Senator Sam Nunn of Georgia, another vocal critic of the administration's defense budgets. In 1979 Carter vetoed another resolution calling for defense spending to increase at an annual rate of at least 5 percent plus inflation.[17]

Jackson's hawkish view on military preparation gained ground when a new regime in Iran took American diplomats hostage on November 4, 1979. Shortly thereafter, to obtain Senate ratification of a treaty with the Soviet Union limiting certain kinds of nuclear weapons, Carter agreed to back a sustained 6 percent after-inflation increase in defense spending.[18] Then, on Christmas Eve 1979, the Soviet Union invaded Afghanistan, initiating a new phase of the Cold War.

Jackson's efforts were backed by the influential Committee on the Present Danger. That organization included Ronald Reagan, who later would appoint more than thirty of its members to positions in his administration. Several leaders of the committee, including Donald Rumsfeld and Jackson staff member Paul Wolfowitz, would help shape military policy well into the twenty-first century.

In the last fiscal year of Carter's administration, the federal government spent $157 billion for national security—$60 billion more than in the final year of the Ford administration from four years earlier.[19] Jackson and Reagan sought to spend even more.

From Tax Reform to Tax Revolt

The federal tax system inherited from World War II no longer produced revenues sufficient to pay for both higher Cold War spending and other existing bipartisan federal commitments, such as Medicare, within a balanced budget. In 1979 House Ways and Means Committee Chairman Ullman and Senate Finance Committee Chairman Long called for a radical overhaul of the federal tax system. They proposed a value-added tax—a form of sales tax—in order to broaden the federal tax base. Many tax experts and most businesses favored a shift to greater taxation of consumption rather than income from production.

By 1980 federal taxation of corporate income yielded revenues of only 2.4 percent of national income, down from 6 percent in 1952.[20] In the mid-1950s corporate taxes provided 30 cents out of every dollar spent in the federal funds budget; in 1980 those revenues covered only ten cents of each federal dollar spent, the lowest relative contribution of the corporate tax since before World War I.[21]

Declining corporate tax revenues were principally the result of international competition, though some elected officials instead blamed deductions that they called "loopholes." Rules on the deduction of business outlays often were intended to bring the taxable income of capital-intensive industry in line with their actual cash flows and the cost of equity financing.[22]

The challenge of international competition became more visible in the 1970s, when Japan flourished as American productivity and trade balances deteriorated. Productivity rose alongside greater educational achievement and capital investment per worker. Nations such as Japan, Korea, and Taiwan improved the skills of their workforces, and devoted a larger share of their national income to business investment than did the United States. Foreign nations used tax systems that weighed more heavily on consumption than investment as a means to encourage growth.

In the 1970s Congress frequently passed new investment incentives. Those efforts resulted in a tax code so complex that Carter labeled it repeatedly as a "disgrace to the human race."[23]

In prior eras a sweeping tax proposal from the leaders of the powerful House and Senate tax committees would have prompted a serious national debate. Long and Ullman's sales tax initiative in 1979, however, died a quiet death. Its obituary included Ullman's defeat for reelection in 1980.

As corporate income tax revenues declined as a share of national income, the federal government relied more heavily on personal income taxes. By 1980 those taxes had reached the limit that many Americans were willing to endure. Americans in the top bracket of 70 percent had always chafed at a tax rate that made tax-planning a part of every investment decision. Far more Americans felt squeezed when high World War II tax brackets began to apply to households with middle incomes in the late 1970s. At the end of World War II only fairly wealthy Americans earned $25,000 to $50,000 a year; 70 percent of taxable income in that range came from investments—proprietary business profits, dividends, interest, and capital gains.[24] Even in the mid-1960s investments produced half the taxable income of taxpayers in the $25,000 to $50,000 bracket. The price and wage inflation of the late 1970s pushed wage-earning workers into that tax bracket. By 1980 salaries and wages accounted for more than 80 percent of income earned by taxpayers earning $25,000 to $50,000.[25] Married couples filing a joint return with $25,000 in net taxable income, after deductions, were subject to a tax rate of 32 percent rate, a rate once reserved only for wealthy families.[26] Inflation had also eroded the value of the standard deduction that once exempted all of the earnings of taxpayers with low wages.

Revenues from personal income taxes jumped from 7.21 percent of national income in 1976 to 8.75 percent of national income in 1980, the largest spike since World War II.[27] The "effective" rate of personal income taxation—average personal tax revenue as a percentage of average revenue on the top line of tax returns—also jumped. In 1953, the end of the Korean War, the effective rate was 13 percent. It dipped a bit in the early 1960s before returning to 14 percent courtesy of the Vietnam War surtax. Federal personal income taxes remained between 13 and 14 percent of gross income until 1978, and then climbed to 15.6 percent in 1980 and a record 16 percent in 1981.[28]

Americans with middle incomes also felt pressed by payroll taxes supporting Social Security pensions and Medicare hospitalization insurance. Payroll tax rates climbed from 6 percent of covered payroll in 1961 to 10.7 percent of covered payroll in 1973 to 13.3 percent of covered payroll in 1981.[29]

A revolt against state taxes started in California in 1978 and soon spread to many other states. The share of national income consumed by state and local government spending and taxes had grown steadily for three decades. Most Americans valued the services provided by local governments, such as law enforcement, garbage collection, and schools for the massive Baby Boom. State constitutions and city charters, however, prohibited borrowing to pay for operating costs, so state and local governments had to either raise taxes or cut services their citizens valued.

By 1980 public opinion surveys showed that most Americans favored lower federal income tax rates, though not at the cost of greater federal borrowing. Since lower tax revenues without new debt required lower spending, where would the federal government cut? Rising interest expense on debts remaining from World War II, Vietnam, and the mid-1970s downturn made it quite difficult to answer that question.

In the 1970s many members of Congress had come to rely on strong presidential leadership—exemplified by the frequent use of vetoes by Nixon, Ford, and Carter—to enforce budget discipline. Presidential advisor and economic historian Herbert Stein noted of the era: "It was the president who took responsibility for . . . restraining deficits. . . . Presidents felt this responsibility and also felt that the public would hold them responsible. So it was presidents who resisted tax cuts, who pressed for tax increases . . . and who vetoed appropriations and impounded funds."[30] The nation would soon find out what happened when a president asked Congress to spend more and tax less.

The Emergence of Ronald Reagan

Just as New Deal programs and civil rights legislation came to symbolize Democratic ideals, so too did the Reagan administration's tax cuts and high defense spending define the GOP's identity by the late 1990s. This particular legacy would have surprised most observers of Reagan's first year as governor of California. The retired actor campaigned for governor in 1966 as an outsider, a "citizen-politician." Reagan won the race with the support of many blue-collar Democrats. Lou Cannon, an admiring biographer, could not find any gubernatorial campaign speech in which Reagan referred to himself as a "conservative."

The newly elected governor immediately faced a projected gap between spending and taxes in a state with a constitution that required a balanced budget. Governor Reagan proposed closing the gap with higher taxes on sales, personal income, alcohol, tobacco, and businesses. Cannon observed that "Reagan's proposal had the distinction of being the largest tax hike ever proposed by any governor in the history of the United States."[31] During Reagan's eight years as California's governor, the state's personal income tax rates rose from 7 percent to 11 percent, corporate income tax rates rose from 5.5 percent to 9 percent, and the sales tax rate rose from 3 percent to 4.75 percent.[32] Reagan never attempted to borrow to pay for routine state expenses.

Governor Reagan tried to restrain the growth in state spending, which nevertheless rose rapidly during his eight years in office. He was particularly successful in cutting the growth in mental health services, which contributed to a significant rise in the homeless population. The governor backed off from an attempt to purge the rolls of California's Medicaid program—one of the most generous in the nation—after his first year in office.

Professional football player Jack Kemp worked as an intern in Reagan's office in 1967 before returning to training camp. In 1970, when he retired from football after a knee injury, Kemp ran for Congress in Buffalo, New York—where he had earlier led the Bills to championships. Kemp instantly became a national GOP star after winning in a district with a blue-collar Democratic constituency. His passionate support for federal civil rights legislation and belief in a strong public social safety net distinguished him from many traditional conservatives.

The charismatic congressman attracted a circle of friends committed to altering the direction of the Republican Party. They included Congressman

David Stockman of Michigan and editorial writer Jude Wanniski. Wanniski developed his own theory of American budget politics after reading Herbert Stein's account of mid-twentieth-century fiscal history, *The Fiscal Revolution in America*. Wanniski's "two Santa Claus theory" tried to explain why Republicans had been a congressional minority for all but four years since the onset of the Great Depression. He noted that when Republicans last obtained an enduring congressional majority—in the 1920s—party leaders such as Andrew Mellon and Calvin Coolidge promised lower tax rates. Democrats became the majority when they offered more services during the New Deal. Wanniski believed this history framed a potential competition between two different political Santa Clauses—a Democratic one delivering more services and a Republican one delivering lower taxes. Wanniski faulted Republicans for not playing their role more adeptly. By giving a priority to balanced budgets rather than tax cuts, Republicans were perceived to be more like Scrooge than Santa. The editorial pages of the *Wall Street Journal* and Kemp's speaking tours helped publicize Wanniski's views.

Many other Republicans were troubled by their party's lack of a clear budget policy. Nixon had embraced greater federal responsibilities and spending. Ford had gained ground in Republican primaries by attacking Reagan on his proposal to slash federal support for education, cancer research, Medicaid, and other popular programs. If balanced budgets precluded tax cuts, and many Republicans agreed to fund Cold War defense and other large federal financial commitments, then what was the distinctive vision of the modern GOP?

The energetic Kemp, who called cuts in social spending "barbaric," offered a straightforward answer. Republicans should cut tax rates and not worry so much about the level of spending. Just when soaring inflation pushed vast numbers of middle-income Americans into higher brackets, Kemp sponsored a bill to cut all personal income tax rates by 30 percent. An unofficial "Kemp for President" bandwagon began to roll and stopped only when presidential candidate Reagan agreed to embrace Kemp's tax plan in exchange for the congressman's endorsement.

Reagan's economic advisors were relieved by calculations showing that revenues lost as a result of the lower rates would be offset by revenue gains from inflation that pushed taxpayers into higher brackets. By assuming a high future rate of inflation, Reagan could promise tax cuts while avoiding the political problem of slashing federal spending. Another 1980

Republican presidential candidate, the onetime congressman and former CIA director George H. W. Bush of Texas, was not so sure. Before Bush became Reagan's running mate, he derided Reagan's plan to increase defense spending, cut taxes, and balance a budget already in deficit as "voodoo economics."[33]

Carter trailed Reagan in the polls, especially after a failed attempt to rescue the hostages from Iran, the tightening of consumer credit, and the economic downturn in the spring of 1980. Reagan's plan, drafted by a polling expert, appealed to Democratic voters by emphasizing social themes—such as the preservation of families and neighborhoods—rather than budget issues. The campaign plan stated that "people act on the basis of their perception of reality; there is, in fact, no political reality beyond what is perceived by the voters."[34] That was particularly true for a candidate who did not have to govern or cast votes in Congress while running for the presidency.

As the election neared, journalists and business leaders pressed the former California governor for a budget plan with concrete numbers. Editorial writers pressed Reagan to explain how he could balance the budget with Kemp's tax cuts and Jackson's ambitious boost in military spending. Despite the ongoing hostage crisis and a slowing economy, by early September 1980 Carter began gaining momentum. Reagan's campaign chairman, William Casey, and campaign manager, James Baker, set out to allay doubts about whether the former Hollywood actor was prepared to be president. Casey arranged for Reagan to give a speech on budget policy buttressed by a "fact sheet" circulated to the press.

On September 8, 1980, after Reagan signed off on the text of the speech, Baker noticed that the fact sheet showed a rise in the projected deficit to $50 billion in the first fiscal year of his prospective presidency.[35] Baker, a former conservative Democrat from Texas, pointedly asked how Reagan could hope to be elected as a conservative if his proposed budget incurred more debt than did Carter's. The fact sheet's author, economic advisor Martin Anderson, was asked to rework it in order to reduce the projected deficit.

Anderson prepared to confront the hard trade-off between Reagan's commitments on tax cuts and military spending. He ultimately escaped the choice by relying on a Senate Budget Committee forecast showing that sustained high rates of inflation and economic growth would produce a phenomenal 80 percent rise in nominal national income within five years.

With those assumptions, federal tax revenues were projected to soar from $610 billion in fiscal 1981 to $1.1 trillion in 1985. The Senate Budget Committee's forecast already included a planned Pentagon buildup on the scale advocated by Reagan. Anderson's revised fact sheet outlined a budget for the fiscal year beginning October 1, 1981, with a modest deficit of $21 billion, a 10 percent cut in tax rates, and a freeze in all nondefense spending.[36] Anderson later referred to the fact sheet as "the essence of the original Reaganomics program."[37]

That fact sheet laid the groundwork for the momentous budget decisions a few months later. Unfortunately, the projections used by both the Senate Budget Committee and Reagan's advisors rested on assumptions with flaws that should have become more obvious with each passing month. Estimates for the fiscal year beginning October 1, 1980, showed far higher federal revenues than would actually be collected; every successive month's record of tax collections should have made that more apparent.

The premises underlying the fact sheet also contradicted the economic theories espoused by Reagan himself. The fact sheet rested on the assumption that rapid economic growth occurred even with high tax rates and that the Federal Reserve's restriction of the money supply had little impact on either growth or inflation. Moreover, the fact sheet included a freeze on much spending in the unified budget—combining the federal funds budget with trust fund budgets—and therefore confused the relationship between various types of federal taxes and the spending paid for by each of those taxes. One could not freeze Social Security pension benefits and count on surplus payroll taxes to balance the federal funds budget; certainly no mainstream politician supported the diversion of payroll taxes for that purpose. If one removed trust funds interest and defense from a proposed spending freeze, balancing the federal funds budget would require cutting a third of domestic spending, not just a spending freeze.[38]

After Reagan's weak performance in the first presidential debate, speech coach Roger Ailes encouraged the candidate return to his polished style of storytelling. Reagan used this talent at the next debate when responding to criticism from Congressman John Anderson of Illinois, the Republican-turned-Independent candidate. When Anderson pressed Reagan to require that tax cuts be conditioned on spending cuts, Reagan quipped that the best way to discipline a spendthrift teenager was to cut his allowance. That analogy made less sense if the teenager could use a credit card. Reagan had used the same analogy when advocating a cap in the growth of taxes during his second term as governor, when California's constitution prohibited the use of debt to fund operations.

On the night of Reagan's victory in November 1980, a CBS News/ *New York Times* exit poll showed that voters were most concerned about "inflation and economy" (33 percent); "jobs and employment" (24 percent); and "balancing the federal budget" (21 percent). Only 10 percent identified tax cuts as the highest priority. By a margin of 53 percent to 30 percent, voters rejected the idea that "cutting taxes is more important than balancing the federal budget."[39] Reagan won by more than a two-to-one among voters who identified balancing the budget as a top priority. Reagan reassured them by evoking the values underlying the American Fiscal Tradition in his inaugural address: "You and I as individuals can, by borrowing, live beyond our means, but only for a limited period of time. Why should we think that collectively, as a nation, we are not bound by that same limitation?"[40]

CAMPAIGN COMMITMENTS AND FLAWED PROJECTIONS

At Kemp's urging, Reagan chose the thirty-four-year-old congressman David Stockman to serve as budget director. Stockman, who had served as an unofficial budget expert for a group of House Republicans, worked nonstop to prepare a budget incorporating Reagan's tax and spending commitments. That budget for fiscal year 1982, beginning in October 1981, assumed an annual inflation rate of 7.7 percent and economic growth at the extraordinary rate of 5.2 percent. Budget insiders called that projection "the Rosy Scenario."[41] Estimates based on those premises showed that tax revenues would skyrocket without a cut in tax rates, much like projected revenues in Anderson's fact sheet. While in hindsight those projections may seem like a ploy to ease the passage of Reagan's agenda, both the Congressional Budget Office and Carter's outgoing Office of Management and Budget used similar assumptions.

The Federal Reserve's restrictive monetary policy was, however, dropping the rate of inflation and slowing down the economy. Estimates of tax revenues should have declined as those trends pushed less taxable income into higher tax brackets.

Stockman cut some federal spending, notably for research and development of alternative energy sources. Members of Reagan's cabinet resisted most other cuts. Budget cuts proposed by the Reagan administration were dwarfed by the higher requested spending for national security—the single largest component of the federal funds budget.

In January 1981 Secretary of Defense Caspar Weinberger, a former assistant federal budget director, convinced Stockman to increase defense spending for fiscal year 1982 by a larger amount than Reagan had promised during the campaign. Stockman only later realized that he had failed to fully account for the impact of the massive increase in defense spending for fiscal 1981.

Even with the optimistic revenue estimates, Stockman's budget contained a projected deficit greater than the one listed in the September 1980 fact sheet. The young budget director reviewed a draft of his budget with Senate Budget Committee Chairman Pete Domenici, Senate Finance Chairman Bob Dole, and Senate Majority Leader Howard Baker. Baker agreed that the budget would need to show savings of at least $44 billion from unspecified sources—a "magic asterisk"—in order to create the appearance of a lower deficit.[42] The Senate Budget Committee—including its Republican majority—did not accept magic asterisk accounting and voted down the resolution containing Reagan's budget. The committee recoiled at the prospect of a debt-financed tax cut.

On March 30, 1981, President Reagan was shot. Americans admired the grit and grace that he demonstrated during his recovery.

The president delivered a moving speech before a large television audience on April 28. Members of Congress greeted him with a long and emotional standing ovation. Reagan began by noting that his health had improved, but the economy had not. After criticizing the size of the national debt, he called on Congress to lower tax rates. Members of Congress were about to return home for their Easter recess, and Reagan framed the question he asked them to pose to their constituents: "Our choice is not between a balanced budget and a tax cut. Properly asked, the question is, 'Do you want a great big raise in your taxes this coming year or, at the worst, a very little increase with the prospect of a tax reduction and a balanced budget down the road a ways?'"[43]

Majority Leader Jim Wright had been lining up votes for a Democratic budget alternative. After Reagan's speech, Wright confided to his diary that the president's aura of heroism had left those opposing him "outflanked and outgunned."[44] Congressman Jack Kemp pushed forward without even the promise of a balanced budget "down the road a ways."

He told the House Budget Committee: "The Republican Party no longer worships at the altar of a balanced budget."[45]

Stockman was unable to replace the magic asterisk with real cuts. At one point he proposed to freeze the level of Social Security benefits, though that action would not close the gap in the federal funds budget and validated fears that the administration intended to compensate for tax cuts by reducing pensions. A Senate resolution condemning Stockman's idea passed unanimously.

NEW CONGRESSIONAL TAX LEADERSHIP

Never in the nation's history had a president proposed large, simultaneous spending increases and tax cuts when the federal budget already had a deficit. For decades powerful House and Senate chairmen like Wilbur Mills and Harry Byrd had killed tax initiatives that threatened fiscal discipline. In 1981, however, both the House and Senate tax committees had new chairmen, and each was busy trying to consolidate support in Congress for his leadership.

The new Democratic chairman of the Ways and Means Committee, Representative Dan Rostenkowski of Chicago, knew how to count votes. He had joined the Ways and Means Committee five years after being elected to Congress at age thirty. For years Rostenkowski had deferred to Mills and to Mayor Richard Daley of Chicago. He earned a reputation as an effective negotiator, and he would need that skill—and more—to maximize his bargaining power in the conference committees that reconciled differences between the House and Senate tax bills. Since the Republican-led Senate Finance Committee had the backing of the White House, Rostenkowski had to count on solid support from House Democrats. In 1981 most House Democrats represented districts in or bordering the South, where Reagan had a strong following.

Before the assassination attempt and the president's comeback speech, Rostenkowski declared that Reagan's plan for large, multiyear tax cuts was "dead."[46] He planned to compete with Reagan by offering a less costly tax cut rather than insisting on a balanced budget.

Quick-witted senator Bob Dole of Nebraska had replaced Russell Long as chairman of the Senate Finance Committee. Dole, a disabled veteran with a national profile from his stint as Ford's running mate, was a traditional conservative who questioned the wisdom of debt-financed tax cuts.

In 1981, however, he was unwilling to fight his party's new president or allow the House to dominate tax policy.

Rostenkowski and the rest of the Democratic House leadership endured a stunning loss in the first round of the budget fight after Reagan's speech. Republicans and an allied group of Southern Democrats found an innovative way to use the budget reconciliation procedure created by Congress the previous year. That procedure gave a majority in Congress the power to direct committees—including the Ways and Means Committee—to prepare legislation conforming to revenue estimates and spending ceilings adopted in the annual budget resolution. On May 7, 1981, House members working with Stockman won a close vote amending the House Budget Committee's resolution. Their amendment, which passed over the opposition of the Speaker and every single committee chairman, bound the Ways and Means Committee to prepare legislation that included at least the first year of Reagan's proposed tax cut.

Afterwards the Senate and House tax committees devised more tax reductions for businesses than had been proposed by the White House, a process observers characterized as a bidding war. However, while the Reagan administration had sought to phase in reductions in tax rates over three years, Rostenkowski's Ways and Means Committee conditioned the third installment on a balanced budget.

In June 1981 a worried Stockman showed the president projections of rising future deficits, a prospect Reagan said he could not "accept."[47] Reagan met in the White House with House Republican leaders and Congressman Kent Hance from Lubbock, Texas, an organizer of the thirty-one-member Conservative Democratic Forum that had helped the White House win the reconciliation resolution. Hance and many conservative members in both parties represented districts with a large number of seniors, veterans, and farmers who depended on federal programs that had largely escaped budget cuts. Hance told the president that if the White House insisted on lower spending, its tax bill would "be in a heap of trouble."[48] Reagan backed down on the issue of additional spending cuts.

On July 27 the president delivered a nationally televised speech opposing the House plan to link the third installment of the tax cut to a balanced budget. Based on the assumption that high inflation would continue to push taxpayers into ever higher brackets, the president held up a chart showing Americans that their taxes would go up "22 percent in three years" without his tax plan.[49] After the speech, Hance successfully amended the House tax bill to remove the restriction on the third install-ment of the tax cut. Debt would have to replace the foregone tax revenues. The House passed the tax bill with a bipartisan vote, 323–107.

A young Republican in West Texas whom Hance had beaten to enter Congress just three years earlier, George W. Bush, closely followed the 1981 budget debate. After that defeat, the vice president's son vowed never again to be "good ol' boyed" by a populist like Hance. In prior decades the district in which both Hance and Bush lived had reelected George Mahon, the conservative former chairman of the House Appropriations Commit-tee. Mahon had always given priority to balanced budgets. Bush's father had gained little traction with sound arguments based on budget math during his primary challenge of Reagan. Perhaps something was changing in the definition of a fiscal conservative.

One sign of that change occurred shortly after passage of the tax bill; Stockman warned his former colleagues in the Republican House leader-ship about the need to slash spending in order to avoid record peacetime borrowing. The chairman of the House Republican Policy Committee, Representative Dick Cheney of Wyoming, replied to Stockman: "The deficit isn't the worst thing that could happen."[50]

BORROWING FOR UNSPECIFIED PURPOSES

The debate over the budget in August 1981 did not indicate a deliberate decision to incur vast debts. Official budget estimates at that time had not yet incorporated the effects of a deteriorating economy and lower infla-tion. The House budget resolution, passed in the spring, projected a $24.8 billion deficit—the lowest in years. The final budget resolution emerging from the conference committee forecasted an only slightly larger $37.6 billion deficit.[51] Moreover, the multiyear budget forecast showed that the budget could be balanced by 1984.

Unexpected deficits were nothing new. For decades good faith esti-mates by professionals in the White House Budget Office had failed to correctly anticipate the precise levels of spending and tax revenues for the next fiscal year.[52]

With polls that showed overwhelming public support for a constitu-tional amendment requiring a balanced budget, few in Congress embraced routine borrowing as a matter of policy. As the size of the budget gap be-came more apparent in the fall of 1981, Republican Senate and House leadership did not publicly justify debt as a means of paying for tax cuts and higher defense spending. Then, and throughout his presidency, Reagan consistently denied that the federal government borrowed for those purposes.

In late 1981, Stockman and senior Senate Republicans tried once more to curb future borrowing. Slowing the rate of the military buildup offered the most obvious means of cutting the deficit, yet Stockman largely failed to reduce defense spending in his three meetings with the president and Secretary of Defense Weinberger from July through September 1981. The increase in Department of Defense spending in fiscal year 1981 was so large that Pentagon planners scrambled to develop new programs. Pentagon spending, even excluding larger outlays for foreign military assistance and veterans, would increase from $134 billion in fiscal year 1980 to $253 billion in 1985.[53] The Reagan administration asked for even more money for the military than Congress appropriated every fiscal year after 1982.

Senate Republicans offered the president their own concrete plan to balance the budget. At a White House meeting, Budget Committee Chairman Pete Domenici spoke for the group, which included Majority Leader Baker, Finance Committee Chairman Dole, and the president's closest political friend, Senator Paul Laxalt of Nevada. Domenici told the president that the budget included money "for feeding babies, for building roads, for cancer research, for the national parks, the FBI. We'll help you squeeze 'em, but we can't bleed 'em. You're just going to have to have some more revenue."[54] He proposed to balance the budget by scaling back tax cuts and imposing new spending cuts split equally between domestic and defense programs. Reagan replied curtly, "We can't solve it with more of tax and spend."[55] The Reagan administration instead opted to borrow and spend.

Early in 1981, Stockman had projected a balanced budget by 1984. By November he was forecasting a record $146 billion deficit in 1984 and $700 billion over five years.[56] In later interviews he acknowledged the flawed early budget projections and the failure to link spending and taxes, but he commented that he stayed on the job "to help correct the enormous fiscal error that I had done so much to bring about. . . . There was no longer any revolution to betray, only a shambles to repair."[57]

The American Fiscal Tradition suffered a setback in 1981, though support for its underlying principles had not collapsed. Some of the borrowing during a severe recession that began in late 1981 could be considered a traditional use of debt. The nation was ready for cuts in personal income tax rates, since many Americans felt that the top marginal tax rate of 70 percent, or a rate of 32 percent that reached those considered to be middle class, was unfair and excessive in the absence of an emergency. After 1981 no prominent federal leader in either party advocated a reversion to the 1980 income tax rates. The fiscal year 1982 budget did, however, sever the tight link between spending and tax policies. The traditional pillar of "pay as you go" budget planning would take years to be rebuilt.

By the end of 1981 Reagan recognized that something had gone wrong. He publicly announced that he was "ready to veto any bill that abuses the limited resources of the taxpayers," though he rarely vetoed spending bills as the deficit continued to widen.[58] In his diary he mused: "We who were going to balance the budget face the biggest budget deficits ever."[59]

15

THE TRADITION SURVIVES, THOUGH ITS PILLARS ERODE

1982–1989: Years when deficits exceeded debt service = 8
(1982–1989, higher spending on
interest expense and the Cold War)

THE FIGHT TO RESTORE FISCAL DISCIPLINE

For almost two centuries the federal government had borrowed for four clearly understood purposes. After 1981, however, federal leaders negotiated limits on the amount of annual borrowing but could not agree on a rationale for the debt incurred. This shift eroded a critical pillar of the American Fiscal Tradition: explicit congressional authorization of debt for a temporary and defined purpose. Democrats blamed projected deficits on Reagan's tax cuts and rising military budgets, though many in their party voted for those tax cuts and the Carter administration planned defense spending in line with the amounts Congress appropriated in the 1980s. Reagan blamed the deficits on domestic spending, though most domestic spending programs did not rise as a share of national income and the president never vetoed any formula-based entitlement spending. Both the president and members of Congress tried to avoid the stigma associated with *explicit* debt financing of their favored policies and programs.

President Reagan's initial speeches on economic policy emphasized fiscal discipline and the need to avoid pushing the nation's total debt to a trillion dollars. For example, in his State of the Union address in February 1981 he lamented that a debt of a trillion dollars would be "a stack of thousand-dollar bills 67 miles high."[1] As debt ballooned to over $2 trillion within a few years, the president dropped that illustration. Instead, he referred to a "structural deficit" in the budget.[2] Budget commentators adopted the phrase to describe a gap between federal commitments and revenues that would persist even with normal economic growth. The phrase conveniently implied that the budget had a "structure" independent of Congress's annual votes or bills signed by the president.

By the second year of the Reagan presidency, financial markets—and many senators—recoiled at spiraling federal debt. When Reagan submitted a budget with an estimated $100 billion deficit, the Senate Budget Committee rejected it by a vote of 20 to 0.[3] Ways and Means Chairman Dan Rostenkowski waited for presidential leadership to close the budget gap. Instead, Reagan pushed for a constitutional amendment requiring a balanced budget but never submitted a budget to Congress that balanced. Senate Finance Committee Chairman Bob Dole stepped in to fill the budget leadership vacuum.

The Constitution requires that tax legislation originate in the House, an obstacle Dole circumvented by amending a minor House bill to add significant tax increases. He called the tax provisions "revenue enhancement" and lined up every single Republican senator to vote for it.[4] Ways and Means Chairman Rostenkowski cooperated with Dole by moving the amended bill directly to a conference committee. Dole and Rostenkowski, with the help of Chief of Staff James Baker, enlisted votes on the House floor for the bill emerging from the conference committee. After delivering a televised address in which he complained about the deficit and applauded "tax reform," Reagan worked to secure the votes of a majority of House Republicans and agreed to send a letter thanking each Democrat who voted for it.[5] Speaker Tip O'Neill and Rostenkowski gathered enough Democratic votes to pass the bill, which the president signed without comment.

The Tax Equity and Fiscal Responsibility Act of 1982 did not quite live up to the promise of its name. Much of the bill's tax increase resulted from undoing certain corporate tax reductions passed the year before. The law also required that income tax be withheld from dividend and interest payments and raised cigarette taxes and taxes for unemployment insurance. In late 1982 Congress also doubled gasoline taxes dedicated to the highway and transit fund and imposed strict controls on hospital costs reimbursed by Medicare Part A. Despite these actions to raise revenues, the deficit continued to rise as a result of soaring interest on expense, higher defense costs, and high unemployment. With November 1982 midterm elections looming and the deficit growing, senators sought political cover by passing a constitutional amendment to balance the budget.

The eventual political success of Reagan's presidency was not apparent in late 1982. Reagan ended the year with a public approval rating of 41 percent, down from 68 percent following the assassination attempt.[6] Democrats gained twenty-seven seats in the House in the November midterm election. The remaining Republican House members, largely elected from districts with little Democratic competition, were more intensely partisan than Senate Republicans. An upstart young congressman from Georgia, Newt Gingrich, called Senator Dole the "tax collector for the welfare state" because of the senator's work to reduce the use of debt to finance routine spending.[7]

Treasury secretaries have, for the most part, served as guardians of fiscal discipline. Treasury Secretary Donald Regan, however, disparaged Dole's efforts as being "Keynesian," a term no economist—including those on the White House Council of Economic Advisers—would have applied to the efforts to reduce deficit spending.

Other members of the senior White House staff, led by James Baker, tried to restore fiscal discipline. Reagan's staff warned the president that the administration's "current long-term fiscal policy" would not "generate tax revenues to finance [proposed spending] even under ideal economic performance."[8] Budget Director David Stockman briefed the president on every federal program and asked for direction on where he should cut. Reagan identified annual cuts of less than $1 billion, a small dent in borrowing that had soared to well over $100 billion per year.[9]

Public support for the tradition of limited borrowing exerted an invisible but powerful pressure on post-1981 budget negotiations. When Reagan was told in early 1983 that the proposed White House budget for the next fiscal year would contain a $188.8 billion deficit, he said that he could not "go to the country with these deficits."[10] Congress responded with bipartisan applause when the president, in his 1983 State of the Union address, asked for a "standby-tax"—a three-year tax raising federal revenues by 1 percent of national income—combined with limits on federal spending. Later that year the House adopted a Democratic budget resolution with its own $174 billion deficit.[11]

Neither Reagan's senior economic advisors nor congressional leaders defended the practice of allowing interest on growing debt to absorb a greater share of future budgets. Conservative economist William A. Niskanen, who served on Reagan's Council of Economic Advisers, later concluded that "the administration did not have a deficit policy. It had a spending policy and a tax policy, and the deficit was an outcome rather than a target of these policies."[12] The president's first chairman of the Council of Economic Advisers, Murray Weidenbaum, commented upon his resignation, "On balance, we really haven't cut the budget. Instead, the much-publicized reduction in non-military programs . . . has been fully offset by the unprecedented growth in military spending. When you add that to the big tax cuts, you get . . . horrendous deficits."[13] His successor, Martin Feldstein, a market-oriented economist, also spoke frankly about the need to reduce annual borrowing. He told reporters that "we can't grow our way out of these deficits."[14]

BALANCING THE SOCIAL SECURITY BUDGET

Two pillars of the American Fiscal Tradition—"pay as you go" budget planning and explicit congressional votes on the purpose of new debt—started to crack in the 1980s. But a third pillar, the use of self-sustaining trust funds, remained strong enough to force hard choices about Social Security pensions.

The post-1972 automatic cost-of-living adjustments to Social Security benefits jeopardized the balance in the program's trust fund; high inflation and two recessions had caused benefits to rise faster than payroll tax revenues in an economy with both high inflation and sluggish growth. By 1981 Social Security actuaries concluded that the pension system would exhaust its funding within a year. Moreover, Congressman Jake Pickle of Texas, who chaired the Ways and Means Subcommittee on Social Security, warned of the need to prepare for the eventual retirement of Baby Boomers.

Chief of Staff James Baker advised the president to create a bipartisan panel to recommend a plan to restore the actuarial balance to the Social Security system. The National Commission on Social Security Reform included five members selected by Speaker Thomas "Tip" O'Neill, five by the Senate, and five by the White House. Alan Greenspan, a conservative economist, chaired the commission. As the Greenspan Commission approached the 1982 year-end deadline for its work, its members had agreed on goals and financial projections, but not on a specific legislative solution.[15] Baker and Greenspan held daily White House meetings with members of the commission to craft common ground on specific recommendations. Within weeks, twelve of the fifteen Greenspan Commission members agreed on a plan to raise payroll taxes, expand coverage to some public and nonprofit employees, impose income taxes on pensions, reduce benefits for early retirement, and gradually increase the retirement age from sixty-five to sixty-seven. The plan called for a measured rise in taxes for Social Security pensions and Medicare hospitalization to a level of 15.3 percent of covered payroll by 1990.

Despite organized opposition, Congress passed many of the Greenspan Commission's ambitious reforms in April 1983. President Reagan praised the bipartisan effort and noted that it demonstrated "for all time our nation's commitment to Social Security."[16] The Social Security Reform Act of 1983 showed that federal leaders could plan a generation ahead. The legislation enabled the pension trust fund to accumulate large pension reserves—a surplus of revenues over expenses—during the working years of Baby Boomers, to finance pensions for that generation.[17]

A large pension reserve for Baby Boomers placed the Social Security trust fund in actuarial balance, but the continued use of a unified budget disguised the amount of debt and annual borrowing in the federal funds budget, just as Senator Arthur Vandenberg had feared would happen. Since federal accounting included the revenues earmarked for pension reserves in the unified budget, it understated the deficit. The practice of subtracting the debt of trust funds from total debt—leaving a smaller reported "debt held by the public"—obscured the future obligations of the federal funds budget. There was nothing necessarily wrong or misleading about investing trust fund reserves in Treasury debt, which is a common practice of well-managed private firms offering annuities. But that investment should not allow the federal government to reduce its reported level of debt.

To prevent such abuse, the Greenspan Commission recommended that the trust funds be removed from the normal federal budget. Congress and the White House, however, were not anxious to highlight increasing debt. The legislation addressed the problem by requiring that trust funds for

Social Security and Medicare hospitalization be removed from the budget beginning ten years later. A few years later even that requirement was quietly dropped.[18]

The Greenspan Commission used reasonable assumptions in its actuarial projections, though one of them—concerning future income distribution—would prove to be inaccurate. The commission forecasted that the trust fund would continue to be in balance as long as the annual wage base subject to payroll taxes rose at the same rate as the liability for future benefits. The commission assessed payroll taxes at a level covering 90 percent of overall payroll in 1983 and indexed the annual increase in the wage ceiling to the average—rather than the median—rise in annual income from wages and salaries.[19] Before 1983 median income in America had risen in line with average income, and the Greenspan Commission's actuaries assumed that this historical linkage would continue. After 1983, however, total wages grew significantly faster than average wages. Incomes of Americans with at least one four-year college degree grew faster than the incomes of other employees, so average wages did not rise as much as incomes of workers above the ceiling on payroll taxes. As a result, by 2005 the Social Security wage base represented only 85 percent of wages and salaries, not the 90 percent the Greenspan Commission had assumed.[20] Much of the existing actuarial imbalance in the Social Security trust fund could be fixed using an adjustment of either the wage ceiling or benefits to compensate for that difference.

Contrary to popular belief, the commission accurately forecasted the ratio of retirees to workers. It also addressed a common criticism that wealthy Americans received pensions that they did not need. Workers with high incomes already received benefits at far lower levels in proportion to their contributions than others, and the 1983 reform applied a high tax rate to those Social Security benefits.

Social Security pensions had lifted many elderly citizens out of poverty. People can judge for themselves whether the pensions are too generous: the average Social Security pension in 2013 was about $1,100 a month, an amount that provided the principal source of income for many older Americans.[21]

Today it is common to hear that the "real problem" with balancing the budget is the growth of "entitlements," including Social Security. In fact, the balance between revenues and spending in the Social Security trust fund is far better than in the federal funds budget, which excludes trust funds.

BUDGET BLAME AND SEQUESTRATIONS

Though the economy grew during the third through fifth fiscal years of the Reagan administration, taxes paid for only $1.354 trillion of the $2.121 trillion in federal funds spending.[22] In short, the United States borrowed to pay for one out of every three dollars it spent apart from trust fund revenues. This gap represented about 5.5 percent of national income, a level of borrowing comparable to that during the Great Depression.[23] In the words of Federal Reserve Chairman Paul Volcker, "the deficit ate up a lot of our private savings, which were awfully low to start with by world standards and even by our own past performance."[24]

Reagan's budgets—like those during the New Deal—spawned partisan myths. Contrary to the view of some "supply side" analysts, President Reagan and his most senior advisors never believed that the tax cuts would somehow "pay for themselves" through increased economic growth. During his January 1983 State of the Union address, Reagan proposed a "standby" tax—not a new tax cut—to reduce deficits.[25]

A second pervasive myth is that the Reagan administration made significant cuts in New Deal and Great Society programs. The largest of these programs—Social Security pensions and Medicare—grew rapidly. As expressed by Reagan loyalist and principal domestic policy advisor Martin Anderson: "On the whole, President Reagan set spending records right and left."[26] The Reagan administration, however, did succeed in reducing spending in four much smaller programs: development of alternative energy technologies (a Ford and Carter initiative), community and regional development (a Johnson and Nixon initiative), training and employment (largely a Democratic congressional initiative), and general revenue sharing (a Nixon initiative).[27] Federal funds outlays during the eight fiscal years of the Reagan administration amounted to about 16.5 percent of total national income, while the average during Carter's four years was 15.5 percent.[28] During the Reagan administration federal funds spending as a share of national income far exceeded the level during the Clinton administration.

House Democratic leadership declined to force the president and the nation to choose between cutting back on popular domestic programs such as Medicare Part B or imposing higher taxes to pay for them. In one of the most unusual episodes in budget history, the House defeated seven different proposed budget resolutions in early 1983. Three of them attempted to balance the budget: one from moderate Democrats that cut all spending and raised revenues in equal amounts, one from "small government" Republicans that slashed domestic spending, and one from the Black Caucus that raised taxes and cut defense spending. The House finally adopted a budget that included less borrowing, more domestic spending, and lower military appropriations than did Reagan's budget. That budget allowed Democrats to highlight their domestic priorities but abdicated the high ground of a budget that actually balanced.

Former vice president Walter Mondale, in his televised speech accepting the Democratic presidential nomination in 1984, proclaimed that chronic borrowing would "hike interest rates, clobber exports, starve investment, [and] kill jobs."[29] He then proposed to cut the deficit by two-thirds in four years, in part by raising taxes. The idea of only gradually tapering off debt-financing belied the urgency and moral imperative of avoiding routine borrowing. If mortgaging future taxes to pay today's bills was so bad, why not immediately balance the budget?

As economic growth revived in 1984, so did the president's public approval rating. Yet Reagan's large reelection margin that year was hardly a partisan victory. Democratic candidates received a substantial majority of all votes cast for Congress. In the absence of a concrete plan by either party to immediately balance the budget, there was no clear mandate on how to do so.

The president and members of Congress had, however, heard public concerns about rising debt. In 1985 Republican senators, with some Democratic support, fought to restore budget discipline. The Senate failed by only one vote to pass a constitutional amendment—subject to state ratification—that required a balanced budget. Senate Appropriations Committee Chairman Mark Hatfield, a Republican, voted against it, explaining that Congress could always balance the budget by simply cutting spending.

Senators Pete Domenici and Bob Dole then crafted a budget resolution that limited the growth in defense spending and froze most other federal spending for a year, a freeze that eliminated the next annual inflation adjustment for Social Security pensions. Senate Republican leaders designed their plan to cut the budget deficits projected during Reagan's second term by at least half, a goal that had been embraced by both Reagan and Mondale during the 1984 presidential campaign. The Senate budget resolution reduced growth in future spending by more than any budget proposal adopted by the House or Senate since 1964.

The Democratic House responded with its own plan, which retained the inflation adjustment for Social Security while cutting military spending by a larger amount than did the Senate's. Reagan and Defense Secretary Caspar Weinberger bridled at congressional limits on defense spending. After the president and House Speaker O'Neill compromised by eliminating cuts to defense and pensions, an angry and frustrated Senate majority delayed action on the White House's request to raise the statutory debt ceiling above $2 trillion.[30]

This impasse led Congress to adopt the new budget procedures, in the form of the Gramm-Rudman-Hollings Balanced Budget and Emergency Deficit Act. The legislation, passed in late 1985, set annual limits on new debt that could be incurred in each of the next five years. That limit dropped by $36 billion a year until it reached zero.[31] Amounts borrowed from trust funds were excluded from that annual limit on debt.[32] The act included a distinctive enforcement mechanism: the controller—an unelected officeholder—was directed to "sequester," or not spend, certain amounts Congress had already appropriated in order to comply with the annual ceilings on debt. (Later, the sequestration authority was transferred to the White House.) The Gramm-Rudman-Hollings Act passed by lopsided margins in both the House and the Senate.[33] Those debt ceiling targets triggered potential sequestrations during five of the next six fiscal years. In each case, Congress and the White House reached some compromise that reduced the amounts scheduled to be sequestered and raised the limit on the debt ceiling.

In preparation for the 1985 budget, virtually all of the president's senior White House staff and economic advisors sought to shrink the administration's annual requests for military spending. Secretary Weinberger defended his proposed budget by showing the president two posters: one depicting a muscular G. I. Joe and the other a scrawny, shabbily clothed soldier. Weinberger prevailed with the president but not members of Congress, who slowed the growth in military spending.

Interest on the debt was the fastest growing component of federal spending in the late 1980s. Annual interest expense grew by $50 billion from 1986 through 1989.[34] In 1989 interest expenses were equal to half of the total amount of all federal funds spending in 1980.[35]

REFORMING THE
WORLD WAR II TAX SYSTEM

In 1986 the Treasury Department and Congress completed the most ambitious reform of the income tax system since World War II. While that
effort did not address the deferred tax bill accumulating as debt, but it
did remove significant economic distortions that had resulted from high
marginal rates of taxation on earned (noninvestment) income. The initiative was the brainchild of Senator Bill Bradley of New Jersey, a moderate
Democrat who cast the lone vote in the Senate Finance Committee against
the massive tax cut bill in 1981. The thoughtful Bradley was a former
professional basketball player who had observed firsthand how attempts
to shelter income from high tax rates skewed economic decisions. Professional athletes and others with high salaries could lower their net income
subject to taxes by making investments that generated early losses while
building asset value. Despite almost annual changes in the tax code, for
decades the average tax rate paid on the top line of personal income tax
returns had been about 13.5 percent.[36] In theory, personal income tax revenues could remain the same if Congress lowered tax rates while eliminating an adequate amount of exclusions and deductions.

Bradley's bill dropped the top tax rate from 50 percent to 30 percent
and made up the lost revenue by raising the tax rate on capital gains and
limiting the ability to lower taxable income with deductions for investment-
related expense.[37] For many years senators considered Bradley's proposal to
be naïve. The concept of broadening the tax base seemed easy in theory, but
income after deductions would have to double in order to offset the loss in
revenues from a one-third cut in tax rates. Moreover, most of the provisions
referred to as loopholes had once been enacted as beneficial incentives.

President Reagan called for tax reform in his 1984 State of the Union
address. Members of Congress responded with laughter, however, when
the president promised to recommend reforms only *after* the election
eleven months later. Reagan's 1981 tax initiative had, however, changed
the politics of federal income taxation. Many elected officials in both parties openly acknowledged that a top rate of 50 percent inevitably led to
attempts to shelter taxable income.

Following the 1984 election Secretary Regan and his Treasury Department staff presented their plan to lower personal tax rates and reduce deductions that had been designed as investment incentives. The Treasury

plan faltered after the president publicly questioned its net increase in corporate taxation. Republican Senate Finance Committee Chairman Bob Packwood believed that it did not "make sense" to pass tax legislation "without a dime's dent in the deficit."[38]

After White House Chief of Staff James Baker switched jobs with Treasury Secretary Regan in early 1985, he and Deputy Treasury Secretary Richard Darman prepared a new plan for tax reform. It did not close the budget gap but at least preserved the level of revenues projected under existing law while lowering personal tax rates on earned (noninvestment) income. Half the members of the Senate signed a letter opposing the consideration of such a revenue neutral tax reform until the federal government reduced its planned borrowing.[39]

Televised speeches by the president and the House Ways and Means Committee's Rostenkowski in May 1986 revived the prospects of tax reform. Rostenkowski crafted a plan that limited deductions and dropped the top tax rate from 50 to 38 percent.[40] With support from House Democrats and the White House, Rostenkowski's bill passed the House on a voice vote. Senate Finance Committee Chairman Packwood then reversed course and embraced the House initiative with certain changes.[41] Packwood and Rostenkowski personally negotiated a compromise that passed Congress with large bipartisan margins. The Tax Reform Act of 1986 lowered the top tax rate on personal income to 28 percent, though a phase-out of deductions for people with higher incomes made the top effective rate 33 percent.

When evaluating calls for tax reform or "closing loopholes" within the context of the fiscal crisis in the early twenty-first century, it is worth recalling some of the consequences of the celebrated 1986 tax reform.[42] Congress reduced personal income tax rates by imposing higher taxes on investment income, even though by the late 1980s national savings rates had fallen to a historic low. Immediately after the Tax Reform Act of 1986 raised the tax rate applied to capital gains, pressure mounted to lower it.

The act also produced an unintended consequence that haunted the budgets of Reagan's successor, George H. W. Bush. Commercial real estate prices and development collapsed after the legislation eliminated tax shelter incentives. Borrowers could not make payments on real estate loans, triggering claims on federal deposit insurance for savings and loans that would soon cost more than $200 billion.

From the end of the Korean War in 1953 through 1989, personal income taxes as a share of adjusted gross income ranged from a low of 11.5

percent in 1965 to a high of 15.7 percent in 1981.[43] During the Reagan administration the effective tax rate fell in the middle of that range. In the 1980s the share of gross income paid in federal personal income tax by the half of American taxpayers with the lowest incomes fell from 6.2 percent to 5.1 percent; the corresponding share for taxpayers with the highest incomes fell from 17.3 percent to 14.5 percent.[44] Most taxpayers did not experience a net reduction in federal taxes, however, because they paid higher payroll taxes in support of dedicated trust funds.[45] The other major revenue source for the federal funds budget—corporate income taxes— stagnated largely as a result of international competition. Federal leadership failed to either identify a replacement source of the revenues provided by corporate taxation or curtail the spending that had once been sustained by corporate taxation.

A MEDICARE IMPASSE

Americans have never liked to pay taxes. Ways and Means Chairman Robert Doughton noted early in the Korean War that everyone "wanted to do their full part in producing the revenue necessary . . . [but] claimed that any additional revenue should come from some other source."[46] The total payroll tax supporting pensions and Medicare hospitalization was scheduled to rise to 15.3 percent of covered payroll in 1990, an amount considered to be the upper limit by all federal leaders in each party.[47] So when Secretary of Health and Human Services Otis Bowen began exploring how Medicare could cover longer hospital stays, hospice care, and expensive prescription drugs, federal officials agreed that any new such services should be financed by taxes on the people who would be eligible for those benefits. The idea of a debt-financed expansion of Medicare remained far outside the political mainstream.

Passage of the Medicare Catastrophic Coverage Act of 1988 initially appeared to be a bipartisan triumph much like the Tax Reform Act of 1986. Medical providers and the American Association of Retired Persons endorsed the legislation's expansion of coverage paid for with a new tax on high-income seniors.

Yet many Medicare beneficiaries became enraged upon learning that the law required retirees to pay a higher share of Medicare costs, even though the tax applied only to beneficiaries with high incomes. Congress repealed the act in 1989. Politicians and budget officials squarely confronted the inevitable dilemma: if payroll taxes for Medicare Part A had reached their tolerable limit, and retired Americans would not pay premiums greater than 25 percent of the cost of Medicare Part B, who would pay the other 75 percent of the program's escalating costs?

Congress did not repeal a provision of the Medicare Catastrophic Coverage Act that required state-administered Medicaid programs to pay premiums and copays for seniors with very low incomes. Many seniors with long-term disabilities, such as dementia, would soon rely on this dual eligibility to pay for long-term, institutionalized care. Within a decade, seven million people with dual eligibility accounted for an annual cost of $50 billion from Medicare (24 percent of Medicare costs) and $63 billion from Medicaid (35 percent of Medicaid costs).[48]

Medicaid had evolved from the grant programs originally backed by conservative Robert Taft and the American Medical Association. By the late 1980s the program become a means of paying for long-term care for impoverished elderly and disabled Americans. This role for Medicaid in part reflected the modern sensitivity to the plight of citizens with age-related disabilities.[49] The federal mandate that required the use of matching state funds to pay Medicare premiums for Americans in nursing homes did, however, squeeze state budgets. Bill Clinton, governor of Arkansas, expressed the frustration of other governors when he criticized the federal attempt to obtain "universal coverage using the states' credit cards as the financing mechanism."[50]

By the end of the Reagan administration, tax policy had reached a stalemate. By then federal leaders in both parties acknowledged the importance of avoiding the distortions caused by the highest marginal tax rate. Republicans never defended debt-financed tax reduction as a matter of principle, yet they allowed the historical bond between spending and tax policies to fray. In 1988 Vice President Bush beat back a strong primary challenge from Bob Dole using a television ad attacking the senator for refusing to sign a pledge against higher taxes. Bush promised to limit future borrowing with a "flexible freeze" on federal spending. Bush courted antitax activists by punctuating his vow to oppose any tax increase with the phrase "read my lips."[51]

After Bush won the 1988 presidential election, former presidents Nixon, Ford, and Carter privately advised him to close the budget gap with a combination of lower spending and higher taxes. The president-elect also had to decide how to respond to the ongoing work of the National Economic

Commission, created by Congress and chaired by Drew Lewis, a former corporate executive and Reagan cabinet member, and Robert Strauss, a former chairman of the Democratic National Committee. Lewis and Strauss worked quietly to develop consensus balancing the budget by cutting spending and raising tax revenue. But in 1989 Bush refused to repudiate his tax pledge.

Bush's own cabinet wanted more flexibility and less freeze when he tried to implement the campaign promise of a "flexible freeze" on federal spending. Secretary of Housing and Urban Development Jack Kemp wanted to revitalize affordable housing programs. Secretary of Defense Dick Cheney asked for a larger military budget, and Secretary of State James Baker argued for financial assistance to help the Soviet Union move toward a market economy and a closer relationship with the West. The president himself championed federal leadership in making higher education more accessible. A spending freeze with so many exceptions was not so different from budget business as usual.

Ways and Means Committee Chairman Rostenkowski met with the president-elect shortly after the election. The chairman promised to give Bush a one-year grace period for pressing new tax legislation, but House Republicans gave the president little leeway. Despite a large deficit, they tried to cut the tax rate on capital gains. Senate Democrats felt betrayed when the president endorsed the House-sponsored tax legislation rather than considering tax legislation only as part of any overall plan to balance the budget.

Many senior economic officials pushed for a return to traditional budget discipline. Federal Reserve Chairman Alan Greenspan warned that he would not expand the money supply to finance continued deficits. Budget Director Richard Darman, a powerful figure in the Bush White House, explained the stakes: "Our deficits are disproportionately financing current consumption rather than investment in future productive capacity. . . . And unless this is corrected, our long-term economic future cannot be what Americans have traditionally hoped for and expected."[52]

Federal borrowing appeared to be out of control. The president—at heart a traditional fiscal conservative—had had enough of what he once termed "voodoo economics."

16

TRADITIONALISTS BATTLE BACK

*1990–2000: Years when deficits exceeded debt service = 7
(1990–1996, structural deficit)*

FIGHTING TO RESTORE FISCAL DISCIPLINE

Ways and Means Chairman Dan Rostenkowski and President Bush had starkly different political pedigrees. Bush was a Connecticut Yankee, the Yale-educated son of a Republican investment banker and US senator, while the Polish American Rostenkowski had learned politics from his father, an alderman in Chicago's Democratic machine. But they had some shared experiences. Both had been superb young baseball players and also were rookies in 1965 on Wilbur Mills's powerful team, the House Ways and Means Committee. They liked and trusted one other.

On March 6, 1990, Rostenkowski told Bush that he intended to get the ball rolling on a plan to close the budget gap. Rostenkowski's proposal—which included a freeze on all cost-of-living adjustments for federal benefits and a higher gasoline tax—would undoubtedly generate controversy. Budget realities and a sense of responsibility for the nation's future soon moved the president to do more than watch Rostenkowski's initiative from the sidelines. A slowing economy and obligations arising from federal deposit insurance had pushed projected deficits to record levels. Without congressional action, the Gramm-Rudman-Hollings debt ceilings would soon require the president to sequester an estimated $100 billion appropriated by Congress for the following fiscal year.[1] That spring Bush invited congressional leaders from both parties to a series of White House budget meetings.

Progress stalled. Democratic senators refused to make any new budget proposals until the president publicly endorsed the elements of a realistic plan to balance the budget. On June 26, 1990, the White House released a statement calling for "entitlement and mandatory program reform; tax revenue increases; growth incentives; discretionary spending reductions; orderly reduction in defense expenditures; and budget process reform."[2] Although the president's chief of staff, John Sununu, tried to distinguish "tax revenue increases" from higher taxes, Bush could not deny the clear implication of his statement. That shift produced turmoil in the ranks of House Republicans, many of whom learned first from journalists about the demise of the "read my lips" campaign promise.

Previous presidents had carefully rallied public support for balanced budgets by unambiguously stating that peacetime borrowing threatened the nation's future. The sacrifices required to actually balance the budget and the record of the Reagan administration required Bush to finesse the issue.

After secret negotiations, acrimonious debate, a brief shutdown of the government, and an initial defeat in the House, Congress passed and Bush signed the Omnibus Budget Reconciliation Act of 1990. The act affirmed the influence of the traditional fiscal constitution while also revealing a challenge from some House Republicans who preferred to tolerate deficits—a form of deferred taxation—rather than vote for an immediate tax increase. They were led by Newt Gingrich, a former Rockefeller Republican who had become a partisan hero after bringing down Democratic Speaker of the House Jim Wright in 1989. In the 1990 budget negotiations Gingrich told Budget Director Richard Darman that he intended to discredit the federal government, including President Bush, and "in four years" ride the resulting backlash to the House speakership.[3] In doing so, Gingrich forced the president to give greater weight to the priorities of House Democrats in order to muster a congressional majority.

The Omnibus Budget Reconciliation Act of 1990 raised revenues and set multiyear limits on annual growth in federal funds spending for defense and all domestic programs except for those funded by formula, such as Medicare. It also significantly reformed budget procedures. One portion of the legislation—the Budget Enforcement Act of 1990—allowed members of Congress to block proposed new appropriations or tax legislation that would raise spending or lower revenues relative to annual targets.

The Budget Enforcement Act proved to be the single most effective budget reform since the Budget and Accounting Act of 1921. It required Congress to confine defense appropriations and a large portion of domestic spending to annual ceilings.

The Congressional Budget Office (CBO) projected that the Omnibus Budget Reconciliation Act of 1990 would cut federal borrowing by almost $500 billion over five years compared to the benchmark of "business as usual."[4] The CBO estimated that the act reduced planned growth in defense spending by $125 billion, raised various sales taxes and user fees by slightly more than $100 billion, limited Medicare payments by $37 billion, and increased both income taxes and payroll taxes by $40 billion.[5] The act's effectiveness was not immediately apparent, however, since its adoption coincided with a recession, spiraling costs of deposit insurance for savings and loans, and a spike in Medicare spending for home health care. The 1990 budget agreement did, however, create a framework for the restoration of fiscal discipline in the ensuing decade.

THE EMERGENCE OF H. ROSS PEROT

Public frustration with the ballooning federal debt played a critical role in the 1992 election. Two candidates for the Democratic presidential nomination—Paul Tsongas and Bob Kerrey—called for a return to traditional budget discipline. Another candidate, Bill Clinton, had balanced budgets as governor of Arkansas and chaired the centrist Democratic Leadership Council. The young governor's six-page "Plan for America" endorsed more spending for medical insurance, education, and infrastructure—all financed with higher taxes for Americans with incomes over $200,000—and middle-class tax relief.[6] Tsongas was not impressed with Clinton's approach, and accused him of running for "Santa Claus." By March 1992, Clinton's superior organization and tenacity had produced an insurmountable lead in the race for the nomination.

A remarkable new political force then burst onto the national stage and highlighted the power of the American Fiscal Tradition. Texas businessman H. Ross Perot was not even an official candidate for the presidency when he began to ride a tidal wave of support. With the demeanor of a no-nonsense businessman, Perot evoked the fundamental values underlying a balanced budget. Because all mainstream politicians agreed with the ideal of a balanced budget, they appeared incompetent when they failed to obtain one. On March 6, when pressed by talk show host Larry King about his presidential ambitions, Perot said he would run if volunteer organizations qualified him for the ballots in all fifty states. More than a million volunteers responded. By May Perot, who just two months earlier had been largely unknown to a majority of Americans, led both Clinton and President Bush in the polls.[7]

Perot used memorable language to remind Americans of how routine borrowing compromised the future, diverted savings from investment, and made the United States more dependent on foreign creditors. No major presidential candidate in recent history had so unequivocally defended the American Fiscal Tradition.

Perot promised to use his business experience to balance the budget "without breaking a sweat."[8] When challenged to provide more details, he committed to do so "in 60 days."[9] Since balancing the budget would require hard choices, Perot cautioned Americans that "if you want Lawrence Welk music, I'm not your man."[10] Perot's support began to falter in June and early July, when he stumbled on other issues and had trouble managing tensions between campaign professionals and his army of volunteers.

Clinton's campaign scrambled to release a new budget plan ahead of Perot. Clinton's plan retained the spending limits imposed by the Omnibus Budget Reconciliation Act of 1990 and pledged to expand federal medical insurance by finding savings in Medicare. It also assumed faster economic growth than other forecasts and endorsed an undefined new tax on the profits of foreign corporations. The Clinton campaign claimed its plan would cut the deficit in half within four years.

As the incumbent, President Bush would have to be more specific than Clinton when responding to Perot's budget challenge. He had little room to maneuver, however, since the 1990 budget agreement had already set limits on federal funds spending apart from formula-based programs such as Medicare. Budget Director Darman noted that Medicare costs could be lowered by tighter ceilings on reimbursements and higher premiums and copayments for beneficiaries; President Bush characterized those ideas as being simply options when pressed on the issue.[11]

Clinton surged past Bush after Perot bowed out of the contest on July 16, at the end of the Democratic National Convention. Clinton's candidacy received a boost when Perot attributed his departure from the race in part to a "revitalized Democratic Party."[12]

The restless Perot found it difficult to remain on the sidelines. Weeks after his July withdrawal, he challenged Bush and Clinton to adopt the forthright budget policies outlined in his best-selling book, *United We Stand*. Perot's proposal extended the 1990 ceilings on growth of federal funds spending, imposed higher income tax rates and payroll taxes on the wealthiest Americans, limited tax deductions, raised premiums for Medicare Part B, increased fuel taxes, and cut planned spending for defense and agricultural programs. Many of those ideas would be enacted in the following years.

Perot reentered the race on October 1. Though polls showed that the Texan's popularity had plummeted following his abrupt summer withdrawal, his communication skill and quirky candor commanded public attention. Perot's thirty-minute televised budget briefings—"infomercials"—attracted large prime-time audiences. A plurality of Americans thought Perot "won" three presidential debates in which he reminded citizens of the need to end routine federal borrowing. According to Perot, "for 45 years we were preoccupied with the Red Army," and "now our number one preoccupation is red ink."[13] His closing statement in the final debate, which he replayed as his last television ad, urged Americans to vote for the candidate they would trust "to take care of your children if something happened to you."[14] Many Americans agreed with Perot's approach to the budget even as they voted for Bush or Clinton.

Clinton won the election with only 43 percent of the vote and did not forget the economic appeal of Perot's candidacy.[15] Before Clinton's inauguration he convened an economic summit at which participants emphasized the priority of lower deficits. Federal Reserve Chairman Alan Greenspan counseled the president-elect that fiscal discipline would lead to lower interest rates and greater long-term job growth. According to Greenspan, any debt-financed stimulus would backfire by raising interest rates, since financial markets feared that continued borrowing would lead to inflationary monetary expansion. Greenspan predicted a severe financial crisis in the late 1990s unless the federal government reduced routine borrowing.

Greenspan later wrote that although he "hadn't put it in so many words, the hard truth was that Reagan had borrowed from Clinton, and Clinton was having to pay it back."[16] When Clinton took office, budget experts projected that business-as-usual unified budgets would produce deficits rising to $360 billion in 1997 and $500 billion in 2000.[17] Federal funds borrowing would rise by even more.

Clinton's two senior budget advisors, Secretary of the Treasury Lloyd Bentsen and Budget Director Leon Panetta, helped set the new administration's fiscal tone. They knew budget politics as well as anyone in Washington. Bentsen, a fiscally conservative Democrat, had been a successful businessman before serving for two decades in the Senate, including six years as chairman of the Senate Finance Committee. The tall, thin, and reserved Texan provided a physical contrast to the squat and amiable Panetta, who had worked to limit deficits while serving as a California congressman. In early 1993 Panetta and Democratic House leaders warned the president that unless he took the initiative in cutting planned future federal spending, Congress would do so on its own terms. Many new House Democrats had been elected from districts where Perot had strong support.

Panetta and Bentsen crafted a plan to cut the projected deficit in the unified budget by $140 billion—about 40 percent—within four years.[18] That plan included a controversial new tax on energy use. Members of Clinton's political staff were disappointed that the draft budget made little progress on the campaign's pledges of greater access to medical insurance and federal investments in economic growth. Clinton responded that the White House could not "lie about the deficit."[19] He personally reviewed the budget in an attempt to find savings to offset the new costs of the spending proposed during his campaign. Once, in frustration, he complained that budget realities forced him to govern like an Eisenhower Republican.

Financial markets responded positively to the emphasis on fiscal discipline in the president's first budget address. Clinton's budget itself, however, included new spending for "stimulus" and "investments" that exceeded the annual ceiling on domestic spending imposed by the 1990 budget agreement. Senate Majority Leader Robert Byrd tried to maneuver around that ceiling, but was blocked in the spring of 1993 by Senate Minority Leader Bob Dole's filibuster.

In August 1993, by a one-vote margin in both the House and the Senate, Congress approved a budget that confined spending to the 1990 ceiling and raised revenues with a higher top income tax rate and a modest increase in the tax on motor fuels. That budget legislation also secured funding for Medicare Part A by eliminating the ceiling on income subject to its payroll tax.

Some Republican leaders incorrectly predicted that the tax increases would trigger a recession. The financial markets responded positively; the interest rate on ten-year federal bonds fell from 7 percent to less than 5.5 percent during the ten months between Clinton's election and the budget vote.

President Clinton then sought to expand medical coverage with a plan that required most employers to provide insurance through managed care plans and offered a subsidy to pay for a portion of that cost. Clinton and his talented wife, Hillary, hoped to reduce the net price of the program to the federal government by combining the purchasing power of the federal government, states, and private insurers to stem rising prices for medical services.

There was nothing radical about the notion of trying to restrain medical costs that continued to rise—for both federal programs and private insurance—at a faster rate than national income. By 1993 a broad-based coalition of large business employers sought to require more employees to obtain insurance as a means of reducing the average level of premiums. Many Republicans embraced that employee mandate as an alternative to Clinton's plan.

Clinton's insurance plan was never able to muster the support of a majority in the House or Senate. Some blamed its legislative failure on the insurance industry's attack ads and lobbying. In fact, budget realities played a critical role in the outcome. The Congressional Budget Office calculated that the plan's insurance subsidies would cost more than the estimated savings in Medicare and new taxes. As a result, the plan would push federal spending above the multiyear budget ceilings established in 1990.

Later medical services legislation showed how economics rather than ideology imposed the greatest barrier to the future expansion of medical services. A central feature of the Clinton program—federal premium subsidies to managed care plans—became the lynchpin of various conservative plans to reform Medicare. The Republican alternative to the Clinton plan for expanding coverage—a mandate for uninsured individuals to buy insurance—was eventually used as the basis for both Governor Mitt Romney's reforms in Massachusetts and Obama's 2010 Affordable Care Act.

GINGRICH, CLINTON, AND "PAY AS YOU GO"

In 1994 Republicans won a House majority for the first time since 1952. Their thirty-two-seat gain accelerated a decade-long trend of Republican progress in the South. Polls showed that Republican congressional candidates attracted votes from many former Perot supporters. Perot himself applauded the House Republican campaign platform, the "Contract with America."[20] Its author, Newt Gingrich, became the Speaker of the House in January 1995.

Gingrich's rise enhanced the influence of his allies, a coalition of Washington-based political strategists and lobbyists. Grover Norquist presided over a weekly Wednesday morning strategy meeting of conservative organizations ranging from the National Rifle Association to various groups with religious affiliations. Norquist had begun his career as a political operative by mobilizing support for a constitutional amendment to balance the budget. Then, in 1985, conservative activist Peter Ferrara recruited him to run the nonprofit Americans for Tax Reform, which backed the Reagan administration's initiative to lower personal income tax rates largely by raising taxes on investment income. After the passage of the Tax Reform Act of 1986, Norquist transformed Americans for Tax Reform into a vehicle for opposing tax increases for any purpose and at any time. He publicized this goal by challenging political candidates to pledge their opposition to all tax increases. Initially 110 state and federal candidates signed the pledge. As that number steadily grew, the pledge played an increasingly important role in Republican primaries.

Norquist acknowledged that spending rather than taxes ultimately determined the size and scope of government, but he asked: "Just how could one create a pledge on spending[?] 'I promise to oppose too much spending.' How much is too much? The power of the taxpayer protection pledge comes from its clear and binary nature. A politician votes for or against a tax hike. Yes or no. Hero or bum."[21]

Norquist's "Taxpayer Protection Pledge" inspired Gingrich's Contract with America, which 185 Republican congressional candidates signed in a ceremony in front of the Capitol on September 27, 1994. The Contract with America backed a constitutional amendment to balance the budget. Gingrich, a former history professor, explained that there was "a deep historic commitment to balancing the budget," which was "a goal that gives people a hard yardstick against which to measure their behavior."[22]

Though relatively few voters knew the details of the Contract with America, Gingrich emerged from the election as the televised face of his party. Speaker Gingrich also set the agenda for the House of Representatives. He supplemented that power with a network of national organizations invested in his success. Rivals of Gingrich for national party leadership in early 1995 fell in line. Senate Majority Leader Dole, who had sparred with Gingrich and Norquist for years, agreed to sign the pledge against new taxes.

Clinton let the new House leaders take the initiative in drafting a proposal to balance the budget. Speaker Gingrich seized the opportunity and used value-laden rhetoric to embolden congressional Republicans. He described a balanced budget as "the only thing that gives you the moral imperative to change the whole structure of the welfare state."[23] At a meeting in February 1995, House Republican leaders—including the new chairmen of the Ways and Means and Appropriations Committees—committed to prepare a plan that would balance the unified budget by 2002. House Budget Committee chairman, young John Kasich of Ohio, warned that such a plan would require fundamental changes to Medicare, which enjoyed broad, bipartisan support. Gingrich replied: "You only get the moral authority to truly change things if you're offering something that is as definitive as balance."[24] Both Kasich and Gingrich would prove to be correct.

The House quickly passed a constitutional amendment to balance the unified budget by 2002.[25] When the amendment failed by one vote in the Senate on March 2, 1995, Gingrich announced that he would use the existing constitutional powers of Congress over spending and taxation to balance the unified budget by 2002.

Clinton respected the authority of a balanced budget and acknowledged the need for a credible plan to achieve that goal, although he proposed to do so in ten years rather than Gingrich's seven. Some White House staff members expressed concern that any definite plan to balance the budget would require substantial reductions in the projected growth of Medicare and Medicaid, since the 1990s budget ceilings had already capped the growth of defense and most other domestic programs. The president insisted, however, that he intended to offer a realistic plan to balance the budget in order to get Americans to "listen to me about progressive programs."[26]

Gingrich successfully united Republicans in Congress in support of a single budget plan. He invited Republican House members to a retreat that featured a discussion of options for balancing the budget, briefings on budget math, shadow votes on hard trade-offs, and coaching from poll-sters on how best to describe their plans to reduce the rate of growth in medical programs. Republican members of Congress, however, had not campaigned on a platform to cut Medicare. In light of a 1995 annual re-port from the Medicare Trustees predicting that hospitalization insurance would exceed its payroll tax revenues by 2002, Republican congressional leaders decided to claim that their plan would "strengthen" Medicare.

Gingrich also proposed to extend the budget ceilings imposed by the Budget Enforcement Act of 1990, which he had voted against. Majority Leader Dole and Budget Committee Chairman Domenici welcomed Gin-grich's embrace of a balanced budget and spending restraint, but they har-bored reservations about his commitment to a $500-per-child tax credit pushed by Norquist and a coalition of organizations with religious ties.[27] This "pro-family" tax cut would require corresponding cuts in Medicare to balance the budget. Dole found it difficult to publicly oppose a tax credit that had been endorsed by both the Speaker and Senator Phil Gramm of Texas, who was then considered the Kansas senator's principal rival for the Republican presidential nomination in 1996. As a result, Dole acquiesced to the tax credit and other cuts totaling $245 billion over the seven-year period.[28]

In order to balance the budget, those tax cuts forced Republican con-gressional leadership to further reduce planned Medicare and Medicaid spending. The White House responded with a multiyear balanced budget plan containing smaller tax cuts and accordingly smaller cuts in Medicare and Medicaid.

Gingrich's bold budget plan gained momentum during the summer of 1995. He could count on a solid majority in the House, a bare majority in the Senate, and a president who would not contest the goal of a balanced budget. Because Clinton agreed with the concept of balancing the budget within a fixed period of time, by August 1995 Gingrich asserted that he and Clinton were merely "arguing detail." Gingrich would soon learn that Americans viewed the trade-off between taxes and medical services as an extraordinarily important detail. In 1995 the old "pay as you go" budget planning principle had forced federal leaders to offer realistic alternatives for bringing federal spending in line with estimated revenues.

Congressional Democrats complained that the president had con-ceded budget leadership to Gingrich, but Clinton's genuine commitment to restoring fiscal discipline commanded respect from some Republicans. Senator Barry Goldwater encouraged Gingrich to work with Clinton: "He's a Democrat, but I do admire him. I think he is doing a good job."[29]

The process for building consensus on top-line budget numbers had distracted congressional committees from the job of writing the specific appropriations required to fund the government during the fiscal year beginning October 1, 1995. Republicans who chaired committees were forced to grapple with harsh choices in order to meet overall budget goals. To cut Medicaid, for example, they had to choose between cutting funds for either assisted living facilities for Americans with severe disabilities or prenatal services for pregnant women. When the new fiscal year began on October 1, Congress had passed only two of the thirteen required appropriations bills. It voted for a six-week extension. During the extension Congress funded the government with a continuing resolution, which maintained funding at the levels of the prior year's budget. At the end of the six weeks, Congress still had not passed the necessary appropriations bills. House Majority Whip Tom DeLay, who had become an effective enforcer of partisan discipline, stated that if the president vetoed another continuing resolution and shut "the government down, we'll keep it shut down until the president signs a bill or an agreement in writing about what he will do."[30]

MEDICARE VERSUS TAX CUTS

The battle between competing plans for balancing the budget focused public attention on the trade-off between taxes and the cost of Medicare and Medicaid. The principal difference between the White House and Republican plans was clear: the Republicans wanted lower taxes and more cuts in medical services. Gingrich expressed his belief that "if [Republicans] solve Medicare," the party would be able to "govern for a generation."[31]

In prior sessions of Congress policy experts had outlined ideas for constraining medical outlays without restricting services or eligibility. Realistic options to do so were limited. For decades federal administrators and private insurers had tried new techniques to limit the rise in medical costs. Even when their efforts made progress, costs still rose as a result of new types of medical treatments and the care of a population that lived longer. Some attempts to cut short-run costs could drive up the cost of services in the long run. For example, pressures to reduce fraud led to expensive record-keeping and billing systems, while incentives to shift patients with chronic conditions to care outside of hospitals contributed to the explosive growth in home health care.[32]

As a result, the drive to curb costs inevitably led to a choice between limiting payments to providers or shifting more costs to the beneficiaries. And at some point even those alternatives would affect services, either because low reimbursement rates would discourage physicians from offering services or because beneficiaries could not afford higher costs.

In September 1995 House leadership unveiled the Medicare Preservation Act, which reduced projected Medicare outlays by an estimated 30 percent, or $270 billion, over seven years.[33] The bill sought to replace Medicare's direct reimbursements to physicians with payments to insurers that offered managed care policies to older Americans. Because the bill limited the annual Medicare subsidy (premium support) to an amount that rose less than the estimated future costs of medical services, rising medical expenses would have to be borne through higher premiums and larger beneficiary copays.

In the fall of 1995, Gingrich and Dole attempted to rally conservative support by occasionally departing from their scripted goal of "strengthening" Medicare. In meetings with conservative activists, Dole expressed pride in his vote against the original Medicare legislation, and Gingrich claimed that his plan would let Medicare "wither on the vine."[34]

In contrast, the Clinton administration proposed to retain existing Medicare while imposing new limits on the reimbursement rates for various categories of medical services. Medicare beneficiaries could continue to see the doctors they preferred rather than those who participated in a particular managed care plan. While Republicans tried to cap the annual increase in Medicaid grants at 5 percent a year, the Clinton administration proposed ceilings on the annual increase in Medicaid costs per beneficiary. The administration's plan reduced projected Medicaid costs by $54 billion over seven years, substantially less than the $180 billion called for by the Republican plan.[35] Governors in each party objected to the Medicaid limits proposed by Republican congressional leaders.

Gingrich's options had narrowed. He could not agree to increase spending for medical services without sacrificing either various tax cuts or the commitment to balance the budget by 2002. He told the president that he would use the House's constitutional power over appropriations and the statutory debt ceiling to shut down the federal government unless the president refrained from exercising his veto power. Because Congress had not yet passed bills to appropriate spending for the fiscal year beginning on October 1, 1995, in November Congress passed a continuing resolution that Gingrich conditioned on higher premium rates for Medicare Part B.[36] On November 13, 1995, the president vetoed that resolution.

The resulting shutdown of many federal activities dominated national headlines. The budget trade-off was framed even more starkly: Republicans wanted to raise Medicare premiums to offset their planned income tax cuts, while Democrats wanted to hold the line on premium increases and reduce taxes by less.[37] Public opinion came down on Clinton's side.

Gingrich tried to shift the debate by claiming that Clinton had refused to talk to him while they traveled to the funeral of Israeli leader Yitzhak Rabin. "It's petty, but I think it's human," he said of the alleged snubbing. "They ask you to get off the plane by the back ramp. . . . Where is their sense of courtesy?"[38] These comments seemed particularly petty after the White House released photographs of Clinton and Gingrich talking during the flight.

Despite the tide of public opinion, Congress passed a bill that cut projected Medicare spending by $270 billion and converted Medicaid into a block grant.[39] Gingrich called it "the most decisive vote on the direction of the government since 1933."[40] On December 6, 1995, Clinton vetoed the bill using the pen President Johnson had used to sign the original Medicare bill in 1965. He expressed his willingness to sign a bill that balanced the budget in seven years without the Medicare cuts and tax cuts.

Public support for Gingrich's approach to the budget further diminished after the second federal shutdown, from December 16, 1995, to January 6, 1996. The shutdown ended when Majority Leader Dole took over negotiations for the Republicans and agreed to an unconditional continuing resolution, the extension of the 1990 budget ceilings, and an increase in the debt ceiling. Gingrich vowed to implement the House budget plan one year at a time.

Accounts of the 1995 budget showdown, which strengthened public approval of Clinton's job performance, often focus on political tactics and style. That type of analysis underestimates the impact of the public's verdict on the trade-off between taxation and medical services. Gingrich engaged in high-profile debate with Clinton about that trade-off, and experienced the consequences of defending a minority opinion. The following year Gingrich would ride the power imparted by strong public support when he worked with Clinton, and against many congressional Democrats, to pass a bill ending federal public assistance to many unemployed mothers of dependent children.

In his 1996 State of the Union address, Clinton proclaimed the end of "the era of big government."[41] Later that year he beat Bob Dole decisively in the presidential election, and Democrats picked up seats in both the House and Senate. Perot received 5 percent of the presidential vote, but the impact of his 1992 campaign endured, since leaders of both major parties had embraced his signature issue of a balanced budget.

After the election, Gingrich said he would focus on "four years of incremental achievements" rather than "four years of obstruction while we scream about values."[42] The president told his economic team that he was determined to balance the budget in his second term.

The president, Chief of Staff Erskine Bowles, and Republican congressional leaders including Senator Domenici revived negotiations to balance the budget by fiscal year 2002. Budget math in 1997 again compelled federal leaders to try to address projected growth of Medicare and Medicaid. The White House and congressional Republicans agreed to give Medicare beneficiaries the option—but not the obligation—to participate in managed care plans, or HMOs, which would receive subsidies based on average Medicare reimbursements. Their agreement also curbed the annual growth in payments to doctors and clinics to the level of growth in the economy.

The administration softened its opposition to a hard limit on annual Medicaid spending when bipartisan leadership in Congress found a new source of revenues to support medical care for impoverished children. Senators Ted Kennedy and Orrin Hatch crafted legislation that would levy higher tobacco taxes to pay for a separate Medicaid grant program for poor children; they fell just short of winning a vote to raise that tax high enough to pay for the entire program.[43]

In the spring of 1997, the White House and Republican negotiators reached a tentative agreement on a plan to balance the budget within four years. Each side was nervous, however, about whether their compromise would be acceptable to other leaders in each party. Speaker Gingrich wanted some form of tax cut to get his caucus on board, while the White House worried about Democratic opposition to a hard cap on Medicaid spending. They both remembered that a coalition of liberal Democrats and conservative Republicans had defeated the first version of the 1990 budget agreement.

A special report in May 1997 from the Congressional Budget Office (CBO) facilitated a compromise on the difficult tax and Medicaid issues. Monthly tax collections had been exceeding projections, prompting the CBO to raise its five-year revenue forecasts by more than $200 billion.[44] The new projections allowed negotiators to lower the tax rate on capital gains and maintain a more flexible Medicaid ceiling. The Balanced Budget Act of 1997 passed in August with bipartisan support. It capped so-called discretionary spending—appropriations not driven by a legal formula—for five years and extended "pay as you go" procedural rules to enforce those limits.

The legislation's most remarkable new feature was its restriction on the growth of Medicare reimbursements. That limit—the Sustainable Growth Rate—allowed prices for many medical services to rise no more than the rate of growth in national income. If any large category of federal spending always grows faster than tax revenues, someday it could consume all available revenues. However, the Sustainable Growth Rate would force the rationing of services if providers could not recover their costs or if the demand for their services grew faster than national income.[45] Federal leaders appointed a bipartisan commission to outline reforms to develop a long-term plan to contain Medicare costs within the ceilings.

Medicare and Medicaid costs barely rose in the two years following the implementation of the Balanced Budget Act of 1997. Medicare costs actually declined in fiscal year 1998—the first time in the program's history. That success arose from caps on payment rates rather than from the managed care insurance alternative (Medicare Part C) inserted in the bill by Republicans. By 1999 only six million out of thirty-nine million total Medicare recipients participated in managed care plans, which never produced significant savings for the federal government.[46]

In fiscal year 1998 the unified budget balanced for the first time since 1969. The federal funds budget did not yet balance, but trends were headed in that direction. The Omnibus Budget Reconciliation Acts of 1990 and 1993, along with the Balanced Budget Act of 1997, had succeeded in restraining routine borrowing. The American Fiscal Tradition had endured.

SURPLUS AND SCANDAL

In January 1998 the Congressional Budget Office published a ten-year projection that showed large future surpluses, under certain assumptions, in the unified budget. In each biannual report from January 1998 until January 2001, the CBO increased its estimate of the size of a potential ten-year budget surplus. News of this progress weakened the resolve of many in Congress to institutionalize "pay as you go" budget planning. Speaker Gingrich and Senate Majority Leader Trent Lott began to call for cuts in federal funds taxes well before the federal funds budget actually experienced a surplus.

Senator Kent Conrad, a fiscally conservative budget expert from North Dakota, warned of the illusory nature of the surplus created by merging Social Security surpluses with the federal funds budget. Herbert Stein, a traditional fiscal conservative, commented that "we have ahead of us a period of very large deficits as the baby boomers come into their Social Security and Medicare benefits. We shouldn't dissipate the surpluses for tax cuts or new spending."[47]

The willingness of Republican leaders to collaborate with Clinton diminished in the wake of reports in January 1998 that the president had a sexual relationship with a White House intern. Republican House members led by Majority Whip Tom DeLay pressed aggressively for Clinton's impeachment, a prospect that forced the president to solidify his relationships with Democratic House members. Chief of Staff Bowles later commented that the scandal ended the productive budget collaboration between Clinton and Gingrich. Plans for long-term reforms of Medicare and Social Security yielded to budget issues with more symbolic than financial significance. Clinton obtained an increase of $1.1 billion in spending for public school teachers and environmental programs, while Gingrich raised spending—largely for the military—by $8 billion.[48]

After Republicans overplayed their hand on impeachment, Democrats picked up five House seats in the 1998 midterm elections. Gingrich lost support for his reelection as Speaker; his farewell speech called his critics within his own party "cannibals."[49]

On January 6, 1999, Clinton announced an end to "the era of big deficits."[50] In order to counter a future threat to fiscal discipline, he proposed to remove the Social Security and Medicare trust funds from the unified budget and to pay two-thirds of anticipated federal funds surpluses into those trust funds in advance of the retirement of the Baby Boomers. The president's plan—had it succeeded—would have clarified federal accounting.

In the late 1990s Federal Reserve Chairman Greenspan also argued that surplus revenues should be used to pay down debt before the Baby Boomers began to retire. He warned that projections of future surpluses depended on faster economic growth than had actually occurred, on average, since World War II.

In fiscal year 2000, for the first time since Eisenhower's last budget, the federal funds budget ended with a slight surplus.[51]

No one can predict what might have happened if the bipartisan drive to balance the budget in 1997 had retained its momentum. Once the federal funds budget balanced in 2000, it would have been much easier to restore traditional budget practices. Budget accounting would have been more transparent if the trust funds had been separated from the rest of the budget as Clinton intended. The Sustainable Growth Rate provided a solid foundation for additional reforms designed to make the Medicare trust funds self-sustaining. Continuation of the "pay as you go" rules in the 1990 Budget Enforcement Act could have restored the historical link between tax and spending policies. Once the federal government had brought annual appropriations in line with its annual commitments to the amount of annual revenues, votes on the debt ceiling could have become a more practical tool for limiting new debt.

Of course, there still would have been heated political battles concerning the level at which spending and taxes balanced. Elections would inevitably shift the balance in one direction or another. But those decisions would have been made within the framework of the unwritten fiscal constitution. The fact that the United States came within reach of restoring traditional budget practices in the late 1990s should give heart to those who still seek to do so today.

THE ILLUSION OF LARGE SURPLUSES

In light of changing circumstances, Dwight Eisenhower often commented that planning was indispensable even though plans themselves were worthless. Long-term budget plans demonstrate the value of Eisenhower's insight. Until recent decades, federal leaders made budget decisions principally based on concrete information about the previous year's budgets and revenue estimates for the current budget year. Formula-based federal funds spending for medical services resulted in greater reliance on long-term budget projections. Since 1976 the Congressional Budget Office (CBO) has provided five-year projections, or "baseline" forecasts, evaluating the impact of new legislation.

Those CBO projections had a poor track record in predicting future deficits and surpluses. In 2000, analysts working for the Federal Reserve compared the CBO's historical projections of deficits and surpluses five years out from a given date with what had actually occurred during those years. That straightforward calculation showed that "there is no relationship between the CBO's projections and the actual surplus/deficit. . . . [A] large deficit was as likely to occur when the CBO projected a surplus as it was when the CBO projected a deficit."[52] Though flawed, these projections nevertheless played a critical role in the 2000 presidential campaign.

In 1998, when the CBO first projected surpluses in the unified budget, the federal funds budget continued to run a deficit.[53] By January 2000 the CBO had begun to project modest and rising surpluses in the federal funds budget. Based on the extension of the 1990 spending caps, higher revenues from the Alternative Minimum Tax, strong economic growth, extraordinary revenue from taxes on investment gains, and the retention of caps on medical reimbursements, CBO projections showed surpluses rising until shortly after 2010—at which point federal spending for Medicare and deficits would soar. Because of those Baby Boom Medicare liabilities, economist Paul Krugman wisely pointed out in 2001 that the use of a ten-year projection was far more misleading than those for either a shorter or a longer time horizon.

The consolidation of trust funds in the unified budget also led to a misleading account of interest expense on federal debt. From 2000 to 2010, rising Social Security trust fund reserves for Baby Boomers would be invested in more federal debt. As a result, the unified budget in some years was projected to incur no "net" interest expense, even though the federal funds budget was borrowing from the trust funds. To understand that dynamic, consider a hypothetical budget of a government that begins with no debt and for ten years spends $50 annually, paid for with $40 in tax revenues and $10 in loans from trust funds. Each year the government borrows more from the trust funds to pay the annual interest due to those same trust funds. At the end of ten years, the $40 in federal funds tax revenues must service a debt of $100 plus the amounts borrowed to pay interest. But the unified budget for that government would show zero debt and zero interest expense. The official unified budget numbers for fiscal years 1998–2000, still available on the White House website, show a surplus.[54] Yet the Treasury borrowed $274 billion during those years.[55]

The flaw in the unified budget would have been obvious if Congress had voted to authorize specific amounts of debt for defined purposes. Not everyone can master accounting, but most people can understand the questionable nature of a reported surplus when the federal government is forced to borrow to pay its bills. Projections prepared by the White House Office of Management and Budget recognized this problem and in 2000 showed virtually no future surpluses after removing the Social Security Trust Fund from its calculations and allocating additional federal funds after fiscal year 2005 to a "Medicare solvency debt reduction reserve."[56] The CBO did not.

The CBO forecast relied on other questionable assumptions. It assumed no growth beyond inflation in the cost of federal programs. To the extent that some categories of cost—notably for medical expenses and new military technologies—tend to rise faster than inflation, the CBO's "baseline forecast" implied steadily declining levels of many federal services. In addition, the CBO projected the continuation of high levels of income tax revenues from investment gains. Roughly half of the surge in revenues above the levels originally forecasted for 1997 to 2000 had resulted from higher rates of economic growth, and the other half resulted from sharply higher incomes of the wealthiest Americans. By 2000 the CBO raised the projected rate of annual economic growth after inflation from 2.1 percent to 3 percent per year—a level well above the average long-term growth rate. That assumption contributed to projections of high levels of investment income and related taxes.[57]

Changes in the American economy had indeed caused federal personal income tax revenue to rise faster than economic growth in the 1990s. Taxpayers with incomes in the top 1 percent, who typically had at least one college degree, did well in the global economy. Their share of the nation's adjusted total gross income rose from 13.8 percent in 1993 to 20.8 percent in 1998, while their share of personal income taxes had grown from 29 percent to 37.4 percent.[58]

The relative prosperity of Americans with high incomes was an awkward reality for politicians as well as forecasters. Democrats did not campaign on promises to create more opportunity for the wealthiest

Americans. Republicans found it more difficult to contend that the 1993 tax increases would destroy incentives and investment. Experts who prepared budget forecasts had problems estimating future revenues from investment gains. A bull market in the late 1990s contributed to higher tax collections, including those from taxes paid on the exercise of stock options in the red-hot market for stock in technology-based companies.[59] Nonetheless, the CBO forecast in 2000 continued to assume high revenues from investment income even after the tech bubble burst and stock prices began to fall.

THE 2000 PRESIDENTIAL CAMPAIGN

Texas Governor George W. Bush became the early front-runner for the Republican presidential nomination in 2000. Many Americans respected his parents, whose circle of friends provided a solid fundraising base. The younger Bush had demonstrated the ability to appeal to a broad range of voters in his two gubernatorial elections. He intrigued Republicans, who yearned for a winner.

Bush's presidential campaign tried to mimic the economic themes of Reagan's presidency. For that purpose, he could not rely on his budget record as governor of Texas. State budgets when Bush was governor had balanced largely as a result of a flood of revenues from a strong economy. In 1997 Bush—over the opposition of the chairman of the state's Republican Party—backed the unsuccessful push of the Democratic-led Texas House of Representatives to expand the tax base in order to fund the future educational needs of the state's growing population of young people.

Bush's brilliant campaign strategist, Karl Rove, carefully built a national organization, while the other leading candidates—Senator John McCain of Arizona and wealthy publisher Steve Forbes—concentrated on a handful of early primary states. Forbes grounded his campaign on a plan to reduce tax rates and focused on the Iowa caucuses that chose the first delegates. McCain had alienated many of his party's leaders on issues such as campaign finance reform, the taxation of tobacco, and the use of budgetary earmarks by Republican colleagues. But McCain soared in the polls after winning the New Hampshire primary.

Grover Norquist and his allied groups helped reverse McCain's momentum after the senator's New Hampshire primary victory. Norquist and Washington-based conservative advocacy groups loathed McCain and vice versa. Bush courted the antitax activists by condemning his father's 1990 budget agreement and promising to reduce personal income tax rates to a maximum rate of 28 percent and provide a new tax credit for each dependent child.[60] The Texas governor estimated that his plan would cost $1.6 billion over ten years and could be funded out of surpluses. Norquist's coalition played a critical role in turning the tide toward Bush in South Carolina, after which the Forbes and McCain campaigns collapsed.

Throughout 2000 Bush maintained only a slight lead in the polls over the Democratic presidential nominee, Vice President Al Gore. Gore refused to treat Social Security reserves as a surplus and vowed to use any federal funds surplus to increase Medicare reserves, expand Medicare coverage for prescription drugs, and reduce taxes for middle-income Americans. Bush also endorsed an expansion to include Medicare coverage of prescription drugs and attacked Gore late in the campaign for failing to do so as vice president during the Clinton administration. Gore, in turn, challenged Bush to pledge not to count Social Security and Medicare trust fund reserves when determining whether the budget balanced after a tax cut. Bush avoided making that commitment.

A heated presidential campaign was a poor forum for explaining the complexities of federal accounting. Gore tried to simplify the issue by calling for revenues from Social Security and Medicare to be placed in a "lockbox." He repeated the "lockbox" metaphor so often that it became fodder for late-night television comedy. Federal law had long prevented the diversion of trust fund balances; the "lockbox" concept was simply meant to illustrate that trust fund revenues and spending should be separated from the remainder of the budget.

Gore won the popular vote but lost in the Electoral College vote following a dispute over the election's outcome in Florida. As a result, Bush could hardly claim a mandate to abandon traditional fiscal policies.

By 2000 federal leaders had succeeded in restoring the "pay as you go" budget planning that served as a principal pillar of the American Fiscal Tradition. They accomplished that goal in part by restraining the growth in federal spending. From fiscal year 1991 through 2001, federal funds spending had grown by only $377 billion, while national income grew by $4.3 trillion.[61] Presidents George H. W Bush and Bill Clinton and congressional leaders in both parties could take justifiable pride in that accomplishment.

Bush's inauguration marked only the first time in thirty-eight years when Republicans had control of the White House and both houses of Congress. The last time that happened—in 1953—President Eisenhower had used the opportunity to balance the budget by slashing military spending and delaying a tax cut. In January 2001 few expected that in the next four years federal funds spending would rise by over half a trillion dollars, absorb a quarter of all growth in the economy, and be paid for by an unprecedented level of borrowing from foreign creditors.

17

THE TRADITION COLLAPSES

2001–2006: Years when deficits exceeded debt service = 5
(2002–2006, debt without principled limits)

GEORGE W. BUSH AND CONGRESS BORROW

While the world watched the noisy courtoom battle over the outcome of the 2000 election, no one seemed to notice that the surplus quietly vanished. The federal funds budget had just balanced at the end of fiscal year 2000, which ended only weeks before the election. Spending in the fiscal year that began October 1, 2000, was scheduled to rise only modestly, but income tax revenues from capital gains declined with the sharp drop in the value of technology-related stocks. That fact did not stop the Congressional Budget Office from projecting an even larger surplus for the next ten years than had been shown in its forecast a year earlier. That surplus consisted primarily of Social Security reserves being accumulated in advance of the retirement of Baby Boomers.[1] Budget projections extending beyond ten years showed a sharp increase in federal spending and deficits once Baby Boomers began to retire and become eligible for Medicare, beginning in 2010.

President George W. Bush outlined his budget priorities in his first State of the Union address, delivered on February 27, 2001. He decried the country's "unprecedented amount of public debt" and invoked traditional values: "We owe it to our children and grandchildren to act now, and I hope you will join me to pay down $2 trillion in debt during the next 10 years." The president vowed to set aside $1 trillion "as a contingency fund for emergencies or additional spending needs." After quoting Yogi Berra—"When you come to a fork in the road, take it"—he asked for tax cuts. Those tax cuts, he said, were needed to deplete the projected surplus: "The growing surplus exists because taxes are too high and government is charging more than it needs. The people of America have been over-charged and on their behalf, I am here to ask for a refund."[2] His speech-writer worried about public reaction to this request in light of polls that showed that voters did not place a high priority on tax relief, a which had been a centerpiece of Bush's presidential campaign.

The administration's budget proposal for the next fiscal year, beginning on October 1, 2001, reflected the ambivalence of Bush's "fork in the road" quip. The revenue projections assumed strong economic growth, but the budget materials urged prompt action on the proposed tax cut in order to stimulate the economy. The written budget referred to a $231 billion sur-plus in fiscal year 2002 and an "unprecedented $1.4 billion reserve."[3] The tables near the end of the budget document, however, showed that debt would rise by almost $300 billion during the next few fiscal years.[4] Where, then, would the trillions of dollars for debt reduction and the contingency reserve come from?

There were other problems with the math. The White House bud-get proposal noted that the $2 trillion target represented "the maximum amount of deficit reduction possible over ten years."[5] Treasury Secretary Paul O'Neill, a former corporate CEO who had been a budget profes-sional in the Nixon and Ford administrations, pointed out that there was no such $2 trillion maximum and that nothing prevented a greater reduc-tion in debt.

The White House did not identify the spending cuts required to achieve ambitious targets for debt reduction. The president's budget in-cluded a 4 percent rise in outlays not governed by legal formulas. That rate of growth was greater than the average during the Clinton administration, but modest compared to the increase proposed in Bush's later budgets. Bush administration officials brushed aside questions on the math. Chief of Staff Andrew Card characterized the estimates of a surplus before the tax cuts as "very conservative," while administration spokesman Ari Fleischer added that the government was "awash in surplus money."[6]

The claims of a large existing surplus were difficult to corroborate or challenge because the federal budget no longer conformed to Thomas Jef-ferson's standard of being clear and intelligible. For several years before

Bush's inauguration, President Clinton, Federal Reserve Chairman Alan Greenspan, and Senator Kent Conrad had highlighted the need to remove trust funds when considering the balance of federal spending and revenues. President Bush and Congress did not heed those warnings in 2001. Greenspan later remarked that, at the time, "little value was placed on rigorous economic policy debate or the weighing of long-term consequences."[7]

The House Ways and Means Committee approved legislation that slashed tax rates even before Congress passed a budget resolution that set a ceiling on spending for the following fiscal year, 2002. Democratic congressional leaders countered with a plan to reduce taxes by an amount less than Bush had proposed, but still by far more than the Republican tax bill that Democrats had opposed—and Clinton had vetoed—two years earlier. At least half of the Senate favored some mechanism for making tax cuts more dependent on achieving of budget milestones. Under strong pressure from the White House, the Senate in May voted 50–49 to reject that approach.

That summer Congress approved the Economic Growth and Tax Relief Act of 2001, which cut taxes regardless of the level of federal spending and tax revenues. Out of forty-nine Democrats in the Senate, twelve voted for Bush's tax cut, while seven did not vote or voted "present." Only two Republican members in either chamber, Senators John McCain of Arizona and Lincoln Chafee of Rhode Island, voted against the bill. Sponsors of the act reduced its estimated impact on long-term deficits by setting a December 31, 2010, date for the tax cuts to expire. The Congressional Budget Office estimated that the bill would result in a "net decrease in the budget surplus" of $1.35 trillion over ten years.[8] However, a surplus in the federal funds budget no longer existed when the tax cut was enacted.

Four years earlier, in May 1997, the CBO released a special report when monthly tax receipts were higher than projected just months before. In May 2001 the CBO and the White House remained silent as they watched tax collections fall short of estimates. Benjamin Franklin, in arguing that denial and deception tend to accompany debt, once said "lying rides upon debt's back."[9] For at least the first eight months of 2001, Franklin's rider assumed the form of misleading budget projections. President Bush's fiscal year 2002 budget assumed that in fiscal year 2001, already well underway, the federal government would collect $1.073 trillion in personal income taxes and $213 billion in corporate taxes.[10] By at least early summer the administration knew that tax collections would not reach those levels. The

White House and leaders in Congress did not publicize the severe revenue shortfall until the end of the fiscal year. In fiscal year 2001 the federal government received $994 billion in personal income taxes and $151 billion in corporate income taxes.[11] A large public corporation would have faced fraud suits from shareholders if it waited until the end of a fiscal year to disclose that its revenues had dropped more than 10 percent from public estimates it repeated throughout the fiscal year.

Without "pay as you go" budget planning, this massive change in current and expected federal revenues had no apparent effect on any tax or spending legislation. According to one senior White House staff member, the president's first six months in office had been drafted in advance in the same manner that a "smart head coach" would "script the first dozen plays of a football game."[12] The surplus had been like having a lead on the scoreboard at the beginning of the game; the game plan did not change when that presumed lead disappeared.

By August 2001, after final passage of the tax bill, the CBO lowered its estimate of a surplus in the unified, ten-year budget by $2.2 trillion and projected a federal funds deficit of more than half a trillion dollars from fiscal 2001 through fiscal 2008.[13] The size of this drop is highlighted by the fact that *all* personal income taxes paid in 2001 and 2002 would not exceed $2.2 trillion.[14]

At a press conference on August 24, 2001, Bush explained his administration's budget policy: "We have the tax relief plan, which is important for fiscal stimulus, coupled with Social Security being off limits except for—except for emergency. That now provides a . . . fiscal straightjacket for Congress."[15] He described the straightjacket—the end of the surplus—as "incredibly positive news" and a tool for "fiscal sanity."[16] Prior generations of fiscal conservatives had viewed presidential vetoes and the onerous requirement of taxation to back new spending as straightjackets on the growth of government. For six years Bush failed to veto a single spending bill.

Though the president claimed to keep Social Security trust funds "off limits," the Bush administration—like previous administrations—relied heavily on the trust funds to finance federal borrowing. This fact was eventually conceded by Bush's senior assistant on economic policy.[17]

Nothing exemplified the brave new world of federal budget policy better than the Treasury's distribution of checks to about ninety million households in August and September 2001.[18] Federal leaders called the payments, which ranged from $300 to $600, "tax rebates," when in fact they were financed using debt.

On September 26, 2001, the Congressional Budget Office reported that tax revenues for the fiscal year ending four days later would be far less than estimated during the final consideration of the tax bill passed a few months earlier. Ordinarily that announcement would have been big news, since the president had referred to his proposed tax cut as a "demand for a refund" from a surplus. Yet late September 2001 was far from ordinary. Americans grieved and expressed their anger in response to terrorist attacks on the World Trade Center and the Pentagon.

Defense Secretary Donald Rumsfeld warned of an impending War on Terror that would require Americans to "forget about 'exit strategies'" because the country was "looking at a sustained engagement" without "deadlines."[19] On October 7, 2001, the United States deployed troops to Afghanistan for the purposes of replacing the government of the tribal nation, expelling the terrorist organization al-Qaeda, and capturing al-Qaeda's leader, Osama bin Laden. By then Congress had also voted unanimously to appropriate $40 billion for new antiterrorism and homeland security activities.[20]

Financing War with Lower Taxes

President Bush's public approval ratings soared in the wake of the 9/11 attacks. Americans applauded his earnest resolve to retaliate against al-Qaeda and its sponsors. The president did not, however, ask Americans to demonstrate their resolve to adversaries by financing the War on Terror with higher tax revenues. After the House quickly passed a tax cut, White House staff reprimanded Treasury Secretary O'Neill for referring to it pejoratively as "show business."[21] The Senate hesitated to lower tax revenues again in light of the rising deficit, leading Bush to demand a "stimulus bill on my desk by the end of November."[22]

When Democratic Senate Majority Leader Tom Daschle of South Dakota criticized the rising budget deficits, Bush—according to a principal White House speechwriter—"was only too delighted to play Roosevelt to Daschle's Hoover."[23] Of course, Roosevelt had actually criticized Hoover for borrowing *too much* and prodded Congress to raise taxes when the nation went to war. In early 2002 a bipartisan majority in Congress complied with the president's demand by enacting debt-financed tax breaks and higher spending on health benefits for unemployed Americans.

The slide into debt accelerated. Bush applauded the passage of "compassionate" legislation that raised farm subsidies by $90 billion over five years.[24] The Farm Security and Rural Investment Act of 2002 reversed the phased reduction in those farm subsidies, a reduction that was considered a triumph of fiscal restraint by Republican congressional leadership in 1996. The administration asked for a 12 percent increase in Department of Defense spending, plus another $10 billion for "contingencies."[25] By the end of fiscal year 2003, national security spending had increased by more than one-third, or $104 billion, from the level it had been when Bush took office.[26]

The 2002 spending binge took place in spite of the further deterioration of federal finances. In early 2002 the CBO estimated that the federal funds deficit would be $1.811 trillion over ten years, before rising even more with the retirement of Baby Boomers.[27] Any extension of the 2001 tax cuts past their planned December 2010 expiration would require increased borrowing thereafter. Compared to its projections in January 2001, the CBO projected $4 trillion in lower revenues and higher spending—an amount equivalent to almost four full years of personal income tax revenues.[28] The CBO attributed 29 percent of the estimated drop in forecasted revenues to a weaker economy; tax cuts, higher spending, and various mistaken revenue assumptions accounted for the balance of the $4 trillion change in the budget outlook.[29]

Federal Reserve Chairman Greenspan and Secretary of the Treasury Paul O'Neill, whose predecessors had used their offices to defend fiscal discipline, seemed helpless to stem the rising tide of red ink. In September 2002 Greenspan pleaded with Congress to extend spending caps and the "pay as you go" rules imposed by the 1990 Budget Enforcement Act. When Congress allowed the Budget Enforcement Act to expire in the fall of 2002, Greenspan made a note that "budget discipline in Washington" had "[given] up the ghost."[30] Secretary O'Neill warned the president that growing deficits would preclude any new debt-financed initiatives.

Political strategist Karl Rove encouraged Republicans to frame the 2002 midterm election as a referendum on the defense against terrorist attacks. Republicans picked up a few seats in the House and two Senate seats. The day after the election, senior economic officials met in Vice President Cheney's office to discuss cutting tax rates on corporate dividends.

When O'Neill referred to the mounting deficits, the vice president asserted that "Reagan proved deficits don't matter."[31] Cheney claimed that the election—in which popular vote for Republican candidates exceeded the Democratic vote by 4 percent—had given Congress a mandate for further tax cuts.[32]

The administration's senior economic and political advisors met days later to discuss next year's budget with the president. O'Neill and Budget Director Mitch Daniels reminded the group that large budget deficits already stretched as far as the eye could see. Then the direction of the conversation veered far outside the boundaries of "pay as you go" budget planning. The group did not address how to offset the costs of the expected war in Iraq or their plans to expand Medicare to cover prescription drugs. Instead, the conversation turned toward cutting taxes on investment income. The president decided to press for lower taxes on dividends and capital gains, and Rove advised him to scale up the size of the requested tax cut because Congress—which then had a Republican majority—might try to reduce its overall size. O'Neill, who had long questioned the wisdom of debt-financed tax cuts, was asked to resign.

Years later Bush blamed terrorism for the collapse of budget discipline: "And then 9/11 hit, which required more tax cuts to stimulate the private sector."[33]

DEBT WITHOUT LIMIT: 2003

In January 2003 the president asked Congress for a tax cut estimated to cost $2.7 trillion in debt, or more than $20,000 of additional debt for every household.[34] Even greater amounts of debt would accumulate if the tax cut was extended beyond 2010. The concept of lower taxes on investment was not radical; for decades many tax experts had observed that the US corporate income tax discouraged investment and resulted in double taxation of corporate income used to pay dividends. Workers ultimately bear much of the burden of the corporate income tax, since it limits investments that contribute to productivity. There was, in fact, only one good reason to continue to tax corporate income: to pay the government's bills.

The House, then led by Majority Leader Tom DeLay, quickly passed the requested tax cuts. The potential cost of a war in Afghanistan and the planned invasion of Iraq did not slow Congress down. In fact, DeLay asserted that "nothing is more important in the face of war than cutting taxes."[35] Fiscal conservatives worked to reduce the size of the tax cut in order to lower the deficit.

Senator John McCain argued against considering a tax bill until Congress had a better understanding of the full cost of the war in Iraq, which had begun on March 20, 2003. McCain, who had been a prisoner of war for nearly six years in Vietnam, knew of the historic tendency to underestimate costs early in military conflicts. McCain was one of only four Republicans in the House or Senate who voted against the massive tax cut, the first to be enacted during war in American history.

Paul O'Neill's replacement as treasury secretary, Jack Snow, assured lawmakers that the nation could "afford the war."[36] Wartime taxes and public bond drives had historically been used as a means for showing the public support for war and enlisting civilians in the war effort. However, when the fiscally conservative Senator Fritz Hollings of South Carolina introduced legislation authorizing a wartime 2 percent value added tax—a kind of sales tax—he could not find a Senate cosponsor.

Prior to the Bush administration, the Pentagon relied on what some called the Weinberger Doctrine to guide recommendations on whether to commit the nation's armed forces to combat. Named for Reagan's defense secretary, Caspar Weinberger, this doctrine's criteria for military intervention included a clear statement of the mission, a prior definition of the result that would trigger troop withdrawal, and—thanks to a later modification from General Colin Powell—the availability of overwhelming force. President Bush, Vice President Cheney, and Secretary of Defense Rumsfeld did not feel bound by the Weinberger Doctrine.

Rather than using overwhelming force, Rumsfeld sought to exploit the Pentagon's advantages in mobility, information technology, and communications. Though Iraqi dictator Saddam Hussein was forced into hiding, the United States lacked a viable strategy for preventing the emergence of hostile unconventional forces or the collapse of civil institutions within Iraq. Newly unemployed Sunni Muslim soldiers, who had been dismissed without pay, reorganized as a resistance movement. Shiite Iraqis established their own militia.[37] Nonetheless, on May 1, 2003, Bush and Rumsfeld proclaimed the end of combat operations in Iraq and Afghanistan. For months after that announcement, the Bush administration did not ask Congress for funding to continue those wars.

Instead, the administration requested the largest expansion of Medicare since 1972. In early 2003 Congress had already increased the cost of Medicare by loosening limits on the reimbursement rates imposed by the Balanced Budget Act of 1997. The Sustainable Growth Rate would have required a drop of 4.8 percent in the average medical reimbursement in 2003. The budget resolution H.J. Res. 2 suspended that ceiling after passing with a large bipartisan margin. Rarely has a fiscal shift with such long-term budgetary consequences occurred with so little fanfare. Congress routinely suspended the applicable annual ceiling in the following fiscal years.

In June 2003 House Speaker Dennis Hastert introduced the administration's bill to require the federal government to pay for most of the expense of prescription drugs for Medicare recipients. A quarter of the cost of the proposed benefit would, like Medicare Part B, be financed with premiums paid by beneficiaries. Federal debt—described by some Medicare officials with the misleading phrase "general revenues"—would cover the rest of the cost.

The idea of subsidized insurance coverage of prescription drugs was nothing new. It made little sense to providers and beneficiaries that Medicare covered expensive hospitalization and drugs used in hospitals, but not drugs that could keep patients with chronic conditions out of the hospital. There was one good reason to exclude Medicare coverage of the cost of prescription drugs: there was no money to pay for it. Eventually, of course, debt itself would have to be repaid with tax revenues. Like Medicare Part A and B, the cost of any new Medicare coverage would soar when the massive Baby Boom generation reached the age of eligibility for Medicare.

Since before taking office, President Bush had consistently made the case for "modernizing" Medicare with prescription drug coverage and more "choices" for Medicare beneficiaries. His argument for greater "choice" gained little traction, since Medicare already allowed patients to choose their own providers or managed care policies. In contrast, public interest in prescription drug coverage was high. The consumption and cost of prescription drugs had grown faster than had the level of Social Security pensions, which remained the principal source of income for most Americans over sixty-five. In 2003 the White House called for a Medicare prescription drug benefit that would cost $400 billion over ten years. Some Democrats advocated a more expensive program.[38]

Democratic Senator Ted Kennedy, a longtime champion of federal medical services, worked with the White House to obtain Senate passage of prescription drug coverage. In June 2003 the Senate Finance Committee sent a bill to the floor with a bipartisan 16–5 vote. The House passed Speaker Hastert's bill with a margin of one vote, and that occurred only after House leaders bolstered Republican support by passing a parallel bill that reduced taxes on income placed in medical savings accounts. That tax benefit was estimated to require an additional debt of $174 billion over ten years.[39]

Another feature of the House bill provides an important lesson for people considering proposals that require all Medicare beneficiaries to use privately administered insurance plans. The House bill limited the prescription drug benefit to privately administered plans covering all Medicare services. Beneficiaries, however, did not want to be forced into a relationship with an insurer, and there was scant proof—based on the experience with Medicare vouchers after 1997—that privately administered plans reduced costs. The conference committee, with approval by the White House, dropped the House bill's expensive tax break as well as the requirement that beneficiaries be forced to participate in private Medicare plans in order to receive the prescription benefits. But the conference committee did agree to subsidize Medicare private plans at a higher—not lower—level than the average cost per beneficiary of the traditional program of direct payment to providers.

On November 22, 2003, a majority in the House voted against the conference committee bill during the time regularly allotted for a record vote. Speaker Hastert and Majority Leader DeLay kept the final vote count open for hours, during which time they convinced several members to switch their positions. Within two months of the passage of the Medicare Prescription Drug Improvement and Modernization Act, the ten-year cost estimates for the new drug benefit, Medicare Part D, increased to $536 billion.[40] Medicare's actuary later admitted that he had believed that the legislation would cost more than estimates published at the time the bill was passed, and that he had been threatened with termination if he shared his conclusions with Congress.[41] By 2005 the Medicare actuary predicted that the ten-year cost would exceed $1 trillion and that the present value of its cost (the amount of current dollars that would have to be reserved and invested in Treasury debt to fund general revenue costs) would be $8.7 trillion, more than the total federal debt at the time.[42] In 2013 the Medicare Trustees estimated that $164 billion will be paid for prescription drug benefits in 2022, an amount significantly greater than the total of $104 billion expected to be paid to physicians under Medicare Part B.[43]

Other than premiums covering 25 percent of costs, there was no funding—other than debt—for the prescription drug benefit. Budget experts had repeatedly warned the White House and Congress that Medicare spending would sharply increase after the first of the Baby Boomers reached age sixty-five in 2010. The decade from 2001 to 2010, when many Baby Boomers were in their prime earning years, represented the last good opportunity to reserve funds for their medical costs. During that decade the increase in population between the ages of forty-five to sixty-five was two times greater than the growth in the population in all other age brackets combined.[44]

Congressman John Boehner of Ohio, who then chaired the Republican House Policy Committee, tried to overcome doubts of House Republicans about the direction of their party after its expansion of Medicare. He argued that "the American people did not want a major reduction in government."[45] Majority Leader DeLay declared that there simply was no "fat left to cut in the federal budget."[46]

The debt-financed spending binge in 2003 culminated in congressional approval that September of the administration's request for $87 billion to reconstruct and fund military operations in Iraq and Afghanistan.[47] Most Democrats supported an amendment that would have reversed a portion of the 2001 tax cuts in order to finance part of that request. Senator Conrad, the ranking Democrat on the Senate Budget Committee, explained to his colleagues that the federal funds budget was already borrowing at a rate of $700 billion a year, the highest level "as a percentage of GDP . . . since World War II."[48] The Senate tabled the amendment by a vote of 57 to 42. Not a single Republican voted in support of raising taxes to pay for the war's continuing costs. When the nation went to war after Pearl Harbor, Congress passed the Revenue Act of 1942 with only two dissenting votes.

Supplemental requests—apart from the initial budget—were typical during the first year of wars, though it was unprecedented for an administration to make its largest funding request months after announcing the end of combat. By the second year of other conflicts, prior administrations included estimates of war-related costs in their annual budgets. Although initial war costs were uncertain, members of Congress had always expected officials to at least have some military plan that could be used to estimate war-related spending. Until his last year in office, however, President Bush consistently excluded such estimates from his annual budget submissions and, instead, made emergency requests for war spending weeks or months after Congress began reviewing all other parts of the budget.[49] This practice undermined the congressional process for setting budget priorities and made any attempt at "pay as you go" budget planning impossible.

In the fiscal year ending September 30, 2003—even before passage of the legislation expanding Medicare and the appropriation of funds for the reconstruction of Iraq—federal tax revenues apart from dedicated trust funds equaled 9.2 percent of national income.[50] That level of federal funds revenues as a share of national income was lower than at any time since the attack on Pearl Harbor. These revenues could only support two-thirds of the federal funds spending, which amounted to 14.2 percent of national income.[51] The gap rose the following fiscal year. Using the balanced budget of 2000 as a benchmark, wars in Iraq and Afghanistan accounted for a quarter of the 2004–2005 deficit.[52] Debt-financed tax reduction and military spending apart from war were responsible for most of the new debt.

Bush was the fourth Republican president to face a massive potential budget deficit during his third year of office. The first, Abraham Lincoln, asked for a massive tax increase to reduce federal borrowing. The second, Herbert Hoover, also asked for higher taxes. The third, Ronald Reagan, asked for a standby tax surcharge combined with spending limits to curb further borrowing. In contrast, when faced with massive deficits in 2003, President Bush asked Congress to pass debt-financed tax cuts, an expansion of Medicare, and substantial funding for the reconstruction of two nations occupied by American forces.

Without the traditional link between spending and tax policies, federal politicians found it harder to say no to spending requests. In fiscal years 1996 and 1997, when federal leaders worked hard to balance budgets, action on appropriations bills had been highly contentious. From 2001 to 2006, however, appropriations bills sailed through Congress with lopsided bipartisan majorities and no threat of a presidential veto.[53]

After the demise of the traditional fiscal constitution, voters began asking congressional candidates variations of the basic question: "If Congress can find money to reconstruct Iraq, why can't it find any money for domestic needs?" The absence of a defined limit on borrowing made that question difficult to answer.

EASY CREDIT AND THE
CONSERVATIVE IDENTITY CRISIS

The traditional taboo against mortgaging large amounts of US tax revenues to foreign creditors no longer constrained federal borrowing. No massive bond drives, like those during prior wars, reminded Americans of the cost and sacrifices required for the War on Terror and the occupation of two nations. Foreign creditors, federal trust funds, and the Federal Reserve absorbed the additional federal debt incurred during the initial years of the Bush administration. In President Clinton's last term, foreign ownership of federal debt had declined from $1.231 trillion to $992 billion; by the end of fiscal year 2004, foreign creditors held $1.795 trillion of that debt.[54]

Easy access to credit did not give rise to the borrowing binge, since credit had been readily available to the federal government since at least 1879. The laws of supply and demand could not be repealed, so obviously the sharp rise in federal borrowing raised interest rates to a level higher than they would have been otherwise. One 2003 study concluded that the sharp swing from projected surplus to deficit in 2001–2003 raised interest rates by 99 basis points.[55] Federal officials had balanced budgets throughout history and, as recently as the 1990s, tried to balance budgets in order to impart greater confidence in financial markets. But neither the plunge in equity markets in 2002 and 2003 nor the decline in bond prices in 2005 and 2006 restrained the use of debt to finance even routine government operations.

Incumbents were naturally reluctant to explain to the public that foreign trade competitors purchased federal debt in order to suppress the value of their currencies and thereby reduce the prices of goods exported to the United States. China used the dollars it accumulated through a rising trade surplus to invest in Treasury debt. Master investor Warren Buffett compared the use of capital inflows to offset a chronic trade deficit to the circumstance of a family of farmers who sold off land to maintain income until they eventually became sharecroppers. The American trade balance deteriorated after 2000. Domestic manufacturing employment—which from 1966 to 2000 had remained in a stable range of 16.6 million (June 1966) to 19.5 million (June 1979)—fell to 13.8 million in 2007. By 2013, after the Great Recession, only 11.9 million American manufacturing jobs were left.[56]

The collapse of traditional fiscal limits opened the door to ideas that would once have been considered radical. The poorly understood proposal to borrow more than a trillion dollars to reform Social Security, sometimes referred to as "privatization," is a prime example. This initiative began when the president appointed a commission in May 2001 and noted that "large budget surpluses over the next ten years" would "provide an opportunity to move to a stronger Social Security system."[57] The notion of Social Security reform sounded prudent in 2001, since the long-run actuarial balance of the Social Security Old-Age and Survivors Insurance Trust Fund had deteriorated. Actuaries calculated that the gap, largest in the later years of a seventy-five-year projection, could be closed by an additional tax or a reduction in the value of benefits between 1 to 1.9 percent of covered payroll, an amount equal to 1 percent or less of national income. The size of that potential shortfall was dwarfed by the growing deficit in the federal funds budget.[58] Though the president asserted that the longer lives of Americans posed risks to Social Security, the demographic trends had actually improved relative to the assumptions used as the basis for the Greenspan Commission's 1983 reforms.[59]

Bush had requested that his Commission to Strengthen Social Security present policy options for funding a new system of personal retirement accounts that would supplement the current pension system. A group of Republican activists rallied in support of a plan to incur over a trillion dollars in debt to fund "private accounts." After his reelection in 2004, President Bush toured the nation to promote the concept of personal accounts. In his State of the Union address in January 2005, Bush claimed that the existing system was "headed toward bankruptcy."[60] He dramatized his claim by visiting a Social Security office, where he claimed that the amount invested in Treasury bonds was only a ledger entry. He asserted during his visit that "there is no 'trust fund.'" In fact most holdings of Treasury bonds, like checking accounts, are electronic ledger entries and federal law required the payment of all amounts owed.

Proponents of private accounts did not, of course, publicize the extensive use of debt to finance their plan. Because the Social Security trust fund had no actuarial surplus, any diversion of dedicated payroll tax revenues would inevitably require the use of debt—directly or indirectly—to fund future benefits at existing levels. That is why Federal Reserve Chairman Greenspan and Treasury Secretary O'Neill had earlier warned the White House that any plan to reduce pension obligations through the funding of private accounts—which both favored—would require a large surplus in the federal funds budget.

In 2004, "almost two-thirds of U.S. retirees relied on Social Security for most of their income, largely due to the decline in traditional pensions in recent decades."[61] To allay public suspicions about the risk of stock market investment, Republican congressional leaders insisted that the new personal accounts would not reduce future guaranteed benefits. Contrary to the perceptions of many traditional conservatives and liberal critics, the reform or privatization plan as described by the president did not entail a significant reduction in future benefits. In March 2006 a bill to fund personal accounts with Social Security reserves held for the retirement of Baby Boomers died with a perfunctory vote, 46 to 53, in the Senate. That bill, had it passed, would have resulted in more than a trillion dollars in additional federal debt—about $10,000 per working American. In hindsight, that defeat was a blessing for the Republican Party. If the Social Security trust fund had been depleted to fund personal accounts holding stocks or various stock index funds, the GOP might have been struggling for its very survival during the stock market crash that accompanied the Great Recession of 2008.

The majority of midterm voters in 2006 held Republicans accountable for the mismanaged wars and domestic failures such as the chaotic response to Hurricane Katrina in 2005. Record deficits incurred during the Bush administration made it difficult for Republicans to cast themselves as guardians of the Treasury. The massive borrowing by the Bush administration invited obvious comparisons with the reduction in annual borrowing during the Clinton administration. Echoing a powerful and traditional theme, one of the Democrats' rising stars, Senator Barack Obama, tried to make the case for budget discipline: "We are mortgaging our future. We're taking a credit card for our children, in our children's name and our grandchildren's, and we're running up the card and being completely irresponsible."[62] Democrats controlled the House for the first time in a dozen years after the 2006 election. Democratic leaders would soon be tested on the strength of their commitment to restore traditional fiscal discipline.

18

THE GREAT RECESSION AND BUDGET STALEMATE

*2007–2013: Years when deficits exceeded debt service = 7
(recession, war, medical services
and extension of tax cuts)*

ON THE PRECIPICE

Upon taking office in 2001 George W. Bush pledged to reduce total debt by $2 trillion and create a $1 trillion contingency reserve. Paying down the debt would allow the nation some flexibility in the event of an economic emergency. His initial goals were consistent with the proud traditions of his party, including the debt reduction following the end of World War I and the Civil War. By 2007, even excluding the cost of two wars, the original Bush fiscal plan was in shambles.

Republicans incurred trillions of dollars of debt to lower tax rates and raise base military spending apart from war. Ultimately that debt would have to be repaid, with interest. Republicans could not realistically expect that future debt service would somehow be borne by the 70 percent of households with 10 percent of the nation's wealth rather than the 5 percent of households with 80 percent of the wealth.[1] The War on Terror entailed a sustained investment in the capacity to detect and respond to potential attacks by groups operating anywhere in the world. The United States could not continue to forever fund its antiterrorism efforts with debt.

Leaders of the new Democratic majority in the House in 2007 faced a stark political dilemma. They took pride in contrasting the Clinton administration's balanced budgets with the red ink of the Bush administration, but congressional Democrats could only balance the budget by slashing federal spending. They were not prepared to cross that bridge.

The new House leadership initially vowed that any tax cut or spending increase would have to be accompanied by corresponding spending cuts or new revenues. The Senate, however, did not offset a loss of revenues when passing legislation that limited the application of the Alternative Minimum Tax. Only a relatively small group of traditional fiscal conservatives—largely "Blue Dog" Democrats from Republican-leaning districts—opposed final House passage of that debt-financed tax cut in 2007.

Most Democrats were also unwilling to insist that new taxes be levied to pay for the wars in Iraq and Afghanistan. The Democratic congressional majority tried to condition war funding on a timetable for withdrawal, but dropped that requirement following a veto by President Bush. The pace of debt-financed wartime spending continued to accelerate as the administration deployed more ground forces as part of a new strategy to reduce violence against Iraqi civilians and thereby stabilize the country's government.

The American Fiscal Tradition allowed for the use of debt in response to severe economic downturns. The need to preserve debt capacity for economic emergencies provided a strong justification for otherwise limiting the use of debt. Downturns are, of course, difficult to forecast. The significance of the ominous clouds that began to appear in 2007 became visible to most experts only in hindsight. Total mortgage debt grew from $6.7 trillion in 2000 to $14.6 trillion in 2008. Total consumer debt rose from 100 percent of annual national income in 2000 to about 140 percent in 2008.[2] Then, in 2007, the number of homeowners who missed mortgage payments soared, and some mortgage lenders failed.

As the decline in the housing market began to slow overall economic growth, the Federal Reserve slashed interest rates in the final months of 2007. The White House and Congress also sought to bolster the economy. In early 2008 the Bush administration joined House Speaker Nancy Pelosi and Minority Leader John Boehner in support of a plan for the federal government to borrow $168 billion and distribute it to Americans as "tax rebates."[3] It would have been more difficult to maintain the fiction of this "tax rebate" if members of Congress had been required to vote separately to authorize additional debt for that purpose. Generations of prior federal leaders would have ridiculed the idea of borrowing money to distribute cash to Americans during a war. Wisely enough, Americans saved the borrowed dollars rather than following the president's recommendation that they spend them.[4]

The risks posed by large pools of mortgage debt and related synthetic debt became clearer when two enormous financial institutions, Freddie Mac and Fannie Mae, became insolvent in the summer of 2008. The erosion of one of the old pillars of the American Fiscal Tradition—clear accounting—contributed to that crisis. For years the federal government had eschewed traditional limits on debt by allowing Freddie Mac and Fannie Mae to foster the perception of a federal guaranty, though Congress had never voted to guarantee their debt. The potential bankruptcy of Freddie Mac and Fannie Mae threatened the survival of banks, insurers, and pension funds that held their debt. In August 2008 the federal government guaranteed the debt of Freddie Mac and Fannie Mae and put both institutions into receivership.

That episode illustrated the risk of dependence on foreign creditors. Even before Congress acted on the guaranty, Treasury Secretary Hank Paulson had to reassure the Chinese government that the United States would stand behind the debts of its two large mortgage lenders. Russian officials tried to convince their Chinese counterparts to begin liquidating bonds issued by Fannie Mae and Freddie Mac as a means of forcing federal assumption of this debt.

BORROWING TO PREVENT DEPRESSION

Wall Street's financial giant Lehman Brothers filed for bankruptcy protection on September 9, 2008. Immediately afterward the world's oldest money market fund became illiquid. If depositors withdrew funds from financial institutions, the credit system of the United States and much of the world would be destroyed.

Much has already been written on the Great Recession of 2008, the world's narrow escape from a global depression. Three lessons from that experience highlight the peril of the current federal debt crisis. First, arcane accounting disguised the size of the debt. Second, creditworthy financial institutions borrowed excessively in pursuit of growth. Third, the danger of high debt became apparent only suddenly, when buyers of mortgage debt disappeared. Creditors loaned freely to the world's largest banks when it was inconceivable that they would be unable to repay; that lending ended abruptly when the inconceivable became a real possibility.

Federal Reserve Chairman Ben Bernanke, a student of the Great Depression, concluded later that "we came very close in October 2008 to Depression 2.0."[5] Bernanke's Federal Reserve functioned as a lender of last resort, and its powerful status as a virtual fourth branch of government—another feature of the nation's unwritten constitution—helped it to preserve the continuity of federal policies when leadership of the executive branch changed hands after the November 2008 election.

Bernanke asked the Treasury to borrow in order to help fund the commercial banking system. In a televised address on September 14, 2008, President Bush told Americans that "without immediate action by Congress . . . America could slip into a financial panic" endangering "our entire economy."[6] Senator John McCain, the Republican presidential nominee, suspended his campaign to attend a White House meeting with President Bush, congressional leaders, and the Democratic presidential nominee, Senator Barack Obama. They urged Congress to move quickly to help prevent a financial collapse.

The idea of federal borrowing to support big banks was difficult to sell to the American public. Taxpayers understood quite well the fact that many federal officials had been reluctant to acknowledge since 2000: federal debt—at least amounts that were not monetized—would have to be repaid by someone, namely American taxpayers. On October 3, after an initial defeat in the House that was followed by a market crash, Congress reluctantly appropriated $680 billion for the Troubled Asset Relief Program, which made loans and equity investments to financial institutions and the auto industry.[7] Though borrowing on this scale and speed had not occurred since World War II, the use of debt for relief from depression was consistent with the American Fiscal Tradition. Bernanke told Congress on October 20, 2008, that while additional deficit spending could "burden future generations and constrain future policy options," it seemed "appropriate in light of the downturn."[8] Never before, however, had borrowing during a downturn begun with a level of debt already so high in relation to national income.

Senators Obama and McCain had both pledged during the campaign to stimulate the economy with plans that required over $100 billion in debt. After Obama's election, as economic activity continued to fall faster than at any time since the Great Depression, most economists urged even greater debt-financed stimulus.[9]

The new president noted the reality of large inherited debts. He explained to the Congressional Democratic Caucus that debt had doubled since 2000 and was "wrapped in a big bow waiting for me as I stepped into the Oval Office."[10] The Congressional Budget Office forecasted a deficit of $1.2 trillion for fiscal year 2009, which was three and a half months underway when President Obama took office.[11] In fact, tax revenues were falling faster than predicted. The deficit in the federal funds budget for fiscal year 2009, which ended on June 30, 2009, turned out to be $1.54 trillion, a larger percentage of national income than at any time except during World War II.[12]

President Obama urged Congress to raise spending and reduce taxes in order to compensate for an estimated trillion dollar contraction of national income. In February Congress passed the $787 billion American Recovery and Reinvestment Act of 2009. It consisted primarily of tax cuts and spending for infrastructure and unemployment relief spread over several fiscal years.[13]

Up to that point in early 2009, the Bush and Obama administrations' responses to the downturn had followed precedents set by the Hoover and Roosevelt administrations. They, along with the Federal Reserve, tried to avoid the mistake of doing too little too late, as in 1929–1933. However, the budget for fiscal year 2010 failed to create a clear line between extraordinary spending for recovery-related efforts and some normal level of spending. The Obama administration's proposed budget for that year, which Congress largely adopted, increased formula-based spending by 14.9 percent and other federal spending by 13.8 percent. The White House estimated that level of spending would require additional debt of $1.1 billion in the unified budget.[14] As in the prior fiscal year, tax revenues during the year turned out to be lower than expected, and borrowing was higher than initially forecasted.

By the summer of 2009 the economy began growing again, though from a much lower level of private sector employment than before the Great Recession.[15] Debt-financed federal spending and tax cuts had placed a floor under economic activity. In the twenty-four months between October 1, 2008, and September 30, 2010, the federal funds budget consisted of $5.37 trillion in spending, $2.42 billion in tax revenues, and almost $3 trillion in new debt, the equivalent of approximately $20,000 of debt for every employed citizen and $30,000 per household.[16]

Senator Kent Conrad, the Senate's budget expert and a harsh critic of chronic deficit spending, warned the president that the deficit resulted from an imbalance between tax and spending policies that predated the recession. Obama replied that he would be willing to make hard decisions to reduce the deficit even if it meant he would be "a one-term president."[17] In January 2010 the Senate defeated a bill, advocated by Conrad, to appoint a bipartisan commission that would make specific recommendations on actions to close the budget deficit. The Senate vote on the measure was 46 in favor and 54 opposed; 6 Republicans who had sponsored the bill voted against it. Obama used an executive order to appoint a commission with a similar purpose.

Republican congressional leaders criticized annual deficits, but did not propose to balance the budget through any combination of spending cuts and tax increases. Republican activist Grover Norquist considered opposition to higher taxes to be his party's "brand" and likened Republicans who voted for any tax increase to "rat heads in a Coke bottle. . . . They damage the brand for everyone else."[18]

MEDICAL SPENDING

Greater access to medical insurance had become a goal that embodied the values of the Democratic Party. The debate over health care during the 2008 campaign focused far more on the expansion of medical coverage than on how to pay for existing Medicare. Most Americans believed it made no sense that a person just a few months younger than those who were eligible for Medicare could face death or financial ruin because of a serious medical condition, while Medicare beneficiaries received some of the finest medical care in the world. There was, of course, a straightforward—though politically awkward—reason for this situation: it was difficult to expand coverage when the federal government lacked sufficient revenues to pay for existing Medicare. Politicians in both parties tended to sidestep this inconvenient truth, which posed the inconvenient question of how they intended to pare down Medicare or increase taxes to fill the funding gap.

No public figure can match the president's power to frame an issue for public debate, but even a president must clearly define and repeat any goal in order to move public opinion. President Obama had the opportunity to explain the goals of paying for Medicare or paying for coverage of workers too young for Medicare. The administration recognized the challenge posed by debt-financed Medicare. White House Budget Director Peter Orszag had warned for years of that problem.

There were few options for finding additional revenues for Medicare. The president had repeatedly pledged not to raise taxes for households making less than $250,000, or roughly 97 percent of taxpayers. In 2010 taxpayers earning more than $250,000 already paid about 50 percent of all personal income taxes.[19]

Many Democrats in Congress were more interested in passing legislation to expand coverage than in closing the Medicare funding gap. On July 14, 2009, House leadership introduced a bill that expanded coverage by borrowing a trillion dollars over ten years, according to Congressional Budget Office estimates. Days later, after faulting the prior administration for "the enactment of two tax cuts, primarily for the wealthiest Americans, and a Medicare prescription program, none of which were paid for," the president vowed that "health-insurance reform . . . will be paid for."[20] As long as the federal government was borrowing heavily to pay for *existing* medical services, it would inevitably have to borrow to pay for any additional services. All but a handful of Senate Republicans criticized the alternatives for increasing access to medical services, though they did not propose to end the debt-financing of Medicare.

The Affordable Care Act, enacted by a razor-thin vote in March 2010, expanded Medicaid, required many people to purchase health insurance, subsidized certain insurance premiums, and placed new caps on Medicare reimbursements. Somewhat less than half of the cost of the Affordable Care Act was paid for using revenues from new Medicare taxes on high incomes, taxes on insurance with high premiums, and civil penalties on workers without health insurance. The act limited the growth in Medicare's reimbursable fees for services to about 2 percent a year, far less than the average historical growth rate and less than even the projected rise in costs borne by physicians.[21] Congressional Republicans opposed the Affordable Care Act, but incorporated its projected reduction in Medicare reimbursements into their own budget plan. The absence of a tax-funded budget or a congressional vote on the amount of debt used to fund specific appropriations confused the issue of how much debt would actually be required to pay for Medicare, Medicaid, and the coverage under the Affordable Care Act.

Unlike the 2003 Medicare Prescription Drug Improvement and Modernization Act, the Affordable Care Act's net cost was reduced by additional taxes and planned reductions in Medicare reimbursement rates. Yet, by making the expansion of medical insurance its signature domestic policy initiative, the Obama administration found it difficult to balance the total outlays and revenues available for medical services.

Unemployment had remained higher for a longer period than after other downturns since the Great Depression. On November 3, 2010, the Federal Reserve announced that it would expand credit by making "large scale asset repurchases," initially $75 billion in Treasury debt for each of eight consecutive months.[22] Bernanke referred to this monetization of debt as "credit easing," though most observers called it "quantitative easing."[23] The expansion of the monetary base also lowered interest rates. Republican leaders who had once embraced budgets financed substantially by foreign central banks now objected to purchases of federal debt by the central bank of their own nation.

Debt-Financed Compromise

A Republican landslide in 2010 returned control of the House of Representatives to the GOP. Afterwards, John Boehner—the Ohio congressman who would become the new Speaker—obtained the president's agreement to extend tax cuts enacted by Congress in 2001 and 2003 that were set to expire at the end of 2010. Boehner, in return, acquiesced to the president's proposal to extend unemployment benefits and temporarily reduce payroll taxes. The Tax Relief, Unemployment Insurance Reauthorization and Job Creation Act of 2010, passed in December, required additional debt of $900 billion over ten years, an amount greater than the controversial stimulus plan in 2009.[24]

The use of trust funds to support popular types of spending within revenues provided by dedicated taxes had been one of the pillars of the American Fiscal Tradition. The reduction in payroll taxes supporting the Social Security Old Age and Survivors Trust Fund was a novel departure from both traditional budget practices and long-standing Democratic policy. President Roosevelt had vowed to maintain tax rates at a level that preserved the program's actuarial balance. The payroll taxes supporting pensions for older Americans were first collected in 1937, even though the nation was still suffering from the Great Depression. Workers accepted that taxation and realized that the popular pension program was not "free."

More recently, the Clinton administration had urged that the Social Security trust funds be removed from the federal budget and that federal debt be retired to preserve the capacity to meet future pension obligations. At the Obama administration's initiative, however, for 2011 and 2012 Congress lowered employee payroll withholding by 30 percent and replaced that revenue with a debt-financed payment from the federal funds budget.

In a political atmosphere characterized by heightened concerns about soaring federal debt, in early 2011 administration officials and Republican congressional leaders began negotiating the terms on which Congress would raise the debt ceiling. Voting to approve trillions of dollars in additional debt posed a particular political challenge for those Republican House members who had been backed by Americans who attended Tea Party rallies. The House could, of course, restore "pay as you go" budget planning and vote to spend no more than the estimated amount of tax revenues. That would require large cuts in outlays for Medicare and defense and highlight the consequences of tax reductions favored by House Republicans. Instead of trying to quickly balance the budget, Speaker Boehner said he would back a higher debt ceiling as part of a plan to reduce the growth in spending projected over ten years. Vice President Joe Biden chaired a group of senior congressional leaders that worked to identify $2 trillion in spending cuts over a decade, an amount equal to the additional borrowing projected to occur through the 2012 election.[25]

On July 17, 2011, the president and Speaker tentatively agreed to lower projected Medicare and Medicaid spending by $450 million and other spending by even more, and to raise $800 billion in tax revenue compared to projections at existing tax rates.[26] The $800 billion increase in tax revenues could have resulted from a partial expiration of those tax cuts set to lapse at the end of 2012. (The complete expiration of those tax cuts would generate $3.5 trillion in revenues over ten years.[27])

The numbers discussed by Obama and Boehner were soft. The president wanted to retain existing Medicare and Medicaid services while reducing the growth in spending for those services, a concept he called "bending the cost curve." Yet, if the administration believed it could lower medical costs without affecting services, it had every reason to do so immediately, with or without any budget bargain.[28] Boehner, for his part, never specified how he intended to increase revenues without raising tax rates. Ultimately the White House and House leadership agreed to impose caps on the rise of spending for defense and various categories of domestic spending over ten years. That agreement resulted in the Budget Control Act of 2011, which also increased the debt ceiling by $2.1 trillion.[29]

For the next fiscal year, beginning on October 1, 2011, the Budget Control Act provided for a reduction in projected outlays of $25 billion, a sum sufficient to cover only a day of federal funds borrowing.[30] Future savings would arise from a process that combined elements of the Budget Enforcement Act of 1990 and the Gramm-Rudman-Hollings Act of 1985: Congress required the executive branch to sequester, or refrain from spending, the full amount that Congress appropriated above two annual limits on spending—one for domestic spending and the other for defense spending apart from the direct costs of war.

There was no effort to define appropriate uses for the borrowed funds or develop a plan to balance the budget over the span of a decade.

Two votes on the House budget resolution in March 2012 dramatized the extent of the collapse of the American Fiscal Tradition. Democrat Jim Cooper of Tennessee and Republican Steven LaTourette of Ohio sought to amend that budget resolution to conform to what they called the "Simpson-Bowles" budget plan. That label referred to recommendations made by the majority of the fourteen-person Commission on Fiscal Responsibility, appointed by the president in April 2010. The amendment offered by Cooper and LaTourette proposed to lower the growth in Medicare spending, although—like the commission's report—it was vague on how that would be accomplished. On March 28, 2012, the House defeated the amendment, 382 to 38. The following day the House's Republican majority passed a budget resolution sponsored by House Budget Committee Chairman Paul Ryan of Wisconsin. The Congressional Budget Office calculated that Ryan's plan would perpetuate routine federal borrowing until sometime after 2040.

THE 2012 CAMPAIGN AND FISCAL CLIFF

By mid-2012 national income and federal funds revenues had been restored to their peak before the downturn. Emergency outlays authorized by the American Recovery and Reinvestment Act of 2009 were winding down. Yet a large gap still remained between tax revenues and routine federal spending, even after excluding the ongoing cost of the wars in Iraq and Afghanistan.

During the 2012 presidential campaign, President Obama and Republican nominee Mitt Romney presented plans to balance the budget in some distant year while borrowing aggressively during the next presidential term. In a major speech on the deficit during the 2011 debate over the budget ceiling, the president had clearly described the need to close the gap in Medicare funding for the Baby Boom generation. Neither candidate in 2012, however, proposed to end borrowing for Medicare. In fact, Romney sought to repeal existing ceilings on Medicare reimbursement.

Budget agreements in 2010 and 2011 had postponed tax increases and extended some emergency spending until January 1, 2013, a date commentators characterized as the "fiscal cliff."[31]

After Obama's reelection, the White House and Republican congressional leaders extended the Bush-era tax cuts for over 99 percent of taxpayers.[32] They agreed on a plan that increased income tax rates for individuals with incomes above $400,000 and couples with incomes above $450,000, ended the debt-financed reduction in payroll taxes, and postponed the spending sequestration mandated by the Budget Control Act of 2011 for three months. Compared to existing law, that compromise was estimated to add debt of $3.9 billion within ten years.[33] Congress adopted the American Taxpayer Relief Act on January 1, 2013, by a lopsided margin. Despite dire predictions about the impact of higher taxes and scheduled sequestrations, there was no discernible change in the path of economic growth.

By 2013 the four pillars of the Tradition—clear accounting, "pay as you go" budget planning, self-funded independent trust funds, and borrowing for a specific purpose defined by Congress—had fallen into disrepair.

Incumbent leaders in each major political party acknowledged the virtue of balancing the budget in the distant future, but denied they had the ability to do so any time soon without impairing economic growth. Many Democrats maligned efforts to bring levels of spending in line with revenues as a form of "austerity." Republican leaders disparaged efforts to substitute tax revenue for debt as a "job killer."

As explained in more detail in Chapter 22, American economic history does not support the idea that a strong economy depends on chronic federal borrowing. Employment was slow to recover after the Great Recession of 2009. From December 2007 through April 2013 the employment of college graduates increased by 9 percent, while employment of workers with only high school diplomas fell by 9 percent. Individuals without a high school degree fared even worse; their employment decreased by 14 percent.[34] Not all college graduates found jobs for which they had been educated, but workers with more education generally fared much better than other citizens.

Many Americans expect federal leaders to seek greater opportunities for those left behind in the changing global economy. Candidates reinforce that expectation by asserting that they will "create jobs" if elected. The desire to improve American competitiveness is a tenuous rationale for using debt instead of tax revenue to pay for routine defense, medical, and other kinds of federal spending.

The Nation's Sixth and Current Debt Crisis

By 2014 virtually all mainstream federal elected officials agreed that excessive federal debt posed a real risk. Several features of this sixth national debt crisis highlight the unusual nature of those risks.

First, the amount of federal debt soared to record levels in relation to the size of annual income realistically available for taxation. Total unmonetized federal debt in 2014 roughly equals annual national income, so annual interest on the debt may absorb much of the nation's economic growth. That puts the nation in a situation similar to that of an employee who receives annual pay raises but cannot improve his or her standard of living because of the need to pay rising debt service to creditors.

Second, since the Great Recession of 2008, tax revenues available for debt service have been no more than 11 percent of the total debt, which is the lowest sustained level since the inauguration of Thomas Jefferson in 1801. Even after the nation's other severe debt crises—following the Civil War and World War II—federal debt was much lower in relation to the amount of annual tax revenues available to pay principal and interest.

Third, interest on federal debt has compounded since 2002. Except in emergencies, the United States rarely borrowed more than it paid in annual interest expense during its first 180 years. The inexorable math of compound interest explains how a person who starts with a penny and doubles it each day would have more than $10 million in a month.

Compound interest can seem like a miracle for a person who saves and invests, but it can be a curse for a debtor.

Fourth, interest rates are likely to rise from the extraordinarily low levels of 2009 to 2013. In contrast, interest rates usually fell or remained stable after the nation's five previous debt crises. Since federal debt has an average maturity of about five years, rising interest rates will increase the future cost of trillions of dollars of refinanced debt.

Fifth, current demographic trends make it difficult to outgrow the burden of federal debt. Population grew rapidly after the earlier spikes in debt—more than 150 percent in the thirty-five years at the beginning of the Republic, more than 100 percent in the thirty-five years after the end of the Civil War, and more than 65 percent in the decades following World War II.[35] The number of female workers also rose from eighteen million in 1950 to sixty-five million in 2000, helping the United States outgrow debt incurred during World War II and the Cold War.[36] After 2000, however, the workforce grew more slowly. The retirement of Baby Boomers—almost one in four citizens born from 1946 through 1964—will result in continuing slow workforce growth in the absence of radical immigration reforms.[37]

Sixth, since 2000 the United States has depended—to an unprecedented degree—on foreign banks and governments to finance its debt. By 2020 interest payments to foreign creditors could consume an amount equal to all federal taxes paid for the domestic operations of US corporations. The nation's largest foreign creditor—the People's Bank of China—has bought federal debt to soak up dollars from its trade surplus. Nations that become dependent on international creditors find it difficult to avoid greater foreign influence on their economic and foreign policies.

Seventh, since 2000 federal officials have relied on budget projections with overly optimistic assumptions. Official forecasts now assume that future members of Congress will vote for substantially lower levels of public services than will the current majority. That kind of assumption calls to mind young St. Augustine's prayer in *The Confessions*: "Oh Lord, give me chastity, but do not give it yet."

Economists debate the approximate level at which national public debt will trigger slower growth.[38] However, it is clear that any nation with higher debt will tend to use relatively more of its tax revenues for debt service. Suppose, for example, that:

- the average interest rate applicable to federal debt returns to its historical average of 4.7 percent (significantly less than the post–World War II average of 5.3 percent),
- federal debt equals annual national income, and
- federal fund revenues are 11 percent of federal debt.

In this case, 42 cents of every tax dollar would pay for interest on prior debt, leaving only 58 cents of that dollar to be spent on national defense and current services. An interest rate spike like the one around 1980 can be devastating. Ask Greece.

What the Nation Borrowed to Pay for After 2000

The most unusual feature of the twenty-first-century debt crisis cannot be measured in numbers. American voters now find it difficult to determine the purpose for which the nation borrowed. In contrast, citizens in prior eras could easily recognize when a war began and ended, which made it easy for voters to identify when war-related borrowing should also cease. For the dozen years after 2000 the federal government incurred half its debt for the traditional purposes of waging war and responding to a severe downturn. The other half financed other types of spending and tax reduction.

When the federal funds budget last balanced in fiscal year 2000, federal funds tax revenues and spending each amounted to 13.3 percent of national income.[39] These percentages were in line with those in fiscal year 1965, immediately before the escalation of the Vietnam War. In fact, since 1961 federal funds revenues have not exceeded 13.8 percent of national income, and federal funds outlays have not fallen below 13.2 percent.[40] (As a result, those figures reflect a rough national consensus on the lower limit of spending and upper limit on taxes for half a century.)

Chart 1 compares spending and revenues against the benchmark level of 13.3 percent of national income, the level at which the United States last balanced its budget.[41] The area between the top and bottom lines represents the extent of new debt. Because the nation lacks an itemized, tax-financed portion of the federal funds budget, one literally cannot trace a borrowed dollar to a particular payment. The balanced budget in 2000, however, is the best available benchmark for demonstrating the use of debt incurred after 2000.

Chart 1: Federal Funds Spending as a Share of National Income

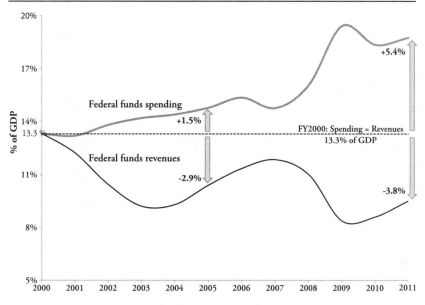

From Fiscal 2000 baseline: $1.32 trillion, 13.3% of GDP

Chart 2 shows the categories of spending that increased as a share of national income since 2000.[42] So, for example, in 2011 the nation borrowed about 1.1 percent of national income to finance ongoing wars and an additional 1.1 percent to pay for higher levels of military spending apart from war ("base" military spending). Debt also paid for the cost of medical services that had risen by 1.5 percent of national income. Borrowing for the four-year stimulus begun in 2010—the American Recovery and Reinvestment Act and the federal funds portion of extended unemployment benefits—accounted for 1.2 percent of national income in 2011 and ended in 2013. All other federal spending rose by just over half a percent of national income from 2000 to 2011. "All other" domestic federal funds spending has been declining since 2011.

The use of debt to pay for base defense (apart from war) and medical services departed from long-standing precedent. The policies of cutting taxes during war or funding new medical services with debt were so far outside the unwritten fiscal constitution that nothing similar had ever previously been considered.

Chart 2: What New Debt Paid For as a Share of National Income

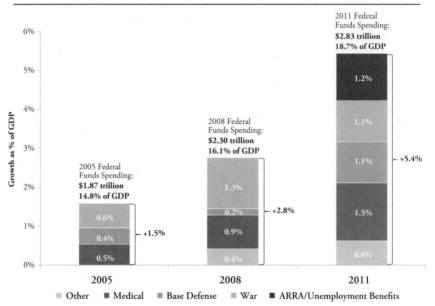

Other   Medical   Base Defense   War   ARRA/Unemployment Benefits

Federal funds revenue supported 24.6 percent of federal Medicare costs in 1970, 23.4 percent in 1980, 27.9 percent in 1990, and 27.8 percent in 2000.[43] The share of federal funds revenue required to support escalating costs of Medicare had grown to 44 percent, about $233 billion out of $530 billion, by 2010—the very year that Baby Boomers first became eligible for the program.[44]

Chart 3 shows the components of federal funds revenues that declined as a share of national income after 2000.[45] Tax legislation in 2001 and 2003 led to the substitution of debt for some tax revenues.

Much of the drop in revenues between 2008 and 2011 resulted from the economic downturn. Even with robust economic growth, the White House Office of Management and Budget projects that by 2014 federal funds tax revenues will recover to 11.4 percent of national income, or 11.0 percent of total debt. When interest payments rise to 3.5 percent of national income, revenues of about 8 percent of national income must support national security, medical costs, and everything else not funded with dedicated trust fund revenues.

A dozen years after the collapse of the American Fiscal Tradition, federal funds tax revenues could not support anything close to the existing

Chart 3: Federal Funds Revenue as a Share of National Income

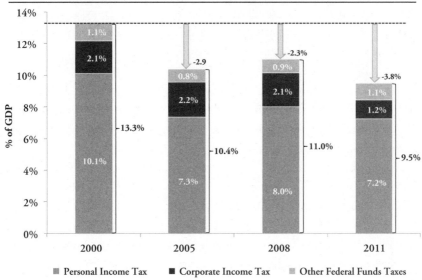

Legend: ■ Personal Income Tax ■ Corporate Income Tax ■ Other Federal Funds Taxes

level of spending on national security, medical services, and everything else outside of trust funds.

Federal Leadership at a Crossroads

By 2014 the consequences of rising debt had exposed the fragility of the debt-financed achievements of federal elected officials in each party.

Republican-sponsored tax reductions did not reduce the size of the federal government. Even apart from outlays occasioned by wars and recession, outlays for the base defense budget and medical programs had climbed sharply. After the 2012 election, Republican congressional leaders agreed not to block the scheduled rise in the tax rate applicable to the highest tax bracket. They had no politically viable alternative. Expenditures for national security—the single category of spending most valued by many conservatives—faced massive cuts as a result of the Budget Control Act of 2011, which Republican leaders had agreed to as a condition for raising the debt ceiling.

Democratic accomplishments also rested on thin ice, as the rising cost of medical services began crowding out other domestic spending. The Budget Control Act of 2011, negotiated by a Democratic president with strong progressive credentials, gradually dropped the share of nonmedical domestic federal funds spending to its lowest level in fifty years. Rising medical and interest expenses threatened future federal commitments to education, job training, nutrition, medical research, affordable housing, urban transit, and renewable energy. Recovery from the Great Recession of 2008 and withdrawal from two wars made it more difficult to hide the use of debt to pay for routine expenses. By 2014, however, incumbent leaders in each party found it hard to act decisively to balance the budget without violating campaign pledges.

Most voters and elected officials profess agreement with the ideal of balancing the budget. Federal candidates can, however, feel pressured by some influential activists and intellectuals—exemplified by Grover Norquist on the right and Paul Krugman on the left—who question the importance of that objective. Norquist and Krugman consider the focus on annual federal borrowing to be a distraction from what they regard as the more significant fight over the size and responsibilities of the federal government. In general, Norquist believes that spending should be reduced to the level of current tax revenues, while Krugman believes that tax revenues should rise to the level of current spending minus newly monetized debt. Norquist and Krugman treat the drive for balanced budgets as pressure to strike what each would consider an unacceptable compromise.

A group of business leaders have organized the Committee for a Responsible Federal Budget to provide some counterweight to the voices who oppose compromises designed to reduce borrowing. The gap between federal revenues and expenditures is so great, however, that even the committee embraced budget plans that allow annual borrowing for routine expenses. The committee seeks to limit the growth of debt to less than the growth in nominal national income. So, for example, if nominal income (not adjusted for inflation) is estimated to grow at 4 percent a year, debt could grow at 3 percent a year. Since the federal government will certainly borrow additional funds during future downturns or wars, a budget rule that condones the use of debt—rather than tax revenues—for recurring expenses runs the risk of debt growing faster than projected. Chronic borrowing also undermines the Jeffersonian principle of confining government to the price that the public is willing to pay in taxes.

PART VI

RESTORING THE TRADITION

19

REVIVING TRADITIONAL
BUDGET PRACTICES

MODERN APPLICATION OF TRADITIONAL PRACTICES

Ending the addiction to debt takes more than political courage. Four pillars of the American Fiscal Tradition—clear accounting, "pay as you go" budget planning, trust funds financed entirely with dedicated revenues, and explicit congressional approval of debt for specific amounts and purposes—once curbed the temptation to borrow. These practices helped federal leaders reduce debt for a minimum of ten out of eleven straight years after each of the nation's first four peaks in debt. After the fifth debt spike (in 1945), traditional budget practices helped steadily reduce the burden of debt for three decades. Modern variations of time-tested practices could help federal leaders respond to the nation's current debt crisis.

Reform 1: A Separate, Tax-Financed Federal Funds Budget

Driving a car without a dashboard and transparent windshield is dangerous, and so is budget planning without a clear view of the relationship between annual spending and revenues. Thomas Jefferson insisted that federal budgets be "clear and intelligible" to "any man of any mind."[1] Today federal accounting often disguises the level of borrowing, the use of borrowed funds, and the actual burden of existing debt. For this reason, the president should submit, and Congress should be required to vote on, a federal funds budget—apart from a trust fund budget—with spending limited to estimated revenues. A separate trust fund budget would encompass all the spending supported entirely by dedicated trust fund revenues. Any spending to be funded with debt should be excluded from the trust fund budget.

A tax-financed budget would help minimize distracting debates—such as those in the 1980s and after 2000—about what borrowed money paid for. Separation of federal funds and trust funds budgets would eliminate complexities of actuarial accounting from much of the federal funds budget and reduce the temptation of federal officials to count social insurance revenues as income without accruing a related liability. Use of a separate trust funds budget is hardly radical; it conforms to the procedure in place before fiscal year 1969.

A tax-financed federal funds budget would also highlight the cost of debt service and, in doing so, serve as a reminder that debt is not free. Citizens today have difficulty even finding the federal interest expense payable annually from federal funds revenues. For example, in fiscal year 2011, the federal funds budget paid $418 billion in net interest, an amount $188 billion higher than the amount shown in the unified budget.[2] A tax-financed budget would also make the consequences of tax cuts more visible by explicitly linking the relationship between spending and taxes. No one likes taxes, and the only reason to tax is to pay for public spending.

Even though enactment of a separate tax-financed budget would not preclude a separate authorization of debt, it would strengthen the political and management skills required to link spending and tax policies. Those skills have atrophied.

Even good faith revenue estimates will, of course, sometimes miss the mark. To reduce this risk, revenue estimates should be adjusted more frequently than twice a year, the current practice. Large corporations adjust their internal revenue forecasts at least monthly and announce any changes to their estimates quarterly.

Reform 2: Tax Financing of Debt Service and Essential Defense

The tax-financed budget should pay for all interest expenses and at least a basic level of national defense. Debt service and some level of national security are federal functions that cannot simply be performed by state and local governments. A requirement that tax revenues be reserved to pay for interest and some level of defense should remove the temptation to fund other items first and then claim that the United States must borrow to pay its creditors or defend itself. A tax-financed federal funds budget that preserves essential federal functions would make the legal debt ceiling a far more realistic tool for enforcing fiscal discipline.

The president and Congress would have to define the appropriate scope of security-related activities worth funding with tax dollars. That funding is likely to encompass programs within the Department of Defense, nuclear weapons programs in the Department of Energy, and various intelligence activities. The president and Congress would likely give priority to the use of taxes for defense-related functions such as homeland security.[3]

Reform 3: Votes on Debt-Financed Appropriations

Congressional procedures now divorce votes on spending from votes on how to pay for that spending. Congress considers amendments to the debt ceiling only *after* it has voted to spend more than available tax revenues. As a result, debates on the debt ceiling have become a form of bad political theater, a bizarre combination of tragedy and farce.

Votes to authorize debt should accompany votes to spend any amount greater than available revenue. Congress should require separate record votes on the portion of any appropriation expected to be financed with debt. Citizens would then be able to determine the amount and purposes of debt voted for by each member of Congress. The total of debts approved to pay for all appropriations would, in essence, constitute a more visible debt-financed budget.

Congress constrained debt more effectively when it voted to incur debt only for specified purposes. Before World War I, each bond issue could be traced to a defined purpose, such as financing the Civil War, the Spanish-American War, and the Panama Canal. Congress established an overall ceiling on debt used to fund World War I, and the level of that provided a context for the amount of ceiling for debt incurred during the Great Depression. Congress raised the limit on authorized debt for the clear purpose of financing World War II. The final wartime debt ceiling, $300 billion, was never exceeded until after the 1961 Berlin Crisis.[4] In contrast, after 2000 it has been far more difficult to identify the rationale for new debt.

The use of a total debt ceiling unrelated to congressional appropriations is misleading as well as ineffective. To understand why, consider the fact that the executive branch could not borrow at all if Congress repealed what is commonly called a "ceiling." Some members of Congress would prefer to characterize votes on the debt ceiling as a fight with the president, and presidents are accustomed to asking Congress to authorize more debt. In fact, the executive branch does not have an independent constitutional power to borrow a dime, and only money Congress votes to spend can be paid for with debt.

A legal debt limit established apart from specific appropriations breeds cynicism and hypocrisy, since many members of Congress have voted against higher debt ceilings after first voting for a level of spending greater than the revenues produced by their tax legislation.

The House and Senate each vote annually on about thirteen appropriations bills—legislation funding various functions of the federal government—and again for related appropriations following compromises in conference committees. Every session, subcommittees of the Appropriation Committee in the House and Senate prepare the details of those bills within the allocated spending ceilings or "marks." A tax-financed federal funds budget could be implemented by giving each appropriations subcommittee two ceilings, one for an amount financed with tax revenue and another for any use of debt.

Separate debt-financed and tax-financed appropriations would give members of Congress the ability to vote only to spend an amount limited to estimated tax revenues. A president could then approve tax-financed spending for some purpose while vetoing debt-financed spending. Presidents and members of Congress should be allowed to explain that they support a particular program, but only to the extent that it can be funded by existing or new tax revenues.

Many incumbents fear political attacks if they vote against any annual appropriations bill because they object to the method of financing rather than the object of the appropriation. So, for example, a member of Congress who strongly supports both agricultural programs and a balanced budget has difficulty explaining to constituents today why he or she voted against an agricultural appropriation that would be funded with an unspecified amount of debt. Members of Congress ought to be given the opportunity to vote only for tax-funded appropriations.

Federal leaders have always had a long list of spending items or tax cuts they would support only if they could be funded with available tax revenue. The nation's Founding Fathers deferred many of their own cherished plans until the nation paid off its debts. Many Americans now respect President Truman for his foresight in calling for a program of hospital insurance for older Americans and armed forces capable of backing American international leadership. But Truman never endorsed debt-financed peacetime military spending or health insurance.

With policy guidance from elected officials, congressional staff should be able to provide estimates of the amount of tax revenues available to pay for various spending bills. Budget professionals for state legislatures, county governments, and city councils all routinely certify the amount of tax revenues available for each appropriation.

The combination of a "pay as you go" federal funds budget and specific authorizations of debt would allow the federal government to send each taxpayer an itemized receipt showing the pro-rata uses of tax dollars and debt incurred on behalf of the taxpayer. Consumers receive itemized receipts from even small retailers, and credit card companies manage to send reports showing spending, unpaid balances, and interest charges. The federal government should be accountable in the same manner.

Reform 4: Tax Financing of Medicare

Wilbur Mills created a tax-financed trust fund for hospitalization and a trust fund for outpatient services financed partially using premiums charged to beneficiaries and partially by federal funds revenues. Though President Johnson assured Mills that there was enough room in the budget to pay for half of the outpatient services in Medicare Part B, the use of federal funds to finance a portion of Medicare did depart from the traditional practice of paying for social insurance entirely with dedicated revenues. The plan to use federal funds revenue to cover a portion of Medicare Part B might have worked—for at least a decade—if not for the cost of the Vietnam War. Other federal obligations and rising medical costs forced Congress to support Medicare Part B with higher taxes, cuts in other programs, and—eventually—debt.

In 1997 President Clinton and Congress addressed this issue with legislation that limited the rate of growth in Medicare Part B reimbursements to the rate of growth in national income. After the collapse of the American Fiscal Tradition, however, Congress cut federal funds revenues, suspended the reimbursement ceilings, and added a prescription drug benefit—Medicare Part D—financed primarily with debt.

In 1983 Congress followed the customary practice for financing social insurance when it brought the Social Security trust fund into actuarial balance well in advance of the retirement of Baby Boomers. The failure to do the same thing for Medicare may be water under the bridge, but it is not too late to place Medicare on a "pay as you go" basis before the tidal wave of Baby Boom retirements arrives in full force. It will be difficult, if not impossible, to balance the federal funds budget after 2010 without sufficient tax revenues to cover the federal funds portion of Medicare Parts B and D.

Traditional budget practices would require Congress to dedicate sufficient tax revenues to fully support the obligations of the Medicare trust funds. Citizens have a variety of views concerning the appropriate level and costs of services provided by Medicare. No one, however, can justify adding a layer of compound interest to the already high cost of medical services.

"Pay as you go" Medicare will make clear to the public precisely how the popular program is financed. Many citizens mistakenly believe that they have fully paid for Medicare with their payroll tax contributions and annual premiums. The very idea of "medical insurance" funded with loans incurred on behalf of taxpayers borders on fraud. What would you call it if an insurer paid a medical bill and then reimbursed itself with a loan to be paid by the families of all patients?

Reform 5: A National Bond Election

Polls show that most voters strongly prefer a budget that balances without higher taxes *or* cuts in the largest categories of spending, such as Medicare. These polling results do not mean that the public is altogether unwilling to choose between practical alternatives. A reasonable consumer might express a preference for a Mercedes and then buy a Chevy if that is all he or she can afford. Americans need to be told just what medical services are available at various levels of premiums and taxation. Many federal officials are well aware of the trade-offs, though they fear that they will experience the fate of the proverbial messenger if they bring bad news to voters.

It is difficult to solve an ill-defined problem. Voters find it hard to grasp the purpose of federal borrowing after years of confusing and conflicting explanations. Members of Congress feel they cannot raise taxes or cut programs that drive federal spending if their opponents in the next election can so easily mischaracterize the available alternatives. The challenge, then, is how to best enlist public participation in decisions on budget trade-offs.

That type of participation occurs thousands of times every year, when cities, counties, school districts, and states seek voter authorization to incur debt supported by general tax revenues. Voters are told the amount of requested debt and how it is to be used. Public officials tell rating agencies and voters whether tax rates would need to be raised to service the debt. State and local officials prepare budgets in light of the need to preserve future revenues available for the coverage of debt service. Bond elections are as routine as Fourth of July parades.

Nothing prevents Congress from holding a national referendum on whether to incur federal debt for specific purposes and amounts. Such a national referendum would allow conservative advocates of smaller government to make the case for bringing expenditures in line with the level of tax revenues. Progressive leaders could then make the case for taxes required to finance needed services. If enough members of Congress push for a national bond election, those who resist will have to explain why voters should be blocked from being heard on such a critical decision.

Since 1970 state and local debt has increased at half the rate of federal debt.[5] The requirement of bond elections has helped enforce that discipline.

The Practicality of Budget Reforms

The foregoing five budget reforms will help overcome political obstacles to balancing the budget. The time is right for this type of change. Contrary to the views of cynics, most citizens elected to the presidency and Congress do care about their nation's future and financial independence. Congress has been willing to impose fiscal limits on itself.

The first four budget reforms are modeled after practices that worked for generations. Budget experts were expected to provide realistic revenue estimates, and then officials in Congress or the executive branch whittled down their wish lists to the amount of those revenues. Trust fund spending was confined to the amounts of dedicated revenues and Congress-approved specific authorizations of debt. These basic budget practices remained intact even while partisan control of the White House and Congress shifted back and forth.

New political dynamics should now empower budget reformers. By 2013 both traditional conservatives and progressives in Congress were dealing with the consequences of the post-2000 borrowing binge. Many conservatives now recognize that debt-financed government failed to restrain the overall size of government or—by 2013—the tax rates applied to the highest incomes. And the very idea of borrowing for routine expenses goes against the grain of business managers who have been a core Republican constituency for over a century. Progressives in Congress recognize that even with high tax rates on the wealthiest Americans, all domestic programs will be cannibalized by interest on debt, basic national defense, and medical expenses.

The timing is right for "pay as you go" Medicare reforms. Virtually all Republican and Democratic members of Congress have pledged to support Medicare while exploring ways to constrain the growth in its cost. Democrats have been frustrated by Republican efforts to reduce federal funds revenues without paying the political price that would accompany the corresponding level of Medicare cuts. Republicans have been unable to overcome the resistance to limitations on average spending per beneficiary. Attempts to make Medicare more sustainable have been thwarted by the illusion that the debt-financed portion of Medicare is free. Republicans and Democrats should be able to agree on the principle of "pay as you go" Medicare and still have plenty of opportunity to rally their constituencies behind plans with varying levels of cost.

Long-term "deficit reduction plans" that push hard choices into the distant future are no substitute for plans to balance the budget within several years. The principle of living within one's means is well understood. Few urgent problems are best solved slowly over decades. Federal officials succeeded in balancing budgets when they explained to the public the need to protect future opportunities and preserve national independence. Elected officials who continue to borrow undermine the credibility of that message. An elected official who warns of the danger of debt while proposing a plan to borrow trillions of dollars more is like a television evangelist who preaches personal virtue but leads a tawdry private life.

Budget plans that call for sacrifices in ten years, but not now, also run a serious economic risk. The race against compound interest, which accelerates over time, must be won as a sprint rather than a marathon. The longer the nation borrows to pay for routine spending, the more likely that an emergency—war or recession—will disrupt any deficit reduction plan that is stretched out over decades. As compound interest accelerates— or "snowballs," to use George Washington's metaphor—it has a greater impact when it hits the wall imposed by the willingness of creditors to lend.

A tax-financed budget is likely to spur more effective management of formula-based spending, described in budget jargon as "nondiscretionary spending," "mandatory spending," and "entitlements." Each of those terms has a distinct legal definition, but they generally refer to spending that is driven by formula, budgeted as an estimate, and made in the form of a payment to a beneficiary or service provider.

Budget reforms enacted in the last several decades have focused on limits to spending outside of formulas—"discretionary spending." Those reforms include the Gramm-Rudman-Hollings Act of 1985 (sequestration after debt limits), the Budget Enforcement Act of 1990 (caps on annual appropriations), and the Budget Control Act of 2011 (sequestration above spending caps). The distinction between federal funds discretionary spending and nondiscretionary spending should not automatically determine what should be funded with tax revenues rather than debt. Consider, for example, the trade-off between a new benefit for veterans (nondiscretionary) and an adjustment in the compensation of active-duty soldiers (discretionary). The decision on how to allocate tax revenues between those two alternatives should not depend primarily on their classification as discretionary or nondiscretionary.

Competent federal managers should be able to avoid running out of money near the end of a year and leaving the beneficiaries and service providers of a formula-based program in the lurch. Well-managed corporations—including insurers—track actual-to-budget variances and manage cash reserves available to pay costs that are difficult to predict in advance. If the federal government cannot rely on management practices required to function within an annual spending ceiling, how can it expect to manage costs over multiple years?

CONSTITUTIONAL AMENDMENT

Madison was right: it makes more sense to limit debt with broad principles enforced by voters than with specific constitutional language enforced by courts. Yet, over several decades, many states have passed some form of resolution endorsing a constitutional requirement for balanced budgets. Such an amendment in 1995 fell one Senate vote short of the required two-thirds vote of the House and Senate. A lively debate has occurred in recent years concerning the relative desirability of a "clean" amendment limiting the use of debt and a version that would restrict the use of tax increases to accomplish that purpose.[6]

A balanced budget constitutional amendment would still necessitate reforms in congressional budget procedures. For example, the constitutional amendment that almost passed in 1995 stated that "Congress shall enforce and implement this article by appropriate legislation, which may rely on estimates of outlays and receipts."[7]

Proposed balanced budget amendments have difficulty specifying how best to retain the traditional ability to borrow during economic downturns. Few mainstream political leaders believe that the federal government should take actions such as raising taxes, laying off military personnel, or reducing the social safety net whenever federal revenues drop during recessions. For this reason, the constitutional amendment that almost passed Congress in 1995 allowed debt to be authorized by a vote of at least 60 percent of the House and the Senate. The requirement of a super-majority is intended to give the federal government flexibility during economic emergencies. However, history shows that the requirement for a 60 percent vote gives a minority the ability to use that bargaining power to actually increase spending or lower taxes in a manner that requires more debt.

For example, in budget negotiations during the 1980s President Reagan and Congress obtained a bipartisan majority by trading higher defense spending in exchange for higher domestic spending. The pivotal budget bills passed in 1990 and 1993 would have resulted in greater debt if they had been stripped of additional revenues in order to obtain a 60 percent vote. Even with rising concern about the level of debt in recent years, congressional leaders could find it harder to enact any combination of lower spending and higher tax revenues if their efforts could be blocked by 40 percent of the members of the House or Senate.

In short, a constitutional amendment requiring a supermajority vote for debt is no substitute for the budget practices that helped impose discipline in the past: clear accounting, "pay as you go" budget planning, separate budgeting for trust funds, and explicit congressional authorization of the purpose and amount of each new debt.

BUDGETS CAN BE BALANCED at various levels of spending and taxation. Traditional limits on debt have never dictated the relative priority of various categories of spending or the mix of taxes levied to balance the budget. As described in the next two chapters, in the foreseeable future the budget cannot be balanced until the United States aligns the levels of spending with tax revenue available for the two largest components of the federal funds spending: national security and medical services.

20

BALANCING THE
NATIONAL SECURITY BUDGET

THE COST OF GLOBAL MILITARY LEADERSHIP

The American Fiscal Tradition helped preserve the debt capacity needed to wage wars. Limits on borrowing also forced generations of federal leaders to carefully weigh the cost of international commitments.

Since the end of World War II, steady annual investments in military and intelligence capabilities have supported America's exceptional international leadership. In the early 1970s President Nixon sought to relax tensions with the Soviet Union in part based on his belief that Americans could not indefinitely bear Cold War sacrifices. Nixon correctly anticipated the diminishing public tolerance for Cold War tax rates. Federal revenues were insufficient to fund the new phase in that Cold War that began in 1979, following a Soviet buildup in nuclear missiles and invasion of Afghanistan.

The United States maintained a global security umbrella even after the collapse of the Soviet threat. The US-led liberation of Kuwait in 1991 and intervention in the Balkans in 1999 demonstrated the singular role of American military strength in the international order that emerged from the Cold War.

The War on Terror beginning in 2001 represented a costly new chapter in the history of US military spending. Its full budgetary implications unfolded over several fiscal years. Since the end of the Korean War, base military spending—apart from direct war costs and expressed in inflation-adjusted dollars—had remained in a fairly stable band. By 2005 the base defense budget burst through its historical upper range. If Osama Bin Laden's goal was to saddle American families with massive debt, he certainly succeeded.

Public debate over Pentagon budgets after 2000 tended to focus on the strategy and conduct of the two ongoing wars. Once US forces in Afghanistan and Iraq broke the grip of repressive regimes, they remained there to prevent chaos before new governments took root. After 2000 the United States also invested more in mobile forces that could respond effectively against terrorist groups and rogue nations. Since counterterrorism does not end with a climactic battle, the capacity to make steady annual investments in preparedness and new technologies is critical. The Bush administration never addressed the inherent conflict between that prolonged need for spending and its use of unsustainable annual borrowing to finance its military buildup.

The use of debt to pay for post-2000 military commitments made it inevitable that either future base military budgets would come down or future taxes would go up. Through 2013 the direct military costs of the wars in Afghanistan and Iraq exceeded $1.5 trillion.[1] Medical costs of discharged active duty and retired combat veterans also continued to increase. Those costs, plus the compound interest on war-related debt, raised total debt associated with those wars to more than $2 trillion, almost $20,000 per American household. After 2020 annual interest on debts related to the wars in Iraq and Afghanistan might surpass the peak annual spending for the wars themselves.

A rough bipartisan consensus on military spending had emerged in support of the Department of Defense 2012 Future Years Defense Program, which envisioned military spending as a smaller share of national income than it had been from 2003 to 2010. Even that level of defense outlays soon seemed unaffordable when Baby Boomers began to be eligible for Medicare and interest rates proceeded to rise.

The Budget Control Act of 2011 limited the growth in the base Pentagon expenditures to levels well below those proposed for the Future Years Defense Program. The top line of Chart 4 shows the Congressional Budget Office's estimate of the cost of the 2012 Future Years Defense Program, and the bottom line shows spending after the effect of the Budget Control Act's sequesters.[2]

The Budget Control Act of 2011 mandated spending cuts of about $52 billion annually—or 10 percent—from the Future Years Defense Program.[3] That difference—depicted as the gap between the top and bottom

Chart 4: Costs of DoD's Plans in the Context of the Budget Control Act (BCA)

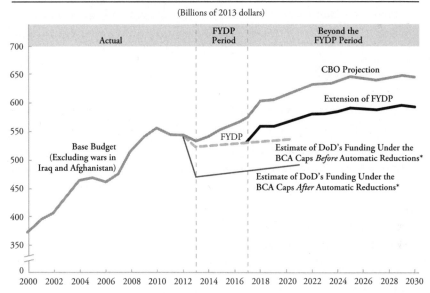

(Billions of 2013 dollars)

FYDP = Future Years Defense Program

*Assumes that DoD receives the same share of funding for national defense under the BCA that it has over the past 10 years.

Source: CBO, *Long Term Implications of the Future Years Defense Program* (July 2012)

lines—represents a significant loss in military capabilities. That reduction in spending occurred without any serious debate over whether and how to scale back US international commitments.

ALTERNATIVE LEVELS OF DEFENSE SPENDING

Four different scenarios illustrate alternative approaches for matching defense spending with Pentagon missions. The approximate cost of each, expressed as a share of national income, excludes security-related outlays for veterans and homeland security.

Alternative 1: Border Defense with Some Capacity for Retaliation

This alternative requires the armed services to sharply reduce the number of uniformed personnel, as well as naval and land-based international deployments. Technological investments would be designed to maintain a defined capacity for airborne retaliation rather than the ability to occupy foreign soil. This alternative would cost less than 2 percent of national income. It would be consistent with a foreign policy outside the current mainstream.

Alternative 2: National Defense

This alternative accomplishes more than basic border security but provides less than the capacity for combat in more than one region at a time or for occupation of a large territory. It would entail significant cuts in the current planned levels of procurement and personnel. A purely "national defense" alternative would, for example, reduce the deployment of a new generation of tactical aircraft and decrease the number of existing naval carrier task forces.[4] The United States would have to concentrate most of its military forces to engage in major combat operations. This defense posture could cost less than 3 percent of national income.

Alternative 3: The Current Consensus

This alternative is consistent with the 2012 Future Years Defense Program. The United States would retain the ability to rapidly deploy overwhelming force in a major regional war. South Korea, Taiwan, Israel, and the Persian Gulf would all remain in the US security perimeter. This alternative costs more—in inflation-adjusted dollars—than it did in 2000 because expenses for items such as health benefits and fuel have risen faster than inflation. This alternative allows the United States to intervene on the ground to counter a hostile nation's development of nuclear weapons. This alternative costs between 3 and 4 percent of national income.

Alternative 4: A Military Capable of Interventions to Replace Hostile Regimes

This alternative reflects the continuation of the type of base defense budget in place from 2003 to 2012. Spending on this scale would support a foreign policy that retains the option of sustained combat in nations such as Iran, Pakistan, or Syria. This alternative costs about 4 to 5 percent of national income. Like Alternative 1, this alternative lacks broad-based public support. It could be funded only by imposing much higher taxes.

The estimated cost for each of the four preceding alternatives should be adjusted upward to account for other defense-related outlays. For the remaining lives of the veterans of Vietnam, Iraq, and Afghanistan, it would be reasonable to estimate that spending for veterans—contained in the budgets of the Veterans Administration and various other federal departments—will consume at least 0.5 percent of national income. Adding that amount to the bottom limit of the current consensus—Alternative 3 above—yields an estimated cost of at least 3.5 percent of national income. That share of national income for defense and veterans is near the post–World War II low. Homeland security and other costs of national security, intelligence, cyberdefense, and aid to allies in the budgets of the State Department and other agencies will amount to another one-half to 1 percent of national income.

Many long-term forecasts—including those produced by the White House and CBO—envision that the Pentagon budget will decline to less than 3 percent of national income by 2020. That assumption may be overly optimistic so long as the United States continues to accept its unique leadership role in international affairs. The cost per soldier for maintaining a high level of operational readiness has consistently grown faster than national income. New weapons, cyberthreats, and greater global mobility all pose risks that may justify steady annual investments in defense. Technological superiority is expensive. Paradoxically, those costs may rise when more potent weapons become more accessible at lower costs to potential adversaries. From 1999 to 2001, defense spending did decline to 3 percent of national income, but that occurred in large part because of the sharp drop in activities related to nuclear weapons developed for the Cold War. There appears to be nothing similar on the horizon.

TAX REVENUES TO SUSTAIN THE "CONSENSUS"

The American Fiscal Tradition once forced the United States to explicitly weigh its commitments to allies against their cost in taxes. Today the level of commitments that taxpayers are willing to fund is, at best, unclear. An unusual partisan alignment has complicated the formation of a new national consensus on that trade-off. The Republican coalition in recent years includes both voters attracted to the vision of smaller government and culturally conservative voters who support an exceptional—albeit costly—American role in international affairs. Most Republican leaders in Washington have used debt to bridge the gap between conflicting demands for a high level of military spending and a low level of taxes.

Federal tax law in place as of 2013 is unlikely to yield revenues that would fully fund military spending in line with the third alternative—the current consensus—presented above. In 2000 the federal funds budget balanced with spending and revenues each at 13.3 percent of national income. At that time personal income tax revenues amounted to a higher share of national income than at any time since the end of World War II.[5] In 2007, before the Great Recession, federal funds revenues were 11.9 percent of national income; in fiscal year 2014 federal funds revenues are projected to be 11.4 percent of national income.[6] If interest expense consumes tax revenues of 3 to 4 percent of national income, a base budget for national defense, homeland security, and veterans of 4.5 percent of national income would require large cuts in existing federal funds spending for Medicare and everything else.

A cut in national security outlays equal to 1 percent of national income might not seem large in the abstract, but it does impair the ability to retain existing military capabilities and keep a step ahead of new threats. Reducing the Pentagon's planned budgets by one-fourth would produce less than three-fourths of the combat strength. There are large fixed costs for items such as global intelligence and retiree health benefits. Because of fixed costs for research, development, and manufacturing capacity for a new weapons system, a cut in the number of new weapons purchased will raise the average cost per unit. The same type of cost increase occurs when federal officials stretch out the procurement schedule. In addition, costs contributing less directly to combat capabilities are often the hardest to constrain. Commitments made to retirees and for the medical care provided for military personnel and their families have a strong ethical dimension that makes them difficult to pare down in any budget year.

Likewise, it is no small hurdle to raise personal income tax revenues by 1 percent of national income. In fiscal year 2014, for example, the White House estimated that personal income tax receipts will amount to 8.1 percent of national income, so an additional 1 percent—bringing the total to 9.1 percent—would require 12 percent more revenue.[7] An increase in personal income tax rates to generate revenue of that magnitude has not occurred since the Korean War.

The United States is unlikely to preserve the existing level of global security by complaining that other nations should be doing more. Allies with armed services designed primarily for territorial defense and limited roles within multinational deployments have long relied on the United States to provide needed intelligence, communications, precision targeting, control of the sea, and logistical support for substantial foreign military operations.

Only a handful of countries have the economic strength to invest in capabilities such as carrier task forces, elite special forces capable of rapid deployment anywhere, and airborne precision-guided munitions operating within a global satellite grid. Developed nations with aging workforces are unlikely to invest significantly more of their national incomes in support of international security. Japan and Germany, with the world's third and fourth largest national economies, occasionally have interests that differ from those of the United States. For example, dependence on exports to China and oil imported from the Persian Gulf could temper the commitments of those nations to the security of Taiwan and Israel.

China, with the world's second largest economy, has the economic capacity to expand its military and shares some interests—such as freedom of the seas—with the United States. Chinese policy does, however, diverge from that of the United States on issues such as international commercial bribery, intellectual property, violations of human rights, and preferential access to raw materials. In the months preceding the 2012 transfer of the Chinese presidency, Chinese leaders and the national press stoked the flame of old grievances with Japan, a key US ally. The People's Republic is less interested in providing a security umbrella for South Korea, Israel, and—of course—Taiwan.

Rather than presuming to prescribe an optimal level of military spending, this chapter has sketched several budget alternatives in broad strokes. However, if the United States is to restore effective "pay as you go" budget planning and confine debt to its traditional uses, citizens who favor a stronger military should urge their fellow citizens to pay the corresponding price of taxation. With a global economy, the fate of Americans has never depended so much on events beyond our borders. The case for retaining military spending at the level of the current consensus is well summarized by Robert Kagan in *The World America Made*. Kagan asserts, however, that "even the most draconian cuts in the defense budget would produce annual savings of only $50 to $100 billion, a small fraction . . . in the annual deficits the United States is facing."[8] To some this number may appear to be small, but budgets projected for many years after 2013 do not contain revenues to pay for that amount and other important federal obligations. Like many others, Kagan dismisses "runaway deficits" as a product of "ballooning entitlement spending." In fact—as shown in the previous chapter—since the budget last balanced in 2000, the nation has borrowed principally for a combination of higher costs for base military budgets, wars, tax cuts, and Medicare. Payroll taxes have paid for the rise in Social Security pensions, and no one believes that the public will support the diversion of those taxes from trust funds to military procurement.

There has always been a division of public opinion on the proper balance between taxes and military spending. That trade-off has been debated since George Washington's administration. The willingness of citizens to tax themselves to pay for military spending strengthens the bond between civilians and soldiers, conveys national resolve to potential adversaries, and preserves credit needed during war. Robust American defense budgets for over half a century have protected the nation's values abroad as well as its citizens at home. These values include a belief in democracy. The very principle of democratic self-governance is undermined when political leaders mortgage the future in order to spend more for international security than the amount they ask the public to pay for with tax dollars.

21

PAYING FOR MEDICAL CARE

THE RISE OF PUBLICLY SUBSIDIZED
MEDICAL INSURANCE

The cost of medical services has grown far faster than federal revenues, and the federal government has borrowed since 2001 to fill the gap. Despite that fact, one can search in vain for a speech by a federal candidate entitled: "Why We Should Mortgage Tomorrow's Taxes to Pay for Today's Medical Bills." People sometimes justify debt-financed tax incentives or spending on education and infrastructure as means of enhancing economic growth. No one touts the economic benefits of borrowing to pay for routine medical expenses.

Federal medical programs arose from the desire to bridge the gap between the cost of medical insurance and the amount of premiums that some people—especially retired and disabled Americans—could afford to pay. Public demand for insurance rose along with the costs and effectiveness of medical services in the late twentieth century.

People dread putting a price on the health of a loved one, and patients often lack the expertise to calculate the trade-off between the price and quality of medical alternatives. Medical insurance helps solve these problems by separating decisions on cost from the process of diagnosis and treatment. Insurance also reduces the financial risk of unexpected or very high medical bills. These advantages of insurance, however, give rise to its principal disadvantage: patients and physicians who worry less about the payment of bills will also be less likely to economize on costs.

By its very nature, insurance redistributes the financial burden of medical services. Premiums paid by people with fewer or less severe medical needs subsidize the cost of caring for those with greater or more immediate needs. As a result, the average premium depends on the total costs incurred for people in an insurance pool. Private insurers, including nonprofits, do not borrow funds they use to pay medical costs because interest on debt would increase their costs.

Hospitals and doctors—not politicians—originated American medical insurance. In 1929 Dallas hospitals created a nonprofit insurance plan, Blue Cross, to secure more stable funding. That same year doctors in Los Angeles began to enroll municipal employees into a plan financed with monthly premiums.

By the 1940s employers competed for skilled workers by offering medical insurance. Federal tax law made medical benefits more attractive to employees, since they were not required to pay income tax on premiums paid on their behalf. Dramatic improvements in medicine have since increased both the cost and the value of these benefits.

Medicare gave older Americans a form of insurance comparable to group health insurance available to employees.[1] Through 2000 dedicated revenues from premiums and payroll taxes covered about three-quarters of the program's cost. After 2000 the cost of Medicare Part B and the new Part D grew much faster than dedicated revenues. Because other existing federal obligations already absorbed every penny of federal funds revenues, debt filled Medicare's funding gap.

For decades federal officials have tried to restrain growth in medical costs. They implemented ambitious reforms including advance payment systems, fixed price schedules, extensive audits, managed care, and incentives to shorten hospital stays. For brief periods of time, those efforts succeeded. Ultimately, the results of cost-saving initiatives were overwhelmed by costs associated with the increased use of services and the greater sophistication of medical diagnosis protocols and treatment.

Everyone applauds greater efficiency, though that concept often is difficult to apply to the delivery of medical services. For example, there is no accepted means of assigning an economic value to the benefit of a diagnostic test that might save one life out of several hundred patients tested.

Decisions that may diminish the length or quality of life involve basic values that transcend politics. Ideology is often used as a tool to help politicians and voters simplify the alternatives for dealing with complex problems, but it offers little realistic guidance to those seeking to reduce medical costs. For example, conservatives frequently blocked actions that would have limited costs by intruding on the relationship between provider and patient, while progressives resisted efforts to restrict eligibility or services.

Between the collapse of the American Fiscal Tradition in 2001 and the onset of the Great Recession in 2008, medical services accounted for almost the entire rise in domestic federal funds spending as a percentage of national income. By 2010 the total cost of all medical care consumed 17.9 percent of national income, or $8,400 per person on average. Medicare and Medicaid—including premiums and payroll taxes dedicated to trust funds—paid for more than a third of that amount.[2] Employer-based health insurance premiums paid for another third. By 2010 Medicare and Medicaid within the federal funds budget rose to about 3.1 percent of total national income, a fifth of all federal funds spending.[3] Then Baby Boomers began to become eligible for Medicare.

THE IMPACT OF BABY BOOMERS

The phrase "perfect storm" refers to a combination of unrelated and unusual meteorological conditions that result in a weather disaster. That overused metaphor is not an appropriate way to describe the combined effect of aging Baby Boomers, new medical treatments, higher prices for the medical services, and federal debt. Weather events cannot be forecasted years in advance, while the budgetary impact of those medical, demographic, and financial trends has been predicted for decades.

Chart 5 depicts the challenge.

Between 2011 and 2021 the number of Americans eligible for Medicare will increase by a third. Moreover, every year the population over the age of eighty-four grows as a percentage of all retired Americans. A combination of Medicaid and Medicare pays for the residential care of millions of Americans with severe age-related and other disabilities, a number that will rise as the population continues to age.[4]

The American Fiscal Tradition once confined federal medical services to the availability of tax revenues. Because there were no spare revenues or tolerance for greater taxation, by the late 1970s various plans for expanded medical coverage included mandates on employers or employees. Those plans were intended to broaden participation in group health insurance.

Chart 5: US Population 65 Years and Older and 85 Years and Older, 1980–2040

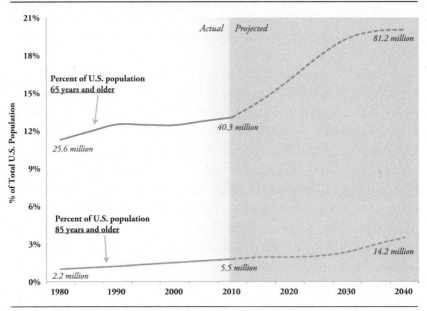

Source: US Census Bureau, Population Division.

That left the challenge of how to subsidize some portion of premiums for those people who could not afford to pay them. In addition, employers in some competitive labor-intensive businesses who did not offer insurance could obtain a cost advantage by not offering group coverage.

Alice Rivlin, one of the leading experts on the federal budget, noted that "we have never directly confronted the question of how much, in a resource-constrained world, we are individually and collectively willing to devote to health care, and how much to all other goods and services."[5]

Debt-financed Medicare violates the original premise of social insurance. Insurance shifts some part of today's medical bills to a population with less than average medical needs. Federal borrowing to pay for current medical bills is akin to passing an unpaid medical bill—plus interest—on to a future, older population with even greater medical needs.

The search for more efficient medical services does not justify the use of debt to fund Medicare. If anything, a tax-financed system should induce greater urgency and realism in the pursuit of cost reduction. Debt itself raises the ultimate cost of medical care by adding a layer of interest payments. Like cancer, the growth of compound interest is difficult to detect in its early stages and more difficult to cure once the pain becomes acute.

Balancing the Budget for Medicare

Three basic alternatives illustrate the type of choices required to balance the budget for Medicare.

Alternative 1: Reduce Medicare Spending to Existing Dedicated Revenues

This alternative would require an immediate 40 percent reduction in payments for Medicare services.[6] Some services would be rationed or unavailable if reimbursement rates are set below the cost of providers. This option is outside the political mainstream, but the prospect of such a cut might prompt an honest debate about the other alternatives.

Alternative 2: Medicare with Strict Cost Ceilings and Higher Tax Revenues

Someone has to pay the medical cost of an aging population. The Medicare payroll tax, now 2.9 percent for most taxpayers, would need to double in order to produce revenues sufficient to cover the program's cost past 2020. Legislation passed in 2007, 2010, and 2012 increased the Medicare premiums and taxation for people with high incomes, so it is unlikely that those taxpayers alone would bear the additional cost of closing the funding gap. This alternative would require the dedication of taxes amounting to, say, 2 percent of national income.[7] If strict cost controls on reimbursement levels eventually discourage medical providers from offering their services, then access to the most costly services or the shift of some costs to beneficiaries may be required in order to avoid further increases in Medicare taxation.

Alternative No. 3: Medicare with Higher Tax Revenues

This alternative retains Medicare with reimbursement rates based on the realistic estimates of the cost of providing services. It will be more expensive than Alternative 2 and might entail some new form of taxation because it might require revenues greater than those produced by the payroll and personal income tax systems.

"PAY AS YOU GO" MEDICARE

Long-term budget plans now embraced by leaders in each party perpetuate the use of debt to fund a large part of Medicare's cost. As of 2013, Republican and Democratic leaders have pledged to retain coverage of the same services for the same beneficiaries, resulting in an estimated average annual cost per beneficiary of about $15,000 by 2020.[8]

Congressional leaders have exaggerated the differences and relative benefits of favored partisan alternatives for restraining the growth of Medicare costs. Most Republican members of Congress endorse a plan that would pay insurance administrators a defined annual amount per beneficiary, while most Democratic members of Congress prefer to curb costs through direct restrictions on the prices paid to providers. Versions of both of these approaches were incorporated into the Balanced Budget Act of 1997. That legislation limited the rise in Medicare costs for several years but also demonstrated the weakness of cost controls and managed care plans without also changing Medicare services or eligibility. No insurance administrator can limit annual costs unless it either puts a lower cap on payment for various services or shifts costs to someone else. Similarly, no direct controls on reimbursement rates can force providers to offer services at a lower price than they are willing to accept.

Nevertheless, politicians still claim that they can lower the growth in Medicare costs without ultimately diminishing the quality of care. Elected officials are used to campaigns that tend to blur the line between hope and reality. They are not the only ones who fail to distinguish between realistic and specific legislation and wishful thinking. A wide variety of expert plans to balance the budget simply *assume* future Medicare costs per beneficiary will not rise after 2020. That assumption recognizes that Medicare costs cannot continue to rise faster than national income during the remaining lives of most Baby Boomers. A premise, however, is hardly a plan. Any plan that surprises the public with unadvertised cuts in services would likely be repealed or delayed. Politicians who believe that the federal government should impose a strict ceiling on Medicare costs per beneficiary should try to do so immediately rather than touting "plans" that will not be implemented until sometime after 2020.

Budget commentators who complain about rising costs of "entitlements" without describing how they would immediately restrain the cost of Medicare shed more heat than light. And glib anecdotes are no substitute for honest debate. For example, many people have heard about the substantial share of total medical costs incurred during the last year of life of patients, but that observation alone does not prescribe a method for reducing those costs. Obviously patients who suffer from more severe illnesses receive more care. In fact, younger Medicare patients receive more extensive and expensive medical care in their last year of life than do older patients. No acceptable system would fail to treat patients simply because their acute conditions make it more likely that they could die.

There are many alternatives—all with human costs—for limiting public funding for the most expensive treatments. Debt-financed denial postpones that choice. When taxes finance medical care, the patient and his or her family are not the only ones with something at stake in making decisions with extreme costs.

"Pay as you go" Medicare reform might just break the partisan stalemate over the program's cost and financing. Republicans oppose higher taxes for Medicare while denying they have any intention to limit services. Democrats oppose restricting benefits and deny asking 98 or so percent of current and future beneficiaries to close the funding gap by paying more. Public opinion polling shows a high level of public support for Medicare—consistently over 70 percent—yet neither Democratic nor Republican leaders suggest a realistic means of substituting revenues for debt to pay for it.[9]

In May 2013 the CBO projected a rise in dedicated payroll tax revenues supporting Medicare from $90 billion in 2013 to $170 billion a decade later.[10] Even assuming an unlikely drop in Medicare reimbursement rates in 2014 and aggressive ceilings on fees afterwards, the CBO projected that—in the same period—Medicare spending (net of premiums) will increase from $586 billion to $1.064 trillion.[11] The CBO expects those outlays will be financed with a combination of debt and a reduction in the portion of national income and tax revenues devoted to all other federal funds spending.

Imagine for a moment that the leadership of either party proposed "pay as you go" funding for Medicare, based on *whatever* level of premium and tax funding a majority in Congress could agree on. They could then challenge others to either justify debt-financed Medicare or offer their own plan that balanced revenues and related services. No one can predict with confidence the ultimate trade-off between taxes and services preferred by a majority of voters. Some will conclude that preserving health is more important than the level of taxation. Others will decide that the burden of extra taxation requires hard limits on reimbursement over the lifetime of patients. The Constitution prescribes a proven technique for resolving precisely that type of conflict: an election. Debt imposes a high price for suppressing that conflict and deferring its resolution.

CRITICAL CHOICES FOR MEDICAID

Since the mid-1990s many Republican congressional leaders have proposed to limit the annual growth of Medicaid grants to a fixed annual percentage. Each state would then have to choose between paying more or discontinuing services if costs rose faster than federal grants. In order to avoid weakening the mandated priority for services to elderly and disabled Americans and pregnant women and their babies, Democrats have favored ceilings linked to the number of beneficiaries and some minimal cost of providing services.

There is no good reason to borrow to fund Medicaid costs that rise faster than federal revenues. For that reason, in 1997 the Clinton administration and congressional Republicans nearly agreed to a hard annual limit on the growth of Medicaid grants. Reasonable limits on the growth of Medicaid would require both Republicans and Democrats to compromise on one of their cherished policy positions.

Republicans would have to reconsider their long-term plan—as reflected in various House budget resolutions adopted after 2010—to balance the budget far into the future by spending a smaller and smaller share of national income on Medicaid. It is hard to imagine that most Americans want millions of citizens with special needs to be evicted from their residential institutions or pregnant women to deliver babies without using modern medical facilities. Since state payments to support long-term care already allow little more than minimum wages to be paid to the employees of providers, few expect some brilliant idea to, for example, lower Medicaid's cost of long-term care for citizens with Alzheimer's disease. It seems disingenuous to count on cutting services for impoverished disabled or elderly citizens to future levels below that which Congress, including current Republican members, is now willing to fund.

Democrats should consider eliminating the feature of the Affordable Care Act that, for a three-year period, allows states to avoid paying a matching share in order to receive grants for Medicaid coverage extended to workers with low incomes. If elected state governments are unwilling to impose taxes to pay for a portion of the cost of a program that benefits their citizens, why should the federal government assume additional debt to fund it? If one believes that the program should be entirely a federal responsibility, then why not wait until the federal government has tax revenue sufficient to replace the matching requirement for all Medicaid coverage?

The principle of "pay as you go" provides the framework for a reality-based national conversation about financing federal medical services. Every day patients and family members have difficult conversations about the health of loved ones. Medical providers deliver unwelcome but honest news to patients. Physicians and patients communicate honestly about medical conditions without resort to partisanship. Insurers do not handicap medical risk based on the ideology of those insured. Adult citizens understand that medical care is not free. Baby Boomers, whose parents bore an enormous tax burden to pay for their children's education and a safer world, have no desire to bequeath their children a legacy of unpaid bills in the form of federal debt.

22

GROWTH, TAXES, AND THE FEDERAL RESERVE

THE MIRAGE OF DEBT-FINANCED GROWTH

Strong economic growth helped reduce debt's burden after five previous spikes in debt. After each use of those emergency borrowings, the federal government balanced budgets and usually paid down debt.

Debt-financed federal spending is not necessary for economic growth. It might temporarily help in a downturn so severe that traumatized citizens and business are reluctant to consume or invest. In that circumstance, however, debt can be monetized with little risk of inflation. Modest federal borrowing during less severe downturns should not interfere with long-term growth as long as the debt is repaid or can be monetized without inflation after recovery. The goal of balancing budgets across each economic cycle was a modern variation of traditional "pay as you go" budget planning. The concept worked better in theory than in practice because federal officials were reluctant to conclude that any economic recovery was complete enough to justify moving a budget into surplus.

There are, of course, ways in which the public sector can contribute to economic growth without mortgaging the future. State laws foster durable contracts and property rights. State and local governments provide a reasonable measure of safety from crime and build most infrastructure. Few doubt that broad-based improvements in knowledge and skills can raise productivity and promote long-run growth, even though many believe that state and local investments in public education can be made more efficiently.

One could argue that all Americans contribute to the economy by waking up each day, but staying alive is hardly a prescription for growth. Similarly, various federal activities make valuable contributions to national welfare and can be justified without exaggerated claims concerning their contribution to growth.

Federal programs that do facilitate growth—such as the funding of an interstate highway system, airports, marine facilities, regulation of the spectrum used for wireless communication, and scientific research—are often funded using trust funds financed with dedicated taxes and account for only a small percentage of overall federal funds spending. Annual federal expenditures supporting economic development—such as investments in education and infrastructure—should not require debt financing.

Strong economic growth has often occurred when the federal government balanced its budgets. The nation grew rapidly in its first thirty-six years, a period in which it paid off its debt entirely. The economy also experienced high rates of growth when surpluses were used to pay down debt in 1844–1857, 1878–1893, 1900–1915, and 1921–1929. Since World War II the nation experienced three long periods of economic growth: 1946–1957, 1961–1974, and 1984–2000. In each of those periods the share of national income devoted to all federal taxes—federal funds and trust fund revenues—rose modestly as a share of national income as the economy grew. In contrast, during 2001–2012 private sector employment stagnated despite higher borrowing levels and lower federal tax receipts as a share of national income.

Bursts of economic expansion at times accompanied spikes in wartime debt (e.g., 1917–1918, 1941–1945, and 1965–1974) or recovery from severe downturns (e.g., 1933–1937, 1976–1979, 1984–1989, and after 2009). Those circumstances do not justify routine borrowing in, say, 2013, when national income hit a record high.

Long-run economic growth depends on factors that do not require federal debt, most notably an increase in the size and productivity of the workforce. Federal borrowing will not change the plight of citizens who have fallen behind in international competition for high wage jobs. Taxing domestic employment in order to pay foreign creditors cannot possibly generate greater long-run opportunities for American workers. Public borrowing that diverts savings from private investment does not enhance productivity.

Despite the verdict of history, many Democratic and Republican leaders now assert that balancing the budget in the near future would cripple the economy. The fig leaf of claimed harm to the economy serves to hide the naked reality of the federal dependence on debt. In some sense, of course, any nation can use debt to shift consumption from the future to the present and create an illusion of sustainable growth. The prodigal son of the New Testament parable seemed prosperous until he finished spending his inheritance. When debt-financed consumption stops, there may be an adjustment similar to that of a consumer who stops writing checks on an account with insufficient funds. But living within one's means is hardly tantamount to damaging the economy.

American history highlights the unusual nature of the recent conversion of conservatives to the idea that federal spending should be financed with debt rather than tax revenues in order to foster economic growth. Fiscal conservatives in both parties successfully fought to amend the Employment Act of 1946 to remove language that could have been interpreted as condoning that very idea. Conservatives pushed for a constitutional amendment to balance the budget for years before Congress nearly passed it in 1995. In contrast, in 2011 various conservative organizations pressured Congress to kill that very constitutional amendment. This shift cannot be attributed to a plan to reduce the size of the federal government by "starving the beast" of tax revenues. History and common sense plainly refute the notion that debt-financed spending diminishes the size of government.

The attitude of many Democrats concerning post-2001 debt was—for a time—less remarkable. They could blame a significant portion of new debt on tax cuts passed at the initiative of a Republican president and Congress, the extended occupation of two foreign countries, and the most severe economic downturn since the Great Depression. Democrats proposed to reduce deficits by raising tax rates on the very highest incomes and phasing out spending for the wars in Iraq and Afghanistan. By 2013 that program had been implemented, yet the White House continued to estimate federal funds borrowing in fiscal year 2014 of more than $800 billion, about $5,000 per employed American and 30 percent of federal funds spending.[1]

The Limit of Income Taxation

The federal personal income tax has generated revenue amounting to a remarkably stable level of national income since the end of the Korean War in 1953. Since then, Americans have paid personal income taxes within a range between 6.7 percent (in 1965) and 9.5 percent (in 2000) of national income.[2] Personal income tax revenues in fiscal year 2014 are projected to be 8.1 percent of national income, in line with the post-1953 average.[3] Personal income tax revenues expressed as a percent of reported gross taxable income—the top line of tax returns—has also fallen in a relatively stable range between 11.6 percent (in 1954) to 15.1 (in 2000).[4] The average has been about 13 percent of gross taxable income.

There has been some political barrier, reflecting public opinion, when personal income taxation approaches 10 percent of national income. President Franklin Roosevelt insisted on higher personal income tax revenues than that when he vetoed a tax bill in 1944. Congress easily overrode that veto even though Americans at the time were willing to make enormous sacrifices in support of the war effort.

Federal personal income taxes have always been based on the ability to pay. So a personal income tax that yields 10 percent of national income and 15 percent or so of gross taxable personal income (before deductions) signifies much higher tax rates applicable to high incomes. Five percent of households with the greatest taxable incomes in 2010—6.7 million households out of 135 million filing returns—earned a third of adjusted gross income and paid three-fifths of all federal income taxes.[5] When they are allocated a portion of the corporate income tax based on their share of capital income, in 2009 that top 5 percent paid 27.9 percent of all their income in federal income taxes.[6] Marginal tax rates on earned income are much higher, even excluding the burden of federal payroll taxes or state and local taxes.

The Affordable Care Act of 2010 and the Taxpayer Relief Act (passed on January 1, 2013) raised the marginal tax rates on earned income for Americans in the highest income bracket to over 40 percent (39.6 percent on earned income, plus an extra .9 percent for Medicare, plus the impact of a phaseout of various deductions).[7] Some view higher tax rates for the "top 1 percent" as class warfare, while others consider them long overdue. Regardless of one's perspective, federal funds revenues will continue to cover only 70 percent of federal funds spending in fiscal year 2014.

Tax rates well above the mid-30 percent range will inevitably incentivize activity designed to defer or reduce taxes. Investors can postpone selling investments for a gain, and a tax system that imposes extraordinary penalties on the sale and reinvestment of capital impairs the efficient allocation of capital. No nation can tax business income made and reinvested in another nation, a fact particularly important in a world of mobile capital. To avoid these and other unintended effects on investment decisions, the United States and other nations tax investment income at lower rates than those applied to salaries and wages. That pragmatic policy, in turn, limits the ability to tax earned income at vastly higher rates without creating artificial incentives to convert income from fees or salaries into equity. The limit on efficient taxation of domestic investment income also implies some upper limit on taxation of earned income, since most people consider it unfair to tax income from salaries at double the rate applied to investment income.

The persistent gap between spending and revenues is unlikely to be closed by higher corporate taxation. Corporate tax revenues as a share of national income steadily diminished between 1953 and 1983. Since 1983 those revenues have leveled out to within half a percent above or below an average of slightly more than 2 percent of national income.[8] Corporate tax revenues are estimated to yield 2 percent of national income in 2014.[9] The decline in the contribution of corporate tax revenues from pre-1983 levels results largely from the effect of international competition for investment and the necessary ability of corporations to substitute debt for equity in their capital structures.

By 2012 income after taxes of US-based corporations accounted for roughly 10 percent of national income, the highest level since shortly after World War II.[10] That amount, however, includes record earnings of US-based corporations from foreign operations not subject to federal taxation if reinvested abroad. The United States cannot stop other nations from setting tax rates that attract production facilities and corporate headquarters; it cannot even prevent its own states from competing against one other using tax breaks. When the federal government has tried to capture more foreign income by taxing corporate profits brought back into the United States, it has unintentionally discouraged the domestic reinvestment of those profits. Today the practical desire to attract greater domestic investment fosters far more pressure to lower corporate tax rates than to raise them.

If personal income tax revenues remain below their post-1953 high of 10 percent of national income, and corporate tax revenues remain at their thirty-year average of 2 percent of national income, then—even with other existing taxes—it will be difficult for federal funds revenues to return to or exceed the level of 13.3 percent of national income obtained in 2000. In light of rising expenses for medical services and interest on the debt, federal funds revenue of less than 13.3 percent of national income is unlikely to cover the cost of maintaining existing levels of national security and all other federal services. (That level of federal taxation could, however, cover those costs without the interest expenses on prior debt, most of which was incurred after 2000.)

Tax Reform?

Federal income tax law has often been reformed. Another round of tax reform may be desirable for a variety of reasons, but it is unlikely to close the budget gap. The word "reform" connotes improvement—generally greater simplicity and fairness. Those concepts are attractive and polls show that the public likes "tax reform" far better than a "tax increase."

New members of Congress quickly find out that simplification and fairness often conflict. For example, some tax reformers seek to simplify tax reporting by reducing the number of tax brackets. On close examination, however, greater gaps between the tax rates applicable to adjacent income tax brackets do not seem more equitable and taxpayers will still need calculators to fill out tax forms. A "flat tax" system, or at least one with fewer rates and a lower top rate, seems simpler but less fair when tax rates applied to lower income brackets must rise in order to replace the loss in revenue from a lower top rate.

Federal personal income taxation has always been based on the ability to pay. A standard deduction eliminated taxes on the lowest incomes and higher tax rates applied to higher incomes. A majority of citizens support the principle of ability to pay and voters are unlikely to change their views in the wake of several decades in which taxpayers with the highest incomes have fared better than other Americans. The average taxable income of one-fifth of taxpayers filing tax returns with the lowest income was $23,500 in 2009, compared to $17,400 in inflation-adjusted dollars thirty years earlier.[11] Americans making $23,500 will hardly consider it fair to increase their income tax rate in order to lower rates applicable to higher incomes.

And their share of national income is so small that the additional tax revenues will do very little to close the budget gap.

It also seems unreasonable to believe—as some tax reformers do—that all corporations should pay the same amount of taxes in any year in which they have the same pretax income as calculated using standard financial accounting. Corporate income statements do not account for losses in prior years or higher costs of equity in industries with large and recurrent capital expenditures that consistently reduce annual cash flow available to investors.

Tax reform is often the banner for efforts to raise tax revenues by reducing exclusions and deductions. That approach was recommended in 2010 by a majority of the members on the National Commission on Fiscal Responsibility and Reform (Simpson-Bowles) and is typical of many balanced budget plans crafted by unelected experts. Simple math accounts for the interest in plans to raise revenue without raising tax rates: only 60 percent of national income—as estimated by economists—qualifies as gross income subject to personal taxation, and less than that is taxable after deductions.

Yet—since the refinement in the income tax system in the decade following increased the passage of the Revenue Act of 1917—tax reform has rarely raised revenue. People have strong and reasonable disagreements about what should be treated as a loophole or "tax expenditure." Most taxpayers consider it unfair to pay taxes on some categories of income— as defined by economists—that are not readily available for payment of taxes. That includes the largest categories of exclusions from personal income taxation, which were designed to encourage investments for retirement and the availability of employer-based health insurance. A nation that saves too little will hesitate to raise taxes on savings that are not available to taxpayers until retirement. A government that borrows too much for federal medical services will be reluctant to reduce the attraction of employer-based health insurance.

Without a doubt, some aspects of tax law are difficult to justify with an economic rationale; the stepped-up basis on capital gains at the time of death comes to mind. That fact does not mean that most exclusions or deductions are poorly conceived "tax expenditures." Consider, for example, the case of a person earning $30,000 a year who works for an employer who self-insures employee medical expenses. After she is injured in a fall at home, her employer pays $10,000 in medical bills. A tax reform purist may call it a "tax expenditure" because she does not owe income taxes on the $10,000 in "noncash compensation" paid by her employer. Most voters, for good reason, would not view it in that way.

Many budget experts advocate the adoption of a new form of taxation. Often their attention turns to some type of consumption or sales tax, since most economists agree that taxes on consumption restrict economic growth less than do taxes on work and investment. Other nations typically rely more heavily than the United States does on consumption taxes, rebated for exports, to support government outlays.

It exceeds the scope of this book to weigh the merits or probablility of a new tax system. A new tax system can raise new revenues, but the United States has only replaced its tax regime in response to the fiscal exigency of war.

Expansive claims of benefits from a new consumption tax system warrant skepticism. The complexity of the current federal tax system results in part from the fact that it has already become a hybrid system of income and consumption taxation. A government can tax consumption by imposing taxes at a point of sale or by taxing income used for consumption. The current system has many features of the latter type of consumption taxation. Gains in the value of property or investments are not taxed as income until sale. Income earned on certain retirement savings and pension earnings is not taxed until distribution. Taxpayers can deduct some income not available for consumption, such as the amounts paid for state and local taxes or contributed to charity. The value of nontaxable employer-based medical insurance is unavailable for consumption except to respond to medical needs. No wonder that most advocates of a federal sales or value-added tax propose that these taxes replace a portion of the federal income tax. Substitution of one tax for another has never raised federal revenues.

Voters have complained to the people they elected to Congress about the federal income tax system. Congress frequently amends tax law. All tax law has been passed with a majority vote of the House and Senate and received a presidential signature. Anyone who believes lobbyists have coerced powerful members of Congress to relinquish large streams of federal revenue has little idea about how Congress actually works. Lobbyists are afraid of long-serving incumbents, not vice versa. Elected members of tax-writing committees, and their expert staffs, have considered every conceivable idea for tax reform. Every tax discourages something, and no one likes to pay. Federal tax law can and will be improved. But the vision that much greater revenue will be gathered from picking the low-hanging fruit of "reform" rather than by "raising taxes" may be a mirage. The most pressing tax reform of all would be the reduction in the use of taxation hidden by deferral, in the form of debt, to fund routine spending.

The federal government has most effectively raised taxes to pay for its spending when federal leaders clearly tell voters what the nation can and cannot afford with additional revenues.

For example, the previous chapter described the merits of "pay as you go" Medicare. Merely dedicating existing income tax revenue to Medicare cannot fund the program without creating a hole of an equivalent size somewhere else in the budget. In light of the reasonable limits on corporate and personal income taxation, suppose the president and Congress considered adjusting Medicare benefits to a level fully funded with a higher payroll tax. The Medicare payroll tax is now the broadest form of federal taxation, covering 2.9 percent of income from salaries, wages, and investments, and 3.8 percent of all income above $250,000 for a couple filing jointly. Though some progressives criticize the Medicare tax for not applying even higher rates for high incomes, they should recognize that taxpayers cannot deduct payroll tax from the income subject to taxation, so Americans pay twice on income subject to the Medicare tax: first through payroll withholding and then by application of a progressive personal income tax.

THE ROLE OF THE FEDERAL RESERVE

The Federal Reserve can play a constructive role in the future—as it has at times in the past—in restoring the American Fiscal Tradition. Though many people complain about the power of the Federal Reserve, it has earned credibility in financial markets. The independence of the Federal Reserve has evolved into a part of the nation's unwritten constitution.

In 1977 Congress mandated that the Federal Reserve foster economic growth "so as to promote effectively the goals of maximum employment, stable prices and moderate long-term interest rates."[12] Restoration of the American Fiscal Tradition will complement the Federal Reserve's ability to discharge those responsibilities. Excessive debt can jeopardize long-term employment growth and moderate interest rates. Price stability could be threatened if a run on federal debt forced the Federal Reserve to monetize large amounts suddenly.

Rising levels of debt held by foreign creditors potentially weaken the effectiveness of the Federal Reserve's open market transactions, an indispensable tool it uses to accomplish its mandated mission. Foreign creditors could, in essence, implement a competing monetary policy through market sales or purchases of large holdings of Treasury debt.

Members of Congress often complain about pressure from the Federal Reserve to balance budgets, but they do at times lean on external constraints when justifying hard decisions. Citizens concerned about the nation's fiscal future should rally to defend the independence of the Federal Reserve when it is attacked for "meddling" in budget politics with actions that support fiscal discipline.

The monetization of some amount of debt by the Federal Reserve might play a role in creating a realistic and durable plan to balance the budget. Monetized debt reduces the net cost of debt service.

The dollar's status as an international store of value and medium of exchange can at times give the Federal Reserve the ability to monetize some amount of debt without destabilizing consumer pricing. Conservatives who resist higher taxation should think carefully about their opposition to monetization in the form of "quantitative easing." It may make more sense to retire a portion of the debt from the two recent wars and a severe downturn by monetization rather than raising a corresponding amount of tax revenue or watching the central banks of other nations monetize that debt. Obviously the extent of monetization must be tempered by careful analysis of the risks of inflation. Yet the options available with $17 trillion in federal debt are not optimal.

23

REFORMING THE POLITICAL PARTIES

REFORMING THE PARTIES

The political environment is right for Democratic and Republican voters, activists, and candidates who are willing to fight to restore their parties' traditional fiscal discipline. Fear, as much as courage, gave generations of federal elected officials the will to balance budgets. "Pay as you go" has always been popular. The principle reflects the public's desire to preserve opportunities for the future and maintain national independence.

Elected officials who were unable to balance peacetime budgets still labored to demonstrate their commitment to the American Fiscal Tradition. For example, the vast majority of Franklin Roosevelt's record 635 vetoes were designed to restrain debt-financed spending. Public loathing of debt still compels many members of Congress to vote against increasing the debt ceiling even to pay for appropriations that they previously voted for.

Candidates who address debt forthrightly can command national attention. When sounding the alarm on the risks of debt in 1992, H. Ross Perot compared federal debt to "a crazy aunt" well known to neighbors but whom "nobody wants to talk about."[1] When Perot talked about debt and vowed to balance the budget, Americans listened to him.

Bipartisan support for balanced budgets need not diminish partisan competition on issues such as the level and nature of federal taxation, the strength of the social safety net, and the scope of American commitments abroad. For example, as leaders of both major parties embraced the balanced budget in the years following World War II, they fought with bare fists concerning the federal regulation of labor–management relations.

Americans still believe in the values underlying their nation's traditional fiscal constitution. In 2013 a phenomenal 74 percent of Americans were "very worried" about the impact of foreign holders of federal debt.[2] Other polling showed that Americans opposed an increase in the debt ceiling based on concerns about the nation's future.[3]

Large political changes can occur within the span of one or two election cycles. Because of the math of compound interest, the nation cannot wait for a decade before reformers in each party fight to restore fiscal discipline.

THE TIME IS RIGHT FOR DEMOCRATIC BUDGET REFORMERS

All but one Democratic president who left office with a strong peacetime economy managed to balance the budget. Franklin Roosevelt believed in the progressive ideal of social insurance, but only if it could be paid for with broad-based taxation. Harry Truman, the last president to proudly identify himself as a "liberal," insisted on submitting budgets with spending confined to estimated tax revenues. The Clinton administration balanced the budget and proposed a plan to earmark surpluses to fund social insurance for Baby Boomers. President Barack Obama reminded Democrats that "if we truly believe in a progressive vision of our society, we have an obligation to prove that we can afford our commitments."[4]

Too often since 2001, however, many Democrats have been content to preserve federal programs they cared about rather than insisting that spending be limited to the available revenues. As a result, future funding for domestic priorities such as education will have to be cut to make room for higher interest payments. Democrats allowed Republicans to reduce taxes without forcing them to pay the electoral price of making corresponding cuts in national defense, Medicare, law enforcement, and many other federal programs with a broad base of public support. By failing to explicitly link tax cuts and spending cuts, Democratic leaders reinforced the stereotype that they somehow like taxes.

Democratic leaders strayed from their party's heritage when they acquiesced to the use of debt to finance Medicare after 2000. The Medicare bill passed in 1965 was intended to be financed primarily with a sustainable combination of premiums and dedicated payroll taxes. Progressives championed the idea of social insurance programs financed by broad-based taxation—proportionate to income—of the ultimate beneficiaries. The Democratic national platform adopted the year before Medicare passed expressed a traditional progressive goal: "a balanced budget within a balanced economy."[5] In 2000 President Clinton and presidential candidate Al Gore sought to assign more revenue from existing taxes to the trust funds to reduce the risk of future borrowing to sustain Medicare benefits. Democrats, including Barack Obama, repeatedly criticized the Bush administration's use of debt to pay for Medicare Part D.

The cost of two wars and the drop in revenues and employment following the Great Recession of 2008 made it difficult to balance the budget for several years. The prospect of rising interest rates and debt service makes "pay as you go" financing of Medicare even more important today. The increasing cost of medical services has already begun to squeeze out future investments in other domestic programs such as education grants, scientific research, public safety, child nutrition, clean energy, and environmental enforcement. Holes in the safety net of medical services should not be patched with the rope that other Americans rely on to climb toward a better standard of living. Democrats should argue for balancing the budget for Medicare. If Medicare must be cut severely because of Republican opposition to obtaining sufficient tax revenue, voters are likely to rectify that problem in the next election.

Abandoning the traditional limits on debt has compromised the most cherished of all Democratic ideals: a nation in which each generation has opportunities greater than the one that preceded it. That vision guided party leaders who built the world's first comprehensive system of public and higher education and who removed barriers imposed by racial, gender, and other forms of discrimination. Democratic leaders championed a program that set aside funds to allow older Americans to retire in dignity without leaving their children and grandchildren a pile of unpaid medical bills or federal debt.

Grassroots Democrats strongly believe in affordable education as a ladder providing upward mobility, yet the cost of future debt service shackles the future of the very people who receive that education. Foreign purchasers of federal debt have sustained trade deficits and limited the opportunities of American workers in industries competing with imports. Workers as well as business owners benefit when balanced budgets free more savings for use in direct investment in the economy rather than federal debt.

No nation ever borrowed its way to long-term prosperity. As Democratic vice presidential candidate Lloyd Bentsen noted in his criticism of Republican policies in 1988, anyone "could give the illusion of prosperity" by writing "$200 billion of hot checks every year."[6] Franklin Roosevelt explained in a radio address that "any government, like any family," could temporarily "spend a little more than it earns. But you and I know a continuation of that habit means the poorhouse."[7]

Democrats must accept the fact that a majority of voters may not support the taxes needed to fund certain types of humanitarian programs. Moreover, if 98 percent of voters are unwilling to pay for a new program with higher taxes, then there will be a limit on what can fairly be funded by the 2 percent of Americans with the highest incomes.

Democrats hold a wide variety of opinions on public policy issues, but the party's reformers should insist on several basic principles that are consistent with their party's historic traditions. In the absence of war or recession, the federal budget should limit spending to available revenues. Tax rates should be based on the ability to pay. Congress should vote to authorize each new use of debt every time it votes for a debt-financed spending bill.

THE TIME IS RIGHT FOR REPUBLICAN BUDGET REFORMERS

Between the Civil War and the 1970s no Republican president or congressional majority authorized borrowing a dime to pay for federal expenses except for those directly attributable to wars and downturns. Republican "pay as you go" budgets freed national savings for private investments in long-term economic growth. When Republicans gained control of the House of Representatives in 1947 and 1953, they cut total spending from the level of the prior year in order to balance budgets.

When confronted with a large deficit, President Reagan called on Congress to freeze nondefense spending, raise Social Security tax rates, tax Social Security income for the first time, and impose a new tax equal to 1 percent of national income. Republicans who gained control of Congress in 1995 almost passed a constitutional amendment requiring a balanced budget.

Until relatively recently, conservative Republicans sought to limit the growth of government by insisting that new domestic spending programs be paid for with higher taxes. "Pay as you go" budgets made the cost of new federal programs clear to voters.

After 2000 Republican voters continued to believe in balanced budgets, but many party leaders followed a different course. A Republican president and Congress used debt to finance tax reduction, an expansion of Medicare, two wars, a higher base military budget apart from war, expanded agricultural assistance programs, and much more. Republican fiscal policy continued to stray from its historic course after George W. Bush left the White House. The 2012 Republican presidential nominee, Mitt Romney, pledged that he would not accept a budget that reduced the deficit by raising a dollar of tax revenue for every ten dollars in spending cuts.[8]

Some Republican political consultants may think that small-government conservatives have no other place to go. In fact, traditional fiscal conservatives can win Republican primaries and regain control of the party. Republicans who believe in individual responsibility yearn for candidates who will vote against appropriations funded with debt. Debt-financed spending is not conservative. Republican incumbents who have never once voted to appropriate less spending than estimated tax revenues will be hard-pressed to explain why the budget should be balanced in ten to thirty years rather than in two or three years.

President Reagan once noted that doing the right thing is not complicated; it just is not always easy. "Pay as you go" for routine spending is not complicated. Republican reformers in Congress should insist on separate votes on debt-financed appropriations in order to let voters know what debt is used for and which members of Congress voted to incur debt.

The goal of a balanced budget can help focus the Republican approach to Medicare. No mainstream Republican leader supports abolishing Medicare. Republicans have made little headway with their favored plan to limit the cost per beneficiary by requiring that coverage be purchased in the form of subsidized plans offered by private insurers. That and other proposals to limit rising Medicare costs would be more persuasive if they were grounded in the principle that the program should cost no more than available tax revenues. It is better to give taxpayers a greater stake in the efforts to reduce the program's costs than to complain about "entitlements" that members of Congress in both parties vote annually to fund. It is unrealistic to expect members of Congress in either party to ignore the public's long-standing support for taxation based on the ability to pay. It is, however, reasonable to insist that Medicare be paid for with broad-based taxation.

Debt-financed military spending undermines national security. If and when the United States intervenes abroad, the nation's balance sheet should not be encumbered by an excessive level of peacetime debt. Republican primary voters will gravitate to candidates who embrace those simple truths.

Edmund Burke—the quintessential conservative—once said that constituents deserve the judgment of each elected official. Conservative heroes have often resisted the trend of the moment in order to defend traditional principles. Conservatives may not win every fight to reduce the scope of government. If they lose because most voters are unwilling to reduce the level of federal services and national defense, then Republicans should insist that their opponents be forthright with constituents about the price expressed in taxation. Even when they are in a minority, conservatives will have a greater impact when they defend convictions that have stood the test of time.

A SELF-EVIDENT TRUTH

The United States has incurred high levels of debt five times in its history and then quickly balanced its budget—usually while maintaining surpluses to reduce debt—for a decade or more. It can do so again. The history described in this volume should give heart to voters and candidates who are willing to work for the political changes needed to protect the nation's future.

Americans today—like those of prior generations—recognize that the use of debt to fund routine spending compromises the prospects of young citizens, the ability to be independent of foreign creditors, and the capacity to use national savings to invest in private sector jobs. Voters are capable of understanding a basic premise of democratic governance: citizens should expect only the level of government services that they are willing to pay for and understand that someone must eventually pay for every public dollar spent.

ACKNOWLEDGMENTS

I LEARNED THAT MY wife, Andrea, a writer, is a splendid editor. My prose is not good enough to fully express my gratitude for her encouragement, edits, and tolerance of rooms in our home filled with obscure books and articles. Shay Everitt worked by my side every day for over two years, organizing sources, deciphering my notes, and correcting my frequent mistakes. Another colleague, Shiju Thomas, devoted hundreds of hours to research. He deserves credit for appendices that include the best available summary of the historical levels of federal debt calculated with consistent accounting.

My friend Michael Zilkha helped me find my excellent agents, Ike Williams and Katherine Flynn, who introduced me to an outstanding publisher, Perseus, and its fine staff. My editor at PublicAffairs, John Mahaney, is a consummate professional. John and Collin Tracy at Perseus and Beth Wright of Trio Bookworks put up with an excessive number of late edits from their author.

Nancy Smith's review and editing made the first complete draft far more readable and taught me the importance of transitions. This book is in much better form as a result of Virginia Northington's thoughtful and rigorous copyediting and fact-checking.

Thanks to my friends Scott Atlas, Franci Crane, Becky Ferguson, Elena Marks, Paul Hobby, Rich Kinder, and Carrin Patman for reviewing early chapters. Scott patiently and thoroughly read and commented on drafts for a year. His friendship and support lifted my spirits when the magnitude of this undertaking began to dawn on me.

I am grateful to my colleagues at Lazard. We help senior management, owners, and boards of businesses place their challenges in a broader context. This book was written in the spirit of that culture.

My parents worked hard to try to give me the skills and values needed to write history. My father, who died before the completion of this book, filled my childhood home with great history books. My mother, a longtime English teacher, taught me and so many others the lost art of diagramming sentences. Their lives and those of my grandparents encompassed half of US history to date. Their sacrifices exemplified the values of entire generations who changed world history and paid for public bills with taxes in order to avoid leaving their children with a mountain of debt.

A couple of sources offered insights that helped shape this book's thesis. Richard Hofstadter's *The American Political Tradition* illuminated the depth and continuity of currents running through the course of American history. The correspondence of Jefferson and Madison can still inspire citizens who seek a principled basis for making budget choices.

Many residents of Houston, Texas, deserve special thanks. Hundreds of them—from disparate backgrounds and with a variety of political views—listened to my description of the book and shared their reactions. They gave me confidence that Americans still have the will to defend our nation's future by limiting its use of federal debt.

And a final thanks to my children, Will, Elena, and Stephen. They accept their responsibilities as citizens and respect idealism. This book has been written with them and—with luck—any grandchildren in mind.

Notes

Chapter 1

1. "From George Washington to Samuel Washington, 12 July 1797," Founders Online, National Archives, http://founders.archives.gov/ documents/Washington /06-01-02-0209, ver. 2013-06-26. Source: *The Papers of George Washington, Retirement Series*, vol. 1, *4 March 1797–30 December 1797*, ed. W. W. Abbot (Charlottesville: University Press of Virginia, 1998), 247–249.

2. George Washington quoted in Hormats, *The Price of Liberty*, xvi–xvii.

3. James Madison to Thomas Jefferson, February 4, 1790, in Madison, *Letters and Other Writings,* vol. 1, 506.

4. Reeves, *President Kennedy*, 622–623.

5. Compare "Table 7.1—Federal Debt at the End of Year: 1940–2018," Historical Tables of the White House Office of Management and Budget, http://www .whitehouse.gov/omb/budget/historicals with United States Bureau of Labor Statistics, "Current Employment Statistics," Table B-1a, http://www.bls.gov/web/empsit /ceseeb1a.htm.

6. See Appendix B.

7. Harry S. Truman quoted in Donovan, *Tumultuous Years*, 132.

8. Robert Taft quoted in Patterson, *Mr. Republican*, 435.

9. Zelizer, *Taxing America: Wilbur D. Mills, Congress, & the State, 1945–1975* (Cambridge: Cambridge University Press, 1998), 75.

10. Schlesinger, *The Coming of the New Deal*, 309.

11. Quoted in Altermeyer, *Formative Years of Social Security*, 89.

12. OMB, Historical Tables, "Table 2.1–Receipts by Source: 1934–2018." See also Appendix C.

13. Pachand Richardson, *The Presidency of Dwight D. Eisenhower*, 77.

14. Dwight D. Eisenhower quoted in Mayer, *The Eisenhower Years*, 191.

15. George W. Bush quoted in Kotlikoff and Burns, *The Coming Generational Storm*, 55.

16. OMB, Historical Tables,"Table 1.4—Receipts, Outlays, and Surpluses or Deficits (-) by Fund Group: 1934–2018."

17. *Budget, Fiscal Year 2003*, 101.

18. Tom DeLay quoted in Surowiecki, "A Cut Too Far."

19. Congressional Budget Office estimate on the 2003 tax cut. See also Bureau of Labor Statistics, "Overview of BLS Statistics on Unemployment."

20. John Boehner quoted in Greenspan, *The Age of Turbulence*, 243.

21. Peterson, *Running on Empty*, 82.

22. Benjamin Franklin, *The Way to Wealth* (1774), 13.

CHAPTER 2

1. George Washington to Benjamin Harrison, January 18, 1784, *The Papers of George Washington*.

2. Washington, "Speech to Officers at Newburgh," March 15, 1783, in *Rediscovering George Washington*.

3. Higginbotham, *George Washington*, 121.

4. George III quoted in Brookhiser, *Founding Father*, 103.

5. Weintraub, *General Washington's Christmas Farewell*, 157.

6. In the seventeenth century, Dutch cities had pioneered the modern form of public debt. European royalty had previously financed wars in part with mortgages of property, including assignment of the rights to rent. The innovative Dutch cities created notes secured by mortgages on future tax revenues. By the 1780s, the Dutch Republic had been crippled by excessive use of public debt.

7. Johnson, *Righteous Anger*, 1.

8. Ibid., 85.

9. Madison, *Writings*, vol. 2, 398.

10. Madison, *Notes of Debates*, 10.

11. Berkin, *A Brilliant Solution*, 25.

12. Madison to Washington, November 8, 1786, in Madison, *Letters and Other Writings*, vol. 1, 255.

13. Caplan, *Constitutional Brinksmanship*, 26. After a majority of states had agreed to send delegates, and months after the Annapolis call to action, Congress pathetically called for the Philadelphia meeting to draft amendments to the Articles of Confederation for later consideration by the body.

14. Madison, *Writings*, vol. 2, 404–405.

15. Beard, *An Economic Interpretation*, 297.

16. Johnson, *Righteous Anger*, 75.

17. Franklin, "Speech to the Federal Convention."

18. DeRose, *Founding Rivals*, 237.

19. *Reports of the Secretary of the Treasury*, 14, https://fraser.stlouisfed.org/docs/publications/?pid=194.

20. Johnson, *Righteous Anger*, 41.

21. Madison made the case for the import taxes with the help of spreadsheets prepared by Jefferson that showed the amount of debt owed to Europeans and related schedules for debt service. Jefferson also passed along advice from Dutch bankers that a 5 percent tax on the value of imports would raise enough money to pay foreign creditors.

22. Chernow, *Washington*, 597.

23. Jefferson to Madison, August 28, 1789, in Jefferson, *Memoirs*, 25.

24. Jefferson felt the issue of hereditary rights helped define the War of Independence itself. He felt so strongly about the principle that, in 1776, Jefferson had proposed that the earlier Saxon leaders of England be depicted on the Great Seal of the United States, reflecting his belief that feudal doctrines had compromised the principles of the early Saxon rulers of England.

25. Jefferson to Madison, September 6, 1789, in Jefferson, *Memoirs*, 30–31.

26. Ibid., 32.

27. Miller, *The Business of May Next*, 19.

28. Madison to Jefferson, February 4, 1790, in Madison, *Letters and Other Writings*, vol. 1, 506.

29. Madison quoted in Sloan, *Principle & Interest*, 178.

30. Jones quoted in Sloan, *Principle & Interest*, 179.

31. Wright, *One Nation Under Debt*, 134. Though once Hamilton commented that national debt could be a "blessing," in context he was actually expressing appreciation for creditworthiness arising from the repayment of debt and an effective credit system.

32. Jefferson to James Monroe, June 20, 1790, in Jefferson, *Works: Volume VI*, 78–79.

33. Alexander Hamilton, "Report on the Public Credit," in *Reports of the Secretary of Treasury*, 14–15, https://fraser.stlouisfed.org/docs/publications/treasar/AR_TREASURY_1790.pdf.

34. In 1789–1790 there was no good estimate of state debts from the Revolution. The battle over the assumption of state debts at times was less a dispute over philosophy than a product of fear and confusion. North Carolina, for example, delayed ratification of the Constitution and opposed assumption of state debts because of its concern that Congress would require taxes to be paid in scarce gold or silver. Ultimately the state was a net creditor of other states.

35. In 1783, when Hamilton and Madison had worked on means of paying Washington's soldiers, Madison had proposed that the Continental Congress assume responsibility for the war debts of the states. Madison, in his notes at that time, underlined his premise: "Justice requires that the debts be paid." Five years later, though, in the tough fight for ratification of the Constitution, he had to assure

Virginians that the Constitution did not obligate the federal government to pay those debts. Even in late 1789, when Hamilton asked for Madison's views on paying the Revolutionary War debts, Madison said he had not formed "any precise ideas." He did tell Hamilton that he favored paying off the debt, in part, to avoid it "slid[ing] into the hands of foreigners."

36. Madison to Jefferson, March 8, 1790, in Madison, *Letters and Other Writings*, vol. 1, 511.

37. One Massachusetts Congressman, Theodore Sedgwick, angrily said that any attempt to collect taxes in Massachusetts without the federal assumption of debt would lead to violence. In the weeks leading up to the Constitutional Convention, Madison realized that one of the principal challenges of the convention would be to create some system that would allow tax collection to be enforced by courts against individuals, rather than by the use of military force against a delinquent state.

38. Jefferson quoted in Winik, *The Great Upheaval*, 162.

39. Madison to Monroe, April 17, 1790, Founders Online, National Archives, http://founders.archives.gov/documents/Madison/01-13-02-0109.

40. Jefferson quoted in Kaplan, *Thomas Jefferson*, 77–78.

41. Jefferson quoted in Sloan, *Principle & Interest*, 178.

42. Hamilton, "Report on the Public Credit," 14–15.

43. Ibid., 14.

44. For GDP, see McCusker, "Estimating Early American Gross Domestic Product," and http://www.measuringworth.com/datasets/usgdp/result.php. For population, see Bureau of the Census, *First Census of the United States*. See also Blodgett, *Economica*, 60.

45. See Appendix F for the history of trade balances. The United States was consistently a net importer for almost ninety years, until 1878. For most of the ninety years after 1878 it was a net exporter.

46. Jefferson had written to Madison about the need for a ban on monopoly charters in the Bill of Rights. British laws were designed to encourage private investment projects with a public purpose, such as bridges or toll roads or even shipping companies, in return for an implied monopoly. This monopoly privilege was treated as a form of property by those receiving it. Since a corporate charter had been understood as creating an implied, exclusive property right, the charter of a competing new corporation was considered as a potential violation of the rights against government taking of property or as the impairment of contract rights. As a result, while the party of Jefferson and Madison *did* oppose certain uses of federal power by Hamilton, many who write of the early Republic are too simplistic in characterizing opposition to the Bank as *simply* an objection to the scope of federal activities.

47. Jefferson to Madison, May 12, 1793, in Jefferson,*Writings: 1792–1794*, 251.

48. Madison quoted in Wood, *Empire of Liberty*, 161.

49. Jefferson to Madison, June 21, 1792, in Jefferson, *Works: Volume VII*, 125.

50. Appendix B shows this measure of the burden of federal debt throughout the nation's history, which was the reason for Jefferson's fears in the nation's first decade and also for the exceptional nature of the debt crisis by 2010.

51. Jefferson quoted in Perkins, *American Public Finance*, 211.

52. Hamilton quoted in Johnson, *Righteous Anger*, 255.

53. Gallatin, *Writings: Volume 1*.

54. Walters, *Albert Gallatin*, 118.

55. White, "Biographical Notice."

56. Chernow, *Washington*, 722.

57. Federal budgets were based on a calendar year until 1843. The first fiscal year encompassed the partial years 1789 and 1791. In 1792, the federal government "expensed" a $2 million investment in stock of the Bank of the United States, which appreciated. Net of this amount, the federal government had modest budget deficits in 1792, 1794, and 1795, totaling $4.25 million. During Hamilton's four years as treasury secretary, interest payments accounted for half of all federal spending. The loan balance of the nation to the Bank of the United States was repaid by a credit for surrender of the federal investment in the bank. The net amount owed was offset in part by cash balances in the bank. The bank's directors became nervous about the unplanned loan to the United States, and it was paid down with surrender of the federal investment in the bank.

58. Walters, *Albert Gallatin*, 89.

59. Ibid.

60. Ibid., 91.

61. Gallatin, *Writings: Volume 3*, 150.

62. Walters, *Albert Gallatin*, 90.

63. Adams, *The Life of Albert Gallatin*, 156.

64. Before becoming foreign minister, Talleyrand—a former Catholic bishop—had unsuccessfully tried to make money on land speculation while living in exile in the United States for two years. Talleyrand considered it amazing that Secretary Hamilton would resign to make money practicing law rather than simply accepting bribes. Talleyrand had been brought back to France on the recommendation of a childhood friend of Gallatin's, Madame Germaine de Stael, who lived in Paris.

65. Adams, *The Life of Albert Gallatin*, 170, 189.

66. Department of the Treasury, *National Loans*, 43–44. These navy bonds were sold at 8 percent interest. Congress was afraid that the rate would be even higher if it had waited until a declaration of war before borrowing for the navy. A small navy had been built to deal with pirates, and Hamilton had paid for some ships with interest-bearing notes issued to shipbuilders.

67. Jefferson, *Writings: Volume IV*, 259.

68. Jefferson to Gallatin, April 1, 1802, in *Oxford Dictionary of American Quotations*, 206.

69. Jefferson to Gallatin in Gallatin, *Writings: Volume 1*.

70. In 1800, before the change in the administration, Gallatin's allies in Congress had mandated that the secretary of the treasury report to Congress annually "on the subject of finance, [with] estimates of the public revenues and public expenditures, and plans for improving and increasing the revenues from time to time for the purpose of giving information to Congress in adopting modes of raising the money requisite to meet the public expenditures."

71. President Jefferson responded to congressional objections by restoring some of the military cuts, so Gallatin settled for a budget allocating half of all revenues for debt reduction and confining all other spending to the remaining half. As revenues grew, Gallatin succeeded in devoting two-thirds of budgets to debt service, including reductions in the principal amount of the debt. After Jefferson's first term, Gallatin reported total expenditures of $49.6 million and revenues of $1 million more. Interest on debt totaled $16.2 million, and principal payments totaled $19.2 billion. If accounted for using modern budget accounting, the $19.2 billion in debt reduction, net of additional borrowing, would be treated as a budget surplus.

72. Gallatin understood better than even Hamilton the central bank functions of the Treasury Department. Gallatin believed that federal debt obligations of over $70 million far exceeded the need for debt as currency. Gallatin thought that short-term notes, with little or no interest, would circulate freely while US debt obligations bearing the interest rates set in 1790 would be held for investment, possibly in Europe. Gallatin also believed that the United States would pay lower interest rates for debt with a fixed maturity, while Hamilton had imitated the British practice of issuing debt instruments without fixed terms.

73. Wright, *One Nation Under Debt*, 171.

74. Jefferson quoted in Hofstadter, *The Idea of a Party System*, 151.

75. See Appendix A.

Chapter 3

1. Thomas Jefferson quoted in Cerami, *Jefferson's Great Gamble*, 58.

2. DeConde, *This Affair of Louisiana*, 150.

3. Malone, *Correspondence*, 60, 62.

4. DeConde, *This Affair of Louisiana*, 136.

5. American diplomats did not know that Great Britain had bribed Talleyrand in 1803 to maintain tension between France and the United States. Ambassador Livingston had also paid Talleyrand, an action authorized by Secretary of State Madison, as a standard, though distasteful, means of receiving an audience.

6. Kukla, *Wilderness So Immense*, 268–269.

7. DeConde, *This Affair of Louisiana*, 164.

8. Adams, *The First Administration*, 322–323, and Kukla, *Wilderness So Immense*, 274–175.

9. Kukla, *Wilderness So Immense*, 278–280.

10. Gallatin, *Writings: Volume 1*, 256. Jefferson and later Monroe used this ambiguity over the status of Texas in their bargaining attempts with Spain to buy part of the Floridas.

11. Adams, *The Life of Albert Gallatin*, 318.

12. Walters, *Albert Gallatin*, 154.

13. Bureau of the Census, *Historical Statistics, 1789–1945*, Series B at 99–108 and 301.

14. Jefferson to John C. Breckinridge, August 12, 1803, in Jefferson, *Memoirs*, 521.

15. Adams, *The First Administration*, 83.

16. Adams, *The Life of Albert Gallatin*, 270.

17. Perkins, *American Public Finance*, 263.

18. Jefferson quoted in Kimmel, *Federal Budget and Fiscal Policy*, 16.

19. On November 21, 1806, after victories in central Europe, Napoleon issued the Berlin Decree, which banned the importation of British goods into the ports of his European allies. A year later, British foreign secretary George Canning secured Orders of Council that forbade trade with France and its allies and instructed the Royal Navy to blockade French ports.

20. Jefferson quoted in Sloan, *Principle & Interest*, 203.

21. Jefferson to Pierre Samuel Du Pont de Nemours, April 15, 1811, Founders Online, National Archives, http://founders.archives.gov/documents/Jefferson/03-03-02-0432.

22. Jean-Baptiste Say quoted in Forsythe, *Taxation and Political Change*, 380.

23. Madison to Jefferson, March 6, 1812, Founders Online, National Archives, http://founders.archives.gov/documents/Madison/03-04-02-0238.

24. Perkins, *American Public Finance*, 17.

25. Department of the Treasury, *National Loans*, 52–53.

26. Kearny, *Sketch of American Finances*, 92.

27. Ibid.

28. Adams, *Administrations of James Madison*, 1077.

29. Borneman, *1812*, 251.

30. Madison, "Sixth Annual Message."

31. Ammon, *James Monroe*, 340.

32. Gouverneur Morris quoted in Ketcham, *James Madison*, 592.

33. Rothbard, *The Panic of 1819*, 2–3.

34. Dallas, *Alexander James Dallas*, 235–237.

35. Dewey, *Financial History*, 134.

36. Walters, *Albert Gallatin*, 286.

37. Macdonald, *A Free Nation Deep in Debt*, 349–350.

38. Mahon, "The Negotiations at Ghent in 1814."

39. Lord Liverpool quoted in Adams, *The Life of Albert Gallatin*, 539.

40. Andrew Jackson quoted in Goodwin, *Andrew Jackson*, 158.

41. On January 1, 1815, there had been obligations on Treasury notes due but unpaid of $2,799,220. Dallas still had to accept received bank notes, selling at a discount to the dollar value of gold coins, in subscriptions of federal debt. The month before getting news of the peace treaty, House Ways and Means Chairman and Jefferson's son-in-law John Eppes asked a leading Federalist congressman, William Gaston of North Carolina, whether the Federalists would "take up the government if we give it to them?" Gaston said they would decline the gift.

42. Department of the Treasury, *National Loans*, 58; Studenski and Krooss, *Financial History*, 79.

43. See Appendix A.

44. Coxe, *A Statement*, liv.

45. John C. Calhoun quoted in Niven, *John C. Calhoun*, 54.

46. Bureau of the Census, *Historical Statistics, 1789–1945*, Series P 89–98 at 298.

47. Adams, *Administrations of James Madison*, 1264–1275. See also Morris, "The First Congress."

48. Ricardo, *Works*, 539.

49. The bank had assets of $41 million in outstanding loans and $2.5 million in silver and gold reserves, with offsetting liabilities of $13 million in deposits and $10 million in outstanding paper notes at the beginning of 1818.

50. McCraw, *The Founders and Finance*, 251.

51. Rohrbough, *The Land Office Business*, 141.

52. Bureau of the Census, *Historical Statistics, 1789–1945*, Series P 89–98 at 298.

53. Dangerfield, *The Era of Good Feelings*, 183.

54. Rohrbough, *The Land Office Business*, 141. Though overextended bank balance sheets made the Panic of 1819 worse, most historical writing about the Panic tends to ignore the inevitable impact of the European recession and the US trade deficit. When export demand for cotton and tobacco declined sharply, US citizens and merchants had to import less to avoid the total loss of gold reserves. Exports fell from $93 million in 1818 to $54 million in 1821. Imports fell from $122 million to $54 million during the same period, eliminating the trade deficit.

55. Madison, *Letters and Other Writings*, vol. 3, 166.

56. Ammon, *James Monroe*, 469.

57. Bureau of the Census, *Historical Statistics, 1789–1945*, Series P 89–98 at 298.

58. Lipscomb, *The Writings of Thomas Jefferson*, vol. 15, 296–297.

59. The federal government dropped the price of land while restricting new land loans. It instituted a loan forgiveness program for those not able to make payments on the old $2 per acre minimum purchase price.

60. Monroe, "Eighth Annual Message."

61. Malone, *Correspondence*, 40.

Chapter 4

1. Dangerfield, *The Era of Good Feelings*, 349.

2. Van Buren, *Autobiography*, 195.

3. Adams, "First Annual Message."

4. James Monroe quoted in Hofstadter, *The Idea of a Party System*, 200.

5. Hofstadter, *The Idea of a Party System*, 244.

6. Van Buren's failed attempt in 1824 to work within the old system of electing a president had taught him some valuable lessons. He had backed the early front-runner, Treasury Secretary William Crawford, in hopes that his Albany Regency and Virginia's dominant "Richmond Junto" would create momentum for Crawford in the informal congressional caucus. Even after a stroke rendered Crawford blind and mute fourteen months before the election, Van Buren secured the nomination of the congressional caucus for him. Nevertheless, most congressmen declined to attend an event that marked the demise of the process that many critics had derided as the "King Caucus." Van Buren did manage to deliver just enough of New York's electoral votes for Crawford to place third and disqualify Henry Clay, who placed fourth, from being considered for the presidency by the House of Representatives.

7. After the passage of the Twelfth Amendment to the Constitution in 1806, voters were required to cast one vote for president and one vote for vice president. (Prior to the Twelfth Amendment, two votes were cast for president, and the vice president was the person who received the second highest number of votes.) However, without a party nominating process, there was not yet a formal procedure in place for fashioning a "ticket."

8. Martin Van Buren quoted in Remini, *Life of Andrew Jackson*, 161.

9. Thomas Jefferson quoted in Brands, *Andrew Jackson*, 97.

10. Parton, *Andrew Jackson*, vol. 2, 354.

11. Van Buren himself explained, in memoirs published after his death, that "by adding the General's personal popularity to the strength" of Jefferson's old party, he hoped to overcome the power and patronage of an incumbent administration enjoying the benefits of economic prosperity. As for Jackson's political views, Van Buren said he would have to rely on "good fortune" that Jackson's Jeffersonian principles from the 1790s would have survived into the 1820s.

12. John Randolph quoted in Graham, *Free, Sovereign and Independent States*, 207.

13. Brands, *Andrew Jackson*, 70.

14. Jackson, "First Inaugural Address."

15. "Report on the Finances: December 1829," in *Reports of the Secretary of the Treasury*, vol. 3, 17.

16. Larson, *Internal Improvement*, 191. Federal budgets during the nineteenth century routinely included public works projects in the appropriations of the Department of the Army, which supervised construction through the Corps of Engineers.

Historians would do well to review those budgets rather than political speeches to determine the scale of spending on public works.

17. Andrew Jackson quoted in Brands, *Andrew Jackson*, 478.

18. Remini, *Life of Andrew Jackson*, 197.

19. Thomas Hart Benton quoted in Remini, *Andrew Jackson: Lessons*, 180.

20. See Appendix B.

21. Jackson deposited the surplus funds, without interest, into various favored state banks. Since Jackson's Treasury required deposits to be made in banks with gold reserves, banks in New York—the center of international commerce that required substantial gold reserves—received a third of the funds. Ironically, the populist Jackson accelerated the rise of Wall Street.

22. The states treated the distributed surplus as a grant. To avoid any constitutional challenge, the federal government treated the surplus payments as loans without interest or any defined maturity. This distribution was similar to the no-interest deposits that had long been used to support the commercial banking system.

23. The budget crisis in Great Britain at the same time gave rise to a set of fiscal policies that became known as "liberal." Those policies included cuts in spending and import taxes on food products and higher income taxes.

24. Bureau of the Census, *Historical Statistics, 1789–1945*, Series L 1–14 (Prices) and Series N 19–26 at 263 (Bank Note Circulation).

25. Ibid., Series P 89–98 at 297.

26. Shultz and Caine, *Financial Development*, 216 and 232. See also *Annual Reports of the Secretary of Treasury*.

27. See Appendix C.

28. See Appendix C.

29. Van Buren, "Special Session Message."

30. John C. Calhoun quoted in Timberlake, *Monetary Policy*, 73.

31. Secretary of the Treasury Levi Woodbury reported to Congress that in 1837–1839, the Treasury had issued notes of $11.79 bearing low or little interest and interest-bearing notes of $7.44 million. Though the short-term notes allowed the administration to deny that it had increased long-term debt to banks, the Treasury was forced to keep recirculating those notes when they came back to the Treasury in payment of taxes. However, most of these amounts were paid off, or redeemed, by January 1, 1840, when after two years of cutting expenses the Treasury reported that only $1.5 million in long-term debt and $1.08 million in notes remained outstanding.

32. Kimmel, *Federal Budget and Fiscal Policy*, 22.

33. Dewey, *Financial History*, 255.

34. Polk, "Second Annual Message."

35. Secretary of the Treasury, *National Loans*, 73–74.

36. Miller, *Great Debates*, vol. 12, 77.

37. North, *Economic Growth*, Table 7 at 98 compared to census data.

38. Ibid., Table H-IX at 255.

39. Ibid., Series P 89–98 at 297.

40. Ibid., Series I at 233.

41. Ibid., Series P 89–98 at 297.

42. See Appendix A.

43. Van Buren quoted in Wilentz, *The Rise of American Democracy*, 615.

44. Salmon Chase quoted in Wilentz, *The Rise of American Democracy*, 610.

45. Frederick, "Buffalo Platform," 20.

46. In the summer of 1848 upstate New York would be the site of yet another remarkable convention, this one organized by women. The Seneca Falls Convention passed a Declaration of Sentiments urging female suffrage.

47. Chase, "An Appeal."

CHAPTER 5

1. Sherman, *Recollections of Forty Years*, 45.

2. Smith, *History of the Republican Party*, 22.

3. Tom Ewing quoted in Gienapp, *The Origins of the Republican Party*, 91.

4. Salmon Chase quoted in Gienapp, *The Origins of the Republican Party*, 114.

5. Sherman, *Recollections*, 111–112.

6. Ibid., 110.

7. Buchanan, "Inaugural Address."

8. Huston, *The Panic of 1857*, 114–117.

9. By fiscal year 1857 postal expenses amounted to almost one-sixth of federal spending. After the Civil War, "on budget" postal expenses were reduced at a high "off budget" price when the United States granted more than one hundred million acres of federal land to railroads in return for lower rates for postal transportation. The postal service since 1974 has been financed with dedicated trust funds from its own revenues.

10. Huston, *The Panic of 1857*, 183–184.

11. Ibid., 193.

12. Ibid., 43.

13. Cross, *Justin Smith Morrill*, 46.

14. Ibid.

15. Sherman, *Recollections*.

16. Flaherty, "Incidental Protection," 112.

17. William Fessenden quoted in Foner, *Free Soil, Free Labor, Free Men*, 213.

18. Fessenden, *Life and Public Services*, 128–129.

CHAPTER 6

1. *Sherman: Memoirs*, 221.

2. Ibid. In April 1862, at Shiloh, Tennessee, Sherman proved his toughness by holding a position against waves of assaults. He had four horses shot out from under him.

3. Davis, *Confederate Government*, vol. 1, 416.

4. Bureau of the Census, *Historical Statistics, 1789–1945*, Series P 89–98 at 297 Series P 99–108 at 300.

5. Lincoln, "July 4th Message."

6. Bureau of the Census, *Historical Statistics, 1789–1945*, Series N 152–165 at 276.

7. Studenski and Krooss, *Financial History*, 140–141.

8. Ibid., 142–143.

9. Ibid., 141–142.

10. Sherman, *Recollections*, 281.

11. Ibid., 279.

12. Niven, *Salmon P. Chase*, 262.

13. Ibid., 269.

14. Cleveland, *Alexander H. Stephens*, 727.

15. The Confederate Congress in 1861 did enact import taxes (similar to those in the 1846 Walker Tariff) and even some export taxes. Because of the US embargo on trade from the Confederacy, and the unwillingness of smugglers to pay taxes, the Confederate states collected less than $4 million in import taxes—less than a couple of weeks of military spending.

16. Taussig, *Tariff History*, 167.

17. Cross, *Justin Smith Morrill*, 61–62.

18. Seligman, *The Income Tax*, 436.

19. Dewey, *Financial History*, 305.

20. Seligman, *The Income Tax*, 472.

21. Bureau of the Census, *Historical Statistics, 1789–1945*, Series P 89–98 at 297.

22. President Lincoln used Walker in other ways. He sent the former Mississippi senator to Great Britain with the assignment of shutting down Confederate financing and maintaining US trade credit. Walker assured British bankers that the United States would pay its debt in currency convertible to gold as soon as possible after the war. He also reminded them that his own state of Mississippi, home of Confederate president Jefferson Davis, had repudiated its debts from the 1830s. Walker would play one more significant role in US history, when he lobbied for Russia to arrange the sale of Alaska.

23. Burton, *John Sherman*, 14.

24. Bureau of the Census, *Historical Statistics, 1789–1945*, Series P 99–108 at 300.

25. Dewey, *Financial History*, 308. (Net increase in debt minus non–interest-bearing demand notes, legal tender notes, fractional currency, temporary loans, and certificates of indebtedness.)

26. Grant, *Mr. Speaker!*, 105.

27. McCulloch, *Men and Measures*, 206.

28. Cross, *Justin Smith Morrill*, 85.

29. John Sherman quoted in Gould, *Grand Old Party*, 54.

30. Noyes, *Forty Years of American Finance*, 16–17.

31. McCulloch, *Men and Measures*, 208.

32. Savage, *Balanced Budgets*, 127.

33. From 1867 to 1869, the Treasury refunded more than $800 million in Civil War bonds, at yields ranging between 4.16 and 5.87 percent. "Repayment was promised in 'coin' and not in gold, which opened the way for the silver controversy of the last decades of the century" (Homer and Sylla, *Interest Rates*, 408).

34. Stabile and Cantor, *Public Debt*, 59.

35. Within three years of the war's end, Congress lowered taxes on imported coal and low-grade iron, as well as taxes on professions, transactions, and the gross receipts of corporations. Excise taxes were retained on oil, gas, whiskey, and tobacco. Congress also eliminated the unpopular taxes on tea and coffee, which produced steady revenue.

36. Studenski and Krooss, *Financial History*, 167n5.

37. John Sherman quoted in Seligman, *The Income Tax*, 464.

38. Taussig, *Tariff History*, 173.

39. From 1868 to 1873 rail construction and related debt exploded. The bonded debt of US railroads increased from $416 million in 1867 to over $2.2 billion in 1874, an amount equal to the interest-bearing federal debt.

40. According to the federal Bureau of Economic Statistics, the United States from 1873 to 1879 was part of a worldwide depression, one particularly severe in England. The downturn's duration would qualify as a depression, but it is referred to in this text as a recession because US output actually increased in the period. For more on this subject, see Wicker, *Banking Panics*, 3. One scholar estimated unemployment at 570,000, a small fraction of the relative level of unemployment experienced during the most severe downturns, especially the Great Depression (Frels, "The Long Wave Depression," 72).

41. Bureau of the Census, *Historical Statistics, 1789–1945*, Series P 89–98 at 297.

42. Ibid., Series P 99–108 at 300.

43. Stampp, *The Era of Reconstruction*, 128.

44. Grant, "First Inaugural Address."

45. Brands, *American Colossus*, 167.

46. Noyes, *Forty Years of American Finance*, 29.

47. This interest rate is calculated by dividing the gross interest on debt paid each fiscal year by the beginning and ending balance of outstanding interest-bearing debt. For gross interest, see Department of the Treasury, *Statistical Appendix* (1970), 8–5. For interest-bearing debt, see Appendix A and note 3.

48. In 1873 Congress authorized the minting of only gold coins because silver coinage had disappeared. After the price of silver dropped, advocates of silver coinage claimed that this decision resulted from a gold conspiracy.

49. Noyes, *Forty Years of American Finance*, 45.

50. Davis, "U.S. Industrial Production Index."

51. Bureau of the Census, *Historical Statistics, 1789–1945*, Series B 304–330 at 33.

52. See Appendix A.

53. Debt reduction combined with high import taxation on consumer goods lowered both the relative price of capital goods and financial investment (Williamson, "Watersheds and Turning Points"). Economic output accelerated after the Civil War, with more extensive production of capital goods and an increasing share of workers employed in manufacturing (Gallman, "Commodity Output").

54. Associations of banks in the largest urban centers developed into mature "clearinghouses." Interbank balances that had been reconciled every Friday began clearing daily. As envisioned by the National Bank Act, New York banks became the "lenders of last resort" for regional banks. By 1880 New York banks supported surging US international trade and became a major hub in the world's financial system.

CHAPTER 7

1. Kelley, *The Transatlantic Persuasion*, 287.

2. William Gladstone quoted in McCulloch, *Men and Measures*, 220.

3. Republican leader James Blaine formulated his party's response to Tilden's policy of retrenchment. The impressive orator defended federal spending for higher military pensions and survivor benefits, as well as the import taxes used to pay for that spending. Blaine and other congressional leaders tried to separate themselves from both the corrupt patronage machines and the reformers who supported Tilden and his predecessor as New York's governor, liberal Republican Carl Shurz.

4. Cleveland later worked with Roosevelt on a bill to protect the rights of exploited workers who made cigars by hand in New York City. The cigar union's young organizer, Samuel Gompers, would go on to shape the American labor movement. Gompers's organizing efforts thrived when he obtained medical benefits for his workers.

5. See Appendix A.

6. Dewey, *Financial History*, 432.

7. Ibid., 430.

8. From the opening of the gold window in 1879 until the outbreak of World War I, various treasury secretaries supplemented expansion of bank credit with silver and gold certificates that were issued in exchange for private deposits of precious metals. The Treasury Department listed these certificates as part of calculated "gross debt" even though they earned no interest and served essentially

as another form of currency. Appendix A distinguishes between interest-bearing and non–interest-bearing debt. The "official" historical statistics found to this day on the Treasury's website inflate the amount of debt by including all paper money.

9. Quoted in Kelley, *The Transatlantic Persuasion*, 325.

10. Jeffers, *An Honest President*, 194.

11. Kelley, *The Transatlantic Persuasion*, 326.

12. McMath, *American Populism*, 26.

13. White, *Railroaded*, 68.

14. Veblen, "The Price of Wheat," Tables of Prices of Wheat and Other Articles at 156.

15. Hofstadter, *The Age of Reform*, 174.

16. Cleveland, "Third Annual Message."

17. Ibid.

18. The political battle over import taxes became more heated even as their size and significance diminished as a percent of the total national income and total federal revenues. In 1866 federal customs collections were $179 million and rose in the next thirty-four years to $233 million. They fell to a low of $130 million in 1878—at the tail end of a recession—then jumped to a high of $220 million in 1882 before leveling off. In contrast to revenues from import taxation, revenues from sales taxes, principally taxes on alcohol and tobacco, rose steadily with national income.

19. Cleveland, "Fourth Annual Message."

20. Sherman could also count on some support from Western "Silver Republicans," a faction that tried not to anger the powerful Farmers Alliance. Between 1889 and 1890 six new Western states—Idaho, Montana, Washington, Wyoming, and the two Dakotas—joined the Union, adding to the region's power in the Senate and Electoral College.

21. McMath, *American Populism*, 141.

22. Adams, *Johnson's Universal Cyclopaedia*, 521.

23. Studenski and Krooss, *Financial History*, 228–229, and Jeffers, *An Honest President*, 281–283.

24. John Sherman quoted in Sundquist, *Dynamics of the Party System*, 147.

25. Brands, *American Colossus*, 474.

26. Bryan quoted in Witte, *Federal Income Tax*, 73.

27. *Pollock v. Farmers Loan & Trust Co.*, 15 S. Ct. 673, 695 (1895) (Justice Field, dissenting).

28. Hobbs and Stoops, *Census 2000 Special Reports*, 11.

29. See Appendix A.

30. Bureau of the Census, *Historical Statistics, 1789–1945*, Series P 99–108 at 299.

31. Taus, *Central Banking Functions*, 96.

32. Faulkner, *Politics, Reform, and Expansion*, 266.

33. Mark Hanna quoted in Samuels and Samuels, *Teddy Roosevelt at San Juan*, 21.

Chapter 8

1. Parker, *Recollections*, 250.

2. Davis, *Financial History*, 486–487.

3. Theodore Roosevelt quoted in Chace, *1912*, 99.

4. Bureau of the Census, *Historical Statistics, 1789–1945*, Series P 99–108 at 300.

5. Roosevelt to General Leonard Wood, March 9, 1905, in Bishop, *Theodore Roosevelt*, 366.

6. Dalton, *Theodore Roosevelt*, 334.

7. William McKinley's speech in Buffalo, New York, on September 5, 1901, in Peck, *Twenty Years of the Republic*, 654.

8. Bureau of the Census, *Historical Statistics, 1789–1945*, Series P 89–98 at 296.

9. Ibid., Series P 99–108 at 300.

10. Roosevelt's speech in Minneapolis, on April 4, 1903, in Roosevelt, *Compilation*, 255.

11. Roosevelt quoted in Morris, *Theodore Roosevelt*, 444.

12. Weisman, *The Great Tax Wars*, 202.

13. Roosevelt, "Sixth Annual Message."

14. Bruner and Carr, *The Panic of 1907*, 67.

15. Willoughby, *The Problem of a National Budget*, 137.

16. Ibid., 138.

17. Stewart, *Budget Reform Politics*, 184.

18. Weisman, *The Great Tax Wars*, 216.

19. Nelson Aldrich quoted in Chernow, *The Warburgs*, chap. 10, "Shy Warrior."

20. Kimmel, *Federal Budget and Fiscal Policy*, 85.

21. Wilson, *Constitutional Government*, xxx.

22. US Censuses of Population and Housing, "Table 1. United States Resident Population by State: 1790–1850," http://lwd.dol.state.nj.us/labor/lpa/census/1990/poptrd1.htm.

23. Wilson, *A Day of Dedication*, 103.

24. Chace, *1912*, 166. These proposals were also part of the contemporaneous platforms of British Liberals led by Lloyd George and Winston Churchill, a reformer just eight years younger than Theodore Roosevelt.

25. Appendix A shows historical debt in comparable terms by subtracting "paper money" in the form of greenbacks and gold and silver certificates from the national debt. After 1913 their functions were replaced by the Federal Reserve note, or modern "paper money," and those notes were no longer included in the debt account. From the Civil War until World War I, the "official" debt statistics on the US Treasury's website are not meaningful for historical comparisons because they include non–interest-bearing notes serving as currency, including notes issued for gold and silver deposited at the Treasury.

26. Studenski and Krooss, *Financial History*, 144–145.

27. Witte, *Federal Income Tax*, 75–79.

28. See Appendix A.

CHAPTER 9

1. Morgan, *Deficit Government*, 7.

2. Claude Kitchin quoted in Tindall, *The Emergence of the New South*, 42.

3. Witte, *Federal Income Tax*, 8.

4. Kitchin quoted in Tindall, *The Emergence of the New South*, 43.

5. McAdoo, *Crowded Years*, 369.

6. Kitchin quoted in Keith, *Rich Man's War, Poor Man's Fight*, 14.

7. Kitchin quoted in Tindall, *The Emergence of the New South*, 53.

8. Woodrow Wilson quoted in Gilbert, *American Financing of World War I*, 84.

9. Ibid., 83.

10. Emergency Loan Act of April 24, 1917.

11. Gilbert, *American Financing*, 84–91.

12. William McAdoo quoted in Mehrota, "Lawyers, Guns, and Public Moneys," 184.

13. McAdoo quoted in Ippolito, *Why Budgets Matter*, 101.

14. Kitchin quoted in "Kitchin Excuses New Tax Bill."

15. A commitment to taxes based on ability to pay was shared by other powerful members of tax-writing committees, including Senator Furnifold Simmons from North Carolina, chairman of the Senate Finance Committee; Senator John Williams of Mississippi, chairman of the Subcommittee on Income and Estate Taxation; and Representative Cordell Hull of Tennessee, who had drafted the original income tax.

16. Gilbert, *American Financing*, 94. An excellent source for monthly revenues and outlays can be found in Firestone, *Federal Receipts*, Table A-3.

17. Gilbert, *American Financing*, 96–97.

18. Firestone, *Federal Receipts*, Table A-3.

19. Gilbert, *American Financing*, 91.

20. William McAdoo quoted in Gilbert, *American Financing*, 90.

21. Studenski and Krooss, *Financial History*, 295–296.

22. Mellon, *Taxation*, 13.

23. Bureau of the Census, *Historical Statistics, 1789–1945*, Series P 144–151 at 307.

24. Studenski and Krooss, *Financial History*, 288–292.

25. James Macdonald, *A Free Nation Deep in Debt: The Financial Roots of Democracy* (Princeton, NJ: Princeton University Press, 2006), 403.

26. Gilbert, *American Financing*, Table 40 at 135.

27. Kimmel, *Federal Budget and Fiscal Policy*, 86.

28. Department of the Treasury, *Statistical Appendix*, Table 32 at 155–159.

29. Bureau of the Census, *Historical Statistics, 1789–1945*, Series P 152–165 at 375.

30. Shultz and Caine, *Financial Development*, 558.

31. Macdonald, *A Free Nation Deep in Debt*, 422.

32. See Appendix C.

33. Department of the Treasury, *Annual Report*, 4.

34. Hofstadter, *The Age of Reform*, 275.

35. Wilson quoted in Chace, *1912*, 269.

36. James Cox quoted in Smith, *FDR*, 180.

37. McGerr, *A Fierce Discontent*, 312.

38. Mellon, *Taxation*, 9, 25.

39. Ibid., 94.

40. Commission on Economy and Efficiency, "The Need for a National Budget," 10.

41. After the Civil War, Congress created appropriations committees that obtained spending authority historically exercised by the Senate Finance Committee and House Ways and Means Committee. The control of spending by appropriators was then eroded by "reforms" in 1884 designed to spread spending power among more committees. The House Ways and Means Committee and Senate Finance Committee retained jurisdiction over all tax bills.

42. Stewart, *Budget Reform Politics*, 205.

43. O'Brien, "Charles Gates Dawes," 102.

44. Dawes, *The First Year*.

45. Hicks, *Republican Ascendancy*, 49.

46. Murphy, "The Business of America."

47. Dawes, "Business Organization of the Government," 117–118.

48. Bureau of the Budget, *Report to the President*, 10–11.

49. Bureau of the Census, "Corporate and Personal Income," in *Historical Statistics, 1789–1945*, Series P 89–98 at 296.

50. OMB, Historical Tables, "Table 2.3—Receipts by Source as Percentages of GDP: 1934–2018."

51. Dewey, *Financial History*, 515.

52. Studenski and Krooss, *Financial History*, 349.

53. Mellon, *Taxation*, 133.

54. Waltman, *Political Origins*, 95.

55. Bureau of the Census, *Statistical Abstract*.

56. Compare Bureau of the Census, *Historical Statistics, 1789–1945*, Table Series P 144–151 and 307, with Mellon, *Taxation*, 34.

57. Bureau of the Census, *Historical Statistics, 1789–1945*, 307.

58. Ibid.

59. Tax Policy Center, "Historical Individual Tax Parameters," 2013, http://www.taxpolicycenter.org/taxfacts/displayafact.cfm?Docid=543.

60. Ibid.

61. In the 1920s, as federal tax rates came down, so did the premium paid for tax-exempt bonds. From 1921 to 1931 the annual yields on high-grade corporate bonds ranged from a high of 5.16 percent in 1921 to a low of 4.04 percent in 1928. During those same years, the average annual yield of high-grade municipal bonds ranged from 5.02 percent in 1921 to 3.97 percent in 1928. Homer and Sylla, *Interest Rates*, Table 47 at 349–350.

62. Andrew Mellon quoted in Cannadine, *Mellon*, 358.

63. Bureau of the Census, *Historical Statistics, 1789–1945*, Series 144–151 and P 152–164. Americans who reported making less than $25,000—all but the wealthiest—paid a total of $103 million. Investment income accounted for 60 percent of reported taxable income in 1926, since by then only wealthy Americans had any tax liability. These estimates of revenues are based on the fiscal year 1926, and the share of personal taxes by income group and personal investment is based on the calendar year 1927.

64. Mellon, *Taxation*, 30.

65. Ibid., 80–82.

66. Walton and Rockoff, *History of the American Economy*, Table 22–1 at 472.

67. Schlesinger, *The Age of Roosevelt*, vol. 1, 68.

68. Hicks, *Republican Ascendancy*, 18.

69. Coolidge, "Inaugural Address."

70. Dickson and Allen, *The Bonus Army*, 29.

CHAPTER 10

1. Schlesinger, *The Age of Roosevelt*, vol. 1, 159.

2. Committee on Economic Security, "Estimates."

3. Hoover, "Address."

4. Firestone, *Federal Receipts*, Table A-4 at 151–152.

5. Dewey, *Financial History*, 535–537.

6. Bureau of the Census, *Historical Statistics to 1970*, Series P 89–98 at 295–296. In 1930 the federal government collected $1.146 billion in personal income taxes, $1.263 billion in corporate income taxes, $537 million in customs receipts, and $270 million in interest and principal owed to the United States by Europe for World War I debts. Revenues from those four sources almost equaled the $3.4 billion in spending before debt retirement. Just three fiscal years later, with much higher taxes, 1933 personal income tax receipts had fallen to $427 million, corporate income tax to $629 million, customs receipts to $327 million, and receipts from foreign debt to zero. Revenue from personal and corporate income taxes did not recover to pre-Depression levels until 1939.

7. Herbert Hoover quoted in Savage, *Balanced Budgets*, 168.

8. Board of Governors, "Industrial Production Index."

9. Committee on Economic Security, "Estimates."

10. Hoover, *Memoirs*, vol. 3, 135–137.

11. Robert Doughton quoted in "Robert Doughton."

12. By 1933 bank reserves and the money supply had dropped by more than 30 percent. Half of US banks closed between 1929 and 1933. The percentages of banks failing each year were: 1930, 5.6 percent; 1931, 10.5 percent; 1932, 7.8 percent; and 1933, 12.9 percent.

13. Hoover cited in footnote 83 in Meltzer, *A History of the Federal Reserve*, 347.

14. Timmons, *Portrait of an American: Charles G. Dawes*, 313.

15. Todd, "Reconstruction Finance Corporation."

16. Calvin Coolidge quoted in Leuchtenburg, *Franklin D. Roosevelt*, 28.

17. Schlesinger, *The Age of Roosevelt*, vol. 1, 176, 204.

18. Brown, *Public Relief*, 89–90.

19. Ratchford, *American State Debts*, 369–370.

20. Brown, *Public Relief*, 124.

21. "Democratic Party Platform of 1932."

22. Roosevelt, "Campaign Address on the Eight Great Credit Groups."

23. Roosevelt, "Campaign Address on the Federal Budget."

24. Hoover, *Memoirs*, vol. 2, 274–275.

25. "Smith Lays Charge."

26. Bureau of the Census, *Historical Statistics to 1970*.

27. Board of Governors, "Industrial Production Index."

28. See Appendix B.

29. Stein, *The Fiscal Revolution*, 45.

30. Kimmel, *Federal Budget and Fiscal Policy*, 178.

31. Rosentreter, "Roosevelt's Tree Army."

32. Benjamin Franklin quoted in Beer, *To Make a Nation*, 154.

33. Stein, *The Fiscal Revolution*, 59.

34. Studenski and Krooss, *Financial History*, 407. For a breakdown of the various categories of spending classified as "ordinary" and "recovery and relief" during the first years of the Roosevelt administration, see Shultz and Caine, *Financial Development*, 715.

35. The combined deficit for those two fiscal years was $7.7 billion. Relief—not including large public works but including public service jobs—was $4.7 billion. The cost of the veterans' bonus and loss of the processing fee more than exceeded the difference.

36. Studenski and Krooss, *Financial History*, Table 75 at 417.

37. Henry Morgenthau quoted in Zelizer, *Governing America*, 142.

38. Brown, *Public Relief*, 204 (relief), and Bureau of the Census, *Historical Statistics to 1970*, Series A 177–133 at 12 (national income).

39. Roosevelt quoted in Leuchtenberg, *Franklin D. Roosevelt*, 122–123, 124.

40. Amenta, *When Movements Matter*, 84.

41. DeWitt, Béland, and Berkowitz, *Social Security*.

42. Hoover, *Memoirs*, vol. 2, 313.

43. Perkins, *The Roosevelt I Know*, 280.

44. Thomas Jefferson quoted in Peterson, *Running on Empty*, 214.

45. Studenski and Krooss, *Financial History*, Table 78 at 428.

46. Livingston, *U.S. Social Security*, 13.

47. Vandenberg, "The $47,000,000,000 Blight."

48. Alf Landon quoted in Leuchtenberg, *Franklin D. Roosevelt*, 179.

49. Kimmel, *Federal Budget*, 187.

50. Roosevelt quoted in Stein, *The Fiscal Revolution*, 98.

51. Kimmel, *Federal Budget*, 227.

52. See Appendix B.

CHAPTER 11

1. Studenski and Krooss, *Financial History*, 437–438.

2. Adolf Hitler quoted in Hormats, *The Price of Liberty*, 148.

3. Evans, *The Third Reich at War*, 332–333.

4. Roosevelt, "State of the Union Address."

5. Henry Morgenthau quoted in Hormats, *The Price of Liberty*, 160.

6. Patterson, *Mr. Republican*, 256.

7. Witte, *Federal Income Tax*, 117–118; "Marginal Rates of Federal Corporate Income Taxation, 1942–2010," Tax Policy Center, http://www.taxpolicycenter.org/taxfacts/displayafact.cfm?Docid=64; "U.S. Individual Income Tax: Personal Exemptions and Lowest and Highest Tax Rates and Tax Base for Regular Tax, Tax Years 1913–2013," Tax Policy Center, http://www.taxpolicycenter.org/taxfacts/displayafact.cfm?Docid=543.

8. Brownlee, *Federal Taxation*, 112.

9. "Ninety Years of Individual and Income Tax Statistics," SOI Tax Stats–Individual Time Series Statistical Tables, 2012, Tables 1 and 1A, http://www.irs.gov/uac/SOI-Tax-Stats-Individual-Time-Series-Statistical-Tables.

10. Derived from "Ninety Years of Individual and Income Tax Statistics."

11. Ibid.

12. Steuerle, *The Tax Decade*, Figure 2.2 at 20.

13. During the war, enrollment in group hospital plans grew from seven million to twenty-six million, with about three-quarters enrolled in nonprofit Blue Cross programs. In the five years after the war, enrollment in employer plans continued to explode, and by the end of 1954, more than 60 percent of American workers had some form of employer-based hospital insurance. That year Congress made clear that employers' payments for medical insurance were properly excluded from the taxable income of beneficiaries.

14. Ledbetter, "Comparison of BEA Estimates." For current relative amounts of various exclusions and deduction, see also OMB Budget, Fiscal Year 2012:

Analytical Perspectives, http://www.whitehouse.gov/sites/default/files/omb/budget/fy2012/assets/spec.pdf. That $900 billion accounted for about a third of all exclusions representing the difference between $7.4 trillion in reported gross income and $10.3 trillion in personal income as estimated by economists for that year. Postwar debates on personal income taxes focused more on tax rates than on expanding the tax base.

15. Bureau of the Census, *Historical Statistics, 1789–1945*, Series P 141–155 at 307.

16. Studenski and Krooss, *Financial History*, 446n2.

17. Roosevelt, "Veto of a Revenue Bill."

18. Henry Morgenthau quoted in Blum, *Years of War*, 21.

19. Studenski and Krooss, *Financial History*, Table 86 at 452.

20. Stabile and Cantor, *Public Debt*, 95.

21. Meltzer, *A History of the Federal Reserve*, vol. 1, Table 7.2 at 298.

22. This interest rate is calculated by dividing the gross interest on debt paid each fiscal year by the beginning and ending balance of outstanding interest-bearing debt. For gross interest, see Department of the Treasury, *Statistical Appendix*, 8–15. For interest-bearing debt, see Appendix A and note 3.

23. Derived from Appendix C. According to one comprehensive analysis of wartime debt, in the five fiscal years from July 1, 1941, through June 30, 1946, out of $383 billion spent by the federal government, taxes provided $169 billion and debt, $214 billion. See also the Committee on Public Debt Policy, *Our National Debt*, at 54.

24. See Appendix B.

25. See Appendix B.

26. Wallace, *Sixty Million Jobs*, 3, 10–11, 184, 190.

27. Harry S. Truman quoted in Patterson, *Mr. Republican*, 440.

28. Donovan, *Conflict and Crisis*, 62.

29. Harry S. Truman quoted in Stein, *The Fiscal Revolution*, 207.

30. James Forrestal quoted in Donovan, *Tumultuous Years*, 59.

31. Truman, "Statement by the President Announcing Revised Budget Estimates."

32. Gaddis, *The United States and the Origins of the Cold War*, 312.

33. Bostdorff, *Proclaiming the Truman Doctrine*, 101.

34. Truman, "Address in Chicago on Army Day."

35. Gaddis, *The United States and the Origins of the Cold War*, 344.

36. Committee on Public Debt Policy, *Our National Debt*, 31.

37. Truman, "Special Message to the Congress on Greece and Turkey."

38. See Appendix C.

39. Witte, *Federal Income Tax*, 134–135.

40. Hoopes and Brinkley, *Driven Patriot*, 365.

41. Lucius Clay quoted in "Learning to Estimate, 1948."

42. Donovan, *Tumultuous Years*, 58.

43. Millis, *The Forrestal Diaries*, 498–99.

44. Truman, *Off the Record*, 134.

45. Millis, *The Forrestal Diaries*, 498–99.

46. Ibid., 526.

47. Smith, *Thomas E. Dewey*, 547.

48. Kirk and McClellan, *Robert A. Taft*, 132–133.

49. Arthur Vandenberg quoted in Brands, *The Strange Death of American Liberalism*, 60.

50. Harry S. Truman quoted in Donovan, *Tumultuous Years*, 58.

51. Brownlee, *Federal Taxation*, 121.

52. See Appendix C.

53. Studenski and Krooss, *Financial History*, Table 90 at 463.

54. Taft-Radcliffe amendment quoted in "The Growing Debt."

55. The act declared it the "policy and responsibility of the Federal Government to use all practical means . . . to coordinate and utilize its plans, functions, and resources for the purpose of creating and maintaining . . . conditions under which there will be afforded useful employment, for those able, willing and seeking to work."

56. Friedman, "A Monetary and Fiscal Framework," 249.

57. Committee for Economic Development, *Taxes and the Budget*.

CHAPTER 12

1. May, *American Cold War Strategy*, 74–75.

2. Chace, *Acheson*, 269.

3. Dean Acheson quoted in Gaddis, *We Now Know*, 76.

4. Leffler, *A Preponderance of Power*, 373.

5. OMB, Historical Tables, "Table 1.1–Summary of Receipts, Outlays, and Surpluses or Deficits: 1789–2018."

6. See Appendix C.

7. Truman, "Special Message to the Congress Recommending a 'Pay as We Go' Tax Program."

8. Truman quoted in Hormats, *The Price of Liberty*, 184.

9. Joseph Stalin quoted in Gellately, *Stalin's Curse*, 340.

10. Smithies, *The Budgetary Process*, 124.

11. Livingston, *U.S. Social Security*, 16.

12. Zelizer, *Taxing America*, 75.

13. Unlike the House, the Senate did not include coverage of workers who had contributed to the system but had to leave work before the age of sixty-five because of disabilities. Two years later, the House again overwhelmingly supported a partial pension for younger but disabled workers, as advocated by Doughton. The aging

chairman planned to retire that year and challenged critics of the proposal by asking, "What political motives could I have?" The Senate again deleted disability coverage in conference committee.

14. Brownlee, *Funding the Modern American State*, 163.

15. Smith and Moore, *Medicaid Politics and Policy*, 35.

16. Eisenhower, "Special Message."

17. Lawrence Lindsey quoted in Noah, "Meme Watch."

18. Bush, "Second Inaugural Address."

19. Kotlikoff and Burns, *The Coming Generational Storm*, 240.

20. US National Center for Health Statistics, *Vital Statistics of the United States: 1957*, http://www.cdc.gov/nchs/products/vsus.htm.

21. Bell and Miller, "Actuarial Study No. 120."

22. Werner, *The Older Population*.

23. US Census Bureau, 2010 Census, http://www.census.gov/2010census/.

24. "Monthly Statistical Snapshot, June 2013: Table 2," Social Security Administration, http://www.ssa.gov/policy/docs/quickfacts/stat_snapshot/.

25. Excellent accounts of the ensuing agreement include Melzer, *The History of the Federal Reserve*, 691–712, and Robert Heltzer and Ralph Leach, "The Treasury-Fed Accord: A New Narrative Account," Federal Reserve Board of Richmond *Economic Quarterly* 87, no. 1 (2001).

26. Marriner Eccles quoted in Hetzel and Leach, "The Treasury-Fed Accord," 43.

27. Truman, "Statement by the President in Response to a Joint Announcement."

28. This interest rate is calculated by dividing the gross interest on debt paid each fiscal year by the beginning and ending balance of outstanding interest-bearing debt. For gross interest, see Department of the Treasury, *Statistical Appendix*, 8–15. For interest-bearing debt, see Appendix A and note 3. The interest rate on new long bonds rose even more, from 2.32 in 1950 to 4.01 in 1960. See also Homer and Sylla, *Interest Rates*, Table 5.1 at 375.

29. See Appendix A.

30. OMB, Historical Tables, "Table 2.1–Receipts by Source: 1934–2018."

31. Eisenhower, "State of the Union," January 5, 1956.

32. Eisenhower, "The President's News Conference."

33. Eisenhower, "Radio and Television Address."

34. Quoted in Stein, *The Fiscal Revolution*, 395.

35. Morgan, *Eisenhower Versus 'The Spenders'*, 87–88.

36. Harry Byrd quoted in Heinemann, *Harry Byrd*, 364.

37. Goldwater, *Conscience of a Conservative*, 38.

38. Stein, *The Fiscal Revolution*, 333.

39. Anderson, "Financial Policies for Sustainable Growth," 132–133.

40. Eisenhower, "State of the Union," January 7, 1960.

41. OMB, Historical Tables, "Table 3.1—Outlays by Superfunction and Function: 1940–2018."

42. Rose, *Interstate*, 31.

43. Ibid., 70.

44. Ibid., 71.

45. The first major American scholar to make this point was Henry Vethake in his work *The Principles of Political Economy* in 1838. However, his analysis did not draw on later economic work concerning the efficient allocation of resources used by Buchanan.

46. Eisenhower, *Mandate for Change*, 129.

47. Eisenhower, "Chance for Peace."

48. Pach and Richardson, *Eisenhower*, 80.

49. Perret, *Eisenhower*, 462.

50. Gaddis, *We Now Know*, 248.

51. Pach and Richardson, *Eisenhower*, 214.

52. Ibid., 221.

53. For an excellent summary of inflation-adjusted defense budgets by category, see Meeker, *A Basic Summary*.

54. Eisenhower, "Farewell Address."

55. Kennedy, "Statement by Senator John F. Kennedy."

56. Bureau of the Census, *Statistical Abstract*, Table 567 at 369.

57. Jacoby, "The Fiscal Policy of the Kennedy-Johnson Administration."

58. Reeves, *President Kennedy*, 331.

59. "JFK on the Economy and Taxes."

60. Reeves, *President Kennedy*, 319.

61. Douglas Dillon quoted in "Treasury Secretary Says US Can't Afford Tax Cut."

Chapter 13

1. Kennedy, "Letter to the Chairman."

2. Stein, *The Fiscal Revolution*, 452–453.

3. Johnson, *The Vantage Point*, 36.

4. Ibid., 37.

5. Johnson, "State of the Union Address (January 8, 1964)."

6. Al Gore Sr. quoted in Reeves, *President Kennedy*, 434.

7. Mann, *Legacy to Power*, 220.

8. Lowndes, "The Revenue Act of 1964," 667.

9. OMB, Historical Tables, "Table 1.4—Receipts, Outlays, and Surpluses or Deficits by Fund Group: 1934–2018."

10. OMB, Historical Tables, "Table 3.1—Outlays by Superfunction and Function: 1940–2018."

11. The administrative or federal funds budget excludes trust funds, such as those for pensions and highways. Federal grants to states for education, health, and housing had been championed by former conservative leader Robert Taft. From

Eisenhower's last budget to Johnson's first, spending for those programs had grown from $3.2 billion to $5 billion. By contrast, spending for defense, veterans, and space programs amounted to $62 billion.

12. Starr, *Remedy and Reaction: The Peculiar American Struggle over Health Care Reform* (New Haven, CT: Yale University Press, 2011), 44.

13. Reagan, "Ronald Reagan Speaks Out Against Socialized Medicine."

14. Manley, *The Politics of Finance*, 148.

15. Wilbur Mills quoted in Zelizer, *Taxing America*, 174.

16. Ibid., 236.

17. Mills quoted in Kennon and Rogers, *The Committee on Ways and Means*, 343.

18. Johnson quoted in Loker, *The History and Evolution of Healthcare in America*, 171.

19. Lyndon B. Johnson, telephone call with John McCormack, Wilbur Mills, Wilbur Cohen, and Carl Albert, March 23, 1965, in "Recordings and Transcripts of Conversations," Citation 7141, LBJ Presidential Library.

20. Mills quoted in Smith and Moore, *Medicaid Politics and Policy*, 44.

21. Starr, *Remedy and Reaction*, 410.

22. Johnson, "Remarks with President Truman."

23. The original Medicare Part A reimbursement formulas helped fuel rising costs by reimbursing the capitalized costs of the hospital room and equipment, spurring new construction. By 1990 hospitalization costs, adjusted for normal inflation and even after price controls imposed in 1983, were 165 percent higher than originally estimated by the chief actuary, Robert Myers.

24. Smith and Moore, *Medicaid Politics and Policy*, 75–76.

25. Vladeck, *Unloving Care: The Nursing Home Tragedy* (New York: Basic Books, 1980), 49.

26. "Medicare and Medicaid Statistical Supplement: 2012 Edition," Centers for Medicare & Medicaid Services, Tables 13.4, 13.8, and 13.9, http://www.cms.gov/Research-Statistics-Data-and-Systems/Statistics-Trends-and-Reports/MedicareMedicaidStatSupp/2012.html.

27. US National Center for Health Statistics, *Vital Statistics of the United States: 1965*, http://www.cdc.gov/nchs/products/vsus.htm. See also Kotlikoff and Burns, *The Coming Generational Storm*.

28. From time to time states that underestimated the costs of programs financed by matching grants had "purged their rolls" in violation of their own eligibility requirements. In *Goldberg v. Kelly*, 397 U.S. 254 (1970), Justice Brennan said that "such benefits are a matter of statutory entitlement to those eligible to receive them." By 1965 federal law also dramatically changed the operation of some hospitals receiving Medicare payments by prohibiting racial discrimination.

29. Daggett, *Costs of Major U.S. Wars*.

30. OMB, Historical Tables, "Table 3.1—Outlays by Superfunction and Function: 1940–2018."

31. Wilbur Mills quoted in Zelizer, *Taxing America*, 337.

32. Johnson, *Vantage Point*, 450.

33. Wilbur Mills quoted in Zelizer, *Taxing America*, 211.

34. Ibid., 272.

35. Assistant Treasury Secretary Samuel Surrey found it odd that in order to close the deficit, the Ways and Means Committee would use a tax bill to control federal spending rather than eliminating tax deductions or exclusions. This experience led Surrey to develop the phrase "tax expenditures," a phrase used routinely by President Obama.

36. McChesney Martin quoted in Green, *Changing America*, 57.

37. Johnson, "President Lyndon B. Johnson's Address to the Nation."

38. Ibid.

39. Johnson, *Vantage Point*, 457.

40. Johnson quoted in Brundage, *The Bureau of the Budget*, 254.

41. See Appendix C.

42. See Appendix A.

43. Stabile and Cantor, *Public Debt*, 135.

44. See Appendix B.

45. Nixon, "Inaugural Address."

46. Matusow, *Nixon's Economy*, 57–58.

47. Ibid., 4.

48. Ibid., 49–50.

49. Ibid., 77.

50. Ibid., 77–78.

51. OMB, Historical Tables, "Table 7.3–Statutory Limits on Federal Debt: 1940–Current." For an overview of the debt ceiling, see Austin and Levit, *The Debt Limit*.

52. Matusow, *Nixon's Economy*, 59. For a good record of how Nixon conveyed these views, see Abrams, "How Richard Nixon Pressured Arthur Burns."

53. See Appendix A and its note 4.

54. See Appendix A and its note 4.

55. Timberlake, *Monetary Policy*, 345–347.

56. Marmor, *The Politics of Medicare*, Tables 7.1 and 7.2 at 98.

57. *2013 Annual Report, Federal Hospital Insurance*, Tables V.B1, V.B3, and V.B5 from 191–199.

58. Federal funds support of outpatient services would grow to $2.3 billion in 1975 and $6.9 billion by 1980, largely as a result of higher prices for medical services and limits on the premium share paid by beneficiaries. These outlays grew to $33.2 billion in 1990 and $61.7 billion in 1996. Medicaid spending, paid for entirely with federal funds, would increase to $14.5 billion in 1980 and $41.1 billion by 1990.

59. Zelizer, *Taxing America*, 312.

60. Tax Policy Center, "Historical Social Security Tax Rates."

61. Zelizer, *Taxing America*, 324. See also Hacker, *The Divided Welfare State*, 142.

62. Moon, *Medicare*, 55.

63. Ibid.

64. Shaviro, *Do Deficits Matter?*, 80.

65. Tax Policy Center, "Historical Social Security Tax Rates."

66. Robert Ball quoted in Hacker, *The Divided Welfare State*, 143.

67. Nixon, "Annual Budget Message."

68. Nixon, "Radio Address."

69. Stein, *The Fiscal Revolution*, 573–575.

70. Gould, *Grand Old Party*, 400.

71. See Greene, *Gerald Ford*, and Reichley, *Conservatives in an Age of Change*.

72. Greene, *Gerald Ford*, 75–76.

73. Ibid., 79, and Reichley, *Conservatives in an Age of Change*, 392–393.

74. Cannon, *Governor Reagan*, 408. For background on the speech, see also Shirley, *Reagan's Revolution*, 80–85.

75. Ronald Reagan quoted in Cannon, *Governor Reagan*, 408.

76. Gould, *Grand Old Party*, 410.

77. Jimmy Carter quoted in Stabile and Cantor, *Public Debt*, 151.

Chapter 14

1. Carter, "The President's News Conference."

2. Carter, *Keeping Faith*, 82.

3. Homer and Sylla, *Interest Rates*, 383.

4. See Appendix C and "Consumer Price Index: All Urban Consumers," United States, Bureau of Labor Statistics, ftp://ftp. bls.gov/pub/special.requests/cpi/cpiai.txt.

5. Biven, *Jimmy Carter's Economy*, 204.

6. See Appendix C.

7. Peterson, "The New Politics of Deficits."

8. Morgan, *The Age of Deficits*, 67.

9. Homer and Sylla, *Interest Rates*, Table 51 at 376.

10. Volcker and Gyohten, *Changing Fortunes*, 172.

11. OMB, Historical Tables, Table 3.2, Account 901.

12. Peterson, "The New Politics of Deficits," 594.

13. The program, which offered competitive grants to nonprofits and state and local governments, replaced a variety of federal job training programs. CETA combined job training, including subsidies paid to employers for "work experience," and funding for public service jobs for those with lower skills who had experienced chronic unemployment. See Baumer and Van Horn, *The Politics of Unemployment*, for an excellent analysis of CETA programs.

14. Ibid., 103, 91.

15. Ibid., 89.

16. White and Wildavsky, *The Deficit and Public Interest*, 37.

17. Kaufman, *Henry M. Jackson*, 389.

18. Ibid.

19. OMB, Historical Tables, "Table 3.1–Outlays by Superfunction and Function: 1940–2018."

20. OMB, Historical Tables, "Table 2.3–Receipts by Source as Percentages of GDP: 1934–2018."

21. See OMB, Historical Tables, "Table 2.2–Percentage Composition of Receipts by Source: 1934–2018."

22. One study attributed about half of the decline in corporate income tax revenues from 1960 to 1985 to falling profits and the other half to various new incentives in tax law. See Alan Auerbach and James Polerba, "Why Have Corporate Tax Rates Declined," NBER working paper 2118 (January 1987).

23. Carter quoted in Mears, "Tax Code Overhaul."

24. Hollenbeck and Kahr, "Ninety Years of Individual Income and Tax Statistics," Table 1 at 144–145.

25. Ibid.

26. "U.S. Federal Individual Income Tax Rates History."

27. OMB, Historical Tables, "Table 2.3–Receipts by Source as Percentages of GDP: 1934–2018."

28. See Appendix H.

29. Tax Policy Center, "Historical Social Security Tax Rates."

30. Herbert Stein, "The Fiscal Revolution in America, Part II," in Brownlee, *Funding the Modern American State*, 256.

31. Cannon, *Governor Reagan*, 194.

32. Ibid., 199.

33. George H. W. Bush quoted in Bannon, "Bush Tax Cuts Turn 10."

34. Phillips-Fein, *Invisible Hands*, 252.

35. Anderson, *Revolution*, 122–129.

36. Ibid., Table 1 at 135.

37. Ibid., 134.

38. The actual federal budget Reagan would inherit, for the federal fiscal year 1981 beginning October 1, 1980, can be best understood if broken into four major parts: spending financed with dedicated taxes, spending on interest on the debt, spending on defense, and everything else. Anderson's hasty calculations for Reagan's budget plan assumed that the budget for fiscal year 1981 had revenues of $610 billion and outlays of $633 million. In reality, however, Reagan's proposals to increase defense spending and cut taxes affected only the federal funds budget, exclusive of trust fund spending and revenues. The actual federal funds revenues for fiscal 1981 would be $410 billion, and spending would be $496 billion.

Subtract from both receipts and spending $251 billion devoted to defense, veterans, and interest payments in that fiscal year, and you are left with $161 billion in receipts, and $245 billion in outlays.

39. Darman, *Who's in Control?*, 77.

40. Reagan, "Inaugural Address."

41. Feldstein, *American Economic Policy*, 287.

42. Howard Baker quoted in Stockman, *The Triumph of Politics*, 166.

43. Reagan, "Address on the Program for Economic Recovery."

44. Jim Wright quoted in Hayward, *The Age of Reagan*, 150.

45. Jack Kemp quoted in Stabile and Cantor, *Public Debt*, 178.

46. "Reagan's Tax Cut Proposal Called All But Dead."

47. Stockman, *The Triumph of Politics*, 213.

48. Kent Hance quoted in ibid.

49. Reagan, "Address on Federal Tax Reduction Legislation."

50. Dick Cheney quoted in Stockman, *The Triumph of Politics*, 311.

51. Savage, *Balanced Budgets*, Table 20 at 248.

52. Peterson, *Running on Empty*, 591.

53. OMB, Historical Tables, "Table 3.1–Outlays by Superfunction and Function: 1940–2018."

54. Pete Domenici quoted in Stockman, *The Triumph of Politics*, 351.

55. Ibid.

56. Ibid., 343.

57. Stockman, *The Triumph of Politics*, 557.

58. Reagan, "The President's News Conference."

59. Reagan, *The Reagan Diaries*, vol. 1, 90.

Chapter 15

1. Reagan, "Address Before a Joint Session."

2. Reagan, "Remarks at the Annual Convention."

3. Feldstein, *American Economic Policy*, 278.

4. Schick, *The Federal Budget*, 145.

5. Reagan, "Address to the Nation."

6. Newport, Jones, and Saad, "Ronald Reagan from the People's Perspective."

7. Newt Gingrich quoted in Gillon, *The Pact*, 52.

8. Hormats, *The Price of Liberty*, 238.

9. Stockman, *The Triumph of Politics*, 356–357.

10. Ronald Reagan quoted in Savage, *Balanced Budgets*, 268.

11. Savage, *Balanced Budgets*, 269–271.

12. Niskanen, *Reaganomics*, 106.

13. Shuman, *Politics and the Budget*, 155.

14. Martin Feldstein quoted in Reeves, *President Reagan*, 211.

15. For simplicity the text refers to a trust fund, though there are two for the system: one paying old-age and survivors' benefits and another for disability payments.

16. Reagan quoted in Grant, *The New American Social Compact*, 42.

17. In the remaining five years of Reagan's presidency, payroll tax revenues rose from $209 billion to $359 billion and transformed an $8 billion deficit in 1982 to an annual Social Security trust fund surplus of $52 billion by 1989. The tax remained at 15.3 percent of payroll until 2010. Most went to the Social Security old-age pension and disability trust funds; a tax of 2.9 percent of payroll funded the Hospitalization Insurance Trust Fund, supporting Medicare Part A.

18. The Gramm-Rudman-Hollings Act, officially entitled the Balanced Budget and Emergency Deficit Control Act of 1985, eliminated the planned removal of the Hospitalization Fund from the unified budget. As reported by the General Accounting Office (GAO) in 1988, "most public reporting" included the various trust funds in budget totals. The GAO also reported on a deliberate slowdown of spending in the Highway and Airport Trust Funds, financed with user fees, to reduce the reported level of the deficit. See GAO, *Budget Issues*.

19. Bivens, "Social Security's Fixable Financing Issues."

20. Ibid.

21. "Monthly Statistical Snapshot, June 2013: Table 2," US Social Security Administration, http://www.ssa.gov/policy/docs/quickfacts/stat_snapshot/.

22. OMB, Historical Tables, "Table 1.4–Outlays by Agency: 1962–2018."

23. See Appendix B.

24. Volcker and Gyohten, *Changing Fortunes*, 178.

25. Reagan, "State of the Union Address."

26. Anderson, *Revolution*, 179.

27. Cuts in these programs accounted for most of the reduction in domestic spending during the eight years of the Reagan administration. The cuts amounted to just over 1 percent of national income. See Charles Schultze, in Martin Feldstein, *American Economic Policy*, 284, especially Table 4.16. Reagan's domestic budgets did, however, devote far more to agricultural programs than did President Carter's. For a detailed comparison of Carter's actual and proposed budgets and Reagan's actual and proposed budgets in his first years, see Savage, *Balanced Budgets*, 270.

28. See Appendix B.

29. Walter Mondale quoted in Savage, *Balanced Budgets*, 229.

30. Rudman, *Combat*, 79–89.

31. Ibid.

32. The law set targets for reducing the deficit from an estimated $171.9 billion in fiscal 1986 to zero in 1991. These targets referred to the deficit in the unified budget, which included Social Security surpluses. An amendment to the law in 1987 stretched out the reduction, from $154 billion in fiscal year 1988 to zero in fiscal 1993.

33. After the Supreme Court ruled that the Gramm-Rudman-Hollings Act gave unconstitutional power over budgets to the controller, Congress passed an altered version of the bill that extended the deadline for a balanced budget by two years and assigned sequestration authority to the White House. Both the 1985 and 1987 versions of the act raised the statutory debt ceilings to allow additional borrowing.

34. This interest rate is calculated by dividing the gross interest on debt paid each fiscal year by the beginning and ending balance of outstanding interest-bearing debt. For gross interest, see OMB, Historical Tables, Table 3.2, Account 901. For interest-bearing debt, Appendix A and note 3.

35. Compare Table 2.2 with OMB, Historical Tables, Table 1.4.

36. See Appendix H.

37. Birnbaum and Murray, *Showdown at Gucci Gulch*, 31.

38. Bob Packwood quoted in ibid., 189.

39. Birnbaum and Murray, *Showdown*, 193.

40. Ibid., 153.

41. White and Wildavsky, *The Deficit and Public Interest*, 487–488.

42. For example, the 2010 National Commission on Fiscal Responsibility and Reform, often referred to as "Simpson-Bowles," has called for aggressive actions to increase tax revenues by eliminating deductions and exclusions: http://www.fiscal-commission.gov/sites/fiscalcommission.gov/files/documents/TheMomentofTruth 12_1_2010.pdf

43. See Appendix H.

44. Logan, "Summary of Latest Income Tax Data," Table 5.

45. Eugene Steuerle provides an excellent summary of the net effect of all tax changes from 1981 through 1990. According to his calculations, the net effect of Reagan-era changes was to reduce federal taxes from what would have been $1.167 trillion to $1.053 trillion at the end of the decade. However, the effect on federal funds revenues was much greater, because taxes for dedicated trust funds increased. See Steuerle, *The Tax Decade*, 186–187.

46. Robert Doughton quoted in Kennon and Rogers, *The Committee on Ways and Means*, 311.

47. Tax Policy Center, "Historical Social Security Tax Rates."

48. Smith and Moore, *Medicaid Politics*, 207.

49. Two other costly mandates had been imposed by fiscally conservative Southern Democrats. Senator David Boren of Oklahoma had authorized a requirement for payments to nursing homes sufficient to allow them to recover the cost of meeting minimum standards, and Senator David Pryor of Arkansas sponsored legislation creating federal standards. As popular governors, both Boren and Pryor learned firsthand the challenge of sustaining life with dignity for many seniors in nursing homes.

50. Bill Clinton quoted in Starr, *Remedy and Reaction*, 71.

51. George H. W. Bush quoted in Balz and Brownstein, *Storming the Gates*, 130.

52. Darman, *Who's in Control?*, 207.

CHAPTER 16

1. Morgan, *The Age of Deficits*, 138.

2. George H. W. Bush quoted in Rosenthal, "Bush Now Concedes."

3. Newt Gingrich quoted in Darman, *Who's in Control?*, 283.

4. Pollack, *Refinancing America*, 69.

5. Steuerle, *The Tax Decade*, Table 11.1 at 177. The balance of the deficit reduction consisted of $57 billion in unspecified other cuts and reduced interest from reduced borrowing. A good summary and analysis can be found in *The Tax Decade*, 177–183. The highest tax rate rose to 31 percent. In reality, the top rate was higher because of the phaseout of deductions for taxpayers in the top bracket.

6. Clinton for President Committee, *A Plan for America's Future*.

7. Also in March 1992, congressional "deficit hawks" flexed their muscles in a vote whose significance was overshadowed by the presidential race. The 1990 Balanced Budget Agreement had created separate annual ceilings on defense and discretionary—non–formula-driven—domestic spending. The Democratic House leadership tried to raise the level of domestic spending above the required ceiling, but Congressman Tim Penny and other Democrats joined with Republicans to defeat the measure.

8. Perot quoted in Shaviro, *Taxes*, 76.

9. Perot quoted in Rapoport and Stone, *Three's a Crowd*, 65.

10. Hager and Pianin, *Mirage*, 202.

11. Marmor, *The Politics of Medicare*, 124–125.

12. Chen, "Perot Quits Presidential Race."

13. Perot quoted in Rapoport and Stone, *Three's a Crowd*, 67.

14. Bush, "Presidential Debate in East Lansing."

15. Toner, "Clinton Captures Presidency."

16. Greenspan, *The Age of Turbulence*, 147.

17. Woodward, *The Agenda*, 71.

18. Ibid., 113.

19. Clinton quoted in ibid., 119.

20. Gingrich, "The Republican Contract with America."

21. Norquist, *Leave Us Alone*, 294–295.

22. Gingrich quoted in Hager and Pianin, *Mirage*, 15.

23. Gingrich quoted in Morgan, *The Age of Deficits*, 179.

24. Gingrich quoted in Hager and Pianin, *Mirage*, 15.

25. The amendment set a low bar for what counted by including trust fund revenues collected as a reserve for the post-2010 retirement of the Baby Boom generation.

26. Clinton quoted in Morgan, *The Age of Deficits*, 184.

27. Morgan, *The Age of Deficits*, 182.

28. Ibid.

29. Phillips-Fein, *Invisible Hands*, 265.

30. DeLay quoted in Morgan, *The Age of Deficits*, 186.

31. Smith, *Entitlement Politics*, 71.

32. Moon, *Medicare*, 66–67.

33. Marmor, *The Politics of Medicare*, 139.

34. Dole quoted in Morgan, *The Age of Deficits*, 183.

35. Morgan, *The Age of Deficits*, 182–183.

36. Perot had advocated that premium rates rise from 25 percent to 35 percent of Medicare Part B's total costs. Clinton's first budget had raised the contribution rate to 31.5 percent, but that level was set to revert to 25 percent in January 1996. Republican leaders feared that their Medicare plan, with premium rates of 31.5 percent, would encounter greater public resistance if it jumped from a 25 percent base.

37. The White House and Congressional Republicans had skirmished about the time period for balancing the budget and whether to assume a 2.3 percent or a 2.5 percent rate of economic growth. Eventually Clinton accepted the seven-year timetable and the assumption of the lower rate of economic growth.

38. Gingrich quoted in "Gingrich Says 'Snub' Contributed to Shutdown."

39. Balz and Brownstein, *Storming the Gates*, 157.

40. Gingrich quoted in Morgan, *The Age of Deficits*, 188.

41. Clinton, "State of the Union."

42. Gingrich quoted in Morgan, *The Age of Deficits*, 193.

43. In Massachusetts Republican governor William Weld and state Democratic leaders had paid for expanded medical coverage with a sharp increase in tobacco taxes. A new federal Children's Health Insurance Program (CHIP) was based on that precedent. Rather than creating a new "entitlement," Congress gave the states the option of either incorporating greater coverage for children in Medicaid or crafting their own program with a block grant. The president and others had long feared that poor children would be hurt the most by annual ceilings on Medicaid growth, since no state would be willing to endure the backlash from evicting elderly and disabled Americans from nursing homes.

44. Joyce, *The Congressional Budget Office*, 75–76.

45. Hahn and Mulvey, "Medical Physician Payment Updates," contains an excellent overview of this issue.

46. Marmor, *The Politics of Medicare*, 150.

47. Herbert Stein quoted in Pianin, "Seeing Budget in Balance."

48. Gillon, *The Pact*, 252.

49. Gingrich quoted in Seelye, "The Speaker Steps Down."

50. Clinton, "Remarks on the Budget Surplus."

51. The White House had not *predicted* a federal funds surplus in fiscal 2000. See OMB, Historical Table 1.4 (2000), reprinted in Meyer, *Evolution of United States Budgeting*.

52. Kliesen and Thorton, "The Expected Federal Budget Surplus."

53. That projection showed the first surplus in the unified budget in fiscal year 2001 and continuing deficits of more than $100 billion a year in the federal funds budget. Before 1998, the CBO had routinely projected budget deficits for the next year and rising deficits five years out. The CBO had last predicted large surpluses in 1980, when it estimated a surplus of $578 billion over five years; the actual deficit in the unified budget during those years was $800 billion and over $1 trillion for the federal funds budget. When the books were closed on fiscal year 1999, federal leaders celebrated a $124 billion surplus in the unified budget, up from $69 billion in 1998. The federal funds budget, however, had a deficit of $88 billion, down only slightly from $92 billion the previous year.

54. OMB, Historical Tables, "Table 1.1–Summary of Receipts, Outlays, and Surpluses or Deficits (-): 1789–2018."

55. See Gross Debt in Appendix A.

56. "Table 13" in *Budget, Fiscal Year 2001*.

57. CBO, *Budget, Fiscal Years 2001–2010*, Summary Table 6 and xxxiii.

58. Logan, "Summary of Latest Federal Income Tax Data," Tables 5 and 6.

59. In 1998 the White House Council of Economic Advisers had warned that a lower tax rate could prompt a short spurt in revenues as investors rushed to cash in gains and lower long-run revenues as investors depleted the pool of long-term capital gains or the stock market fell. Experts debated just how to estimate the level of future capital gains. See Kasten, Weiner, and Woodward, "What Made Receipts Boom," and Parcell, "Challenges and Uncertainties."

60. Forbes proposed a flat tax rate of 17 percent on all earned income with a standard deduction of $13,000 for each taxpayer and $5,000 for each dependent. Because of the exemption of investment income from taxation, the Forbes plan was essentially a consumption tax.

61. Compare Table 1.4 with OMB, Historical Tables, Table 1.2.

CHAPTER 17

1. The CBO predicted a $5.6 trillion surplus over the next ten years, up $1 trillion from its forecast six months earlier. Nearly half of the CBO's projected surplus resulted from the practice of including trust fund surplus revenues in the unified budget without accounting for the related liabilities.

2. Bush, "Address Before a Joint Session."

3. *Budget, Fiscal Year 2002*, 7.

4. OMB Historical Tables, Table 7.1 (FY 2002), http://www.gpo.gov/fdsys/pkg/BUDGET-2002-TAB/pdf/BUDGET-2002-TAB.pdf.

5. *Budget, Fiscal Year 2002*, 7.

6. Ari Fleischer quoted in Joyce, *The Congressional Budget Office*, 97.

7. Greenspan, *The Age of Turbulence*, 217.

8. "H.R. 1836," 1.

9. Franklin, *The Way to Wealth*, 13.

10. OMB Historical Tables, Table 2.1 (FY 2002), http://www.gpo.gov/fdsys/pkg/BUDGET-2002-TAB/pdf/BUDGET-2002-TAB.pdf.

11. OMB, Historical Tables, "Table 2.1, Receipts by Source: 1934–2018." In future fiscal years revenues would fall even more relative to prior projections. For the next fiscal year, 2002, Clinton's OMB had projected individual income tax revenues of $1.097 trillion *before* the tax cut. Bush's budget projected collections of $1.079 trillion *with* a tax cut. In fact, in fiscal year 2002 only $858 billion in personal income taxes were collected. The Clinton and Bush budget offices projected corporate income tax revenues of $214 billion and $218 billion, respectively, for fiscal year 2002. The actual figure would be $148 billion.

12. McClellan, *What Happened*, 91.

13. CBO, *Budget: Update*, Table 1–9 and Table 1.3.

14. In addition to revenues lost from the tax cuts, more than $400 billion resulted from "changed economic conditions" and mistaken assumptions ("technical adjustments") that had been detected since the preceding May. Another amount, totaling over $400 billion, represented interest on larger debt. See CBO, *Budget: Update*.

15. Bush quoted in Brownlee, *Federal Taxation*, 227.

16. Sanger, "President Asserts Shrunken Surplus May Curb Congress."

17. Television journalist Brit Hume confronted White House economic advisor Larry Lindsey on the issue by asking, "Isn't it the case that the [Social Security] money will be very much touched and it will be loaned back to the government? Social Security will get IOUs or government securities and what will happen is the money will be used to pay down other government debt, correct?" Lindsey said, "That's correct."

18. Tax Policy Center, "Quick Facts."

19. Donald Rumsfeld quoted in Bacevich, *The Limits of Power*, 4.

20. Campbell, Rockman, and Rudalevige, *The George W. Bush Legacy*, 175.

21. Paul O'Neill quoted in Pollack, *Refinancing America*, 134.

22. Greene and Hosler, "Bush Pushing for Fast Relief."

23. Frum, *The Right Man*, 213.

24. Bush quoted in Tanner, *Leviathan on the Right*, 157.

25. *Budget, Fiscal Year 2003*, 101.

26. See OMB, Historical Tables. In 2002 dollars, adjusted for inflation, the administration requested $372 billion for fiscal year 2003, an amount much higher than the 1992–2001 average of about $310 billion annually in 2002 dollars. In nominal dollars, the administration requested $379 billion. When it took office, the administration projected a fiscal 2003 military budget of $334 billion in nominal dollars.

27. CBO, *Budget: Fiscal Years 2003–2012*, Table 1.6 at 16.

28. Ibid., 3.

29. Ibid., 45.

30. Greenspan, *The Age of Turbulence*, 235.

31. Suskind, *The Price of Loyalty*, 291.

32. In his memoirs, Cheney states that he was trying to put deficits "in context." He then explained that the Reagan budget had created a "peace dividend . . . increased federal revenues and, eventually, lower deficits" (Cheney, *In My Time*, Ch. 10).

33. "Taxes, Trade, Social Security and More."

34. Brownlee, *Federal Taxation*, 237.

35. DeLay quoted in Surowiecki, "A Cut Too Far."

36. Snow quoted in Hormats, *The Price of Liberty*, 278.

37. For an excellent overview of the initial planning for the war in Iraq, see Ricks, *Fiasco*.

38. Maranto, Iansford, and Johnson, *Judging Bush*, 112.

39. Thomas, Lee, and Lipton, "A Political History."

40. Ibid.

41. Ibid.

42. *2005 Annual Report*, 107–112.

43. *2013 Annual Report, Federal Old-Age and Survivors Insurance* , 111.

44. US Census Bureau, 2000 Census Summary File 1, and 2010 Census Summary File 1. Between 2000 and 2010, the population increased by 27.3 million. The number of Americans ages forty-five to sixty-four increased by 19.5 million.

45. Boehner quoted in Greenspan, *The Age of Turbulence*, 243.

46. DeLay quoted in Yarrow, *Forgive Us Our Debts*, 16.

47. Peterson, *Running on Empty*, 82.

48. Kent Conrad quoted in 108 Cong. Rec. (October 2, 2003), at 24036.

49. See Hormats, *The Price of Liberty*, for an excellent analysis of the difference between budgeting for the wars in Iraq and Afghanistan and standard American practice in all previous wars.

50. See Appendix C.

51. See Appendix C.

52. See Chapter 18, Chart 1.

53. For tables summarizing House and Senate votes by party for selected years, see Schick, *The Federal Budget*, 223–227.

54. See Appendix D.

55. Lauback, "New Evidence on the Interest Rate," 7. Later in the decade the Federal Reserve calculated that the spike in borrowing during the downturn pressed rates up by as much as an entire percentage point.

56. Bureau of Labor Statistics, "Databases, Tables, & Calculators."

57. Bush, "Remarks by the President."

58. SSA, *2001 OASDI Trustees Report*, Table II.D3.

59. The Greenspan Commission had anticipated the aging of the population and had slightly underestimated the positive impact of higher immigration on the trust fund. The perceived deterioration in the balance in the trust fund consisted of (1) the use of average wages rather than median wages to raise the annual limit on total wages subject to the tax and (2) a smaller increase in worker productivity than had been assumed between 1984 and 2004. See the excellent analysis in Bivens, "Social Security's Fixable Financing Issues."

60. Quoted in Altman, *The Battle for Social Security*, 273 and 282.

61. 108 Cong. Rec. (September 24, 2004), at 792.

62. Obama quoted in Yarrow, *Forgive Us Our Debts*, xii.

Chapter 18

1. For statistics on distribution of wealth, see Fry and Taylor, "A Rise in Wealth for the Wealthy."

2. Council of Economic Advisers, *Economic Report*, 280.

3. Herszenhorn, "Bush and House in Accord," and Herszehorn and Stout, "$168 Billion Stimulus Plan."

4. The legislation allowed payments up to $600 for individuals with incomes of up to $75,000. Those numbers were doubled for those filing joint returns. Presidential candidate Obama opposed the plan. Economic research showed that Americans had also saved, rather than spent, cash distributions, called "tax rebates," that were paid out of borrowed federal funds in 1975 and 2001. Former Reagan economic advisor Martin Feldstein, who originally supported the 2008 rebate plan, concluded later that Americans saved rather than spent money intended for consumer spending. See Feldstein, "The Tax Rebate."

5. Bernanke quoted in Wessel, "Inside Dr. Bernanke's E.R."

6. Bush, "Speech on the Economic Crisis."

7. Herszenhorn, "Bailout Plan Wins Approval."

8. *Economic Outlook and Financial Markets: Before the Committee on the Budget, U.S. House of Representatives*, 110th Cong. (October 20, 2008) (statement of Ben Bernanke, Chairman of the Federal Reserve).

9. Even Martin Feldstein, a conservative economist who had opposed large deficits when serving as President Reagan's economic advisor, made the case for some combination of federal spending and tax cuts to put the brakes on the economic free fall (www.project-syndicate.org/print/the-case-for-fiscal-stimulus).

10. Obama quoted in "Obama Fires Up House Democrats."

11. CBO, *The Budget Outlook, Fiscal Years 2009–2019*, 1.

12. OMB, Historical Tables, "Table 1.4—Receipts, Outlays, and Surpluses or Deficits by Fund Group: 1934–2018."

13. Herszenhorn, "A Smaller, Faster Stimulus Plan."

14. *Budget, Fiscal Year 2010*, 117–120.

15. The number of private sector jobs had dropped from the level a decade

earlier. For a comprehensive review of various stimulus measures, and their effects, see Blinder and Zandi, "Great Recession."

16. Compare Appendix A, Appendix C, and United States Census data.

17. Obama quoted in Woodward, *The Price of Politics*, Ch. 3.

18. Norquist, *Leave Us Alone*, Ch. 20, section titled "No One Votes on Total Spending."

19. Extrapolated from Logan, "Summary."

20. "Obama Makes Fresh Appeal."

21. Oliver, Lee, and Lipton, "A Political History," 323. Those two types of "savings"—for Medicare payments and subsidies for Medicare Part C private plans— were estimated to total about a half a trillion dollars over a decade. Another $87 billion "savings" was simply an illusion. A new program was established for long-term care insurance programs, in which workers could pay premiums for long-term assisted care, which may be needed when they were elderly. In the early years of the program, premiums exceeded expenses, and these were counted as savings, despite the fact that the premiums were to be set at a rate determined by actuaries to cover no more than the cost. One of the most prominent "savings"—$57 billion over ten years— consisted of reducing payments by Medicare and Medicaid to hospitals that provide a disproportionately larger share of services to people with low incomes and no private health insurance. See CBO, *CBO's Analysis of the Major Health Care Legislation*.

22. Federal Reserve Board of Governors, "Press Release November 3, 2010," http://www.federalreserve.gov/newsevents/ press/monetary/20101103a.htm.

23. Coy, "Credit and the Bernanke Code."

24. "Obama Signs Tax Deal."

25. Mascaro, "Budget Talks."

26. Hirschfeld-Davis, "'Gang of Six.'" See also Bai, "Obama vs. Boehner."

27. CBO, *2011 Long-Term Budget Outlook*.

28. Ungar, "New Data."

29. CBO, *CBO's Analysis of the Debt Ceiling*.

30. Ibid., Table 1.

31. CBO, *Economic Effects*, Table 2 at 6.

32. Nitti, "Secrets of the Fiscal Cliff Deal."

33. Congressional Research Service, *The "Fiscal Cliff"*, 4, 2.

34. Rampell, "College Graduates Fare Well."

35. Bureau of the Census, *Historical Statistics of the United States, 1789-1945*, Series B 26-30 and B 31-39 at 25-26.

36. Toossi, "A Century of Change."

37. See Chart 5 in Chapter 21 and its cited sources.

38. Compare Reinhart and Rogoff, "Growth in a Time of Debt"; Kumar and Woo, "Public Debt and Growth"; and Greenlaw, Hamilton, Hooper, and Mishkin, "Crunch Time," with Herndon, Ash, and Polin, "Does High Debt Consistently Stifle Economic Growth?"

39. The 13.3 percent figure is derived from OMB, Historical Tables, "Table

1.4—Receipts, Outlays and Surpluses or Deficits by Fund Group: 1934–2018," and "Table 10.1—Gross Domestic Product and Deflators Used in the Historical Tables: 1940–2018." Note that these percentages differ slightly from those in Appendix C because percentages used in the appendices are for calendar years, for which estimates are available from 1789.

40. Ibid.

41. See notes on Charts 2 and 3.

42. "Medical" includes federal funds contributions to the SMI Trust Fund (2011 Medicare Trustee Report) funding Medicare Plan B, Medicaid, CHIP, Other Mandatory Healthcare (OMB, Historical Tables, FY 2013 Table 8.5), and non-Medicare Discretionary Healthcare (OMB, Historical Tables, FY 2013 Table 8.7). It excludes Federal Employee Health Benefits and Veterans Health. "Base Defense" includes National Defense, International Security Assistance, and Veterans Benefits and Services (OMB, Historical Tables, FY 2013, Table 3.2) and is net of statistics on War. "War" is also known as "Overseas Contingency Operations" and is found in annual White House Defense Budgets as well as in CBO, *Budget: Fiscal Years 2012–2022*, 71, Box 3–2. ARRA (American Recovery and Reinvestment Act of 2009) funds are spread throughout various years, mostly 2009–2011, and 2011 estimates can be found in ibid., 8, Box 1–1. Figure excludes 2011 Medicaid contribution of $12 billion, as this is reflected in the Medical category. The Unemployment Benefits data found in OMB Historical Tables include trust fund monies. Data presented here reflects only 2011 federal funds payments to the Unemployment Trust Funds and is found in the OMB, *Analytical Perspectives of the White House Budget Fiscal Year 2013*, 247–248. Note: In 2005 there was a slight decrease in "other" spending relative to the growth in national income and 2000 spending.

43. *2013 Annual Report, Federal Hospital Insurance*, Table V.B5 at 199.

44. Ibid., and Table V. B1 at 191.

45. See OMB, Historical Tables, Table 2.1. Other Federal Funds Taxes is derived from Federal Funds Receipts net of Personal and Corporate Income Taxes. Tables 1.4, 2.3, 2.4, and 2.5 give detail related to specific federal fund and trust funds receipts.

Chapter 19

1. Thomas Jefferson, letter to Treasury Secretary Albert Gallatin, April 1, 1802, in *Oxford Dictionary*, 206.

2. Despite vast volumes of budget materials published by the Congressional Budget Office and White House Office of Management and Budget, the net federal funds annual interest expense is difficult to find in any accessible publication and must be recreated from ledgers. In 2011 the federal funds budget paid $453 billion in interest. After subtracting interest paid to various federal funds balances held by the Treasury, $45 billion, the net interest expense of federal funds was $418 billion. The unified budget distorts both interest payable on federal debt and the funds available for debt service. In 2011, at record low interest rates, federal interest

amounted to 29 percent of federal funds revenue. "Net interest" appears to be only 10 percent of revenues from the unified budget. OMB, *Historical Tables*, Table 3.2, Account 901, adjusted by interest paid as recorded in various US Treasury ledgers.

3. In fiscal year 2011 the base defense budget, i.e., apart from the wars, was $546 billion, and an additional $124 billion was spent for the Veterans Administration, $46 billion for homeland security, and $12 billion for international military assistance.

4. "Statutory Limits on Federal Debt: 1940–Current," The White House, www .whitehouse.gov/sites/default/files/omb/budget/ . . . /hist07z3.xls.

5. See Appendix E.

6. Hooper, "Pence Lobbies Leaders."

7. *H.J. Res 22: Proposing an Amendment to the Constitution of the United States to Require a Balanced Budget*, 104th Cong., January 4, 1995. http://www.govtrack.us /congress/ bills/104/hjres22/text.

Chapter 20

1. National Priorities Project, "Cost of War."

2. CBO, *Long-Term Implications*.

3. Alexander, "Budget Cuts."

4. In *Putting "Defense" Back into U.S. Defense Policy*, Eland notes that the United States would have to rely on regional alliances to fill a vacuum in military power.

5. See Appendix H.

6. Appendix C and OMB, Historical Tables, "Table 1.4—Receipts, Outlays, and Surpluses or Deficits by Fund Group: 1934–2018."

7. OMB, Historical Tables, "Table 2.3—Receipts by Source as Percentages of GDP: 1934–2018."

8. Kagan, *The World America Made*, 129.

Chapter 21

1. When Medicare was enacted, only a quarter of Americans over sixty-five had medical insurance. Premiums for Medicare Part B were set at levels designed to encourage widespread participation by even healthier older Americans, to assist in spreading risks.

2. *Health, United States, 2012*, Tables 111 and 114, http://www.cdc.gov/nchs /data/hus/hus12.pdf#111.

3. For Medicare, see *Medicare Trustees Report*, Table V.B1 at 191 and V.B5 at 199 ($594 billion times 43.1 percent federal funds revenues), http://downloads.cms .gov/files/TR2013.pdf and OMB, Historical Tables, "Table 10.1" ($16.2 trillion). For Medicaid ($265 billion), see CBO, *Medicaid Spending*.

4. CMMS, *National Health Expenditure Projections*. By 2020, if expanded by the Affordable Care Act, Medicaid is expected to account for about a fifth of all federal medical spending.

5. Rivlin and Antos, *Restoring Fiscal Sanity 2007*, 70.

6. It would be a 50 percent reduction if Medicaid were included. See Meeker, *Basic Summary*, 274.

7. An increase in the personal income tax rates to make up the balance would be equivalent to undoing all the tax reductions in 2001 and 2003 for Americans at all income levels.

8. *2013 Annual Report, Federal Hospital Insurance*, Table V.D1 at 13, www.socialsecurity.gov/oact/tr/2013/tr2013.pdf.

9. See, for example, polling on Medicare compiled at http://www.pollingreport.com/health3.htm.

10. CBO, *Updated Budget Projections*.

11. Ibid.

Chapter 22

1. To check on the most recent estimate, go to Table 1.4 at http://www.whitehouse.gov/omb/budget/historicals.

2. See Appendix H.

3. OMB, Historical Tables, "Table 2.3—Receipts by Source as Percentages of GDP: 1934–2018."

4. Derived from Appendix H.

5. McBride, "Summary of Latest Federal Income Tax Data," Tables 2, 5, and 6.

6. Tax Policy Center, "Historical Average Federal Tax Rates."

7. Congressional Research Service, *The "Fiscal Cliff,"* 7.

8. OMB, Historical Tables, "Table 2.3—Receipts by Source as Percentages of GDP: 1934–2018."

9. Ibid.

10. "FRED: Economic Data."

11. Tax Policy Center, "Historical Income Distribution."

12. 12 USC § 225a, November 16, 1977, http://www.federalreserve.gov/about thefed/section2a.htm.

Chapter 23

1. Perot, *United We Stand*, 8.

2. Mendes, "Americans Fear Impact."

3. Newport, "In Their Own Words."

4. Obama, "Remarks by the President"

5. "Democratic Party Platform of 1964."

6. Bentsen quoted in Stengel, "Ninety Long Minutes."

7. Roosevelt, "Radio Address."

8. "Complete Text of the Iowa Republican Debate."

Bibliography

Aaron, Henry J., Barry P. Bosworth, and Gary Burtless. *Can America Afford to Grow Old?: Paying for Social Security*. Washington, DC: Brookings Institution, 1989.

Abrams, Burton A. "How Richard Nixon Pressured Arthur Burns: Evidence from the Nixon Tapes." *Journal of Economic Perspectives* 20, no. 4 (Fall 2006): 177–188.

Adams, Charles Kendall, ed. *Johnson's Universal Cyclopaedia: Volume 6*. New York: A. J. Johnson Company, 1895. Google Books edition.

Adams, Henry. *The First Administration of Thomas Jefferson*. Vol. 2 of *The History of the United States*. New York: Charles Scribner's Sons, 1909. Google Books edition.

———. *History of the United States of America During the Administrations of James Madison*. 2 vols. New York: Library of America, 1986.

———. *History of the United States of America During the Administrations of Thomas Jefferson*. 9 vols. New York: Library of America, 1986.

———. *The Life of Albert Gallatin*. Philadelphia: Lippincott, 1880. Google Books edition.

Adams, John Quincy. "First Annual Message (December 6, 1825)." The Miller Center, University of Virginia. http://millercenter.org/president/speeches/detail /3514.

Alexander, David. "Budget Cuts Have Left U.S. Forces Unbalanced, Less Prepared: General." *Chicago Tribune*, July 18, 2013.

Allen, W. B. *George Washington: America's First Progressive*. New York: Peter Lang, 2008.

Altermeyer, Arthur J. *Formative Years of Social Security*. Madison: University of Wisconsin Press, 1966.

Altman, Nancy J. *The Battle for Social Security: From FDR's Vision to Bush's Gamble*. Hoboken, NJ: John Wiley & Sons, 2005.

Amar, Akhil Reed. *America's Unwritten Constitution*. New York: Basic Books, 2012.

Ambler, Thomas Henry. *Thomas Ritchie: A Study in Virginia Politics.* Richmond, VA: Bell Book & Stationary, 1913. Google Books edition.

Amenta, Edwin. *When Movements Matter: The Townsend Plan and the Rise of Social Security.* Princeton, NJ: Princeton University Press, 2006.

Ammon, Harry. *James Monroe: The Quest for National Identity.* Charlottesville: University of Virginia Press, 1990.

"An Address from the United States in Congress Assembled to the Legislatures of the Several States." In *Documents from the Continental Congress and the Constitutional Convention, 1774–1789.* October 6, 1786. Library of Congress. http://memory.loc.gov/cgibin/query/r?ammem/bdsdcc:@field%28DOCID +@lit%28bdsdcc20801%29%29.

Anderson, Martin. *Revolution: The Reagan Legacy.* Stanford, CA: Hoover Institution Press, Stanford University, 1990.

Anderson, Robert B. "Financial Policies for Sustainable Growth." *Journal of Finance* 15, no. 2 (May 1960): 127–139.

Arnett, Alex Mathews. *Claude Kitchin and the Wilson War Policies.* New York: Russell & Russell, 1971.

Ashby, LeRoy. *The Spearless Leader: Senator Borah and the Progressive Movement in the 1920's.* Urbana: University of Illinois Press, 1972.

Austin, D. Andrew, and Mindy R. Levit. *The Debt Limit: History and Recent Increases.* Washington, DC: Congressional Research Service, 2013.

Auten, Brian J. *Carter's Conversion: The Hardening of American Defense Policy.* Columbia: University of Missouri Press, 2008.

Bacevich, Andrew J. *The Limits of Power: The End of American Exceptionalism.* New York: Metropolitan Books, 2008.

Bai, Matt. "The Game Is Called Chicken." *New York Times Magazine.* April 1, 2012.
———. "Obama vs. Boehner—Who Killed the Debt Deal?" *New York Times,* March 28, 2012.

Bailey, Stephen Kemp. *Congress Makes a Law: The Story Behind the Employment Act of 1946.* Westport, CT: Greenwood, 1980.

Balogh, Brian. *A Government Out of Sight: The Mystery of National Authority in Nineteenth-Century America.* Cambridge: Cambridge University Press, 2009.

Balz, Dan, and Ronald Brownstein. *Storming the Gates: Protest Politics and the Republican Revival.* Boston: Little, Brown, 1996.

Banks, Robert. *The Life and Administration of Robert Banks, Second Earl of Liverpool, K. G.: Volume 2.* Edited by Charles Duke Yonge. London: Macmillan, 1868. Google Books edition.

Bannon, Brad. "Bush Tax Cuts Turn 10: Wall Street Celebrates, Americans Suffer." *U.S. News and World Report,* June 7, 2011.

Bartlett, Bruce. *Impostor: How George W. Bush Bankrupted America and Betrayed the Reagan Legacy.* New York: Doubleday, 2006.

Bartlett, Irving H. *John C. Calhoun: A Biography.* New York: Norton, 1993.

Baumer, Donald C., and Carl E. Van Horn. *The Politics of Unemployment.* Washington, DC: CQ Press, 1985.

Beard, Charles A. *An Economic Interpretation of the Constitution of the United States.* Mineola, NY: Dover, 2004.

Beer, Samuel H. *To Make a Nation: The Rediscovery of American Federalism.* Cambridge, MA: Belknap Press of Harvard University Press, 1993.

Beland, Daniel. *Social Security: History and Politics from the New Deal to the Privatization Debate.* Lawrence: University Press of Kansas, 2005.

Bell, Felicitie C., and Michael L. Miller. "Actuarial Study No. 120: Life Tables for the United States Social Security Area 1900–2100." Social Security Administration. http://www.ssa.gov/oact/NOTES/as120/LifeTables_Tbl_10.html#wp1041324.

Berkin, Carol. *A Brilliant Solution: Inventing the American Constitution.* Boston: Houghton Mifflin, 2002.

Berkowitz, Edward D. *America's Welfare State from Roosevelt to Reagan.* Baltimore: Johns Hopkins University Press, 1991.

Bernanke, Ben S. *Essays on the Great Depression.* Princeton, NJ: Princeton University Press, 2000. Kindle edition.

———. *The Federal Reserve and the Financial Crisis.* Princeton, NJ: Princeton University Press, 2013. Kindle edition.

Bernstein, Aaron. "Commentary: Why the Greenspan Fix Didn't Work: Slower-Than-Expected Wage Growth and Soaring Inequality Have Wreaked Havoc." *BusinessWeek.* May 30, 2005. http://www.businessweek.com/print/magazine/content/05_22/b3935100_mz057.htm?chan=gl.

Birnbaum, Jeffrey H., and Alan S. Murray. *Showdown at Gucci Gulch: Lawmakers, Lobbyists, and the Unlikely Triumph of Tax Reform.* New York: Vintage Books, 1987.

Bishop, Joseph Bucklin. *Theodore Roosevelt and His Time: Shown in His Own Letters.* Vol. 1. New York: Charles Scribner's Sons, 1920. Google Books edition.

Biven, Carl W. *Jimmy Carter's Economy: Policy in an Age of Limits.* Chapel Hill: University of North Carolina Press, 2002.

Bivens, L. Josh. "Social Security's Fixable Financing Issues: Shortfall in Funds Is Not Inevitable." *Economic Policy Institute Issue Brief*, no. 207 (April 2005): 1–9. http://www.epi.org/publication/ib207/.

Blevins, Sue A. *Medicare's Midlife Crisis.* Washington, DC: Cato Institute, 2001.

Blinder, Alan S. *After the Music Stopped: The Financial Crisis, the Response, and the Work Ahead.* New York: Penguin, 2013.

———, and Janet L. Yellen. *The Fabulous Decade: Macroeconomic Lessons from the 1990s.* New York: Century Foundation Press, 2001.

———, and Mark Zandi. "How the Great Depression Was Brought to an End." Moody's Analytics. July 27, 2010. http://www.economy.com/mark-zandi/documents/End-of-Great-Recession.pdf.

Bliss, William D. P., ed. *The Encyclopedia of Social Reform*. New York: Funk & Wagnalls, 1897. Google Books edition.

Blodgett, Samuel, Jr. *Economica: A Statistical Manual for the United States*. Washington, DC: Printed for the author, 1806. Google Books edition.

Blum, John Morton. *Woodrow Wilson and the Politics of Morality*. Boston: Little, Brown, 1956.

———. *Years of War, 1941–1945: From the Morgenthau Diaries*. Boston: Houghton Mifflin, 1967.

Blumenthal, David, and James A. Morone. *The Heart of Power: Health and Politics in the Oval Office*. Berkeley: University of California Press, 2009.

Blyth, Mark. *Austerity: The History of a Dangerous Idea*. New York: Oxford University Press, 2013. Kindle edition.

Board of Governors of the Federal Reserve System. "Industrial Production Index." St. Louis Federal Reserve. Accessed July 16, 2013. http://research.stlouisfed.org/fred2/data /INDPRO.txt.

Borneman, Walter R. *1812: The War That Forged a Nation*. New York: HarperCollins, 2004.

Bostdorff, Denise M. *Proclaiming the Truman Doctrine: The Cold War Call to Arms*. College Station: Texas A&M University Press, 2008. Google Books edition.

Bowen, Catherine Drinker. *A Miracle at Philadelphia*. Boston: Little, Brown, 1966.

Bowers, Claude G. *Beveridge and the Progressive Era*. Cambridge, MA: Riverside, 1932.

———. *The Tragic Era: The Revolution After Lincoln*. Cambridge, MA: Riverside, 1957.

Brands, H. W. *American Colossus: The Triumph of Capitalism, 1865–1900*. New York: Doubleday, 2010. Kindle edition.

———. *Andrew Jackson: His Life and Times*. New York: Anchor Books, 2006. Google Books edition.

———. *The Strange Death of American Liberalism*. New Haven, CT: Yale University Press, 2003. Google Books edition.

Brant, Irving. *James Madison: Secretary of State, 1800–1809*. Indianapolis: Bobbs-Merrill, 1953.

Bremner, Robert P. *Chairman of the Fed William McChesney Martin Jr. and the Creation of the American Financial System*. New Haven, CT: Yale University Press, 2004.

Brennan, Mary C. *Turning Right in the Sixties: The Conservative Capture of the GOP*. Chapel Hill: University of North Carolina Press, 1995.

Brookhiser, Richard. *Founding Father: Rediscovering George Washington*. New York: Simon & Schuster, 1997. Google Books edition.

Brown, Harold. *Thinking About National Security: Defense and Foreign Policy in a Dangerous World*. Boulder, CO: Westview, 1983.

Brown, Josephine Chapin. *Public Relief, 1929–1939*. New York: Octagon Books, 1971.

Brownlee, W. Elliot. *Federal Taxation in America: A Short History*. Cambridge: Cambridge University Press, 2004.

———. *Funding the Modern American State, 1941–1955: The Rise and Fall of the Era of Easy Finance*. Cambridge: Cambridge University Press, 1996.

Brundage, Percival Flack. *The Bureau of the Budget*. New York: Praeger, 1970.

Bruner, Robert F., and Sean D. Carr. *The Panic of 1907: Lessons Learned from the Market's Perfect Storm*. Hoboken, NJ: John Wiley & Sons, 2007.

Buchanan, James M. *The Collected Works of James M. Buchanan*. Vol. 2, *Public Principles of Public Debt: A Defense and Restatement*. Indianapolis: Liberty Fund, 1999.

———. "Inaugural Address (March 4, 1857)." The Miller Center, University of Virginia. http://millercenter.org/president/speeches /detail/3554.

Buchanan, James M., and Richard E. Wagner. *The Collected Works of James M. Buchanan*. Vol. 8, *Democracy in Deficit: The Political Legacy of Lord Keynes*. Indianapolis: Liberty Fund, 1999.

Budget of the United States Government: Fiscal Year 2001. Washington, DC: Office of Management and Budget, 2001.

Budget of the United States Government: Fiscal Year 2002. Washington, DC: Office of Management and Budget, 2002. http://www.gpo.gov/fdsys/pkg/BUDGET -2002-BUD/pdf/BUDGET-2002-BUD.pdf.

Budget of the United States Government: Fiscal Year 2003. Washington, DC: Office of Management and Budget, 2003. http://georgewbush-whitehouse.archives. gov/omb/budget/fy2003/budget.html.

Budget of the United States Government, Fiscal Year 2010. http://www.gpo.gov /fdsys/pkg/BUDGET-2010-BUD/pdf/BUDGET-2010-BUD.pdf.

Buel, Richard, Jr. *America on the Brink: How the Political Struggle over the War of 1812 Almost Destroyed the Young Republic*. New York: Palgrave Macmillan, 2005.

Bureau of the Budget. *Report to the President of the United States by the Director of the Bureau of the Budget*. Memphis: General Books, 2010.

Bureau of the Census. *First Census of the United States*. 1790. http://www2.census .gov/prod2/decennial/documents/1790m-02.pdf.

———. *Historical Statistics of the United States, Colonial Times to 1970*. 2 vols. Washington, DC: Department of Commerce, 1975. http://www.census.gov /compendia/statab/past_years.html.

———. *Historical Statistics of the United States, 1789–1945*. Washington, DC: Government Printing Office, 1949.

———. *Statistical Abstract of the United States: 1947*. 68th ed. Washington, DC: Government Printing Office, 1947. Google Books edition.

Bureau of Economic Analysis. *Balance of Payments Statistical Supplement*. Washington, DC: Government Printing Office, 1958.

Bureau of Labor Statistics. "Databases, Tables, & Calculators by Subject." http:// www.bls.gov/data/.

———. "Overview of BLS Statistics on Unemployment." March 14, 2012. http:// www.bls.gov/bls/employment.htm.

Burner, David. *The Politics of Provincialism: The Democratic Party in Transition, 1918-1932*. Cambridge, MA: Harvard University Press, 1986.

Burton, Theodore Elijah. *John Sherman*. Boston: Houghton Mifflin, 1908. Google Books edition.

Bush, George H. W. "Presidential Debate in East Lansing, Michigan." October 19, 1992. *The American Presidency Project*. http://www.presidency.ucsb.edu /ws/?pid=21625.

Bush, George W. "Address Before a Joint Session of the Congress on Administration Goals." February 27, 2001. *The American Presidency Project*. http://www. presidency.ucsb.edu/ws/?pid=29643.

———. *Decision Points*. New York: Random House Digital, 2010. Kindle edition.

———. "Remarks by the President in Social Security Announcement." May 2, 2001. http://www.ssa.gov/history/gwbushstmts.html.

———. "Second Inaugural Address (January 20, 2005)." The Miller Center, University of Virginia. http://millercenter.org/ president/speeches/detail/4463.

———. "Speech on the Economic Crisis" (transcript). *New York Times*, September 25, 2008. http://www.nytimes.com/2008/09/25/business/worldbusiness /25iht24textbush.16463831.html.

Byrd, Robert C. *Committee on Appropriations, United States Senate, 1867–2008*. Washington, DC: Government Printing Office, 2008. Kindle edition.

Califano, Joseph A., Jr. *The Triumph and Tragedy of Lyndon Johnson: The White House Years*. New York: Simon & Schuster, 1991.

Calleo, David P. *The Bankrupting of America: How the Federal Budget Is Impoverishing the Nation*. New York: William Morrow, 1992.

Campbell, Colin, Bert A. Rockman, and Andrew Rudalevige, eds. *The George W. Bush Legacy*. Washington, DC: CQ Press, 2008.

Canellos, Peter S., ed. *Last Lion: The Fall and Rise of Ted Kennedy*. New York: Simon & Schuster, 2009.

Cannadine, David. *Mellon: An American Life*. New York: Vintage Books, 2008.

Cannon, Lou. *Governor Reagan: His Rise to Power*. New York: PublicAffairs, 2003.

———. *President Reagan: The Role of a Lifetime*. New York: PublicAffairs, 2000. Kindle edition.

———, and Carl M. Cannon. *Reagan's Disciple: George W. Bush's Troubled Quest for a Presidential Legacy*. New York: PublicAffairs, 2008.

Caplan, Russell L. *Constitutional Brinksmanship: Amending the Constitution by National Convention*. Oxford: Oxford University Press, 1988.

Caro, Robert A. *The Years of Lyndon Johnson.* Vol. 4, *The Passage of Power.* New York: Knopf, 2012. Kindle edition.

Carosso, Vincent P., and Robert Sobel, eds. *Public Debts: An Essay in the Science of Finance (Wall Street and the Security Markets).* New York: Arno, 1975.

Carter, Jimmy. *Keeping Faith: Memoirs of a President.* Fayetteville: University of Arkansas Press, 1995.

———. "The President's News Conference." April 15, 1977. *The American Presidency Project.* http://www.presidency.ucsb.edu/ws/?pid=7357.

Centers for Medicare & Medicaid Services. *National Health Expenditure Projections 2010–2020.* https://www.cms.gov/NationalHealthExpendData/downloads/proj2010.pdf.

Cerami, Charles A. *Jefferson's Great Gamble: The Remarkable Story of Jefferson, Napoleon and the Men Behind the Louisiana Purchase.* Naperville, IL: Sourcebooks, 2003.

Chace, James. *1912: Wilson, Roosevelt, Taft & Debs—The Election That Changed the Country.* New York: Simon & Schuster, 2004.

———. *Acheson: The Secretary of State Who Created the American World.* Cambridge, MA: Harvard University Press, 1998.

Chase, Salmon P. "An Appeal of the Independent Democrats in Congress to the People of the United States." In *The Library of Original Sources: 1833–1865,* edited by Oliver Joseph Thatcher, 144–159. New York: University Research Extension, 1907. Google Books edition.

Chen, Edwin. "Perot Quits Presidential Race: Clinton's Goal: The Revitalizing of America." *Los Angeles Times,* July 17, 1992.

Cheney, Dick. *In My Time: A Personal and Political Memoir.* New York: Threshold Editions, 2011. Kindle edition.

Chernow, Ron. *Alexander Hamilton.* New York: Penguin, 2010.

———. *The House of Morgan: An American Banking Dynasty and the Rise of Modern Finance.* New York: Grove, 1990.

———. *The Warburgs: The Twentieth-Century Odyssey of a Remarkable Jewish Family.* New York: Vintage Books, 1994. Google Books edition.

———. *Washington: A Life.* New York: Penguin, 2010.

Cherny, Robert W. *A Righteous Cause: The Life of William Jennings Bryan.* Boston: Little, Brown, 1985.

Chinn, Menzie D., and Jeffry A. Frieden. *Lost Decades: The Making of America's Debt Crisis and Long Recovery.* New York: Norton, 2011.

Clark, Champ. *My Quarter Century of American Politics.* New York: Harper & Brothers, 1920.

Cleveland, Grover. "Third Annual Message (December 6, 1887)." The Miller Center, University of Virginia. http://millercenter.org/president/speeches/detail/3757.

———. "Fourth Annual Message (December 3, 1888)." The Miller Center, University of Virginia. http://millercenter.org/president/speeches/detail/3758.

Cleveland, Henry. *Alexander H. Stephens: In Public and Private*. Philadelphia: National, 1866. Google Books edition.

Clinton for President Committee. *A Plan for America's Future*. 1992. http://www.ibiblio.org/pub/academic/political-science/speeches/clinton.dir/c60.txt.

Clinton, William J. "Address Before a Joint Session of the Congress on the State of the Union." January 23, 1996. *The American Presidency Project*. http://www.presidency.ucsb.edu/ws/?pid=53091.

———. "Remarks on the Budget Surplus for Fiscal Year 1999." January 6, 1999. *The American Presidency Project*. http://www.presidency.ucsb.edu/ws/?pid=56390.

Coit, Margaret L. *John C. Calhoun: An American Portrait*. Cambridge, MA: Riverside, 1950.

Commission on Economy and Efficiency. "The Need for a National Budget." *House Documents* 118 (December 4, 1911, to August 26, 1912). Washington, DC: Government Printing Office, 1912. Google Books edition.

Committee for Economic Development. *The New Congressional Budget Process and the Economy: A Statement*. New York: CED Publications, 1975.

———. *Taxes and the Budget: A Program for Prosperity in a Free Economy: A Statement on National Policy*. New York: CED Publications, 1947.

Committee on Economic Security. "Estimates of Unemployment in the United States." Chapter 3 in *Social Security in America*. 1937. Social Security Administration. http://www.ssa.gov/history/reports/ces/cesbookc3.html.

Committee on Public Debt Policy. *Our National Debt: Its History and Its Meaning Today*. New York: Harcourt, Brace, 1949.

"Complete Text of the Iowa Republican Debate on Fox News Channel." *Fox News Insider*. August 12, 2011. http://foxnewsinsider.com/2011/08/12/full-transcript-complete-text-of-the-iowa-republican-debate-on-fox-news-channel.

Congressional Budget Office (CBO). *The Budget and Economic Outlook: An Update*. August 2001. http://www.cbo.gov/publication/13249.

———. *The Budget and Economic Outlook: Fiscal Years 2001–2010*. January 2000.

———. *The Budget and Economic Outlook: Fiscal Years 2003–2012*. January 2003.

———. *The Budget and Economic Outlook: Fiscal Years 2012–2022*. January 2012.

———. *The Budget Outlook: Fiscal Years 2009–2019*. Washington, DC: Congressional Budget Office, 2009.

———. *CBO's Analysis of the Debt Ceiling Agreement*. August 1, 2011. http://www.cbo.gov/publication/42210.

———. *CBO's Analysis of the Major Health Care Legislation Enacted in March 2010*. March 30, 2011. http://www.cbo.gov/publication/22077.

———. *Economic Effects of Reducing the Fiscal Restraint That Is Scheduled to Occur in 2013*. May 2012. http://www.cbo.gov/sites/default/files/cbofiles/attachments/FiscalRestraint_0.pdf.

———. *2011 Long-Term Budget Outlook.* June 2011. http://www.cbo.gov/sites/default/files/cbofiles/attachments/06–21-Long-Term_Budget_Outlook.pdf.

———. *Long-Term Implications of the 2013 Future Years Defense Program.* July 11, 2012. www.cbo.gov/publication/43428.

———. *Medicaid Spending and Enrollment Detail for CBO's May 2013 Baseline.* http://www.cbo.gov/sites/default/files/cbofiles/attachments/44204_Medicaid.pdf.

———. *Updated Budget Projections: Fiscal Years 2013 to 2023.* May 2013, Table 2 at 11. http://www.cbo.gov/publication/44172.

Congressional Research Service. *The "Fiscal Cliff" and the American Taxpayer Relief Act of 2012.* January 4, 2013.

Cooke, Jacob E. *Tench Coxe and the Early Republic.* Chapel Hill: University of North Carolina Press, 1978.

Cooke, Jay. "The National Debt: Its Amount, Rate of Growth, and Estimated Aggregate at the Close of the War." Prepared by Dr. William Elder. *New York Times.* May 6, 1865. http://www.nytimes.com/1865/05/06/news/national-debt-its-amount-rate-growth-estimated-aggregate-close-war-american.html.

Coolidge, Calvin. "Inaugural Address (March 4, 1925)." The Miller Center, University of Virginia. http://millercenter.org/president/speeches/detail/3569.

Council of Economic Advisers. *Economic Report of the President.* Washington, DC: Government Printing Office, 2011.

Council on Foreign Relations. *Independent Task Force Report No. 67: U.S. Trade and Investment Policy.* New York and Washington, DC: Council on Foreign Relations Press, September 2011.

Coxe, Tench. *A Statement on the Arts and Manufactures of the United States.* Philadelphia: A. Cornman, 1814.

Coy, Peter. "Credit and the Bernanke Code." *Businessweek.* November 4, 2010. http://www.businessweek.com/magazine/content/10_46/b4203012812548.htm.

Croly, Herbert D. *Marcus Alonzo Hanna.* New York: Chelsea House, 1983.

Cross, Coy F., II. *Justin Smith Morrill, Father of the Land-Grant Colleges.* East Lansing: Michigan State University Press, 1999.

Cross, Whitney R. *The Burned-Over District: The Social and Intellectual History of Enthusiastic Religion in Western New York, 1800–1850.* Ithaca, NY: Cornell University Press, 1950.

Culver, John C., and John Hyde. *American Dreamer: A Life of Henry A. Wallace.* New York: Norton, 2000.

Daggett, Stephen. *Costs of Major U.S. Wars.* Congressional Research Service. June 29, 2010. http://www.fas.org/sgp/crs/natsec/ RS22926.pdf.

Dallas, George Mifflin. *Life and Writings of Alexander James Dallas.* Philadelphia: Lippincott, 1871. Google Books edition.

Dalton, Kathleen. *Theodore Roosevelt: A Strenuous Life*. New York: Vintage Books, 2002. Google Books edition.

Dangerfield, George. *The Era of Good Feelings*. Chicago: Elephant Paperback, 1989.

Darman, Richard. *Who's in Control? Polar Politics and the Sensible Center*. New York: Simon & Schuster, 1996.

Davis, Jefferson. *The Rise and Fall of the Confederate Government*. Vol. 1. New York: Da Capo, 1990.

Davis, Joseph H. "U.S. Industrial Production Index 1790–1915." The National Bureau of Economic Research. 2004. http://www.nber.org/data/industrial -production-index/.

Dawes, Charles G. "Business Organization of the Government." In *America Speaks: A Library of the Best Spoken Thought in Business and the Professions*, ed. Basil Gordon Byron and Frederic Rene Coudert. New York: J. J. Little & Ives, 1928.

———. *The First Year of the Budget of the United States*. New York: Harper & Brothers, 1923.

DeConde, Alexander. *This Affair of Louisiana*. Baton Rouge: Louisiana State University Press, 1976.

"Democratic Party Platform of 1932." June 27, 1932. *The American Presidency Project*. http://www.presidency.ucsb.edu/ws/?pid=29595.

"Democratic Party Platform of 1964." August 24, 1964. *The American Presidency Project*. http://www.presidency.ucsb.edu/ws/?pid=29603.

Department of the Treasury. *Annual Report of the Secretary of the Treasury on the State of the Finances for the Fiscal Year Ended on June 30, 1920*. Washington, DC: Government Printing Office, 1920. Google Books edition.

———. *The National Loans of the United States, From July 4, 1776, to June 30, 1880*. Washington, DC: Government Printing Office, 1881.

———. *Statistical Appendix to the Annual Report of the Secretary of Treasury on the State of Finances*. Charleston, SC: Nabu, 1970.

———. *Statistical Appendix to the Annual Report of the Secretary of Treasury on the State of Finances*. Washington, DC: Government Printing Office, 1980.

DeRose, Chris. *Founding Rivals: Madison vs. Monroe, the Bill of Rights, and the Election That Saved a Nation*. Washington, DC: Regnery, 2011.

Dewey, Davis Rich. *Financial History of the United States*. New York: Longmans, Green, 1934.

DeWitt, Larry, Daniel Béland, and Edward Berkowitz, eds. *Social Security: A Documentary History*. Washington, DC: CQ Press, 2008.

Dickson, Paul, and Thomas B. Allen. *The Bonus Army: An American Epic*. New York: Walker, 2004.

Donovan, Robert J. *Conflict and Crisis: The Presidency of Harry S. Truman, 1945–1948*. Columbia: University of Missouri Press, 1996. Google Books edition.

———. *Tumultuous Years: The Presidency of Harry S. Truman, 1949–1953*. Columbia: University of Missouri Press, 1982.

Douglas, Paul H. *Social Security in the United States: An Analysis and Appraisal of the Federal Social Security Act*. New York: Whittlesey House, 1936.

Dull, Jonathan R. *A Diplomatic History of the American Revolution*. New Haven, CT: Yale University Press, 1985.

Dungan, Nicholas. *Gallatin: America's Swiss Founding Father*. New York: New York University Press, 2010.

Easton, Nina J. *Gang of Five: Leaders at the Center of the Conservative Ascendancy*. New York: Touchstone, 2000.

Eberstadt, Nicholas. *A Nation of Takers: America's Entitlement Epidemic*. West Conshohocken, PA: Templeton, 2012.

Eisenhower, Dwight D. "Annual Message to the Congress on the State of the Union." January 5, 1956. *The American Presidency Project*. http://www.presidency.ucsb.edu/ws/?pid=10593.

———. "Annual Message to the Congress on the State of the Union." January 7, 1960. *The American Presidency Project*. http://www.presidency.ucsb.edu/ws/?pid=12061.

———. "Chance for Peace (April 16, 1953)." The Miller Center, University of Virginia. http://millercenter.org/president/speeches/detail/3357.

———. "Farewell Address (January 17, 1961)." The Miller Center, University of Virginia. http://millercenter.org/president/speeches/detail/3361.

———. *Mandate for Change, 1953–1956*. Garden City, NY: Doubleday, 1963.

———. "The President's News Conference." February 23, 1955. *The American Presidency Project*. http://www. presidency.ucsb.edu/ws/?pid=10418.

———. "Radio and Television Address to the American People on the Tax Program." March 15, 1954. *The American Presidency Project*. http://www.presidency.ucsb.edu/ws/?pid=10181.

———. "Special Message to the Congress Transmitting Proposed Changes in the Social Security Program—August 1, 1953." Eisenhower's Statements on Social Security, Social Security Administration. http://www.ssa.gov/history/ikestmts.html.

Eisner, Robert. *How Real Is the Federal Deficit?* New York: Free Press, 1986.

Eland, Ivan. *Putting "Defense" Back into U.S. Defense Policy: Rethinking U.S. Security in the Post-Cold War World*. Westport, CT: Praeger, 2001.

Elkins, Stanley, and Eric McKitrick. *The Age of Federalism: The Early American Republic, 1788–1800*. Oxford: Oxford University Press, 1993.

Ellwood, John W. "The Politics of the Enactment and Implementation of Gramm-Rudman-Hollings: Why Congress Cannot Address the Deficit Dilemma." *Harvard Journal on Legislation* 25, no. 2 (Summer 1988): 553–575.

Evans, Richard J. *The Third Reich at War*. New York: Penguin, 2009.

Farris, Scott. *Almost President: The Men Who Lost the Race but Changed the Nation.* Guilford, CT: Lyons, 2011.

Faulkner, Harold U. *Politics, Reform, and Expansion 1890–1900.* New York: Harper & Row, 1959.

Feldstein, Martin, ed. *American Economic Policy in the 1980s.* Chicago: University of Chicago Press, 1994.

———. "The Tax Rebate Was a Flop; Obama's Stimulus Plan Won't Work Either." *Wall Street Journal.* August 6, 2008.

Fellman, Michael. *The Making of Robert E. Lee.* Baltimore: Johns Hopkins University Press, 2000. Google Books edition.

Fels, Rendings. "The Long-Wave Depression, 1873–97." *Review of Economics and Statistics* 31, no. 1 (1949): 69–73.

Fenberg, Steven. *Unprecedented Power: Jesse Jones, Capitalism, and the Common Good.* College Station: Texas A&M University Press, 2011.

Ferguson, E. James. *The Power of the Purse: A History of American Public Finance, 1776–1790.* Chapel Hill: University of North Carolina Press, 1961.

Ferguson, James M., ed. *Public Debt and Future Generations.* Chapel Hill: University of North Carolina Press, 1964.

Fessenden, Francis. *Life and Public Services of William Pitt Fessenden.* Boston: Houghton, Mifflin, 1907.

Finan, Christopher M. *Alfred E. Smith: The Happy Warrior.* New York: Hill and Wang, 2002.

Firestone, John M. *Federal Receipts and Expenditures During Business Cycles, 1879-1958.* Princeton, NJ: Princeton University Press, 1960.

Flaherty, Jane. "Incidental Protection: An Examination of the Morrill Tariff." *Essays in Economic and Business History* 19 (2001): 103–118.

Foner, Eric. *Free Soil, Free Labor, Free Men: The Ideology of the Republican Party Before the Civil War.* Oxford: Oxford University Press, 1995.

Forsythe, Dall W. *Taxation and Political Change in the Young Nation, 1781–1833.* New York: Columbia University Press, 1977.

Franklin, Benjamin. "Speech to the Federal Convention, September 17, 1787." In Colleen A. Sheehan and Gary L. McDowell, eds. *Friends of the Constitution: Writings of the "Other" Federalists, 1787–1788.* Indianapolis: Liberty Fund, 1998.

———. *The Way to Wealth.* 1774. Reprint, New York: Leavitt, Trow, 1948. Google Books edition.

Franklin, Grace A., and Randall B. Ripley. *CETA: Politics and Policy 1973–1982.* Knoxville: University of Tennessee Press, 1984.

"FRED: Economic Data." Economic Research of the Federal Reserve Bank of St. Louis. http://research.stlouisfed.org/fred2/graph/?g=cSh.

Frederick, J. M. H., ed. "Buffalo Platform." *National Party Platforms.* Akron, OH: Werner, 1896. Google Books edition.

Freeman, Douglas Southall. *R. E. Lee: A Biography*. Vol. 1. New York: Charles Scribner's Sons, 1936.

Frels, Rendigs. "The Long Wave Depression, 1873–97." *Review of Economics and Statistics* 31, no. 1 (February 1949).

Friedman, Milton. "A Monetary and Fiscal Framework for Economic Stability." *American Economic Review* 38, no. 3 (1948): 245–264.

Frum, David. *The Right Man: An Inside Account of the Bush White House*. New York: Random House, 2005. Google Books edition.

Fry, Richard, and Paul Taylor. "A Rise in Wealth for the Wealthy; Declines for the Lower 93%: An Uneven Recovery, 2009–2011." Pew Research. April 23, 2013. http://www.pewsocialtrends.org/2013/04/23/a-rise-in-wealth-for-the -wealthydeclines-for-the-lower-93/.

Gaddis, John Lewis. *The United States and the Origins of the Cold War, 1941– 1947*. New York: Columbia University Press, 1972.

———. *We Now Know: Rethinking Cold War History*. Oxford: Clarendon, 1997.

Gage, Lyman J. *Memoirs of Lyman J. Gage*. New York: House of Field, 1937.

Galbraith, John Kenneth. *The Great Crash 1929*. Boston: Houghton Mifflin, 1954.

Gallatin, Albert. *Selected Writings of Albert Gallatin*. Edited by James E. Ferguson. Indianapolis: Bobbs-Merrill, 1967.

———. *Suggestions on the Banks and Currency of the Several United States, in Reference Principally to the Suspension of Specie Payments*. 1841. Reprint, N.P.: General Books, 2009.

———. *The Writings of Albert Gallatin: Volume 1, 1788–1816*. Edited by Henry Adams. Philadelphia: Lippincott, 1879. Kindle edition.

———. *The Writings of Albert Gallatin: Volume 3*. Edited by Henry Adams. Philadelphia: Lippincott, 1879. Google Books edition.

Gallatin, James. "The Financial Economy of The United States with Suggestions for Restoring Specie Payments." A letter to President Andrew Johnson (1868). Google Books edition.

———. *A Great Peace Maker: The Diary of James Gallatin, Secretary to Albert Gallatin, 1813–1827*. New York: Charles Scribner's Sons, 1914.

Gallman, Robert E. "The United States: Commodity Output, 1839–1899." In *Trends in the American Economy in the Nineteenth Century: A Report of the National Bureau of Economic Research, New York*, Conference on Research in Income and Wealth: Studies in Income and Wealth, vol. 24, 13–72. Princeton, NJ: Princeton University Press, 1960.

Garraty, John A. *Silas Wright*. New York: Columbia University Press, 1949.

Garvy, George. "Keynes and the Economic Activists of Pre-Hitler Germany." *Journal of Political Economy* 83, no. 2 (1975): 391–405.

Gellately, Robert. *Stalin's Curse: Battling for Communism in War and Cold War*. New York: Borzoi, 2013. Google Books edition.

General Accounting Office (GAO). *Budget Issues: Trust Funds and Their Relationship to the Federal Budget.* September 1988.

Gerhardt, Michael J. *The Forgotten Presidents: Their Untold Constitutional Legacy.* New York: Oxford University Press, 2013. Kindle edition.

Gienapp, William E. *The Origins of the Republican Party: 1852–1856.* New York: Oxford University Press, 1987.

Gilbert, Charles. *American Financing of World War I.* Westport, CT: Greenwood, 1970.

Gillon, Steven M. *The Pact: Bill Clinton, Newt Gingrich, and the Rivalry That Defined a Generation.* Oxford: Oxford University Press, 2008.

Gingrich, Newt. "The Republican Contract with America." Prentice Hall Documents. 1994. http://cwx.prenhall.com/bookbind/pubbooks/dye4/medialib/docs/contract.htm.

"Gingrich Says 'Snub' Contributed to Shutdown." *Moscow-Pullman Daily News* (Moscow, ID). November 16, 1995.

Goldberg, Robert Alan. *Barry Goldwater.* New Haven, CT: Yale University Press, 1995.

Goldman, Peter, Thomas M. DeFrank, Mark Miller, Andrew Murr, and Tom Matthews. *Quest for the Presidency 1992.* College Station: Texas A&M University Press, 1994.

Goldwater, Barry. *The Conscience of a Conservative.* 1960. Reprint, Blacksburg, VA: Wilder Publications, 2009.

Goodheart, Adam. *1861: The Civil War Awakening.* New York: Knopf, 2011. Kindle edition.

Goodwin, Philo A. *Biography of Andrew Jackson: President of the United States.* New York: R. Hart Towner, 1837. Google Books edition.

Gordon, General John. *Reminiscences of the Civil War.* Chicago: Acheron, 2012. Kindle edition.

Gordon, John Steele. *An Empire of Wealth: The Epic History of American Economic Power.* New York: HarperCollins E-Books, 2008. Kindle edition.

———. *Hamilton's Blessing: The Extraordinary Life and Times of Our National Debt.* New York: Walker, 2010. Kindle edition.

Gould, Lewis L. *Grand Old Party: A History of the Republicans.* New York: Random House, 2003.

———. *The Most Exclusive Club: A History of the Modern United States Senate.* New York: Basic Books, 2005.

Graham, John Remington. *Free, Sovereign and Independent States: The Intended Meaning of the American Constitution.* Gretna, LA: Pelican, 2009. Google Books edition.

Grant, James. *Mr. Speaker! The Life and Times of Thomas B. Reed, the Man Who Broke the Filibuster.* New York: Simon & Schuster, 2011.

Grant, Jane A. *The New American Social Compact: Rights and Responsibilities in the Twenty-First Century.* Lanham, MD: Lexington Books, 2008. Google Books edition.

Grant, Ulysses S. *The Complete Personal Memoirs of Ulysses S. Grant.* N.P.: Seven Treasures Publications, 2009. Kindle edition.

———. "First Inaugural Address (March 4, 1869)." The Miller Center, University of Virginia. http://millercenter.org/president/speeches/detail/3556.

Green, Mark J., ed. *Changing America: Blueprints for the New Administration.* New York: Newmarket, 1992.

Greene, David L., and Karen Hosler. "Bush Pushing for Fast Relief." *Baltimore Sun*, November 1, 2001.

Greene, John Robert. *The Presidency of Gerald R. Ford.* Lawrence: University Press of Kansas, 1995.

Greenlaw, David, James Hamilton, Peter Hooper, and Frederic Mishkin. "Crunch Time: Fiscal Crises and the Role of Monetary Policy." US Monetary Policy Forum. February 13, 2013.

Greenspan, Alan. *The Age of Turbulence: Adventures in a New World.* New York: Penguin Books, 2008. Kindle edition.

"The Growing Debt." *Oakland Tribune* (Oakland, CA). October 13, 1945.

Hacker, Jacob S. *The Divided Welfare State: The Battle over Public and Private Social Benefits in the United States.* Cambridge: Cambridge University Press, 2002.

Hager, George, and Eric Pianin. *Mirage: Why Neither Democrats Nor Republicans Can Balance the Budget, End the Deficit, and Satisfy the Public.* New York: Times Books, 1997.

Hahn, Jim, and Janemarie Mulvey. "Medical Physician Payments and the Sustainable Growth Rate." Congressional Research Service, December 27, 2011. https://www.astro.org/uploadedFiles/Content/Advocacy/CRS%20Report%20-%20Medicare%20Physician%20Payment%20Updates%20and%20the%20SGR.pdf.

Hamilton, Holam. "Texas Bonds and Northern Profits: A Study in Compromise, Investment, and Lobby Influence." *Mississippi Valley Historical Review* 43, no. 4 (1957): 579–594.

Hayward, Steven F. *The Age of Reagan: The Fall of the Old Liberal Order, 1964–1980.* Roseville, CA: Prima, 2001.

Health, United States, 2012: With Special Feature on Emergency Care. Hyattsville, MD: National Center for Health Statistics, 2013.

Heckscher, August. *Woodrow Wilson.* New York: Collier Books, 1991.

Heidler, David S., and Jeanne T. Heidler. *Henry Clay: The Essential American.* New York: Random House, 2010.

Heinemann, Ronald L. *Harry Byrd of Virginia.* Charlottesville: University of Virginia Press, 1996.

Heller, Walter W. *New Dimensions of Political Economy*. New York: Norton, 1976.

Helms, Robert B. "The Tax Treatment of Health Insurance: Early History and Evidence, 1940–1970." In *Empowering Health Care Consumers Through Tax Reform*. Edited by Grace-Marie Arnett. Ann Arbor: University of Michigan Press, 1999.

Hendrix, Henry J. *Theodore Roosevelt's Naval Diplomacy: The U.S. Navy and the Birth of the American Century*. Annapolis, MD: Naval Institute Press, 2009.

Herndon, Thomas, Michael Ash, and Robert Polin. "Does High Debt Consistently Stifle Economic Growth?: A Critique of Reinhart and Rogoff." Political Economy Research Institute, University of Massachusetts–Amherst. April 15, 2013.

Herszenhorn, David M. "Bailout Plan Wins Approval; Democrats Vow Tighter Rules." *New York Times*. October 3, 2008.

———. "Bush and House in Accord for $150 Billion Stimulus." *New York Times*, January 25, 2008.

———. "A Smaller, Faster Stimulus Plan, but Still with a Lot of Money." *New York Times*. February 13, 2009.

———, and David Stout. "$168 Billion Stimulus Plan Clears Congress." *New York Times*. February 7, 2008.

Hetzel, Robert L. *The Monetary Policy of the Federal Reserve*. Cambridge: Cambridge University Press, 2008. Kindle edition.

———, and Ralph F. Leach. "The Treasury-Fed Accord: A New Narrative Account." *Federal Reserve Bank of Richmond Economic Quarterly* 87, no. 1 (Winter 2001): 33–55.

Hicks, John D. *The Populist Revolt: A History of the Farmers' Alliance of the People's Party*. Lincoln: University of Nebraska Press, 1961.

———. *Republican Ascendancy, 1921–1933*. New York: Harper & Row, 1960.

Higginbotham, Don. *George Washington: Uniting a Nation*. Oxford: Rowman & Littlefield, 2004. Google Books edition.

Hiltzik, Michael. *The New Deal: A Modern History*. New York: Free Press, 2011. Kindle edition.

Hirschfeld-Davis, Julie. "'Gang of Six' Debt Plan Helps Derail Boehner's Deal with Obama." Bloomberg. July 24, 2011.

Hobbs, Frank, and Nicole Stoops. *Census 2000 Special Reports: Demographic Trends in the 20th Century*. Washington, DC: US Census Bureau, 2002. www.census.gov/prod/2002pubs/censr-4.pdf.

Hoffer, William James Hull. *To Enlarge the Machinery of Government: Congressional Debates and the Growth of the American State, 1858–1891*. Baltimore: Johns Hopkins University Press, 2007.

Hoffman, Ronald, and Peter J. Albert. *Peace and the Peacemakers: The Treaty of 1783*. Charlottesville: University of Virginia Press, 1986.

Hofstadter, Richard. *The Age of Reform from Bryan to F.D.R*. New York: Vintage Books, 1955.

————. *The American Political Tradition and the Men Who Made It*. New York: Vintage Books, 1948.

————. *The Idea of a Party System: The Rise of Legitimate Opposition in the United States, 1780–1840*. Berkeley: University of California Press, 1969.

Hollenbeck, Scott, and Maureen Keenan Kahr. "Ninety Years of Individual Income and Tax Statistics, 1916–2005." *Statistics of Income Bulletin* (Winter 2008). http://www.irs.gov/pub/irs-soi/16-05intax.pdf.

Hollings, Ernest F. *Making Government Work*. With Kirk Victor. Columbia: University of South Carolina Press, 2008.

Holt, Michael F. *The Rise and Fall of the American Whig Party: Jacksonian Politics and the Onset of the Civil War*. Oxford: Oxford University Press, 1999.

Homer, Sidney, and Richard Sylla. *A History of Interest Rates*. Hoboken, NJ: John Wiley & Sons, 2005.

Hooper, Molly K. "Pence Lobbies Leaders for a 'Clean' Balanced-Budget Amendment." *The Hill*. July 27, 2011. http://thehill.com/homenews/house/173759-pence-lobbies-leaders-for-a-clean-balanced-budget-amendment

Hoopes, Townsend, and Douglas Brinkley. *Driven Patriot: The Life and Times of James Forrestal*. Annapolis, MD: Naval Institute Press, 1992.

Hoover, Herbert. "Address to the Chamber of Commerce of the United States." May 1, 1930. *The American Presidency Project*. http://www.presidency.ucsb.edu/ws/?pid=22185.

————. *The Memoirs of Herbert Hoover*. Vol. 2: *The Cabinet and the Presidency, 1920–1933*. New York: Macmillan, 1952.

————. *The Memoirs of Herbert Hoover*. Vol. 3: *The Great Depression, 1929–1941*. New York: Macmillan, 1952.

Hoover, Kevin D., and Mark V. Siegler. "Taxing and Spending in the Long View: The Causal Structure of U.S. Fiscal Policy, 1791–1913." *Oxford Economic Papers* 52, no. 4 (2000): 745–773.

Hormats, Robert D. *The Price of Liberty: Paying for America's Wars*. New York: Times Books, 2007.

Howe, Daniel Walker. *What God Hath Wrought: The Transformation of America, 1815–1848*. New York: Oxford University Press, 2007.

"H.R. 1836." Congressional Budget Office Pay-As-You-Go Estimate. June 4, 2001. http://www.cbo.gov/sites/default/files/cbofiles/ftpdocs/28xx/doc2867/hr1836omb.pdf.

Huston, James L. *The Panic of 1857 and the Coming of the Civil War*. Baton Rouge: Louisiana State University Press, 1987.

Ippolito, Dennis S. *Why Budgets Matter: Budget Policy and American Politics*. University Park: Pennsylvania State University Press, 2003. Google Books edition.

Irwin, Douglas A., and Richard Sylla, eds. *Founding Choices: American Economic Policy in the 1790s*. Chicago: University of Chicago Press, 2011.

Irwin, Neil. *The Alchemists: Three Central Bankers and a World on Fire*. New York: Penguin, 2013.

Isaacson, Walter. *Benjamin Franklin: An American Life*. New York: Simon & Schuster, 2003. Kindle edition.

Jackson, Andrew. "First Inaugural Address (March 4, 1829)." The Miller Center, University of Virginia. http://millercenter.org /president/speeches/detail/3485.

Jacob, Kathryn Allamong. *King of the Lobby: The Life and Times of Sam Ward, Man About-Washington in the Gilded Age*. Baltimore: Johns Hopkins University Press, 2010.

Jacoby, Neil H. "The Fiscal Policy of the Kennedy-Johnson Administration." *Journal of Finance* 19, no. 2 (May 1964): 353–369.

Jeffers, H. Paul. *An Honest President: The Life and Presidencies of Grover Cleveland*. New York: HarperCollins, 2000.

Jefferson, Thomas. *Memoirs, Correspondence, and Private Papers of Thomas Jefferson: Volume 3*. Edited by Thomas Jefferson Randolph. London: Henry Colburn and Richard Bentley, 1829. Google Books edition.

———. *The Works of Thomas Jefferson: Volume VI*. New York: Cosimo Books, 2009. Google Books edition.

———. *The Works of Thomas Jefferson: Volume VII*. New York: Cosimo Books, 2009. Google Books edition.

———. *The Writings of Thomas Jefferson: 1792–1794*. New York: G. P. Putnam's Sons, 1895. Google Books edition.

———. *The Writings of Thomas Jefferson: Volume IV*. New York: Derby & Jackson, 1859. Google Books edition.

Jefferson, Thomas, and William Dunbar. *Documents Relating to the Purchase and Exploration of Louisiana*. 1904. Reprint, Whitefish, MT: Kessinger, 2007.

Jellison, Charles A. *Fessenden of Maine: Civil War Senator*. Syracuse, NY: Syracuse University Press, 1962.

Jenkins, Roy. *Gladstone: A Biography*. New York: Random House, 2002. Kindle edition.

"JFK on the Economy and Taxes." John F. Kennedy Presidential Library and Museum. http://www.jfklibrary.org/JFK/JFK-in-History/JFK-on-the-Economy-and-Taxes.aspx.

Johnson, Calvin. *Righteous Anger at the Wicked States: The Meaning of the Founders' Constitution*. Cambridge: Cambridge University Press, 2009.

Johnson, Lyndon Baines. "President Lyndon B. Johnson's Address to the Nation Announcing Steps to Limit the War in Vietnam and Reporting His Decision Not to Seek Reelection." March 31, 1968. Lyndon B. Johnson Presidential Library. http://www.lbjlib.utexas.edu/johnson/archives.hom/speeches.hom/680331.asp.

———. "Remarks with President Truman at the Signing in Independence of the Medicare Bill." July 30, 1965. Lyndon B. Johnson Presidential Library. http://www.lbjlib.utexas.edu/johnson/archives.hom/speeches.hom/650730.asp.

———. "State of the Union Address (January 8, 1964)." The Miller Center, University of Virginia. http://millercenter.org/president/speeches/detail /3382.

———. *The Vantage Point: Perspectives of the Presidency, 1963–1969*. New York: Holt, Rinehart and Winston, 1971.

Johnson, Simon, and James Kwak. *White House Burning: The Founding Fathers, Our National Debt, and Why It Matters to You*. New York: Pantheon Books, 2012. Kindle edition.

Joyce, Philip G. *The Congressional Budget Office: Honest Numbers, Power, and Policymaking*. Washington, DC: Georgetown University Press, 2011.

Kagan, Robert. *The World America Made*. New York: Knopf, 2012.

Kaplan, Lawrence S. *Thomas Jefferson: Westward the Course of Empire*. Wilmington, DE: Scholarly Resources, 1999.

Kasten, Richard A., David J. Weiner, and G. Thomas Woodward. "What Made Receipts Boom and When Will They Go Bust." *National Tax Journal* 52 (1999): 22–247.

Kastor, Peter J. *The Nation's Crucible: The Louisiana Purchase and the Creation of America*. New Haven, CT: Yale University Press, 2004.

Katznelson, Ira. *Fear Itself: The New Deal and the Origins of Our Time*. New York: Liveright, 2013.

Kaufman, Robert G. *Henry M. Jackson: A Life in Politics*. Seattle: University of Washington Press, 2000.

Kazin, Michael. *A Godly Hero: The Life of William Jennings Bryan*. New York: Anchor Books, 2007. Kindle edition.

Kearny, John Watts. *Sketch of American Finances, 1789–1835*. New York: G. P. Putnam's Sons, 1887.

Keith, Jeanette. *Rich Man's War, Poor Man's Fight: Race, Class, and Power in the Rural South During the First World War*. Chapel Hill: University of North Carolina Press, 2004. Google Books edition.

Keith, Robert. "Submission of the President's Budget in Transition Years." *CRS Report for Congress* (September 2008).

Kelley, Robert. *The Transatlantic Persuasion: The Liberal-Democratic Mind in the Age of Gladstone*. New Brunswick, NJ: Transaction, 1990.

Kenneally, James J. *A Compassionate Conservative: A Political Biography of Joseph W. Martin, Jr., Speaker of the U.S. House of Representatives*. Lanham, MD: Lexington Books, 2003. Google Books edition.

Kennedy, John F. "Commencement Address at Yale University." June 11, 1962. *The American Presidency Project*. http://www.presidency.ucsb.edu/ws/?pid =29661.

———. "Letter to the Chairman, House Ways and Means Committee, on Tax Reduction." August 21, 1963. *The American Presidency Project*. http://www. presidency.ucsb.edu/ws/?pid=9375.

———. "Statement by Senator John F. Kennedy on Balance of Payments, Philadelphia, PA." October 31, 1960. *The American Presidency Project*. http://www.presidency.ucsb.edu/ws/?pid=74301.

Kennon, Donald R., and Rebecca M. Rogers. *The Committee on Ways and Means: A Bicentennial History, 1789–1989*. Washington, DC: Government Printing Office, 1989.

Ketcham, Ralph. *James Madison: A Biography*. Charlottesville: University of Virginia Press, 1990.

Kimmel, Lewis H. *Federal Budget and Fiscal Policy, 1789–1958*. Washington, DC: Brookings Institution, 1959.

Kindleberger, Charles P. *Manias, Panics, and Crashes: A History of Financial Crises*. New York: John Wiley & Sons, 2000.

Kirk, Russell, and James McClellan. *The Political Principles of Robert A. Taft*. 1967. Reprint, New Brunswick, NJ: Transaction, 2010.

"Kitchin Excuses New Tax Bill as War Measure." *New York Times*. May 11, 1917.

Klein, Edward. *Ted Kennedy: The Dream That Never Died*. New York: Crown, 2009.

Kliesen, Kevin L., and Daniel L. Thorton. "The Expected Federal Budget Surplus: How Much Confidence Should the Public and Policymakers Place in the Projections." *Federal Reserve Bank of St. Louis* (March/April 2001): 16.

Kotlikoff, Laurence J., and Scott Burns. *The Coming Generational Storm: What You Need to Know About America's Economic Future*. Cambridge, MA: MIT Press, 2005.

Kramer, Michael, and Sam Roberts. *"I Never Wanted to Be Vice President of Anything!" An Investigative Biography of Nelson Rockefeller*. New York: Basic Books, 1976.

Krueger, Anne O., ed. *The Political Economy of American Trade Policy*. Chicago: University of Chicago Press, 1996.

Krugman, Paul. *Fuzzy Math: The Essential Guide to the Bush Tax Plan*. New York: Norton, 2001.

Kukla, Jon. *Wilderness So Immense: The Louisiana Purchase and the Destiny of America*. New York: Anchor Books, 2003.

Kumar, Manmohan, and Jaejon Woo. "Public Debt and Growth." IMF Working Paper. 2010.

Kuznets, Simon. "National Income Estimates for the United States Prior to 1870." *Journal of Economic History* 12, no. 2 (Spring 1952): 115–130.

Larson, John Lauritz. *Internal Improvement: National Public Works and the Promise of Popular Government in the Early United States*. Chapel Hill: University of North Carolina Press, 2001.

Laubach, Thomas. "New Evidence on the Interest Rate Effects of Budget Deficits and Debt." *Finance and Economics Discussion Series 2003–13 of the Board of Governors of the Federal Reserve System* (May 2003). www.federalreserve.gov/pubs/feds/2003/200312/200312 pap.pdf.

"Learning to Estimate, 1948." Central Intelligence Agency. March 12, 2008. https://www.cia.gov/news-information/featured-story-archive/2008-featured-story-archive/learning-to-estimate-1948.html.

Lears, Jackson. *Rebirth of a Nation: The Making of Modern America, 1877–1920.* New York: Harper Perennial, 2010.

Ledbetter, Mark. "Comparison of BEA Estimates of Personal Income and IRS Estimates of Adjusted Gross Income, New Estimates for 2005." *Survey of Current Business* (November 2007). http://www.bea.gov/scb/pdf/2007/11%20November/1107_pi_agi.pdf.

Leff, Mark. *The Limits of Symbolic Reform: The New Deal and Taxation, 1933–1939.* New York: Cambridge University Press, 2002.

Leffler, Melvyn P. *A Preponderance of Power: National Security, the Truman Administration, and the Cold War.* Stanford, CA: Stanford University Press, 1992.

Lekachman, Robert. *The Age of Keynes.* New York: Random House, 1966.

Lence, Ross M., ed. *Union and Liberty: The Political Philosophy of John C. Calhoun.* Indianapolis: Liberty Fund, 1992.

Leuchtenburg, William E. *Franklin D. Roosevelt and the New Deal.* New York: Harper & Row, 2009.

Levy, Herbert. *Henry Morgenthau, Jr.: The Remarkable Life of FDR's Secretary of the Treasury.* New York: Skyhorse, 2010.

Lincoln, Abraham. "July 4th Message to Congress (July 4, 1861)." The Miller Center, University of Virginia. http://millercenter.org/president/speeches/detail/3508.

Lipscomb, Andrew A., ed. *The Writings of Thomas Jefferson.* Washington, DC: Thomas Jefferson Memorial Association of the United States, 1904.

Livingston, Steven G. *U.S. Social Security: A Reference Handbook.* Santa Barbara: ABC-CLIO, 2008.

Lizza, Ryan. "Fussbudget: How Paul Ryan Captured the G.O.P." *New Yorker.* August 6, 2012, 24–32.

Logan, David S. "Summary of Latest Federal Income Tax Data." Tax Foundation. October 24, 2011. http://taxfoundation.org/article/summary-latest-federal-individual-income-tax-data-0.

Loker, Thomas W. *The History and Evolution of Healthcare in America: The Untold Backstory of Where We've Been, Where We Are, and Why Healthcare Needs Reform.* Bloomington, IN: iUniverse Books, 2012. Google Books edition.

Longley, Kyle. *Senator Albert Gore, Sr.: Tennessee Maverick.* Baton Rouge: Louisiana State University Press, 2004.

Love, Robert A. *Federal Financing: A Study in the Methods Employed by the Treasury in Its Borrowing Operations.* New York: AMS, 1931.

Lowndes, Charles L. B. "The Revenue Act of 1964: A Critical Analysis." *Duke Law Journal,* no. 4 (Autumn 1964): 667–705.

Lubove, Roy. *The Struggle for Social Security, 1900–1935*. Cambridge, MA: Harvard University Press, 1968.

Lyon, E. Wilson. *The Man Who Sold Louisiana*. Norman: University of Oklahoma Press, 1974.

Macdonald, James. *A Free Nation Deep in Debt: The Financial Roots of Democracy*. Princeton, NJ: Princeton University Press, 2006.

Madison, James. *Letters and Other Writings of James Madison*. Vol. 1, *1769–1793*. Philadelphia: Lippincott, 1865. Google Books edition.

———. *Letters and Other Writings of James Madison*. Vol. 3, *1816–1828*. Philadelphia: Lippincott, 1865. Google Books edition.

———. *Notes of Debates in the Federal Convention of 1787*. With an introduction by Adrienne Koch. New York: Norton, 1987.

———. "Sixth Annual Message." September 20, 1814. *The American Presidency Project*. http://www.presidency.ucsb.edu/ws/?pid=29456.

———. *The Writings of James Madison*. Vol. 2, *1783–1787*. New York: G. P. Putnam's Sons, 1901. Google Books edition.

Mahon, A. T. "The Negotiations at Ghent in 1814." *American Historical Review* 11 (October 1905–July 1906): 85.

Maier, Pauline. *Ratification: The People Debate the Constitution, 1787–1823*. New York: Simon & Schuster, 2010.

Malone, Dumas, ed. *Correspondence Between Thomas Jefferson and Pierre Samuel du Pont de Nemours, 1798–1817*. Boston: Riverside, 1930. Kindle edition.

———. *Jefferson and His Times*. Vol. 6, *Jefferson the President: First Term, 1801–1805*. Boston: Little, Brown, 1970.

Manley, John F. *The Politics of Finance: The House Committee on Ways and Means*. Boston: Little, Brown, 1970.

Mann, Bruce H. *Republic of Debtors: Bankruptcy in the Age of American Independence*. Cambridge, MA: Harvard University Press, 2002.

Mann, Robert. *Legacy to Power: Senator Russell Long of Louisiana*. New York: Paragon House, 1992.

Maranto, Robert, Tom Iansford, and Jeremy Johnson, eds. *Judging Bush: Studies in the Modern Presidency*. Stanford, CA: Stanford University Press, 2009.

Marcus, Robert D. *Grand Old Party: Political Structure in the Gilded Age, 1880–1896*. New York: Oxford University Press, 1971.

Marmor, Theodore R. *The Politics of Medicare*. Hawthorne, NY: DeGruyter, 2000.

Martenson, Chris. *The Crash Course: The Unsustainable Future of Our Economy, Energy, and Environment*. Hoboken, NJ: John Wiley & Sons, 2011.

Martin, Cathie J. *Shifting the Burden: The Struggle over Growth and Corporate Taxation*. Chicago: University of Chicago Press, 1991.

Martin, Joe. *My First Fifty Years in Politics*. New York: McGraw-Hill, 1960.

Martin, John Bartlow. *Adlai Stevenson of Illinois: The Life of Adlai E. Stevenson*. New York: Doubleday, 1976.

Mascaro, Lisa. "Budget Talks Identify $1 Trillion in Budget Cuts." *Los Angeles Times.* May 25, 2011. http://articles.latimes.com/2011/may/25/nation/la-na -congress-debt-20110525.

Matusow, Allen J. *Nixon's Economy: Booms, Busts, Dollars, & Votes.* Lawrence: University Press of Kansas. 1998.

May, Ernest R., ed. *American Cold War Strategy: Interpreting NSC 68.* Boston: Bedford Books, 1993.

Mayer, George H. *Republican Party, 1854–1966.* 2nd ed. New York: Oxford University Press, 1967.

Mayer, Michael S. *The Eisenhower Years.* New York: Facts on File, 2010. Google Books edition.

McAdoo, William G. *Crowded Years: The Reminiscences of William G. McAdoo.* Boston: Houghton Mifflin Company, 1931.

McBride, William. "Summary of Latest Federal Income Tax Data." Tax Policy Foundation, November 29, 2012. http://taxfoundation.org/article/summary -latest-federal-income-tax-data-2012.

McClellan, Scott. *What Happened: Inside the Bush White House and Washington's Culture of Deception.* New York: PublicAffairs, 2008.

McCormick, Richard P. *The Second American Party System: Party Formation in the Jacksonian Era.* New York: Norton, 1973.

McCoy, Drew R. *The Last of the Fathers: James Madison & the Republican Legacy.* Cambridge: Cambridge University Press, 1991.

McCraw, Thomas K. *The Founders and Finance: How Hamilton, Gallatin, and Other Immigrants Forged a New Economy.* Cambridge, MA: Belknap Press of Harvard University Press, 2012.

McCulloch, Hugh M. *Men and Measures of Half a Century.* New York: Charles Scribner's Sons, 1888.

McCullough, David. *Truman.* New York: Simon & Schuster. 1992.

McCusker, John J. "Estimating Early American Gross Domestic Product." *Historical Methods* 33 (Summer 2000): 155–162.

McFaul, John M. *The Politics of Jacksonian Finance.* Ithaca, NY: Cornell University Press, 1972.

McGerr, Michael. *A Fierce Discontent: The Rise and Fall of the Progressive Movement in America, 1870–1920.* New York: Free Press, 2003.

McMath, Robert C., Jr. *American Populism: A Social History: 1877–1898.* New York: Hill and Wang, 1993.

McNamara, Robert S. *In Retrospect: The Tragedy and Lessons of Vietnam.* New York: Random House, 1995.

Meacham, Jon. *American Lion: Andrew Jackson in the White House.* New York: Random House, 2008. Kindle edition.

Mears, Walter R. "Tax Code Overhaul Not in Sight." *Lawrence Journal World.* November 26, 1977.

Meeker, Mary. *A Basic Summary of America's Financial Statements*. USA, Inc. February 2011. images.businessweek.com/mz/11/10/1110_mz_49meekerusainc.pdf.

Mehrota, Ajay K. "Lawyers, Guns, and Public Moneys: The U.S. Treasury, World War I, and the Administration of the Modern Fiscal State." *Law and History Review* 28, no. 1 (February 2010): 173–225.

Mellon, Andrew W. *Taxation: The People's Business*. New York: Macmillan, 1924.

Meltzer, Allan H. *A History of the Federal Reserve, Volume 1: 1913–1951*. Chicago: University of Chicago Press, 2003.

Mendes, Elizabeth. "Americans Fear Impact of Foreign-Held Debt on Economy." Gallup. March 9, 2012. http://www.gallup.com/poll/153179/Americans-Fear-Impact-Foreign-Held-Debt-Economy.aspx.

Merriner, James L. *Mr. Chairman: Power in Dan Rostenkowski's America*. Carbondale: Southern Illinois University Press, 1999.

Merry, Robert W. *A Country of Vast Designs: James K. Polk, the Mexican War, and the Conquest of the American Continent*. New York: Simon & Schuster, 2009.

Meyer, Annette E. *Evolution of United States Budgeting: Changing Fiscal and Financial Concepts*. New York: Greenwood, 1989.

———. *Evolution of United States Budgeting: Revised and Expanded Edition*. Westport, CT: Praeger, 2002. Kindle edition.

Meyerson, Michael I. *Liberty's Blueprint: How Madison and Hamilton Wrote the Federalist Papers, Defined the Constitution, and Made Democracy Safe for the World*. New York: Basic Books, 2008. Google Books edition.

Miers, Earl Schenck. *The General Who Marched to Hell: Sherman and the Southern Campaign*. New York: Dorset, 1990.

Miller, Marion Mills, ed. *Great Debates in American Taxation*. Vol. 12, *Revenue: The Tariff and Taxation*. New York: Current Literature, 1913. Google Books edition.

Miller, William Lee. *The Business of May Next: James Madison and the Founding*. Charlottesville: University of Virginia Press, 1994.

Millis, Walter, ed. *The Forrestal Diaries*. New York: Viking, 1951.

Monroe, James. "Eighth Annual Message (December 7, 1824)." The Miller Center, University of Virginia. http://millercenter.org/president/speeches/detail/3606.

Moon, Marilyn. *Medicare: A Policy Primer*. Washington, DC: Urban Institute Press, 2006.

———. *Medicare Now and in the Future*. Washington, DC: Urban Institute Press, 1996.

Mooney, Chase C. *William H. Crawford, 1772–1834*. Lexington: University Press of Kentucky, 1974.

Moore, James, and Wayne Slater. *Bush's Brain: How Karl Rove Made George W. Bush Presidential*. Hoboken, NJ: John Wiley & Sons, 2003.

Moore, John Robert. "Senator Josiah W. Bailey and the 'Conservative Manifesto' of 1937." *Journal of Southern History* 31, no. 1 (1965): 21–39.

Morgan, H. Wayne. "Populism and the Decline of Agriculture." In *The Gilded Age: Essays on the Origins of Modern America*. Edited by H. Wayne Morgan. Syracuse, NY: Syracuse University Press, 1970.

Morgan, Iwan W. *The Age of Deficits: Presidents and Unbalanced Budgets from Jimmy Carter to George W. Bush*. Lawrence: The University Press of Kansas, 2009.

―――. *Deficit Government: Taxing and Spending in Modern America*. Chicago: Ivan R. Dee, 1995.

―――. *Eisenhower Versus 'The Spenders': The Eisenhower Administration, The Democrats, and the Budget, 1953–60*. London: Printer Publishers, 1990.

Morris, Edmund. *The Rise of Theodore Roosevelt*. New York: Modern Library, 2002. Google Books edition.

Morris, Robert. "The First Congress, on $6 a Day." *New York Times*. March 2, 1989.

Murphy, Kevin C. "The Business of America." Chap. 9 in *The Fortunes of Progressivism, 1919–1929*. 2013. http://www.kevincmurphy.com/uatw-business -brooms.html#11.

Myers, Robert J. *Medicare*. Homewood, IL: McCahan Foundation, 1970.

National Priorities Project. *Cost of War*. http://costofwar.com.

Neal, Steve. *Dark Horse: A Biography of Wendell Willkie*. Garden City, NY: Doubleday, 1984.

Newport, Frank. "In Their Own Words: Americans' Views on Raising Debt Ceiling." Gallup Politics. July 18, 2011. http://www.gallup.com/poll/148547/ Own-Words-Americans-Views-Raising-Debt-Ceiling.aspx#2.

Newport, Frank, Jeffrey M. Jones, and Lydia Saad. "Ronald Reagan from the People's Perspective: A Gallup Poll Review." Gallup. June 7, 2004. http://www .gallup.com/poll/11887/ronald-reagan-from-peoples-perspective-gallup -poll-review.aspx.

Newton, Jim. *Eisenhower: The White House Years*. New York: Doubleday, 2011.

Niemi, Albert W., Jr. *U.S. Economic History*. 2nd ed. Lanham, MD: University Press of America, 1980.

Niskanen, William A. *Reaganomics: An Insider's Account of the Policies and the People*. Oxford: Oxford University Press, 1988.

Nitti, Tony. "Secrets of the Fiscal Cliff Deal." *Forbes*. January 2, 2013. http://www .forbes.com/sites/anthonynitti/2013/01/02/secrets-of-the-fiscal-cliff-deal.

Niven, John. *John C. Calhoun and the Price of Union: A Biography*. Baton Rouge: Louisiana State University, 1993. Google Books edition.

―――. *Salmon P. Chase: A Biography*. Oxford: Oxford University Press, 1995.

Nixon, Richard. "Annual Budget Message to the Congress, Fiscal Year 1974." January 29, 1973. *The American Presidency Project*. http://www.presidency.ucsb .edu/ws/?pid=3908.

———. "Inaugural Address." January 20, 1969. *The American Presidency Project.* http://www.presidency.ucsb.edu/ws/?pid =1941.

———. "Radio Address: 'The New Budget': Charting a New Era of Progress." January 28, 1973. *The American Presidency Project.* http://www.presidency.ucsb.edu/ws/?pid=3897.

Noah, Timothy. "Meme Watch: Bushies Take the Bait." *Slate.* December 16, 2002. http://www.slate.com/articles/news_and_politics/chatterbox/2002/12/meme_watch_bushies_take_the_bait.html.

Norquist, Grover. *Leave Us Alone: America's New Governing Majority.* New York: HarperCollins, 2008. Kindle edition.

North, Douglass C. *The Economic Growth of the United States: 1790–1860.* New York: Norton, 1966.

Noyes, Alexander Dana. *Forty Years of American Finance: A Short Financial History of the Government and People of the United States Since the Civil War, 1865–1907.* New York: G. P. Putnam's Sons, 1909.

Obama, Barack. "Remarks by the President on Fiscal Policy." April 13, 2011. http://www.whitehouse.gov/the-press-office/2011/04/13/remarks-president-fiscal-policy.

"Obama Fires Up House Democrats to Help Push Through Stimulus Bill." CNN. February 6, 2009. http://www.cnn.com/2009/ POLITICS/02/06/obama.stimulus/.

"Obama Makes Fresh Appeal on Health Care at Prime-time News Conference." *PBS NewsHour.* July 22, 2009. http://www.pbs.org/newshour/updates/health/july-dec09/obamapresser_07-22.html.

"Obama Signs Tax Deal into Law." CNN. December 17, 2010.

Oberlander, Jonathan. *The Political Life of Medicare.* Chicago: University of Chicago Press, 2003.

O'Brien, Steven G., ed. "Charles Gates Dawes." In *American Political Leaders: From Colonial Times to the Present.* Princeton, NJ: Visual Education, 1991. Google Books edition.

O'Driscoll, Gerald P., Jr. "The Ricardian Nonequivalence Theorem." *Journal of Political Economy* 85, no. 1 (February 1977): 207–210.

Office of Management and Budget (OMB), White House. Historical Tables. http://www.whitehouse.gov/omb/budget/historicals.

Officer, Lawrence H. *Two Centuries of Compensation for U.S. Production Workers in Manufacturing.* New York: Palgrave Macmillan, 2009.

O'Hanlon, Michael E. *Budgeting for Hard Power: Defense and Security Spending Under Barack Obama.* Washington, DC: Brookings Institution Press, 2009.

———. *Defense Policy Choices for the Bush Administration.* Washington, DC: The Brookings Institution Press, 2001.

Oldaker, Nikki. *Samuel Tilden: The Real 19th President.* With John Bigelow. Clearwater, FL: Show Biz East Productions, 2006. Kindle edition.

Oliver, Thomas R., Philip R. Lee, and Helene L. Lipton. "A Political History of Medicare and Prescription Drug Coverage." *Milbank Quarterly* 82, no. 2 (2004): 283–354.

Olson, Laura Katz. *The Politics of Medicaid.* New York: Columbia University Press, 2010.

O'Neill, Tip. *Man of the House: The Life and Political Memoirs of Speaker Tip O'Neill,* with William Novak. New York: Random House, 1987.

Oxford Dictionary of American Quotations. 2nd ed. Edited by Margaret Miner and Hugh Rawson. Oxford: Oxford University Press, 2006. Google Books.

Pach, Chester J., Jr., and Elmo Richardson. *The Presidency of Dwight D. Eisenhower.* Lawrence: University Press of Kansas, 1991.

Parcell, Ann. "Challenges and Uncertainties in Forecasting Federal Individual Income Tax Receipts." *National Tax Journal* 52 (1999): 325–338.

Parker, George Frederick. *Recollections of Grover Cleveland.* New York: Century, 1909. Google Books edition.

Parsons, Lynn Hudson. *The Birth of Modern Politics: Andrew Jackson, John Quincy Adams and the Election of 1828.* New York: Oxford University Press, 2009. Google Books edition.

Parton, James. *The Life of Andrew Jackson,* vol. 2. Cambridge, MA: Riverside, 1888. Google Books edition.

Patterson, James T. *Mr. Republican: A Biography of Robert A. Taft.* Boston: Houghton Mifflin, 1972.

Patton, Eugene B. "Secretary Shaw and Precedents as to Treasury Control over the Money Market." *Journal of Political Economy* 15, no. 2 (February 1907): 65–87.

Paulson, Henry M., Jr. *On the Brink: Inside the Race to Stop the Collapse of the Global Financial System.* New York: Business Plus, 2010.

Pauly, Mark V., and William L. Kissick, eds. *Lessons from the First Twenty Years of Medicare: Research Implications for Public and Private Sector Policy.* Philadelphia: University of Pennsylvania Press, 1988.

Peck, Harry Thurston. *Twenty Years of the Republic, 1885–1905.* New York: Dodd, Mead, 1920. Google Books edition.

Penner, Rudolph G., and Alan J. Abramson. *Broken Purse Strings: Congressional Budgeting, 1974–88.* Washington, DC: Urban Institute Press, 1988.

Perkins, Bradford. *Castlereagh and Adams: England and the United States, 1812–1823.* Berkeley: University of California Press, 1964.

Perkins, Edwin J. *American Public Finance and Financial Services, 1700–1815.* Columbus: Ohio State University Press, 1994.

Perkins, Frances. *The Roosevelt I Know.* New York: Penguin Group, 2011.

Perot, Ross. *United We Stand: How We Can Take Back Our Country.* New York: Hyperion, 1992.

Perret, Geoffrey. *Eisenhower.* Holbrook, MA: Adams Media Corporation, 1999.

Peterson, Paul. "The New Politics of Deficits." *Political Science Quarterly* 100, no. 4 (Winter 1985–1986): 593.

Peterson, Peter G. *Running on Empty: How the Democratic and Republican Parties Are Bankrupting Our Future and What Americans Can Do About It.* New York: Farrar, Straus, and Giroux, 2004.

Phillips-Fein, Kim. *Invisible Hands: The Making of the Conservative Movement from the New Deal to Reagan.* New York: Norton, 2009.

Pianin, Eric. "Seeing Budget in Balance, CBO Projects a Decade of Surpluses." *Washington Post.* January 8, 1998. http://www.washingtonpost.com/wp-srv /politics/special/budget/stories/010898.htm

Poen, Monte M. *Harry S. Truman Versus the Medical Lobby: The Genesis of Medicare.* Columbia: University of Missouri Press, 1979.

Polk, James K. "Second Annual Message." December 8, 1846. *The American Presidency Project.* http://www.presidency.ucsb.edu/ws /?pid= 29487.

Pollack, Sheldon D. *Refinancing America: The Republican Antitax Agenda.* New York: State University of New York Press, 2003.

Potter, David M. *The Impending Crisis, 1848–1861.* New York: Harper Perennial, 1976.

Rampell, Catherine. "College Graduates Fare Well in Jobs Market, Even Through Recession." *New York Times.* May 4, 2013.

Rapoport, Ronald B., and Walter J. Stone. *Three's a Crowd: The Dynamic of Third Parties, Ross Perot, and Republican Resurgence.* Ann Arbor: University of Michigan Press, 2005.

Rappleye, Charles. *Robert Morris: Financier of the American Revolution.* New York: Simon & Schuster, 2010.

Ratchford, B. U. *American State Debts.* New York: AMS, 1966.

Rauchway, Eric. *Murdering McKinley: The Making of Theodore Roosevelt's America.* New York: Hill and Wang, 2011. Kindle edition.

Reagan, Ronald. "Address Before a Joint Session of the Congress on the Program for Economic Recovery." February 18, 1981. *The American Presidency Project.* http://www.presidency.ucsb.edu/ws/?pid=43425.

———. "Address on Federal Tax Reduction Legislation (July 27, 1981)." The Miller Center, University of Virginia. http://millercenter.org/president /speeches/detail/5676.

———. "Address on the Program for Economic Recovery (April 28, 1981)." The Miller Center, University of Virginia. http://miller center.org/president /speeches/detail/5446.

———. "Address to the Nation on Federal Tax and Budget Reconciliation Legislation." August 16, 1982. Ronald Reagan Presidential Library Archives. http://www.reagan.utexas.edu/archives/speeches/1982/81682a.htm.

———. "Inaugural Address." January 20, 1981. *The American Presidency Project.* http://www.presidency.ucsb.edu/ws/?pid=43130.

———. "The President's News Conference." November 10, 1981. *The American Presidency Project.* http://www.presidency.ucsb.edu/ws/?pid=43228.

———. *The Reagan Diaries.* Vol. 1, *January 1981–October 1985.* Edited by Douglas Brinkley. New York: HarperCollins, 2010. Google Books edition.

———. "Remarks at the Annual Convention of the National League of Cities in Los Angeles, California." November 29, 1982. Ronald Reagan Presidential Library Archives. http://www.reagan.utexas.edu/archives/speeches/1982/112982c.htm.

———. "Ronald Reagan Speaks Out Against Socialized Medicine." Speech to the American Medical Association. 1961.

———. "State of the Union Address (January 25, 1983)." The Miller Center, University of Virginia. http://millercenter.org/president/speeches/detail/5680.

"Reagan's Tax Cut Proposal Called All But Dead." *News and Courier* (Charleston, SC). March 26, 1981.

Reeves, Richard. *President Kennedy: Profile of Power.* New York: Touchstone, 1993. Kindle edition.

———. *President Reagan: The Triumph of Imagination.* New York: Simon & Schuster, 2005.

Rediscovering George Washington. Website. The Claremont Institute and PBS, 2002. http://www.pbs.org/georgewashington/index.html.

Regan, Donald T. *For the Record: From Wall Street to Washington.* New York: St. Martin's, 1989.

Reichley, James. *Conservatives in an Age of Change: The Nixon and Ford Administrations.* Washington, DC: Brookings Institution, 1981.

Reinhart, Carmen, and Kenneth S. Rogoff. "Growth in a Time of Debt." *National Bureau of Economic Research Working Paper, No. 15639* (January 2010).

———. *The Time Is Different: Eight Centuries of Financial Folly.* Princeton, NJ: Princeton University Press, 2009.

Remini, Robert V. *Andrew Jackson: The Course of the American Empire.* Vol. 1, *1767–1821.* Baltimore: Johns Hopkins University Press, 1998.

———. *Andrew Jackson: Lessons in Leadership.* New York: Palgrave Macmillan, 2008. Google Books edition.

———. *The House: The History of the House of Representatives.* New York: Harper Collins, 2006.

———. *The Life of Andrew Jackson.* New York: HarperCollins, 2001. Google Books edition.

Renehan, Edward J., Jr. *Dark Genius of Wall Street: The Misunderstood Life of Jay Gould, King of the Robber Barons.* New York: Basic Books, 2005.

Reports of the Secretary of the Treasury. Vol. 3, *1829–1836.* Washington, DC: Blair & Rives, 1837. Google Books edition.

Ricardo, David. *The Works of David Ricardo.* London: John Murray, 1846. Google Books edition.

Richardson, William A. *Practical Information Concerning the Public Debt of the United States: With the National Banking Laws: For Banks, Bankers, Brokers, Bank Directors, and Investors.* Washington, DC: W. H. & O. H. Morrison, 1873. Google Books edition.

Ricks, Thomas. *Fiasco: The American Military Adventure in Iraq.* New York: Penguin, 2006.

Rivlin, Alice M., and Joseph R. Antos. *Restoring Fiscal Sanity 2007: The Health Spending Challenge.* Washington, DC: Brookings Institution Press, 2007.

"Robert Doughton, House Tax Leader Under FDR, Truman." *Toledo Blade.* October 1, 1954.

Roberts, Paul Craig. *Supply-Side Revolution: An Insider's Account of Policymaking in Washington.* Cambridge, MA: Harvard University Press, 1984.

Robertson, David. *A Political Biography of James F. Byrnes.* New York: Norton, 1994.

Rohrbough, Malcolm J. *The Land Office Business: The Settlement and Administration of American Public Lands, 1789–1837.* New York: Oxford University Press, 1968.

Rohrer, Wayne C., and Louis H. Douglas. *The Agrarian Transition in America: Dualism and Change.* Indianapolis: Bobbs-Merrill, 1969.

Roosevelt, Franklin D. "Annual Message to Congress." January 3, 1938. *The American Presidency Project.* http://www.presidency.ucsb.edu/ws/?pid=15517.

———. "Campaign Address on the Eight Great Credit Groups of the Nation at St. Louis, Missouri." October 21, 1932. *The American Presidency Project.* http://www.presidency.ucsb.edu/ws/?pid=88401.

———. "Campaign Address on the Federal Budget at Pittsburgh, Pennsylvania." October 19, 1932. *The American Presidency Project.* http://www.presidency.ucsb.edu/ws/?pid =88399.

———. "Radio Address on the National Democratic Platform from Albany, New York." July 30, 1932. *The American Presidency Project.* http://www.presidency.ucsb.edu/ws/?pid= 88406.

———. "State of the Union Address." January 6, 1942. *The American Presidency Project.* http://www.presidency.ucsb.edu/ws/?pid=16253.

———. "Veto of a Revenue Bill." February 22, 1944. *The American Presidency Project.* http://www.presidency.ucsb.edu/ws/?pid=16490.

Roosevelt, Theodore. *A Compilation of the Messages and Speeches of Theodore Roosevelt, 1901–1905.* Edited by Alfred Henry Lewis. Washington, DC: Bureau of National Literature and Art, 1906. Google Books edition.

———. "New Nationalism Speech." August 31, 1910. *The White House Blog.* http://www.whitehouse.gov/blog/2011/12/06/archives-president-teddy-roosevelts-new-nationalism-speech.

———. "Sixth Annual Message (December 3, 1906)." The Miller Center, University of Virginia. http://millercenter.org/president/speeches/detail/3778.

Rose, Mark H. *Interstate: Express Highway Politics, 1939–1989*. Knoxville: University of Tennessee Press, 1990.

Rosenberg, Charles E. *The Care of Strangers: The Rise of America's Hospital System*. Baltimore: Johns Hopkins University Press, 1995.

Rosenthal, Andrew. "Bush Now Concedes a Need for 'Tax Revenue Increases' to Reduce Deficit in Budget." *New York Times*. June 27, 1990.

Rosentreter, Roger L. "Roosevelt's Tree Army: Michigan's Civilian Conservation Corps." Michigan Department of Natural Resources. August 18, 2010. http://www.michigan.gov/dnr/0,4570,7-153-54463_18595_18602-53515--,00.html.

Ross, Earl Dudley. *The Liberal Republican Movement*. New York: AMS, 1971.

Rothbard, Murray N. *The Panic of 1819: Reactions and Policies*. Auburn, AL: Ludwig von Mises Institute, 2007.

Rudman, Warren B. *Combat: Twelve Years in the U.S. Senate*. New York: Random House, 1996.

Sage, Leland L. *William Boyd Allison: A Study in Practical Politics*. Cedar Rapids, IA: Torch, 1956.

Samuels, Peggy, and Harold Samuels. *Teddy Roosevelt at San Juan: The Making of a President*. College Station: Texas A&M University Press, 1997. Google Books edition.

Sanders, Elizabeth. *Roots of Reform: Farmers, Workers, and the American State, 1877–1917*. Chicago: University of Chicago Press, 1999.

Sanger, David E. "President Asserts Shrunken Surplus May Curb Congress." *New York Times*. August 25, 2001.

Savage, James D. *Balanced Budgets & American Politics*. Ithaca, NY: Cornell University Press, 1988.

Schauffler, Robert Haven, ed. *Washington's Birthday*. New York: Moffat, Yard, 1910.

Schick, Allen. *The Federal Budget: Politics, Policy, Process*. Washington, DC: Brookings Institution Press, 2000.

Schlesinger, Arthur M. *The Age of Roosevelt*. Vol. 1, *1919–1933: The Crisis of the Old Order*. Boston: Houghton Mifflin, 159.

———. *The Age of Roosevelt*. Vol. 2, *1933–1935: The Coming of the New Deal*. Boston: Houghton Mifflin, 1986.

Schoenwald, Jonathan M. *A Time for Choosing: The Rise of Modern American Conservatism*. Oxford: Oxford University Press, 2001.

Schultze, Charles L. *The Politics and Economics of Public Spending*. Washington, DC: Brookings Institution, 1968.

Schwantes, Carlos A. *Coxey's Army: An American Odyssey*. Lincoln: University of Nebraska Press, 1985.

Secretary of the Treasury. *National Loans of the United States*. Washington, DC: Department of Treasury, 1882.

Seelye, Katharine Q. "The Speaker Steps Down: Facing a Revolt, Gingrich Won't Run for Speaker and Will Quit Congress." *New York Times*. November 7, 1998.

Seligman, Edwin Robert Anderson. *The Income Tax*. New York: Macmillan, 1911.

Shaviro, Daniel. *Do Deficits Matter?* Chicago: University of Chicago Press, 1997.

———. *Taxes, Spending, and the U.S. Government's March Towards Bankruptcy*. Cambridge: Cambridge University Press, 2007.

Sherman, John. *Recollections of Forty Years in the House, Senate and Cabinet. An Autobiography*. Chicago: Werner, 1895. Google Books edition.

Sherman, William Tecumseh. *Sherman: Memoirs of General W. T. Sherman*. New York: Library of America, 2013. Kindle edition.

Shirley, Craig. *Reagan's Revolution: The Untold Story of the Campaign That Started It All*. Nashville: Nelson Current, 2006.

Shlaes, Amity. *Coolidge*. New York: HarperCollins, 2013.

Shultz, George P., and Kenneth W. Dam. *Economic Policy Beyond the Headlines*. Chicago: University of Chicago Press, 1998.

Shultz, William J., and M. R. Caine. *Financial Development of the United States*. New York: Prentice-Hall, 1937.

Shuman, Howard E. *Politics and the Budget: The Struggle Between the President and the Congress*. Englewood Cliffs, NJ: Prentice Hall, 1988.

Silbey, Joel H. *Martin Van Buren and the Emergence of American Popular Politics*. Lanham, MD: Rowman & Littlefield, 2002.

Simon, William E. *A Time for Truth*. New York: Reader's Digest Press, 1978.

Skidelsky, Robert. *Keynes: The Return of the Master*. New York: PublicAffairs, 2009. Kindle edition.

Skocpol, Theda. *Protecting Soldiers and Mothers: The Political Origins of Social Policy in the United States*. Cambridge, MA: Belknap Press of Harvard University Press, 1992.

Sloan, Herbert E. *Principle & Interest: Thomas Jefferson and the Problem of Debt*. New York: Oxford University Press, 1995.

Smith, David G. *Entitlement Politics: Medicare and Medicaid, 1995–2001*. New York: De Gruyter, 2002.

———, and Judith D. Moore. *Medicaid Politics and Policy, 1965–2007*. New Brunswick, NJ: Transaction, 2008.

Smith, James Morton, ed. *The Republic of Letters: The Correspondence Between Thomas Jefferson and James Madison, 1776–1826*. 3 vols. New York: Norton, 1995.

Smith, Jean Edward. *FDR*. New York: Random House, 2008. Google Books edition.

Smith, Joseph Patterson. *History of the Republican Party in Ohio*. Chicago: Lewis, 1898. Google Books edition.

Smith, Justin H. *The War with Mexico: The Classic History of the Mexican-American War*. St. Petersburg, FL: Red and Black, 2010. Kindle edition.

"Smith Lays Charge of Bigotry to Republicans." *Berkeley Daily Gazette*. October 28, 1932.

Smith, Richard Norton. *Thomas E. Dewey and His Times: The First Full-Scale*

Biography of the Maker of the Modern Republican Party. New York: Simon & Schuster, 1982.

Smith, Rixey, and Norman Beasley. *Carter Glass: A Biography*. Freeport, NY: Books for Libraries, 1970.

Smithies, Arthur. *The Budgetary Process in the United States*. New York: Simon & Schuster, 1855.

———. "Reflections on the Work and Influence of John Maynard Keynes." *Quarterly Journal of Economics* 65, no. 4 (November 1951): 578–601.

Social Security Administration (SSA). *2001 OASDI Trustees Report*. http://www.ssa.gov/OACT/TR/TR01/II_project.html#83100.

"Speaker Carlisle Talks." *Columbus Daily News*. May 4, 1887.

Stabile, Donald R., and Jeffrey A. Cantor. *The Public Debt of the United States: An Historical Perspective, 1775–1990*. New York: Praeger, 1991.

Stampp, Kenneth M. *The Era of Reconstruction, 1865–1877*. New York: Vintage Books, 1965.

Starr, Paul. *Remedy and Reaction: The Peculiar American Struggle over Health Care Reform*. New Haven, CT: Yale University Press, 2011.

———. *The Social Transformation of American Medicine: The Rise of a Sovereign Profession and the Making of a Vast Industry*. New York: Basic Books, 1982.

Stein, Herbert. *The Fiscal Revolution in America: Policy in Pursuit of Reality*. Washington, DC: AEI, 1996.

Stengel, Richard. "Ninety Long Minutes in Omaha." *Time*. October 17, 1988.

Steuerle, C. Eugene. *The Tax Decade: How Taxes Came to Dominate the Public Agenda*. Washington, DC: Urban Institute.

Stewart, Charles III. *Budget Reform Politics: The Design of the Appropriations Process in the House of Representatives, 1865–1921*. Cambridge: Cambridge University Press, 1989.

Stiglitz, Joseph E., and Linda J. Bilmes. *The Three Trillion Dollar War: The True Cost of the Iraq Conflict*. New York: Norton, 2008.

Stiles, T. J. *The First Tycoon: The Epic Life of Cornelius Vanderbilt*. New York: Vintage Books, 2009.

Stockman, David A. *The Great Deformation: The Corruption of Capitalism in America*. New York: PublicAffairs, 2013.

———. *The Triumph of Politics: Why the Reagan Revolution Failed*. New York: HarperCollins, 1986.

Studenski, Paul, and Herman E. Krooss. *Financial History of the United States*. New York: McGraw-Hill, 1963.

Sundquist, James L. *Dynamics of the Party System: Alignment and Realignment of Political Parties in the United States*. Washington, DC: Brookings Institution, 1983. Google Books edition.

Surowiecki, James. "A Cut Too Far." *New Yorker*. April 21, 2003. http://www.newyorker.com/archive/2003/04/21/030421ta_talk_surowiecki.

Suskind, Ron. *Confidence Men: Wall Street, Washington, and the Education of a President*. New York: HarperCollins, 2011.

———. *The Price of Loyalty: George W. Bush, the White House, and the Education of Paul O'Neill*. New York: Simon & Schuster, 2004.

Tanner, Michael D. *Leviathan on the Right: How Big Government Conservatism Brought Down the Republican Revolution*. Washington, DC: Cato Institute, 2007.

Tanous, Peter, and Jeff Cox. *Debt, Deficits, and the Demise of the American Economy*. Hoboken, NJ: John Wiley & Sons, 2011.

Taus, Esther Rogoff. *Central Banking Functions of the United States Treasury, 1789–1941*. New York: Columbia University Press, 1943.

Taussig, F. W. *The Tariff History of the United States*. New York: Capricorn Books, 1964.

"Taxes, Trade, Social Security and More—George Bush Speaks Out." *Forbes*. May 21, 2012.

Tax Policy Center. "Historical Average Federal Tax Rates for All Households." October 2012. http://www.taxpolicycenter.org/taxfacts/displayafact.cfm?Docid=456.

———. "Historical Income Distribution for All Households." October 2012. http://www.taxpolicycenter.org/taxfacts/displayafact.cfm?Docid=458.

———. "Historical Social Security Tax Rates." February 26, 2013. http://www.taxpolicycenter.org/taxfacts/displayafact.cfm?Docid=45.

———. "Quick Facts: Fiscal Stimulus." Urban Institute and Brookings Institution. 2010. http://www.taxpolicycenter.org/taxtopics/quick_fiscal_stimulus.cfm.

Taylor, Donald H., Jr. *Balancing the Budget Is a Progressive Priority*. New York: Springer, 2012. Kindle edition.

Temin, Peter. *The Jacksonian Economy*. New York: Norton, 1969.

Thomas, Thomas R., Philip R. Lee, and Helene L. Lipton. "A Political History of Medicare and Prescription Drug Coverage." *Milbank Quarterly* 82, no. 2 (2004): 283–354.

Thompson, Kenneth W., ed. *The Budget Deficit and National Debt*. Vol. 1. Lanham, MD: University Press of America, 1997.

Thorndike, Rachel Sherman. *The Sherman Letters*. New York: Charles Scribner's Sons, 1894.

Tilden, Samuel J. *Letters and Literary Memorials of Samuel J. Tilden*. Edited by John Bigelow. New York: Harper & Brothers, 1908. Google Books edition.

Timberlake, Richard H. *Monetary Policy in the United States: An Intellectual and Institutional History*. Chicago: University of Chicago Press, 1993.

Timmons, Bascom N. *Portrait of an American: Charles G. Dawes*. New York: Henry Holt, 1953.

Tindall, George B. *The Emergence of the New South, 1913–1945*. Baton Rouge: Louisiana State University Press, 1967.

Todd, Richard Cecil. *Confederate Finance*. Atlanta: University of Georgia Press, 2009.

Todd, Walker F. "History of and Rationales for the Reconstruction Finance Corporation." *Federal Reserve Bank of Cleveland Economic Review* (1992): 25. www.clevelandfed.org/research/review/1992/92-q4-todd.pdf.

Toll, Ian W. *Six Frigates: The Epic History of the Founding of the U.S. Navy*. New York: Norton, 2006.

Tompkins, C. David. *Senator Arthur H. Vandenberg: The Evolution of a Modern Republican, 1884–1945*. East Lansing: Michigan State University Press, 1970.

Toner, Robin. "Clinton Captures Presidency with Huge Electoral Margin; Wins a Democratic Congress." *New York Times*. November 4, 1992.

Toossi, Mitra. "A Century of Change: The U.S. Labor Force, 1950–2050." *Monthly Labor Review* (May 2002): 15–29. http://www.bls.gov/opub/mlr/2002/05/art2full.pdf.

"Treasury Secretary Says US Can't Afford Tax Cut." *Ocala Star-Banner* (Ocala, FL). March 19, 1962.

Truman, Harry S. "Address in Chicago on Army Day." April 6, 1946. *The American Presidency Project*. http://www.presidency.ucsb.edu/ws/?pid=12625.

———. *Off the Record: The Private Papers of Harry S. Truman*. Edited by Robert H. Ferrell. Columbia: University of Missouri Press, 1997. Google Books edition.

———. "Special Message to the Congress on Greece and Turkey: The Truman Doctrine." March 12, 1947. *The American Presidency Project*. http://www.presidency.ucsb.edu/ws/?pid=12846.

———. "Special Message to the Congress Recommending a 'Pay as We Go' Tax Program." February 2, 1951. *The American Presidency Project*. http://www.presidency.ucsb.edu/ws/?pid=13976.

———. "Statement by the President Announcing Revised Budget Estimates." April 11, 1946. *The American Presidency Project*. http://www.presidency.ucsb.edu/ws/?pid=12628.

———. "Statement by the President in Response to a Joint Announcement by the Treasury Department and the Federal Reserve System." March 3, 1951. Harry S. Truman Library and Museum. http://trumanlibrary.org/publicpapers/viewpapers.php?pid=261.

Tucker, Garland S., III. *The High Tide of American Conservatism: Davis, Coolidge, and the 1924 Election*. Austin: Emerald, 2010.

2005 Annual Report of the Boards of Trust of the Federal Hospital Insurance and Federal Supplementary Medical Insurance Trust Funds. March 23, 2005. http://www.cms.gov/Research-Statistics-Data-and-Systems/Statistics-Trends-and-Reports/ReportsTrustFunds/downloads/tr2005.pdf.

2013 Annual Report of the Board of Trustees of the Federal Old-Age and Survivors Insurance and Federal Disability Insurance Trust Funds. Social Security Administration. 2013. www.socialsecurity.gov/oact/tr/2013/tr2013.pdf.

2013 Annual Report of the Boards of Trustees of the Federal Hospital Insurance and Federal Supplementary Medical Insurance Trust Funds. http://downloads.cms. gov/files/TR2013.pdf.

Unger, Harlow Giles. *John Quincy Adams.* Cambridge, MA: Da Capo, 2012.

Ungar, Rick. "New Data Suggests Obamacare Is Actually Bending the Cost Curve." *Forbes.* February 12, 2013.

"U.S. Federal Individual Income Tax Rates History, 1862–2013 (Nominal and Inflation-Adjusted Brackets)." The Tax Foundation. 2013. http://taxfounda tion.org/article/us-federal-individual-income-tax-rates-history-1913–2013 -nominal-and-inflation-adjusted-brackets.

Van Buren, Martin. *The Autobiography of Martin Van Buren.* Edited by John Clement Fitzpatrick. Washington, DC: Government Printing Office, 1920.

———. "Special Session Message (September 4, 1837)." The Miller Center, University of Virginia. http://millercenter.org/ president/speeches/detail/3724.

Vandenberg, Arthur H. "The $47,000,000,000 Blight." *Saturday Evening Post* 209, no. 43 (April 24, 1937).

———. *The Private Papers of Senator Vandenberg.* Edited by Arthur H. Vandenberg Jr. Cambridge, MA: Riverside, 1952.

Van Deusen, Glyndon G. *The Jacksonian Era, 1828–1848.* Prospect Heights, IL: Waveland 1992.

Veblen, Thorstein. "The Price of Wheat Since 1867." *Journal of Political Economy* 1, no. 1 (December 1892).

Vethake, Henry. *The Principles of Political Economy.* Philadelphia: Nicklin & Johnson, Law Booksellers, 1838. Reprint, Charleston, SC: BiblioLife, 2009.

Vietor, Richard H. K. *How Countries Compete: Strategy, Structure, and Government in the Global Economy.* Boston: Harvard Business School Press, 2007.

Villard, Henry H. *Deficit Spending and National Income.* New York: Farrar & Rinehart, 1941.

Vladeck, Bruce C. *Unloving Care: The Nursing Home Tragedy.* New York: Basic Books, 1980.

Volcker, Paul, and Toyoo Gyohten. *Changing Fortunes: The World's Money and the Threat to American Leadership.* New York: Random House, 1992.

Walker, David M. *Comeback America: Turning the Country Around and Restoring Fiscal Responsibility.* New York: Random House, 2009.

Walker, Robert J. "Review of Our Finances, and of the Report of Hon. S. P. Chase, Secretary of the Treasury." *Continental Monthly.* December 19, 1862, 129–144.

Wallace, Henry A. *Sixty Million Jobs.* New York: Stratford, 1945.

Walters, Raymond, Jr. *Albert Gallatin: Jeffersonian Financier and Diplomat.* New York: Macmillan, 1957.

———. *Alexander James Dallas: Lawyer–Politician–Financier, 1759–1817.* Philadelphia: University of Pennsylvania Press, 1943.

Waltman, Jerold L. *Political Origins of the U.S. Income Tax*. Jackson: University Press of Mississippi, 1985.

Walton, Gary M., and Hugh Rockoff. *History of the American Economy*. 9th ed. Ft. Worth, TX: South-Western Educational, 2002.

Wanniski, Jude. *The Way the World Works*. Washington, DC: Regnery, 1998.

Washington, George. *The Papers of George Washington*. Charlottesville: University of Virginia, 2007.

Watkins, T. H. *Righteous Pilgrim: The Life and Times of Harold L. Ickes, 1874–1953*. New York: Henry Holt, 1990.

Watts, Steven. *The Republic Reborn: War and the Making of Liberal America, 1790–1820*. Baltimore: Johns Hopkins University Press, 1987.

Webber, Carolyn, and Aaron Wildavsky. *A History of Taxation and Expenditure in the Western World*. New York: Simon & Schuster, 1986.

Weinberger, Caspar W., and Gretchen Roberts. *In the Arena: A Memoir of the 20th Century*. Washington, DC: Regnery, 2001.

Weintraub, Stanley. *General Washington's Christmas Farewell: A Mount Vernon Homecoming, 1783*. New York: Plume, 2004.

Weisman, Steven R. *The Great Tax Wars: Lincoln to Wilson—The Fierce Battles over Money and Power That Transformed the Nation*. New York: Simon & Schuster, 2002.

Werner, Carrie A. *The Older Population: 2010*. Bureau of the Census. November 2011. http://www.census.gov/prod/cen2010/briefs/c2010br-09.pdf.

Wessel, David. *In Fed We Trust: Ben Bernanke's War on the Great Panic*. New York: Three Rivers, 2009.

———. "Inside Dr. Bernanke's E.R." *Wall Street Journal*. July 24, 2009.

———. *Red Ink: Inside the High-Stakes Politics of the Federal Budget*. New York: Crown Business, 2012.

Whalen, Christopher. *Inflated: How Money and Debt Built the American Dream*. Hoboken, NJ: John Wiley & Sons, 2011.

White, Joseph, and Aaron Wildavsky. *The Deficit and Public Interest: The Search for Responsible Budgeting in the 1980s*. Berkeley: University of California Press, 1989.

White, Richard. *Railroaded: The Transcontinentals and the Making of Modern America*. New York: Norton, 2011.

White, Thomas W., ed. "Biographical Notice of H. H. Brackenridge." *Southern Literary Messenger* 7, no. 1 (January 1842).

Wicker, Elmus. *Banking Panics of the Gilded Age*. Cambridge: Cambridge University Press, 2000.

Widmer, Ted. *Martin Van Buren*. New York: Times Books, 2005.

Wiebe, Robert H. *The Search for Order, 1877–1920*. New York: Hill and Wang, 1967.

Wilentz, Sean. *The Rise of American Democracy: Jefferson to Lincoln.* New York: Norton, 2005.

Williamson, Jeffrey G. "Watersheds and Turning Points: Conjectures on the Long-Term Impact of Civil War Financing." *Journal of Economic History* 34, no. 3 (1974): 636–661.

Willoughby, William F. *The Problem of a National Budget.* New York: Appleton, 1918.

Wilson, George C. *This War Really Matters: Inside the Fight for Defense Dollars.* Washington, DC: CQ Press, 2000.

Wilson, Joan Hoff. *Herbert Hoover: Forgotten Progressive.* Boston: Little, Brown, 1975.

Wilson, Woodrow. *Constitutional Government in the United States.* New Brunswick, NJ: Transaction Publishers, 2006. Google Books edition.

———. *A Day of Dedication: The Essential Writings and Speeches of Woodrow Wilson.* Edited by Albert Fried. London: Macmillan, 1965. Google Books edition.

Winik, Jay. *The Great Upheaval: America and the Birth of the Modern World, 1788–1800.* New York: HarperCollins, 2007.

Wirls, Daniel. *Buildup: The Politics of Defense in the Reagan Era.* Ithaca, NY: Cornell University Press, 1992.

Witte, John F. *The Politics and Development of the Federal Income Tax.* Madison: University of Wisconsin Press, 1986. Google Books edition.

Wood, Gordon S. *Empire of Liberty: A History of the Early Republic, 1789–1815.* Oxford: Oxford University Press, 2009.

Wooddy, Carroll Hill. *The Growth of the Federal Government, 1915–1932.* New York: McGraw-Hill, 1934.

Woodward, Bob. *The Agenda: Inside the Clinton White House.* New York: Simon & Schuster, 2005.

———. *Maestro: Greenspan's Fed and the American Boom.* New York: Simon & Schuster, 2000. Kindle edition.

———. *The Price of Politics.* New York: Simon & Schuster, 2012. Kindle edition.

———. *The War Within: A Secret White House History, 2006–2008.* New York: Simon & Schuster, 2008.

Wright, Robert E. *One Nation Under Debt: Hamilton, Jefferson, and the History of What We Owe.* New York: McGraw-Hill, 2008.

———, and David J. Cowen. *Financial Founding Fathers: The Men Who Made America Rich.* Chicago: University of Chicago Press, 2006.

Yarrow, Andrew L. *Forgive Us Our Debts: The Intergenerational Dangers of Fiscal Responsibility.* New Haven, CT: Yale University Press, 2008.

Zelizer, Julian E. *Governing America: The Revival of Political History.* Princeton, NJ: Princeton University Press, 2012. Google Books edition.

———. *Taxing America: Wilbur D. Mills, Congress, & the State, 1945–1975.* Cambridge: Cambridge University Press, 1998.

APPENDICES

Appendix A

US Treasury Debt, 1790–2013

[Millions of dollars, $US]

Year[1]	Gross Federal Debt[2]	Interest-Bearing Treasury Debt[3]	Federal Reserve Holdings of Treasury Debt[4]	Monetized Debt[5]	Net Unmonetized Debt[6]
1790	76	-	-	-	76
1791	77	-	-	-	77
1792	80	-	-	-	80
1793	78	-	-	-	78
1794	81	-	-	-	81
1795	84	-	-	-	84
1796	82	-	-	-	82
1797	79	-	-	-	79
1798	78	-	-	-	78
1799	83	-	-	-	83
1800	83	-	-	-	83
1801	81	-	-	-	81
1802	77	-	-	-	77
1803	86	-	-	-	86
1804	82	-	-	-	82
1805	76	-	-	-	76
1806	69	-	-	-	69
1807	65	-	-	-	65
1808	57	-	-	-	57
1809	53	-	-	-	53
1810	48	-	-	-	48
1811	45	-	-	-	45
1812	56	-	-	-	56
1813	82	-	-	-	82
1814	100	-	-	-	100
1815	127	-	-	-	127
1816	124	-	-	-	124
1817	104	-	-	-	104
1818	96	-	-	-	96
1819	91	-	-	-	91

Year[1]	Gross Federal Debt[2]	Interest-Bearing Treasury Debt[3]	Federal Reserve Holdings of Treasury Debt[4]	Monetized Debt[5]	Net Unmonetized Debt[6]
1820	90	-	-	-	90
1821	94	-	-	-	94
1822	91	-	-	-	91
1823	90	-	-	-	90
1824	84	-	-	-	84
1825	81	-	-	-	81
1826	74	-	-	-	74
1827	68	-	-	-	68
1828	58	-	-	-	58
1829	49	-	-	-	49
1830	39	-	-	-	39
1831	24	-	-	-	24
1832	7	-	-	-	7
1833	5	-	-	-	5
1834	0	-	-	-	0
1835	0	-	-	-	0
1836	0	-	-	-	0
1837	3	-	-	-	3
1838	10	-	-	-	10
1839	4	-	-	-	4
1840	5	-	-	-	5
1841	14	-	-	-	14
1842	20	-	-	-	20
1843	33	-	-	-	33
1844	24	-	-	-	24
1845	16	-	-	-	16
1846	16	-	-	-	16
1847	39	-	-	-	39
1848	47	-	-	-	47
1849	63	-	-	-	63
1850	64	-	-	-	64
1851	68	-	-	-	68
1852	66	-	-	-	66
1853	60	60	-	-	60
1854	42	42	-	-	42

Year[1]	Gross Federal Debt[2]	Interest-Bearing Treasury Debt[3]	Federal Reserve Holdings of Treasury Debt[4]	Monetized Debt[5]	Net Unmonetized Debt[6]
1855	36	35	-	-	35
1856	32	32	-	-	32
1857	29	29	-	-	29
1858	45	45	-	-	45
1859	59	58	-	-	58
1860	65	65	-	-	65
1861	91	90	-	-	90
1862	524	365	-	159	365
1863	1,120	708	-	412	708
1864	1,816	1,360	-	455	1,360
1865	2,678	2,218	-	458	2,218
1866	2,756	2,322	-	429	2,322
1867	2,650	2,239	-	409	2,239
1868	2,583	2,191	-	391	2,191
1869	2,545	2,151	-	389	2,151
1870	2,437	2,036	-	397	2,036
1871	2,322	1,921	-	399	1,921
1872	2,210	1,801	-	401	1,801
1873	2,151	1,696	-	403	1,696
1874	2,160	1,725	-	432	1,725
1875	2,156	1,709	-	436	1,709
1876	2,131	1,697	-	430	1,697
1877	2,108	1,698	-	393	1,698
1878	2,159	1,781	-	373	1,781
1879	2,299	1,888	-	374	1,888
1880	2,091	1,710	-	373	1,710
1881	2,019	1,626	-	387	1,626
1882	1,857	1,450	-	391	1,450
1883	1,722	1,324	-	390	1,324
1884	1,625	1,213	-	393	1,213
1885	1,579	1,182	-	392	1,182
1886	1,556	1,132	-	414	1,132
1887	1,466	1,008	-	452	1,008
1888	1,385	937	-	446	936
1889	1,250	816	-	432	816

Year[1]	Gross Federal Debt[2]	Interest-Bearing Treasury Debt[3]	Federal Reserve Holdings of Treasury Debt[4]	Monetized Debt[5]	Net Unmonetized Debt[6]
1890	1,122	711	-	409	711
1891	1,006	611	-	394	611
1892	968	585	-	380	585
1893	961	585	-	374	585
1894	1,017	635	-	380	635
1895	1,097	716	-	379	716
1896	1,223	847	-	374	847
1897	1,227	847	-	378	847
1898	1,233	847	-	384	847
1899	1,437	1,046	-	389	1,046
1900	1,263	1,023	-	239	1,023
1901	1,222	987	-	233	987
1902	1,178	931	-	246	931
1903	1,159	915	-	244	915
1904	1,136	895	-	239	895
1905	1,132	895	-	236	895
1906	1,143	895	-	246	895
1907	1,147	895	-	251	895
1908	1,178	898	-	276	898
1909	1,148	913	-	232	913
1910	1,147	913	-	231	913
1911	1,154	915	-	237	915
1912	1,194	964	-	228	964
1913	1,193	966	-	226	966
1914	1,188	968	-	219	968
1915	1,191	970	8	228	962
1916	1,225	972	57	309	914
1917	2,976	2,713	71	320	2,642
1918	12,455	12,198	259	497	11,939
1919	25,485	25,237	232	468	25,005
1920	24,299	24,063	336	566	23,726
1921	23,978	23,739	257	485	23,482
1922	22,963	22,710	557	784	22,154
1923	22,350	22,007	135	379	21,872
1924	21,251	20,981	431	670	20,550

Year[1]	Gross Federal Debt[2]	Interest-Bearing Treasury Debt[3]	Federal Reserve Holdings of Treasury Debt[4]	Monetized Debt[5]	Net Unmonetized Debt[6]
1925	20,516	20,211	353	628	19,858
1926	19,643	19,384	385	631	18,998
1927	18,512	18,253	370	615	17,883
1928	17,604	17,318	235	476	17,083
1929	16,931	16,639	216	457	16,423
1930	16,185	15,922	591	823	15,331
1931	16,801	16,520	668	898	15,852
1932	19,487	19,161	1,784	2,050	17,377
1933	22,539	22,158	1,998	2,313	20,160
1934	27,053	26,480	2,432	2,950	24,049
1935	28,701	27,645	2,433	3,258	25,212
1936	33,779	32,989	2,430	3,050	30,559
1937	36,425	35,800	2,526	3,032	33,274
1938	37,165	36,576	2,564	3,011	34,012
1939	40,440	39,886	2,551	2,962	37,335
1940	42,968	42,376	2,458	2,844	39,918
1941	48,961	48,387	2,180	2,549	46,207
1942	72,422	71,968	2,640	2,996	69,328
1943	136,696	135,380	7,149	8,324	128,231
1944	201,003	199,543	14,899	16,158	184,644
1945	258,682	256,357	21,792	23,849	234,565
1946	269,422	268,111	23,783	24,718	244,328
1947	258,286	255,113	21,872	24,814	233,241
1948	252,292	250,063	21,366	23,315	228,697
1949	252,770	250,762	19,343	21,107	231,419
1950	257,357	255,209	18,331	20,214	236,878
1951	255,222	252,852	22,982	24,840	229,870
1952	259,105	256,863	22,906	24,730	233,957
1953	266,071	263,946	24,746	26,573	239,200
1954	271,260	268,910	25,037	26,950	243,873
1955	274,374	271,741	23,607	25,651	248,134
1956	272,751	269,883	23,758	25,960	246,125
1957	270,527	268,486	23,035	24,547	245,451
1958	276,343	274,698	25,438	26,486	249,260
1959	284,706	281,833	26,044	28,440	255,789

Year[1]	Gross Federal Debt[2]	Interest-Bearing Treasury Debt[3]	Federal Reserve Holdings of Treasury Debt[4]	Monetized Debt[5]	Net Unmonetized Debt[6]
1960	286,331	283,241	26,523	29,168	256,718
1961	288,971	285,672	27,253	30,203	258,419
1962	298,201	294,442	29,663	32,984	264,779
1963	305,860	301,954	32,027	35,622	269,927
1964	311,713	307,357	34,794	38,855	272,563
1965	317,274	313,113	39,100	42,969	274,013
1966	319,907	315,431	42,169	46,337	273,262
1967	326,221	322,286	46,719	50,370	275,567
1968	347,578	344,401	52,230	55,154	292,171
1969	353,720	351,729	54,095	55,625	297,634
1970	370,919	369,026	57,714	59,241	311,312
1971	398,130	396,289	65,518	67,037	330,771
1972	427,260	425,360	71,426	72,947	353,933
1973	458,142	456,353	75,181	76,714	381,173
1974	475,060	473,238	80,648	82,193	392,590
1975	533,189	532,122	84,993	85,722	447,129
1976	620,433	619,254	94,714	95,433	524,540
1977	698,840	697,629	105,004	105,753	592,625
1978	771,544	766,971	115,480	116,266	651,491
1979	826,519	819,007	115,594	116,438	703,413
1980	907,701	906,402	120,846	121,752	785,556
1981	997,855	996,495	124,466	125,420	872,029
1982	1,142,034	1,140,883	134,497	135,228	1,006,386
1983	1,377,210	1,375,751	155,527	156,247	1,220,225
1984	1,572,266	1,559,570	155,122	155,812	1,404,448
1985	1,823,103	1,821,010	169,806	170,478	1,651,204
1986	2,125,303	2,122,684	190,855	191,532	1,931,829
1987	2,350,277	2,347,750	212,040	212,739	2,135,710
1988	2,602,338	2,599,877	229,218	229,933	2,370,660
1989	2,857,431	2,836,309	220,088	220,817	2,616,222
1990	3,233,313	3,210,943	234,410	235,168	2,976,533
1991	3,665,303	3,662,759	258,591	259,369	3,404,168
1992	4,064,621	4,061,801	296,397	297,239	3,765,404
1993	4,411,489	4,408,567	325,653	326,602	4,082,913
1994	4,692,750	4,689,524	355,150	356,258	4,334,375

Year[1]	Gross Federal Debt[2]	Interest-Bearing Treasury Debt[3]	Federal Reserve Holdings of Treasury Debt[4]	Monetized Debt[5]	Net Unmonetized Debt[6]
1995	4,973,983	4,950,644	374,114	375,423	4,576,529
1996	5,224,811	5,220,790	390,924	392,449	4,829,865
1997	5,413,146	5,407,528	424,518	426,397	4,983,010
1998	5,526,193	5,518,681	458,182	460,435	5,060,499
1999	5,656,271	5,647,241	496,644	499,292	5,150,597
2000	5,674,178	5,622,092	511,413	514,431	5,110,679
2001	5,807,463	5,762,186	534,135	537,639	5,228,051
2002	6,228,236	6,216,252	604,191	608,297	5,612,061
2003	6,783,231	6,769,795	656,116	660,492	6,113,679
2004	7,379,053	7,364,191	700,341	705,010	6,663,850
2005	7,932,710	7,913,715	736,360	741,574	7,177,355
2006	8,506,974	8,455,063	768,924	774,639	7,686,139
2007	9,007,653	8,959,209	779,632	785,758	8,179,577
2008	10,024,725	10,004,689	491,127	494,696	9,513,562
2009	11,909,829	11,891,535	769,160	770,626	11,122,375
2010	13,561,623	13,543,760	811,669	813,009	12,732,091
2011	14,790,340	14,772,741	1,664,660	1,666,041	13,108,081
2012	16,066,241	15,993,827	1,645,285	1,646,665	14,347,162
2013	16,738,184	16,720,634	NA	NA	NA

NOTES

1. Figures at the end of the fiscal year. For 1790–1842, fiscal years end December 31; for 1843–1976, fiscal years end June 30; from 1977 on, fiscal years end September 30.

2. Before 1970: Department of the Treasury, *Statistical Appendix* (1970), 60–61. After 1970: Department of the Treasury, Bureau of Public Debt, Monthly Statement (June editions prior to 1977 and September editions afterwards). For years except 1809, 1852, 1982, 1983, 1984, and 1986, this data is consistent with those found in Bureau of the Census, Historical Statistics (2006).

3. Interest-bearing debt for 1853–1980, Department of the Treasury, *Statistical Appendix* (1980), 61–63; for 1981–2011, Department of the Treasury, Bureau of Public Debt, Monthly Statement (September editions). Interest-bearing is not separately listed since 2001, but the figure can be calculated by subtracting (a) amounts in the "other" category of nonmarketable and matured but outstanding securities, from (b) "total public outstanding debt." A historical record of non–interest-bearing debt and matured debt still outstanding—which was used to verify the above methodology and calculations—can be found for 1790–1970 in Department of the Treasury, *Statistical Appendix* (1970), 60–61, and for 1971–2011, Department of the Treasury, Bureau of Public Debt, Monthly Statement (June editions prior to 1977 and September editions afterwards)

4. For 1915–1939: Federal Reserve Bulletin, various editions (1915–1920: August publication; 1920–1939: September publication). For 1915–1920, figures represent US debt holdings on different dates between June 28 through July 2. For 1940–2012: OMB, Historical Tables, "Table 7.1—Federal Debt at the End of Year: 1940–2018."

5. Monetized debt equals non–interest-bearing debt plus debt held by the Federal Reserve.

6. Net unmonetized debt equals gross federal debt minus matured debt minus monetized debt. That also equals interest-bearing US Treasury debt minus monetized debt.

APPENDIX B

Unmonetized Debt Compared to National Income and Tax Revenues, 1790–2012

[Millions of dollars, $US]

Year[1]	Unmonetized Debt[2]	Unmonetized Debt (% of GDP[3])	Federal Funds Revenues[4]	Federal Fund Revenues (% of Unmonetized Debt)
1790	76	39.9%	N/A	N/A
1791	77	37.5%	4	N/A[5]
1792	80	35.7%	4	4.6%
1793	78	31.2%	5	5.9%
1794	81	25.6%	5	6.7%
1795	84	21.9%	6	7.3%
1796	82	19.7%	8	10.2%
1797	79	19.4%	9	11.0%
1798	78	19.0%	8	10.1%
1799	83	18.8%	8	9.1%
1800	83	17.3%	11	13.1%
1801	81	15.7%	13	16.0%
1802	77	17.1%	15	19.5%
1803	86	17.7%	11	12.8%
1804	82	15.4%	12	14.4%
1805	76	13.5%	14	17.9%
1806	69	11.2%	16	22.5%
1807	65	11.1%	16	25.2%
1808	57	8.8%	17	29.9%
1809	53	7.7%	8	14.6%
1810	48	6.8%	9	19.6%
1811	45	5.9%	14	31.9%
1812	56	7.1%	10	17.5%
1813	82	8.4%	14	17.6%
1814	100	9.3%	11	11.2%
1815	127	13.8%	16	12.4%
1816	124	15.1%	48	38.6%
1817	104	13.5%	33	32.0%
1818	96	13.0%	22	22.6%

Year[1]	Unmonetized Debt[2]	Unmonetized Debt (% of GDP[3])	Federal Funds Revenues[4]	Federal Fund Revenues (% of Unmonetized Debt)
1819	91	12.5%	25	27.0%
1820	90	12.7%	18	19.9%
1821	94	12.7%	15	15.6%
1822	91	11.3%	20	22.3%
1823	90	11.9%	21	22.7%
1824	84	11.1%	19	23.1%
1825	81	9.9%	22	26.9%
1826	74	8.5%	25	34.1%
1827	68	7.4%	23	34.0%
1828	58	6.5%	25	42.4%
1829	49	5.2%	25	51.1%
1830	39	3.8%	25	63.5%
1831	24	2.3%	29	117.4%
1832	7	0.6%	32	455.2%
1833	5	0.4%	34	707.3%
1834	0	0.0%	22	57347.4%
1835	0	0.0%	35	93236.8%
1836	0	0.0%	51	15082.2%
1837	3	0.2%	25	756.2%
1838	10	0.7%	26	252.9%
1839	4	0.2%	31	874.5%
1840	5	0.3%	19	367.5%
1841	14	0.8%	17	124.0%
1842	20	1.2%	20	98.9%
1843	33	2.1%	8	25.4%
1844	24	1.4%	29	124.8%
1845	16	0.9%	30	188.5%
1846	16	0.8%	30	190.4%
1847	39	1.6%	26	68.3%
1848	47	1.9%	36	76.0%
1849	63	2.6%	31	49.5%
1850	64	2.5%	44	68.7%
1851	68	2.5%	53	77.0%
1852	66	2.2%	50	75.3%
1853	60	1.8%	62	103.3%

Year[1]	Unmonetized Debt[2]	Unmonetized Debt (% of GDP[3])	Federal Funds Revenues[4]	Federal Fund Revenues (% of Unmonetized Debt)
1854	42	1.1%	74	175.5%
1855	35	0.9%	65	184.5%
1856	32	0.8%	74	232.8%
1857	29	0.7%	69	242.0%
1858	45	1.1%	47	104.3%
1859	58	1.3%	53	91.7%
1860	65	1.5%	56	86.7%
1861	90	1.9%	42	45.9%
1862	365	6.3%	52	14.2%
1863	708	9.2%	113	15.9%
1864	1,360	14.2%	265	19.5%
1865	2,218	22.2%	334	15.0%
1866	2,322	25.6%	558	24.0%
1867	2,239	26.6%	491	21.9%
1868	2,191	26.6%	406	18.5%
1869	2,151	27.2%	371	17.2%
1870	2,036	26.1%	411	20.2%
1871	1,921	25.1%	383	20.0%
1872	1,801	21.7%	374	20.8%
1873	1,696	19.2%	334	19.7%
1874	1,725	20.1%	305	17.7%
1875	1,709	20.7%	288	16.9%
1876	1,697	20.2%	294	17.3%
1877	1,698	19.7%	281	16.6%
1878	1,781	21.0%	258	14.5%
1879	1,888	20.0%	274	14.5%
1880	1,710	16.3%	334	19.5%
1881	1,626	13.8%	361	22.2%
1882	1,450	11.8%	404	27.8%
1883	1,324	10.6%	398	30.1%
1884	1,213	10.2%	349	28.7%
1885	1,182	10.1%	324	27.4%
1886	1,132	9.2%	336	29.7%
1887	1,008	7.6%	371	36.9%
1888	936	6.7%	379	40.5%

Year[1]	Unmonetized Debt[2]	Unmonetized Debt (% of GDP[3])	Federal Funds Revenues[4]	Federal Fund Revenues (% of Unmonetized Debt)
1889	816	5.8%	387	47.4%
1890	711	4.7%	403	56.7%
1891	611	3.9%	393	64.3%
1892	585	3.5%	355	60.7%
1893	585	3.8%	386	66.0%
1894	635	4.4%	306	48.2%
1895	716	4.5%	325	45.3%
1896	847	5.4%	338	39.9%
1897	847	5.2%	348	41.0%
1898	847	4.6%	405	47.8%
1899	1,046	5.3%	516	49.3%
1900	1,023	4.9%	567	55.4%
1901	987	4.4%	588	59.5%
1902	931	3.8%	562	60.4%
1903	915	3.5%	562	61.4%
1904	895	3.5%	541	60.4%
1905	895	3.1%	544	60.8%
1906	895	2.9%	595	66.5%
1907	895	2.6%	666	74.4%
1908	898	3.0%	602	67.1%
1909	913	2.8%	604	66.2%
1910	913	2.7%	676	74.0%
1911	915	2.6%	702	76.7%
1912	964	2.6%	693	71.9%
1913	966	2.4%	714	74.0%
1914	968	2.6%	725	74.9%
1915	962	2.5%	683	71.0%
1916	914	1.8%	761	83.3%
1917	2,642	4.4%	1,101	41.7%
1918	11,939	15.6%	3,645	30.5%
1919	25,005	31.6%	5,130	20.5%
1920	23,726	26.6%	6,649	28.0%
1921	23,482	31.6%	5,571	23.7%
1922	22,154	29.9%	4,026	18.2%
1923	21,872	25.4%	3,853	17.6%

Year[1]	Unmonetized Debt[2]	Unmonetized Debt (% of GDP[3])	Federal Funds Revenues[4]	Federal Fund Revenues (% of Unmonetized Debt)
1924	20,550	23.4%	3,871	18.8%
1925	19,858	21.7%	3,641	18.3%
1926	18,998	19.4%	3,795	20.0%
1927	17,883	18.5%	4,013	22.4%
1928	17,083	17.4%	3,900	22.8%
1929	16,423	15.7%	3,862	23.5%
1930	15,331	16.6%	4,058	26.5%
1931	15,852	20.5%	3,116	19.7%
1932	17,377	29.2%	1,924	11.1%
1933	20,160	35.2%	1,997	9.9%
1934	24,049	36.0%	2,926	12.2%
1935	25,212	33.9%	3,578	14.2%
1936	30,559	36.0%	3,871	12.7%
1937	33,274	35.8%	4,794	14.4%
1938	34,012	38.9%	5,477	16.1%
1939	37,335	39.9%	4,822	12.9%
1940	39,918	38.8%	4,929	12.3%
1941	46,207	35.7%	6,900	14.9%
1942	69,328	41.8%	12,336	17.8%
1943	128,231	63.1%	21,117	16.5%
1944	184,644	82.2%	40,466	21.9%
1945	234,565	102.8%	41,875	17.9%
1946	244,328	107.3%	36,357	14.9%
1947	233,241	93.3%	35,380	15.2%
1948	228,697	83.2%	37,822	16.5%
1949	231,419	84.8%	35,849	15.5%
1950	236,878	78.9%	35,334	14.9%
1951	229,870	66.2%	46,183	20.1%
1952	233,957	63.6%	59,989	25.6%
1953	239,200	61.4%	63,085	26.4%
1954	243,873	62.4%	62,774	25.7%
1955	248,134	58.2%	58,168	23.4%
1956	246,125	54.7%	65,594	26.7%
1957	245,451	51.7%	68,847	28.0%
1958	249,260	51.7%	66,720	26.8%

Year[1]	Unmonetized Debt[2]	Unmonetized Debt (% of GDP[3])	Federal Funds Revenues[4]	Federal Fund Revenues (% of Unmonetized Debt)
1959	255,789	49.0%	65,800	25.7%
1960	256,718	47.3%	75,647	29.5%
1961	258,419	45.9%	75,175	29.1%
1962	264,779	43.8%	79,700	30.1%
1963	269,927	42.3%	84,013	31.1%
1964	272,563	39.7%	87,511	32.1%
1965	274,013	36.8%	90,943	33.2%
1966	273,262	33.5%	101,428	37.1%
1967	275,567	32.0%	111,835	40.6%
1968	292,171	31.0%	114,726	39.3%
1969	297,634	29.2%	143,322	48.2%
1970	311,312	28.9%	143,159	46.0%
1971	330,771	28.3%	133,785	40.4%
1972	353,933	27.6%	148,846	42.1%
1973	381,173	26.7%	161,357	42.3%
1974	392,590	25.3%	181,228	46.2%
1975	447,129	26.5%	187,505	41.9%
1976	524,540	27.9%	201,099	38.3%
1977	592,625	28.4%	241,312	40.7%
1978	651,491	27.6%	270,490	41.5%
1979	703,413	26.7%	316,366	45.0%
1980	785,556	27.4%	350,856	44.7%
1981	872,029	27.2%	410,422	47.1%
1982	1,006,386	30.1%	409,253	40.7%
1983	1,220,225	33.5%	382,432	31.3%
1984	1,404,448	34.8%	420,391	29.9%
1985	1,651,204	38.0%	460,307	27.9%
1986	1,931,829	42.1%	474,123	24.5%
1987	2,135,710	43.9%	538,705	25.2%
1988	2,370,660	45.1%	561,446	23.7%
1989	2,616,222	46.2%	615,320	23.5%
1990	2,976,533	49.8%	635,937	21.4%
1991	3,404,168	55.1%	641,618	18.8%
1992	3,765,404	57.6%	656,339	17.4%
1993	4,082,913	59.4%	705,523	17.3%

Year[1]	Unmonetized Debt[2]	Unmonetized Debt (% of GDP[3])	Federal Funds Revenues[4]	Federal Fund Revenues (% of Unmonetized Debt)
1994	4,334,375	59.3%	775,095	17.9%
1995	4,576,529	59.7%	838,922	18.3%
1996	4,829,865	59.6%	917,242	19.0%
1997	4,983,010	57.9%	1,010,435	20.3%
1998	5,060,499	55.7%	1,113,614	22.0%
1999	5,150,597	53.3%	1,164,569	22.6%
2000	5,110,679	49.7%	1,325,979	25.9%
2001	5,228,051	49.2%	1,256,733	24.0%
2002	5,612,061	51.1%	1,109,164	19.8%
2003	6,113,679	53.1%	1,025,357	16.8%
2004	6,663,850	54.3%	1,101,077	16.5%
2005	7,177,355	54.8%	1,310,397	18.3%
2006	7,686,139	55.5%	1,517,766	19.7%
2007	8,179,577	56.5%	1,661,404	20.3%
2008	9,513,562	64.6%	1,571,828	16.5%
2009	11,122,375	77.1%	1,166,960	10.5%
2010	12,732,091	85.1%	1,248,560	9.8%
2011	13,108,086	84.4%	1,431,513	10.9%
2012	14,347,162	88.3%	1,545,860	10.8%

NOTES

1. Debt and federal fund receipt figures are based on fiscal years (see Footnote 1 of Appendix A). GDP figures are for calendar years. For comparison with GDP in fiscal years since 1940, use OMB, Historical Tables, "Table 10.1."

2. Appendix A.

3. GDP from Measuring Worth, http://www.measuringworth.com (accessed October 10, 2013).

4. See Appendix C, note 2.

5. Data for 1791 includes the data for 1789–1791.

AUTHOR'S NOTE

The burden of a particular amount of debt should always be measured against something else, principally the value of the currency and the ability to pay. A public debt of $54 million may seem small today, but it was large in relation to the purchasing power of the dollar and national income in 1790.

This appendix compares unmonetized debt with the levels of both national income and federal funds revenues. Those revenues are the only ultimate source of payment of debt.

Frequently budget commentators refer to "debt owed to the public as a percentage of national income." That percentage grossly understates the burden of debt on taxpayers, since the numerator—"debt held by the public"—excludes debt owed to trust funds. Debt owed to trust funds is a real claim on federal funds revenues. To understand why, consider the accounting if trust funds exchanged their holdings of federal debt for an equivalent amount of debt issued by large corporations, state and local governments, and foreign governments. Even though the "debt held by the public" would appear to soar, the amount owed by the US Treasury—the claim on federal funds revenues—would not change.

National income, commonly measured as Gross Domestic Product or GDP, is an artificially large measure of the capacity to repay debt. GDP includes the value of estimated output that will not be available to service debt, such as black market activities or earnings from certain foreign operations that pay taxes abroad. In addition, there would be little economic activity if the government confiscated all income to pay debt service, and a revolution would occur well before then.

As shown in Appendices G and H, since World War II there are distinct limits to the amount of federal revenues that Americans are willing to pay. A relatively small share of all American households pays most of the taxes available for debt service. In 2010, for example, 13.8 million households—10 percent of households filing tax returns—paid for 71 percent of personal income tax revenues. See McBride, "Summary of Latest Federal Income Tax Data." Regardless of whether one considers the progressive tax system to be fair or unfair, as a matter of math a tax system based principally on the ability to pay will—by definition—rest on a somewhat smaller tax base to service debt.

APPENDIX C

Federal Funds Revenues, Outlays, and Surplus/Deficit
1789–2013

Year[1]	Federal Funds Revenues[2]	Federal Funds Outlays[3]	Surplus / (Deficit)	Federal Funds Revenues	Federal Funds Outlays	Surplus / Deficit
	[Thousands of dollars, $US]			[As percentage of GDP[4]]		
1789–91	4,419	4,269	150	1.1%	1.1%	0.0%
1792	3,670	5,080	(1,410)	1.6%	2.3%	–0.6%
1793	4,653	4,482	171	1.9%	1.8%	0.1%
1794	5,432	6,991	(1,559)	1.7%	2.2%	–0.5%
1795	6,115	7,540	(1,425)	1.6%	2.0%	–0.4%
1796	8,378	5,727	2,651	2.0%	1.4%	0.6%
1797	8,689	6,134	2,555	2.1%	1.5%	0.6%
1798	7,900	7,677	223	1.9%	1.9%	0.1%
1799	7,547	9,666	(2,119)	1.7%	2.2%	–0.5%
1800	10,849	10,786	63	2.3%	2.2%	0.0%
1801	12,935	9,395	3,540	2.5%	1.8%	0.7%
1802	14,996	7,862	7,134	3.3%	1.7%	1.6%
1803	11,064	7,852	3,212	2.3%	1.6%	0.7%
1804	11,826	8,719	3,107	2.2%	1.6%	0.6%
1805	13,561	10,506	3,055	2.4%	1.9%	0.5%
1806	15,560	9,804	5,756	2.5%	1.6%	0.9%
1807	16,398	8,354	8,044	2.8%	1.4%	1.4%
1808	17,061	9,932	7,129	2.6%	1.5%	1.1%
1809	7,773	10,281	(2,508)	1.1%	1.5%	–0.4%
1810	9,384	8,157	1,227	1.3%	1.2%	0.2%
1811	14,424	8,058	6,366	1.9%	1.1%	0.8%
1812	9,801	20,281	(10,480)	1.2%	2.6%	–1.3%
1813	14,340	31,682	(17,342)	1.5%	3.3%	–1.8%
1814	11,182	34,721	(23,539)	1.0%	3.2%	–2.2%
1815	15,729	32,708	(16,979)	1.7%	3.5%	–1.8%
1816	47,678	30,587	17,091	5.8%	3.7%	2.1%
1817	33,099	21,844	11,255	4.3%	2.8%	1.5%
1818	21,585	19,825	1,760	2.9%	2.7%	0.2%
1819	24,603	21,464	3,139	3.4%	3.0%	0.4%
1820	17,881	18,261	(380)	2.5%	2.6%	–0.1%

Year[1]	Federal Funds Revenues[2]	Federal Funds Outlays[3]	Surplus / (Deficit)	Federal Funds Revenues	Federal Funds Outlays	Surplus / Deficit
	[Thousands of dollars, $US]			[As percentage of GDP[4]]		
1821	14,573	15,811	(1,238)	2.0%	2.2%	−0.2%
1822	20,232	15,000	5,232	2.5%	1.9%	0.6%
1823	20,541	14,707	5,834	2.7%	1.9%	0.8%
1824	19,381	20,327	(946)	2.6%	2.7%	−0.1%
1825	21,841	15,857	5,984	2.7%	1.9%	0.7%
1826	25,260	17,036	8,224	2.9%	2.0%	0.9%
1827	22,966	16,139	6,827	2.5%	1.8%	0.7%
1828	24,764	16,395	8,369	2.8%	1.8%	0.9%
1829	24,828	15,203	9,625	2.7%	1.6%	1.0%
1830	24,844	15,143	9,701	2.4%	1.5%	0.9%
1831	28,527	15,248	13,279	2.7%	1.4%	1.3%
1832	31,866	17,289	14,577	2.8%	1.5%	1.3%
1833	33,948	23,018	10,930	2.9%	2.0%	0.9%
1834	21,792	18,628	3,164	1.8%	1.5%	0.3%
1835	35,430	17,573	17,857	2.6%	1.3%	1.3%
1836	50,827	30,868	19,959	3.4%	2.1%	1.3%
1837	24,954	37,243	(12,289)	1.6%	2.4%	−0.8%
1838	26,303	33,865	(7,562)	1.6%	2.1%	−0.5%
1839	31,483	26,899	4,584	1.9%	1.6%	0.3%
1840	19,480	24,318	(4,838)	1.2%	1.5%	−0.3%
1841	16,860	26,566	(9,706)	1.0%	1.6%	−0.6%
1842	19,976	25,206	(5,230)	1.2%	1.6%	−0.3%
1843	8,303	11,858	(3,555)	0.5%	0.8%	−0.2%
1844	29,321	22,338	6,983	1.7%	1.3%	0.4%
1845	29,970	22,937	7,033	1.6%	1.2%	0.4%
1846	29,700	27,767	1,933	1.4%	1.3%	0.1%
1847	26,496	57,281	(30,785)	1.1%	2.4%	−1.3%
1848	35,736	45,377	(9,641)	1.5%	1.9%	−0.4%
1849	31,208	45,052	(13,844)	1.3%	1.9%	−0.6%
1850	43,603	39,543	4,060	1.7%	1.5%	0.2%
1851	52,559	47,709	4,850	1.9%	1.8%	0.2%
1852	49,847	44,195	5,652	1.6%	1.4%	0.2%
1853	61,587	48,184	13,403	1.9%	1.5%	0.4%
1854	73,800	58,045	15,755	2.0%	1.6%	0.4%
1855	65,351	59,743	5,608	1.6%	1.5%	0.1%

Year[1]	Federal Funds Revenues[2]	Federal Funds Outlays[3]	Surplus / (Deficit)	Federal Funds Revenues	Federal Funds Outlays	Surplus / Deficit
	[Thousands of dollars, $US]			[As percentage of GDP[4]]		
1856	74,057	69,571	4,486	1.8%	1.7%	0.1%
1857	68,965	67,796	1,169	1.6%	1.6%	0.0%
1858	46,655	74,185	(27,530)	1.1%	1.8%	−0.7%
1859	53,486	69,071	(15,585)	1.2%	1.6%	−0.4%
1860	56,065	63,131	(7,066)	1.3%	1.4%	−0.2%
1861	41,510	66,547	(25,037)	0.9%	1.4%	−0.5%
1862	51,987	474,762	(422,775)	0.9%	8.1%	−7.2%
1863	112,697	714,741	(602,044)	1.5%	9.3%	−7.8%
1864	264,627	865,323	(600,696)	2.8%	9.1%	−6.3%
1865	333,715	1,297,555	(963,840)	3.3%	13.0%	−9.7%
1866	558,033	520,809	37,224	6.1%	5.7%	0.4%
1867	490,634	357,543	133,091	5.8%	4.2%	1.6%
1868	405,638	377,340	28,298	4.9%	4.6%	0.3%
1869	370,944	322,865	48,079	4.7%	4.1%	0.6%
1870	411,255	309,654	101,601	5.3%	4.0%	1.3%
1871	383,324	292,177	91,147	5.0%	3.8%	1.2%
1872	374,107	277,518	96,589	4.5%	3.3%	1.2%
1873	333,738	290,345	43,393	3.8%	3.3%	0.5%
1874	304,979	302,634	2,345	3.6%	3.5%	0.0%
1875	288,000	274,623	13,377	3.5%	3.3%	0.2%
1876	294,096	265,101	28,995	3.5%	3.2%	0.3%
1877	281,406	241,334	40,072	3.3%	2.8%	0.5%
1878	257,764	236,964	20,800	3.0%	2.8%	0.2%
1879	273,827	266,948	6,879	2.9%	2.8%	0.1%
1880	333,527	267,643	65,884	3.2%	2.6%	0.6%
1881	360,782	260,713	100,069	3.1%	2.2%	0.9%
1882	403,525	257,981	145,544	3.3%	2.1%	1.2%
1883	398,288	265,408	132,880	3.2%	2.1%	1.1%
1884	348,520	244,126	104,394	2.9%	2.1%	0.9%
1885	323,691	260,227	63,464	2.8%	2.2%	0.5%
1886	336,440	242,483	93,957	2.7%	2.0%	0.8%
1887	371,403	267,932	103,471	2.8%	2.0%	0.8%
1888	379,266	267,925	111,341	2.7%	1.9%	0.8%
1889	387,050	299,289	87,761	2.8%	2.1%	0.6%
1890	403,081	318,041	85,040	2.6%	2.1%	0.6%

Year[1]	Federal Funds Revenues[2]	Federal Funds Outlays[3]	Surplus / (Deficit)	Federal Funds Revenues	Federal Funds Outlays	Surplus / Deficit
	[Thousands of dollars, $US]			[As percentage of GDP[4]]		
1891	392,612	365,774	26,838	2.5%	2.4%	0.2%
1892	354,938	345,023	9,915	2.1%	2.1%	0.1%
1893	385,820	383,478	2,342	2.5%	2.5%	0.0%
1894	306,355	367,525	(61,170)	2.1%	2.6%	–0.4%
1895	324,729	356,195	(31,466)	2.1%	2.3%	–0.2%
1896	338,142	352,179	(14,037)	2.2%	2.3%	–0.1%
1897	347,722	365,774	(18,052)	2.1%	2.2%	–0.1%
1898	405,321	443,369	(38,048)	2.2%	2.4%	–0.2%
1899	515,961	605,072	(89,111)	2.6%	3.1%	–0.5%
1900	567,241	520,861	46,380	2.7%	2.5%	0.2%
1901	587,685	524,617	63,068	2.6%	2.3%	0.3%
1902	562,478	485,234	77,244	2.3%	2.0%	0.3%
1903	561,881	517,006	44,875	2.1%	2.0%	0.2%
1904	541,087	583,660	(42,573)	2.1%	2.3%	–0.2%
1905	544,275	567,279	(23,004)	1.9%	2.0%	–0.1%
1906	594,984	570,202	24,782	1.9%	1.8%	0.1%
1907	665,860	579,129	86,731	1.9%	1.7%	0.3%
1908	601,862	659,196	(57,334)	2.0%	2.2%	–0.2%
1909	604,320	693,744	(89,424)	1.9%	2.1%	–0.3%
1910	675,512	693,617	(18,105)	2.0%	2.1%	–0.1%
1911	701,833	691,202	10,631	2.0%	2.0%	0.0%
1912	692,609	689,881	2,728	1.8%	1.8%	0.0%
1913	714,463	714,864	(401)	1.8%	1.8%	0.0%
1914	725,117	725,525	(408)	2.0%	2.0%	0.0%
1915	683,417	746,093	(62,676)	1.8%	1.9%	–0.2%
1916	761,445	712,967	48,478	1.5%	1.4%	0.1%
1917	1,100,500	1,953,857	(853,357)	1.8%	3.2%	–1.4%
1918	3,645,240	12,677,359	(9,032,119)	4.8%	16.6%	–11.8%
1919	5,130,042	18,492,665	(13,362,623)	6.5%	23.4%	–16.9%
1920	6,648,898	6,357,677	291,221	7.5%	7.1%	0.3%
1921	5,570,790	5,061,785	509,005	7.5%	6.8%	0.7%
1922	4,025,901	3,289,404	736,497	5.4%	4.4%	1.0%
1923	3,852,795	3,140,287	712,508	4.5%	3.6%	0.8%
1924	3,871,214	2,907,847	963,367	4.4%	3.3%	1.1%
1925	3,640,805	2,923,762	717,043	4.0%	3.2%	0.8%

Year[1]	Federal Funds Revenues[2]	Federal Funds Outlays[3]	Surplus / (Deficit)	Federal Funds Revenues	Federal Funds Outlays	Surplus / Deficit
	[Thousands of dollars, $US]			*[As percentage of GDP[4]]*		
1926	3,795,108	2,929,964	865,144	3.9%	3.0%	0.9%
1927	4,012,794	2,857,429	1,155,365	4.2%	3.0%	1.2%
1928	3,900,329	2,961,245	939,084	4.0%	3.0%	1.0%
1929	3,861,589	3,127,199	734,390	3.7%	3.0%	0.7%
1930	4,057,884	3,320,211	737,673	4.4%	3.6%	0.8%
1931	3,115,557	3,577,434	(461,877)	4.0%	4.6%	−0.6%
1932	1,923,892	4,659,182	(2,735,290)	3.2%	7.8%	−4.6%
1933	1,996,844	4,598,496	(2,601,652)	3.5%	8.0%	−4.5%
1934	2,926,000	6,558,000	(3,632,000)	4.4%	9.8%	−5.4%
1935	3,578,000	6,427,000	(2,849,000)	4.8%	8.7%	−3.8%
1936	3,871,000	8,335,000	(4,464,000)	4.6%	9.8%	−5.3%
1937	4,794,000	7,620,000	(2,826,000)	5.2%	8.2%	−3.0%
1938	5,477,000	6,689,000	(1,212,000)	6.3%	7.7%	−1.4%
1939	4,822,000	8,718,000	(3,896,000)	5.2%	9.3%	−4.2%
1940	4,929,000	8,974,000	(4,045,000)	4.8%	8.7%	−3.9%
1941	6,900,000	13,260,000	(6,360,000)	5.3%	10.2%	−4.9%
1942	12,336,000	34,831,000	(22,495,000)	7.4%	21.0%	−13.6%
1943	21,117,000	78,765,000	(57,648,000)	10.4%	38.8%	−28.4%
1944	40,466,000	92,284,000	(51,818,000)	18.0%	41.1%	−23.1%
1945	41,875,000	94,846,000	(52,971,000)	18.4%	41.6%	−23.2%
1946	36,357,000	56,204,000	(19,847,000)	16.0%	24.7%	−8.7%
1947	35,380,000	34,803,000	577,000	14.2%	13.9%	0.2%
1948	37,822,000	28,988,000	8,834,000	13.8%	10.5%	3.2%
1949	35,849,000	37,686,000	(1,837,000)	13.1%	13.8%	−0.7%
1950	35,334,000	38,389,000	(3,055,000)	11.8%	12.8%	−1.0%
1951	46,183,000	43,732,000	2,451,000	13.3%	12.6%	0.7%
1952	59,989,000	64,994,000	(5,005,000)	16.3%	17.7%	−1.4%
1953	63,085,000	73,006,000	(9,921,000)	16.2%	18.7%	−2.5%
1954	62,774,000	65,924,000	(3,150,000)	16.1%	16.9%	−0.8%
1955	58,168,000	62,341,000	(4,173,000)	13.6%	14.6%	−1.0%
1956	65,594,000	64,281,000	1,313,000	14.6%	14.3%	0.3%
1957	68,847,000	67,189,000	1,658,000	14.5%	14.1%	0.3%
1958	66,720,000	69,737,000	(3,017,000)	13.8%	14.5%	−0.6%
1959	65,800,000	77,071,000	(11,271,000)	12.6%	14.8%	−2.2%
1960	75,647,000	74,856,000	791,000	13.9%	13.8%	0.1%

Year[1]	Federal Funds Revenues[2]	Federal Funds Outlays[3]	Surplus / (Deficit)	Federal Funds Revenues	Federal Funds Outlays	Surplus / Deficit
	[Thousands of dollars, $US]			[As percentage of GDP[4]]		
1961	75,175,000	79,368,000	(4,193,000)	13.3%	14.1%	−0.7%
1962	79,700,000	86,546,000	(6,846,000)	13.2%	14.3%	−1.1%
1963	84,013,000	90,643,000	(6,630,000)	13.2%	14.2%	−1.0%
1964	87,511,000	96,098,000	(8,587,000)	12.8%	14.0%	−1.3%
1965	90,943,000	94,853,000	(3,910,000)	12.2%	12.8%	−0.5%
1966	101,428,000	106,592,000	(5,164,000)	12.4%	13.1%	−0.6%
1967	111,835,000	127,544,000	(15,709,000)	13.0%	14.8%	−1.8%
1968	114,726,000	143,100,000	(28,374,000)	12.2%	15.2%	−3.0%
1969	143,322,000	148,192,000	(4,870,000)	14.1%	14.5%	−0.5%
1970	143,159,000	156,327,000	(13,168,000)	13.3%	14.5%	−1.2%
1971	133,785,000	163,681,000	(29,896,000)	11.5%	14.0%	−2.6%
1972	148,846,000	178,142,000	(29,296,000)	11.6%	13.9%	−2.3%
1973	161,357,000	187,040,000	(25,683,000)	11.3%	13.1%	−1.8%
1974	181,228,000	201,372,000	(20,144,000)	11.7%	13.0%	−1.3%
1975	187,505,000	248,169,000	(60,664,000)	11.1%	14.7%	−3.6%
1976	201,099,000	277,236,000	(76,137,000)	10.7%	14.8%	−4.1%
1977	241,312,000	304,467,000	(63,155,000)	11.6%	14.6%	−3.0%
1978	270,490,000	342,366,000	(71,876,000)	11.5%	14.5%	−3.0%
1979	316,366,000	375,427,000	(59,061,000)	12.0%	14.3%	−2.2%
1980	350,856,000	433,487,000	(82,631,000)	12.3%	15.1%	−2.9%
1981	410,422,000	496,213,000	(85,791,000)	12.8%	15.5%	−2.7%
1982	409,253,000	543,473,000	(134,220,000)	12.2%	16.2%	−4.0%
1983	382,432,000	613,306,000	(230,874,000)	10.5%	16.9%	−6.3%
1984	420,391,000	638,663,000	(218,272,000)	10.4%	15.8%	−5.4%
1985	460,307,000	726,764,000	(266,457,000)	10.6%	16.7%	−6.1%
1986	474,123,000	757,243,000	(283,120,000)	10.3%	16.5%	−6.2%
1987	538,705,000	761,053,000	(222,348,000)	11.1%	15.6%	−4.6%
1988	561,446,000	814,348,000	(252,902,000)	10.7%	15.5%	−4.8%
1989	615,320,000	891,441,000	(276,121,000)	10.9%	15.8%	−4.9%
1990	635,937,000	977,118,000	(341,181,000)	10.6%	16.3%	−5.7%
1991	641,618,000	1,022,590,000	(380,972,000)	10.4%	16.6%	−6.2%
1992	656,339,000	1,042,678,000	(386,339,000)	10.0%	15.9%	−5.9%
1993	705,523,000	1,060,960,000	(355,437,000)	10.3%	15.4%	−5.2%
1994	775,095,000	1,073,602,000	(298,507,000)	10.6%	14.7%	−4.1%
1995	838,922,000	1,102,133,000	(263,211,000)	10.9%	14.4%	−3.4%

Year[1]	Federal Funds Revenues[2]	Federal Funds Outlays[3]	Surplus / (Deficit)	Federal Funds Revenues	Federal Funds Outlays	Surplus / Deficit
	[Thousands of dollars, $US]			[As percentage of GDP[4]]		
1996	917,242,000	1,139,294,000	(222,052,000)	11.3%	14.1%	−2.7%
1997	1,010,435,000	1,158,261,000	(147,826,000)	11.7%	13.5%	−1.7%
1998	1,113,614,000	1,205,541,000	(91,927,000)	12.3%	13.3%	−1.0%
1999	1,164,569,000	1,251,689,000	(87,120,000)	12.0%	12.9%	−0.9%
2000	1,325,979,000	1,324,350,000	1,629,000	12.9%	12.9%	0.0%
2001	1,256,733,000	1,357,246,000	(100,513,000)	11.8%	12.8%	−0.9%
2002	1,109,164,000	1,469,320,000	(360,156,000)	10.1%	13.4%	−3.3%
2003	1,025,357,000	1,581,334,000	(555,977,000)	8.9%	13.7%	−4.8%
2004	1,101,077,000	1,706,442,000	(605,365,000)	9.0%	13.9%	−4.9%
2005	1,310,397,000	1,865,490,000	(555,093,000)	10.0%	14.2%	−4.2%
2006	1,517,766,000	2,055,037,000	(537,271,000)	11.0%	14.8%	−3.9%
2007	1,661,404,000	2,070,799,000	(409,395,000)	11.5%	14.3%	−2.8%
2008	1,571,828,000	2,296,449,000	(724,621,000)	10.7%	15.6%	−4.9%
2009	1,166,960,000	2,706,938,000	(1,539,978,000)	8.1%	18.8%	−10.7%
2010	1,248,560,000	2,665,399,000	(1,416,821,000)	8.3%	17.8%	−9.5%
2011	1,431,513,000	2,828,155,000	(1,396,642,000)	9.2%	18.2%	−9.0%
2012	1,545,860,000	2,722,687,000	(1,176,827,000)	9.5%	16.7%	−7.2%
2013	1,700,877,000	2,741,429,000	(1,040,522,000)	NA	NA	NA

NOTES

1. Receipts and expenditures are for fiscal years (see note 1 of Appendix A). GDP figures are for calendar year. GDP for 1789–1791 only includes data for 1790 and 1791.

2. For 1789–1933, see Department of the Treasury, *Statistical Appendix* (1970), 8–13. For 1934–2011, see OMB, Historical Tables, "Table 1.4—Receipts, Outlays, and Surpluses or Deficits (-) by Fund Group: 1934–2018." Figures for 2013 appear as estimates.

3. For 1789–1933, see Department of the Treasury, *Statistical Appendix* (1970), 8–13. For 1934–2011, see OMB, Historical Tables, "Table 1.4—Receipts, Outlays, and Surpluses or Deficits (-) by Fund Group: 1934–2018." Figures for 2013 appear as estimates.

4. See Appendix B, note 3.

APPENDIX D

Foreign Holdings of US Debt, 1976–2011

[Billions of dollars, $US]

Year[1]	Foreign and International[2]	Change yr-over-yr, $	Change yr-over-yr, %	Total Privately Held Debt[3]	Foreign Ownership as % of Total Privately Held Debt
1976	78.1	–	–	409.5	19.1%
1977	109.6	31.5	40.3%	461.3	23.8%
1978	133.1	23.5	21.4%	508.6	26.2%
1979	119.0	–14.1	–10.6%	540.5	22.0%
1980	129.7	10.7	9.0%	616.4	21.0%
1981	136.6	6.9	5.3%	694.5	19.7%
1982	149.5	12.9	9.4%	848.4	17.6%
1983	166.3	16.8	11.2%	1,022.6	16.3%
1984	205.9	39.6	23.8%	1,212.5	17.0%
1985	224.8	18.9	9.2%	1,417.2	15.9%
1986	263.4	38.6	17.2%	1,602.0	16.4%
1987	299.7	36.3	13.8%	1,731.4	17.3%
1988	362.2	62.5	20.9%	1,858.5	19.5%
1989	391.8	29.6	8.2%	1,958.3	20.0%
1990	463.8	72.0	18.4%	2,207.3	21.0%
1991	506.3	42.5	9.2%	2,498.4	20.3%
1992	562.8	56.5	11.2%	2,782.2	20.2%
1993	619.1	56.3	10.0%	2,989.3	20.7%
1994	682.0	62.9	10.2%	3,130.0	21.8%
1995	820.4	138.4	20.3%	3,286.0	25.0%
1996	993.4	173.0	21.1%	3,393.2	29.3%
1997	1,230.5	237.1	23.9%	3,401.6	36.2%
1998	1,224.2	–6.3	–0.5%	3,313.2	36.9%
1999	1,281.4	57.2	4.7%	3,175.4	40.4%
2000	1,038.8	–242.6	–18.9%	2,936.3	35.4%
2001	992.2	–46.6	–4.5%	2,779.7	35.7%
2002	1,188.6	196.4	19.8%	2,924.8	40.6%
2003	1,443.3	254.7	21.4%	3,267.9	44.2%
2004	1,794.5	351.2	24.3%	3,607.1	49.7%

Year[1]	Foreign and International[2]	Change yr-over-yr, $	Change yr-over-yr, %	Total Privately Held Debt[3]	Foreign Ownership as % of Total Privately Held Debt
2005	1,929.6	135.1	7.5%	3,864.9	49.9%
2006	2,025.3	95.7	5.0%	4,074.2	49.7%
2007	2,235.3	210.0	10.4%	4,269.7	52.4%
2008	2,802.4	567.1	25.4%	5,332.0	52.6%
2009	3,570.6	768.2	27.4%	6,782.7	52.6%
2010	4,324.2	753.6	21.1%	8,211.1	52.7%
2011	4,904.6	580.4	13.4%	8,462.4	58.0%

NOTES

1. Calendar year-end figure for 1976–1988. Fiscal year ending September 30 for 1989–2011.

2. Years 1976–1988 from Council of Economic Advisors, *Economic Report of the President* (1995), Table B-89 at 378. Years 1989–1997 from Council of Economic Advisors, *Economic Report of the President* (2000), Table B-87 at 408. Years 1998–2010 from Council of Economic Advisors, Economic Report of the President (2012), Table B-89 at 422. Year 2011 data from Department of Treasury, "Treasury International Capital System." NB: Includes nonmarketable foreign series, Treasury securities, and Treasury deposit funds. Excludes Treasury securities held under repurchase agreements in custody accounts at the Federal Reserve Bank of New York. Estimates reflect benchmarks to this series at differing intervals. For further detail, see Department of Treasury, "Treasury International Capital System." http://www.treasury.gov/resource-center/data-chart-center/tic/Documents/mfh.txt.

3. Same as above except 2011, which is from the *Economic Report of the President (2012)*. Note that privately held debt excludes Federal Reserve and intragovernmental holdings.

Appendix E

US State and Local Debt, 1970–2009[1]

[Millions of dollars, $US]

Year	State & Local	State	Local	% of Unmonetized Federal Debt[2]
1970	143,571	42,008	101,563	46.06%
1971	158,827	47,793	111,034	47.97%
1972	175,158	54,453	120,705	49.44%
1973	188,485	59,375	129,110	49.42%
1974	206,616	65,296	141,320	52.59%
1975	219,925	72,127	147,798	49.15%
1976	240,532	84,825	155,707	45.82%
1977	259,658	90,200	169,458	43.78%
1978	280,433	102,569	177,864	42.80%
1979	304,103	111,740	192,363	42.83%
1980	335,603	121,958	213,645	42.70%
1981	363,892	134,847	229,045	41.71%
1982	404,579	147,470	257,109	40.18%
1983	454,501	167,290	287,211	37.22%
1984	506,330	186,377	319,953	35.75%
1985	568,633	211,917	356,716	34.41%
1986	658,875	247,715	411,160	34.07%
1987	727,132	265,551	461,580	34.02%
1988	755,034	276,786	478,247	31.83%
1989	799,077	295,500	503,577	30.31%
1990	858,006	318,254	539,752	28.62%
1991	915,711	345,554	570,157	26.89%
1992	975,610	372,319	603,290	25.90%
1993	1,017,686	389,721	627,965	24.91%
1994	1,074,660	410,998	663,662	24.78%
1995	1,115,370	427,239	688,131	24.25%
1996	1,169,714	452,392	717,322	24.21%
1997	1,221,501	456,657	764,844	24.49%
1998	1,283,560	483,117	800,443	25.33%

Year	State & Local	State	Local	% of Unmonetized Federal Debt[2]
1999	1,369,253	510,486	858,767	26.54%
2000	1,451,815	547,876	903,939	28.12%
2001	1,554,018	576,494	977,524	29.47%
2002	1,681,377	636,796	1,044,582	29.90%
2003	1,812,667	697,929	1,114,738	29.58%
2004	1,976,588	779,542	1,197,046	29.60%
2005	2,085,026	810,852	1,274,174	28.97%
2006	2,204,016	870,032	1,333,984	28.48%
2007	2,404,698	936,008	1,468,691	29.23%
2008	2,552,522	1,005,311	1,547,210	26.77%
2009	2,683,668	1,045,340	1,638,328	24.09%

NOTES

1. US Census Bureau, "Census of Governments," http://www.census.gov/govs/.
2. Unmonetized debt from Appendix A.

Appendix F

Trade Balances, 1790–2010[1,2]

[Millions of dollars, $US]

Year[3]	Balance of Goods and Services	Unilateral Transfers, net[4]	Current Account balance
1790	1	-	(1)
1791	(5)	-	(8)
1792	(4)	-	(8)
1793	6	-	2
1794	14	(1)	9
1795	(9)	(1)	(13)
1796	2	(1)	(4)
1797	(6)	-	(11)
1798	4	-	(2)
1799	20	-	15
1800	3	-	(2)
1801	7	-	2
1802	12	-	7
1803	13	(11)	(3)
1804	17	-	12
1805	(6)	-	(10)
1806	(4)	-	(7)
1807	(1)	-	(5)
1808	(11)	-	(17)
1809	18	-	12
1810	12	-	7
1811	41	-	35
1812	(18)	-	(21)
1813	20	-	15
1814	(6)	-	(9)
1815	(11)	-	(15)
1816	(53)	-	(58)
1817	(4)	-	(11)
1818	(20)	-	(25)
1819	(9)	-	(15)
1820	4	1	2

Year[3]	Balance of Goods and Services	Unilateral Transfers, net[4]	Current Account balance
1821	9	1	5
1822	(4)	-	(9)
1823	7	-	2
1824	6	1	-
1825	11	1	7
1826	1	1	(3)
1827	12	2	10
1828	(10)	2	(12)
1829	3	2	-
1830	11	2	8
1831	(11)	1	(14)
1832	(7)	5	(7)
1833	(14)	5	(14)
1834	(18)	6	(18)
1835	(27)	3	(30)
1836	(60)	10	(58)
1837	(19)	7	(21)
1838	3	3	(4)
1839	(40)	4	(49)
1840	39	4	30
1841	(4)	4	(8)
1842	8	6	7
1843	26	2	22
1844	7	4	-
1845	6	6	4
1846	(1)	11	1
1847	11	16	19
1848	(3)	13	(2)
1849	3	10	2
1850	(32)	16	(28)
1851	(7)	15	(5)
1852	(18)	17	(16)
1853	(59)	19	(56)
1854	(43)	21	(42)
1855	0	8	(14)
1856	3	8	(12)

Year[3]	Balance of Goods and Services	Unilateral Transfers, net[4]	Current Account balance
1857	(15)	14	(16)
1858	33	7	24
1859	(8)	6	(26)
1860	25	8	7
1861	(79)	(1)	(104)
1862	32	-	-
1863	17	3	(12)
1864	(80)	3	(111)
1865	(19)	5	(59)
1866	(40)	(4)	(95)
1867	(92)	4	(145)
1868	(9)	4	(73)
1869	(105)	(3)	(175)
1870	(21)	1	(100)
1871	(17)	-	(101)
1872	(159)	4	(242)
1873	(81)	14	(167)
1874	41	(11)	(72)
1875	(1)	(14)	(113)
1876	115	(11)	9
1877	189	(13)	89
1878	294	(11)	207
1879	280	(8)	194
1880	193	(4)	110
1881	225	(5)	132
1882	29	(13)	(68)
1883	77	(22)	(34)
1884	31	(24)	(83)
1885	98	(27)	(15)
1886	16	(28)	(105)
1887	(59)	(28)	(185)
1888	(119)	(30)	(256)
1889	(49)	(44)	(210)
1890	(25)	(45)	(195)
1891	45	(50)	(140)
1892	123	(54)	(74)

Year[3]	Balance of Goods and Services	Unilateral Transfers, net[4]	Current Account balance
1893	20	(44)	(163)
1894	212	(54)	44
1895	(1)	(55)	(182)
1896	156	(49)	(15)
1897	259	(41)	91
1898	576	(44)	400
1899	551	(68)	359
1900	574	(75)	394
1901	526	(104)	334
1902	338	(105)	153
1903	412	(115)	225
1904	350	(137)	142
1905	367	(133)	165
1906	358	(147)	149
1907	362	(177)	119
1908	498	(192)	235
1909	90	(187)	(161)
1910	110	(204)	(158)
1911	350	(224)	50
1912	331	(212)	45
1913	447	(207)	167
1914	111	(170)	(114)
1915	1,684	(150)	1,598
1916	2,970	(150)	2,952
1917	3,225	(205)	3,270
1918	2,108	(268)	2,190
1919	4,279	(1,044)	3,824
1920	3,047	(679)	2,844
1921	1,782	(509)	1,613
1922	432	(352)	645
1923	132	(365)	477
1924	729	(364)	987
1925	345	(403)	684
1926	73	(381)	445
1927	332	(357)	716
1928	572	(365)	1,012

Year[3]	Balance of Goods and Services	Unilateral Transfers, net[4]	Current Account balance
1929	339	(377)	771
1930	287	(342)	690
1931	(30)	(319)	197
1932	15	(238)	169
1933	36	(208)	150
1934	299	(172)	429
1935	(238)	(182)	(54)
1936	(184)	(208)	(93)
1937	15	(235)	62
1938	906	(182)	1,109
1939	755	(178)	888
1940	1,365	(210)	1,509
1941	2,053	(1,136)	1,274
1942	6,057	(6,336)	77
1943	10,684	(12,907)	(1,869)
1944	12,040	(14,142)	(1,690)
1945	5,683	(7,113)	(1,072)
1946	7,316	(2,991)	4,885
1947	10,857	(2,722)	8,992
1948	5,906	(4,973)	2,417
1949	5,367	(5,849)	873
1950	1,188	(4,537)	(1,840)
1951	3,788	(4,954)	884
1952	3,531	(5,113)	614
1953	3,259	(6,657)	(1,286)
1954	3,514	(5,642)	219
1955	2,786	(5,086)	430
1956	4,618	(4,990)	2,730
1957	6,141	(4,763)	4,762
1958	2,466	(4,647)	784
1959	69	(4,422)	(1,282)
1960	3,508	(4,062)	2,824
1961	4,195	(4,127)	3,822
1962	3,370	(4,277)	3,387
1963	4,210	(4,392)	4,414
1964	6,022	(4,240)	6,823

Year[3]	Balance of Goods and Services	Unilateral Transfers, net[4]	Current Account balance
1965	4,664	(4,583)	5,431
1966	2,940	(4,955)	3,031
1967	2,604	(5,294)	2,583
1968	250	(5,629)	611
1969	91	(5,735)	399
1970	2,254	(6,156)	2,331
1971	(1,303)	(7,402)	(1,433)
1972	(5,443)	(8,544)	(5,795)
1973	1,900	(6,913)	7,140
1974	(4,292)	(9,249)	1,962
1975	12,404	(7,075)	18,116
1976	(6,082)	(5,686)	4,295
1977	(27,246)	(5,226)	(14,335)
1978	(29,763)	(5,788)	(15,143)
1979	(24,565)	(6,593)	(285)
1980	(19,407)	(8,349)	2,317
1981	(16,172)	(11,702)	5,030
1982	(24,156)	(16,544)	(5,536)
1983	(57,767)	(17,310)	(38,691)
1984	(109,073)	(20,335)	(94,344)
1985	(121,880)	(21,998)	(118,155)
1986	(138,538)	(24,132)	(147,177)
1987	(151,684)	(23,265)	(160,655)
1988	(114,566)	(25,274)	(121,153)
1989	(93,142)	(26,169)	(99,486)
1990	(80,864)	(26,654)	(78,968)
1991	(31,135)	9,904	2,898
1992	(39,212)	(36,636)	(51,613)
1993	(70,310)	(39,812)	(84,806)
1994	(98,493)	(40,265)	(121,612)
1995	(96,384)	(38,074)	(113,567)
1996	(104,065)	(43,017)	(124,764)
1997	(108,273)	(45,062)	(140,726)
1998	(166,140)	(53,187)	(215,062)
1999	(263,159)	(50,428)	(301,656)
2000	(376,749)	(58,767)	(416,338)

Year[3]	Balance of Goods and Services	Unilateral Transfers, net[4]	Current Account balance
2001	(361,771)	(64,561)	(396,603)
2002	(417,432)	(64,990)	(457,248)
2003	(490,984)	(71,796)	(519,089)
2004	(605,356)	(88,243)	(628,519)
2005	(708,624)	(105,741)	(745,774)
2006	(753,288)	(91,515)	(800,621)
2007	(696,728)	(115,061)	(710,303)
2008	(698,338)	(125,885)	(677,135)
2009	(381,272)	(123,280)	(376,551)
2010	(500,027)	(136,095)	(470,898)

NOTES

1. The current account balance represents the difference between imports and exports of goods, services, and transfers. Mathematically it is represented by the following: Balance of Goods and Services + Balance of Income (income receipts net of income payments) + Unilateral Transfers = Current Account balance. For 2010, Current Account balance = (500,027) + 165,224 + (136,095) = (470,898).

2. For 1790–1918: US Office of Business Economics, unpublished data. For 1919–1945: US Bureau of Economic Analysis, *Statistical Supplement (1958)*, 10–13. For 1946–1959: Council of Economic Advisors, *Economic Report of the President* (1997), 414–415. For 1960-2010: Bureau of Economic Analysis, Survey of Current Business, Table 1: US International Transactions, http://www.bea.gov/scb/date_guide.asp. See also *Historical Statistics* (2006), Table Ee1-21.

3. Data for 1900 is the average of two data points. One figure is comparable with data before 1900 while the other set is comparable with data after 1900.

4. "Unilateral Transfers, net" includes (a) transfers of goods and services under military grant programs, (b) government transfers of goods and services (or cash) for which payment by the foreign country is not made, is not expected, or has not been specified, (c) and estimates of personal remittances of the foreign-born population in the United States.

APPENDIX G

Corporate Income Tax: Effective Rates and Share of National Income, 1960–2009[1]

Year	Corporate Income Tax Receipts ($ billions)	Corporate Income Subject to Tax ($ billions)	Effective Tax Rate[2]	Corporate Income Tax[3] (% of GDP)	Corporate Income Tax[4] (% of Federal Funds Outlays)
1960	21.5	47.2	45.5%	4.0%	28.7%
1961	21.0	47.9	43.7%	3.7%	26.4%
1962	20.5	51.7	39.7%	3.4%	23.7%
1963	21.6	54.3	39.7%	3.4%	23.8%
1964	23.5	60.4	38.9%	3.4%	24.4%
1965	25.5	70.8	36.0%	3.4%	26.8%
1966	30.1	77.1	39.0%	3.7%	28.2%
1967	34.0	74.8	45.4%	3.9%	26.6%
1968	28.7	81.4	35.2%	3.0%	20.0%
1969	36.7	81.2	45.2%	3.6%	24.8%
1970	32.8	72.4	45.3%	3.1%	21.0%
1971	26.8	83.2	32.2%	2.3%	16.4%
1972	32.2	95.1	33.8%	2.5%	18.1%
1973	36.2	115.5	31.3%	2.5%	19.3%
1974	38.6	144.0	26.8%	2.5%	19.2%
1975	40.6	146.6	27.7%	2.4%	16.4%
1976	41.4	183.5	22.6%	2.2%	14.9%
1977	54.9	212.5	25.8%	2.6%	18.0%
1978	60.0	239.6	25.0%	2.5%	17.5%
1979	65.7	279.4	23.5%	2.5%	17.5%
1980	64.6	246.6	26.2%	2.3%	14.9%
1981	61.1	241.5	25.3%	1.9%	12.3%
1982	49.2	205.2	24.0%	1.5%	9.1%
1983	37.0	218.7	16.9%	1.0%	6.0%
1984	56.9	257.1	22.1%	1.4%	8.9%
1985	61.3	266.1	23.0%	1.4%	8.4%
1986	63.1	276.2	22.9%	1.4%	8.3%
1987	83.7	311.8	26.9%	1.7%	11.0%

Year	Corporate Income Tax Receipts ($ billions)	Corporate Income Subject to Tax ($ billions)	Effective Tax Rate[2]	Corporate Income Tax[3] (% of GDP)	Corporate Income Tax[4] (% of Federal Funds Outlays)
1988	94.2	383.2	24.6%	1.8%	11.6%
1989	103.0	371.1	27.8%	1.8%	11.6%
1990	93.0	366.4	25.4%	1.6%	9.5%
1991	97.5	350.0	27.9%	1.6%	9.5%
1992	99.9	377.9	26.4%	1.5%	9.6%
1993	116.6	436.8	26.7%	1.7%	11.0%
1994	139.7	494.0	28.3%	1.9%	13.0%
1995	156.4	564.7	27.7%	2.0%	14.2%
1996	171.5	639.8	26.8%	2.1%	15.1%
1997	182.3	683.8	26.7%	2.1%	15.7%
1998	188.6	663.4	28.4%	2.1%	15.6%
1999	184.7	693.7	26.6%	1.9%	14.8%
2000	207.3	760.4	27.3%	2.0%	15.7%
2001	151.1	635.3	23.8%	1.4%	11.1%
2002	148.0	600.6	24.7%	1.3%	10.1%
2003	131.9	699.3	18.9%	1.1%	8.3%
2004	189.4	857.4	22.1%	1.5%	11.1%
2005	278.3	1,201.3	23.2%	2.1%	14.9%
2006	353.9	1,291.4	27.4%	2.6%	17.2%
2007	370.2	1,248.3	29.7%	2.6%	17.9%
2008	304.3	978.2	31.1%	2.1%	13.3%
2009	138.2	894.9	15.4%	1.0%	5.1%

NOTES

1. For corporate income tax after credits, see OMB, Historical Tables, "Supplemental Materials: Receipts," http://www.whitehouse.gov/omb/budget/Supplemental. These amounts exclude trust fund receipts for the hazardous substance superfund. For corporate income subject to tax, see IRS, "SOI," Historical Table 15, for all years except 2008 and 2009. Information for 2008 and 2009 is from IRS, "SOI," Historical Table 13, http://www.irs.gov/uac/SOI-Tax-Stats-SOI-Bulletin-Historical-Tables-and-Appendix.

2. The effective tax rate is a percentage derived by dividing corporate income tax revenues (after credits) by the corporate income subject to taxation.

3. See Appendix B, note 3.

4. For federal funds outlays, see Appendix C.

APPENDIX H

Personal Income Tax: Effective Rates and Share of National Income, 1950–2010

Year	Personal Income Tax Receipts ($ billions)	Adjusted Gross Income ($ billions)	Effective Tax Rate[2]	Personal Income Tax[3] (% of GDP)	Personal Income Tax[4] (% of Federal Funds Outlays)
1950	18.4	179.1	10.3%	6.1%	47.9%
1951	24.2	202.3	12.0%	7.0%	55.3%
1952	27.8	215.3	12.9%	7.6%	42.8%
1953	29.4	228.7	12.9%	7.5%	40.3%
1954	26.7	229.2	11.6%	6.8%	40.5%
1955	29.6	248.5	11.9%	6.9%	47.5%
1956	32.7	267.7	12.2%	7.3%	50.9%
1957	34.4	280.3	12.3%	7.2%	51.2%
1958	34.3	281.2	12.2%	7.1%	49.2%
1959	38.6	305.1	12.7%	7.4%	50.1%
1960	39.5	315.5	12.5%	7.3%	52.8%
1961	42.2	329.9	12.8%	7.5%	53.2%
1962	44.9	348.7	12.9%	7.4%	51.9%
1963	48.2	368.8	13.1%	7.5%	53.2%
1964	47.2	396.7	11.9%	6.9%	49.1%
1965	49.6	429.2	11.6%	6.7%	52.3%
1966	56.1	468.5	12.0%	6.9%	52.6%
1967	63.0	504.8	12.5%	7.3%	49.4%
1968	76.7	554.4	13.8%	8.1%	53.6%
1969	86.6	603.5	14.3%	8.5%	58.4%
1970	83.9	631.7	13.3%	7.8%	53.7%
1971	85.4	673.6	12.7%	7.3%	52.2%
1972	93.6	746.0	12.5%	7.3%	52.5%
1973	108.1	827.1	13.1%	7.6%	57.8%
1974	123.6	905.5	13.6%	8.0%	61.4%
1975	124.5	947.8	13.1%	7.4%	50.2%
1976	141.8	1,053.9	13.5%	7.6%	51.1%
1977	159.8	1,158.5	13.8%	7.7%	52.5%

Year	Personal Income Tax Receipts ($ billions)	Adjusted Gross Income ($ billions)	Effective Tax Rate[2]	Personal Income Tax[3] (% of GDP)	Personal Income Tax[4] (% of Federal Funds Outlays)
1978	188.2	1,302.4	14.5%	8.0%	55.0%
1979	214.5	1,465.4	14.6%	8.1%	57.1%
1980	250.3	1,613.7	15.5%	8.7%	57.7%
1981	284.1	1,772.6	16.0%	8.8%	57.3%
1982	277.6	1,852.1	15.0%	8.3%	51.1%
1983	274.2	1,942.6	14.1%	7.5%	44.7%
1984	301.9	2,139.9	14.1%	7.5%	47.3%
1985	325.7	2,306.0	14.1%	7.5%	44.8%
1986	367.0	2,524.1	14.5%	8.0%	48.5%
1987	369.0	2,813.7	13.1%	7.6%	48.5%
1988	412.8	3,124.2	13.2%	7.9%	50.7%
1989	432.8	3,298.9	13.1%	7.7%	48.6%
1990	447.1	3,451.2	13.0%	7.5%	45.8%
1991	448.3	3,516.1	12.8%	7.3%	43.8%
1992	476.2	3,680.6	12.9%	7.3%	45.7%
1993	502.7	3,775.6	13.3%	7.3%	47.4%
1994	534.8	3,961.1	13.5%	7.3%	49.8%
1995	588.3	4,244.6	13.9%	7.7%	53.4%
1996	658.1	4,590.5	14.3%	8.1%	57.8%
1997	727.3	5,023.5	14.5%	8.4%	62.8%
1998	788.5	5,469.2	14.4%	8.7%	65.4%
1999	877.3	5,909.3	14.8%	9.1%	70.1%
2000	980.5	6,424.0	15.3%	9.5%	74.0%
2001	888.0	6,170.6	14.4%	8.4%	65.4%
2002	797.0	6,033.6	13.2%	7.3%	54.2%
2003	748.0	6,207.1	12.1%	6.5%	47.3%
2004	832.0	6,788.8	12.3%	6.8%	48.8%
2005	934.8	7,422.5	12.6%	7.1%	50.1%
2006	1,023.9	8,030.8	12.7%	7.4%	49.8%
2007	1,115.6	8,687.7	12.8%	7.7%	53.9%
2008	1,031.6	8,262.9	12.5%	7.0%	44.9%
2009	865.9	7,626.4	11.4%	6.0%	32.0%
2010	944.5	8,045.0	11.7%	6.3%	35.4%

NOTES

1. For 1950–1985: IRS, "SOI," Table 8: Personal Income per National Income and Product Accounts (NIPA), and Taxable Income and Individual Income Tax per SOI and Table 5: Total Adjusted Gross Income Estimated from National Income and Product Accounts (NIPA) and as Reported on Individual Income Tax Returns per SOI, http://www.irs.gov/uac/SOI-Tax-Stats-SOI-Bulletin-Historical-Tables-and-Appendix. For 1986–2000: IRS, "SOI," Table 5: Personal Income and Total Adjusted Gross Income Based on Individual Income Tax Returns per National Income and Product Accounts (NIPA), http://www.irs.gov/uac/SOI-Tax-Stats-SOI-Bulletin-Historical-Tables-and-Appendix. For 2001–2010: IRS, "SOI," Table 3: Number of Individual Income Tax Returns, Income, Exemptions and Deductions, Tax, and Average Tax, by Size of Adjusted Gross Income, http://www.irs.gov/uac/SOI-Tax-Stats-SOI-Bulletin-Historical-Tables-and-Appendix.

2. The effective rate is a percentage derived from dividing personal income tax revenues by personal adjusted gross income.

3. Appendix B, note 3.

4. For federal funds spending, Appendix C.

INDEX

Bill White is senior advisor at Lazard, a firm advising corporate leaders and governments worldwide. He served as Houston's mayor and was twice re-elected with an average vote of 88 percent. He also served as the deputy secretary of energy of the United States. He received the prestigious John F. Kennedy Profiles in Courage Award for his leadership in response to Hurricane Katrina and the Governing Official of the Year Award by *Governing* magazine. He has worked as the CEO of a successful business and as a member of numerous corporate boards. In 2010 he received more votes for governor of Texas than any Democratic candidate in the state's history.

PublicAffairs is a publishing house founded in 1997. It is a tribute to the standards, values, and flair of three persons who have served as mentors to countless reporters, writers, editors, and book people of all kinds, including me.

I. F. STONE, proprietor of *I. F. Stone's Weekly*, combined a commitment to the First Amendment with entrepreneurial zeal and reporting skill and became one of the great independent journalists in American history. At the age of eighty, Izzy published *The Trial of Socrates*, which was a national bestseller. He wrote the book after he taught himself ancient Greek.

BENJAMIN C. BRADLEE was for nearly thirty years the charismatic editorial leader of *The Washington Post*. It was Ben who gave the *Post* the range and courage to pursue such historic issues as Watergate. He supported his reporters with a tenacity that made them fearless and it is no accident that so many became authors of influential, best-selling books.

ROBERT L. BERNSTEIN, the chief executive of Random House for more than a quarter century, guided one of the nation's premier publishing houses. Bob was personally responsible for many books of political dissent and argument that challenged tyranny around the globe. He is also the founder and longtime chair of Human Rights Watch, one of the most respected human rights organizations in the world.

· · ·

For fifty years, the banner of Public Affairs Press was carried by its owner Morris B. Schnapper, who published Gandhi, Nasser, Toynbee, Truman, and about 1,500 other authors. In 1983, Schnapper was described by *The Washington Post* as "a redoubtable gadfly." His legacy will endure in the books to come.

Peter Osnos, *Founder and Editor-at-Large*